ml

This book is to be returned on or before
the last date stamped below.

EARLY EUROPEAN AGRICULTURE

BRITISH ACADEMY MAJOR RESEARCH PROJECT

The Early History of Agriculture

Management Committee:
  Professor J. G. D. Clark, Sc.D., F.B.A.
  Professor Sir Joseph Hutchinson, C.M.G., Sc.D., F.R.S.
  Dr G. H. S. Bushnell, Ph.D., F.S.A.
  Dr R. G. West, Ph.D., F.R.S.
  E. S. Higgs, M.A., B.Comm. (Director)

Assistant Director, British Academy Fellow:
  M. R. Jarman, M.A.

Documentary Secretary:
  H. N. Jarman, B.A.

The following people were associated with the Project and have
contributed to this volume:
  Atholl Anderson, Department of Anthropology, University of
    Otago, Dunedin, New Zealand
  Paul Bahn, Department of Prehistoric Archaeology, University
    of Liverpool
  Geoff Bailey, Department of Archaeology, University of
    Cambridge
  Jan Bay-Petersen, Department of Archaeology, University of
    Leicester
  Coinneach Maclean, South Uist, Outer Hebrides
  Margaret Sakellaridis, Cambridge
  Claudio Vita-Finzi, Department of Geography, University
    College, London
  Derrick Webley, Bangor, Gwynedd

EARLY EUROPEAN AGRICULTURE

ITS FOUNDATIONS AND DEVELOPMENT

being the third volume of Papers in Economic Prehistory
by members and associates of the British Academy Major
Research Project in the Early History of Agriculture

written in honour of ERIC HIGGS

edited by

M. R. JARMAN

G. N. BAILEY and H. N. JARMAN

CAMBRIDGE UNIVERSITY PRESS

CAMBRIDGE
LONDON   NEW YORK   NEW ROCHELLE
MELBOURNE   SYDNEY

Published by the Press Syndicate of the University of Cambridge
The Pitt Building, Trumpington Street, Cambridge CB2 1RP
32 East 57th Street, New York, NY 10022, USA
296 Beaconsfield Parade, Middle Park, Melbourne 3206, Australia

© Cambridge University Press 1982

First published 1982

Printed in Great Britain at The Pitman Press, Bath

Library of Congress catalogue card number: 81–17960

British Library cataloguing in publication data

Early European agriculture: its foundations and
development.
1. Agriculture – Europe – Origin
2. Agriculture – Europe – History
I. Jarman, M. R.   II. Bailey, Geoff N.
III. Jarman, H. N.   IV. Higgs, Eric
630'.94   GN799.A4

ISBN 0 521 24359 9

CONTENTS

Figures 71, 72 and 73 reproduced with the permission of Corvina Press, Budapest.

Figure 105 reproduced with the permission of Duckworth, London.

INTRODUCTION

This book stems largely from the work of, and is entirely a tribute and memorial to, Eric Higgs. At the time of his sadly lamented death in October 1976 he was in the process of drawing to its conclusion the British Academy Major Research Project on the Early History of Agriculture. He became so intimately associated with the Project's work and the thinking which it represented that the man and institution became synonymous in many peoples' minds, denoting a powerful and individual conception of prehistoric studies. The personality and originality of the man, no less than the force of his arguments, affected generations of his students. It is thus that the present volume remains Eric's book, despite the fact that it existed only as a sketchy outline at the time of his death; for the contributors have a more than ordinary academic debt to acknowledge.

Many people have contributed to the volume in different ways and different degrees. It has been jointly written by a small number of Project members, but over the years we have, of course, drawn data and ideas from a wider circle of friends and colleagues. In the nature of things it has not proved possible to produce a book of this scope and size with total unanimity. Broadly speaking, the general and theoretical chapters, and the outlines of our approach represent the views of the Project as a whole and of all our principal contributers. Such disagreement as has arisen has been confined to specific pieces of data and their interpretation, and the weight and balance given to different points of argument. Where controversy proved intractable, the view represented is that of the senior editor.

The general responsibility for the first three chapters, Chapters 6, 7, and the concluding section lies with M. R. Jarman; that for Chapter 4 with G. N. Bailey, that for Chapter 5 with H. N. Jarman. Within this framework there has been an inextricable degree of cross-fertilisation. These authors aside, we received direct contributions, or access to unpublished original research, from the following: Athol Anderson (Sweden), Paul Bahn (French Pyrenees, megaliths), Jan Bay-Petersen (Northern Poland, French and Italian littoral), Coinneach Maclean (Romania), Nigel Mills (Provence), Margaret Sakellaridis (Switzerland),

Claudio Vita-Finzi (Dordogne), Derrick Webley (penetrometer studies, Britain), Marek Zvelebil (Finland).

Our thanks are due to these and to the many people who assisted in ways less easy to acknowledge. These include Grahame Clark and Sir Joseph Hutchinson who gave generously of their time and encouragement; the large number of people who allowed us on to their excavations and into their museum storerooms; the countless farmers and agricultural labourers who answered our insistent – and often impertinent and incomprehensible – questions concerning modern and historic agriculture; and Michael Young, who tolerantly overlooked our importunities and drew the figures. We are especially grateful to Bill Powell for his concept of the urban caveman, whose absence from these pages results purely from lack of space rather than lack of relevance. We are also glad to acknowledge our indebtedness to the organisations and institutions that supported our work financially. The British Academy has been our major sponsor since the Project's inception in 1967. Generous financial contributions have also been received from the Wenner-Gren Foundation for Anthropological Research, the British Council, and the Deutscher Akademischer Austauschdienst. The Department of Archaeology in the University of Cambridge kindly provided us with rooms in which to work and other necessary services.

The volume is organised in terms of the analysis of three primary exploitation zones: the coastal zone, the lowland zone, and the upland zone. There are alternatives. The two most obvious are either a chronological scheme (in which one would analyse the development of European agriculture as a whole at a series of time horizons) or a geographical scheme (in which one would take the subject country by country or area by area). It was felt that, as the literature abounds with syntheses based on one or both of these latter principles, more might be gained by a different approach. Far more important, as our work progressed we became ever more convinced that these three primary zones embodied potentials and constraints of immense significance in the development and regulation of economic behaviour. These factors, which override chronological and national boundaries, encapsulate the crucial determinants which link certain kinds of economy, tending to the existence of observable uniformities. Given our conviction that archaeology must (among other things) seek to recognise and analyse regularities and organising principles, we felt that this was a most appropriate way in which to arrange this volume.

This scheme has not been without its problems, as will clearly emerge from Chapters 4–6. One most obvious difficulty is that of repetition and duplication. It is a basic tenet that the primary resource zones were interrelated, resources from one area being integrated with those of another by various mechanisms. In our attempt to deal with this within our chosen framework there has been some unavoidable duplication of information. It is also true that within each particular zone we have been frequently forced to the conclusion that the important economic and environmental variables were remarkably similar from area to area: another kind of repetitiveness. In view of our professed preoccupation with regularities in the archaeological record this is, perhaps, to be expected.

In addition to our concern with primary exploitation zones we have developed the concept of *economic niches*, which describe the way in which human populations behave with respect to these zones, and the ways in which the unequal resources they offer are integrated. These are to be seen as elements which together make up the total exploitation of a region; and they comprise the mobile, mobile-cum-sedentary, and sedentary niches. The mobile niche integrates widespread complementary resources by means of transhumance or stock transference (in the case of pastoralism) or by seasonal movements which may on occasion have been less structured among certain hunting and gathering economies. The mobile-cum-sedentary niche incorporates both a mobile and sedentary element; a characteristic example being a lowland agricultural economy with a pastoral element which requires a degree of seasonal mobility for its effective management. The sedentary niche is largely a phenomenon of the lowland resource zone, and typically concerns agricultural economies. In certain rare instances, as we shall see later, coastal economies may also occupy the sedentary economic niche.

We make no apology for including, where it has seemed to us helpful, data from the Mesolithic, Upper Palaeolithic, or even Middle Palaeolithic periods, along with our consideration of Holocene agricultural economies. We are profoundly convinced that a crucial and often overlooked aspect of archaeological data concerns long-term continuity. In Chapter 3 we outline

some of our reasons for recognising long-term regularities in economic forces and organisation. In the later chapters, as was mentioned above, we frequently see these regularities reflected in site locations and territories, and the ways in which the various resources were integrated.

One limitation of all general syntheses is that they cannot be exhaustive in their treatment of the material. This is no less true of the present volume, and it is certain that many will feel its usefulness to be greatly restricted because particular examples and areas are omitted, or because it is felt that undue weight has been placed on a relatively small sample of the total available evidence. Naturally, care has been taken to overcome this problem as far as possible, but a number of significant constraints have limited our coverage. The total permanent staff of the project has never been large, reaching a maximum of seven for a short period, and latterly reduced to one. Of the nine years of active research (the last few months having been entirely devoted to the preparation of this volume) it appears with the benefit of hindsight that the first three were almost entirely given over to ground clearance: to the proposal of objectives and approaches which seemed at once theoretically valid and practically feasible. The results of this initial stage emerged as *Papers in Economic Prehistory* (1972). The second stage, the tentative first development of this theme, was published as a somewhat disparate collection of papers, *Palaeoeconomy* (1975). In attempting the final stage of synthesis, we are only too aware of the degree to which our restricted time and resources have forced us to be selective.

We hope, of course, and believe that we have gone some way to overcoming this limitation by the particular choices we have made as to approach and study area. The central objective has been to arrive at principles of economic behaviour which are stable in the long term, and which have far-reaching evolutionary importance. If we have in any way succeeded, then these ought to apply as much in areas we have been unable to consider as they do in those from which we have a great deal of information.

Be that as it may, many areas are not dealt with here in any detail. We were unable to study much of Scandinavia at first hand. This limitation is to some extent mitigated by the fact that we were fortunate in having access to recent palaeoeconomic work in that area, and also by the region's environment, which places most of it beyond the limits of many systems of farming. Equally it has not proved possible to conduct any field work in European Russia. Other major geographical gaps are East Germany, Czechoslovakia, and Yugoslavia.

Another important limitation has been the impossibility of conducting major campaigns of excavation, most of the field work having concentrated on surveys. Shortage of time and resources has precluded any more ambitious field operations, and we have been forced to make use of earlier work, or of cooperative ventures with excavators who frequently had very different archaeological objectives to ours, but who offered the best opportunity of access to material in certain crucial areas. Many of our hypotheses can only be adequately tested when on-site archaeological data are available that have been collected with those propositions in mind. Thus to a very real degree the success or failure of this volume rests with a future generation of archaeological research. It is satisfying to note that a number of detailed area studies is now being conducted by research students with this objective in mind.

Free will is for history only an expression connoting what we do not know about the laws of human life.

Leo Tolstoy, *War and Peace*

And in truth, the period of time covered by history is far too short to allow of any perceptible progress in the popular sense of Evolution of the Human Species.

George Bernard Shaw, Notes to *Caesar and Cleopatra*

1. PHILOSOPHY AND BASIC PRINCIPLES

This volume, the culmination of ten years' work of the British Academy's Major Research Project on the Early History of Agriculture, attempts to draw together into a coherent whole the main theoretical themes advanced in our previous publications, and to illustrate their operation through a consideration of early agricultural development in Europe.

Our last major publication, *Palaeoeconomy*, proposed reasons for the development of the study of palaeoeconomy as a specifically formulated approach to prehistory. Reaction to this suggestion has, predictably, been mixed, and many readers seem to have misunderstood our intent. In an effort to provide some elucidation, and because of their crucial bearing on the present volume, some rehearsal of the arguments is now necessary.

Perhaps the commonest criticism has been levelled at the apparent arrogance of a proposal which seemed to claim pre-eminence for one approach to the subject by disparaging other competing viewpoints. This is an important question, which requires discussion. Unfortunate though it may be, this problem is bound to arise to some extent in any attempt to proselytise. If existing approaches were not deficient in some respects there would be no need to propose others. It was never the intention, however, to imply that palaeoeconomy offered the only acceptable framework for the treatment of archaeological data. Our concern was rather to establish its right to be considered as one valuable and distinct approach; and one that avoided some of the difficulties and limitations, which (it seemed to us) were inherent in other existing approaches. It is axiomatic, of course, that palaeoeconomy, like any selective study, is itself limited. We attempted to give reasons for our belief that these limitations were to a large extent forced upon us by the very nature of archaeological information.

Others argued strongly that palaeoeconomy was simply a part of 'human palaeoecology' or 'cultural ecology' under a different name, and that it was thus already established and in no need of a new name or of elaborate explication. In a way this statement highlights the very point we were trying to make when we suggested that ecological studies were too general in their scope to provide an entirely suitable theoretical framework. For the argument, if pursued rigidly, would suggest that fissioning of subjects would never occur, or at least need not do so. A whole range of modern disciplines – ethology, economics, geography, demography, and a host of others – could equally well be denied separate importance on the argument that they can all be subsumed within the sphere of ecological studies. Yet each of these has derived considerable impetus and advantage from the definition of its own specialised objectives, theoretical structure, and methods. Expressing the case in terms of Clarke's (1972) analysis of the different approaches within the 'New Archaeology' we would hope that a 'palaeoeconomic paradigm' would cull from, and integrate into a more effective whole, the most useful aspects of his 'ecological' and 'geographical paradigms'.

The critical question at issue, and the one that ultimately decides our choice of models, is the nature of archaeology as a discipline: its objectives, and the ways in which it is hoped that these should develop. Do we believe that 'Archaeology . . . is concerned with the recovery, systematic description and study of antiquities' in Clarke's (1968) words? In truth, this rather narrow view does less than justice to his multifarious and original approach, but it *is* representative of a large body of archaeological opinion, as a glance at many of the subject's periodicals will confirm. Is archaeology the time dimension of anthropology? Or are we aiming at a 'who-dunnit' kind of archaeology: an attempt to extrapolate back in time as personalised and 'real' an account of human activity as the wayward data will permit? Or is 'the proper subject of concern the social life of prehistoric man', as one eminent prehistorian has recently emphasised (Clark, J. G. D. 1975)?

Clearly it is vain, given the present state of turmoil in which the subject finds itself, to attempt to lay down a single exclusive gospel as the only route to archaeological salvation; but one can try to isolate those themes and approaches which appear to have more relevance and power for development within the context of the existing climate of thought and available techniques.

One possible avenue which has so far been but little explored is the development of a more specifically scientific framework for the subject, although the current vogue in conceptual models is beginning to change this. Recent technological advances have, of course, placed within the orbit of many archaeologists a whole range of 'scientific' aids, from computers to bulldozers, but these have so far been employed primarily within the traditional framework of the subject and have not impinged greatly upon its theoretical structure. It is, of course, debatable whether archaeology 'should' try to become a science. The very idea is anathema to some. What is undeniable is that at present the subject cannot be described as scientific except in the very broadest definition of that term, and that a scientific archaeology would generate new aims and objectives, and thus would encourage a reappraisal of the data. Perhaps it would be justified for this alone.

An important prerequisite for such a development to take place is that we should start to search for regularities in the material. It seems reasonable to take Braithwaite's (1953) view that 'The function of a science . . . is to establish general laws covering the behaviour of empirical events or objects' and thus to be able to make 'reliable predictions of events as yet unknown'. For most archaeologists, the excitement and stimulus of the subject lies in its hints at uniqueness and individuality; the particular decorative motif which makes the pottery of a certain site or 'culture' unlike that of any other; the percentage of angle burins which makes a Palaeolithic assemblage an exception; the size and orientation of the gateway to the Iron Age hillfort which are hitherto unmatched; these are the focus of interest, and to some degree the measure of success. Little attention or prestige would be accorded the excavation report which stated baldly that the site and its contents were in all essentials identical with half a dozen others of the same age and area. But regularity and predictability are important, for it is they that indicate the laws or principles which may govern and structure the otherwise uncontrollable variety of our observations. They may, indeed, be taken as key indices of a scientific discipline, and a conscious search for them a *sine qua non* of the scientific approach. Most archaeology is unscientific when judged by these criteria, and we may note that Braithwaite excludes history from his corpus of scientific disciplines as being 'concerned merely with the occurrence of particular historical events'.

In recommending a scientific approach to the subject, therefore, we are being unashamedly deterministic, in the broad sense that the postulation of laws presupposes the existence of factors that regulate and determine the way in which the data behave. This does not necessarily mean that we are being deterministic in the more specific sense of excluding *a priori* the possibility of the operation of any random or 'chance' factors. The whole emotive issue of determinism (in its more general sense) reveals itself as a semantic red herring when pushed to its logical extremes. As is so often the case, the source of confusion concerns the relationship between the scale of enquiry and the explanatory devices chosen by the investigator. Carr (1961) neatly illustrated the absurdity of continuing to belabour the determinist *vs* free will debate in historical studies. Hull (1974) points out that whereas 'the basic laws of quantum physics are necessarily statistical' (i.e. non-deterministic) when applied to single particles, they may be deterministic 'for large ensembles of sub-atomic particles'. Our present concern is not really with the philosophical complexities raised by the apparent conflict of deterministic and statistical/probabilistic explanation, however. If archaeology can accept that important aspects of human behaviour are susceptible to scientific enquiry, from which may be derived laws or general principles, we may safely leave aside for the present the question of the precise nature of these principles.

The issue of determinism does have a further significance for us, however. The widespread passionate belief in human uniqueness has led to a situation where the word 'determinist' with regard to human affairs has become a pejorative or term of abuse. Let us at once, and unequivocally agree that man is indeed unique. But then so, of course, are all other organisms, at one level or another. Conversely, few but the most enthusiastic apostles of human free will would deny that there is a broad framework of restraint, of limitation, on our behaviour, which springs from the nature of matter and energy, and the ways in which organisms (including man) can gain access to them. The difficulty arises with the assertion that while all animals are unique, some, like Orwell's pigs, are more unique than others; that the essence of man, the important thing about him, lies in this uniqueness, and that therefore to study him in any other terms is to miss the whole point. Many archaeologists and anthropologists believe that man is raised to such a plane by his intelligence, by his language, and by the fact that much of his evolution is expressed through 'socially transmitted change' rather than through 'biologically or genetically transmitted change', that it is impossible to study him effectively in the same way that other organisms may be studied. From this viewpoint 'the main result of applying the principles of animal behaviour to human societies is to highlight their differences' (Clark, J. G. D. 1975).

This is a value judgement of great emotional appeal. No doubt modern proponents of this view are influenced in some degree by the same feelings which placed the Earth at the centre of the mediaeval universe. What must be accepted, however, is that the proposition can neither be proved nor disproved, although persuasive polemics can be and are marshalled on both sides. There are clearly demonstrable points of close similarity between man and other animals, just as there are distinguishing features. The choice of one of these aspects of humanity as having a pre-eminent significance depends upon objectives and basic philosophical stances, and cannot be justified purely in terms of logical debate. Implicit in the view which gives pre-eminence to human uniqueness is the belief that man is in some degree divine, supernatural; that the most significant part of human behaviour is not subject to the same laws which govern the rest of the universe. This is a proposition based upon faith or inspiration, and not upon data which can be rationally examined and evaluated. 'True' or not, it concerns a subject which by its own definition has placed itself beyond the scope of scientific consideration.

In recommending the development of a scientific archaeology (not as the sole approach, be it noted, but as one valid objective) we are therefore making an important statement about the kinds of behaviour and data that we are attempting to study. It is quite apparent that this will be a selective approach, certain aspects of human behaviour and archaeological data being dismissed as of little or no importance to the particular objectives in view because they cannot be effectively studied by the available techniques within a scientific framework.

ARCHAEOLOGICAL EVIDENCE

This leads us to a consideration of the nature of archaeological evidence. One important aspect of the development of modern archaeology, as with so many subjects, was the particularist nineteenth-century habit of observation, collection, and description as ends in themselves. Consequently the museums of the world are full of trilobites and torques, of butterflies, beads, and beakers, testifying to the energy devoted to that cause, while the libraries are similarly congested with monographs describing these objects. Such activities fulfilled a valuable function at the time, in many instances. Classification of its basic data is an important aspect of the early development of any subject. Archaeology retains perhaps a closer link with this approach to its data than many disciplines, as can be

seen from the enthusiastic devotion of so much in the way of time and resources to 'rescue archaeology'. This work has an important place in the overall framework of the subject. It is hard, on the other hand, to avoid the observation that at present it is all too often motivated exclusively by the understandable desire to grab frantically at what we can while it is still there, when more preliminary thought about basic archaeological objectives might perhaps yield results of greater utility in the long run.

In the definition of these objectives a point of great significance is that archaeology is essentially imprecise in its dating. Contemporaneity of archaeological sites and objects can only rarely be established in other than the most general terms, even with the modern range of sophisticated dating techniques. The further back in time we go, of course, the wider become the margins of chronological error. While in Iron Age Europe one is used to accepting an uncertainty of a few decades or a century, students of the Upper Palaeolithic must cope with potential inaccuracies of several centuries or even millennia; and those working on the Lower Pleistocene development of man are more than thankful if they can on occasion tentatively date a site, skull, or tool, to within a couple of hundred thousand years.

A second major limitation of archaeological evidence is the degree to which it has been destroyed and distorted since its time of origin. The vast preponderance even of those aspects of life which leave solid and unenigmatic remains must have been destroyed or damaged beyond recovery and interpretation. Those realms of human behaviour which leave no solid traces, or those artefacts which are but obscurely and deviously related to the activities which gave rise to them, offer the richest field for speculation, but perhaps the poorest harvest of testable hypotheses. No one could deny the importance in human behaviour of language, religion, art; of social, moral, and psychological systems and values. However, their interrelationship, and their relationships with other factors such as the environment, the economy, and technology are both complex and poorly understood; so that even in a modern context it is not possible to assess the nature and significance of all the various forces with any confidence.

As far as prehistory is concerned this objective becomes absurd, as few if any of the relevant data are available, or could ever be. Prehistoric art exists, of course, but not one of the competing theories purporting to explain it can be substantiated or refuted, nor is it possible to imagine how this could be accomplished short of conversation with the artists. When one considers the confusion which surrounds the nature and purpose of modern art, one wonders indeed if this goal would be brought much nearer even if such conversation were possible. Similarly, religion has clearly exerted considerable force in the past, as it does today; but it is hard to envisage circumstances that would permit us to get much beyond the description of those few aspects of belief which become fossilised in monument or artistic representation.

The question of 'social archaeology' requires especial mention, as it is much in vogue today to maintain that the future of the subject lies in the analysis of the social behaviour of prehistoric man. Again, much depends upon what is meant by this. A leading proponent has stated that 'Social archaeology owes its crucial importance to the elementary but basic fact that all archaeological data are the product of the labours of men who not merely lived in society, but acquired their patterns of behaviour as members of social entities' (Clark, J. G. D. 1975). The 'basic fact' is indeed incontestable, but is expressed in terms too general to take us much further in our attempt to develop an effective approach to archaeological studies. It is so generalised a proposition that a similar form of words could easily be used to justify the primacy of environmental, ecological, geographical, or indeed cultural archaeology. A similar statement could moreover be made with equal accuracy of any of a wide variety of social animals, many of which have complicated repertoires of behaviour that develop and are transmitted within specific social contexts. It is revealing here to contrast Clark's view of the relationship between human and animal behaviour with that of Wynne-Edwards (1962), who asserts that the close affinity of man to other animals is particularly apparent from a study of their social behaviour.

Of course, the development of social archaeology has not rested entirely on truisms. Clark and others have gone on to pursue specific objectives in social archaeology. Many of these involve the attempt to derive descent and kinship structure from a detailed consideration of archaeological data, especially patterning in pottery typology. These studies are united by a number of features: the availability of a wealth of ethnographic evidence as an interpretative aid; relatively complete archaeological information; and an unusually tight control over chronological variables due to the choice of recent periods, where the margin of error is less, and where historical data are frequently available for some of the period under consideration. These advantages immediately place these studies in a most privileged position compared with almost all archaeological situations. Furthermore, recent anthropological opinion

(Allen & Richardson 1971) seems to indicate that the interpretation of even those favoured bodies of data has failed to take account of the complexity and variability of human social behaviour.

Yet more important, from our point of view, is the growing realisation among anthropologists that many social mechanisms are largely reflections of economic activity, and thus act as dependent rather than independent variables. For while Sahlins (1972) argues that '"Economy" becomes a category of culture rather than behavior, in a class with politics or religion', this seems an unnecessarily parochial viewpoint, and one which takes no account of the many successful attempts to view both economy and society in their wider relationships with the environment. Thus Leeds (1961) found that many detailed aspects of Yaruro belief and cosmology were intimately related to their ecological niche, and that 'This ecological balance in turn limits the human population and socio-economic forms. Nor can any immediate desire or fancy of the Yaruro change the limitations which the ecological relationship imposes'. McLoughlin (1970) in his survey of East African peasant society concludes yet more specifically that 'relationships within the immediate family, within the extended kinship group, and within the broader community have developed over time to guide and regulate the decision making systems for food production'. Rappaport (1968) found a similar relationship between the belief systems of the Tsembaga of New Guinea and their environment, concluding that 'ritual operates to keep the trophic demands of the Tsembaga and their pigs within the carrying capacity of their territory'.

The longer the time scale involved, the more apparent becomes the dependence of social upon economic behaviour. It is true that disciplines which focus on modern human behaviour have many significant advantages over archaeology. The range and refinement of the data available to them are incomparably superior to those from even the best of archaeological circumstances, and they have an enviable capacity in these days of sophisticated mathematical models and hardware to design experiments specifically with a view to testing them against data gathered under controlled conditions. Because of the short time scale inherent in these subjects, however, they are in a poor position to assess the evolutionary significance of the processes they study, to sort out short-term factors and random components from those which may be part of longer term developments. Archaeology is in the converse position.

The apparent conflict between the anthropological and archaeological viewpoints emerges as a question of alternative chronological focus occasioned by the differing time scales forced on the subjects by their data. To this extent there is no incompatibility between the two views, which merely concern different facets of the same processes. In medicine physiological changes can frequently be explained in terms of neurology, endocrinology, microbiology, and the external environment. Each explanation may be sound, and even complete within its own frame of reference. The profound differences result from the scope of enquiry and scale of causation which is sought.

Similarly in behavioural studies, the answer to the question 'why did A do B?' is never simple. The reasons why an individual or a society acts in a particular way or evolves in a particular direction may be couched in terms of choice, genes, or environment with equal justification, depending upon the point on the scale between proximate and ultimate causation that has been chosen as the objective of enquiry. The decision as to the appropriate framework for studies of human behaviour rests overwhelmingly on the time scale involved. Prehistory must perforce deal for the most part in terms of evolutionary forces and of guiding principles which operate in the long term, while sociology and kindred subjects are constrained to concentrate upon the short term and proximate causative factors.

In querying the emphasis placed by some archaeologists upon social factors we are thus not denying these all significance or a place in the scheme of things. They do appear, however, to be of secondary rather than primary importance among the long-term determinants of human behaviour, which are the concern of this book. Social behaviour is sufficiently flexible and volatile to vary widely (in its own terms) but on such a local and short-term scale as to place it effectively beyond the reach of archaeological investigation. Examples of this are innumerable. One has only to consider the worldwide impact of industrial upon pre-industrial economies to be aware of the fragility and – necessarily – adaptability of social institutions. We must also remember that a number of social systems may be developed to accommodate a single range of basic economic and environmental variables. Cole & Wolf (1974) point out that 'One finds an effective use of an entire alpine valley by a communal organization whose members hold all resources in common; by a division of a valley into two or more interdependent communities, each of which exploits some aspect of the environment . . . or by a series of independent households, each holding exclusive rights to a portion of each ecological zone'. They then go on to document such variations in the organisation and behaviour of two villages within 2 km of each other in the same valley. Wilson (1975) has suggested that the widespread social flexibility of man is strongly selected for genetically, a factor reinforced by the existence of multiple adaptive peaks appropriate to a number of different social systems. The point is therefore not to question the existence of such variability, or its importance to certain kinds of study; but rather to suggest that such fineness of detail is in most, if not all cases, inaccessible to archaeology, which may more usefully base its enquiries upon more stable phenomena.

PALAEOECONOMY

What are we left with then? It seems that there may be distinguished certain aspects of prehistoric human behaviour that are susceptible to a scientific approach which consciously searches for regularity, for organising principles; and a category of data that is not amenable to this approach. It is important to make this distinction, and to realise that doing so does not imply a judgement as to the relative value of the two approaches. They are simply 'other' and have different interests and objectives.

It is worth re-emphasising, however, that the nature of archaeological information suits it better to some kinds of enquiry than to others. Archaeology's coarse and indeterminate chronology, and the precarious control it has over the quality and completeness of the information available, severely impede the analysis of short-lived or individual phenomena. On the other hand, the subject is uniquely placed among the disciplines which deal with man to observe and analyse long-term trends and factors in past human behaviour which appear to be of abiding significance.

Among the aspects of past human behaviour which are particularly appropriate for analysis in terms of a long-term, evolutionary approach, economic behaviour clearly has a great importance. The economy is the primary adaptation whereby life is maintained and populations survive and grow. It is thus a biological linchpin exposed to the full force of natural selection, and as such it is to be expected that the impact of economic necessity or advantage will be widespread and profound in human behaviour. Many people, and some modern economists among them, would protest that economic necessity is too rare an occurrence to have acted as a stimulus, or to provide us with an explanation of behaviour. Studied in the short term, economic behaviour frequently appears to operate according to 'satisficer' rather than 'maximiser' models.

Satisficer models were primarily developed by economists and geographers dealing with short-term decision-making in industrialised economies and large business corporations. Starting from the realisation that man has neither the sensory nor analytical equipment to compute the precise 'maximal' or 'optimal' strategy in a given set of circumstances, it was found that individuals tend to settle for a 'satisficer' solution to a problem, one which achieves the necessary goals to a level satisfactory to the person concerned, but not necessarily to a level which could not be improved upon.

This is all undisputed. Everything here again depends on the time scale of study, however. The long-term development of economic behaviour seems to be more profoundly influenced by the exigencies of natural selection than by limitations on the mentality of individuals. A particular beetle or bandicoot doubtless operates suboptimally in many cases; and, who knows, may on occasion act in accordance with satisficer models. This does not release them from the biological Sword of Damocles which threatens that if beetles or bandicoots in general fail to tend towards an optimum subsistence strategy, then they will be supplanted by other beetles, bandicoots, or their competitors.

There is a danger that, in looking for adaptiveness and an approximation to the optimum in human economies, we may be interpreted as relying upon a Panglossian argument that all human relationships with their environment are for the best in this best of all possible worlds. This is far from the case. It will certainly be seen that in our discussion of ethnological and archaeological examples we search for the adaptive significance of economic arrangements. This is by no means the same as suggesting that the fit is always perfect, or that maladaptation may not arise and persist for a while. Among human communities, individual and community choice, periods of unusual affluence when economic factors seem of little direct significance, deliberate pursuit of less than profitable goals, these are all observable in the short individual and historical time scale, although perhaps a little less frequently in subsistence economies than might be supposed. It requires a conscious effort to view human behaviour on a longer, evolutionary time scale, but it is a necessary effort. It is easy to be dazzled by the present-day affluence of industrialised societies, and to be blinded by anthropological and historical examples of uneconomic behaviour. Recognition of these should not, however, prevent our perception that there are observable long-term trends, which override the individual and short-term variability. These trends may be attributed to the operation of evolutionary forces, and *from this particular viewpoint* the short-term deviations may be dismissed as 'noise'. As we shall see, the tendency of human as of animal populations to press upon their available resources – to exceed their optimum population level in Sauvy's (1969) terms – is a powerful incentive in the long term for the development and maintenance of well-adapted productive economies.

THE RÔLE OF POPULATION PRESSURE

The proposition that economic behaviour may be seen in evolutionary terms should perhaps be examined a little more closely. What, for example, is there to prevent or even to discourage a community or population from behaving in an 'uneconomic' fashion, even in the long term? Why should not certain societies maintain unproductive economic systems even on a prehistoric time scale? Our view is that, at least as a general rule, they are forced by internal or external population pressure to adopt more productive patterns of exploitation.

Population pressure is inherent in human, as in other animals' existence. This will be taken by many as a most contentious statement, and indeed much recent anthropological dogma proposes the precise contrary. A conclusion frequently drawn from such studies as Lee's now classic work on the !Kung Bushmen (1968, 1972a) is that most 'hunter–gatherers' have the inherent ability to adjust their population size to a level well below the theoretical carrying capacity of their environment, and to maintain this relationship by a variety of social and other mechanisms. In this way a state of quasi-permanent relative affluence is inferred, and this inference is boldly extended to pre-Neolithic man as a whole. Modern industrial man is seen as having lost this capacity for self-regulation, a process believed by many to have originated with the Neolithic 'food-producing revolution'.

Some have sought to support this proposition by pointing to the existence of comparable mechanisms in many species of animals. It is now well-established that there exists a wide range of physiological and behavioural syndromes in the animal kingdom whose overall effect is to regulate population density. These vary widely in their nature, and not all of them are directly density-dependent; but they do all exercise a degree of control on the animal numbers. This evidence has been coupled by some workers with the ethnographic observations to argue for a major dichotomy between on the one hand pre-Neolithic 'natural' man, who, like other animals, was spared the impact of population pressure by the intervention of these barriers to uninhibited population increase; and on the other hand Neolithic and more especially industrial man, who, having in some mysterious and unexplained way lost these evolutionary responses despite their obvious adaptive value, were exposed to continuing and increasing demographic stress.

Let us briefly examine the position. As we have said, there is a growing body of evidence and an increasing degree of acceptance that animal populations are regulated in their numbers by a wide variety of mechanisms. Most workers are agreed that food supply is the overriding ultimate limiting factor, although simple 'Malthusian' control may occur rather infrequently. The proximate cause is often more subtle and complex, operating in such a way that the animal population may be viewed as self-regulating. One authority has even seen the need to control population size as the primary factor giving rise to social behaviour in animals (Wynne-Edwards 1962). Some have taken this to mean that population pressure does not normally occur in animals, as the inhibitory mechanisms to population growth are initiated at levels well below the theoretical carrying capacity, and the population is therefore perpetually buffered against attaining levels where pressure will be experienced.

A number of considerations suggest an alternative view. The first is a general point that may usefully be illustrated by reference to an analogy suggested by the use of the term population *pressure*. Gases are frequently considered as exerting or being at certain pressures, a characteristic which is relevant whether or not the pressure is sufficient to burst the container or to liquefy the gas. Similarly, population pressure need not necessarily predicate far-reaching or cataclysmic reactions in animal populations. From this point of view we may see the very ubiquity and significance of regulatory mechanisms as evidence of the widespread existence of population pressure, rather than as indications that such pressure rarely occurs. This is not simply a semantic device for denying the obvious. Upon close examination it is hard to see the justice of an argument which infers directly from the existence of self-regulatory demographic responses in animals to an absence of any population pressure. How far such a suggestion is from Wynne-Edwards' thesis can be seen from his discussion of periodic population eruptions, such as those studied so extensively in certain Arctic species. Here, emigration is specifically invoked as a 'means of rapidly reducing population density in any area where the optimum has been exceeded'.

This general point aside, other evidence suggests that population pressure must be considered an important potential causative agent in animal behaviour. Indeed, as has been extensively documented by Lack (1954), there are numerous instances of food shortage acting as a limiting factor on animal populations. Lack discusses examples from birds, mammals, fish, and insects. It is perhaps easy to get an impression, in many cases, of a comfortable gap between animal populations and the carrying capacities of their environments. A number of points must be taken into account, however. Seasonal and annual variations in available resources need to be considered. Pressure of population on resources is frequently only experienced at one or two seasons of the year, as in winter, and during the period when the young must be fed. Such pressure may only become acute in particularly poor years, when resources are less abundant than usual. Thus periods of severe stress will be intermittent, and irregular, even though they may occur quite frequently enough to be of great evolutionary significance. Some consideration also needs to be given to the recognition of the relevant factor in the environment. As a broad generalisation, where food is limiting, populations will be related to the abundance of *the least available necessity at the worst time of the year*. It is no use measuring one staple resource and expecting that a close relationship between this and population levels will necessarily emerge.

To some extent the efficiency of exploitation in terms of energetics is also a consideration. A corollary of the concept of an optimum population level is that increased population will automatically result in a fall in economic return per unit of labour input: the 'law of diminishing returns'. Either standards of living will decline, or individuals must work harder to maintain the same level. For this reason considerable pressure can in some circumstances be experienced by an exploiting population long before deleterious effects are necessarily apparent in the resource population. Thus those populations of wolves that subsist mainly upon moose, caribou, or Dall sheep are thought to be limited primarily by the difficulty of catching their prey. Higher wolf populations would be under great population pressure because they would run out of prey they were physically able to catch. They would have to subsist on less food, or devise ways of catching fitter prey, or reduce their own numbers. Nevertheless it is most unlikely that a higher rate of predation, if this were the eventuality, would seriously jeopardise the prey populations, which could adjust to the additional burden of exploitation by an increased rate of reproduction, by maintaining slightly lower population levels, or by surrendering fewer individuals to other causes of mortality.

1. PHILOSOPHY AND BASIC PRINCIPLES

Precisely the same considerations are relevant in the case of human populations. The !Kung Bushmen provide a useful example, both because they have been studied in great detail for a number of years and because extensive use has been made of the resulting data by anthropologists and archaeologists. A number of features of !Kung life led to most interesting conclusions regarding the relationship of their population to its available food resources. Lee (1968, 1972a, 1976) was able to show that, contrary to much established anthropological doctrine, this particular group of 'hunter–gatherers' showed many signs of relative subsistence affluence. Life expectancy was fairly high; infanticide occurred but was not common, while senilicide was very rare. Clinical malnutrition was rare or absent. Food was obtained with remarkably little expenditure of effort, at least in terms of man-hours. Considerable surpluses of the staple mongongo nut were observed to remain unexploited.

This evidence has been interpreted by Lee and others in a number of ways. Two propositions of particular importance have emerged, the two seeming superficially to be very similar, but in fact carrying crucially different implications. The first proposition is that hunter–gatherer populations are characteristically maintained at a level below that which would start to deplete the food supply. This seems to be a perfectly acceptable inference; and indeed, when one considers the general picture, it must be so. If population levels, and thus intensity of exploitation, were as a general rule so high as to diminish the available food supply, then a very few seasons would lead to the classic Lotka–Volterra predator–prey oscillation, with the attendant likelihood of extermination of the predator – man, in this case. Such a crude pattern must have been as rare an occurrence in man as it seems to be for other animals. Human economies must, like other natural exploitation systems, have as a rule been *efficient* in Wilkinson's (1975) terms; that is to say, they will have been regulated so as to ensure sustained yields in the long term.

The second proposition takes the form of an apparently acceptable minor extension of the first. It is argued that 'since food supply appears to be abundant in modern hunters' and that 'since it appears that some observed hunter population densities have become stabilized at a mere fraction of the numbers that could be supported by the food supply' (Lee, 1972b), food supply is not the limiting factor involved, which must thus be sought elsewhere. Various social mechanisms, such as the wide spacing of births, are commonly proposed as the agents involved.

It may be the case that the apparent superabundance of mongongo nuts indicates a surplus of food to !Kung Bushman requirements, although Lee's data are insufficient, in time depth at least, to demonstrate this satisfactorily. As was mentioned above, however, it is of critical importance to take into account fluctuations in the level of resources from season to season, year to year, and decade to decade. Lee himself (1976) obviously realises this:

a hunter–gatherer group may be able to satisfy subsistence requirements within 100 km^2 for four years out of five but it will still go out of business unless it has access to a much larger area during the fifth year. And in order to ride out environmental fluctuation over the course of 50, 100 or 200 years, the area to which the group must maintain access must be even larger. . . . However, little of this long-term perspective is visible to the observer.

The point is, of course, that one simply cannot make a reasonable assessment of population–resource relationships without taking this long-term perspective into account.

In fact, examined closely, much of Lee's own evidence and that of others working on the Bushmen seems to indicate a considerably greater degree of population pressure on food resources than is commonly supposed. The misapprehension seems to have arisen as a result of the failure to take sufficient account of conditions at the lean period of the year and to isolate the true limiting factor involved – which is clearly *not* the availability of the mongongo nut. In a semi-desert area such as the Kalahari it seems likely that water will be one of the most important resources, and indeed Yellen & Lee (1976) state that the 'scarcity of permanent water is the most crucial limiting factor with which the !Kung must contend'. In other, drier parts of the Kalahari, water is even more stringently limiting. Silberbauer (1972) found that the G/Wi Bushmen had surface water available for only six or eight weeks of the year, having to rely on vegetable sources of fluid for the rest of the year. Not only is water shortage itself limiting; it has an important effect upon the availability of food. The dry, lean season of the year lasts for about three months, from August to October. By the end of this period 'The areas within easy walking distance of the waterholes become depleted of choice foods, and diet consists largely of roots, edible gum, and whatever less desirable foods may be found' (Yellen & Lee 1976). Detailed medical examination (Truswell & Hansen 1976) seems to show that, although clinical malnutrition is a rarity among the !Kung Bushmen, a general level of undernourishment is the norm. The people are all thin, and are shorter than their genetic potential would almost certainly allow. Because 'In these lean months, the foods eaten are mostly roots and bulbs, which would be expected generally to contain much water but to have low caloric density', these authors conclude that 'the only nutritional weakness . . . is a shortage of energy (calories) usually in the dry spring season'.

These points illustrate the importance of a careful consideration of seasonal and annual variation, and the other factors involved. It is especially noteworthy that the water shortage acts in two important ways in the case of the Bushmen. Not only is it clearly a limiting factor itself, particularly in years of drought when a number of bands have to share the same waterhole. Just as important, if less obvious, is its effect in restricting the possible range of dry season exploitation to a day's walking distance (round trip) around the few permanent waterholes. During the lean period of the year food supplies beyond this radius are inaccessible, and thus no matter how rich they may be they are irrelevant to the question of the relationship between population and resources.

The ethnographic record supplies many similar instances of populations relatively closely adjusted to the available food resources. Baumhoff (1963) describes such a case from California. Damas (1972) says that 'Famine was not uncommon in the aboriginal period' among the Copper Eskimo, and there was a high incidence of female infanticide. Starvation was widespread among the Inuit Eskimo in the winter of 1957–8 (Hoffman 1976). 'Securing food is a constant problem and a never-ending concern' among the Mistassini Cree, and 'times of starvation are vividly remembered' (Rogers 1972). The Guayaki, according to Clastres (1972), undergo food shortage in their winter lean season. The importance of taking annual variations into account is evident from Gardner's (1972) discussion of the Paliyans. 'Their natural environment in a good year is bounteous far beyond human need . . . While this allows them a wide margin of safety in times of distress, conditions do sometimes become so difficult that inter-regional migrations are necessary.' Carneiro's (1961) work on the Kuikuru is frequently quoted as supporting the suggestion of a general absence of serious population pressure under aboriginal conditions. Here, as with the !Kung, it is questionable whether a sufficiently detailed analysis is available to substantiate the claim. The data certainly seem to support the view that considerably more manioc could be grown, and that thus many more calories could be extracted from the environment. Manioc, however, like most root crops, is so poor in protein as to be a negligible source of this

most essential nutrient. It therefore seems at least possible that the limiting factor involved is availability of protein, which seems to come mainly from fish. This view is certainly suggested by Lathrap's (1968) review of the evidence. Barth (1960) notes that in southern Persia 'the pastures of the whole of Fars are utilised nearly to their total carrying capacity'. Elsewhere in Iran, Salzman (1972) describes a situation in which pressure of population on resources is such that the sale of labour in towns and the cultivation of marginal land are necessary to maintain the mobile pastoral economy through the lean period of the year.

This list could doubtless be expanded endlessly; many of the examples quoted above came from a single publication. On the other hand, there is also a large number of cases in the literature where it is claimed that there is no evidence for a high degree of population pressure on resources. This apparent contradiction illustrates the limitation of ethnographic evidence for our purposes. From the point of view of archaeology's concern with the long term, the time depth of most ethnographic studies is woefully inadequate. For this reason we must depend primarily upon theoretical arguments, although it does also seem that there is considerable ethnographic evidence in support of our view that human populations, like those of other animals, frequently exert considerable pressure upon their food resources.

The significant question, as far as studies of man are concerned, thus emerges not as 'why do human populations experience population pressure, while other organisms do not?' but 'why are many modern human populations apparently less sensitive to the lower levels of pressure than many animal populations, thus critically exceeding the optimum population–resource relationship with such dramatic short-term results?' It seems that an important distinction needs to be made between on the one hand *recurrent (or, on an archaeological time scale, sustained) population pressure*, which occurs so frequently in nature as to be treated as a general rule; and on the other hand, *sustained population increase*, which occurs in rather more specialised circumstances. Human development provides many striking examples of this latter phenomenon.

It must at once be admitted that in the present state of knowledge we can offer little beyond a brief and generalised discussion of the possible reason for this state of affairs. One difference between man and other organisms is the degree to which his subsistence is technologically oriented. An obvious consequence of a technologically rather than a physiologically based economy is the capacity for much greater rates of change and increases in productivity. One should perhaps point out here that radical changes in animal subsistence behaviour, sometimes permitting far higher populations to be maintained, are by no means unknown. The successful exploitation of man-made habitats; the colonisation of inland ecological niches by some species of seagulls; the dramatic expansion in the range of the fulmar (*Fulmarus glacialis*) in Atlantic Europe; these provide well-known instances of successful opportunistic changes in animal behaviour leading to higher overall population levels. Man stands out, however, both by reason of his sustained long-term population increase, and by the degree to which he has been able to raise his economic productivity, and thus his population, per unit area. It is hard to see how this phenomenon can be dissociated from man's technological development, the means whereby this increased productivity has been achieved, and the ever-increasing population levels sustained.

It cannot be overstressed that we do not feel there to be any cogent evidence for the separation of non-agricultural from agricultural and industrial man in these matters. Evidently the rate of technological progress, as the rate of population increase, has accelerated with time, but there seems no reason to suggest that essentially different forces or balances come into being with the development of modern economic systems. Evidence for rising populations from the Neolithic onwards is widespread, if patchy. Some data will be discussed in great detail later in this volume. Evidence from the earlier periods is inevitably more scanty and harder to interpret, but certainly the number of occupation sites known per unit area shows a distinct tendency to increase with time. We must, furthermore, take into account man's dramatic ecological and geographical diversification. From his tropical savannah origins he has successfully colonised an impressive number of land masses and environments, extending his range by a factor of tens if not hundreds. Occasionally more revealing evidence emerges. Wendorf's (1968) excavation of a Late Pleistocene cemetery in Nubia in which about half the bodies showed signs of a violent death is extremely suggestive of warfare. Other hypotheses are of course possible, but perhaps less likely. As Wendorf himself points out, accepting the evidence at face value, localised extremes of population pressure provide a reasonable – in our view the most plausible – explanation.

Indeed, the widespread historical evidence of endemic warfare in parts of North America, both among 'hunters and gatherers' and among agriculturalists,

ought to make us suspicious of any generalised proposition concerning the absence of population pressure or stress at certain levels of economic development. Where the evidence exists, the warfare is as a general rule specifically for economic motives. Hickerson (1965) says that in the Upper Mississippi valley in the eighteenth and nineteenth centuries 'Warfare was a function of competition over game', and was in fact one of the mechanisms whereby the local human populations adjusted to the available resources. After only three years of enforced truce between the Sioux and the Chippewa famine became widespread, resulting eventually in a return to warfare. Larson (1972) has shown that in the southeastern United States 'suitable agricultural lands were a critical resource in some areas . . . during the Mississippi period, constituting a causal factor and the primary objective of the apparently endemic warfare in the area'. There is confirmatory evidence from other areas and time periods. Browman (1976) has argued convincingly that the Wari imperial expansion in the Junin department of Peru, *c* A.D. 400–500, and the economic change from llama pastoralism to potato agriculture which accompanied it, were substantially caused by demographic pressure. Reichel-Dolmatoff (1961) showed that under aboriginal conditions in Colombia populations were so closely adjusted to the available resources that 'the 80-inch isohyet [which divided the zone of single-maize cropping from that of multi-annual cropping] was practically a military frontier'. Warfare was one of the primary mechanisms of population regulation, and 'In many sub-Andean chiefdoms cannibalism was simply part of the food quest'. The intra- and intertribal warfare widespread historically in parts of New Guinea has been explained in terms of competition for land (Brookfield & Brown 1963). Vayda (1961) has suggested that there is generally a sound ecological function for warfare among swidden agriculturalists. Although in individual cases other explanations may be appropriate, it is surely reasonable to view such warfare as an extreme form of intraspecific competition, a phenomenon which seems hardly likely to arise in the absence of considerable and widespread population pressure.

We should similarly reject any too easy assumption that twentieth-century man has lost the capacity to regulate his populations by means of inherent biological mechanisms. The growing worldwide interest in artificial means of birth control and the rise of such groups as the Zero Population Growth movement might be viewed as expressions of these forces. In Formosa, Hong Kong, and Singapore the birth rate dropped significantly and steadily in the early nineteen sixties. In Western Europe overall rates of population increase are below one per cent per annum in most countries, while there is a negative rate of natural increase in some.

It is understandable that attention tends to be focused upon the evident hardship caused by overpopulation in many parts of the world. Starvation is shocking in itself, and modern techniques of mass communication bring home the reality more vividly than ever before. The strength of this emotional impact does not justify the assumption that this is simply a recent phenomenon, however. Not only is there good evidence for episodes of destructively high population pressure at other periods and in other circumstances; it is moreover only an understandable anthropocentrism which makes us more aware of human than of other animals' demographic disasters. The present extreme levels of population pressure in many 'underdeveloped countries' are largely if not wholly due to the explosive effect of medical advance. Technological, demographic, and resource factors vary at differing rates. As Wrigley (1967) has put it 'Populations have . . . a life of their own'. The impact of the demographic changes wrought by medical improvements will be delayed, but inexorable. There is no guarantee that resource levels or economic organisation will develop at the same pace to accommodate the population changes. We are witnessing today the inevitable but (in archaeological and evolutionary terms) short-term consequences of such an imbalance between the rates of demographic and economic development. In due course new unstable equilibria will develop, and a different relationship between population and resources will be established.

It seems then that both from a theoretical and a practical viewpoint we may assume that population pressure has been a constantly repeated factor in human development, and that periods of significant stress upon resources will have been a recurrent feature. Given that there will have been homeostatic plateaux, maintained by a number of different regulatory mechanisms, the long archaeological time scale encourages us to view the long-term trend to population increase as the norm, the focus of attention. Here we find ourselves in agreement with Birdsell (1968) that 'For most Pleistocene situations, the population density should be considered to approximate that of operational saturation' and that 'The intrinsic rate of increase in man is sufficiently high to assure that depleted numbers would be completely restored within a few decades. In Pleistocene time perspectives, the recovery was instantaneous.'

Of course, it is true that in some circumstances a particular population will be protected from significant periods of stress for a considerable time. Populations colonising hitherto unexploited environments such as islands; or in the case of man, the recolonisation of whole continents by technologically advanced populations; or the raising of the carrying capacity by a sudden technological or economic advance; these are typical examples. Characteristically in these cases population levels rise extremely rapidly, leading relatively quickly on a prehistoric time scale to a new plateau, in which situation periodic episodes of stress are again inherent. There are many historical instances of this. The population of the United States of America doubled (partly through immigration) between 1860 and 1890. Following the introduction of the potato to Ireland in the late sixteenth century the population rose from about one million to four millions in 1790, and eight millions in 1845. After the notorious potato famines of the eighteen forties the population rapidly declined again, to about two million.

As far as our consideration of palaeoeconomy is concerned, the main importance of population pressure as a constant factor is that it will have conferred a substantial selective advantage upon those communities with more rather than less productive economies. The economy is in this sense in an identical position to other behavioural or physiological traits. These are favoured if they enhance evolutionary fitness. An increase in productivity generally confers an obvious advantage in individual and population fitness in that it permits higher population levels and thus increased representation of the genotype which gave rise to the behavioural change. In economic development, as in so many aspects of human evolution, the genetic changes are ostensibly swamped by the rapid and dramatic changes at the cultural and behavioural levels. The degree to which these latter are superficial effects of more fundamental evolutionary processes or represent the workings of an autonomous process of 'cultural evolution' is an unresolved and much-disputed issue. In either case the selective value of economic fitness is evident, and the development of economies may thus be expected to be subject to evolutionary processes.

On an archaeological time scale this evolutionary pressure encouraging the success of increasingly productive economies may be seen as an important force tending to produce observable regularity. As we have pointed out, there will certainly have been occasions in the past when circumstances protected particular populations and communities from this force, for a time. In some cases the barriers to significant economic development will have resulted in long periods of relative stability. The fate of, for instance, the indigenous peoples of the Americas, both in the recent historical past and today, provides an eloquent if dispiriting example of the outcome of such episodes.

It follows from the foregoing discussion that effective studies of prehistoric economies must recognise and deal with a number of key variables. Crucial among these are an assessment of the available resources, of the technology whereby the resources were exploited, and of the exploiting population and its distribution. Archaeology can study each of these; in an unsatisfactory and uneven way, perhaps, but sufficiently well nevertheless for the analysis of palaeoeconomies to be a reasonable goal. It is true that there are limits to the precision with which one can make these assessments. The importance of certain resources may be overemphasised, while others of equal importance may have left little trace. Technological capability may frequently have been considerably greater than the surviving evidence implies. Estimates of population levels in particular are extremely difficult to arrive at and are virtually unverifiable when they are achieved. On the other hand, the assessment of past resources is in essence no more difficult than many other palaeoecological studies, and may in practice be easier in many instances; for archaeology has the valuable capacity to analyse both site contents and off-site data, the one providing a measure of check upon the other. Similarly, the artefactual contents of sites provide some basic technological information, and site location patterns can on occasion provide further clues as to exploitative capacity. While population estimates expressed in absolute numbers must be treated with extreme caution, careful use of the sizes and distribution of sites, combined with estimates of the available resources, can provide serviceable *relative* estimates of population levels as between area and area, or one period and another.

We do not feel that we should have done justice to our views if we left this general philosophical statement of objectives and principles without a comment on the relationship between archaeology and 'the real world' of today. We do not take it as axiomatic that all spheres of endeavour must necessarily have a practical justification. Nevertheless, we believe that the study of archaeology has great potential significance for man, beyond its undoubted educational and recreational value. This case should be stated, albeit briefly.

One of the more appreciative reviewers of *Palaeoeconomy* pointed out that the thesis that popula-

tion pressure was a constant, and overpopulation a recurrent, factor in human development has implications for the way in which we approach these matters today. Many, if not all, the world's major political preoccupations can be viewed as being mostly concerned with economics, or at least as having a primary economic element. Even ostensibly ideological concerns are, characteristically, so intimately bound up with economic issues for it to be difficult to perceive where idealism ends and self-interest begins. The relationship of technological development to the 'energy crisis', of overseas aid to overpopulation in 'underdeveloped countries', of harvesting policies to biological resources; these are quite clearly questions of the utmost importance for modern man. A lesson which can be drawn from the study of prehistory is that wars, starvation, exploitation and conservation are not simply moral, ethical, or political issues. There is an important, indeed a primary biological component to these phenomena, *without recognition of which no really effective consideration of them can be made.*

No enlightened modern government would proceed on many of its policy deliberations without consulting a battery of sociologists, economists, and geographers, even if their recommendations are then systematically ignored. The relationship of population density and distribution to social (and anti-social) behaviour is an obvious example of such a question, having been much in the news in industrialised countries in the last few decades. Such consultation is fitting and necessary, indeed. But, as we have argued, many of the crucial factors involved are manifestly operating on a time scale which these disciplines cannot deal with effectively. There are biological and evolutionary forces at work that require a longer span and broader canvas for their appreciation.

We are not sufficiently arrogant to suggest that archaeology is the only discipline that can convey this message; or to believe that our hypothetical reconstructions of Holocene conditions are likely to have any perceptible impact upon today's political decisions. On the other hand, the possible demonstration that there are laws which govern human behaviour in the long term ought to have an effect on the way in which we view our behaviour today, and hence upon our approach to today's provisions for the future. We might perhaps follow Carr (1961) in paraphrasing Sir Charles Snow, and say that good prehistorians have the future in their bones.

We have now reached the point, as we see it, of having justified our choice of goals. These, and the techniques whereby they may be pursued, must now be examined a little more closely. We have identified the interrelationship between population, resources, and technology as having a critical importance. While the resources can in theory be viewed as finite, and setting a ceiling on population, it is the level of technology that determines what proportion of the theoretical resource total can be exploited; and both technological and demographic factors affect the point at which exploitation of a particular resource becomes marginal or unprofitable (be this in terms of commerce or energetics). There is in many cases a reciprocal relationship between population levels and economic systems, such that while a high population density may require intensive and highly productive patterns of exploitation, it is also true to say that these systems frequently can only come into being and be maintained by the high population levels. Once a productive, labour-intensive system exists, there are considerable pressures which tend to maintain the level of output in the short run, quite apart from the tendency discussed above for there to be a long-term trend towards systems of yet higher extractive potential, serving yet higher populations. Failure to maintain the productivity of a subsistence economy at a level sufficient to satisfy the existing population would obviously result in short-term discomfort at best, or if continued in the long term, would necessarily lead to major readjustments in the economic system, population levels, or both.

RESOURCES

It is necessary to make an initial distinction between dietary and non-dietary resources. As this book is centred on the development of agriculture we shall obviously be concerned primarily with the former, although the latter do have significance.

Dietary resources

There is a close relationship between the subsistence economy – those activities surrounding the acquisition of food – and factors of diet and nutrition. The subsistence economy provides the means whereby man acquires the energy and nutrients he needs to live and reproduce, and therefore lies at the very core of survival and evolutionary performance. It is evident that in the long run those animal populations which did not choose or have accessible appropriate foods would have become extinct. Paradoxically, the fact that man, like all animals, must eat to live is so self-evident that food production and diet are often taken for granted in

anthropological studies. For instance, in such books as *Themes in Economic Anthropology* (Firth 1967) the emphasis is on the social and distributive aspects of non-industrial economies, rather than on production and subsistence. The fact that a community exists to be studied at all must mean that it can procure enough of the right sorts of food to maintain its members. Economies which as a rule function efficiently and effectively do not generally attract much anthropological or sociological attention. Thus the way in which long-term, stable systems have evolved is neglected. There are of course exceptions to this generalisation, but, by and large, inferences about prehistoric diet and dietary resources must be based on other types of information.

The most direct source of data about prehistoric dietary resources is the food remains from archaeological sites themselves. In the past such material was collected only haphazardly, but now that that state of affairs is greatly improved, the difficulties of interpretation have become apparent. In particular, the differential preservation and collection of plant and animal remains has fostered the development of a meat *vs* vegetable dichotomy. Clarke's (1976) 'Mesoliths' feast sumptuously on roots, shoots, and pine nuts, while Higgs' transhumant herders roast their red deer or sheep, and millennia later Harris' Aztecs (Harris, M. 1979) eke out their insufficient cereal diet with cannibalism while Lee's (1968) Bushmen stuff themselves with mongongo nuts. Each of these evangelists believes that his particular examples have a broader relevance. It seems unlikely, however, that the organic material alone from sites can ever be interpreted with the precision required to tell us even in the broadest terms how many calories, grams of protein, vitamins, and minerals were consumed by each person per day and what the dietary source of those nutrients was; and in many cases it seems insufficient in itself to allow us to assess the staple food sources.

The case ought to be at least partly clarified by the findings of nutritional science: can man live on roots, shoots, and pine nuts, and especially, can he live for generations on those staples? Unfortunately there is no clear answer from the nutritionists. It is relatively easy to study species with a very narrow range of food that is acceptable to them. Some herbivores will eat only leaves from one or two species of tree; some carnivores exploit only one or two species of animal; many parasites are host-specific. The reasons for these preferences are somewhat obscure and are almost certainly not based upon nutritional requirements alone. Interspecific competition is one obvious additional factor. All mammals require similar nutrients in roughly the same

1. PHILOSOPHY AND BASIC PRINCIPLES

Table 1. Energy and protein requirements of moderately active adult males and females, as assessed by various authorities

	Energy (kcal)				Protein (g)			
	male	female	pregnant	lactating	male	female	pregnant	lactating
FAO[a]	3000	2200	2480	2750	37	29	38	46
United Kingdom[b]	3500	2200	–	–	75	55	–	–
Holland[e]	3000	2400	2700	3100	70	60	80	100
Norway[e]	3400	2500	2900	3500	70	60	85	100
Africa[c]	2820	–	–	–	–	–	–	–
South Africa[e]	3000	2300	2600	–	65	55	80	80
Canadian Council on Nutrition[b]	3582	2390	–	–	47	40	–	–
Food and Nutrition Board, National Research Council, U.S.A.[d]	2900	2100	2300	3100	70	58	78	98
Central America[e]	2700	2000	2500	3000	55	50	75	90
India[e]	2800	2300	2300	2700	55	45	100	110
Japan[e]	3000	2400	2700	3000	70	60	90	95
Australia[e]	2700	2300	2000	2600	37[f]	27[f]	30[f]	42[f]

[a] Passmore *et al.* (1974).
[b] Robson *et al.* (1972).
[c] Clark, C. & Haswell (1967).
[d] Bowes & Church (1966).
[e] Young (1964).
[f] Subject to increment in relation to quality of protein in diet.

proportions, but energy distribution and recycling in the ecosystem takes place within a framework of trophic levels which governs the rate of energy flow through the system and the magnitude of the biomass at different levels. To suggest that the world population of lions could be increased by feeding them grass not only violates the taste sensibilities and digestive capabilities of lions, but attempts to insert them at a trophic level already occupied by cattle, deer, antelopes, and so on, while removing them from a trophic level that helps to regulate the populations of those species.

Man (along with pigs and rats), however, is dietarily an omnivore; he finds a wide range of substances both palatable and nutritionally satisfactory. Thus the computation of human nutritional requirements is immensely complicated. It becomes yet more so when subjected to the question of what is meant by 'requirements'. Is one defining the minimum diet essential to keep people alive; or a diet that will keep them free from clinically diagnosable malnutrition; or a diet which will allow them to cope with rare periods of severe stress; or one which will permit the realisation of their full genetic potential? Ideally, from the point of view of the long-term survival of the species, the dietary requirements should be defined in terms of breeding capability and evolutionary success. It must at

once be admitted that we are in no position to attempt such a definition. The practical barriers preventing the assessment of long-term dietary needs of humans are at the moment insurmountable, and it is the absence of suitable experimental evidence which lies at the root of much nutritional controversy.

Table 1 shows some of the resulting variety in recommendations. Clark, C. & Haswell (1967) have discussed some of the reasons for discrepant figures for energy requirements, and it would probably be fair to say that if one takes into account individual and geographical variations in age, body weight, level of activity and climate, calorific requirements can be measured reasonably accurately and agreed upon nowadays. The actual amount of protein utilised by the human body can also be measured, but the uncertainty about optimal levels of protein intake is illustrated by the wildly different recommendations. The value and palatability of major groups of food as suppliers of protein and other nutrients is also problematic, as the following series of quotations from Davidson, Passmore & Brock (1972) illustrates:

On cereals: 'To make a balanced diet, cereals should be supplemented by animal proteins, minerals and vitamins A and C.'

Table 2. Nutrients contained in groups of foodstuffs (per 100 g)[a]

	Energy (kcal)	Protein (g)	Fat (g)	Carbohydrate (g)	Trp / Pha	Leu / Isl	Lys / Val	Met / Thr	thiamine	niacin	A	riboflavin	ascorbic acid	D	B12	Ca	Fe
LOW ENERGY																	
leafy vegetables	≤50[b]	≤4[c]	≤1	<10	<0.1 / 0.1–0.2	0.1–0.2 / 0.1–0.2	0.1–0.2 / 0.1–0.2	<0.1 / 0.1–0.2			✓	✓	✓				✓
shellfish	50–81	6–12.8	1.2–1.4	3.4–3.7	no data	no data	no data	no data		✓					✓	✓	✓
fruits	≤85	<2	<1	<20	<0.1 / <0.1	<0.1 / <0.1	≤0.1 / <0.1	<0.1 / <0.1					✓				✓
fish (lean)	50–96	7.5–19.2	0.4–3.9	0	<0.2 / 0.7	1.3–1.4 / 0.9	1.5–1.6 / 0.9–1.0	0.5 / 0.8	✓	✓				✓	✓	✓	✓
milk	65–93	1.8–5.2	1.4–6.2	4.0–6.7	<0.1 / 0.2	0.4 / 0.2	0.3 / 0.3	<0.1 / 0.2	✓		✓	✓			✓	✓	
MEDIUM ENERGY																	
roots and tubers	75–125	≤2	<1	18–30	<0.1 / <0.1	≤0.1 / <0.1	≤0.1 / <0.1	<0.1 / 0.1	✓				✓				✓
pulses (cooked)	90–130	6.7–11.0	0.5–5.7	10–24	0.2–0.5 / 0.2–0.5	0.4–0.8 / 0.3–0.6	0.3–0.6 / 0.3–0.7	0.1–0.4 / 0.2–0.5	✓	✓		✓				✓
(dry)	330–339	21.4–34.9	1.0–18.1	35–62	1.1–1.8 /	1.8–2.9 / 1.3–2.0	1.5–2.4 / 1.3–2.0	0.9–1.5 / 0.9–1.5	✓	✓						✓	✓
eggs	158	12.8	11.5	<1	0.2 / 0.8	1.1 / 0.9	0.8 / 1.0	0.4 / 0.6			✓	✓		✓	✓	✓	✓
meat (lean)	122–200	20–22	2.5–12	0	0.3 / 0.8–1.5	1.5–1.9 / 1.5–1.8	1.5–1.8 / 1.0–1.5	0.4–0.5 / 0.9–1.5	✓	✓		✓			✓		✓
fish (fat)	136–203	18.7–22.0	6–12.3	0	0.2 / 0.6–0.8	1.3–1.7 / 0.9–1.1	1.5–2.0 / 0.9–1.2	0.5–0.7 / 0.8–1.0	✓	✓	✓			✓	✓	✓	✓
HIGH ENERGY																	
exceptional fruits[d]	120–335	<2	<1–26	3–73	<0.1 / <0.1	<0.1 / <0.1	<0.1 / <0.1	<0.1 / <0.1				no data					
meat (medium-fat)	220–378	16–28	11–32	0	0.3–0.5 / 0.6–1.6	1.2–3.2 / 0.8–2.0	1.4–3.4 / 0.8–2.2	0.4–1.0 / 0.7–1.7	✓	✓					✓		✓
sugar/honey	300	<1	0	80	0 / 0	0 / 0	0 / 0	0 / 0									
cereals[e]	319–365	6.3–16.3	0.5–7.5	18–80	0.1–0.2 / 0.3–0.8	0.5–1.1 / 0.3–0.7	0.2–0.7 / 0.4–0.8	0.1–0.3 / 0.2–0.6	✓	✓		✓					✓
nuts[f]	560–696	9.4–19	45–75	11–27	<0.2 / 0.5–1.1	0.7–0.9 / 0.8–1.1	0.4–0.6 / 0.8–1.1	0.1–0.3 / 0.3–0.6	✓	✓		✓			✓	✓	✓

Amino acids (g). Vitamins. Minerals.

[a] References: Documenta Geigy 1962, Bowes & Church 1966.
[b] Except artichokes = 51.
[c] Except brussel sprouts = 4.7.
[d] Olives, dates, plantain, avocados, tamarind.
[e] Except fresh maize: energy = 92, protein = 3.2.
[f] Except chestnuts: energy = 213, protein = 3.4.

15

1. PHILOSOPHY AND BASIC PRINCIPLES

On pulses: 'A combination of pulse and cereal proteins may have a nutritive value as good as animal proteins.'

On meat: 'Protein of animal origin is not essential for man . . . Yet as soon as the income of a family or community rises, there is nearly always an increase in the amount of meat they consume.'

On fish: They are a good source of high quality protein and energy. 'Yet, although many fish are delicious, on the whole, fish are less tasty than meat, and a fish diet tends to be montonous.'

On groundnuts: 'As most children know, peanuts are good to eat, but few would care to eat a lot of them.'

On nuts: 'We know of no record of any people who regularly consumed large quantities of nuts, except for some Bushmen in Botswana . . . Most nuts have a high content of fat and protein, but as they are eaten in such small amounts their nutritive value is generally insignificant . . .'

On some foods they are in no doubt:

On vegetables: '. . . man should eat vegetables because he likes them; vegetables may also be good for him . . ., but this should be a secondary consideration.'

On fruits: 'The only essential nutrient in which fruits are rich is ascorbic acid.'

While recognising the complications and uncertainties within nutritional science itself, there are nevertheless some useful generalisations that can be made. Table 2 summarises the nutritive value of major groups of food. Looking at that table, one can say with some confidence that since it takes 2–3 kg of leafy vegetables to supply even 1000 kcal of energy, it is impossible for man, given the size of his stomach, to meet his daily energy requirements with green vegetables. On the other hand, some exceptional fruits, medium-fat meat, sugars, cereals, and nuts are excellent sources of energy, and roots and tubers, pulses, eggs, lean meat, and fat fish are moderately good. Of these, several are also good sources of protein: pulses, eggs, lean meat, fat fish, medium-fat meat, cereals, and nuts. Milk appears to be poor in calories and protein, but since it is usually consumed in larger quantities than 100 g and is readily available to infants, its contribution to human diets is greater than the figures indicate.

Table 3. Minimal daily protein requirement from foods with different proportions of amino acids[a]

Source	Amount of protein (g)
egg	20.0
milk	22.4
soya flour	23.4
mixed food (meat providing one-third nitrogen)	25.4
mixed plant	31.0
white wheat flour	38.7

[a] Reference: Hegsted 1964.

Protein is not, of course, a single uniform substance; it is composed of amino acids which combine in various numbers and proportions to form different proteins. There are eight amino acids which the adult human body cannot manufacture in sufficient quantity and which it must secure in the correct proportions from food in order to make human protein. There is a ninth which is probably essential for children. Cannibalism would presumably provide the ideal proportions of amino acids. Failing such a diet, eggs provide the next best array of amino acids, meat (including fish) and milk products next, cereals, legumes, and nuts next, with the remainder of the plant kingdom containing proportions and quantities of amino acids that differ so greatly from those required by the human body as to be of little or no use in fulfilling human protein needs.

Of the high-protein foods, it cannot be disputed that protein from animal sources provides more of the essential amino acids in more appropriate proportions than does protein from any single plant source. The *minimal* daily protein requirements (in order to maintain nitrogen balance) can be provided by different amounts of protein depending on its source (Table 3). What can be questioned is whether these differences are great enough to be of practical significance. When adequate calories are available from a varied diet, then considerably more than minimal protein requirements are automatically provided. Thus a large proportion of the world population gets its complement of amino acids primarily from a combination of cereals (poor in lysine) and pulses (poor in methionine). However, when food is in short supply, or when most of the dietary energy comes from low-protein foods, then small amounts of meat and other animal products will be more efficacious in correcting the imbalance than a similar quantity of plant protein. In the long term this could give selective advantage to those populations

16

with access even to small amounts of animal protein. Rappaport (1968) demonstrated the critical importance of small amounts of animal protein in a tuber-based economy in Melanesia. We must remember, furthermore, that the success of a species depends upon its breeding success and therefore upon the well-being of its breeding population. Thus the ability of an economy to supply the more demanding requirements of children and pregnant and lactating women is of greater significance than its success at fulfilling the average needs of the over-forties.

In order to assess the importance of foods which are good suppliers of vitamins and minerals, a brief consideration is needed of the concept of staple foodstuffs as opposed to casual or occasional foods. As was stated above, man is an omnivore. He eats a large variety of substances. Even within a single subsistence society the variety of foods consumed is often surprising. If, however, a quantitative dietary study is carried out, such as that by Lee (1968) on the Dobe !Kung Bushmen, it is immediately apparent that the foodstuffs are not all consumed in equal quantities. For example, of some 85 edible plant species, one – the mongongo nut – formed 50 per cent by weight of all the plant food consumed; and 90 per cent of the vegetable diet by weight came from only 23 species. A brief consideration of our own diets would reveal the same pattern. If the contribution of each food to the diet is calculated on the basis of energy and protein value, rather than weight, the difference between staples and casuals becomes yet more marked. This is illustrated in Table 4 by information based on the diets of 128 families in Crete (Allbaugh 1953). Cereals provided 30 per cent of the diet by weight, but furnished nearly 40 per cent of the calories and 50 per cent of the protein. In contrast, an enormous variety of vegetables and fruits comprised 46 per cent of the diet by weight, but provided only 12–15 per cent of the energy and protein. Meat, fish, and eggs made up 6 per cent of the diet by weight and supplied nearly 20 per cent of the protein. It is also notable from Table 4 that in a Neolithic diet without contributions from potatoes and olives (both as fruit and oil), the value of fruits and vegetables as sources of energy and protein would be even lower.

It is not suggested that apples, turnips, marrow, spinach, and so on are unimportant components of our diets. They are, on the contrary, good suppliers of vitamins, minerals, and essential fibre. What the data do show, however, is that while there are only relatively few good sources of protein and calories, there are literally thousands of edible species whose primary nutritional value lies in their vitamin and mineral

Table 4. Sources of energy and protein in the diet (based on diets of 128 Cretan families for one week, autumn 1948)[a]

	Quantity per person per week (pounds)	Energy (%)	Protein (%)
cereals	5.4	39	47
potatoes	2.5	4	4
pulses and nuts	0.8	7	17
milk and cheeses	0.7	3	5
meat, fish, eggs	1.2	4	19
oils and fats	1.3	29	trace
fruits and olives	4.2	8	3
tomatoes and citrus fruits	1.8	1	2
vegetables	2.3	2	3
sugar	0.2	2	trace
beverages except milk	0.4	1	–
total	20.8	100	100

[a] Reference: Allbaugh 1953.

content. If berries don't happen to be in season, apples are; if we live outside the geographic range of chestnut woods, we may live within the range of hazel woods; when leafy greens die down for the winter, roots are available under the soil; when there is nothing humanly edible growing, the Eskimos can obtain their vitamin and mineral requirements from animal livers and by utilising stomach contents of caribou.

It is of course apparent that there are a number of different aspects to be considered in the assessment of the value of a food resource. Among these is the proportion it can contribute to the diet in terms of weight, energy, and protein. Other factors, of an economic rather than a nutritional nature, are also of importance. The rôle and potential of a resource are significantly affected by such things as its reliability, its seasonality, and storability, and the expense involved in its exploitation and processing. Many of these factors are in most cases difficult to analyse accurately in terms of prehistoric data, and hence there is little point in the further elaboration of this theme. Nevertheless, it does seem worth making a basic distinction between *staple resources*, by which we mean the primary sources of energy and protein, and *critical resources*, which refers to the resources which may be numerically negligible in the overall diet but may yet have a crucial significance at a particular season or in certain circumstances. It is easy to imagine a situation in which a resource fulfils a vital rôle in maintaining a population's viability at the lean season of the year – possibly just a matter of a few weeks – while contributing only a very small amount of nutriment to the annual diet. Hoffman (1976) found that freshwater fish contributed only about 15 per cent to the Inuit diet, but that it was a vital complement to the staple caribou in times of shortage. This usage of the term 'critical resource' corresponds closely to that of Wilkinson (1975), although we would perhaps include his 'emergency resource' category within that of critical resources, in view of the difficulty of distinguishing them archaeologically. The exploitation of musk oxen, as Wilkinson describes it, and the use of acorns to provide flour in years of poor grain harvest in Europe, provide good historical examples of critical resources. The vast number of foods consumed occasionally, or as snacks, relishes, and fillers may reasonably be termed *casual resources*.

It was stated earlier that our main reason for studying dietary regimes was to assess the constraints and directives they place upon economic activities, site location, population levels, and, ultimately, on the evolutionary development of the human species. It seems likely that the relatively few sources of staple foods – namely meat, milk products, fish, cereals, and legumes – will always have exerted greater influence over these factors than will the ubiquitous casual resources and sources of vitamins and minerals. For while vegetable sources of minerals and vitamins number thousands of species and are hence widespread and widely available, conditions suitable for the cultivation of cereals and legumes or the support of large animal herds are much more restricted. Human groups who located their sites near herds of animals or good arable soil and gained in addition access to a variety of greens cannot but have had an evolutionary advantage over any communities so ill-advised as to settle near greens without reference to animal or arable resources. It seems justifiable to assume that where food is available in sufficient quantities, man's omnivorous habits will have led him to eat a wide variety of foodstuffs which will automatically have supplied any vitamins and minerals that may have been in short supply in the staple foods comprising his diet. The remainder of this discussion will therefore concentrate on the problem of availability of staple foodstuffs.

So far we have considered man's nutritional needs and have assessed various categories of food in terms of the degree to which they fulfil these needs, assuming them to be available in whatever quantity is required. It is obvious, however, that foodstuffs are not available in unlimited quantities and that some categories are much more abundant than others. The concept of energy pyramids and trophic levels indicates that there must always be more or a greater biomass of herbivores than

carnivores in an ecosystem, and of plants than herbivores. Hence, other things being equal, a given area growing cereals will always have a higher human carrying capacity than the same area growing cattle. Not only will the cereals be inherently the more productive crop, but they represent a tapping of the food chain at the primary producer level before energy has been lost in transfers to higher levels.

Table 5 shows the calorific and protein yield per hectare of cereals, legumes, and meat under intensive production systems. It is interesting to note that although legumes yield roughly the same amount of protein per hectare as cereals, they produce only about 50–70 per cent of the amount of energy. This is clearly one reason for the great importance of cereals in the early development of agriculture. There is no other group of plants which combines high calorific and protein content with high productivity and adaptability; and therefore no other group of plants which could have supported the population increases that occurred.

While emphasising the great importance of the rôle of cereals in human development, one must not lose sight of the fact that without a supplement from legumes and/or animal products they cannot entirely fulfil human dietary requirements. Moreover, there are vast areas of the earth's surface which are not suitable for cereal cultivation – even with modern specially developed varieties and technology – and are either incapable of producing any edible human food or can be exploited for human staples only through the use of grazing animals. Until our technology allows us, and population forces us, to convert the protein in grass into a palatable, digestible form by a more economic means than through herbivores, those animals must continue to form part of our diet, on a world scale.

We are aware, of course, that so far no attention has been given to the importance of root crops. These have considerable importance as suppliers of carbohydrate, and thus energy, in many parts of the world, such as the humid tropics, and were a primary factor in the Irish population explosion of the seventeenth and eighteenth centuries. On the other hand, they have a negligible protein content, and are thus much less well suited to act as basic staples than are cereals, meat, or legumes, which supply significant quantities of both protein and calories. For this reason, in areas where root crops are important in the economy, the population is nevertheless quite likely to be more influenced by the seemingly less significant suppliers of protein, whether plant or animal. It is of interest to note, for instance, that pigs have a considerable economic importance in many of the economies of Southeast Asia which apparently rely

RESOURCES

Table 5. Yield of energy and protein from cereals, legumes, and meat under intensive systems of production in Europe, 1969–71 (source of yields: FAO 1979)

	Energy (Mcal/ha)	Protein (kg/ha)		Energy (Mcal/ha)	Protein (kg/ha)
Austria			**Hungary** (*cont.*)		
wheat	10899	435	peas (dry)	4743	336
beans (dry)	6834	448	lentils	2025	145
peas (dry)	7691	545	**Italy**		
			wheat	7945	317
Bulgaria			beans (dry)	2975	195
wheat	9441	377	peas (dry)	4165	295
beans (dry)	2353	154	lentils	2822	202
peas (dry)	4872	345	**Poland**		
lentils	1746	125	wheat	8185	327
			beans (dry)	5127	336
Denmark			peas (dry)	4223	299
wheat	15238	609	**Romania**		
peas	9700	688	wheat	5841	233
			beans (dry)	245	16
France			peas (dry)	4359	309
wheat	12075	482			
beans (dry)	4257	279	**Spain**		
peas (dry)	11237	797	wheat	4229	169
lentils	4143	297	beans (dry)	2040	134
			peas (dry)	2876	204
W. Germany			lentils	2467	177
wheat	13816	552			
			United Kingdom		
Greece			wheat	14063	562
wheat	6157	246	peas (dry)	10074	714
beans (dry)	3505	230	meat[a]	494	49
peas (dry)	3958	281			
lentils	2874	206	**Yugoslavia**		
			wheat	8222	328
Hungary			beans (dry)	1408	92
wheat	8808	352	peas (dry)	3628	257
beans (dry)	391	26	lentils	2753	197

[a] Source: Duckham & Masefield (1970).

upon root staples. Thus Rappaport (1968) found that in the Tsembaga economy of New Guinea pigs, although apparently highly inefficient to rear in terms of energetics, provided a vital source of high-quality protein, especially crucial in the periodic episodes of stress. He suggests that 'Melanesian pigs . . . cannot be regarded as luxuries. They are a very expensive necessity'. Similarly, Leeds (1961) lists the protein-yielding maize, anteater, alligator, deer, and pigs as among the important dietary elements of the South American Yaruro, usually considered to be primarily dependent upon manioc. One of the main advantages of many root crops is the low demand that they make upon soil fertility. They are thus well adapted to pedologically poor or unstable areas, and represent a means of raising the productivity of otherwise unpromising environments. As far as Europe is concerned, of course, the main root crop of significance as a human food is the potato, a recent introduction from South America, and thus beyond the scope of the main part of this book.

To summarise, the evidence presented shows that, given man's nutritional needs and digestive capacities, and the potential productivity of the various foods, only animal products and cereals combined with legumes easily supply the calorific and protein requirements of large human populations, and thus constitute a staple diet. In some areas root crops are staples in the sense

19

that they supply the majority of the dietary energy, but they are so poor in protein as to need substantial supplementation from other protein-rich foods. In certain very specialised circumstances nuts are available in sufficient abundance and regularity to be exploited as staples, but this appears to be exceptional. It has further been shown that if the dietary staples are secured in adequate quantities the remainder of the requirements (for vitamins and minerals) can usually be provided by readily available casual foods. For these reasons, in our study of prehistoric economy we have focused attention on the means of acquisition of animal products, cereals, and legumes.

Non-dietary resources

The non-dietary resources that most concern us are minerals of various kinds; stone in particular and to a lesser extent metals and clay. There is, of course, a great variety of other non-dietary resources – vegetable and animal products for tool-making and clothing, fuel, building materials, and so on. In some cases it may well have been that important aspects of population density and distribution were affected by the availability of these resources. Neolithic mines and 'workshops' for various stones are well known, for example. It would be a mistake to assume too easily that Grimes Graves, for instance, necessarily represents the activities of a group of full-time miners, however, or that it had a great significance in the overall distribution of population or the nature of the subsistence economy. One characteristic of mineral resources is that they tend to be distributed very unevenly. There is good historical and ethnographic evidence to show that individuals or groups are often prepared to go long distances on occasion to secure valuable and durable resources. Throughout the Holocene, and indeed to some extent in earlier periods, there are indications that sought-after commodities, such as obsidian, were being dispersed from their sources over very long distances, by whatever mechanism.

As a rule, however, it seems most unlikely that non-dietary resources played a basic rôle in determining the nature of early agricultural economies and the populations which these supported. It is hard to see how non-dietary resources can in general have constituted the primary limiting factors on populations. Thus while Damas (1972) suggests that 'Wood was the most prized resource' for the Copper Eskimo, he also notes that in areas lacking woodland the limitation was overcome by trade. In other words, the availability of this resource was less significant than that of dietary

staples in controlling the distribution of population. Of course, non-dietary resources will have had some impact, particularly at a local level, or where they tip the balance in an otherwise relatively uniform environment. Green (1973) notes that the presence of navigable water appears to have importance for the location of Mayan settlements in some areas at least. Significantly, the availability of good agricultural land was found to be another major determinant.

Despite the inevitable exceptions, therefore, we feel that the impact of non-dietary resources is much more likely to have been felt at a secondary than a primary level, in their effect upon architecture and tool production, for instance. It is of course true that the availability of the raw materials necessary for certain kinds of tools and technology may have had an important influence on productive capacity in some cases, at least in the short run. At the low levels of technological complexity which most concern us here this does not seem likely to have been a factor of overriding significance. Needless to say, the more closely one approaches modern times, with urbanised populations and industrial economies, the greater the importance of non-dietary factors, until simple food production comes eventually to play a subsidiary rôle. It must therefore be remembered that here we are dealing primarily with prehistoric subsistence economies supporting relatively low levels of population density and small agglomerations of people.

The means by which the resources available to prehistoric communities may be studied are well established, for the most part. While it cannot be claimed that available procedures leave no gaps and pose no problems in their interpretation, there exists a sufficient body of theory and data to provide a sound background for future work. The site contents themselves provide a vast range of information in the form of organic remains and minerals. A whole battery of techniques is available to archaeologists who are interested to explore the environmental context of their sites. Each of these categories of information has given rise to so vast a literature as to need no further discussion here. Recently, attention has been focused upon techniques which attempt to articulate on-site data with off-site data more successfully than has been possible hitherto. These techniques, *site catchment analysis* and *territorial analysis*, will be discussed in some detail later (Chapter 2).

Of late there has been an increasing vogue for very detailed assessments of resources, based upon a combination of ethnographic, bioarchaeological, and locational considerations. Some, like Jochim (1976), have allied this to a 'systems approach' in an attempt to place precise values on the various factors involved in prehistoric man–land relationships. These studies are of great value for their detailed analysis of the way in which specific systems may have operated. Their weakness, as is so often the case with approaches which lean heavily on ethnographic data and inspiration, is that one frequently has to assume so much that is unknowable in the prehistoric context that the results, while superficially convincing, have to be viewed as hypothetical in the extreme. For instance, as Jochim himself points out, 'One of the major problems . . . is the assessment of the relative importance of each [resource] attribute'. He is forced by his objectives to assume 'in the absence of any empirical information on this point . . . that those attributes deemed pertinent are of equal significance', an assumption manifestly contrary to experience. The difficulty is that, where precise numerical results are the end product, even a slightly different set of assumptions may lead to a very different outcome; and the neatness of the equations and their solutions appears a little illusory. This is not to deny the importance of these experiments, and it is certain that the more general procedures adopted in this volume will require increasingly detailed and precise testing. We should not, however, lose sight of the nature of our basic evidence and the limitations which this imposes upon our interpretations.

TECHNOLOGY

Technology may be viewed for our purposes as a collection of supremely flexible behavioural patterns and their associated artefacts. This is intentionally a broad usage. So much of subsistence behaviour consists of know-how rather than tools, of applied experience rather than hardware, that this loose definition seems preferable to a stricter one. In *Palaeoeconomy* we stressed, as many others have done, the continuity that exists in basic tool types over very long periods of prehistory, sometimes spanning episodes of considerable economic change. This theme recurs in the present volume, and is a further inducement to us to take a broad view of subsistence technology.

The close relationship between technology and population levels on the one hand, and resources on the other, is of great significance in the study of prehistoric economies. Technological levels affect resource utilisation and population in a number of ways. One obvious example is the exclusion from an economy of certain resources due to a lack either of the knowledge or the

means for their exploitation. Metals, even though the ores may exist at the surface, will be inaccessible to communities with inadequate knowledge or industrial capacity. Submarine oil (and deep-sea fish, for that matter), even if their presence is known, are not effective economic resources in the absence of equipment to reach them at an acceptable cost. Another aspect of the complex interrelationship of technology and resources is the rôle of the decline in the availability of one established resource as a goad stimulating the exploitation of alternatives, frequently with attendant technological adjustments. In modern times the rapidly growing interest in, and technology surrounding, the development of nuclear and solar energy has a clear relationship to the increasing cost of exploiting established sources of energy such as coal and oil. In the historic, and doubtless the prehistoric past, pressure of demand upon available resources has similarly stimulated technological development; drainage and irrigation, more powerful or more efficient agricultural tools, selective breeding of plants and animals, and so on.

The cost of exploiting a particular resource frequently has two aspects. Not only is there the cost (whether it is expressed in terms of the expenditure of energy or money) of the extraction of the resource; there is often the less obvious factor of *integration* to be considered. Whether on a local or on a global scale, irregularities and discontinuities in the availability of resources are accommodated by integration, by the movement of people and goods. On the whole, the larger the population and the more advanced the technology, the greater seems to be the importance of long-distance resource integration. Technological changes affect the capability and efficiency of transport, a point which will be considered further below (Chapter 2). Other developments, such as the advent of new methods of preservation of perishable goods, or the appearance of a new industrial process, will clearly have important repercussions on the way in which resources are utilised and integrated.

One reviewer of *Palaeoeconomy* took us to task for having, as he saw it, established in our introductory paper the importance of technology in the study of palaeoeconomies, and then having substantially ignored it thereafter. It must be acknowledged that the criticism is to some extent justified. Similar comments will doubtless be levelled at this volume, and with equal justification; for we are in something of a cleft stick here. Our basic assumptions, logic, and modern and historical experience all lead us to the conclusion that technology is one of the key variables in economic systems. Sadly, generalities apart, our capacity to perceive prehistoric technological levels and abilities is extremely poor, and almost all detailed interpretations rest on the most tenuous of assumptions. The spirit is willing but the data are weak.

The overwhelming preponderance of surviving Palaeolithic and Neolithic artefacts are of stone or pottery. The latter, while relatively clear as to function, are remarkably uninformative as regards more basic economic significance; and most prehistoric stone tools are notoriously ambiguous as regards their function. Some of the most convincing-looking Palaeolithic projectile points appear on the basis of micro-wear analysis more likely to be cutting or scraping tools; while conversely, according to Wendorf's data (1968), 'burins' and indeed 'waste flakes' may in fact have functioned on occasion as projectile points. There is in addition a permanent tendency to underestimate the technological capabilities of prehistoric populations due to lack of direct evidence. The vagaries of pre-servation are such that we cannot assume with any confidence that the earliest surviving bow, or plough, or canoe give any real indication of the date at which these tools first came into use. In this field of enquiry negative evidence must be treated with particular caution.

Fortunately, rather more can be done with the behavioural component of our broadly defined tech-nology. In the record of the botanical and faunal col-lections from sites, the nature of the sites themselves, their distributions, locations, and surroundings, there lies a potentially rich field of enquiry which has received little systematic attention. Necessarily, these sources of information will support only general inferences as to technological levels, but this is something which archaeology must learn to accept. A study of the soils around prehistoric settlements may not tell us for sure whether or not the plough was in use; but it can yield valuable indications as to subsistence priorities, and thus to likely economic strategies. A study of the plant and animal remains will not necessarily illuminate reaping practice or demonstrate the use of byres, but may indicate overall agronomic and pastoral objectives and the way in which the environment was being exploited. We are not suggesting, of course, that artefactual evidence should be ignored where it can be helpful; merely that these situations are sadly rare, as far as concerns palaeoeconomic studies in their present stage of development.

POPULATION

It was argued above that long-term population pressure was an important factor promoting the development of economic systems with increasing extractive potential. We should re-emphasise the crucial distinction between population pressure, which we believe to have been a constant, and population increase which has been a recurrent but irregular phenomenon. We may assert with a fair degree of confidence that population in-crease and economic development went together, both on a prehistoric and an historic time scale. It is perhaps more difficult to be sure as to which was the cause, which the effect. Did population pressure push certain communities towards technological innovation, and thus more productive economies? Or did ingenious inventions raise the demographic ceiling, thus allowing population levels to rise? Arguments have been put forward in favour of each of these hypotheses, and it seems that in the short term both situations arose from time to time, the two processes no doubt reinforcing each other. The longer prehistoric perspective suggests, however, that we may most usefully view the impact of sustained population pressure as the more potent fac-tor.

The very fact that there has existed such a pro-nounced long-term trend towards more productive economies argues for the existence of an equally stable, long-term causative factor or factors. Human genius and inventiveness are unpredictable commodities, and history is littered with examples of inventions which languished unused until situations of stress made their development worthwhile. This is a corollary of the observation made earlier that the development of certain resources and technologies was only economi-cally advantageous in particular circumstances; cir-cumstances which frequently arise as the result of unacceptable pressure upon existing resources.

It is appropriate here to comment briefly on the hypothesis put forward by Binford (1968) and others that the first appearance of agriculture was causally related to an episode of demographic stress. Binford is forced by his interpretation of demographic and etholo-gical theory to explain the sudden occurrence of high population pressure in terms of a speculative recon-struction of demographic and economic relationships existing between populations in the Near East in the Late Pleistocene/Early Holocene period. Reduced to its simplest form the hypothesis runs as follows: (i) the norm is for animal and human populations to be homeostatically regulated at levels where there is no significant pressure upon resources; (ii) this state of affairs was changed by an increased reliance on fish and wildfowl, and an increased tendency to sedentism, which favoured population growth; (iii) population growth increased the incentive for emigration, thus causing population pressure in adjacent areas; and (iv) this population pressure favoured the development of more productive economies, such as agriculture.

We have outlined above our reasons for rejecting the suggestion that population pressure was such a recent or unusual phenomenon in human affairs. In Chapter 3 we shall develop further our reasons for seeing more long-term economic and demographic continuity in the prehistoric record than is envisaged by Binford. Here it suffices to point out that evidence for an increased reliance upon fish and wildfowl, and for a greater degree of sedentism, is scanty and ambiguous in the extreme; and that the relationship between these factors and population increase must also be viewed as putative at best. Yet more important is that Binford's hypothesis leaves unanswered – indeed unremarked – the question as to why the suggested economic and 'socio-cultural' changes took place. What caused the demographically well-adjusted 'Pleistocene hunters' to become relatively maladjusted 'fishers and gatherers'? At best, the focus of ignorance has simply shifted to another term in the equation. The hypothesis favoured in this volume overcomes this particular difficulty by assuming population pressure to be an endemic factor, on the prehistoric time scale. The problem of causation of early agriculture remains, however.

There is much to be said for the suggestion that recognisably modern agricultural economies arose as a response to severe population pressure. It can reasonably be argued that the change from Pleistocene to Holocene climatic conditions may have occasioned a significant decline in the biomass accessible to human exploitation in many environments, thus encouraging more efficient and productive patterns of utilisation. The change from tundra to an increasingly forested vegetation; from dry savannah to semi-desert; and the loss of large areas of coastal lowland due to the eustatic rise in sea level; these could have placed human exploiters adjusted to Late Pleistocene ecosystems in positions of great economic stress. It seems more than likely that this was a most significant factor in the widespread development of modern agricultural economies.

One objection which has been levelled at the 'environmental stress' explanation of agricultural origins is the question of why, in that case, such economies did not develop earlier. As shall be seen in Chapter 3, we do not believe that the techniques of animal and plant husbandry *are* purely a Holocene phenomenon; they do indeed have their origin far back in prehistory. It is true, on the other hand, that economies of far greater productive potential do seem to emerge in the early

Holocene in a number of areas. The apparently intractable question of why these did not arise earlier resolves itself ultimately as a matter of population levels. It is not that there was no selective advantage in economic development at earlier dates, but that it was not until the Late Pleistocene/Early Holocene that population levels relative to resources reached a point which favoured such far-reaching expedients. Prior to that, development took the form of colonisation of new environments and of adaptations in subsistence behaviour which had a less dramatic long-term impact.

Boserup (1965) has done much to encourage archaeological acceptance of population pressure as an independent variable by her documentation of the relationship between population levels and the intensification of agricultural systems in many modern and historical cases. Substantially similar views have more recently been put forward by Gleave & White (1969). However, as Bronson (1972) has pointed out, Boserup's thesis fails to take account of too many of the relevant data for it to be appropriate without modification to all cases. In particular, we may note that its rigid application to some archaeological observations can lead to very suspect conclusions. The long periods of economic stability visible in the prehistoric record have been attributed to the absence of population pressure due to those demographic self-regulating mechanisms discussed above. The persistence in areas such as Australia and California of populations which, prior to the European conquest, pursued extensive 'hunting and gathering' economies despite the fact that they had long been in contact with populations practising more productive agricultural economies, has been similarly explained. It may be doubted whether this is the whole story, however.

We may go a little further in our attempt to understand the relationship between population and economic growth if we recognise that the development of technology is not only a matter of expanding the repertoire of material equipment, but includes – and increasingly demands – a growing expenditure of time and energy: human labour. Furthermore, the more technologically oriented the economy becomes, the greater the importance of *investment activity*, where effort is increasingly diverted from the satisfaction of immediate needs to activities whose aim is the assurance of some future return. There is thus increasingly a time lag between the input of effort and the output of food. The manufacture of elaborate tools is an obvious example of such investment activity, while the cultivation of crops and the herding of animals represent simpler but no less real instances.

1. PHILOSOPHY AND BASIC PRINCIPLES

At certain levels of development the capacity to indulge in investment activity has a critical impact on the economic system. In favourable circumstances the transition from one level of production to a more intensive one can be achieved without major internal disruption or difficulty. Boserup (1965) describes a number of cases of intensification of agricultural production which took place due to internal population pressure by a series of gradual and easily accommodated transformations. On the other hand, this is not always the case. Particularly when the technological leap required to make an effective economic advance is a large one, *and* when the population is already stretching its resources to a point where there is little surplus labour for investment, such development is less likely to be generated internally. Baumhoff (1963) seems to be describing a situation of this nature in California, where the increased investment required to make a significant economic change would have been so large that the indigenous population could not supply the impetus. Leeds (1961) documents an equally appropriate example from the horticultural Yaruro of Venezuela. A precisely similar phenomenon has become a commonplace of today's international economics, where much consideration has been given to the problem of raising certain countries to the take-off point for sustained economic growth. As has recently been pointed out, there is every likelihood that many underdeveloped countries would, left to themselves, remain underdeveloped. But of course they are not, and will not be, left to themselves; and from this point of view the ubiquitous foreign aid programmes may be seen as a form of non-violent external competition.

One should thus beware of the too easy acceptance of population pressure as the independent variable in every case, for all the general value of Boserup's thesis. As we have seen, rigid adherence to the hypothesis poses serious questions about the balance between population and resources in the earlier prehistoric periods. Furthermore, reflection on modern and historical data clearly shows that there can be a distinct feedback from technological change to population levels and their relationship to resources. Medical advances have a direct demographic impact; and changes in agricultural technology can have an equally dramatic effect upon food output. We noted above that modern agriculture may well have been partly stimulated by population stress. We may point out with equal justification that the 'Neolithic' expansion into Europe – regardless of precisely how much movement of populations it represents – probably exemplifies another primary factor in the picture: dramatic demographic response to the sudden raising of the population ceiling by a technological advance.

Given the significance of the population factor, it is obviously of great importance for archaeology to develop adequate means for its consideration from prehistoric data. It has immediately to be admitted that this is by no means within the subject's grasp at present. Broadly speaking, attempts to deal with this aspect can be divided into two kinds. One approach works indirectly from estimates of levels of resources and productivity, to produce carrying capacity figures which put a ceiling on possible past populations. The second approach focuses upon direct archaeological evidence for population levels, such as the size, density and distribution of settlement sites. Both approaches make extensive use of ethnographic and historical analogies to support their particular interpretations.

It is not proposed to undertake a detailed survey of these methods, as a substantial literature on the subject already exists (cf., for example, Cook 1972, Petersen 1975 and his bibliography). We feel, however, that the second approach is more likely to yield useful archaeological results in the foreseeable future. Among the difficulties faced by the former approach are that it is often very difficult to arrive at precise estimates of resource levels (which would themselves have fluctuated considerably from year to year and from decade to decade) and that its practitioners are frequently aiming at the production of precise numerical population estimates – a most hazardous undertaking given the uncertainty surrounding resource levels and the unknown size of the gap between the actual prehistoric population and the theoretical carrying capacity of the environment. One tends thus to be faced with a figure so hedged about with qualifications, or so slenderly justified, as to command little confidence. The second approach, too, has its problems. Differential site preservation and discovery are obvious pitfalls. And this approach, also, can be and has been used to generate absolute population estimates with all their attendant *caveats*. It does seem justified, however, to use this method to arrive at estimates of relative population levels, at least in favourable circumstances. A dramatic increase in the number of settlement sites can on occasion be taken as a reliable indicator of population increase. A spread on to marginal land may reasonably be taken as an indication of high population pressure, and a reversal of such a trend as an indication of the lowering of pressure, whether through population decline or economic advance. Renfrew, C. (1972) has provided a most useful practical example of an attempt to determine past population levels. It is especially interesting to note that the most convincing of his suggestions arise primarily from his inferences regarding population growth and relative levels between different areas and time horizons, rather than from his attempts to put absolute figures to the data. As Renfrew himself notes, the difficulty of reconciling the various estimates of prehistoric populations is 'a healthy reminder of the hypothetical nature of our figures'.

2. TERRITORIES AND MOBILITY

TERRITORIES

We have so far discussed, in very general terms, the basic factors which are involved in the operation and development of economic systems. In order to proceed beyond the general to a more specific treatment of prehistoric case studies it is necessary first to consider in some detail an additional factor: the way in which animal populations are related to and organised within the areas they inhabit. All organisms live in and exploit certain finite regions of space. The fact that these are sometimes difficult to perceive or define does not affect the validity of this proposition. This fundamental relationship between organisms and their surroundings springs quite simply from the need to maintain a favourable energy budget. For the organism to survive and reproduce it must be able to extract more energy from its environment than it expends in obtaining that energy. The first practical effect of this is that there is a limit to the time or distance which can be travelled for subsistence. The more distant the resource to be exploited, the more expensive it is in energy costs, and the more its exploiter is exposed to predation and competition. There is, of course, a bewildering variety of different ways in which animals organise their spatial relationships, but all exhibit this limitation.

Apparent exceptions to this general rule do exist. The most obvious of these are, perhaps, animals such as the filter-feeding marine species which are able to lead essentially stationary lives because they live in an environment which is itself mobile, and brings the food to the exploiting animal. Many micro-organisms, particularly parasites, have a complex relationship with their environment such that they may be highly mobile thanks to the movement of their containing medium or host, but may be essentially stationary as far as volitional movement is concerned or as far as their *effective environment* (in the sense used by Allee *et al*. 1949) is concerned. What is of significance in the present context is the fact that even in these cases there is a limit to the distance from which nutrients are available, even if this limit may on occasion be dependent upon factors totally beyond the influence, or even the consciousness, of the animal in question. From this point of view these examples may perhaps be better viewed as limiting cases than exceptions.

For each individual or group of animals there is thus a specific region from which it habitually gains its subsistence. Such an area is usually called the *home range*. One would expect that as a consequence of competition and other selective pressures home ranges would tend around the optimum size for the individual or community occupying it. Such little direct evidence as there is supports this hypothesis. The sizes of the home ranges of a large number of species have been shown to be correlated with the weight of the animal, the productivity of the environment, and the efficiency of exploitation. In rich environments ranges are smaller than in poorer ones. In some cases the precise energy ratios involved have been measured. Smith (1968) showed that on average the ranges of the *Tamiasciurus* tree squirrel provided only slightly more than the minimum energy necessary to maintain the animals year-round. As has often been pointed out, there are a number of ways in which different intraspecific populations and their home ranges can be articulated. Wynne-Edwards (1962) defines four major types depending on whether the animal concerned is gregarious or solitary, and on whether the home ranges are mutually exclusive or overlapping. As he points out, there are many intermediate examples, and many features of the home range behaviour of some species are flexible, varying with environmental conditions.

A great deal of confusion has arisen in some circles concerning the relationship of home ranges to *territories*. Ethologists now customarily confine the use of the word territory to an area which is actively defended by its occupant or occupants in some circumstances. This single phenomenon of intraspecific aggression has become the focus of attention for many of those who have tried to relate animal territoriality to some aspects of human behaviour. Crook (1968), Wilson (1975), and others have pointed out some of the misapprehensions which have commonly occurred, and have stressed the complexity and variability of territorial behaviour. In some species the exhibition of territorial behaviour is dependent upon ecological and demographic factors. Territorial aggression is hard to distinguish in some cases from the defence of 'individual space', and in others 'territories' appear to be defined in terms of mutual avoidance rather than actual conflict. Territoriality is thus not to be seen as a single specific pattern of behaviour, but as one of the many flexible ways in which organisms are related to each other and their environment. Consequently, the relationship of territories to home ranges is highly variable. While most, if not all, animals have home ranges, territoriality in the ethological sense is much less common. Some species have territories which are identical with their home ranges. The best known examples of this are the breeding territories of certain birds. In other cases only a small core area within the home range is defended – frequently the nesting site among birds – there being varying degrees of overlap between different home ranges. Figures 1–5 illustrate some examples of animal home ranges and territories.

Man is comparable in these respects with many other animals. Home range behaviour seems to be universal in human exploitation, while territoriality seems to occur in certain circumstances. Figures 6–10 illustrate the home ranges of some modern human groups practising subsistence economies. Two features emerge from these which are of particular interest for our present concerns. The first is that, under certain conditions at least, there is a strong tendency for areas of different land use to be arranged around the settlement in a series of roughly concentric zones. This observation was first discussed in detail by von Thünen in his *Der isolierte Staat*, but this and other factors affecting land use have been considered more recently by Chisholm (1968). A number of different variables have

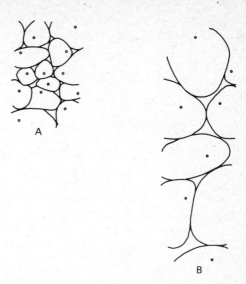

Figure 2. Dunlin nesting territories in Alaska, showing the smaller area per pair in a richer environment (A) as compared with a poorer environment (B). During the breeding season the territories act essentially as home ranges, as most (A) or all (B) of the feeding takes place within the territory. After Holmes (1970).

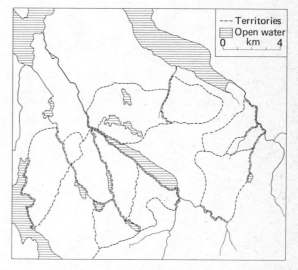

Figure 3. Territories of red deer hinds in part of the western Highlands of Scotland. The territories of the stags infill and cross-cut those of the hinds. After Darling (1937).

an impact on the zonation of land use and on the determination of the sizes of ranges. Among these are the profitability of the resource concerned and the labour costs involved in its exploitation, and the efficiency and cost of transport. This feature of zonation is clearly shown in Figure 9, which shows different land use categories around the village of Soba, in Nigeria. The innermost zone is used for the intensive cultivation of garden crops and tobacco, the next primarily for the permanent cultivation of guinea corn and cotton, the

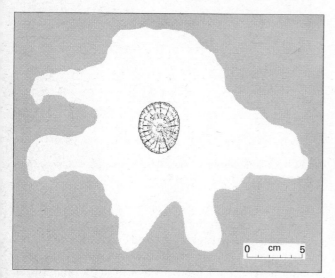

Figure 1. Grazing territory of a limpet. After Moore (1938).

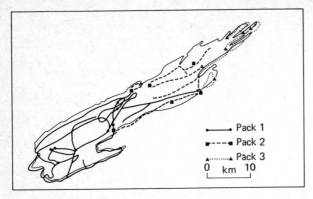

Figure 4. Apparent territoriality shown by the patterns of movement and kill sites of three different wolf packs on Isle Royale in 1966. After Jordan *et al.* (1967).

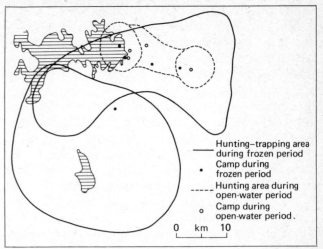

Figure 7. Hunting and fishing territory of a single Inuit family in the course of one year, showing the home bases from which the various areas were exploited. After Hoffman (1976).

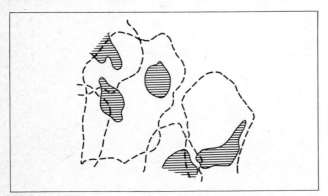

Figure 5. Overlapping baboon home ranges in Nairobi Park, 1959. The core areas are shaded. After De Vore & Washburn (1963).

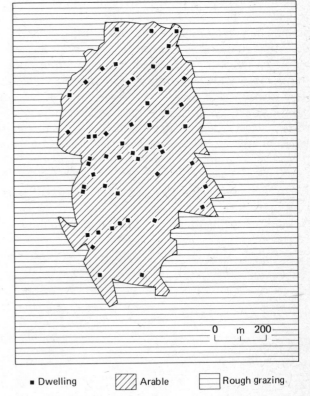

Figure 8. Concentration of arable land around Haya farmsteads in Tanzania. After Reining (1970).

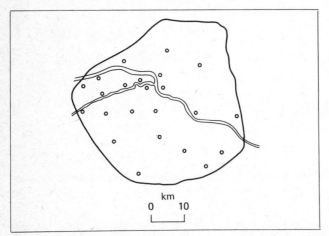

Figure 6. G/Wi Bushmen territory, showing camp sites used in the course of one year. After Silberbauer (1972).

third and fourth being cultivated by rotational bush-fallow and by forest-fallow methods, respectively (Prothero 1957). A much less elaborate zonation is visible in Figure 8, which simply shows the concentration of cultivated land around the Haya farmsteads, with the less intensively exploited grazing land surrounding the dispersed village.

Even in some hunting and gathering economies there is evidence of a rudimentary zonation of land use. Characteristically, vegetable foods are cropped from a smaller area than animal foods. Thus while the Hadza women obtain plant foods from within an hour's walk of the camp, game may be followed for up to a day's

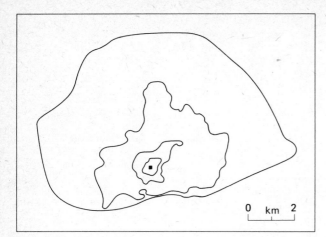

Figure 9. Zonation of land use in the village territory of Soba, Nigeria. After Prothero (1957).

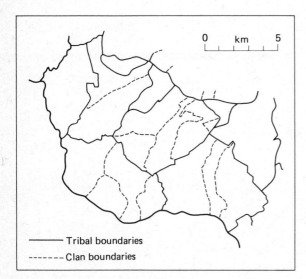

Tribal boundaries
------- Clan boundaries

Figure 10. Tribal and clan territories among the Chimbu in central Papua. After Brookfield & Brown (1963).

Table 6. Intensity of exploitation of plant foods around G/Wi Bushman camps

| | Distance from camp (miles) | | | |
	0–1	1–2	2–3	3–4
number of days supply of plant food per household in sample period	314	423	274	83
number of days supply of plant food per household per square mile	100	45	17.5	3.8

Data from Silberbauer 1972, Figs 7–11.

(although this may perhaps be properly treated as a special case of terrestrial exploitation) seems to take place within a maximum radius of 8–10 km in Eskimo and Koryak economies, and 8 km seems to have been the limit for whaling in *umiaks* (Stefansson 1914, Levin & Potapov 1964). Marine molluscs, like plant foods, are a sedentary resource, relatively easy to locate and harvest. Their value is limited, however, by the high costs of transportation and the high proportion of waste to nutritive value. Whereas one bag-load of mongongo nuts, weighing 12.5 kg, supplies about 5 man-days of calories, an equivalent weight of oysters provides only about 0.5 man-days of calories. Furthermore, the shell-fish are probably more expensive to exploit. Accordingly, shell-gathering seems characteristically to have been confined within a smaller area than other marine exploitation. Meehan (1975) showed that in northern Australia clams were not transported in quantity further than about 3 km, while in South Africa Bigalke (1974) noted maximum distances of 3 and 5 km respectively for the exploitation of mussels and limpets.

Perhaps of greater importance in the present context is the general point that there seem to be modal values, thresholds beyond which certain broad categories of exploitation are not usually pursued. Table 7 shows some figures for limits of certain kinds of exploitation from a wide geographical range. It can be seen that the customary limit of hunting exploitation from any one camp is of the order of 10 km or so. In some instances this limit is considerably exceeded, but in this case temporary overnight stays away from the base camp are the general rule. Thus Woodburn (1968) has said of the Hadza that when a large kill is made at a considerable distance from camp, the camp frequently moves to the kill site rather than *vice versa*. There is little relevant information from extensive pastoralist economies, but these seem on the whole to exploit a slightly smaller area around the settlement. This is to be expected, in that the daily movement of stock over

walk (Woodburn 1968). For the Bushmen, the maximum radius of hunting exploitation quoted varies from area to area and according to seasonal conditions. Usually of the order of 10 km or so, it can be as much as 16–24 km; but in general the bulk of the vegetable food comes from a smaller region around the camp. For instance, a rough analysis of Silberbauer's (1972) Figures 7–11 shows that for the G/Wi, at least as far as that particular set of observations is concerned, by far the bulk of both input of effort and output takes place within the first 3 km of the camp (Table 6). Similarly, Tindale (1972) notes that 5 km is considered the maximum acceptable limit for the gathering of plant food among the Pitjandjara.

Similar principles apply to the exploitation of aquatic resources. Ice hunting of seal with sledge and harpoon

Table 7. Limits of subsistence exploitation

Area/population	Mode of exploitation	Average distance (km)	Usual limit	Extreme limit (km)	Source
Copper Eskimo	winter sealing		8 km		Damas 1972
Ainu	fishing	4–6.5			Watanabe 1972
!Kung	hunting & gathering		2 h/10 km	16–24	Lee 1968, 1972b, 1976
G/Wi	plant gathering		8 km		Silberbauer 1972
	hunting			24	Silberbauer 1972
Hadza	plant gathering		1 h		Woodburn 1968
	hunting		day's return journey		Woodburn 1968
Birhors	hunting		8–16 km		Sinha 1972
Pitjandjara	plant gathering		5 km		Tindale 1972
	hunting		(unspecified, but >5 km)		Tindale 1972
Sudan	extensive grazing		4–5.5 km	10–12	Graham 1969
Uganda	extensive grazing		10.5 km		Dyson-Hudson 1972
Baluchi	extensive grazing		<16 km (?)		Swidler 1972
Hopi	peasant agriculture				
	foot		6.5 km		Bradfield 1971
	burros & tractors		12 km		Bradfield 1971
Kuikuru	peasant agriculture		6.5 km		Carneiro 1961
Yaruro	peasant agriculture		3.5–4 km		Leeds 1961
Sierra Leone	peasant agriculture				
	wet rice		0.8 km		Donald 1970
	dry rice		3.2 km		Donald 1970
Tropical Africa	peasant agriculture		6.5–11 km		Morgan 1969
Mindanao	peasant agriculture	0.5	1 h/1.2 km		Conklin 1957
Finland	peasant agriculture	1.0–1.1			Chisholm 1968
Holland	peasant agriculture	0.8–1.4			Chisholm 1968
Belgium	peasant agriculture	0.3–1.0			Chisholm 1968
Switzerland	peasant agriculture	0.3–1.0			Chisholm 1968
France	peasant agriculture	0.3–2.0			Chisholm 1968
W. Germany	peasant agriculture	0.3–2.0			Chisholm 1968
Bulgaria	peasant agriculture	2.0			Chisholm 1968
Romania	peasant agriculture	0.7–2.5			Chisholm 1968
Spain	peasant agriculture	0.3–6.0			Chisholm 1968
China	peasant agriculture	0.3–1.0	0.5–1.8 km		Chisholm 1968
Punjab	peasant agriculture	0.8–4.0			Chisholm 1968

large distances inhibits their productivity. For example, Graham (1969) points out that in the Sudan when during periods of extreme shortage goats have to be moved as much as 5 or 6 miles for water, 'They remain alive, but under these conditions they cannot provide the milk which is their *raison d'être*'. Higgs & Vita-Finzi (1972) found that daily cattle and goat movements from one particular modern Arab settlement in Israel took place within 4–5 km. Browman (1976) interprets the evidence of settlement distribution as indicating a threshold of *c* 6–7 km for llama pastoralism in Peru in the first century A.D. As far as arable based economies are concerned there is a clear drop in the distance which it is economical to travel for purposes of every-day exploitation. Chisholm (1968) has suggested that in many cases 5 km may be taken as the limit beyond

which the costs in terms of extra labour, travel, and transport begin to offset the advantage of cultivating more land. It is also worth stressing that this is to be viewed as an outside limit in the majority of cases. The overwhelming preponderance of land under cultivation is to be found within a much smaller radius of the settlement, frequently within 1 or 2 km.

As Chisholm has pointed out, it is really time rather than distance itself which is the significant factor in these limits to exploitation. The limit of the !Kung bushman hunting territory is based upon the round-trip distance it is possible to travel while still leaving a reasonable portion of the day actually for hunting. The Hanunóo limit for swiddens is based on 'an hour's walking distance (with a heavy load of grain)' (Conklin 1957). Morgan (1969) says of tropical African agriculture that the limit is set 'by the farmer's estimate of the amount of time he can afford to lose in journeying during the day', cultivation only being worthwhile beyond this limit if a subsidiary or temporary homestead is erected. Bradfield (1971) also stresses that it is the labour involved in transport which 'precluded the use of any considerable acreage of farm land sited more than four miles from the parent village' under aboriginal Hopi conditions. Baumhoff (1963) suggests that the exigencies of transport of the acorn harvest were instrumental in determining the small size of 'tribelet areas' under aboriginal conditions in parts of California.

We are aware, of course, that the detailed records of resource utilisation by individuals or family groups would present a very much more complex picture than that given in our brief synthesis. The mapping of individual peasant land holdings and the uses to which different fields were put, or of particular hunting trips by one specific hunter or group of hunters, often reveals an elaborate and changing palimpsest of land use. Thus the data compiled on Inuit land use by Freeman, M. M. R. *et al.* (1976) show not only that various resources were exploited in different areas and at different levels of intensity, but also the degree to which, in so extreme and unpredictable an environment, the area exploited would change from year to year. These minutiae do not, however, affect the basic principles discussed above, which continue to apply. The Inuit are as constrained by the demands of time, energy, and distance as are other populations, with the consequent restriction of exploitation within an acceptable distance of their home bases. The difference lies mainly in the fact that these have to be shifted frequently. Furthermore, this type of information concerns the kind of short-term detail with which archaeology cannot deal effectively, its data being better adapted to the analysis of the central tendencies of long-term processes.

As implied above, it is the nature of the resources themselves, coupled with the pressure upon them and the means for their exploitation, which together determine these time–distance thresholds. The most land-extensive of the economies considered here, extensive hunting, is forced to operate within large territorial limits because of the relative unpredictability and mobility of the resources concerned. The slightly smaller limits which seem to be typical of extensive pastoralism may be partly attributed to the more controlled and dependable nature of the man–animal relationship, and partly to the fact that if the animals were forced to make daily journeys of up to 20 km (round trip) their

condition would suffer greatly, and they would thus be a less valuable resource. The distinctly narrower limits associated with arable agriculture, the more intensive forms of pastoralism, and certain types of marine exploitation are at least primarily dependent upon the increased labour and transport costs involved in these systems. The complex of forces which combine to determine exploitation thresholds may be termed the *time–distance factor*.

It is of some interest to observe that the impact of the time–distance factor is by no means restricted to subsistence economies. The distances which people are prepared to travel to and from work daily have of course been drastically altered by technological changes in the field of transport. The time involved has not changed nearly so much. One hour to and from work is commonly treated as an acceptable average commuting time by millions of urban workers in industrialised countries; while an hour and a half to two hours is frequently viewed as an undesirable (but sometimes necessary) extreme limit.

There thus seems every reason to believe that there is a broad pattern of restraint upon certain kinds of exploitation, exerted ultimately by the relationship of the input to the output of energy. This holds good for a wide variety of animals and for human economies, and it seems fully justified therefore to make the assumption that similar factors operated in the prehistoric past.

EXPLOITATION TERRITORIES

In view of the widespread significance of the time–distance factor, it is clearly of interest for archaeology to develop some means of dealing with it in archaeological terms. The importance in palaeoeconomic studies of an estimate of the available resources has been discussed earlier. The time–distance factor clearly has considerable significance here, as it is one of the primary determinants controlling which of the various resources existing in a region as a whole are accessible to populations exploiting the area from a particular site. Studies of the general environmental setting of a site or group of sites have a long history in archaeology, and these have frequently been very informative, providing a useful background interpretative aid in the analysis of many of the archaeological data. Their potential is restricted by a number of limitations, however.

Environmental or palaeoecological studies geared to archaeological enquiries have tended on the whole to be of a general nature. There are good reasons for this. The sort of detailed meteorological and palynological evidence commonly used is often not available for the region of the site itself. It is therefore difficult in most cases to obtain a clear impression of the way in which the immediate environment of the site fits into the wider picture. Similarly, without reference to a specifically articulated body of theory there is no effective way of 'weighting' different environmental factors according to their economic importance, or of considering how this weighting may be affected by increasing distance from the prehistoric site. The environment of a site is frequently described in terms of physiographic and vegetational zones, or ecological zones, all of which have been defined on the basis of data collected for other disciplines than archaeology. It is by no means the case that those zones will necessarily provide the best framework for the analysis of past human behaviour. It has frequently been noted that prehistoric sites are often found in ecotonal positions, that is at the edges of ecological zones or where these overlap. Equally, particularly in severe environments, sites will tend to be in exceptional locations rather than in areas typical of the zone as a whole. Thus in deserts water sources will be the foci of settlement, in poorly drained lowlands it will be attracted to eminences, and so on.

This must not be read as a condemnation of such studies in the past. As will be seen, we ourselves continue to make considerable use of general environmental data which form a most necessary aspect of the initial stage of consideration of any prehistoric economy. All we would argue is that more effective and sensitive analyses can be achieved when greater account is taken of specific site location features and of the time–distance factor.

To this end we have developed the technique of territorial analysis, the objective of which is to delimit the *exploitation territories* of archaeological sites. The exploitation territory of a site is defined as that area which was accessible to habitual exploitation by the occupants of the site. The method has been discussed before in some detail (Higgs 1975, Appendix A; Jarman, M. R. 1972a), and need only be summarised here. It is assumed that during the periods with which we are concerned travel will have been primarily if not exclusively by foot. It is further assumed, on the basis of the modern evidence discussed above, that arable agricultural economies are unlikely to have exploited to any great extent land beyond 5 km. The more extensive forms of pastoralism and hunting economies seem frequently to concentrate their exploitation within a maximum radius of about 10 km. As was noted earlier, it is really time and energy which are the critical factors, rather than distance itself. Consequently we have con-

verted these distance figures into time estimates. In reasonably flat terrain the time taken to cover 5 km and 10 km at a moderate walking pace is about 1 hour and 2 hours respectively, and we therefore employ these figures in delimiting exploitation territories. An important advantage of using time rather than distance thresholds is that this takes into account the considerable impact which topography and geographical features such as rivers can have upon movement. In view of the evidence from modern economies we have paid particular attention to the area within the 1 km (10 minute) threshold where arable economies are concerned. While such economic systems can, and frequently do, exploit land further from the site, the vast majority of effort is customarily applied to this much smaller area. The territorial limits are thus determined by a minimum of four walked transects from the site, the distance reached after the appropriate time being plotted on a map.

Once the exploitation territory has been defined it is analysed in terms of land use potential. The key factors to be taken into account are soil quality and texture, vegetation, modern and historical land use, availability of water, and the existence of any other limiting factors due, for example, to topographic or climatic features. It has been assumed on the basis of historical and ethnographic data that soil tractability will have been a factor of great importance in determining prehistoric arable potential. For this reason we have excluded from the 'potentially arable' land use category all areas of heavy soil, even though they may well be under arable exploitation today. This matter is discussed in greater detail in Chapter 5. It is obviously of the first importance to take into account the nature and extent of any geomorphological change which may have taken place since the occupation of the site, or any other significant environmental change. For this reason particular attention must be paid to evidence, such as artefactual remains, which might help to date the development of particular land forms.

Both the theoretical basis and the practice of this technique have been much challenged. We will attempt to answer some of the most commonly raised criticisms later in this chapter, but here it may help if, as a preliminary, we discuss briefly some of the things which are *not* implied by our model. The first point to be stressed is that the exploitation territory is purely an economic concept not an ethological one. It is a measure of the area accessible for day-to-day subsistence, and carries no implication as to whether or not the area would have been defended. To judge from both ethnographic and ethnological data this would have varied depending on factors which are unlikely to be preserved satisfactorily in the archaeological record. Nor can we hope, for similar reasons, to recognise territories such as those dealt with by anthropologists and ethnologists. These frequently incorporate linguistic, sociological, and political phenomena, all of which are beyond the range of most archaeological data. We cannot hope to delineate precise tribal territories, or the areas of land specifically associated with particular families, bands, or moieties.

We cannot even, on the basis of territorial analysis alone, certainly delimit the area which actually was exploited from a particular archaeological site. Two important areas of uncertainty contribute to this unsatisfactory situation. First, we cannot be sure that we have chosen precisely the right time–distance threshold for the population in question. This will indeed have varied, to a small extent, not only from settlement to settlement within any particular population, but also from decade to decade and from generation to generation, as other economic and demographic factors varied. In these circumstances it is clearly impossible for us to achieve precision from archaeological data. The second major limitation springs from the indeterminacy of archaeological chronological estimates. One of the main factors which would have distorted our 'idealised' territories, tending to compress them to some degree, would have been the presence of other sites or populations, competing for some of the same resources. We might hope to take account of this factor effectively in archaeological terms if we could date sites accurately enough to be sure as to which were precisely contemporaneous. Sadly this is only very rarely the case. The best we can do in the vast majority of cases is to hypothesise that certain sites are 'archaeologically contemporaneous' on the basis of radiometric dating or of typological similarity. As we have noted earlier, archaeological contemporaneity involves uncertainties of decades or tens of thousands of years, depending on the context.

Similarly, there is little chance in most archaeological instances of distinguishing exploitation territories which were rigidly defined and mutually exclusive from those which were more flexible and overlapped to a considerable extent. One may be able to guess at these questions either on the basis of ethnographic or historical analogy, or if the site contents themselves give some hint, but such cases are likely to be exceptions.

The kind of difficulty with which we are faced is illustrated in Figures 11 and 12. Figure 11 shows the annual exploitation territories of some modern Bushmen groups. It can be seen that these are of unequal

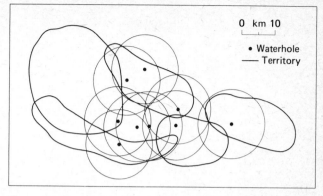

Figure 11. Annual exploitation territories of the !Kung Bushmen. After Yellen (1976).

size, and that they overlap extensively but unevenly. Also shown are the theoretical limits which would result from territorial analysis. They are in this case simply 10 km rings around each of the permanent waterholes, as we have not been able to submit these particular sites to field analysis. We are not concerned here with the fact that the ethnographically observed territories are much larger in some directions than the theoretical territories which might result from archaeological analysis. This arises principally if not entirely from the fact that the ethnographic territories are *annual territories* (see pp. 36–7), not site exploitation territories. The asymmetry of the territories around their 'home bases', the degree of territorial overlap, and the fact that not all the waterholes are foci for particular Bushman populations, are observations of interest, however. It is apparent that while the distribution of archaeological remains might in such a case clearly indicate the critical importance of the permanent water sources for settlement and exploitation patterns, the chances of correctly interpreting the precise distribution of particular human groups at one particular point in time are slight indeed. Nor is one likely to be able to say for certain how many of the sites were occupied simultaneously by different populations, and how many were, on the other hand, occupied at different times by a single population.

This is not to suggest that these problems are always wholly intractable, but only that they represent areas in which we fully realise the technique's limitations. Careful consideration of the available resource levels from both territorial and on-site data will give some clues as to the overall carrying capacity of the region. The recognition of the water sources as the critical factor combined with their uneven distribution would allow one at least to make reasoned guesses as to the likely distribution of territories in the area as a whole. As

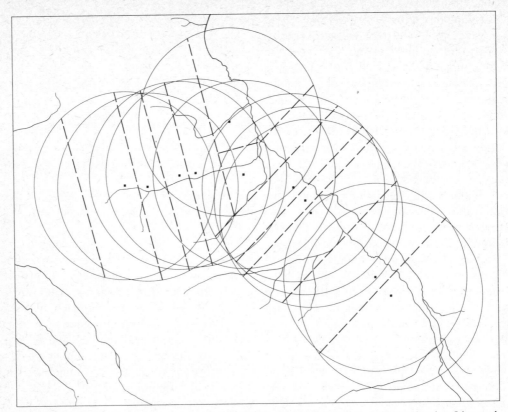

Figure 12. Distribution of Linear Pottery sites on part of the Aldenhovener Platte showing 5 km and hypothetical, mutually exclusive territorial limits.

Dennell & Webley (1975) have shown, some features of site distribution may give information as to which settlements are most likely to have been contemporaneous or successively occupied. In the rare cases where dendrochronology or other sensitive dating methods are applicable this can be assessed with yet more confidence.

Figure 12 illustrates a comparable archaeological example. This shows a markedly asymmetric distribution of Linear Pottery sites on the Aldenhovener Platte of northwest Germany. Theoretical walked territorial limits are shown, as well as a possible interpretation which assumes that all the sites were in occupation at the same time, and that actual exploitation territories did not overlap. It can be seen that the sites are located fairly close together along small river valleys, but with much greater distances separating the settled river valleys than between different sites in the same valley. The observed distribution is a reasonable way of organising the population of the area if it is assumed that there was a considerable premium attached to proximity to the relatively scarce damp valley-bottom grazing areas. It is clear, however, that different assumptions regarding the contemporaneity of sites, or the way in which adjacent territories were articulated,

would yield a very different picture as regards the precise territorial boundaries.

A further source of uncertainty concerns the assumption that we are dealing with foot travel and transport. It must be remembered that in this volume we are dealing primarily with periods in which highly sophisticated means of transport can certainly be ruled out. On the other hand, chariots, carts, and the widespread use of horses as draught animals are in evidence in Europe at least by the end of the Bronze Age. Indeed, there is some evidence (Bahn 1976, 1978) that the control of and use of horses for transport may extend back into the Pleistocene. Similarly, we know both from the colonisation of islands such as Crete and Cyprus, and from the physical remains of paddles and boats, that water transport of some sophistication was available at least from the early Holocene onwards.

Two considerations weigh in favour of our continuing to make the basic assumption of foot travel. Horses are singularly rare in the early Holocene faunal collections of Europe. In many areas they are totally absent between the end of the Pleistocene and the Bronze Age. Where they occur it is usually spasmodically and in very small numbers. In these circumstances it is difficult to argue for their having had a major economic effect on the early agricultural development of the continent. Secondly, it seems that as a general rule the availability of horse transport has most of its impact in the intensification of land use relatively close to the settlement. While lightly laden horses may have a considerably greater travelling speed than man, average speeds of heavily laden beasts of burden are not high. Thus while they have the potential to increase substantially the labour applied to, and profitability of, land at a moderate distance, they do not usually dramatically expand the normal limits of day-to-day agricultural exploitation. It is true that Bradfield (1971) found that the introduction of *burros* and then tractors coincided with an extension of the limits of Hopi cultivation from *c* 6.5–12.0 km at one village. Other factors are also relevant in this case, however. A large area of prime arable land near the village was lost due to geomorphological change, thus putting extreme pressure on the economic system. Furthermore, the majority of the fields still lie within the 6.5 km radius, and Bradfield notes that the capacity for an intensification of the exploitation of these was another result of the introduction of non-human transport. Similarly, we may point out that horses have been available to the farmers in many of Chisholm's examples (see Table 7) for centuries if not millennia, and they have often had the use of motorised equipment in recent years. Yet these examples give the smallest average farm sizes among the sample we discuss. As far as water transport is concerned, we are perhaps fortunate in that few of the areas dealt with in this book show any signs of having given rise to economies dependent upon aquatic resources to any great degree. In this situation it seems reasonable to maintain our basic assumption regarding transport and to deal with exceptions as special cases where they arise.

We are not simply trying to ignore the existence of these exceptions. On the contrary, territorial analysis has proved on occasion to be a most useful tool in pointing to such cases. As is discussed in Chapter 4, territorial studies in Sweden led Anderson (1976) to the conclusion that a deficiency of resources available from the walked territories of sites in Central Norrland could best be explained in terms of the use of water and ski transport. In Chapter 5, Maclean's work on the fauna from the Romanian site at Cascioarele suggests that horses present in the later Gumeliniţa levels may have been used for transport, which could have been one of the reasons for the considerable faunal changes associated with this level. It is of interest to note that the hypothesis is that this aid to efficient transport may have altered the extent to which hunted animals were brought back to the home-base settlement, rather than that it will have engendered radical changes in the economy as a whole or in the size of the area exploited.

To summarise, then, we may say that territorial analysis is a technique that permits us to delimit an area beyond which habitual exploitation from a particular settlement can be excluded. This territory can then be mapped and analysed in detail, and its characteristics related to the on-site data. This provides an invaluable independent assessment of the economic potential available to prehistoric populations, against which the inferences drawn from the on-site faunal and botanical evidence can be tested. This is of the first importance in the analysis of Neolithic economies. A frequent and intractable problem in such studies is the virtual impossibility of assessing accurately the relative importance of the plant and animal components in the diet. As noted above (Chapter 1), even where preservation is good and adequate collection of plant material has taken place (and this is very much the exception rather than the rule), there exists no satisfactory method for making this assessment on the basis of on-site data alone. The factors affecting deposition and preservation of plant and animal remains are so different and so various as to reduce to a minimum the value of a direct numerical comparison. Thus while bones are essentially waste products, seeds, from which most of the botanical data come, are mainly only deposited by accident, having escaped consumption fortuitously. Artefactual evidence is impossible to use in any precise numerical way. Ploughs may indicate an arable component, spear throwers suggest a hunting component, 'milk boilers' imply a pastoral component, net weights a fishing component; but these hints are not quantifiable, even at the crudest level of probability.

Local environmental information has, in fact, always provided the most sensitive means of interpreting the organic contents of sites. One of the main values of the territorial approach is that, in focusing attention on a specific territory rather than an ill-defined zone, it can yield fairly accurate assessments of economic potential. As we shall see in later chapters, important insights into the way in which past populations exploited their environment can result from this study of the relationship between settlements and their immediate surroundings, and the constraints and opportunities which these incorporate.

It should be re-emphasised that the validity of the theory and the success of the method *do not* depend upon our having chosen, by good luck or good judgement, the 'correct' thresholds for the operation of the time–distance factor. The basic hypothesis rests upon an observation so simple and so widespread as to be virtually a truism: that there must be some relationship between the time and energy necessary for the exploitation of a resource and its economic importance to a particular organism or group of organisms. If this premise is accepted, then unless it is suggested that the limits drawn are much too narrow, the method will yield valid and interpretable results in a majority of cases. Critics of the method frequently point out that we cannot be sure that the whole of the exploitation territory was in fact exploited. This is perfectly true. Indeed, as we shall see later, detailed evidence from some areas suggests that for many Neolithic sites the actual area of exploitation may have been distinctly smaller than the theoretical hour's limit. This criticism misses the point, however. The exploitation territories are intended only to represent the potential area of habitual exploitation. Unless elaborate and precise inferences are being drawn concerning the productivity of the whole of a site territory, it matters little whether the limit corresponds exactly to the area actually exploited. This latter will in any case have varied on a short time scale, according to local factors of population pressure, economic success, and environmental conditions. In most, if not all cases, the area immediately adjacent to the site will have been that of prime economic importance.

It is true that the method would be considerably less valuable if it could be shown that there were much likelihood that our theoretical territories were greatly too small. This seems most implausible, however, in view both of modern ethnographic data and of energetics. As we have seen, distance from the settlement is consciously recognised as a limiting factor on exploitation in a number of ethnographic cases. Furthermore, while it is not possible to be categorical in the absence of more substantial data, the nutritional status of many populations with subsistence economies does not encourage the view that they could readily afford the expenditure of a yet higher proportion of energy in daily movement and transport. Rappaport's (1968) estimates suggest that as much as between one-sixth and one-quarter of the total energy needed to cultivate the Tsembaga root crop staples is spent in travel and transport, with most journeys being of only 20–30 minutes. We have already noted that there seems to be a close general approximation among animals to an optimal home range area.

It would be foolish, of course, to suggest that the technique presents no difficulties, that there will be no exceptions to our general propositions, or that there will be unambiguous results from every study. In this volume we are not concerned with the exceptions, however, which are unlikely in any case to have had much long-term impact on economic behaviour. Furthermore, as we have mentioned, the technique itself can be a useful indicator of unusual or aberrant factors operating in particular cases.

ANNUAL TERRITORIES

Site exploitation territories represent only a part of our concern with the spatial aspects of prehistoric subsistence economies. Geographical and seasonal imbalances in resources impose major constraints upon economic behaviour. One of the main adaptations to these imbalances is the widespread mechanism of seasonal mobility. We shall return to this topic in greater detail later on. Here we are primarily interested in its implications for territorial behaviour and theory.

In the simplest terms human groups may conveniently be viewed as inhabiting home bases or *preferred sites*, those occupied for a long period or repeatedly; and *transit sites*, those occupied only fleetingly (Higgs 1975). Many elaborations of this basic classification are possible, and are sometimes necessary. The preferred sites may be permanently or seasonally occupied. A group may change its home base half a dozen times in a year, or may return to a particular site regularly but at intervals greater than one year. The transit sites include a vast range of special function sites, including kill sites, trading posts, defensive and look-out stations, mines, and so on. In the technologically simpler economies of many subsistence populations these transit sites will often have left little discernible archaeological trace. The more complex the economic system, the more complex the nature of population activity and distribution, and the settlement distribution arising from it. In sophisticated economic systems which generate large reliable surpluses the special function sites can often be permanently occupied, despite their divorce from subsistence production in many cases.

A population which moves its home base or makes extensive use of transit sites changes its exploitation territory in doing so. Some areas, hitherto inaccessible, are brought within reach of exploitation; others, previously accessible, are now beyond the limits. It is clear therefore that a consideration of the rôle of mobility is essential to any economic analysis. The accurate analysis of on- and off-site data may give a good picture of the situation at one particular site, but may be a very misleading guide to the economic parameters of the whole economic system of which the site forms a part.

We have hence defined the *annual territory* as the

total area potentially exploitable by a human group in the course of a year. It may contain one or more home bases, or may coincide with a single site exploitation territory. This is a similar concept to that of the *lifetime range* (Jewell 1966) in ethological studies, although we cannot hope to define our archaeological annual territories with comparable precision.

The shape and size of annual territories is highly variable. At the one extreme there is the case of a sedentary population which makes no regular use of transit sites. In this case the annual territory is identical with the site exploitation territory. There are cases of relatively restricted mobility, with a number of home-bases and transit sites, but all occurring within a coherent and relatively compact area. Such cases are illustrated for the Bushmen and Eskimos in Figures 6 and 7. The more highly mobile economies exploit more extensive annual territories. These take a number of forms. Some, like the Basseri (see p. 44), occupy what is essentially a long continuous strip through which they travel in regular, predictable movements. Other groups have essentially two home ranges which form the terminals of the system, and are only connected by the single narrow corridor along which the population travels. This pattern is becoming increasingly common due both to increasing competitive pressure for resources from other economic groups, and to the availability today in some areas of the means of rapid mechanised transport for both the stock and their herders. Finally there are some highly diffuse annual territories, particularly characteristic of some extreme or marginal environments. Where resources are either very scanty, or unreliable, or both, economies are characteristically geared to exploiting the fugitive sources of food as and when they appear. Not all the annual territory is necessarily exploited in any one year; indeed it is frequently only a small fraction which is in use, and a given area may only support herbivore and human populations for a few years out of any generation. Certain arctic and desert economies exemplify this kind of exploitation pattern. The caribou and the camel, for instance, are particularly well adapted to make use of the available resources on a very fluid and mobile basis, as are the economies which depend upon these species. Salzman (1972) describes an example from Iran where a particular area was being exploited for the first time in ten years. Hunting territories also varied greatly from year to year among the Inuit Eskimo (Hoffman 1976).

Even this extreme, it should be noted, is significantly different from the romantic idea of nomadism as totally lacking in regularity, predictability, and territorial con-

straint. It is very doubtful whether this kind of unrestricted mobility has or ever had any existence in reality; if so, it can only have been as an exception of very short duration. The selective advantages conferred by territoriality (in our sense) are such that on a prehistoric time scale any totally unterritorial populations would have been outcompeted by populations making better use of the available resources. The chief advantage is the greater familiarity with the local resources, and thus greater knowledge of their extent and limitations. Similar advantages operate in the rest of the animal world. As Zipf (1965) and Southern (1955) have pointed out, there is also an important increase of efficiency, an economy of effort, which results from intimate knowledge of the surroundings. This knowledge can be of critical importance in crisis situations involving conflict or extreme pressure of population on resources.

We are aware that the definition of annual territories is as fraught with difficulties as that of site exploitation territories, if not more so. It is rare indeed for one to be able to demonstrate with certainty the association of one particular prehistoric site with another. Where this can be done there are usually alternative ways of viewing the association than the model we have briefly outlined above. This does not release us from the necessity of dealing in terms of annual territories, however. Modern and historical data assure us of their widespread significance, and indeed indicate that many economic systems are not comprehensible if the factor of mobility is not taken into account. As will be seen in Chapters 4–6 there is ample evidence in the archaeological record for the existence of these patterns of mobility, and for the integration of different environmental zones which are often at considerable distances from each other. In view of this, and given the generalising aims of palaeoeconomic studies, we need not be too dismayed at the limitations forced on us by the deficiencies of the data. If we can reliably isolate the probable direction and extent of seasonal movements, then the fact that we may remain uncertain as to which particular site in one zone is related to which particular site in another, is perhaps not too significant.

CATCHMENTS

As is discussed in Jarman, M. R. (1972a), the definition and analysis of exploitation territories can be viewed as one aspect of the more general technique of *catchment analysis*. There has been considerable confusion as to the interrelationship of the two, and with the wisdom of hindsight it can be seen that we in our own publications have almost certainly contributed to the confusion by failing to underline sufficiently the distinction between them. Catchment analysis (Vita-Finzi & Higgs 1970, Higgs & Vita-Finzi 1972, Jarman, M. R., Vita-Finzi & Higgs 1972) is concerned with the points and areas of origin of all the various contents of archaeological sites. This encompasses a vast range of information, and involves the different agencies by which the contents have been transported to the site. For we are not solely concerned with objects brought in by man. The geological deposits will have been derived by a variety of processes (Vita-Finzi 1975); different elements within the fauna and flora will have come from different areas and will probably have been incorporated into the deposits by various means (Vita-Finzi & Higgs 1970); and, of course, the different kinds of raw material represented in the artefacts will have come from widely varying sources.

One might thus speak in terms of the geological, zoological, botanical, and artefactual catchments of a site. These different catchments will not be of identical size or shape, of course, and will thus form a complicated palimpsest of overlapping areas, with the site itself probably being the single point held in common by them all. Pollen spectra similarly represent a palimpsest of pollen derived from a number of different sources, directions, and distances.

Catchment analysis is concerned with all these factors, or with a particular aspect of them which has been defined as of interest with respect to a specific objective. The site exploitation territory, on the other hand, would from this point of view represent just a part of what might be termed the economic catchment of the site. Some examples will help to illustrate the kinds of difference involved. Bailey (1975b) analysed certain Australian shell deposits and found that some had markedly different species compositions from others, despite their being geographically close together. One was a natural deposit, the other a product of human exploitation. The discrepancy was explained by the fact that, having derived from different processes, they represented different catchments and selective agencies. Vita-Finzi & Higgs (1970) were able to show that apparent contradictions in the faunal evolution of the Mount Carmel caves could be explained if one took into account the fact that the large mammals would have derived from one or more (larger) catchment areas – the site exploitation territory, whereas the micro-mammals would almost certainly have derived from another (much smaller), possibly representing the hunting range of owls. Flannery (1976) has analysed the varying catchments demonstrated by some of the site

contents of the Formative Period village of San José Mogote in the Oaxaca Valley. He found that while basic food stuffs probably came from within a relatively restricted radius around the site, mineral resources frequently came from much farther away, up to several hundred kilometres for shell and obsidian.

One further difference between catchment and territorial analysis is worthy of comment, although the two clearly have elements of similarity and the distinctions should not be overemphasised. In general, catchment analysis is an *empirical* statement of observations concerning the geographical relationship between an archaeological site and its constituents, and whether these arrived there through geological, meteorological, human, or other biological agencies. Territorial analysis in the sense discussed above also has an empirical, observational element, of course; but it is far more importantly a *theoretical* expression of what we believe to be some norms of human exploitative behaviour. The purely observational aspect is necessarily restricted, as we are frequently concerned with commodities of widespread distributions, rather than with those coming from one or a few point sources. In these circumstances we are forced to rely upon our theoretical construct of the time–distance factor to locate for us roughly the zone of maximum economic effort and return.

Over the past few years a great deal of criticism has been levelled at catchment and territorial analysis. Hodder & Orton (1976) provide a characteristic example. Many criticisms stem from misunderstandings as to the basic objectives, premises, and techniques involved. Some have resulted from the confusion between the two types of analysis. Doubtless some criticisms are a result of the inadequacies in our exposition. Many of the more perceptive criticisms may be applicable to the earliest essays in the field, but are at least far less so to later studies (e.g. Higgs 1975). It is hoped that the discussion above will have allayed some of the doubts and fears. However, as much of the remainder of the volume depends upon the validity of territorial analysis in particular, we feel it worthwhile to attempt brief answers to some of the more frequent objections.

By far the most frequent of these is that in taking modern conditions of environment and land use as a basis from which to work we are failing to take account of changes in these factors since the time of occupation. This, fortunately, is easily answered. It just is not so. The modern situation is indeed taken as one of the critical sources of information, particularly with regard to the land-use potential. Considerable efforts are made to perceive the extent and nature of environmental change during and since the sites' occupation, however. Indeed, such changes formed a critical part of the hypothesis offered in some studies (e.g. Vita-Finzi & Higgs 1970, Dennell & Webley 1975). It may, of course, be the case that in particular instances it will be seen, following more detailed studies, that failure to take account of certain changes will have rendered our explanations false. In view of the fact that we have now carried out hundreds of analyses covering most of the countries of Europe (while colleagues have employed the technique on all the other humanly inhabited continents), it would be most surprising if this did not prove to be so. This will not constitute a valid objection to the theory or method, however, but only a demonstration that they can be poorly used or that they will only provide lasting results in a proportion of cases. Archaeology has after all available to it a whole battery of disciplines and techniques to aid in the interpretation of past environmental change. We probably cannot do better than quote from Flannery (1976) on this point. Of environmental change since the time of a site's occupation he writes that 'this is a question that will always be with us, not merely in site catchment analysis but in all phases of archaeology. One has two choices: He can throw up his hands in defeat, or he can reconstruct the prehistoric environment to the best of his ability and plunge ahead'.

A second group of criticisms focuses on the question of the relationship between land-use potential of a territory and the degree to which this was realised in prehistory. We have assumed that, in the long term, economic potential will tend to have been used to best advantage within the limitations of the current technology; for output to have been optimised. Others have doubted this whether on ethnographic (Hodder & Orton 1976) or archaeological and palaeoeconomic grounds (Flannery 1976). We have discussed in detail our reasons for this assumption in Chapter 1. It is important to realise that our assumption is not expected to apply to each individual site at every point in its development; yet it may remain a valid generalisation. It is equally important to remember that the assumption does not imply that all commodities will have been exploited to produce a maximum yield, or even a maximum sustainable yield. Where a population is limited by the availability of commodity A, there may be little point in overproduction of commodities B and C, even if this can be achieved with little additional effort. It is thus no part of our argument that the economies practised at all prehistoric sites will be accurately reflected in their territories. We are merely searching for, and trying to analyse, a general relationship between sites and their immediate surroundings. There is ample justification for this attempt not only in our own results, but in the findings of geography, ethnography, and ethology.

We have been similarly taken to task for our assumption that subsistence factors will have been of paramount importance in determining site location (and hence the details of the exploitation territories). We have already outlined (Chapter 1) our reasons for considering dietary resources to have been of the first importance. Again, it has never been claimed that this proposition will be justified in all cases. There will be many individual sites which are located for other purposes than subsistence, or for which there are other important elements involved. In fact territorial and catchment analyses can provide most useful indications of this in some cases, as was found at the site of Rivoli (Jarman, M. R. 1976c). There is, however, considerable evidence from a number of disciplines which suggests that for subsistence economies it is generally matters of food supply that are the primary influence upon site location. It is always difficult to document such a contention from the ethnographic data. Most ethnographers are little concerned with the question, and the data thus tend to be absent or to be available only in a haphazard and fortuitous form. Site location factors, where discussed, are very rarely ranked in order of importance. One is also usually faced with the problem of being confronted primarily with evidence as to culturally defined ideals rather than of actual site locations.

However, even a brief and casual survey of some of the literature reveals the great and widespread importance of subsistence in affecting site location. Caribou migration patterns and fishing resources are of paramount importance in determining Inuit site location (Hoffman 1976). For the Guayaki the 'cultivation of *guchu* [larvae found in the pindo palm] . . . exerts a profound influence upon the wandering habits of the Guayaki in that it gives an order to their travels' (Clastres 1972). Other factors are the proximity of water and the fear of lightning. For the G/Wi 'The availability of food plants is the principal factor governing the band's choice of campsite' (Silberbauer 1972) except when surface water is available. Similar considerations govern the choice of !Kung campsites (Lee & De Vore 1976). Tindale (1972) lists availability of water, animal, and plant food among the factors controlling site location for the Pitjandjara. Other factors are the availability of firewood, visibility, presence of warm ground, and the absence of the spiny seeds of *Calotis hispidula* and of too many rocks. For the Birhors (Sinha 1972) proximity of forest resources, water, other competing groups, and of tribal markets are taken into account. The spawning grounds of the dog salmon used to be the critical factor determining Ainu site location (Watanabe 1972). Significantly, when the economy changed to an agricultural one the pattern of site location changed as well. Salzman (1972) lists exclusively economic factors as influencing population movement among the Yarahmadzai in Iranian Baluchistan, among these being the distribution of water and pasture, and the availability of an urban labour market. Conklin (1957) notes that for the Hanunóo a number of factors, including religious prohibitions, and the existing distribution of population and land use have the effect of delimiting the general area available for new swiddens, while soil, climate, and terrain are critical in their precise location. Similarly, among the Yąnomamö of South America, while population pressure and defensibility determine the general pattern of site distribution, 'Once the general area is selected, the specific garden location is decided by topographic features, drainage, water supply and vegetation type' (Chagnon 1968).

Turning to studies of historic and prehistoric site location a similar pattern emerges. Water run-off and the water-retention characteristics of the soil were critical in the choice of the sites for Hopi fields (Bradfield 1971). Green (1973) found that 'agricultural requirements underlay settlement location' for Maya sites in Belize. Soil was chosen for settlement 'which produces the best *milpa* [forest agriculture] today', whereas other soils were specifically avoided. Green also detected a correlation with navigable water, which she interpreted as indicating the importance of transport and trade. This may well have been the case, but it is also worthy of note that not one of her sites is actually on a navigable river, and that therefore some other factor may also be involved. It would be interesting to know how many such rivers there are, for instance, and how far it is possible to get away from them while satisfying other requirements. A further correlation observed was with other sites; in other words sites tended to cluster. Again the 'social advantages' of trade and services provide a possible explanation of this, but as Green points out the correlation may be at least in part due to the distribution of the significant environmental variables. In Veracruz Rossman (1976) observed a comparable strong correlation of sites with the *lomas* soils, which provide the best land for *milpa* cultivation in that area today.

Flannery (1976) quite rightly makes the point that one must take account of seasonal camps which may be used to expand the 'economic catchment' of a site. In our terms, as we have discussed, this involves defining the annual territory of a group, not just the individual site exploitation territories. The apparent difference between Flannery's viewpoint and his interpretation of ours resolves itself purely as a slight confusion between the exploitation territory and the total catchment of a site. As he points out, temporary camps are a means by which resources from outside the exploitation territory of a home base (i.e. beyond the range of day-to-day exploitation) may nevertheless be integrated into the economy. As he also indicates, the existence of such temporary camps may sometimes be reliably inferred from the contents of a home base, even if the camps themselves have not yet been discovered.

A number of minor points can be dealt with less laboriously. It has been objected that we have relied over-much upon the hypothesis of the zonation of exploitation patterns around sites, a hypothesis which may describe special cases rather than the general situation (Hodder & Orton 1976). It is true that we have made considerable use of Chisholm's (1968) discussion of this and other phenomena, but we have been much more concerned with an attempt to define reasonable and practical territorial limits than with the details of zonation which may on occasion have existed within these limits. Suggestions that we have only treated single sites in isolation rather than groups of sites, and that we have failed to relate site distribution patterns to the overall availability of different resources, are dealt with in some of the papers in Higgs (1975). We fully agree with Flannery (1976) that relatively small areas of land of very high productivity can be of great importance; and that a consistent pattern of association of sites with such areas is almost certain to be of significance. As pointed out before, we do not accept his general proposition that villages will have had more land at their disposal than their populations needed, and thus his argument for 'the primacy of social factors in the spacing of villages'. Social factors will necessarily have had an effect, and it is just possible that in his particular study area it was a primary influence. Considerations discussed in Chapter 1 lead us to the conclusion that, in general, social factors will have been of secondary importance, however. Indeed it is revealing that Flannery himself emphasises that 'the social factors may play a frequently unrecognised ecological role' of population regulation, suggesting that they are themselves dependent upon other more crucial forces.

A final group of criticisms, not so far mentioned,

must also be discussed. These have come primarily from those interested in developing the use of some of the established geographical models of spatial analysis in archaeological studies. It seems to us that the criticisms from this quarter are largely the result of misunderstandings of the way in which our techniques were developed, the objectives which we had in mind, and the data with which we are dealing. It is entirely true, as Hodder & Orton (1976) have pointed out, that we have tended to dismiss as noise the non-economic factors in site distribution, and have thus in general assigned a secondary rôle to such matters as trade, defence, building materials, and the social factors involved in determining inter-site distance. This is neither through accident nor oversight. Nor is it by chance that most if not all of the studies in which these factors appear to be of heightened importance concern periods and areas where there have developed complex and sophisticated economies. These cases are commonly characterised by complex site hierarchies, evidence of an 'urban elite', or at least a group of people not primarily dependent upon their own subsistence activities, and by evidence of 'central places' acting as foci of services for a surrounding area rather than as centres for extractive exploitation serving their own populations. These features are among the hallmarks of advanced 'civilised' or 'semi-civilised' societies, in which sufficiently large and dependable economic surpluses are available to support the superstructure of a state.

This brings into operation a comparable but different set of forces operating on the spacing of sites. Energy and distance remain of great importance, but the significant factor is the range over which a centre can effectively transmit certain services, or the distance which people are prepared to travel for certain economic and social benefits. In these circumstances the basic factor of the availability of subsistence products may well be outweighed, or even totally obscured. This distinction is explicitly recognised by Earle (1976) for instance, who found in his consideration of the Valley of Mexico and of southern Veracruz that in the Formative Period 'The founding and spacing of hamlets and small villages followed one set of rules, the growth and spacing of large villages or regional centers followed another'.

The studies which gave rise to the theory and techniques of catchment and territorial analysis, and which are the primary concern of this volume, deal with much simpler levels of economic and social organisation than this. We believe that the principles which we have discussed remain of great significance for much of the

rural population even of advanced societies, and modern studies such as that of Chisholm would seem to justify this belief. We have never suggested that all aspects and levels of site location will conform to the same set of rules, however, and it is of course quite apparent that in a market- and services-oriented economy other factors than subsistence will come increasingly into play. Flannery (1976) indicates our situation precisely when he says in his discussion of complex settlement systems that 'It is unlikely that central place models will ever play a major role in Early Formative archaeology' because of the apparent absence of site hierarchies. In other words, prior to certain stages of regional development, sites *will* as a general rule be located according to the availability of natural resources, and not in terms of 'service catchments'.

MOBILITY

In the consideration of the detailed field analyses which constitute much of this book we shall frequently be presented with situations which in our view are best appreciated in terms of *seasonal mobility*. It is important therefore to set out here in general terms the arguments which have led us to this conclusion.

The most casual appraisal of natural resources indicates that they are not distributed either evenly or at random in the world. There are great variations both spatially and chronologically. As far as chronological variation is concerned, we must deal not only with fluctuations such as are consequent upon long-term climatic and environmental change, but also short-term variations, from year to year and from season to season. It is true, as was emphasised earlier, that archaeological studies are ill-equipped to deal with local and short-term changes, but in as much as they are regular and predictable something can be done. It is of great importance that something should be done, as periodic imbalances in the distribution of resources are among the most crucial factors which influence animal and human behaviour. The most significant aspect of variation for the purposes of the present discussion is that of seasonal change. As has already been pointed out, seasonality of resources can have a critical effect on human territories.

Let us take a simple, generalised, hypothetical example. The mountainous regions of the temperate latitudes of the northern hemisphere are, as a whole, characterised by low temperatures and snow cover in winter. The degree to which these factors are significant varies enormously of course from area to area, according to altitude, aspect, geographical position, and so on; but the generalisation is valid. Again, as a generalisation, one can say that as far as subsistence economies are concerned these regions offer primarily grazing resources, and are relatively poor in arable potential or other sources of plant staples. Thus the mountains as a zone would have tended in the past, as now, to be exploited mainly by animal-based economies. Winter conditions in these areas are clearly hostile to most grazing animals, the only exceptions being those specially adapted to cold and to finding food under appreciable depths of snow. There is thus considerable incentive for the animals to move away from mountainous areas in winter, to areas where these limitations do not apply, or apply less severely. If the herd is under human control the incentive is there for the animals to be herded to such areas. This is not to say that no animals under 'natural' conditions would stay and survive in the mountains throughout the winter, nor that pastoralists have at their disposal no expedients whereby this could be achieved. The pressure for movement remains.

In the summer, by contrast, the mountains are at their best from the point of view of herbivores. Relatively high levels of spring and summer precipitation tend to produce lush and continuous summer plant growth, and in these periods the potential grazing productivity of mountain areas is at its height. These conditions attract grazing animals from other regions, and there is thus an increase of the animal population in summer, whether or not these animals are herded by man.

For many lowland regions, particularly in coastal areas, the converse is true. The lower altitudes (and in some cases the proximity of the sea) moderate the extremes of winter cold and snowfall; while in many lowland areas plant growth is reduced or even ceases altogether for much of the summer and early autumn, due to lack of rainfall. In Western Europe the exceptionally dry summers of 1975 and 1976 indicated dramatically how widespread and important the impact of this seasonal imbalance can be. Such was the shortage of summer grazing that in many areas grazing resources and hay customarily reserved for winter use were exhausted far earlier than this, leading to an unacceptable strain on the economic system and the collapse of many livestock operations. There is thus the reverse tendency of herbivores to move away from the lowlands in summer, into the highlands with their better grazing resources.

We have then a situation in which the uneven seasonal distribution of resources can be overcome by the mechanism of mobility, which integrates the resources of a number of geographical entities. Resources which can be integrated in this way to overcome the limitations inherent in any single area may be termed *complementary resources*. There are, of course, other ways in which animals can adapt to this situation. The most obvious possibility, in theory, would be that animal populations might be maintained at whatever levels could be sustained in a single region at the worst time of the year. This is against all the observed evidence, however, and there are powerful theoretical considerations which make this an unlikely long-term solution. One important index of success in an animal species is in terms of population numbers. Regulation of populations to the level sustainable at the period of least available resources would obviously be extremely wasteful of resources at the period of their maximum availability. Any animal population or species which managed through the mechanism of seasonal movement to make better use of the total available resources, and thus to maintain a higher population, would in the long run outcompete the less efficient populations or species.

Two further possibilities exist. Some species are adapted to fluctuating resources by the extreme flexibility of their population size; others by a variety of storage mechanisms. Species with rapid sexual maturation and thus with the capacity for short-term adjustments in population size can take advantage of periods of glut by higher rates of population increase, lowered breeding rates or a cessation of breeding allowing levels to adjust to the lean periods. Some small rodents are among the obvious examples of this capability. This is not directly relevant to our present concerns, however. Our main interest is in the medium-sized and large herbivores which are of primary economic significance. These are all annual or at most bi-annual breeders, and thus cannot take effective advantage of seasonal surpluses in this way. The squirrel is an obvious example of an animal which makes use of stored food from periods of abundance in order to survive periods of scarcity. In a sense one could view the internal storage of fatty reserves by species which habitually hibernate as an extreme example of a similar process. This adaptation is unknown at any very significant level in grazing animals. They do, of course, store body fat in the late summer which is metabolised for energy during the winter lean season; but this does not happen to anything like the extent which would support long periods of inactivity with zero food intake.

Human food storage, fulfilling exactly the same rôle

of evening out the extremes of abundance and shortage, is a highly developed adaptation. Deposits of mammoth bones at some Ukrainian Palaeolithic sites have sometimes been interpreted as the remains of food stores. Ethnographic evidence indicates the widespread storage of meat and fish by drying and salting, while arctic peoples have the technique of freezing at their disposal. Many plant seeds are relatively easily stored, designed as they are in many cases to withstand several months under natural conditions without spoiling. In the present context it is of more relevance to note that one of the commonest means by which human exploiters of herbivores attempt to even out the seasonal resource distribution of their animals is through the storage of their fodder. Indeed, as will be seen later, there is good reason for supposing that such practices are of great antiquity. It is worth pointing out, however, that at least as far as we can judge from the modern situation, these techniques are seldom if ever sufficient in themselves to make the most of seasonal abundance. They are almost always employed in addition to, not instead of, the primary mechanism of mobility. Storage of winter fodder in the form of hay or foggage tends to be most highly developed in areas where no alternative mechanisms exist, or where these are already fully utilised.

This, then, is the general hypothesis: that important variations in resource distribution have placed great selective value upon mechanisms which permit the integration of complementary resources. Seasonal mobility is of great importance among these, permitting the maintenance of a higher overall population than would be possible through the exploitation of the resources individually by separate populations. The evidence in support of this hypothesis is substantial and varied, and draws on ethological, historical, and ethnographic studies.

The amount of information about animal mobility is too dauntingly large for us even to attempt a general summary here. As Lack (1954) puts it 'Regular, seasonal journeys from one area to another and back again later are made by many birds, whales, seals, bats, fish, cuttlefish, lepidoptera, dragonflies, locusts, and probably hoverflies. Migration has been evolved where it results in a higher reproductive rate or a lower mortality than residence throughout the year, and it is characteristic of areas subject to marked seasonal changes'. We shall concentrate on a number of species of herbivorous animals which have a special interest to us because of their economic importance to man. A number of specific causes has been suggested as creating the need for these movements, but it seems that

food shortage – actual or potential – or the attraction of better food resources in another area is almost always, if not invariably, one of the important factors involved. In a number of cases additional factors, such as avoidance of insects or other parasites, are certainly of significance, but the balance of population to resources seems always to be a major consideration, and may be taken as the general overriding factor in all such behaviour patterns.

The reindeer give one of the clearest and best known examples of seasonal movement among animals. All populations of *Rangifer* are migratory to some extent. It has been argued by Bouchud (1966) and others that certain Pleistocene populations may not have been nearly so mobile as those extant today. Even accepting his interpretation of the evidence, it suggested a minimum seasonal movement of the order of about 60 km, while other arguments can be put forward (Sturdy 1972, 1975) which strongly suggest a more marked seasonal movement.

As far as modern populations of reindeer are concerned the degree of migration varies from population to population and from area to area. In some circumstances these movements are restricted, and cover relatively small distances. This is characteristic of isolated populations on islands, or in other cases where there are natural barriers to movement. Brody (1976) illustrates such a situation on Baffin Island. More usual is the pattern described by Kelsall (1968), in which the Barren Ground caribou (reindeer) regularly travel as much as five hundred miles from their winter to their summer ranges (Figure 13). Precise ranges and migration routes vary from year to year, and it is not necessarily the whole population that moves every year. Migration routes are at their most predictable where rivers, lakes, or other natural features constrict the possible routes, and annually used 'reindeer crossings' result. Some individuals will spend an entire year in the winter range. Nevertheless a broad pattern of seasonal migration is the norm.

The American bison is almost equally renowned for its long-distance migration behaviour. As Roe (1972) has indicated, there must be some doubt as to how much credence can be given to the historical accounts of mass migrations regularly involving tens or even hundreds of thousands of individuals. There seems to be very little doubt as to the mobility of bison herds, however, and the movements seem on the whole to have been related to travel between different seasonal ranges. Meagher (1973) has documented comparable short-distance movements of bison in Yellowstone National Park (Figure 14). Here altitude as much as

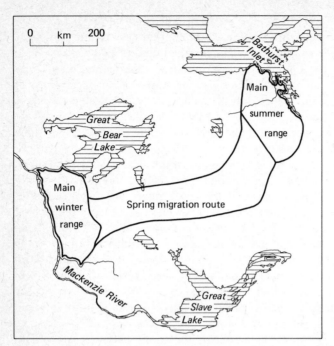

Figure 13. The seasonal range and spring migration route of one herd of barren ground caribou in 1950–51. After Kelsall (1957).

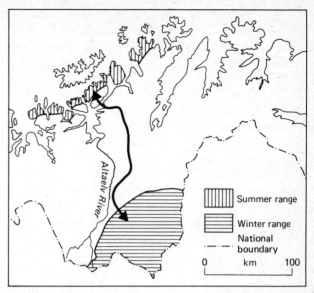

Figure 15. Main summer and winter ranges of reindeer in northern Norway, showing the route taken by one group of Lapps. After Brandon-Cox (1969).

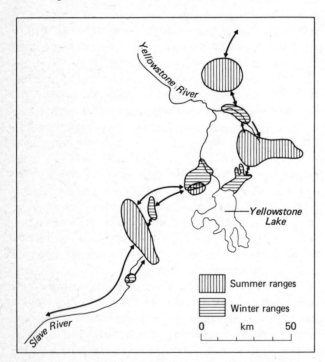

Figure 14. Main summer and winter ranges of bison in Yellowstone National Park. Arrows indicate routes of seasonal movement. After Meagher (1973).

geographical distance seems to be of primary importance.

Many other large and medium-sized herbivores have been shown to undertake comparable seasonal move-

ments. Elk customarily travel from 50–300 km between their summer and winter ranges. Geist's work on the mountain sheep (1971) has given a picture of predictable small scale seasonal movement, as has that of Grubb & Jewell (1966) for the feral Soay sheep. Similar movements are known for the saiga antelope, and for many of the African antelopes, such as the eland and the wildebeest.

As far as human economies are concerned there is an equal range of examples available. The Lapps (Figure 15) are well known for their mobile reindeer pastoralism, with the herders frequently following the animals for as much as 200 km between the summer and winter ranges. Many Near Eastern tribes are equally celebrated for their mobile pastoralism, which sometimes depends on the camel, sometimes on sheep and goats. As Spooner (1972) indicates, the precise nature and extent of mobility is immensely variable, depending both upon environmental variables and upon the animal involved. At one extreme movement is within as small an area as 20 km; while at the other, tribes such as the Qashqai undertake an annual round trip of about 1000 km. The movements are, however, distinguished on the whole by a high degree of regularity and predictability. Figure 16 shows the seasonal movement of one such group, the Basseri.

It is to be emphasised that, as with other animals, human patterns of mobility and migration are geographically ubiquitous, and that they are rarely if ever a matter for choice. They are forced upon many popula-

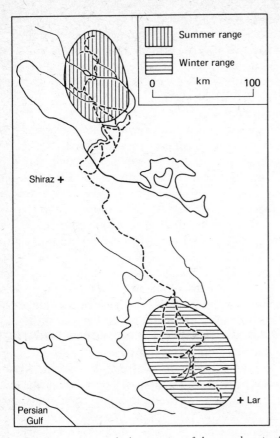

Figure 16. Main summer and winter ranges of sheep and goats of the Basseri tribe in southern Iran, showing main routes of seasonal movement. After Barth (1959–60).

apart from the subarctic and Near Eastern examples mentioned above, it is the dominant mode of subsistence over very large areas of Africa (cf. for example, Evans-Pritchard 1940, Gulliver 1955, Stenning 1959); while Ekvall (1968) has documented the importance in Tibet of similar patterns of mobility. These indeed constitute a crucial aspect of subsistence behaviour throughout much of Central Asia. Seasonal movements of varying lengths form an important part of many European stock-rearing and mixed farming economies. Nor should we imagine that such mobility is an adaptation found only in exclusively animal-based economies. Many pastoralists incorporate an arable element into their subsistence. Moreover the North American 'suitcase farmers' and other comparable migrant workers provide an example of the mobile exploitation of a variety of commercial arable crops.

Thus, to sum up, it is evident that seasonal mobility is a widespread mechanism by which complementary resources are integrated. Animals naturally make use of this adaptation, and man can associate himself with those mobile species, whether as a hunter and gatherer, herd follower, or pastoralist. In this way the human exploiters enjoy the same advantages as the animal species, in maintaining a higher population than would otherwise be possible.

There are many possible ways of classifying mobile economies. Some, such as that of Arbos (1922), are derived from a detailed analysis of modern and historical data, and are specific and complex in nature. As usual, the deficiencies of archaeological data encourage us to adopt a simple and more generalised scheme. We include within the term *transhumance* all mobile economies which practice regular seasonal movements that cover a considerable distance and involve the movement of all or most of the human group. We have sometimes found it useful to distinguish between short-range transhumance, by which we mean systems involving movements of up to 50–60 km, and long-range transhumance, referring to movements of greater amplitude. The term *stock transference* is useful to denote those economies in which only a small section of the human group moves with the animals, often the young men or a specialist group of herders. This form of mobility frequently involves relatively short geographical distances, and is a characteristic of what we have called mobile-cum-sedentary economies (see p. viii).

It must be borne in mind, however, that even this simple classification introduces arbitrary divisions into an endlessly varying spectrum. Even within a single area there is often a continuum both of distances

tions by the same broad environmental exigencies as apply to other species, and confer the same evolutionary benefits. As Barth (1960) points out for the Persian province of Fars, the system of mobile pastoralism in operation allows the pastures 'to support a far higher population than would be supported by any other pastoral pattern of land use.'

Nor are these adaptations limited to one particular kind of economy, but characterise most subsistence economies in environments with seasonal extremes. Seasonal mobility is such a common feature among hunters and gatherers that the rare instances of relative sedentism, such as the Indians of the northwest coast of North America, are often singled out for comment. The Inuit Eskimo (cf. Freeman, M. M. R. *et al.* 1976) at one environmental extreme, and the Wik Monkan Australian aborigines at another (Thomson 1939) practise economies employing a high degree of seasonal movement, while most other hunters and gatherers rely upon such movements to a greater or lesser extent. Mobile pastoralism is so widespread as to preclude any notion of our compiling a comprehensive list. Quite travelled and of degrees of mobility. It is clear that these two factors are closely related. The possibility of effective resource integration within a relatively localised framework is an important aspect of the establishment of stock transference systems which often maintain close links with a sedentary part of the economy. The more that environmental variables require long-range movement, the greater the tendency of whole families or communities to be involved in the transhumance. These two systems may therefore be thought of as 'modal types', despite the fact that there are innumerable integradations linking the distances travelled by long-range transhumants with those travelled by short-range transhumants; and linking these latter with those travelled by peoples practising stock transference. Similarly, it is reasonable to talk in terms of transhumance as defined above, despite the fact that in many cases transhumants will maintain permanent villages in which the sick or the elderly may live the whole year round. The complexity of pastoralist economies in terms of the degree and range of mobility, the herd composition, and the relationships maintained with sedentary groups is admirably illustrated by Ekvall's (1968) description of Tibetan pastoralism. It is also revealing to note that the Tibetans themselves find it worthwhile to make a basic division very much on the lines discussed above. The distinction between the *aBrog Pa* (high pasturage ones) and the *Sa Ma aBrog* (neither soil nor high pasturage) rests largely on the variable but close links which the latter retain with sedentary communities, themselves largely a factor of distance.

SEDENTISM

A similar intergradation is found between sedentary and mobile-cum-sedentary economies. The category 'sedentary' is itself a variable one, implying a range of mobility localised within closely circumscribed limits; while, as pointed out above, sedentary economies frequently incorporate a mobile-cum-sedentary element. The importance of sedentism has traditionally been overstated in prehistoric studies, or, to be more precise, that of mobility has been largely ignored. Sedentism has been assumed *a priori* in the majority of cases, mobility being regarded as a rarity for which there must be strong evidence before its existence can be seriously entertained. The considerable advantages of mobility in many circumstances have already been discussed. Sedentism seems on the whole to be a rare phenomenon among recent hunter and gatherer populations. Of the 29 groups listed by Murdock (1967)

on the northwest coast of America, the classic exemplars of 'primitive' sedentism, less than half lived in 'compact, relatively permanent settlements', and even these included minor or occasional mobile elements in their economy. In view of the advantages of sedentism with respect to the efficient use of energy this scarcity is of some interest.

Where sedentism does occur amongst hunters and gatherers it seems generally to be related to a number of recurrent features. It is probably no coincidence that it is almost exclusively confined to coastal groups, where aquatic resources are available as a seasonal complement to the terrestrial resources. In many cases this is associated with an inaccessible and/or relatively unproductive hinterland, which would not repay intensive exploitation. This is the case for many of the Northwest Coast Indians, and also for the Chugach and the East Greenland Eskimo. Similar limitations are presented by small islands or those with an unproductive hinterland, and this may well have contributed to the existence of relatively sedentary populations in the Aleutians and the islands of the Bering Strait.

Exceptions exist, of course. The North Alaskan Eskimos provide an example of a population which was primarily sedentary despite the presence of an accessible and productive hinterland. The latter was exploited by a separate group. The explanation in this case is perhaps to be seen in the economic dependence upon the bowhead whale. Poor ice formation in this area allows the bowhead to come much closer to the coast than customarily; it is thus accessible within the potential exploitation territory of coastal populations, and was indeed the main dietary staple.

Bowheads are large animals, weighing up to 60 tons each. This circumstance has two interesting consequences, each of which may well have encouraged sedentism. Firstly, they require considerable investment activity for their exploitation. Substantial boats and other equipment are needed, and the time and experience required to hunt such prey successfully must also be considered. Secondly, when dietary resources come in such large but relatively unpredictable parcels, the practice of food storage is necessary both in order to minimise waste and to spread the yield over a sufficient proportion of the year for a whale-based economy to be viable. The arctic climate, and the ease with which the blubber can be rendered down to provide an energy-rich product with good keeping qualities, clearly enhance the possibilities for the use of the bowhead as a staple.

The example of the North Alaskan Eskimo thus brings us to another feature common to most sedentary populations of hunters and gatherers; that is that they all rely to some extent upon food storage. As we have discussed elsewhere, this is a not uncommon adaptation among other animal species, and it is not surprising that it also occurs at all levels of human economic organisation. The advantages of such an adaptation are not necessarily available to all, however. Food storage may be viewed as a means whereby periodic superabundance can be spread and transferred to leaner seasons. The first precondition is thus that there should be periods of substantial surplus. It is also necessary that the conditions and technology for storage should be available. Not all foods can be preserved satisfactorily, and climatic and ecological circumstances also have an impact. It should be remembered, too, that food storage is a form of investment activity and that it thus requires a variable but often considerable input of labour for no immediate return. In some cases (Hoffman 1976, Suttles 1968) the effort involved in storing food can substantially exceed the cost of harvesting. The labour must obviously be available and the expected return sufficiently high and reliable for the investment to be worth it. As we have discussed (Chapter 1), some populations are in economic and ecological situations which make it difficult for them to indulge in substantial investment of labour.

It is worth commenting that trade appears in this context as the spatial analogue of storage, involving the transfer of food in the dimension of space rather than time. The comparability of the two mechanisms is underlined by their apparently reciprocal relationship. For as the importance of seasonal mobility seems to decrease for the bulk of the population with the development of more complex and labour-intensive economies, so the rôle of trade and marketing networks becomes ever more significant. Nevertheless, trade, like storage, is present in some circumstances at all levels of complexity. It is noteworthy that in the example of the North Alaskan Eskimo discussed above, trade in whale oil and caribou skins, combined with occasional movements inland for caribou exploitation and coastwards for the taking of the smaller sea mammals, were important mechanisms which tended to even out disadvantageous fluctuations in the two economies, increasing the flexibility and viability of each.

Despite our belief that sedentism has been unjustifiably and uncritically accepted as the normal mode of settlement for prehistoric man, it remains apparent nevertheless that, as suggested above, it becomes an increasingly prevalent pattern. Certainly there are many more sedentary farmers, proportionately, than there are sedentary hunters and gatherers. The relative

and quantitative growth of sedentary economies deserves comment.

Among the factors involved are the effects of increasing labour and investment costs, and of rising population pressure. We have discussed at some length (pp. 27–36) the effect of high labour costs on the size of exploitation territories. Similarly, the more effort invested in an area or enterprise the greater the incentive to remain sufficiently stationary to protect the investment and reap its reward. Rising population was, and remains a potent force encouraging increased sedentism. Dense populations require correspondingly high levels of food production, and land-extensive mobile economies thus tend in the long run to be supplanted by more intensive systems where these are viable. They characteristically rely upon a high labour input, and frequently upon considerable long-term investment, both factors tending to favour sedentism. While in some cases the mobile and sedentary economies can be integrated successfully, many cases result ultimately in the competition for a resource which is of critical importance for each system. In such circumstances the more powerful and productive economy is inevitably the winner. Countless mobile economies have first retreated, and finally succumbed altogether, to the pressures exerted by sedentary agriculturalists, and as we shall see in Chapter 6 there is evidence to suggest that this process has a long prehistory.

Other factors involved in the proliferation of sedentary populations include the reliable and repeated production of surpluses and the capacity for their storage. It was noted in our discussion of the North Alaskan Eskimo that the large size of the bowhead whales coupled with the possibilities of storage had a crucial effect in this respect. Cereal-based economies face a comparable situation. The main harvest is concentrated in a short space of time, frequently a matter of a few weeks. The population is thus presented with a colossal short-term surplus which it must preserve for consumption over the rest of the year. It is of some significance, however, that cereals are inherently easier to store in most environments than are many other staple resources. This is not to say that there would have been no difficulties or disasters, but whereas untreated meat, for instance, would inevitably start to deteriorate in temperate conditions within a week or so, dry-ripe cereals are adapted to last months without spoiling, and as long as they could be kept dry would present few problems of storage.

It can be seen from the foregoing discussion that a consideration of the degree of mobility or sedentism involved is of considerable importance in the analysis of prehistoric economies. Not only does the question impinge directly on the practical matter of the assessment of exploitation territories, it also carries important implications concerning the general scope of the economy, its productive potential, and its complexity of organisation. We have concentrated so far on modern and recent historical data in an effort to show the wide-ranging relevance, and the adaptive significance, of patterns of population distribution, the relationships of settlements to their immediate surroundings, and the various mechanisms of resource integration between population and population, area and area. In Chapters 4–6 we shall attempt to pursue these matters further with reference to prehistoric data.

3. PALAEOECONOMIC PERSPECTIVES

THEORETICAL CONSIDERATIONS

It became apparent very early in the work of the Project that the study of prehistoric agriculture was greatly influenced by two important beliefs. The first of these was that the origins of domestication lay in the Near East; the second was that it occurred for the first time in the Holocene period, prior to which all men were hunters and gatherers. Close examination of these propositions revealed that they were hypotheses rather than facts; reasonable hypotheses, indeed, but not beyond question. There is ample evidence which indicates the existence of farming economies in the Near East and in the Holocene; there is remarkably little evidence which bears directly upon the nature of exploitation patterns in the Pleistocene, while alternative areas of early agricultural development in the Old World have received very little attention until the past few years.

The study of early domestication has been conducted almost exclusively by zoologists and botanists. This is perhaps less satisfactory than might appear at first sight. Domestication involves plants and animals, it is true; but it also involves man. 'The adjective "domestic" describes human behaviour to the commensal', as Spurway (1955) put it. From this viewpoint it is helpful to have an approach to domestication which focuses on human economic behaviour rather than on the exploited organisms themselves. This ought to be especially relevant to archaeology, given its concern with past human behaviour.

One of the main factors which has tended in the past to encourage a parochial view of early domestication is the hypothesis that only those species which are now domesticated can have been so in the past. In the literature one frequently comes across references to 'potentially domesticable' species, by which is usually meant the modern domesticates of developed agricultural systems. However useful this may originally have been in focusing attention on those species that have become of major worldwide importance this now seems an unnecessarily restrictive and static view of the matter. An emphasis on economic behaviour rather than on particular species of plants and animals encour-

ages the consideration of man's close exploitative relationships with species other than the common domesticates of today. We know of animals such as the onager, and plants such as buckwheat, foxtail millet, and the primitive wheats, which have declined drastically in importance or gone out of domestication altogether when superseded by more effective economic alternatives.

There is no reason to suppose that this flexibility in man–animal and man–plant relationships is solely a recent phenomenon. Evidence for close economic relationships with animals now regarded purely as 'wild' species is discussed later in the chapter. There is eivdence strongly suggestive of an early form of controlled exploitation of members of the *Chenopodium* genus from both the Old and New Worlds (Helbaek 1960, Streuver 1962). Furthermore, all the modern experimental evidence indicates that a vast range of plants and animals is 'potentially domesticable', and can have their behaviour, phenotype, and genotype modified by man for his advantage. Wilkinson (1972) has discussed the evidence for animals in some detail. It thus seems that there is little reason for palaeoeconomy to restrict its enquiries to the common farmyard species, or to assume that no close economic relationships could have been established with other organisms in the prehistoric past.

Once released from the alluring but futile search for the first instance of particular domesticates, we are freer to attempt to trace the development of particular kinds of economic relationship. From this perspective it appears that most of the past discussion of early agriculture has focused upon the evolution of a particular kind of agricultural system – the broadly modern style of mixed farming, as far as Europe is concerned. In this chapter we try to isolate some regularities underlying the variety of close man–animal and man–plant relationships, and briefly discuss some of the possible forerunners to modern agriculture in the light of archaeological evidence. In subsequent chapters we shall return to a discussion of the early development of the distinctive form of agriculture seen in Europe today.

Detailed considerations of the accepted view of

3. PALAEOECONOMIC PERSPECTIVES

agricultural origins, together with possible alternative interpretations, have already been published (Higgs & Jarman 1969, 1972; Jarman, H. N. 1972; Jarman, M. R. 1976a; Jarman, M. R. & Wilkinson 1972). We may conveniently summarise the arguments in terms of terrestrial animal resources, terrestrial plant resources, and marine resources.

TERRESTRIAL ANIMAL RESOURCES

The moment that account is taken of the variability of modern man–animal relationships – in both simple and complex economies – it becomes apparent that the terms 'domestic' and 'wild' each covers a vast range of phenomena. One need only consider the difference in behaviour and relationship to man between a racehorse, a pekinese, and a Hereford bullock, for instance, or between a fox, an elephant, and a field mouse, for this variability to be apparent. It is also true that the borderline between the wild and domestic classes is blurred, there being innumerable gradations between what is thought of as a typical wild and a typical domestic animal. It is for this reason that all efforts to base a classification on any single criterion have failed. Many animals usually thought of as 'domestic' are not selectively bred – some camels, ranch cattle, and many stray cats and dogs, for example – while certain 'wild' animals (like some deer) are selectively bred for features such as antler shape. Many wild animals are tame and habituated to human presence, while hill sheep are anything but tame, and domestic mink are often positively aggressive. Physiological differences between wild and domestic populations are not invariably present, as is shown by such animals as the Indian elephant and some camels and asses. The complexity of man–animal relationships in a modern situation is admirably illustrated by Ingold's (1974) discussion of Lapp–reindeer relationships.

These are not, of course, reasons for abandoning the wild–domestic classification altogether. At certain levels of description and enquiry it is a useful and accurate tool. In studying the way in which closer, more complex, and controlled exploitative relationships arose, however, when almost by definition we are interested in the interface between the 'wild' class and the 'domestic' class, insistence on this division may prove an obstacle rather than an aid to the analysis.

The customary model for the consideration of prehistoric animal exploitation stems from a number of sources. The study of animal domestication is dominated by an approach rooted in zoology, one conse-

quence of which has been that interest has focused on physiological changes in the animals concerned. Attention has been directed away from the behavioural aspects to such a degree that the most commonly accepted definition of domestication requires that detectable physical change should have taken place in the animals as a result of selective breeding. This has some practical merits, particularly where prehistoric material is concerned; after all, there remain only the animal bones of the non-human partner in the relationship, and behavioural inferences must be tentative at best. The apparent efficacy of the approach is enhanced when the bones of prehistoric animal populations are compared with those of today's domesticates, which have frequently changed greatly as the result of millennia of selective breeding.

In order for the zoological distinction between wild and domestic animals to be a practicable and useful procedure, one must be reasonably sure that the physiological (in the case of prehistoric remains, osteological) changes took place relatively rapidly. At the very least it is necessary to be able to make some estimate of the time span involved. It is customary to suppose that early domestic animals were raised as small populations which were reproductively isolated from local wild representatives of the species. Under such conditions the changes in selective pressure undergone by the isolate might be expected to produce visible change within relatively few generations. Experimental evidence as to how rapidly specific kinds of change might have occurred is scarce and ambiguous, however. Everything depends on factors which we cannot assess accurately for the prehistoric past, such as the precise nature and severity of the new selective pressures.

It is here that the palaeoeconomic approach begins to differ clearly from the zoological approach to the problem. There is no way in which we can know that man's early steps in the intensification of his exploitative relationship with animals involved isolation or selective breeding. The accepted stereotype is of one or two immature animals being separated aimlessly, or at least casually, from the wild population; kept captive and as pets; fed poor or inadequate food (thus resulting in loss of size); and maintained in genetic-sexual isolation from the local wild population. It is possible that this occurred. On the other hand, there is little solid evidence to support the hypothesis, and alternatives exist. Indeed, when we think of the difficulty with which many modern zoo animals are persuaded to breed in substantially better conditions, one may wonder whether the envisaged prehistoric circumstances

50

can possibly have given rise to large, healthy populations of domestic stock that rapidly became economic staples. For it is striking that in most cases (with the exception of the dog) the earliest zoologically distinguished domestic animals appear on archaeological sites in large numbers and were clearly of considerable economic importance. We do not, by and large, find sites with small numbers of puny, zoologically domestic animals underlying levels in which these are more frequent, indicating the transition from casual taming to pastoralism.

An equally plausible model, and from an economic point of view a more likely one, is of gradual intensifications of man-animal relationships, involving the whole, or a large part of, a local animal population. The selective pressures operating on a herbivore population exploited by herd-following hunters, and those operating on one exploited by herd-following pastoralists, are not likely to have been sufficiently different in the short term to have given rise to dramatic osteological change. Furthermore, in view of the many modern and historical examples of extensive interbreeding between wild and domestic populations of the same species (Higgs & Jarman 1972, Jarman, M. R. & Wilkinson 1972) – sometimes due to the impracticability of preventing it, sometimes as an intentional measure of animal husbandry – we may reasonably question the assumption that total genetic isolation between wild and domestic populations was the rule in prehistoric times.

These arguments add up to the strong possibility that human economic behaviour may have changed significantly in prehistoric times without causing observable osteological change. The available zoological techniques may be able to show with varying degrees of certainty that animals were domesticated at certain periods and in certain areas, but they cannot show that prior to this period the animals were hunted. In fact, zoology is little concerned with the precise nature of the pattern of exploitation. It may be reasonable to continue employing these criteria for that advanced stage of development where selective breeding is well established and continuous; for this should indeed eventually leave detectable osteological traces. It would be unjustifiable to infer from this that there had been no significant change in economic behaviour at an earlier (possibly much earlier) date, however, and it is not even certain that the zoologically detectable selective breeding was the most important of such changes from the human point of view.

An increasing realisation of the limitations of morphological data in this context has led to the use of other criteria, particularly the evidence of cropping patterns. It has been argued by Ducos (1969, 1976) and others that man-the-hunter will exploit his prey at random and that his crop will thus reflect species, age, and sex compositions roughly in accordance with those available in the vicinity of the site. Man the pastoralist, on the other hand, by virtue of his increased control over his available resources, will be able to crop selectively, and thus maintain a rational and economic pattern of exploitation. Evidence of age- and sex-biased crops has thus been taken by some workers as an indication of domestication. This is unjustified both at the theoretical and the practical level. All the available evidence leads us to conclude that animal predators rarely operate at random on their prey, whatever the specific causes of their selectivity. Selective predation has been documented among wolves, lions, cheetahs, tigers, wild dogs, raptorial birds, and many other species. Some specific examples are quoted in Jarman, M. R. & Wilkinson (1972). Modern human hunters are also often selective in their effect upon prey populations, sometimes fortuitously, sometimes by design. There is no reason to suppose that prehistoric human predation would have been different in this respect. Where it has been collected, archaeological evidence bears this out, indicating a high degree of selectivity of exploitation in many cases. As was pointed out in *Papers in Economic Prehistory* (Jarman & Wilkinson 1972), evidence of prehistoric cropping patterns remains an important aspect of palaeoeconomic analysis, but cannot be used as a simple index of domestication. This point has recently been elaborated by Wilkinson (1976) and Collier & White (1976).

If the term domestication be confined to man–animal relationships employing selective breeding, there is a need for a framework within which to discuss earlier and simpler close man–animal relationships. Here the term 'animal husbandry' may be appropriate, particularly as it describes an important aspect of human behaviour which frequently distinguishes close exploitative relationships. We may further emphasise the significant variability of man's association with the animals he exploits by suggesting a more complex classification than that in current use. There are many possible ways of going about this; the one outlined here (see Jarman, M. R. 1976a) has been designed with economic criteria and archaeological feasibility in mind. It will be seen that one of the main variables is the degree to which the animals' freedom of movement is controlled.

(1) Random predation. The human group makes no effort to control or benefit from the regularity of the

animal behaviour, simply exploiting the animal when it happens to be available. From a theoretical point of view this is unlikely to have been a common exploitation strategy as far as staple resources are concerned; being inefficient it would tend to be superseded by more effective and successful relationships.

(2) Controlled predation. In such a relationship the degree of control exerted on animal movement might be quite considerable at particular times, but would not necessarily amount to a general year-round association between man and prey. The control of animal movement in game drives or by corralling are obvious examples.

(3) Herd following. The human group, or a part of it, echoes the animal movements, maintaining a degree of contact with it, such that a given human population tends to become associated with a given animal population. Such a system could easily develop by a series of gradual intensifications to

(4) loose herding, where more direct control is exerted over animal movement at least at some time or times in the year. In a mobile economy, the spring and autumn movement, for instance, might be initiated by the herders, or controlled so as to ensure a complete transfer of the stock associated with a particular human population. Many modern pastoralist economies fall into this category.

(5) Close herding. This involves close control of animal movement all the year around, and would probably require constant human contact with the herd, and/or the extensive use of fences. This is the relationship that exists in much of Western European commercial livestock exploitation at present, except where it has developed to the stage of

(6) factory farming. Here, characteristically, the animal is kept largely immobile throughout its life, and is maintained in a wholly artificial environment.

It should be stressed that this classification is not viewed as an economic ladder of progress, with one stage inevitably developing towards, and eventually into, the next. As we have said, the first category of relationship is not likely to have been practised in the long term with respect to staple food resources in many cases; while the third and fourth categories represent patterns of exploitation which could have occurred at almost any stage of human development, and on occasion mark the maximum degree of organisation practicable or advantageous. It is also evident that the classification is primarily concerned with man's exploitation of gregarious food-supplying herbivores, and does not take account of many aspects of man's relationships with such animals as the dog and horse.

TERRESTRIAL PLANT RESOURCES

These have traditionally been studied within much the same hypothetical framework as have animal resources (Jarman, H. N. 1972). The primary criterion for assessing the economic status of a prehistoric plant food has been its morphology, with such features as the brittle rachis in cereals denoting a wild form, the tough rachis a domestic crop. Much the same objections apply to this as to purely morphological criteria for assessing animal exploitation. The application of botanical techniques and criteria can give us good evidence of some of the effects of the later stages of plant husbandry; of the point where, either because of their transportation to areas where they could not survive naturally, or because of genetic changes which would be maladaptive in the wild, we must infer large-scale human intervention to explain their survival. Again, however, it is not possible to know how long it took for visible phenotypic changes to become established after changes (which may have been of great economic importance) in human exploitation patterns. It is usual to suggest that the process would have been rapid; but one suspects that this is due as much as anything to the realisation that if it were not, we are left with a long and important period of development which available botanical procedures are powerless to elucidate. There is also the possibility that some of the morphological changes usually thought to occur only under 'domestication' may have been selected by harvesting methods applied to 'wild' plants. For instance, Lynch (1973) has suggested that groups moving from one place to another as part of a transhumant economy may have harvested plants along the way either too early or too late for the best yield, thus inadvertently selecting for either late or early maturing individuals. In the case of cereals, populations with more brittle or less brittle rachises could develop under such selection without ploughing, sowing, weeding, and other activities generally associated with domestication. In fact, as with animals, the degree and rapidity of change depend entirely upon the nature and severity of the changes in selective pressure, and upon the degree to which gene flow is maintained with other populations not thus affected. In the prehistoric context these are factors about which we can usually only speculate.

Some recognition of this state of affairs has been given by workers such as Helbaek (1970) who, while reserving the term 'domestication' for plants whose morphology has changed, used the term 'cultivated' to describe plants which may be the objects of quite sophisticated husbandry practices, but whose morphology is unaltered. It is in this sense that his (Helbaek 1966) otherwise rather confusing description of the barley from Beidha as 'cultivated wild barley' becomes clearer. Unfortunately, some other botanists have used the term 'cultivated' in different senses, or inconsistently, and it is frequently employed as a loose synonym for 'domesticated'. It is worth noting that while for botanists it is the physiological change which is the crucial event, for palaeoeconomists it is the incidence and consequences of husbandry which are of prime interest.

Zoogeographical considerations have been of some importance in the development of the accepted approach to animal domestication, but plant geography has had much more significance for the study of plant domestication. It is pointed out, plausibly, that plants are only likely to have been domesticated initially within their areas of natural distribution. An attempt is then made to determine the past distributions of the plants by reference to their modern distributions, environmental tolerances, and inferred past climatic conditions. This is reasonable enough in principle, but difficulties in the reconstruction of past environments result in the assumption that past wild cereal distributions are substantially the same as those indicated by modern relict populations.

An example of the difficulties to which this can lead, and of the contrast between a botanical and a palaeoeconomic approach, is given by the well-known site of Mureybit (van Zeist & Casparie 1968). The site lies in an area which is today some 100–150 km from the nearest wild einkorn, and is believed to be in an area too dry for this species to grow naturally now or to have done so during the occupation of the site. Plant remains from the site include einkorn which is morphologically 'wild'. Van Zeist and Casparie conclude that the cereal was regularly harvested wild at 100 km or more from the site, and carried back. From an economic point of view this is an extremely unlikely explanation. One cannot rule it out as absolutely impossible, but in terms of the time and labour involved in exploiting a resource at such a distance, it must be deemed highly improbable. This leads us to consider alternative hypotheses, of which two immediately spring to mind. The first is that the climate may have been sufficiently wetter 10 000 years ago to have permitted the existence of a local wild einkorn population. The second is that the occupants of Mureybit, located at the edge of the Euphrates floodplain, were making use of this favoured water-rich area to cultivate einkorn, despite the fact that its morphology was indistinguishable from that of the uncultivated plant (Jarman, H. N. 1972). The same range of possible hypotheses has recently been adopted

by Hillman (1975) in his discussion of plant remains from the site of Tell Abu Hureyra, some 30 km from Mureybit.

The simple wild–domestic classification is thus too crude and inflexible to be entirely adequate for the analysis of early man–plant relationships, just as it is in the case of animals. When one looks at what is really meant by plant domestication, it can be seen that the term customarily implies a whole range of activities and attitudes, including planting, weeding, watering, protection from pests, parasites, and diseases, cultivation of the ground, selection of seed for future crops, and so on. These features do not always occur together; some ethnographic (and, one must presume, prehistoric) cases involve close man–plant relationships which simply involve planting, or occasional weeding, or differential harvesting practices designed to ensure future crops. The Menomini Indians of Wisconsin allow some wild rice to fall back into the water as they harvest it in order to assure a crop the following year (Jenks 1900). The Paiute Indians were known to irrigate otherwise wild plants to increase their yield (Steward 1929). Yarnell (1964) notes several plant species whose range was altered, sometimes intentionally and sometimes not, through the use made of them by Indians. Botanists have focused on morphological change, with its implication of genetic change, as the key criterion of the change of economic relationship. This is for the excellent reason that it is one of the few pieces of evidence available to us from some prehistoric contexts. Nevertheless, we must not let this practical consideration blind us to the fact that phenotypic and genotypic changes may frequently have been of trivial importance by comparison with some of the other behavioural changes which may have left no morphological trace. As a generalisation it seems fair to suggest that from the point of view of the economy the *cultivation* of a crop is of far greater significance than its *domestication* in this narrow botanical sense. As was suggested in Chapter 2, studies of site location and the analysis of exploitation territories have a vital part to play in our attempt to advance our understanding of these elusive but crucial changes in economic behaviour.

We may accordingly envisage a classification of plant exploitation practices which parallels that outlined for animal exploitation.

(1) Casual gathering, in which the resources are exploited simply because they exist in the vicinity of other more important staples. No effort would be made to husband or increase such resources.

(2) Systematic gathering. Here a particular plant or

group of plants becomes the focus of regular and systematic economic activities. The plant distribution might influence site location and population levels, at least at certain times of the year. Some husbanding of the resources may well be a feature of these relationships, so that future crops are assured.

(3) Limited cultivation. Productivity is encouraged and regulated in some way, such as by transplanting, tillage, weeding, irrigation, and so on. Some or other of these activities occur quite commonly among populations considered to be 'gatherers' rather than 'agriculturalists' or 'horticulturalists'. The traces of these activities will frequently be very difficult to perceive in the prehistoric record.

(4) Developed cultivation. This refers to the propagation of crops under human control, and frequently involves situations in which the plants would be unable to propagate themselves without human intervention. Many traditional and peasant farming systems fall into this category.

(5) Intensive cultivation. This concerns sophisticated and technologically complex systems, involving greenhouses and selectively bred plants. The whole environment of the plants is under human control, and the plant varieties are frequently selectively bred for specific features to such an extent that they would be unable to survive at all in any environment unmodified by man.

MARINE RESOURCES

It is commonly assumed that marine resources were 'hunted' or 'gathered' resources in prehistoric times, and that the establishment of closer relationships and more intensive levels of exploitation, amounting to domestication or cultivation, was not achieved until the historical period. Marine resources have therefore received scant attention in theoretical discussions of early husbandry. If it is true, however, that these resources were selected for a closer economic relationship only at a relatively late stage in the long-term development of human economies, this is itself a point of interest which merits more careful investigation. We have discussed above the limitations of the conventional wild–domestic classification of man's relationships with plants and animals. We must now examine the exploitation of marine resources in the light of these considerations.

The major limitations on the extension of human control over marine resources stem from the difficulties of access. The factor of accessibility is indeed one of the primary influences determining the nature of marine exploitation systems, and is discussed in more detail later (Chapter 4).

It is a fundamental characteristic of mobile marine resources that they represent a reservoir of food which is largely inaccessible, but by the same token almost infinite in relation to human needs at low population densities. Human predation, however uncontrolled, affects such a small part of the total population of many species that any losses are easily replenished. With the cod and haddock of the North Sea, for example, a very advanced level of technology had to be reached before any pressure was brought to bear on the population as a whole. Until recently the risk of over-exploitation was low, and the need for measures aimed at conservation of the fish stocks or increases in their intrinsic productivity non-existent. Thus not only is it difficult at simple technological levels to establish close economic relationships with mobile marine resources, but their husbandry may also be unnecessary as a general rule.

The sedentary molluscan resources of the intertidal zone might appear more vulnerable. Here too, however, there are some species whose distributions extend into the sublittoral zone, where increasing depth and distance from the shore put them beyond the effective reach of human exploitation in the absence of an advanced technology. The rich cockle beds of the Maplin Sands off the Essex coast, for example, are some 45 km from land and required sophisticated boats and dredging equipment for their effective exploitation. Where such technological aids are lacking, offshore shell beds act as an untapped reserve which helps to replenish losses from intensively exploited beds closer inshore.

Even where molluscs are confined to the intertidal zone, the amount of effort required to collect a given quantity of calories is relatively high. The substantial costs of exploitation coupled with the fairly low nutritional yield of shellfish result in a steeply declining curve of profitability with increased input of effort. Exploitation beyond the optimum level will normally have the effect of reducing average individual shell size and of increasing the distance that has to be walked to gather a given number of shells. At simple levels of technology, both these effects may be expected to increase sharply the energy cost of shell-gathering, and this in turn may be expected to put a brake on further increases in the level of exploitation. Disincentives of this sort are not invariably sufficient to prevent over-exploitation. Conservation measures involving periodic restriction on shell-gathering may be necessary, such as those recorded among the Maori in New Zealand. This depends on the accessibility of the resource and the available technology. The fact remains, however, that at low levels of technology the diminishing returns which result from increasing difficulties of access generally act as a check on the exploitation of resources of both the open sea and the intertidal zone, without the need for any husbanding or management of resources. With the reduction of the barriers to access due to technological advances this form of regulation may become increasingly inadequate and the need for more elaborate measures of control and conservation more pressing.

Thus technological advance is a primary factor in raising the level of output of marine resources, either increasing extractive efficiency within a given area or through the extension of the total area available to exploitation. Portable containers and boats are obviously important as aids to efficient exploitation. Other simple measures are the construction of fish traps, such as the rudimentary prehistoric stone constructions recorded along parts of the Australian and South African coastlines, which were used to trap fish on the outgoing tide. Nets and communal drives are also used to concentrate fish in shallow water.

In modern systems of marine exploitation a distinction may be made between sea fishing and sea farming. The former is of course closely analogous to the hunting and gathering of terrestrial resources. As with these, it is by no means always the case that patterns of exploitation described as fishing are devoid of all aspects of resource management and conservation. Obvious examples of this include the prohibition of exploitation at certain times of the year, and the regulation or proscription of certain exploitation techniques, such as the use of poison, dynamite, or nets of particular designs. As we have already noted, the relative inaccessibility of many marine resources automatically means that the appearance of such restrictions will be a relatively late phenomenon, characteristic of periods when population pressure and technological sophistication raise the real threat of overexploitation.

With sea farming systems attention is increasingly devoted to the protection and husbandry of resources, and to attempts to maintain artificially high levels of both the resource population and of cropping rates. Thus the farming of molluscs may include some or all of the following activities:

(1) Collection and planting of young shellfish (spat).
(2) Thinning of young shell beds in the early stages of growth and transplantation to new areas for improved growth.
(3) Control of predators, parasites, and disease.
(4) The use of technologically advanced methods of harvesting.

(5) Artificial selection.

At their most developed these practices extend to the creation of an entirely artificial substrate. The *bouchot* system is an example of this, in which stakes are driven into soft mud to provide an attachment for mussels. These can be moved around within the intertidal zone to ensure optimum feeding conditions at all stages of growth. Trays suspended above the bottom are commonly used in oyster cultivation. As well as allowing oysters to thrive in rivers where bottom conditions would otherwise be unfavourable, they also permit the oysters to be placed at precisely the right tidal level for optimum feeding and keep them out of reach of bottom predators such as starfish and boring whelks.

Similar principles apply to the farming of fish. The main differences arise from their mobility and the consequent need to impound stocks in ponds or artificial enclosures. Examples of such systems are provided by the farming of mullet, or such freshwater fish as trout. The controlled feeding of the fish is often an important aspect of such relationships.

It is noteworthy that highly intensive marine farming systems are possible without their necessarily involving any conscious attempt at selective breeding, a point of some interest in view of the importance attached to this aspect of the exploitation of terrestrial resources. Artificial selection is a relatively recent development and has so far been mainly concerned with producing disease-resistant strains. It has yet to make a considerable economic impact on marine exploitation systems.

It seems, then, that aquatic resources are broadly comparable with terrestrial resources in their relationships with their human exploiters. Far from it being possible to perceive a simple clear-cut division into a wild (hunted) class of resources, and a domestic–tame–captive (farmed) class, there are many different elements involved which concern the mobility and control of the resource, its productivity, reliability, and so on. Techniques of exploitation include a variety of measures of husbandry and of ensuring that a return of food can be obtained with a minimum expenditure of effort.

As we have already observed, the difficulty of access to most marine resources has meant that highly intensive and controlled systems are primarily a recent phenomenon. Similarly, selective breeding, so often viewed as the essential characteristic of the domestication of terrestrial resources, has so far made very little impact upon marine exploitation systems, despite the sophistication and highly controlled nature of many of these. As far as the prehistoric past is concerned, it seems most unlikely that farming of aquatic resources played an important economic role. However, even the damming of pools or the construction of traps involve the control of the mobility of a resource to ensure its future availability – a crucial part of the technique of exploitation of many farm animals. The control and husbandry of such fish as carp in the pools of Europe's mediaeval monasteries and the Roman cultivation of oysters should make us beware of the assumption that all early exploitation of such resources was simple, opportunistic, and unregulated.

CATEGORIES OF ECONOMIC BEHAVIOUR

The foregoing discussion has emphasised the diversity and flexibility of man's exploitation of various categories of resources. It was suggested that there is rarely any single characteristic or simple criterion on the basis of which one may readily distinguish wild from domestic organisms. This is especially true of attempts to deal with prehistoric material. Centuries of selective breeding have led in modern times to a situation in which there is a pronounced polarity between wild and domestic forms in many cases. This marked divergence of form and behaviour would have been much less common in the past, and would presumably have been essentially absent in those cases which most concern us, where human economic behaviour toward currently domesticated species was in the early stages of its development.

Nevertheless, within this highly variable collection of economic practices and systems it is possible to perceive a number of unifying factors. These principles are perhaps more easily seen as categories of behaviour and economic objectives than in terms of classes of organisms. Two primary themes are the variation between direct and indirect exploitation, and between opportunistic and controlled exploitation.

The term 'direct exploitation' may be used to describe systems in which the bulk of effort is expended with the objective of obtaining an immediate return of food. The relationship between inputs of human effort and outputs of food is a simple and immediate one. Of course, it is true that any food-getting activity with a technological element involves a degree of deferred gratification. The manufacture of the most simple tool or container diverts energy from the immediate satisfaction of needs in the interest of their more effective or efficient fulfilment in the future. Nevertheless it is useful to distinguish patterns of exploitation in which the technological element is small, and in which the majority of effort devoted to food-getting activities is

directly concerned with the location and extraction of resources, from others which are more technologically oriented.

It is clear that there are patterns of direct exploitation in each of our resource categories. Many simple forms of hunting and gathering can reasonably be described in these terms. The casual collection of molluscs and plant foods, and generalised 'eclectic' hunting and fishing practices frequently seem to fall into this category. Direct exploitation is often associated with casual or subsidiary resources, where an extra investment of labour is not justified by the expected returns. This is not always the case, however. We discussed in Chapter 1 the importance which investment can have in the increase of productivity and the development of more complex economies. It was pointed out that in certain circumstances the investment required for an appreciable change cannot be raised within a particular population or region. Where this happens in technologically simple economies one may expect direct exploitation even of staple resources.

'Indirect exploitation' refers to systems in which a high proportion of time and energy is diverted from the immediate acquisition of food, and is invested in activities designed to assure some future return. This subordination of present gains to future returns can offer a number of benefits. The primary objective is usually to effect a net increase in the overall productivity of a resource. On the other hand it can also result in an increase in predictability of the return; or can increase its availability at periods or in areas where it would otherwise be scarce or absent; or can increase the efficiency of exploitation by lowering the long-term labour costs. With increasing economic complexity this investment activity becomes by far the dominant element in exploitation systems. A smaller and smaller proportion of effort is spent in actually locating and cropping the resource concerned, and a correspondingly greater proportion is spent on technological aids to efficiency and to the control of the resource and the prediction of its behaviour.

It is obvious that even the most simple of human economies includes elements of indirect exploitation. It is also apparent that direct and indirect exploitation constitute the poles of an intergradating series of economic systems rather than strongly divided classes of behaviour. We have already noted that tool manufacture is a simple form of investment. As we shall see below, apparently simple economies sometimes embody quite sophisticated provisions for future prosperity.

Some patterns of exploitation of both terrestrial and

marine resources may conveniently be described as 'opportunistic'. This term denotes economic systems in which no attempt is made to husband the resource or to increase its potential productivity. This does not imply that the exploiter is operating totally at random in his environment, or that he does not apply his often very sophisticated knowledge of the local ecology in order to increase the chances of an economic return. Totally random or catch-as-catch-can exploitation has no economic significance in patterns of exploitation practised by man or other animals, although it may occur with respect to casual and unimportant resources.

Opportunistic exploitation is most characteristic of technologically simple economies, but is by no means restricted to these. Much modern fishing, and for that matter many industrial concerns, operate on an opportunistic basis. Opportunistic exploitation is likely to be inefficient in the long run except in cases where there is for some reason a considerable barrier to overexploitation. For this reason it is not as a general rule found as a long-term strategy for the exploitation of staple resources. In some cases, however, either population levels or the efficiency of exploitation are so severely limited by some other factor or factors in the environment that opportunistic exploitation of staples can be maintained for very long periods without any risk. We argued in Chapter 1, for instance, that the Dobe !Kung can apparently behave in this way with regard to their staple mongongo nut, because their population is limited by shortage of water. Many marine resources could be similarly exploited until technological developments made it possible to exploit them heavily in deep-sea as well as coastal environments. The relative difficulty of human movement, and of maintaining contact with game, may have had much the same effect in those densely forested areas where large-scale clearance by fire was not feasible. In these circumstances the relative inaccessibility of ungulate resources could have made opportunistic exploitation the most effective strategy for very long periods, and a more intensive and controlled exploitation would have been both very difficult to achieve and economically unnecessary.

'Controlled' patterns of exploitation employ a variety of means, often technologically very simple, to regulate the relationship between man and resource so as to husband the resource and ensure its long-term viability. It is clear that those modes of exploitation described today as farming or domestication are highly developed forms of controlled exploitation. It is also quite apparent from the ethnographic record that elementary measures of plant and animal husbandry are widespread among populations usually characterised as 'hunter–gatherers'. These techniques include conservation of resources by the regulation of cropping pressure (sometimes through taboos), or, in the case of plants, by deliberate propagation and fostering of favoured species; the control of animal movement through drives and corrals (applicable to both terrestrial and marine resources); and simple environmental engineering through the use of fire and the control of water. Campbell (1965) discusses a wide range of such practices among the Australian aborigines. The list includes the planting of seeds and sections of such tubers as the yam; the cultivation of an edible grub called the salt-water cobra; the capture and feeding of cassowaries for future slaughter; and widespread environmental manipulation including stream control and the management of vegetation by fire. This latter technique was practised so widely and to such effect that Jones (1969) has suggested that it might reasonably be termed 'fire-stick farming'. Similar practices are evidently to be found in South America. Clastres (1972) documents the raising of monkeys and coatis and the cultivation of the edible *guchu* larvae among the Guayaki, for instance. Among some hunters the husbandry of resources takes the form of a regulated cropping policy, and the guarding of game from exploitation by human competitors.

These techniques are at this level often practised in an unsystematic fashion, and sometimes involve minor resources rather than staples. They represent an attempt to increase the degree of human control over the behaviour and availability of the resource concerned. This control allows the relationship between resource levels and rates of exploitation to be monitored with greater precision and flexibility. Controlled cropping and conservation help to ensure an efficient turnover of stock and the maintenance of a relatively smooth, predictable food supply. The amplitude of the inevitable oscillations between periods of dearth and glut can be reduced, and the total food output can generally be increased. Furthermore, the increased control over the movement or availability of a resource often increases the efficiency of its exploitation. The rudimentary husbandry visible in these technologically simple economies occurs in much more powerful forms and combinations among agriculturalists and pastoralists, in whose economies the controlled patterns of exploitation tend completely to dominate opportunistic practices. In the more highly developed forms of controlled exploitation, such as in battery farming, greenhouse horticulture and hydroponics, and trout farming, the whole of the environment of the exploited organism is controlled by and depends upon the exploiter.

3. PALAEOECONOMIC PERSPECTIVES

PREDATION AND HUSBANDRY

The widespread presence of controlled patterns of exploitation among modern hunter–gatherers suggests that the same measures of resource husbandry may also have existed among Pleistocene hunter–gatherers. Indeed, it seems increasingly likely that the 'origins of agriculture' as customarily defined represent the dramatic results of the combination of a whole range of long-established husbandry techniques focused on peculiarly productive associations of plants and animals, rather than the invention of patterns of economic behaviour which were new in themselves. We briefly discuss some archaeological evidence for this suggestion below, but here it is perhaps just worth recalling that Dart (1967) suggested plausibly that the porcupine may have been domesticated (or at least held captive and husbanded, in our terms) in Middle Palaeolithic times in the Near East. The accumulating evidence of early prehistoric use of fire for the management of grazing and browse (Mellars 1976) is a further indication of sophisticated man-resource relationships.

In view of these conclusions we decided that it would not be possible to study effectively agriculture of the early Holocene without first making a more determined enquiry than was customary into the nature of earlier exploitation patterns. For it is remarkable that, with a few notable exceptions, analyses of Pleistocene economies are restricted to the assertion that the populations concerned were 'hunters and gatherers', supported only by lists of the species which were hunted and gathered. We have argued for a very much more gradual development from simple to complex and controlled exploitation systems than is usually envisaged. From this perspective it seems doubtful whether it is worth searching for the 'origins' of domestication at all. The origins of any phenomenon so diverse and widespread are likely to be similarly various and ubiquitous. At any rate, we felt that the origins, if such exist in identifiable form, certainly lie at least as far back as the Pleistocene, or more probably in much earlier roots of pre-human behaviour. Remarkably close parallels exist between the exploitation patterns exhibited by certain of the social insects and those of man. Wilson (1971) has extensively documented insect relationships that include the exploitation of one species by another either for labour or as living sources of food, or both. In extreme cases the entire economy of the exploiter depends upon the exploited species. These examples suggested strongly that the origins of such close economic interspecific associations may well

have to do with biological circumstances which cannot be narrowly defined as to time and place.

A striking feature of many European Advanced Palaeolithic economies is the degree to which they appear to have concentrated on the exploitation of only one or two species. Economic specialisation on one or two animals does occur earlier, of course, as the high proportion of *Bison* at the Middle Palaeolithic site of Amvrosievka, and of reindeer at Molodova, show; conversely, there are many Advanced Palaeolithic sites which seem to indicate broad-spectrum rather than specialised economies. There is, however, a discernible trend towards an increased dependence on a few resources during the late Pleistocene in Europe. Perhaps the most dramatic examples of this are the many sites which show a long-term dependence upon the exploitation of reindeer or red deer. These are species which were of such economic importance over wide areas and for many millennia that one might reasonably expect that close, controlled, and effective patterns of exploitation would have evolved. One aspect of any such system is likely to have been an element of herd conservation: the regulation of the crop (whether by intent or force of circumstance) to a naturally occurring surplus of the population, the removal of which will not impair its viability and breeding success in the future.

This is no more than to re-emphasise that human economies, like so many other interspecific relationships, are subject to selective pressures at more complex and important levels than the mere fitness or fecundity of individuals. An exploitative relationship is rarely a simple one-sided process. If it is to remain viable in the long term it must be at least tolerable, and is frequently beneficial, to the prey species at the population level. There is no evolutionary value to a predator in becoming so numerous and successful as to diminish seriously the species upon which it depends. In the long run, selection is in favour of efficient, relatively stable, interspecific relationships rather than the overwhelming success of individual species. This is not the blatant contradiction of current theories of population genetics and sociobiology that it might seem. It is really a statement of the obvious, that individuals, populations, and species that became so pre-eminently successful in the short term as to jeopardise the stability of the communities of which they were members, endangered thereby the continuing success of that community, and hence their own existence. Such a pattern of behaviour is clearly maladaptive in the long term, and it is not to be expected that it should have gained much evolutionary currency.

It is indeed noteworthy, when one considers the hundreds of species brought to extinction or to its verges by man, that these are very rarely species of great economic significance. Thus the American bison was not reduced to its remnant populations of the eighteen eighties by the Indians for whom it formed a staple resource; not even when the availability of the horse and firearms increased so dramatically their potential destructiveness. The bison was brought close to extinction by European colonists for whom it had relatively little economic value, and for whom it represented competition for grazing as well as a dangerous encouragement to the independence of the Indians. Between 3.5 and 4 million bison are recorded as having been killed in the three years between 1872 and 1874. Of those, the Indians accounted for less than 5 per cent (Roe 1972).

Just as with many close economic relationships developed by the social insects, so many of those of human groups contain an important *symbiotic* element. Symbiosis may be defined as a group of relationships between organisms of different species in which both partners benefit in some way from the association, or in which one partner benefits while the other is not affected either favourably or adversely. In those close man–animal relationships termed 'domestication' the animals receive a number of benefits. In particular they are cushioned against the hazards of predation, disease, extreme food shortage, and competition. It may be thought that these are trivial advantages in view of the fact that as far as the meat-producing animals are concerned, the relationship terminates abruptly with the slaughter of the animal. The biological advantages are far more apparent, however, when viewed at the population or species level. One of the most important measures of the evolutionary success of a species is in terms of the size and health of its population. By this criterion modern domestic animals and plants are among the most conspicuously successful species in the world today. Their numbers are typically measured in tens or hundreds of millions, in contrast with comparable wild species whose populations are often smaller by factors of tens, and which are frequently declining. This remarkable success is due almost exclusively to the advantages conferred upon these particular species by their association with man, which gives them a colossal advantage by comparison with their wild competitors. Or, to put it another way, their success is due to their ability to capitalise upon man's economic needs, and to adapt themselves to him.

Nor should we think that these subtle but vastly important advantages are necessarily confined to animals in modern 'domestic' associations with man. It has long been known that many herbivores benefit from a regular movement of home range which helps to control various parasites which otherwise tend to infest the pastures and become endemic in the herbivore population. One of the functions of sheep dogs in certain areas is to induce sufficient movement into the flock to inhibit the build-up of parasites to critical levels. Zeuner (1963) pointed out that the natural herding propensities of the wolf may well serve a comparable function. It is also apparent that predation frequently plays an important rôle in population regulation of the prey species. This was eloquently shown by the famous example of the mule deer in various parts of North America. Characteristically, following the control or prohibition of human predation and the extermination of other predators, the numbers of deer rose dramatically to the point where they seriously damaged their grazing resources. Starvation and cataclysmic population decline followed. Similar data are available for caribou and moose, and it seems to be a general rule that herbivore populations are both more stable and healthier if they live in association with predators than if they do not. In addition to this overall population regulatory function, predation frequently has the effect of eliminating unfit and biologically surplus members of a group, to the benefit of the population as a whole. This is well documented, for example, in wolf predation upon bison (Fuller 1962), caribou (Crisler 1956), and moose (Mech 1970), where senile and diseased individuals are differentially removed. Predation by wild dogs upon Thompson's gazelle in the Serengeti was found by Estes & Goddard (1967) to be strongly selective for territorial males, because of their reluctance to leave their breeding territories. This was interpreted as being of major importance in making territories available to younger and more vigorous males. In other species, however, it is individuals unable to maintain territories that seem most vulnerable to predation, and the crucial factor overall may well be the large superfluity of sexually competent males available in most populations of gregarious herbivores. These constitute a naturally occurring biological surplus which can be exploited without affecting the viability of the prey population. It is therefore of some interest to note that differential predation upon males has been recorded in a substantial number of cases.

We see, therefore, that many patterns of animal exploitation are highly complex, and that these and some 'primitive' human economies incorporate strong symbiotic elements and features of controlled exploitation. In view of this it seems that, in our analysis of early agriculture, we should take into consideration earlier economic systems and exploitative relationships which involved species other than the modern farmyard plants and animals.

EARLY MAN–ANIMAL RELATIONSHIPS

We will now discuss briefly aspects of the past exploitation of some large herbivores which are not usually thought to have been domesticated in prehistory. As is shown by the range of man's modern close economic relationships with animals, which encompasses taxa from insects to carnivores, we should not assume too readily that man will only establish such relationships with the more obvious species. There are, however, good reasons for our concentrating initially on the major meat producers. Despite the diversity of domesticates today it is evident that by far the most significant relationships are those which provide important food staples and/or sources of labour. In most cases this comes down in practice to the large- and medium-sized herbivores. Furthermore, there is ample archaeological evidence for the existence of long-lasting and economically crucial relationships with such species far back into the Pleistocene. As we have argued above, where it can be shown that intensive exploitation of a single species has endured for a long period, we are justified in examining seriously the hypothesis that some close and controlled relationships had been established.

The reindeer

The reindeer is unusual in the present context because the mode of its exploitation by Palaeolithic man has been discussed much more fully than has that of most other animal resources. Interest has been aroused by the evidence of considerable economic specialisation on reindeer in late Pleistocene Europe. The cultural extravagance of the later French Magdalenian has, perhaps, served to encourage this preoccupation. Both in the last century and in this, the idea has been mooted of Palaeolithic domestication of the reindeer. The hypothesis has never been effectively destroyed, but has, by and large, foundered on two basic issues. The more significant of these has been the dogma of cultural development which assumes *a priori* that during the Pleistocene all men were hunters and/or gatherers. In addition, it has been pointed out that there is no firm evidence of osteological change in the reindeer populations concerned. From this it is inferred that no systematic selective breeding took place.

As we have discussed in general terms above, neither of these objections really touches the central point of interest as far as palaeoeconomy is concerned. The former is one of the assertions which we are specifically trying to test. The latter assumes far too much about the nature of early forms of animal husbandry to be an effective rebuttal. A look at modern patterns of reindeer exploitation encourages us to examine the question a little more closely.

The first point of significance is that reindeer economies frequently involve little in the way of sophisticated technological aids. Characteristically, the main feature of the exploitation pattern is the behavioural adaptation whereby the human group follows the reindeer more or less closely in its annual migrations. In many cases, as with some Lapps, the reindeer are not herded except at particular times of the year. With the exception of an annual round-up and slaughter, and with minimal control during the major migration, the animals are left to find their own food. The human group follows the deer, but does not maintain close day-to-day contact. Sturdy (1972) found in Greenland that the deer were left alone as much as possible as a conscious measure of husbandry. Ingold (1974) describes a situation in Finland where, partly due to recent changes in economic and social conditions, and partly due to the technological innovation of the snowmobile, control over some of the deer has become so spasmodic that he argues that it represents essentially a return to a hunting economy. These herd-following and loose-herding relationships are often combined with closer and more intensive relationships with a few individual animals. These are used for dairy products and transport, and also as decoys.

The relative simplicity of these relationships means that very little technological hardware is required. Animal movement is controlled largely by their natural tendency to move away from man, and by the use of natural topographic features such as cliffs or large bodies of water. Where necessary, these are supplemented by fences and corrals, which can be extremely simple. The lack of day-to-day control over the movement of individual animals means that breeding is unsupervised and that crossing with wild reindeer is frequent where they are present. In some areas this is actively encouraged.

Some domesticated reindeer are thus exploited in ways which would leave very little unequivocal archaeological evidence to show that they were not hunted. Indeed, at their simplest the kinds of exploitation outlined above differ little from certain forms of hunting, which frequently employ similar techniques of

60

herd-following and corralling. Perhaps the main differences, if they exist at all, lie in the degree to which an individual human population is associated with a specific animal population, and the degree of selectivity applied in cropping procedures.

When we examine the archaeological evidence we find a number of indications that in some cases we may be dealing with a kind of loose-herding and herd-following pastoralism rather than with an opportunistic hunting economy. Sturdy (1972) found in his study of a modern reindeer economy in Greenland that small temporary camps were frequently established in order to control the movement of animals, in particular to prevent their egress from particular ranges. Large blocks of grazing were often roughly delineated by major topographic obstacles, and herding practices concentrated on discouraging the stock from straying from these through natural entry and exit points. In his analysis of Pleistocene reindeer economies (Sturdy, 1975), he coined the term *extended territories* to refer to such areas, which were regularly exploited by the mobile herbivores upon which the human group subsisted, but parts of which might rarely or even never be visited by the human group itself. Sturdy found that in many areas of Europe the locations of sites belonging to Late Palaeolithic reindeer-dependent groups seemed to conform to these principles. That is to say that many of the smaller temporary sites, in particular, seemed to help delimit large discrete blocks of grazing, and to be placed with a view to controlling access to and egress from them. The sites did not, as a rule, provide particularly large territories for hunting, nor were they generally located in especially good 'ambush' positions where maximum advantage could be taken of game drives.

Sturdy argues cogently that the only really effective form of economy for many of the human groups would have involved some kind of herd-following, from winter grazing grounds of the North European Plain to the summer range in the German and Swiss uplands, for instance. Alternative staple resources to the reindeer would not have existed in sufficient quantities outside the coastal region, and an uncontrolled hunting economy would have been too risky an adaptation to have survived so long and so successfully. Herd-following would have permitted the establishment of long-standing associations of particular human groups with specific reindeer populations, with the latter thus becoming habituated to a degree of human control. The argument of Burch (1972) that wild caribou cannot effectively be followed by human exploiters, because of the rapidity and unpredictability of their movements, is not really relevant to us here. Modern European evidence shows conclusively that reindeer can become sufficiently habituated to human exploitation to be loose-herded. These are normally thought of as 'domestic' or 'semi-domestic' reindeer. What we are trying to find out is how far back this kind of relationship may have extended. It does not help to show that caribou, when hunted (usually as a relatively minor resource as far as food is concerned, and not a staple), consistently outdistance their human predators.

At some sites, such as Stellmoor, there are further hints that we may be dealing with a controlled form of exploitation. The slaughter pattern is strongly weighted in favour of males, and is indeed remarkably close to one of the recommended cropping policies for modern reindeer ranching in Scandinavia. While there is, as always, a number of possible explanations for this evidence, it fits very well the hypothesis that a regulated economy was in operation. The evidence, discussed long ago by Rust (1943), for the slaughter of reindeer at close range at such sites as Ahrensburg and Stellmoor, points in the same direction. Whether or not we follow Rust in interpreting the 'Lyngby axe' as having been used for the slaughter of essentially captive animals, the frequency with which the shoulder blades were perforated at the ideal point for the penetration of the heart does argue for a high degree of control.

It must be admitted that the evidence could be accommodated to an hypothesis of selective hunting. An animal which, like the reindeer, tends to migrate in segregated herds, with different age and sex groups passing through an area separately at different times, can be hunted selectively either by intent or fortuitously. If, for instance, it could be shown that the very large Stellmoor fauna represents one vast kill, then this explanation might be thought quite plausible. Furthermore, the evidence for the use by hunters of corrals, and of the killing of caribou at close quarters from canoes at points where they cross major rivers and lakes, allows for a similar explanation of the perforations of the shoulder blades.

It must be accepted, however, that the evidence fits as well or better with the hypothesis of a closer and more controlled form of exploitation than this. The chances that the thousand or more individual reindeer indicated in the Ahrensburgian levels at Stellmoor represent a single kill, or even one season's kill, are remote indeed. We must remember, too, the recurrent finds both here and elsewhere of the antlers of castrated animals. These occur in very small numbers, and are quite reasonably interpreted by most authorities as the results of naturally occurring accidents or hormone deficiencies. We nonetheless do well to bear in mind the maintenance of small numbers of castrated animals as decoys and draft animals in some modern reindeer herd-following economies. As already noted above, site location and territorial evidence are also suggestive of a controlled form of exploitation.

A comparable situation may be represented in the Dordogne region of France. A brief glance at the broad geographical context of the Dordogne shows that it is intermediate between the areas immediately to its east and west in a number of important factors. To the east lies the Massif Central, rising from 300 m to over 1800 m; to the west are the Atlantic lowlands. The climatic and vegetational features of so large an area are, of course, highly complex, but it is fair to generalise that with greater altitude and distance from the coast, winter conditions become increasingly severe and the growing season shorter. Even today, the central area of the Massif Central, much of which is over 1000 m, has only about three months complete freedom from frost, and from three to six months of annual snow cover (Monkhouse 1974). Under the much more extreme climate of the final glaciation, winter conditions here must have been yet more severe. The Dordogne area has less pronounced winter cold and a longer growing season, while the coastal regions to the west have among the most moderate winters in France.

The implications of these topographic and climatic features as far as subsistence is concerned are of some importance. The Massif Central would have offered good summer grazing, but would have been virtually or totally uninhabitable for a long winter period. The Dordogne area would have offered, as the snow melted, grazing resources in the summer and spring earlier than those available to the east, and would also have provided autumn grazing. To what extent winter occupation would have been possible in the Dordogne would have depended largely on the amount and duration of snow cover. Even today winters can be harsh, and during the last glaciation July surface air temperature is estimated to have been about 8 °C lower than today's (Gates 1976). Geological and faunal evidence concur in general in indicating periglacial conditions, and it seems unlikely that the winter forage would have been sufficiently good to provide grazing for large numbers of herbivores. There would thus have been considerable incentives for them to move further west to the more favoured conditions of the Atlantic coast.

Thus for any herbivore population exploiting the summer resources of the Massif Central it would have been essential to move to lower ground for most of the year. As far as the Dordogne area is concerned, there would have been a strong incentive to move in summer to the rich seasonal grazings either to the east, in the Massif Central, or possibly to the south in the High Pyrenees; while in the winter there would have been a tendency to move to the lower altitudes and more maritime climate of the Gironde and Charente region. This latter was in a sense the most favoured in that it could almost certainly have supported a permanent herbivore population. Assuming that we are correct, however, to argue that large numbers of animals were forced into these lowland areas in winter, only a small proportion of this total could have been accommodated permanently, and the summer population, if any, must have been relatively small.

It can thus be seen that important environmental constraints would have encouraged considerable east–west seasonal movement of animals. As Sturdy argued for northern Europe, any human group subsisting primarily on reindeer (as is the case at many Upper Palaeolithic sites in the Dordogne, particularly in the Magdalenian period) would have had powerful incentives to adapt its behaviour to that of the reindeer, and to follow its broad pattern of movement. We might thus expect that the Dordogne sites as a whole represent primarily the spring and autumn occupations of human populations following the herds to and from their main summer and winter grazing areas.

As Bahn (1977) has recently discussed in some detail, there is a considerable amount of evidence that the occupants of the Dordogne caves and shelters were not the basically 'sedentary tribes' envisaged by Bordes and others. Three major sources can be identified for the fossil shells encountered in many of the Dordogne sites. A high proportion of these come from the Anjou and Touraine area of the Loire valley, most of the rest coming from the Bordeaux and Landes regions on the Atlantic coast. A few come from the Mediterranean coastal area of Roussillon. Similar evidence emerges from the study of non-fossil mollusc shells in the Dordogne caves. By far the majority of these are of broadly cold-loving species, which must have come from the Atlantic coast. A few are more typical of warmer waters, and presumably come from the Mediterranean. The existence in some sites of the bones and artistic representations of marine species such as seals also suggests familiarity with coastal regions. All this evidence demonstrates contact with low-lying areas, that is, our presumptive winter grazing zones.

A number of alternative explanations could be devised to explain this evidence. The objects could have been acquired by trade or exchange networks, and doubtless in some cases were. This is perhaps a less plausible hypothesis as regards the bones and teeth of seals, but it is theoretically possible that they represent animals which had come up the rivers 200 km or so from their more usual marine environment. What cannot be contested is that there was clearly an extensive network of contracts over wide areas of southwest France, which involved the movement of shells and other objects. Furthermore, it is at least as likely – perhaps, in view of the general environmental arguments outlined above, more likely – that these represent by-products of the normal, necessary movements of human groups and their herbivore subsistence base, as that they indicate merely the tenuous social relationships of separate, sedentary human populations.

Turning now to a more specific examination of the Les Eyzies area of the Dordogne, a number of sites show a quite remarkable economic reliance upon reindeer. Obvious examples of this are the Abri Pataud, where the proportion of reindeer fluctuates between 85 per cent and 97 per cent, Laugerie Haute, and La Madeleine. In general there seems to be an increasing dependence upon reindeer in the final stages of the last glaciation, particularly in the Magdalenian period, but such specialisation does also occur earlier. It is usually held (Bouchud 1966) that these sites represent the activities of reindeer hunters who exploited the herds on a year-round basis. The sites are thought of as being permanently occupied, or occupied on an intermittent basis throughout the year. It is suggested that confirmation of this can be seen in the faunal evidence, as Bouchud interprets the reindeer antlers and teeth as indicating exploitation at all seasons. This hypothesis has been discussed in detail elsewhere (Sturdy 1975), and it is therefore unnecessary for us to elaborate here. Suffice it to say that the majority of the male antlers are shed, while most of those of fawns and females are attached to the skulls. This is consonant with a predominantly autumn–winter–spring occupation, and certainly any extensive summer occupation would be expected to have left more evidence in the form of shed female and attached male antlers. Similar considerations apply to the dental evidence. Notwithstanding Bouchud's demonstration that occasional kills may have been made at all seasons of the year, there is frequently a significant peak in the ages at certain periods. Bouchud himself recognises this: 'En effet, l'examen des divers graphiques mensuels montre une accumulation privilégiée sur certains mois et cela de façon constante'. Significantly, these peaks tend to coincide with the spring and autumn seasons. As we have already noted, there are basic environmental reasons which would lead one to expect that the area would be most likely to see its major influx of both men and herbivores at these seasons.

It seems at least possible, then, that some of the famous caves and shelters in the Dordogne region may have been the relatively briefly, though repeatedly, occupied sites of herd-followers, rather than the more permanently established camps of 'migration hunters'. Sturdy has discussed the considerable advantages which a herd-following economy offers by comparison with alternatives, for any human group subsisting primarily on reindeer. The same factors would have applied in France as elsewhere in Europe. By the hypothesis suggested here, sites such as Laugerie Haute and La Madeleine would in all likelihood have been major foci of settlement for human groups following the reindeer in their spring and autumn migrations from the coastal lowlands to the Massif Central, and back. It seems worth enquiring whether there were particular factors in the region which contributed to the great importance which it seemed to have in the late glacial period.

One of the most striking topographic features of the Les Eyzies region is the steep sides to the valleys of rivers such as the Vézère and the Beune. These frequently amount to cliffs, which, while not always more than a few metres in height, are sufficiently high and vertical to present a considerable barrier to movement of men or animals. We have already discussed the importance of such natural barriers in the management of reindeer in herd-following economies like that of the Lapps. The coincidence of such a remarkable concentration of reindeer-dominated late glacial sites with a region abounding in natural corrals seems unlikely to be fortuitous. The probability of the use of topographic features in this way obviously suggests the possibility of a relatively high degree of human control over the reindeer.

Figure 17 shows the Les Eyzies region with a number of key sites, their exploitation territories, and sections of river valley where the slopes are sufficiently steep to act as a significant barrier to movement. A number of points are of interest. Firstly, the small size of the exploitation territories suggests that the sites are not well-suited for the practice of a wide-ranging hunting economy. Geomorphological evidence (Vita-Finzi 1974, 1978) indicates that the valleys would, despite the depositional episode during the late glacial period, have been substantially similar in their basic shape to those of today. During spring and early summer they would probably have been sufficiently wet and unstable

3. PALAEOECONOMIC PERSPECTIVES

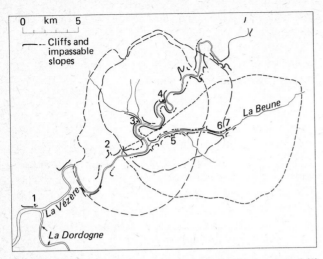

Figure 17. Les Eyzies region of France, showing the location of (1) Gare de Couze; (2) St. Circ; (3) Laugerie-Haute; (4) La Madeleine; (5) Les Combarelles; (6) Cap Blanc; (7) Laussel. Also shown are the 2 hour site exploitation territories of Laugerie-Haute, La Madeleine and Cap Blanc.

(due to snow melt and solifluxion) to have provided a considerable disincentive to movement, if not an absolute barrier. For this reason the reindeer would almost certainly have kept to the ridges as far as possible during the spring migration, although this would not necessarily have been the case during their return in autumn. Equally it means that the valley bottoms could have been used as temporary corrals even more easily in spring than at other periods of the year.

We may summarise the position as follows. A number of different lines of evidence lead us to the conclusion that both man and reindeer were predominantly migratory in their late glacial exploitation of southwest France. The main axis of movement was probably east to west, from the summer grazings of the Massif Central to the winter grazings of the coastal lowlands. The most logical rôle for the whole Dordogne area in this economy is as the main autumn and spring zone, and contrary to the established hypothesis the faunal picture fits well with such a suggestion. It is quite possible, both theoretically and as regards the faunal evidence, that there was a certain amount of occupation throughout the winter. How far this was possible would have depended ultimately upon the availability of grazing and the depth and duration of snow cover. Any winter occupation may thus have involved a small, selected killing herd, as better and more extensive winter grazings would almost certainly have been available in the coastal zone. It is, of course, possible that considerable use would have been made of stored meat by the overwintering human population. Winter

temperatures would probably have been sufficiently low for freezing of meat to be practicable at least during the mid-winter period. Many of the largest sites are notably located where the valley sides offer maximum opportunities for corralling of stock, and it thus seems probable that a high degree of control was being exercised over the reindeer at certain times of the year. It is worth remembering that many modern reindeer economies operate with a single major round-up and slaughter in the year, frequently in the autumn.

The horse

We have discussed the case of the reindeer in some detail both because of its intrinsic interest and because there is a considerable body of relevant information. We will now deal more briefly with some other species. Here the data are more scattered, but those that are available point to patterns of exploitation closely comparable with those discussed in the case of the reindeer. As with the reindeer, the possibility of control or domestication of the horse in Palaeolithic times was mooted in the last century, but has largely been dismissed in favour of the hypothesis of its much more recent domestication. A reappraisal of the situation is worthwhile both because of changes in the theoretical approach to Pleistocene economies, and also because of the discovery of new evidence.

Like the reindeer, the horse was clearly a staple resource for certain human groups in late glacial Europe, some of the levels at the site of Solutré providing the best known and most dramatic examples. As Bahn discussed recently (1976, 1978), there are two main classes of evidence which suggest that, on occasion at least, man developed a close and controlled exploitative relationship with the horse in late glacial France. The first and most widespread of these is the artistic evidence. This includes the celebrated St Michel d'Arudy engraving, which appears to show clearly a horse's head with some kind of rope harness attached. Many other comparable examples exist, but they are not usually so clear or unequivocal as to their interpretation. Such representations are usually dismissed as the stylised depiction of anatomical features, and indeed it is just possible that this is the case. However, it should be borne in mind that since the recent discovery and exhaustive analysis (Pales & St Péreuse 1966) of a similar representation from the site of La Marche, the onus of demonstration has perhaps shifted to those who wish to maintain that the horse was, during the Pleistocene, invariably the object of a hunting economy. Another well-known piece of artistic evidence is the representation of piebald horses at Pech Merle. As Zeuner noted in 1963, such colouring is almost unknown among existing wild horses. The other aspect of evidence concerns the bones of horses from Palaeolithic sites. A particularly intriguing example is the occasional occurrence of a feature of dental wear reputed to arise solely from the 'crib-biting' behaviour of some horses subjected to long-term constraint.

The red deer

The red deer is another species for which we have ample evidence of its having fulfilled a crucial economic rôle for long periods of prehistory. It has never been seriously considered as a potential prehistoric domesticate because its modern status is almost universally that of a wild, hunted animal. On the other hand, it becomes obvious that we should be cautious of this judgement when we consider the historical instances of the use of red deer as draught animals (Jarman, M. R. 1972b, Wilkinson 1972, Plate II) and the semi-domesticated status of deer in parks of many of Europe's large country houses. More significant is the growing interest over the past decade or so in the farming of red deer, which has clearly shown not only that the species (like so many others) is eminently 'domesticable', but also that it can be profitably exploited in close economic relationships with man.

The mere demonstration that they can be domesticated, and that they were so occasionally in historic times, does not of course justify the assumption that red deer were ever subjected to sophisticated management by prehistoric man. Evidence that they may indeed have been so has been discussed in some detail elsewhere (Jarman, M. R. 1972b, 1976a, 1976b) and will only be summarised here. Broadly speaking, where it can be shown that red deer were a staple resource, and where the evidence on cropping patterns is available, the deer have frequently been exploited in a selective fashion. Significantly, as Sturdy found with the reindeer, the kind of selection was economically rational, and reflected fairly closely the sort of exploitation pattern which would result from a controlled 'ranching' of the species for meat. Again, as with the reindeer a number of possible explanations is available. It is certainly true that behavioural characteristics of the animals themselves may lead to a natural weighting in the crop, even if no conscious selection were involved. This point has recently been re-emphasised by Wilkinson (1976). We are more concerned here, however, with the actualities of exploitation patterns, and the economic and behavioural consequences for both the partners in the relationship, than with the more elusive question of the conscious motives and rationalisations of the men involved.

What we can assert with confidence is that the archaeological data are at least as consonant with an hypothesis of a controlled economy that may well have included herding and other husbandry practices, as they are with the customary hypothesis that red deer were simply wild hunted animals, then and now. Indeed, the suggestion (Simmons & Dimbleby 1974) that ivy may have been used as winter fodder for deer in Mesolithic times clearly favours the proposition of a sophisticated pattern of exploitation. Similarly the faunal evidence from Brovst suggests that the island may have been used as a corral for the controlled exploitation of red deer in Ertebølle times (Rowley-Conwy, personal communication).

The fallow deer

Zeuner (1963) pointed out some time ago that fallow deer had been widely introduced by man into many areas of Europe where it did not occur naturally, and that this in itself indicated a degree of control that might amount at least to 'semi-domestication'. Like the other animals we have discussed, the fallow deer was of great economic importance for considerable periods of prehistory. In parts of the Near East it constituted one of the principal dietary staples throughout most of the Upper Pleistocene. Little is known of the way in which it was exploited at that time, apart from the fact that its long-term success implies that a reasonably efficient relationship was in operation.

More specific indications come from the Holocene, particularly from the Neolithic of Cyprus. Here, as on Crete, the available evidence suggests that the island was not colonised during the Upper Pleistocene by man or by the large mammalian fauna characteristic of the adjacent mainland at the time. Both islands seem to have carried an impoverished relict fauna which included dwarf forms of hippopotamus and elephant. With the Holocene came a complete break. The relict fauna disappeared, and was replaced by one which included the domestic farmyard animals and fallow deer. These faunal collections, unlike the earlier ones, are found on large numbers of unquestionable archaeological sites.

Characteristically, the fallow deer was of great economic importance at the earliest human settlements, being by far the commonest species at such sites as Philia (Legge, personal communication). At later sites, and certainly by the Bronze Age, its numbers had declined considerably. There seems little reason to doubt that the common domestic animals, which appear with the first certain signs of human occupation, were introduced to Cyprus by man. It is, of course, possible that the fallow deer just happened to arrive by other means at the same time. Like many deer they can swim strongly, and it is obviously not inconceivable for them to have crossed the 80 km or so from Anatolia. This could have occurred at that particular time either by chance or due to demographic pressure in the mainland deer population. This would seem to be a sufficiently remarkable coincidence, however, for us to prefer the alternative hypothesis: that they were introduced by man, along with the sheep and goats. The introduction of deer in sufficient numbers to act as a breeding stock for the substantial population of which there is archaeological evidence clearly argues for a high degree of control over the animals and for their sophisticated management.

Furthermore, it is surely perverse to suggest that man imported small numbers of sheep and goats, which he herded and husbanded while depending primarily on fallow deer which he also imported, but then released and hunted. It seems overwhelmingly more like that the deer were the objects of the same measures of husbandry as the other imported herbivores, and that they were herded, behaviourally domestic animals until their decline in economic importance some millennia after their first introduction to the island.

As was mentioned above, we have no details whatever as to the nature of the exploitation of fallow deer on the mainland during the preceding periods. Nonetheless, if we are right in our hypothesis that they were introduced into Cyprus as a herded species early in the Holocene, this clearly has most interesting implications regarding the economy of the 'Palaeolithic hunters' of the Near East.

The gazelle

Like the fallow deer, this species was of great economic importance for many millennia in the Near East. Legge (1972) has shown that during the closing stages of the Pleistocene and early Holocene it was the main staple at many sites in the Palestine area. Furthermore, at Nahal Oren it was found that a high proportion of the crop consisted of young individuals, indicating a selective exploitation pattern akin to that discussed above for red deer. Significantly, as far as could be determined, the cropping pattern of gazelle was closely comparable with that of sheep and goats in the same general area and time period.

The barbary sheep

As with so many species, little is known of the way in which *Ammotragus* was exploited in prehistoric times. It has been assumed so widely and so firmly that it was simply hunted that until recently little or no attempt has been made to test or elaborate the hypothesis. It was of great economic importance throughout much of the Upper Pleistocene in the Mediterranean coastal regions of North Africa, forming 50–95 per cent of the faunal remains at such sites as Haua Fteah and Tamar Hat. Saxon (1976) points out that evidence of the exploitation pattern at the latter site can plausibly be explained in terms of the differential cropping of young males and old females; a rational policy for meat production. Again, it seems that a long-lived intensive, and selective relationship had developed. Saxon argues, moreover, that the Barbary sheep must have been subject to constraint and behavioural control, as they are potentially so difficult to hunt as to render this an impracticable means of exploiting them as a staple resource.

All that the foregoing discussion attempts to establish is that archaeologists may have been too hasty, firstly in assuming that no form of herding, or control and husbandry of animals, could have been practised prior to the Neolithic, and secondly in confining their attention so exclusively to the common farmyard species. Whether or not we wish to term such relationships domestication, semi-domestication, animal husbandry, or whatever, we have seen that there is ample reason to believe that relatively sophisticated forms of animal management may have arisen during the Pleistocene, and that these frequently involved species which are today unhesitatingly classified as wild animals. Examples exist other than those which have been discussed above. A number of pre-Neolithic sites have yielded heavy stones perforated or otherwise modified, possibly for the purpose of acting as fetters. Morel (1967) argued that the slaughter pattern of the hartebeest at a North African Capsian site was so biased as to indicate a most rigorous control of the cropping policy, implying either the strictest of hunting codes or the controlled *parcage* of the animals. Palaeopathological evidence indicates the occasional survival of animals which would almost certainly have died from injury, predation, or disease but for (presumably human) intervention. Doubtless many similar examples will emerge once the evidence is sought.

It is worth reiterating here that the essence of these close man–animal relationships seems to us to lie in the increase of human control over the other species in the partnership. This increase of control does not always require great expertise, technological sophistication, or input of effort. Many benefits can result from an increase in human control. Productivity and efficiency may be improved, risks reduced, and the balance of labour shifted from the location and extraction of resources to various measures of husbandry. Selective breeding and physiological change clearly have a place in these developments, but are viewed by us as secondary phenomena, examples of specific responses to circumstances, rather than general and crucial criteria for the definition of classes of economic relationship.

It is perhaps worthwhile to discuss briefly here the scanty and ambiguous 'cultural' evidence of exploitation techniques in pre-Neolithic Europe. Artefactual evidence which unequivocally demonstrates hunting is remarkably rare, considering the assumption that it was the primary economic adaptation for so long. By Magdalenian times in Western Europe spear-throwers, barbed bone points, and arrows are all in evidence, but in relatively small numbers. By and large, Advanced Palaeolithic toolkits are conspicuously lacking in unequivocal projectile tips. It seems paradoxical that the time of maximum florescence of undoubted arrowheads over very wide areas in Europe is the Late Neolithic and Bronze Age periods. Artistic evidence, particularly from the Mesolithic, occasionally indicates what appear to be traditional hunting techniques, with animals being shot by bow and arrow. We should bear in mind, however, that this is evidence of slaughtering practice rather than of the whole economic relationship. Domestic animals are today not infrequently slaughtered by use of firearms, the typical 'hunting' weapon of today. Spears, bows and arrows, and firearms are part of the basic material equipment of many recent and modern pastoralists. Furthermore, the art evidence illustrates structures which can only be interpreted as corrals as early as *c* 12 000 b.p. The use of corrals, while economically ambiguous, would clearly lend itself to the sophisticated management of animals.

The osteological evidence is similarly equivocal. Noe-Nygaard (1974) and others have pointed to wounds caused by projectiles, and sometimes the projectile tips themselves, in bones from prehistoric sites. This evidence is certainly consonant with the hypothesis that those animals were 'hunted', although it cannot be held to demonstrate the case in view of the fact that again it refers to techniques of slaughter rather than to anything more significant economically. Some rare specimens, it is true, indicate the healing of old wounds. It is inferred that these are evidence of early failed attempts at hunting the animal; and they do indeed seem to indicate a situation where human control over the individual animal was small.

It is no part of our argument that no animals were hunted in Advanced Palaeolithic or Mesolithic times. Such a contention would clearly be absurd. Indeed, as was discussed earlier (pp. 56–7) there are some circumstances in which 'hunting' represents the most rational and effective exploitation technique. On the other hand, as we have argued, there are many instances where this is not the case, and these are by no means confined to the most recent prehistoric periods.

It would be satisfying if we could develop this theme equally fully with respect to plant and aquatic resources. For a number of reasons this is not possible. As we have already noted there are fundamental reasons for believing that as a general rule terrestrial animal protein will have been the single most important dietary resource in pre-Neolithic Europe. The number of plant species available in European ecosystems with the nutritional qualifications and availability to challenge the animal species is very small (see Chapter 1). Aquatic resources suffer from difficulties involved in their exploitation which effectively cancel out their advantages in theoretical productivity (see Chapter 4). Thus in our view there are excellent reasons for bias towards large mammals in any discussion of Palaeolithic and Mesolithic economies in Europe. It is also undoubtedly true, however, that circumstances will have unduly favoured the preservation of terrestrial faunal evidence as opposed to that of vegetable resources (which preserve much less well in most environments) and marine resources (many of the coastal sites having been submerged by rising sea levels).

Clarke (1976) has recently argued for a much more important rôle of vegetable foods in Mesolithic Europe. It will be clear from what has been said that we take a different view in this volume, although it is evident that plant foods will on occasion and in certain areas have attained a considerable importance. Direct archaeological evidence from European Mesolithic sites has been discussed in depth by Jacobi (1976). A number of sites, such as Ulkestrup, Holmgaard and Duvensee, have produced large quantities of hazelnut shells, but only sporadic finds of other plant species. Jacobi comes to the conclusion that archaeological evidence, pollen diagrams, and site territorial data from British Mesolithic sites could be interpreted as suggesting a system of land management favouring hazel. Such a possibility is consistent with our other arguments concerning the sophistication of man's relationships with animal species. As we pointed out in Chapter 1, nuts are among the few groups of plants with a high energy and protein content, and would have been the only component of the indigenous European flora that could have served as a staple dietary item. It would therefore not be surprising to find that man had exploited them in a controlled and rational manner. The degree to which they could have been exploited during the Mesolithic would have depended on their availability in postglacial vegetation. Probably neither oak nor hazel would have been abundant prior to the Atlantic pollen zone. Acorns are rare in all Mesolithic sites and hazelnuts are not common until the late Mesolithic. Therefore, the existing evidence seems to support our contention that prior to the introduction of large-grained cereals and pulses, plant foods may have enjoyed local, short-term importance, but that animal products will have usually been of equal or greater significance.

One of Clarke's arguments is difficult to rebut, however, in the almost total absence of direct evidence on the issue. This is the suggestion that, even in the absence of suitable plant staples, the variety and reliability of plant foods would have resulted in their providing the bulk of the diet even if individual species never rose to a dominant importance. If we accept for the moment Clarke's hypothetical assumption that the Mesolithic diet consisted of 60–80 per cent plant food by weight we can estimate the caloric and protein contribution made by plants and animals (Table 8). The actual figures depend on the number of calories required per person per day, the total weight of food consumed per day, and the composition of the local flora and fauna. On the basis of figures given by Clark, C. & Haswell (1967), we have taken 2500 kcal as the average daily energy requirement. Ethnographic evidence indicates that the quantity of food consumed varies greatly from day to day. We have made calculations using three different values: 750 g, the weight of wheat flour required to provide 2500 kcal; 1 kg; and 2 kg, a figure that is almost certainly too high as a daily average, but that shows what happens as quantities increase to an upper limit. For simplicity the local fauna has been assumed to have been red deer. In fact, bones of boar are often common on Mesolithic sites and probably would provide more fat and thus more calories (see, for example, Chapter 4, Table 9). The values for energy contributions from meat are therefore minima. Conversely, the values for nuts are maxima, since we have not taken into account acorns and chestnuts,

which provide considerably fewer calories and less protein than hazelnuts. The rest of the edible flora has been assumed to have been a mixture of leaves and roots whose dietary value might approximate that shown in Table 8.

It is clear from Table 8 that although on these figures they form the bulk of the diet, roots and greens only begin to make a significant contribution of energy and protein when total intake is 2 kg. At lower levels of intake hazelnuts provide the majority of the calories and nuts and meat most of the protein. Put another way, if man were forced to get even a quarter of his daily energy requirement from greens and roots, he would have to eat nearly 1.5 kg of them and still have room left for 200 g of nuts and 400 g of meat to get the other three-quarters of his calories. Thus the *variety* of plants confers little benefit in that, with rare exceptions, they cannot have satisfied energy and protein requirements no matter how widely available they may have been. As pointed out in Chapter 1, only nuts could have provided a staple plant food source prior to the introduction of large-grained cereals and legumes into Europe.

One factor of crucial significance that Clarke scarcely deals with at all is the *efficiency* of exploitation. This is, admittedly, partly due to the lack of adequate data on the subject. It is notable that throughout the paper he emphasises the high risk and low productivity of hunting. It will be evident that the cost and efficiency of animal exploitation depend to a large extent on the nature of the man–animal relationship, and the degree of control exercised by man. As we have noted, there is every reason to suppose that, in some cases at least, the degree of control was considerable, and that the exploitation of animals may have been a much more dependable and profitable undertaking than Clarke infers. Conversely, the 'edible gums, saps, barks, shoots, stems, buds, flowers, fruits, nuts, roots, tubers, rhizomes, corms, bulbs, mosses, seaweeds, waterplants or fungi . . . waiting immobile, predictable, for the plucking', on which Clarke lays so much emphasis, however valuable they may have been as sources of vitamins and minerals, as relishes and famine foods, will in many cases have required more energy to harvest and prepare than they will have yielded in their consumption.

The nature of early man–plant relationships will certainly become clearer as modern techniques for retrieval of plant remains are applied to earlier sites. We would expect to find in some instances strong indications of closely controlled relationships with particular species at least as early as the early Holocene.

Table 8. The dietary contributions of plant and animal food sources to diets consisting of 60 and 80 per cent plant food by weight[a]

	60% plants : 40% meat			80% plants : 20% meat		
	weight (g)	energy (kcal)	protein (g)	weight (g)	energy (kcal)	protein (g)
total consumed	750	2500		750	2500	
plants	450			600		
greens and roots	150	67.5	2.6	277	124.7	4.7
nuts	300	2010	38.1	323	2164.1	41
meat	300	420	60	150	210	30
totals	750	2497.5	100.7	750	2498.8	75.7
total consumed	1000	2500		1000	2500	
plants	600			800		
greens and roots	333	149.9	5.7	500	225	8.5
nuts	267	1788.9	33.9	300	2010	38.1
meat	400	560	80	200	280	40
totals	1000	2498.8	119.6	1000	2515	86.6
total consumed	2000	2500		2000	2500	
plants	1200			1600		
greens and roots	1066	479.7	18.1	1400	630	23.8
nuts	134	897.8	17	200	1340	25.4
meat	800	1120	160	400	560	80
totals	2000	2497.5	195.1	2000	2530	129.2

dietary value of foods used in table (per 100 g edible portion):

		kcal	protein (g)
greens:	dandelion greens	44	2.7
	water cress	22	1.7
roots:	onions	40	1.4
	parsnips	78	1.5
	turnips	32	1.1
average greens & roots		c 45	1.7
nuts = hazelnuts[b]		671	12.7
meat = venison		139	20

[a] Source: Documenta Geigy 1962
[b] Values for other nuts available in the flora are: acorns, 498 kcal, 3.9–6.3 g protein (Baumhoff 1963); chestnuts (fresh), 213 kcal, 3.4 g protein.

We would not, however, expect these to be as prevalent as such relationships with the large herbivores, and think it very unlikely that they would have existed under glacial conditions, for obvious ecological reasons.

THE BIRTH OF MODERN EUROPEAN AGRICULTURE

In what follows in this volume, then, it is taken as axiomatic that the roots of the sophisticated patterns of exploitation which we know as agriculture lie far back in prehistory. This much now seems incontrovertible, and should not in any case be an occasion for surprise when one considers the complexity and sophistication of many animal exploitation systems. We do not, therefore, make any attempt to discuss the origins of European agriculture in the traditional sense. This must not be interpreted as an attempt to evade the problems posed by the data by denying their existence;

to explain away the phenomenon of agriculture by claiming that it does not exist or that it has always done so.

Far from it. It is undeniable that rapid, widespread, and far-reaching economic changes did take place in Europe early in the Holocene, when the distinctive agricultural systems of today first began to develop. It is the primary task of this volume to enquire into this phenomenon. As explained earlier, we do not believe that the evidence supports the hypothesis that modern-style agriculture arose as the result of a number of revolutionary changes in basic exploitative strategies. It is of some importance, therefore, that we should consider what was involved in this development.

A major difficulty arising from the view of agriculture as the product of a relatively sudden series of unique inventions is that this requires us either to propose equally unparalleled causative circumstances or forces, or to discard altogether the hypothesis of rationally explicable causation of the phenomenon. The former approach has failed so far to generate convincing explanations, and we reject the latter for reasons discussed in Chapter 1. Our suggestion that agriculture may better be viewed as the eventual outcome of long-term changes in economic behaviour, involving processes and relationships which had been current throughout the Pleistocene, avoids this particular pitfall whatever its shortcomings in other directions. By attempting to explain the development of agriculture in terms of widely existing evolutionary factors we avoid the need to invoke special cases, and can more easily see these important adaptations within the context of other patterns of economic behaviour among both men and other animals.

The first outstanding change concerns the species which formed the basis of the economy. Over much of Europe, in the relatively short time between about 9000 and 5000 years ago, economies emerged which were based on the modern farmyard animals – sheep, goats, pigs, and cattle – with the addition in some areas of wheat, barley, and pulse crops. This combination of species replaced earlier economies based primarily on large herbivores: reindeer, red deer, equids, and bison (depending on the time and place), with pigs important in many areas in the early Holocene. For a number of reasons the characteristic Neolithic 'subsistence package' represents an extremely powerful economic unit, of great flexibility and productive potential.

As far as the animals are concerned, an initial point is that they are to a substantial degree non-competitive. Sheep and goats, even when grazed together, tend to utilise different sectors of the available plant cover; sheep and cattle are each able to make use of pasture which could not be effectively grazed by the other. Pigs, and to some extent goats, are useful as converters both of human refuse and of woodland resources into high-protein food. A number of other factors enhance the potential of the farmyard animals. Broadly speaking, they seem to tolerate higher stocking rates than can be maintained for the cervids, which were so important prior to the Neolithic, while their reproductive rate is also higher. To some extent this must be treated with caution, however, as the intensive breeding and management applied for many years to the farmyard animals may have influenced these factors. Another important feature is the adaptability of the common farmyard animals with respect to their food. They seem able to do well in a very wide variety of ecological circumstances, thus facilitating the spread of the economic system, and increasing its flexibility.

The plants concerned in Neolithic agriculture also have certain critically important potentials. We have seen that the plants available for exploitation prior to the Neolithic introduction of cereals and pulses were on the whole conspicuously lacking in the nutritional requirements which might encourage their exploitation as staples. The main exceptions to this are the nuts and acorns. Even the value of these as staples is limited by high annual variation in crop levels, most oaks producing good crops only one in two to four years. An even greater limitation is the difficulty of significantly increasing the production and spread of tree crops. Hazel can be, and evidence indicates it was, encouraged by small-scale forest clearance. Oak, beech, and chestnut production is difficult to influence on a time scale of less than a generation or more. On the contrary, the cereal–pulse association combines high nutritive value with reliable minimum yields in a wide range of habitats, and very high yields in optimal habitats. Indeed, in suitable environmental circumstances cereal agriculture offers the highest return per unit area in terms of calories immediately accessible to human consumption. The well-known ability that some pulse crops have of fixing atmospheric nitrogen in the soil through the action of the *Rhizobium* group of bacteria means that, as with the animal component of the economy, it is the integration of different elements which gives the system its great potential. Cereal crops, especially wheat, are expensive of nitrogen, and thus the pulse group is of immense value as a rotation crop, quite apart from its nutritional input to the system. Similarly, the potential for the integration of the arable and pastoral aspects of the economy in many environments increases the productivity and flexibility of the system as a whole. The grazing of stock on fallow fields is an obvious example of this relationship: not only do the stock benefit from the grazing, but their transformation of vegetation to dung increases the efficiency of the re-cycling of nutrients within the ecosystem.

We can thus see that there are considerable economic advantages inherent in the adoption of the modern 'farmyard' economy, in comparison with that which it replaced over such a wide area. A valid question, faced with this phenomenon, is why the change occurred when it did.

One of the most popular explanations of agricultural origins among archaeologists has been in terms of 'cultural' development. Braidwood (1960) suggested that the economic changes were perhaps inevitable once a certain level of 'cultural' attainment was reached, but was unable to isolate the factors or mechanisms involved. Piggott (1965) is perhaps invoking a similar force with his concept of 'innovating societies'. These formulations fail to satisfy because in the absence of a more rigorous analysis of the causal factors involved, they do not really explain anything. Childe (1952) long ago suggested that environmental stimulus in the form of desiccation may have been such a causative factor; and although there has been a general tendency in the past 20 years to play down such hypotheses, more recent work (Wright 1976) seems to suggest that climatic change of a magnitude sufficient to be significant may indeed have taken place in the Near East.

As far as most of Europe is concerned it is easy enough to explain the absence of the arable aspects of agriculture in the period immediately prior to the Holocene, at least as far as the cereals are concerned. With the possible exception of a few favoured areas, under the environmental conditions then prevailing the large-grained cereals could not have grown in economically significant numbers. It is striking, as will be seen later, that in many areas of Europe cereal agriculture appears very soon after the point when environmental conditions first changed sufficiently to permit their successful exploitation.

It seems, then, that environmental influences in all probability had an impact upon the appearance of modern-style agricultural economies in Europe. Nevertheless it is hard to see climatic factors themselves as the ultimate cause. Comparable climatic conditions certainly occurred on many occasions earlier in the Pleistocene, and we are left with the question of why they were so dramatically effective in the Holocene while failing to produce such an impact in the earlier interglacials.

We have considered earlier (Chapter 1) the reciprocal relationship between populations and the economic systems which support them. The appropriateness of exploitation patterns depends greatly upon demographic considerations. Low population densities not only do not require intensive economies of high extractive capacity, they rarely have sufficient man-power to make these possible. Conversely, high levels of population often cannot survive on extensive systems with low levels of return, but have the labour resources to construct and maintain more complex systems. In a number of ways the development of agricultural economies can be seen in these terms. As we have pointed out, most of the mechanisms involved in the change from a typical 'hunting' or 'gathering' pattern of exploitation to a typical 'stock breeding' or 'arable farming' system involve forms of investment: of time, labour, and energy. In the interests of securing a greater and/or more stable and predictable return in the long term, increasing emphasis is placed upon investment strategies for the future, and less upon the direct satisfaction of short-term requirements. In these characteristics they are more appropriate to relatively high population densities than are simpler economies based upon direct exploitation. We might therefore expect the development of more complex and productive systems during periods of increase in population density.

The early development of European agriculture seems in general to support this hypothesis. Precise population figures are of course beyond archaeological retrieval, but all the evidence supports the suggestion that the Early Neolithic in Europe, with its modern-style mixed farming economy, was associated with considerable population increase. Indeed, the substantial loss of coastal lowlands due to eustatic rise in sea level in the millennia prior to this must of itself have created considerable population pressure, in some areas at least. It is thus of interest to note that one of the major elements within the overall economic change was a much more intensive exploitation of the lowland zone through the mechanism of arable agriculture.

To some it will doubtless seem that we are relying too much on a demographic *deus ex machina* in our insistence upon the significance of population pressure. At least, if this is the case, it is a conscious and intentional emphasis which we have given, and not merely an oversight. There is overwhelming evidence for the pre-eminent importance of population density in the evolution of much social and economic behaviour among animals. We are profoundly convinced that the same is true of man, and that evidence of this is to be found in the prehistoric record.

4. COASTS, LAKES, AND LITTORALS

We have chosen to begin our analysis of the early development of modern European agriculture with the coastal zone. This may seem an odd choice at first sight, but it was felt that some aspects of postglacial economic evolution could be better appreciated when this zone had been discussed. We have already referred to the probable significance of environmental change during the late Pleistocene and early Holocene (Chapter 3). Rising sea level was one of the major factors involved, as it would not only have drowned and thus made inaccessible wide areas of coastal lowland, but it would have brought with it profound changes affecting many aspects of the marine and terrestrial environment. Moveover, some of the early Holocene economies which immediately preceded the Neolithic form of farming seem to have been characterised by a degree of dependence upon aquatic resources. This has been seen by many as one of the primary forms of adaptation to the environmental changes, and by others as a fundamental step on the path leading to Neolithic agriculture. The general significance of this phenomenon, as part of an overall trend towards 'broad spectrum' and less mobile economies than those that had been current hitherto has been variously urged by such authors as Binford (1968), Burkill (1960), Clark, J. G. D. (1948), Cohen (1977), Flannery (1969), Hawkes (1969), and Sauer (1952).

Coasts and lake edges frequently embody a number of advantages which attract settlement. These include the diversity of the available resources, drawn from a variety of ecosystems ranging from dry land to open water, and the important effect which large bodies of water exert on local climatic conditions. The greater variety of resources available within a relatively limited area offers a range of alternatives which can greatly improve the stability of the overall food supply, whether on a day-to-day basis or over longer periods of time. This is in accordance with the general ecological proposition that the greater the range of resources exploited by an animal the more stable the relationships involved (Slobodkin 1962). Community stability thus tends to be correlated with the number of energy pathways in operation. Seasonal variability is of particular relevance, since some aquatic resources are most densely concentrated, most easily accessible, or most nutritious during periods of terrestrial food shortage, and therefore form a natural seasonal complement to exploitation on land. They may in many cases be of great importance in times of unusual hardship, without necessarily forming a regular item of diet. The relative predictability with which some return can be expected, coupled with their near-inexhaustability in many subsistence situations, makes aquatic resources especially valuable in this context. Thus Hoffman (1976) notes the crucial importance of fish to the Caribou Eskimo as a 'back-up resource'. While it was usually fed to the dogs, its productivity could reliably be stepped up for human consumption simply by the intensification of effort applied to its exploitation. In some particularly favourable environmental circumstances the potential of marine resources may greatly exceed that of terrestrial resources, a factor which doubtless contributes to the high population densities and relatively small annual territories observed among the Indians of America's northwest coast, for example.

The impact of these advantages was not confined to recent periods of prehistory. Lake edges were crucial in the development of early Pleistocene economies in sub-Saharan Africa. Coastal sites are among the earliest recorded in North Africa and Europe, and it may be that the resources of coastal areas made them attractive routes of dispersal for early hominid populations (Sauer 1962). Many of the technologically simple hunting and gathering communities which survived until recently show a similar involvement with aquatic environments.

THE ETHNOGRAPHIC RECORD

The archaeological view of coastal economies has been greatly influenced by ethnographic studies. In view of this it will be helpful as a preliminary to summarise some of the evidence and see to what extent it supports the archaeological conclusions that have been drawn. We have not attempted a general survey, which would require several volumes in itself and would in any case be of very uneven value. Instead examples have been selected because they seem to throw light on some questions which are of particular interest to us in our analysis of prehistoric economies.

Two themes above all others recur persistently: the view of coastal populations as impoverished 'strand-loopers', and the interpretation of shell middens as the permanent or quasi-permanent habitation sites of coastal communities. Thus Lubbock, in his *Prehistoric Times* (1865), compared the shell middens of Denmark with those of the Canoe Indians of Tierra del Fuego. Ever since then interpretations of the Ertebølle sites of Denmark have tended to emphasise the dependence upon marine resources (particularly shellfish) and the material poverty of the inhabitants. The middens have customarily been viewed as the semi-permanent home bases of a threadbare beachcombing subsistence eked out in a marginal environment. It has in general been ignored that there is evidence of a substantial terrestrial element in the Ertebølle economy, and that evidence of habitation during both summer and winter may indicate an intermittent rather than a year-round occupation.

Mobile economies are by far the most numerous among ethnographic examples of coastal groups. We may distinguish two kinds of mobile coastal economy: one in which movements are made inland at times when coastal resources are in short supply or inaccessible, or when inland resources are particularly rich; and strand-looping, where the marine character of the economy is maintained throughout the year. Strandlooping consists of movements along the coast, different marine resources being exploited at different seasons to provide a year-round subsistence base. Each of these types of economy is exemplified among the Indians of Tierra del Fuego.

The Yahgan and the Alacaluf (Canoe Indians) of the Beagle Channel and the islands and peninsulas of the Pacific coast, lived in an environment of great climatic and topographic severity. The impact of physiographic limitations upon the economy is well summed up by Bird (1938).

. . . there is no place where one can walk along or near the shore without the greatest difficulty. The reason lies not only in the densely tangled forest that clings wherever it can secure a foothold but also in the rough nature of the country – mountains and hills that drop precipitously beneath the sea with little or no foreshore. Beaches are few and widely separated. Glaciers and swift flowing rivers offer further obstacles . . .

For food the natives on the Pacific side necessarily depended almost entirely on what the sea had to offer – a large variety of excellent shellfish, seals, otters, porpoises, and, occasionally, whales . . . On land it is a different story. Only isolated localities have anything to offer . . . Pursuit is arduous and only where the topography favoured the hunters were any deer taken . . .

A harsh and capricious climate add to the difficulties of the terrain. A long period of winter frost, heavy and unpredictable snowfalls, and frequent gales with torrential rainfall have to be accommodated. It thus seems that the hinterland is scarcely habitable even on a seasonal or occasional basis, and that at best the possibilities of inland exploitation are severely limited by the adverse environment.

The inhabitants of the area usually occupied shell middens as their home bases. These were often of considerable size, having accumulated for centuries. Marine resources exploited included seals, sea lions, and birds, as well as molluscs. Fishing was comparatively rare. Plant foods seem to have been of negligible importance. The hunting of deer and guanaco features little in ethnographic accounts, although it seems likely that these were exploited wherever they were available (Bird 1946, Emperaire 1955). Complementary sites seem to have been of two main kinds. Some offered substantially similar resources to those of the home base. These were occupied to make use of a localised abundance of molluscs and marine mammals, a practice which would also have had the function of resting the resources adjacent to the home base. Other sites seem to have been used specifically for sealing, fowling, or hunting, and off-shore islands were exploited in this way from temporary camps.

Further to the east, principally in the Atlantic coastal regions of southern Argentina, were found the Ona, or Foot Indians. The environment remains severe, but is less restricting than for the Canoe Indians. Topography in particular is less of a limiting factor, and the hinterland is characterised by the existence of some relatively open and accessible areas. The home bases were again coastal sites, some, at least, shell middens (Lothrop 1928). On the other hand the more exposed coastline results in a lower level of molluscan resources, and these were thus of less significance here than in the Canoe Indian economy. The staple was the guanaco, and in response to its seasonal movements between the coast (in winter) and inland (in summer), the Ona undertook summer movements into the hinterland (Gusinde 1931). This exploitation of inland resources, permitted by their greater accessibility in comparison with the Pacific coastal area, was further prompted by the scarcity of fresh water in the coastal zone (Bird 1938).

Thus the Canoe Indians hunted game wherever conditions permitted, and the Foot Indians exploited molluscs wherever they were abundant. As far as we can tell the important economic differences appear to stem from crucial variations in the available resources, primarily the accessibility of the hinterland, reinforced perhaps by the greater wealth of coastal resources for the Canoe Indians.

Tasmania presents comparable contrasts. On the west coast, where the narrow plain is backed by a densely forested mountain range, the aboriginal economy was based on strandlooping, with seasonal movements along the shoreline and to offshore islands. In the summer, sealing supported large semi-permanent populations which dispersed into smaller groups in winter, subsisting mainly on molluscs, duck eggs, and mutton birds (Jones 1974). Elsewhere in Tasmania, where inland resources were more easily accessible, complex patterns of seasonal movement linked the coast with the hinterland, with some groups travelling over 100 km from their inland home bases to exploit coastal resources, while other groups remained by the sea for most of the year and undertook only limited movements into the immediate hinterland.

The Seri Indians of the Gulf of California furnish an example of a strandlooping economy in rather different environmental circumstances. Turtles, fish, and shellfish were staple resources. These were supplemented by fruit and terrestrial game, which had for the most part to be exploited within 6 km of the coast (Ascher 1962), although there is some archaeological evidence to suggest that movement may have extended as far as 20 km inland in some places (Bowen 1976). The economy was restricted to this narrow coastal strip by the inland desert, which extends in places almost to the seashore.

By and large, examples of strandlooping are rare, and the general picture seems to be of patterns of seasonal movement, varying according to environmental circumstances, serving to integrate coastal and inland resources. Many of these involve relatively small-scale movements of the order of 30 km, such as those of the Californian Indians (Greengo 1952), the Central Eskimo (Balikci 1968), the Australian Aborigines (White & Peterson 1969, Poiner 1976) and the coastal Bushmen (Parkington 1972). On the other hand, annual movements could extend up to several hundred kilometres in extreme environments, as is shown by the Caribou Eskimo (Birket-Smith 1929) and the Chukchi (Leeds 1969).

Sometimes the detailed disposition of human groups relative to the seasonal variations in resources can be shown to have achieved a highly sensitive adjustment. Bailey (1975b) has documented a case in northern New South Wales. There are three main resource zones and two human groups. Marine resources are at their most abundant in summer, and the larger human group has its home bases on the coast. At this time the immediate hinterland is rendered inaccessible and has a low productivity due to extensive flooding. As the floods dry out, and the productivity of the coastal zone declines, movements are made inland to exploit marsupials and plant foods. A smaller human population has its home bases yet further inland in the foothills of the New England range. Here winter is the lean season, and some groups travel to the coast to exploit the modest resources which are at this season largely ignored by the coast-based group. Similar reciprocal movements are documented elsewhere, as amongst the Caribou and Coastal Eskimo groups, and some California Indians (Kroeber & Barrett 1960), for example.

Three points of interest emerge from the ethnological data discussed. A first conclusion of importance is that strandlooping, far from being the 'typical' coastal economy as has sometimes been inferred, seems rather to occur in special circumstances. Strandlooping economies never seem to arise where there are substantial resources assessible inland, and are an example of an extreme economic adaptation to an unfavourable environment. Even in basically strandlooping economies such as those of the Canoe Indians and Seri Indians exploitation of inland resources is pursued wherever the environmental constraints permit.

Sedentary coastal economies, discussed in some detail in Chapter 2, seem to be of similarly restricted occurrence. Again, use is usually made of inland resources where these are accessible and worthwhile. They are, in a sense, a direct analogue of the strandlooping economies, but in situations of unusually high marine productivity. This permits much higher population densities than in poorer areas, and mitigates or obviates entirely the need for substantial mobility along the coast. Invariably they have to make use of stored food from seasons of surplus to make sedentism possible over the lean periods.

The third point of interest is that shellfish customarily have only a minor role in the overall economy and diet. Rarely if ever do they seem to have been exploited as staples, although they may frequently have acted as critical resources. The Chugach Eskimo, for example, rely on shellfish principally as a reserve when other resources fail (Birket-Smith 1953). Even in areas of exceptional shellfish productivity they seem to have been overshadowed in importance by other resources. Thus Meehan (1977) showed that shellfish contribute only between about 2.5 and 8.9 per cent of the calorie intake of those populations that regularly exploit the prolific shell beds in the tropical bays of northern Australia. Here again they reach their peak of importance in the lean season. In the absence of comparable numerical data elsewhere it is not possible to pursue this point further, although it is worth noting that even for the Yahgan and Alacaluf with their primarily strandlooping economy, the importance of shellfish may have been less than is implied by their shell midden settlements. Bird (1946) noted that deer bones are fairly frequent in their middens. As we shall see below, there are reasons for supposing that the bones of mammals may represent a much larger dietary contribution than might be inferred from the vastly superior bulk of mollusc shells.

THE ARCHAEOLOGICAL RECORD

In view of the high ecological productivity and diversity of many aquatic environments it is tempting to conclude that settlement was primarily attracted to coasts and lakes by the rich potential of the aquatic resources. A number of considerations suggest that we should examine the evidence a little more closely.

One important limitation to be taken into account is that aquatic resources are frequently less accessible than terrestrial resources, and they are thus technologically more demanding, especially in coastal areas. They may present human exploiters with divergent and conflicting claims on time and energy, and may therefore be persistently ignored or exploited at low levels of intensity until the development of a relatively sophisticated technology. We must also remember that despite the apparent richness of many marine environments, most of the species of major economic importance exist at such high levels in the trophic pyramid that they represent an intrinsically inefficient use of ecological energy. As we have already seen, predominantly marine-based economies are comparatively rare in the ethnographic record, and seem to be the product of specific environmental constraints.

It is arguable that shell middens, in particular, occupy a privileged position in the archaeological record. They are durable and often very large, and provide a striking contrast to the usually paltry remains of other economic activities. The middens themselves almost invariably contain substantial evidence of an important terrestrial component to the economy. Furthermore, when factors of preservation are taken into account, it seems certain that the importance of shellfish is exaggerated in comparison with that of the mammals represented in the shell mounds (Parmalee & Klippel 1974, Bailey 1975a, Lubell *et al.* 1975, Osborn 1977). Similar biases may well affect the representation of fish bones, and many recent studies have therefore tended to be cautious in taking the easy inferential step from shell middens to a mollusc-based economy or from coastal sites to a strandlooping pattern of exploitation.

The relatively sudden appearance of shell mounds in the prehistoric record is another factor which may have focused undue attention on them. As has often been pointed out, this phenomenon may well be largely a result of the destruction of earlier sites by sea level changes, rather than of a dramatic shift in exploitative strategies. The further back one goes into the Pleistocene, the greater the degree of uncertainty on this count.

The great emphasis given to aquatic resources has tended to lead to a neglect of the rôle which large bodies of water play in modifying the local terrestrial environment. Typical effects include the raising of water tables and the tempering of climatic extremes. These modifications are sufficiently pronounced to justify our recognition of the *littoral* as a separate resource zone, that is the strip of land adjacent to the water's edge. Littorals often provide especially productive conditions for terrestrial resources and may be expected to have exerted an important determining influence upon the distribution of population and on patterns of exploitation.

COASTAL RESOURCES

Because of its complex mosaic character, we have found it useful to subdivide the coastal exploitation zone into three subsidiary resource zones: the open water zone, the intertidal zone, and the littoral zone. Since the term littoral may also be used to refer to the intertidal zone, it is important to emphasise that this is not the usage employed here. Furthermore, the littoral zone in our sense is not simply a terrestrial appendage to the consideration of aquatic resources but may itself be modified by the proximity of the sea, and therefore forms an integral feature of the coastal exploitation zone.

Further subcategories may be defined within each resource zone to suit local circumstances, for example estuaries and islands in the open water zone, soft and hard shores in the intertidal zone, or marshy and dry ground in the littoral zone. The three major categories, however, are adequate as an overall framework and emphasise features which we believe to be of widespread importance.

The open water zone

This is perhaps the most variable resource zone. Its economic potential is influenced by a number of ecological factors, and it will be useful to examine briefly the variability and distribution of these in European waters.

The ultimate limiting factor on the potential of marine resources is their productivity in terms of biomass per unit area per unit time. This depends on the rate of primary production of phytoplankton, the microscopic marine organisms formed by photosynthesis in the surface waters of the sea. The proximate limitation as far as human economies are concerned is the accessibility of the resources within the limitations of the available technology and the time–distance factor. This was discussed in some detail in Chapter 3. Between these two factors there is an intermediate group of limiting effects imposed by the structure of food webs in the marine ecosystem.

The production of phytoplankton is determined principally by the availability of nitrates and phosphates, whose presence in surface waters is largely dependent on recycling of decomposed tissue from the sea bottom by physical mixing, and also by a favourable combination of temperature and illumination. Broadly speaking the temperate oceans of middle latitudes are the most productive with fairly high rates of primary production in the spring and autumn and good vertical mixing caused by winter cooling of surface waters and storm turbulence. Productivity in high latitudes is limited by the short period of adequate illumination, and in low latitudes by the persistence of temperature gradients which tend to trap nutrients at depths where penetration of sunlight is insufficient for photosynthesis. Upwelling of deep water masses may offset the limitations of inadequate illumination or excess temperature, notably in the Antarctic Ocean.

An important rôle in the productivity of the European marine environment is played by the continental shelf, which consists of a shallow sloping of the sea bed down to a depth of 100–150 m. The rapid recycling of nutrients possible within this zone favours the production of a rich plankton crop which attracts marine animals of every kind. In addition, some photosynthesis can take place on the sea bottom in shallower areas down to a maximum of 20–50 m depending on the translucency of the water. This results in the growth of attached algae such as seaweed and a bottom fauna of molluscs, crustaceans, and bottom-feeding fish, which are especially abundant in the intertidal zone.

Water temperature and water depth, then, are key variables. These have been represented in Figure 18 by the distribution of temperature isohyets and the continental shelf in European waters. By far the most productive waters are those of the North Atlantic, where seasonal temperature variation ensures an effective recharging of nutrients, and the continental shelf is at its most extensive. The richest area within this zone is the North Sea with several off-shore banks and shallows and a bottom fauna biomass two to four times higher than elsewhere (Laevastu 1961). The Baltic Sea, although it is extensive and shallow, represents a pocket of relatively low productivity within a zone of high potential, since the restriction of tidal inflow from the North Sea results in a sluggish turnover of nutrients and a progressive decline in salinity and production of phytoplankton with increasing distance from the North Sea.

The Mediterranean and the Atlantic waters off the Iberian peninsula can be grouped together in a zone of generally low productive potential. The Mediterranean in particular is a deep, steep-sided basin with a narrow continental shelf. Nutrients accumulated on the sea bottom tend to be carried through the straits of Gibraltar by the deep, outflowing bottom current, but are not replaced by the inflowing currents, which are derived from the relatively infertile surface of the mid-Atlantic ocean. Thermoclines put a further brake on primary production, especially in the south and east. The least productive waters are those of the eastern Mediterranean; the most productive are in the northern Adriatic and around the Iberian coast.

The conversion of the primary vegetation into food suitable for human consumption is a less efficient process in the marine ecosystem than on land, mainly because of the microscopic nature of the phytoplankton and the number and complexity of links in the food chains which support the larger marine animals. Even in the heavily fished waters around the British Isles, for example, only 0.05 per cent of the annual production of phytoplankton is harvested as fish (Coull 1972). Almost none of the primary production was accessible to pre-industrial man apart from some species of seaweed; while herbivorous species available for exploitation are confined to molluscs, some small pelagic fish, and the whalebone whales (Mysticeti). The most numerous group of herbivorous animals is the zooplankton, minute free-swimming creatures which form the principal food of small pelagic fish such as herring. These in turn are eaten by larger fish such as cod and haddock and by the toothed whales (Odontoceti) and seals. Thus many of the species of greatest economic importance to man are primary or secondary carnivores. This

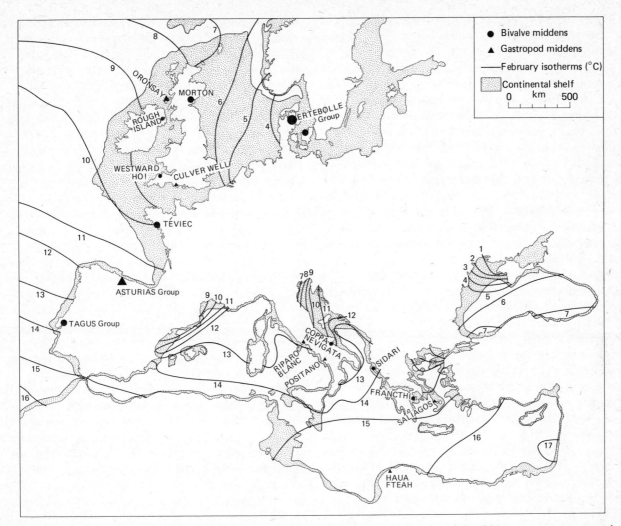

Figure 18. Distribution of coastal shell middens in Europe and the Mediterranean, showing the relationship to sea temperatures and the continental shelf. Size of symbol indicates approximate quantity of mollusc shells.

has vital repercussions on the efficiency of marine exploitation by man, due to energy loss at each change of trophic level.

Thus regional variations in the quantity of marine food available for human consumption depend ultimately on variations in primary production. Nevertheless, local variations in the biology and behaviour of the exploited species, and specifically in their accessibility to man, exert an important proximate limitation on their economic potential.

Resources in the open water zone tend to be mobile, dispersed and wide-ranging. Factors of distance and technology are therefore paramount limitations, and the existence of seasonal concentrations is of particular importance in their mitigation. The effect of these limitations is most clearly seen in areas where the

continental shelf is shallow and extends a long way offshore. In the coastal waters of northwest Europe, for example, fish species of the demersal (bottom-feeding) cod family are found in abundance. Apart from the cod itself (*Gadus callarias*), these include haddock (*Melanogrammus aeglefinus*), whiting (*Gadus merlangus*), saithe (*Pollachius virens*) and hake (*Merluccius merluccius*). Commercial catches are taken by trawl on the spawning grounds, where the adults form large seasonal concentrations. However, these tend to occur at some depth – from about 20–40 m in the case of whiting to 90–180 m in the case of hake. In the North Sea the spawning grounds are thus as much as 300 km from land, distances well beyond the effective range of simple technologies. These species do, however, sometimes make feeding migrations into shallower water, especially when young. In Scotland 10–15 per cent of the demersal catch is taken from within 5 km of land (Perkins 1974).

Perhaps the best compromise between abundance and accessibility at simple levels of technology is to be found on coastlines with a moderately steep continental shelf – not so steep as to impoverish seriously the bottom fauna, but steep enough to bring deeper water within economic reach of land. The west coast of Norway is just such an example, and it is worth noting the presence of a thriving cod fishery in this area from an early period (Clark, J. G. D. 1948). Other Mesolithic fisheries based on the cod family were located on the island of Zealand overlooking the straits which separate it from the Swedish coast (Møhl 1971a), and on the small Scottish offshore island of Oronsay, where saithe is the most frequently recorded fish in the midden remains (Mellars & Payne 1971). These examples of early coastal sites owe their preservation in part to glacio-isostatic uplift, so that they may have undue prominence in the archaeological record simply because of differential preservation. At the same time their locations underline the importance of coastlines where atypical features allowed improved accessibility to mobile marine resources.

A second important demersal group is the flatfish, including sole (*Solea solea*), plaice (*Pleuronectes platessa*), and flounder (*Platichthys flesus*). These feed on muddy or sandy bottoms, often quite close inshore, especially in the vicinity of estuaries. They therefore pose less severe problems of access than do the cod family.

Of the pelagic fish (those, that is, that live in surface shoals and feed on phytoplankton or zooplankton) the most abundant species in northwest Europe are herring (*Clupea harengus*) and mackerel (*Scomber scombrus*). The herring in particular forms immense shoals which pass close to the shore during spawning migrations, while mackerel spawn in deeper water and move closer to the shore only during spring and summer feeding migrations. These species are notoriously rare in prehistoric sites, and this is unlikely to be due solely to the factor of distance, since Perkins (1974) has shown that 80 per cent of the modern Scottish herring catch comes from within 5 km of land. In contrast to the demersal fish, which can be caught with baited lines or speared in shallow water, the small pelagic fish require the use of drift nets if they are to be taken in worthwhile quantities. As Clark, J. G. D. (1948) has observed, it is possible that there was little incentive among small communities to engage in the relatively labour-intensive activity of manufacturing and maintaining such equipment, although the necessary knowledge and technological skills may well have been in existence.

A more accessible group of pelagic fish, and one which is sometimes represented among prehistoric food remains, is the diadromous group, notably the salmon (*Salmo salar*), trout (*Salmo trutta*) and eel (*Anguilla anguilla*). These move between coastal and inland waters during spawning migrations and can be taken in large numbers at these times.

Sea mammals are widely distributed in Atlantic waters. Of the whalebone whales, the right whale family (Balaenidae) are slow-moving creatures and can be approached in a rowing boat and dispatched by a hand-propelled harpoon (Hardy 1959). Among the toothed whales, the common porpoise (*Phocaena phocaena*) and the various species of dolphins, relatively small animals about 2–4 m long, would also have been accessible to simple technologies. The most abundant of the seals is the grey seal (*Halichoerus grypus*), especially accessible to exploitation because of its habit of spending up to 2 months on land during the breeding and mating seasons. Of wider distribution but lesser accessibility is the common seal (*Phoca vitulina*).

In the coastal waters of the Iberian peninsula and the Mediterranean, demersal fish species are less well represented because of the narrower continental shelf. The cod family, with the exception of hake, is in any case largely absent from the Mediterranean because of the higher temperatures. Pelagic species are most important in the modern fisheries of this area. These include mackerel, sardine (*Sardina pilchardus*), anchovy (*Engraulis encrasicholus*), and, above all, the bluefin tuna (*Thynnus thynnus*). The smaller species were apparently not exploited in prehistory, presumably for reasons similar to those suggested to explain the neglect of the herring in northwest Europe. The tuna, however, is a large fish which is known to have been effectively exploited since at least the Neolithic period (Evans & Renfrew 1968). Among the diadromous fish only the sturgeon (*Acipenser sturio*) is of any economic importance. Salmon do not extend further south than the Cantabrian coast of Spain, while the trout and eel, though present, do not exist in the Mediterranean in numbers comparable with the Atlantic populations.

The intertidal zone

The intertidal zone does not form an entirely self-contained ecological or economic unit. At high tides it is essentially an extension of the shallow waters of the continental shelf, while the molluscs and crustaceans exposed at low tide are in some cases only the upper-most part of a distribution which extends well below the low-water mark. The area of exposed shore varies widely with fluctuations in topography and tidal ampli-tude. Certain species of molluscs are especially well adapted to conditions of periodic exposure and are usually found in greatest numbers between tide marks.

Both major groupings of molluscs – the bivalves and gastropods – include edible representatives whose shells are found in large numbers in European prehis-toric middens. The commonest bivalves are oysters (*Ostrea edulis, Crassostrea angulata*), mussels (*Mytilus edulis*), and cockles (*Cardium edule*). The commonest gastropods are limpets (*Patella* spp.) and periwinkles or topshells (*Littorina littorea, Trochus* spp.). All are widely distributed around European shorelines; all are grazing animals which feed directly on phytoplankton or other plant material.

The bivalve species are sedentary filter feeders which burrow into the surface of soft sediments or lie on the surface, and which depend on the flow of water cur-rents for their food supply. They are most abundant in estuaries or sheltered inlets. This is partly because of the presence of a suitable substrate and maximum protection from storm disturbances; partly because the formation of slack water and eddies ensures a dense, concentrated settlement of the larvae; and partly be-cause of the favourable food supply which is main-tained by the extensive ebb and flow of the tides across the shallow river flats and by the presence of plant detritus washed into the river from land.

Gastropods on the other hand predominate on ex-posed rocky shores where they make limited feeding movements in search of weed or algae, which they scrape off the rock surface. As a rule the gastropods represent a less concentrated supply of food for man than the bivalves, although their habitat is generally a more stable one.

Regional variations in the abundance of molluscs follow a pattern similar to the other marine resources. The northwest coasts, with high levels of primary productivity, numerous broad estuaries, and an exten-sive tidal range, support the largest populations. In the shallow waters of the Baltic, extensive beds of mussels and cockles are found, but they show a rapid diminu-tion in individual size with decreasing salinity.

The littoral zone

We define the littoral arbitrarily but loosely as that area most exposed to modification by the sea. We have usually concentrated upon the area within 10 km of the shore, as this coincides with our maximum theoretical limit for daily exploitation in extensive economies and also encompasses the area within which the impact of the sea is most strongly felt. In some cases, of course, the climatic effect of the sea is felt considerably further inland. The principal factors from our point of view include higher water tables, increased and more evenly distributed annual rainfall, warmer winters, and a general moderation of climatic extremes.

The overall consequence of these factors is usually to enhance the potential of this zone as a winter grazing area, although in some circumstances (as in modern Brittany, for instance) the oceanic conditions also increase arable and horticultural potential. The areas of swamp and marsh that are frequently found in coastal regions are remarkable for their high levels of primary productivity. While it is true that many European marsh plants produce humanly edible food (Clarke 1976), the vast preponderance of the productivity is in the form of cellulose-rich grasses, sedges, and reeds. These provide resources which would have been a vital part of the annual grazing succession of both wild and husbanded animals in prehistory, as they are today despite their steady contraction due to drainage. The abundance and quality of marshland grazing is sug-gested by the importance of such areas as Romney Marsh and the East Anglian Fens in historical livestock economies. In the U.S.S.R. more than 50 per cent of the country's hay crop comes from largely unimproved water meadows (Larin 1962). In temperate Europe coastal marshlands frequently carry the first flush of spring vegetation, and are thus of crucial importance at the end of the winter lean period. In the Mediterranean they are of considerable value in maintaining areas of plant growth throughout the year in a region of summer desiccation. Salt marshes, in addition, are of especial value in sheep husbandry, as the snail host of the liver fluke does not breed in salt or brackish waters, and the life cycle of this parasite is thus broken.

The littoral is sometimes rich in other resources such as wildfowl, at least on a seasonal basis. These, while of some local importance, will rarely if ever have approached the significance of the grazing resources and the animals these supported, due both to their lower productivity and poor accessibility.

LACUSTRINE RESOURCES

Lakes are less easy to categorise than coasts since they are patchily distributed across the landscape and their exploitation is more directly influenced by the econo-mic potential of the adjacent terrain. Nevertheless they

4. COASTS, LAKES, AND LITTORALS

share many of the resource characteristics of coasts. The intertidal zone is normally absent, and shells of molluscs, although they are sometimes found in European lake sites, never form the large accumulations typical of coastal middens. The other two resource zones, however, can be adapted with fairly minor modifications to the analysis of lacustrine economies.

The economic potential of the open water zone is determined by general principles similar to those described for European coastal waters. Most lakes in temperate Europe are dimictic, that is the water column is stratified twice during the year – in summer and in winter – and is thoroughly mixed during spring and autumn. The value of this mixing process, however, is tempered by the fact that much of the nutrient supply restored to the surface in autumn is often washed out of the lake during winter before it can be utilised by the main burst of photosynthetic activity in spring and early summer. Primary production is highest in shallow lakes and the shallower parts of deep lakes, but is little affected by regional variations of climate. Local factors are a more significant variable, particularly the character and quantity of nutrients washed into the lake from adjacent land surfaces.

The chief human food resources of this zone are fish, of which there is a variety of species, although especial mention may be made of pike (*Esox lucius*), perch (*Perca fluviatilis*), and trout. Diadromous species such as eel and salmon may also be well represented, depending on the distance of the lake from the sea. These freshwater species spend most of their life as primary carnivores, and therefore represent only about 1 per cent of total primary production (Macan & Worthington 1972). Pike is a secondary carnivore and represents only about 0.1 per cent of primary production. Nevertheless, temperate lakes may produce an annual biomass of up to 30 kg per hectare of fish (Hickling 1971), although much of this would be unsuitable for consumption or inaccessible to exploitation. Considerations of accessibility, technology, and transportation are prominent here as with marine resources. The only lacustrine plant foods which seem likely to have been of much significance are water chestnuts (*Trapa natans*) and water lilies (*Nuphar luteum*). These do occur in large numbers at certain archaeological sites. They are nutritionally limited, but would have contributed carbohydrate to the diet.

The littoral zone is potentially a significant feature, since a strip of marsh or swamp vegetation is sometimes found along lake edges. Also, as in coastal areas, the shores of large lakes often enjoy a milder climate than the region as a whole, since the thermal properties of

the lake water have a moderating influence, although this is more localised than the oceanic conditions which prevail on sea coasts. On the other hand, the small, shallow lakes frequently dotted across the flat landscapes of northern Europe tend to create unfavourable microclimates in the slight depressions that trap cold air, form frost pockets, and delay the onset of the growing season. Since the major lake regions of Europe were formed by glacial action, they tend to occur either at high latitude or at high altitude. These are areas which suffer relatively severe winters, and where the climatic influence of lakes would be especially crucial to economic exploitation.

We turn now to detailed studies of prehistoric sites in the coastal zone along the Baltic in Poland and Denmark and the Atlantic of Cantabrian Spain. Lakeside economies were analysed principally in lowland Denmark and Sweden and in highland areas flanking the central European Alps. A guiding consideration has been to cover as wide a range of environmental conditions as possible and to obtain some balance of representation on either side of the traditional Mesolithic–Neolithic divide. Our coverage is inevitably uneven, as are the data. We have already discussed the ambiguous significance of the shell middens and the difficulty of assessing the degree of vulnerability of coastal sites of different ages to destruction by isostatic and eustatic processes.

These uncertainties do not, of course, present insuperable barriers to analysis. Figure 18 shows the general distribution of the principal shell midden deposits of Mesolithic or earlier date. The largest number of sites is in northwest Europe, notably Denmark. Isolated concentrations of middens are also known from the Iberian peninsula, while the Mediterranean has the fewest middens and the smallest sites in terms of shell content. The abundance of sites in northern Britain and Denmark is almost certainly due, in part, to glacio-isostatic uplift, which has ensured the preservation of early Holocene middens that would otherwise have been submerged by the rising sea. Nevertheless, middens of comparable date have survived elsewhere because of locations on estuaries upsteam from the sea, as with the Tagus middens, or because of locations a little inland from and above the contemporaneous seashore, as in Italy and northern Spain. It is also noticeable that the general decline in size and number of middens from the north Atlantic to the southeast Mediterranean echoes closely the broad variations in marine productivity discussed above. Thus the much sparser distribution of shell middens in southern Europe can be attributed at least as much to poor resource potential as to destruction of evidence, and the surviving archaeological distribution can be assumed to be at least sufficiently representative in broad outline to form a basis for comparative study, even if it is far from complete in detail.

DENMARK

The earliest certain traces of settlement in Denmark following the retreat of the Fenno–Scandian ice sheet date from about 9700 b.c. (Degerbøl & Krog 1959). Initially economic exploitation was based on reindeer and elk, which were progressively replaced by bovid, red deer, and pig with the onset of warmer conditions by the seventh millennium b.c. Fish from inland lakes were exploited at about the same period, but there is little evidence of marine exploitation until the late Atlantic period, when middens incorporating shells of oysters and bones of sea mammals and fish appear in association with the Ertebølle culture from about 3600 b.c. onwards. After about 3000 b.c. there is some evidence of a decline in marine exploitation, along with progressive transformations of the terrestrial landscape and economy occasioned by the spread of farming settlements.

Denmark has a fairly uniform glacial landscape, with low hummocky hills, soils of loamy clay or sand, and marsh- or lake-filled depressions. There is little regional contrast in topography and no point is higher than 150 m above sea level. The major terrestrial changes in the recent prehistoric period concern the sequence of vegetational development in which the landscape carried initially pine and birch woodlands, and subsequently dense climax forest of lime, elm, and oak during Atlantic times, followed by progressive clearance from the Neolithic period onwards.

The coastline is mostly low and easily accessible with sheltered inlets and shallow off-shore waters, except on the exposed west coast. It has been shaped by almost continuous processes of eustatic and isostatic adjustment throughout the postglacial which have affected the total land mass, the character of the marine and intertidal environment, and the preservation of coastal sites. Isostatic uplift since the Ertebølle period has reduced the inflow of salt water from the North Sea to the Baltic, causing lowered salinities and reduced tidal amplitude resulting in a less productive marine environment. There has also been a progressive silting of bays and estuaries since Ertebølle times.

Climate is fairly uniform across the country, with mean temperatures in July of 15–17°C, and in January

of 0°C. Annual rainfall averages between 400 mm and 700 mm and is evenly distributed throughout the year. Snow cover does not last for more than a few days as a rule, although it may persist for weeks at a time in unusually severe winters.

Although overall climatic constraints would have been closely similar during the period which most concerns us, certain differences should be noted. The Atlantic period (c. 6500–3000 b.c.) marks the establishment of peak altithermal conditions. Plant and animal distributions indicate that mean annual temperature was probably 2–3 °C higher than today. Shellfish resources in particular would have benefited from higher temperatures. The transition to the Sub-Boreal period at about 3000 b.c. may have brought a reduction in temperature. This and other changes in the marine environment which are likely to have been initiated at about this time would have adversely affected the viability of some shellfish populations.

Coastal economies of the Ertebølle period

At least 50 shell middens were examined by the Kitchen–Midden Commissions and others during the nineteenth century, and other sites have been recorded or investigated since that time, although many have never been published. The sample considered here encompasses sites of varied size and location and includes coastal deposits lacking mollusc shells and hinterland sites, as well as the better known shell mounds (Figure 19).

At first sight there appears to be a strong case for inferring an economic system primarily concerned with the exploitation of marine resources. All the sites of the littoral zone are located on the immediate shoreline, either along the sea or on estuaries, or would have been so during the Ertebølle period. Some, in northeast Jutland, are separated from the modern seashore by salt marshes or marine deposits as much as 10 km wide. However, this is probably due to isostatic uplift of the coastline since the Ertebølle period (Iversen 1973, Krog & Tauber 1974). Some sites may have had a small area of salt marsh between them and the sea during their occupation, but this would have been so narrow that we may treat the sites as being essentially on the seashore. An obvious result of this is that the exploitation territories include large areas of coast and open sea. Their potential yield of terrestrial resources appears thus to have been considerably less than that available from site locations further inland, while their potential in terms of marine and littoral exploitation was high (Figures 20 and 21). A similar impression is

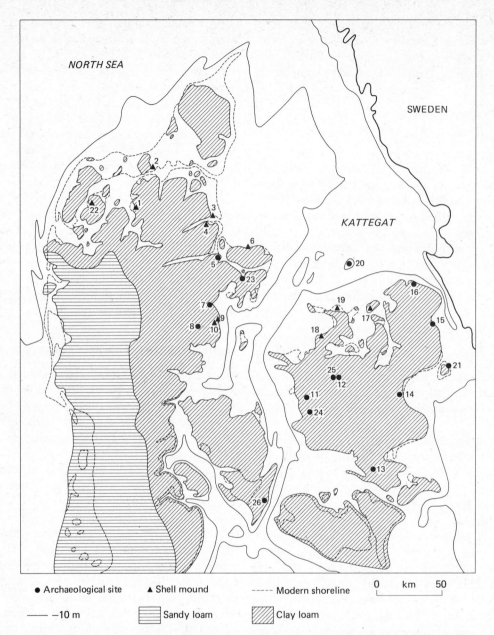

Figure 19. Distribution of sites in Denmark, showing relationship to soil zones and former shorelines. 1, Ertebølle; 2, Brovst; 3, Havnø; 4, Aamølle; 5, Dyrholm; 6, Meilgaard; 7, Brabrand; 8, Ringkloster; 9, Norsminde; 10, Norslund and Flynderhage (two sites immediately adjacent and shown as one symbol on figure); 11, Mullerup; 12, Øgaarde; 13, Svaerdborg; 14, Ølby Lyng; 15, Vedbaek; 16, Villingebaek; 17, Sølager; 18, Faareveile; 19, Klintesø; 20, Hesselø; 21, Carstensminde; 22, Øster Jølby; 23, Barkaer; 24, Store Valby; 25, Muldbjerg; 26, Troldebjerg.

gained from the excavated food remains, of which the impressive number of shells alone seem to show an overwhelming predominance of marine resources in the coastal diet. Closer examination of both types of data, however, suggests that this face-value assessment may overestimate the influence of marine resources on the overall organisation of subsistence and settlement.

Coastal diet: on-site data

The relative representation of excavated food remains is shown in Table 9. Bones of the larger mammals, birds, and fish are expressed in terms of minimum number of individuals as indicated by the most commonly occurring anatomical element, where such data

82

Table 9. Estimated caloric value of food resources found at Danish Ertebølle sites

	Red deer	Roe deer	Pig	Aurochs	Elk	Terrestrial sub-total	Grey seal	Other seal	Fish	Bird (mainly aquatic)	Molluscs	Aquatic sub-total	Total (Mcal)
Meat-weight/animal (kg)	132	11	125	360	300		162	60	0.5	3500	124[b]		
kcal/kg	1400	1400	3500	3000	1400		4000	4000	760	4	600		
Mcal[a]/animal	185	15	438	1080	420		648	240	0.4		74[b]		
Bay sites													
Ertebølle													
MIND[c]	13	33	27	1	2		7	1	9	57	314[d]		
total Mcal	2405	495	11826	1080	840	16646	4536	240	4	228	23236	28244	44890
% total Mcal	5.4	1.1	26.3	2.4	1.9	37.1	10.1	0.5	*	0.5	51.8	62.9	
% non-molluscan Mcal	11.1	2.3	54.6	5.0	3.9	76.9	20.9	1.1	*	1.1	—	23.1	21654
Meilgaard													
MIND	9	7	11				5	2	30(73.5[b])	27	50[d]		
total Mcal	1665	105	4818			6588	3240	480	12(1470)	108	3700	7540	14128
% total Mcal	11.8	0.7	34.1			46.6	22.9	3.4	0.1	0.8	26.2	53.4	
% non-molluscan Mcal	16.0	1.0	46.2			63.2	31.1	4.6	0.1	1.0	—	36.8	10428
% non-molluscan Mcal corrected for recovery of fish remains	14.0	0.9	40.5			55.4	27.3	4.0	12.4	0.9	—	44.6	11886
Faareveile													
MIND	2	10	8				—	—	2	2	75[d]		
total Mcal	370	150	3504			4024	—	—	1	8	5550	5559	9583
% total Mcal	3.9	1.6	36.5			42.0	—	—	*	0.1	57.9	58.0	
% non-molluscan Mcal	9.2	3.7	86.9			99.8	—	—	*	0.2	—	0.2	4033
Ølby Lyng													
no. specimens	646	330	137		1		9	134	3864	303			
Estuary sites													
Aamølle													
MIND	6	7	3	1			2[e]	—	1	8	81[d]		
total Mcal	1110	105	1314	1080		3609	848	—	[0.4]	32	5884	6874	10483
% total Mcal	10.6	1.0	12.5	10.3		34.4	8.1	—	*	0.3	57.2	65.6	
% non-molluscan Mcal	24.7	2.3	29.3	24.1		80.4	18.9	—	*	0.7	—	19.6	4489
Dyrholmen													
MIND	23	17	22	4	1		—	1	—	—	—		
total Mcal	4255	255	9636	4320	420	18886	—	240	—	—	—	240	19126
% total Mcal	22.2	1.3	50.4	22.6	2.2	98.7	—	1.3	—	—	—	1.3	
% non-molluscan Mcal	22.2	1.3	50.4	22.6	2.2	98.7	—	1.3	—	—	—	1.3	19126
Norslund.													
no. specimens	171	86	215	182	5	—	13	18	316	23	n.d.		
Offshore island sites													
Havnø													
MIND	2	2	2	1			3	—	2	17	40[d]		
total Mcal	370	30	876	1080		2356	1944	—	1	68	2960	4973	7329
% total Mcal	5.0	0.4	12.0	14.7		32.1	26.5	—	*	0.9	40.4	67.8	
% non-molluscan Mcal	8.5	0.7	20.1	24.7		54.0	44.5	—	*	1.6	—	46.1	4369
Klintesø													
MIND	6	14	6				2	2	5	36	13[d]		
total Mcal	1110	210	2628			3948	1296	480	2	144	962	2884	6832
% total Mcal	16.2	3.1	38.5			57.8	19.0	7.0	*	2.1	14.1	42.2	
% non-molluscan Mcal	18.9	3.6	44.8			67.3	22.1	8.2	*	2.4	—	32.7	5870

*<0.1%. [a] 1 Mcal = 1000 kcal. [b] Mcal/m³. [c] MIND, minimum number of individuals. [d] number of m³ excavated. [c] includes one neonatal seal (50 kg).

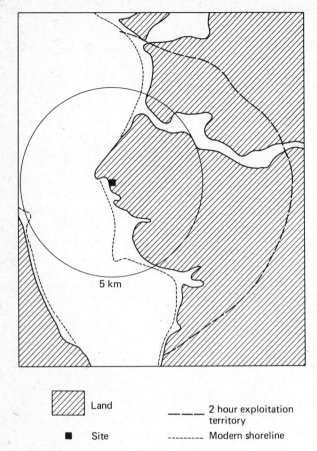

Figure 20. Site exploitation territory of Ertebølle.

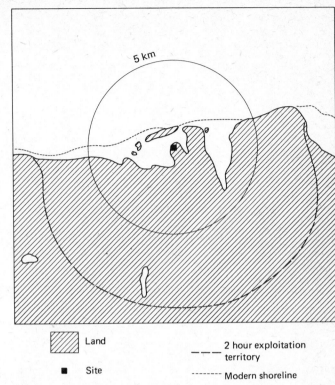

Figure 21. Site exploitation territory of Meilgaard.

are available. These figures are transformed into meat weights and calorific yields using the conversion factors shown. Mammalian meat weights are based on adult weights unless the faunal remains indicate otherwise (Bay-Petersen 1975, 1978). The relative representation of shellfish is based on the total volume of midden from which the non-molluscan fauna was derived, multiplied by a conversion figure of 124 kg/m³ of molluscan meat (Bailey 1975b, 1978). It is assumed that the high blubber content of a seal carcase gives it a higher average calorific yield than that of the fattiest land mammal.

These calculations show that, with the exception of Dyrholmen, marine resources constituted between 40 per cent and 70 per cent of the dietary energy consumed. Even allowing that the values for meat weights and calorific yields arrived at by this method are only rough approximations of the dietary value of the archaeological remains, marine resources appear to have been of major importance. This is especially apparent at the Jutland shell mounds where seal and shellfish account for between 52 per cent and 68 per

cent of the total food remains. Similar percentages are found on the Zealand middens of Faareveile and Klintesø. The more recently excavated coastal site of Ølby Lyng, although it is not a shell midden, yielded an overwhelming predominance of fish bones.

A major potential source of error in the comparison of resources in this way is the possibility of differential preservation. Where only one type of resource is under study, for example large mammal bones, this may not be a serious problem, and relative representation of species in the diet may be inferred with reasonable confidence from the bone remains. Where such disparate types of resources as land mammals, fish, sea mammals, birds, and molluscs are being compared, each affected by different factors of preservation, a more critical assessment is called for.

Many authors have drawn attention to the marked under-representation of bones that could result from the scavenging activities of domestic dogs or other destructive agents (Gifford 1978). It has been shown that only a fraction of the discarded animal bones are normally trodden into the underlying deposit: the remainder are pulverised by carnivore activity and weathering; mollusc shells, by contrast, stand a much better chance of being preserved in the quantities originally collected (White 1968).

These inferences about differential preservation have been tested in several areas by measuring the total quantities of shells incorporated in shell mounds and their average annual rate of accumulation as indicated by radiocarbon dates (Bailey 1975a, 1977, 1978, Clark, J. G. D. 1975). The results compare well with rates of accumulation predicted from local data on modern shellfood yields. On the other hand, the average annual increment of shellfish is usually inadequate to supply more than a relatively small portion of the total annual diet of a hypothetical human group, whatever levels of human population are postulated. Clark, J. G. D. (1975), in a conservative estimate of the Danish evidence, took a single family as the minimum population unit for each midden. Even at this level the molluscs could not have contributed the proportion of the diet which seems to be indicated by their numerical predominance; there simply are not enough shellfish to supply even a single family with the majority of its food. More refined estimates of population size based on midden areas suggest that groups of up to 40 people may have used the large Danish shell mounds. At this population level the gross contribution of shellfood to the annual diet would have been even lower. At Meilgaard, for example, shellfood would have contributed 1.8 per cent of the diet of 40 people, 2.7 per cent if 25 people were involved. This compares with between 26 per cent and 32 per cent for the relative representation of shellfood in the excavated remains (Bailey 1978).

Two alternative suppositions seem to follow from these data. The shell mounds may have been used as transitory sites mainly for exploiting shellfood, while most other subsistence activities were carried out elsewhere and left their remains at other archaeological sites. Alternatively, the shell mounds were major foci of settlement and subsistence, but most of the food remains other than the shells were destroyed. It must be remembered, furthermore, that the use of the 'minimum number of individuals' statistic inevitably and consistently belittles the contribution of these mammalian staples.

These possibilities were carefully considered by the Second Danish Kitchen–Midden Committee, which decided in favour of the latter alternative (Madsen *et al.* 1900). The seasonal indications of migrant birds, deer antlers, and slaughter patterns of juvenile ungulates showed that the shell mounds had been used at a number of seasons, and this was interpreted as showing year-round occupation. The large number of artefacts and the wide range of artefact types were also considered incompatible with the notion of a specialised shell-gathering site. Recent discussion of ecological data suggested that the sustainable annual yield of mammalian resources, both marine and terrestrial, available within the potential exploitation territory of the Meilgaard shell mound would have been sufficient to support communities of up to 40 people throughout the greater part of the year (Bailey 1978).

It seems then that in the shell middens we have sites occupied in more than one season, though not necessarily continuously, and for a large number of years; sites at which for reasons of differential preservation the mammalian remains are underrepresented and the molluscan remains overrepresented. If we assume that the sites represent all or most of the subsistence of the human group for all or most of the year, then it can be calculated that at some sites as little as 6 per cent of the animals originally slaughtered were preserved. We have earlier (Chapters 1 and 3) given our reasons for discounting the notion that plant foods may have made a substantial contribution to the diet. Only hazelnuts qualify for serious consideration as staples, and these, although well preserved in a number of Mesolithic deposits, are recorded in significant quantity only in the hinterland.

If we therefore agree that it is theoretically unacceptable to compare mathematically the molluscan and non-molluscan remains from a shell mound, and further agree that shellfish will not have contributed more than 2 or 3 per cent of the dietary energy, then we can recalculate the figures in Table 9 omitting shellfood entirely without distorting the percentages by very much. The effect, of course, is to reduce considerably the apparent contribution of marine resources to the economy. At all the sites for which figures are given terrestrial resources are at least as important as seal and fish, and at five they contribute more than three-quarters of the dietary energy.

While it seems that the importance of shellfood has usually been overestimated, it is possible that fish are considerably underrepresented in the bone remains. It is arguable that fish bones, being smaller, are either less likely to be preserved than bones of mammals, or less likely to be recovered in excavation. The assumption that fish bones are especially vulnerable to destruction, though commonly voiced, has little to recommend it. Preservation is largely a matter of bone density, which is independent of size, and the ease with which bones are trampled into the underlying deposit. It has recently been shown that large mammal bones tend to remain on the surface longer than small, compact bones, and are therefore more vulnerable to fragmentation or destruction (Gifford 1978). Some parts of the fish skeleton are fragile and easily destroyed, but bones such as the vertebrae are small, compact and easily trodden into the soil. Thus while shell middens may present peculiar conditions for the preservation of bones and further work is certainly needed on this question, it is arguable that fish bones would have had at least as good a chance of archaeological representation as mammalian bones. The former may frequently have been better preserved than the latter, though their small size may have reduced their chances of recovery.

The recently excavated site of Ølby Lyng (Møhl 1971a) gives some support to the idea that many fish bones were missed in the early excavations of middens. Here 3864 of the 5509 identified faunal specimens are of fish, almost all cod. There may be another reason for this high proportion relative to some other sites, however. Adult cod prefer deep water, ascending to shallower water between 20 m and 50 m to spawn and when young. Thus sites with access to relatively deep water within their economic reach would be far more likely to show a degree of dietary dependence on fish than those with access only to the poorer shallow waters. This calls to mind Clark's observation (Clark, J. G. D. 1975) that while all the coastal sites of Zealand contain cod, it has been identified at fewer than half the Jutland coastal sites. Much of northern and eastern Jutland would at best have territories very poor in cod and other deep-water fish, as the in-shore waters tend to be shallow. Zealand, with access to deeper waters relatively close to the coast is much better off in this respect. The classic Jutland site of Ertebølle, on the Limfjord, is particularly impoverished as far as these resources are concerned, and this seems sufficient to explain the small proportion of fish remains at the site. The site of Meilgaard, located near the deeper and more productive waters of the Kattegat, yielded fairly large numbers of fish remains despite its having been excavated in the nineteenth century.

A recent test excavation at Meilgaard seems to confirm our belief that fish were not as a rule among the primary staples. Sieving of 2 m^3 of deposit yielded an average of 3820 fish vertebrae per cubic metre, representing a minimum of 73.5 fish (assuming that they were all cod). Similar quantities have been recovered by similar methods from the east Zealand site of Vedbaek (Albrethsen & Brinch Petersen 1977). Using this larger figure for fish, we may again 'correct' the percentages for Meilgaard in Table 9, which now show fish contributing 12.4 per cent of the calories. This is probably a generous estimate, since most of the fish vertebrae are from small individuals. Large ungulates still provide 55.4 per cent of the calories, with seals

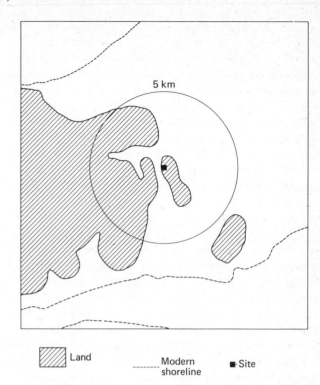

Figure 22. Site exploitation territory of Brovst.

contributing 31.3 per cent. At other sites the contribution from fish would have been even less. If we correct the figures given for fish by the same factor of 100, they would have made up less than 10 per cent of the calories. This is in line with and lends support to our view that fish provide as a rule a relatively poor return of calories per unit of time and effort expended, when compared with terrestrial mammals. Some quantitative support for this view comes from a study of the Cree of central Quebec, where it was found that moose hunting provides five times as much nutrition per man day of hunting as does beaver hunting, ten times as much as fishing, and over thirty times as much nutrition as hunting for small game (Weinstein 1979). Even in instances where one would assume that the primary function of a site was for the exploitation of marine resources, this is not always borne out by the faunal remains. Terrestrial species have been found to predominate at the island site of Brovst (Rowley-Conwy, personal communication). The island is too small (Figure 22) to support viable natural populations of the larger herbivores, and it seems possible that these were maintained there artifically by man, again emphasising the overall importance of the terrestrial economic component.

The significance of birds in the diet is more difficult to evaluate. Their bones are frequently small and

DENMARK

fragile, and they might therefore be thought to be underrepresented. On the other hand, where they do survive they are customarily in a very good state of preservation. Certainly there is no consistent evidence to suggest that they were of any great dietary significance, although the large flocks of seasonal migrants may have encouraged intensive exploitation for brief periods at certain times of year, enhancing the attractions of some littorals and off-shore islands as foci of economic exploitation.

Coastal exploitation territories

On balance, the evidence of food remains indicates that, at best, marine resources might have supplied about half the animal food at the large coastal sites, whereas at major sites such as Ertebølle as little as one-quarter of the dietary energy came from marine sources. Proceeding from this, we must ask why so many sites should be located on the seashore, where much of the potential site territory was taken up by relatively unproductive open water.

One possibility is that the marine resources had an effect on site location out of proportion to their gross contribution to the annual diet. It could be argued that resources that are predictable and dependable on a day-to-day basis, or resources especially costly to extract and transport, would exert a disproportionately large influence on site location.

Molluscs are a predictable resource, and they are also costly to transport over any distance. Sea mammals and fish often require fairly high inputs of time and effort in their location or extraction, particularly in the acquisition and maintenance of specialised equipment. Thus settlements might have been located to provide easiest access to those resources which were most reliable or which required the major inputs of time, effort, and equipment, rather than those which represented the major potential outputs of food. These factors might have been sufficient to outweigh considerations of the optimum location for exploitation of the terrestrial staples.

On the other hand, a site location on the coast normally reduces the area of accessible terrestrial resources, often by as much as half or more, and we should perhaps ask whether other factors may also have been influential. One obvious consideration is that the productivity of terrestrial resources was almost certainly not distributed uniformly, and that the littoral zone may have been particularly favoured in this respect. In such a case the extra terrestrial productivity of the littoral zone might have outweighed the loss of dry land within the territory.

Palynological evidence suggests that much of the Danish landscape, especially in the more fertile coastal areas, was covered with dense deciduous forest during the Atlantic period (Iversen 1973). Dense forest would have provided poor grazing conditions for most ungulates. Even the so-called woodland animals such as roe deer, pig, and elk prefer more open conditions of woodland interspersed with clearings, while red deer and cattle subsist primarily upon grasses and sedges, resorting to browse mainly during periods of winter shortage. At the edge of woodlands and in clearings light penetration and growth of herbs and grasses is at its best. Marshy areas also occur frequently in clearings, and offer areas of favoured grazing. Indeed, in the heavily forested regions of northern Europe these restricted areas of high primary productivity may be regarded as among the major grazing resources. Thus the forest edges would have been not only the most accessible, but probably also the most productive area for terrestrial exploitation. The anomalous location of the Ertebølle coastal sites may therefore be more apparent than real. The locations are in many cases favourable for marine exploitation, but probably also gave good access to the favoured grazing areas of the large ungulates.

In Jutland, for example, Dyrholmen, Norslund, and Flynderhage are situated on narrow river estuaries some distance inland from the open coast (Figures 23 and 24). Norslund and Flynderhage are perhaps better placed for marine exploitation than is Dyrholmen, and all may be described as coastal sites in the sense that they give access by boat to marine resources in more open coastal waters. However, if marine exploitation had been a primary consideration, we would expect locations closer to the sea. Aquatic resource remains are sparsely represented at all three sites (Table 9), while Dyrholmen is sufficiently far inland to have been beyond the effective range of shell-gathering to judge by the absence of humanly collected mollusc shells. Conversely, the upstream location of the sites clearly improves access to terrestrial resources, whether these are measured in terms of the gross area of land within the site territories or the length of the littoral.

Even the large Jutland sites with a high representation of marine resources appear to be located as much for access to terrestrial as marine resources. Ertebølle and Meilgaard are both associated with sinuous coastlines which would maximise the length of littoral within easy reach of the sites. Aamølle, in spite of the large number of mollusc shells in its deposits, is nevertheless

87

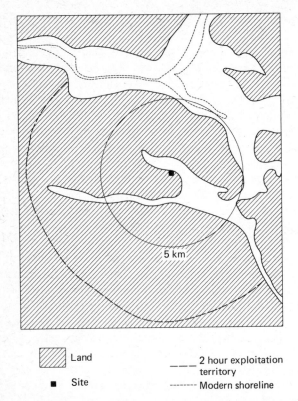

Land
Site
_ _ _ 2 hour exploitation territory
-------- Modern shoreline

Figure 23. Site exploitation territory of Dryholmen.

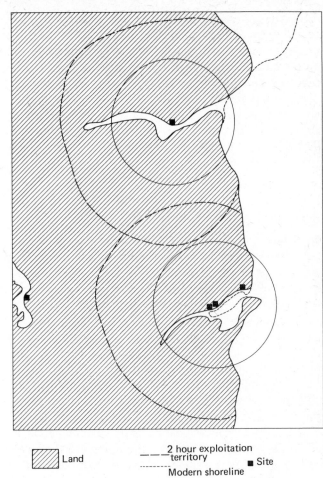

Land
_ _ _ 2 hour exploitation territory
-------- Modern shoreline
Site

Figure 24. Site exploitation territories of Brabrand (upper) and Norslund (lower). The inland site is Ringkloster.

on the inner reaches of a river estuary in a location favourable for the exploitation of littoral resources (Figure 25). Possibly this situation is to be explained by a complementary relationship with the off-shore site of Havnø, which may have served as a subsidiary encampment better placed for the extraction of aquatic resources such as seal and fowl. Some corroboration of this hypothesis may be seen in the small size of the Havnø midden, the small quantity of artefacts, and the good representation of seal and bird remains in comparison with Aamølle.

In general, although they appear to be best located for the maximisation of aquatic and marine resources, the off-shore islands show a considerable representation of terrestrial food remains. In some cases, as at Brovst (see Chapter 3), the island location may actually have been beneficial to the exploitation of terrestrial mammals. In other cases, as we have argued for Havnø, the sites may have served essentially as a temporary encampment linked to home bases on the mainland. The Zealand site of Klintesø might fall into this category also, given its relatively good representation of bird and seal remains in comparison with the mainland site of Faareveile, although the representation of deer and pig at Klintesø might also suggest a hypothesis more in line with that applied to Brovst.

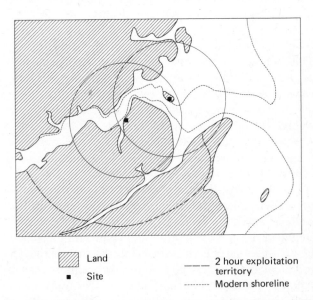

Land
Site
_ _ _ 2 hour exploitation territory
-------- Modern shoreline

Figure 25. Site exploitation territories of Havnø (upper) and Aamølle (lower).

88

In spite of the considerable local and regional variability in resource availability, the general picture appears to be one in which both the on-site and the off-site data show terrestrial resources as the major factor in determining patterns of site location and economic integration.

Economic niches

We must now turn briefly to consider whether there was a relationship between the coastal economy and that of the hinterland. It was pointed out earlier in this chapter that purely coastal economies adjacent to an unexploited hinterland do sometimes exist in diversified coastal environments of the Danish type with littoral, estuarine, and island resources. Such are exemplified ethnographically by certain populations in Tasmania, Tierra del Fuego, and the northwest coast of North America. On the other hand, these are rare and appear to be specific economic responses to a particularly unfavourable combination of conditions inland, in particular the concurrence of a steep and rugged topography with a dense vegetation supporting relatively scanty resources.

These circumstances do not apply to Denmark. The country is conspicuous for its flat landscape and the absence of any substantial topographic barriers. The pollen analyst's view that Denmark presented 'continuous forest, with dangerous swamps as the only openings . . .' (Iversen 1941) almost certainly exaggerates the difficulty of penetrating the Atlantic vegetation, as much as it underestimates the economic value of swamps. Indeed, mature deciduous European woodland frequently has much less understorey than the thinned and coppiced woods of today. In any case, Australian evidence indicates that an environment of swamps and dense rainforest need not present insuperable obstacles to inland penetration by technologically simple economies, where waterways are available for access (Bailey 1975b), as they are in Denmark.

Thus there is little doubt that the hinterland could have been reached and exploited, and the 300 or more inland Mesolithic sites clearly indicate that it was (Christiansen & Skelmose 1963, Matthiassen 1937). Most of these are surface scatters, however, and thus present difficulties of interpretation. Not only are few dated with any accuracy, but in many cases the evidence is confined to the lithic industry. Nevertheless, most of the sites seem broadly to be dated to the Atlantic period, on typological grounds, and Clark, J. G. D. (1975) has recently pointed to the existence of such distinctive Ertebølle artefact types as the tranchet

arrowhead and the flake axe in these inland assemblages. The recent radiocarbon dates from the inland Ertebølle site of Ringkloster (Andersen 1975) establish unequivocally the exploitation of the hinterland contemporary with the major coastal sites. Similar indications have been reported in the Aamosen district of Zealand (Troels-Smith 1966). The occurrence of occasional specimens of marine species such as seals and whale at Rinkloster and at the earlier Maglemosian inland sites of Svaerdborg and Øgaarde demonstrates conclusively that some links existed between the coast and hinterland. The typological and economic data are still too scanty to elucidate the exact nature of this connection, but some movement of people between the two seems likely.

As will be seen elsewhere in this volume, many areas of Europe experience seasonally or topographically induced climatic extremes sufficiently severe as virtually to demand an economic response capable of integrating relatively widespread resources. Typically, summer drought and/or winter cold and snow cover are the primary stimuli. Denmark is much less affected by such factors than are many regions. The evenly distributed rainfall and large amount of surface water greatly reduce the likelihood of serious summer drought, while the oceanic climate mitigates the severity of winter conditions. For these reasons we need not necessarily expect there to have been the kind of rigid seasonal round which is characteristic of some areas.

On the other hand, there are seasonal and geographical variations in resources, and we should see whether there is any evidence of the way in which the human populations adjusted to them. Since there is no clear-cut zonal variation in resources, evidence of seasonality may vary from site to site or area to area, rather than producing a clear coastal–inland dichotomy. An initial point of some importance is that the division of sites into coastal and inland categories is to some extent a distortion in Mesolithic Denmark. Site locations are primarily distinguished by their almost universal preference for water-side situations, whether these are coastal, estuarine, or lake-side. This is doubtless partly a reflection of the value of the aquatic resources themselves, but, as has been pointed out, probably has as much or more to do with the quality of the terrestrial grazing resources at these junctions.

The broad availability of resources would have put winter occupation of coastal sites at a premium. Many of the marine resources are either most accessible or at their best between autumn and spring. The most commonly recorded seal species, the grey seal, which occurs at 16 of the 18 coastal Mesolithic sites that have yielded substantial faunal remains (Møhl 1971b), would have bred either in the spring (as it does under today's conditions in the Baltic) or in the autumn (as it now does in English waters, and as it would presumably have done in the Baltic if the slightly warmer and more saline seas of the Ertebølle period altered the conditions sufficiently). Not only are seals most vulnerable to human predation during the two-month breeding period, but they provide the maximum return of blubber during the autumn and early winter. The harp seal (*Pagophilus groenlandicus*) is also recorded at a number of sites, being represented by 43 specimens at Ølby Lyng. To judge from its modern ecology this species would probably have been available in Danish waters during its southward spring migration. Porpoises, also known from Ølby Lyng, are most easily caught during their winter migrations; while cod, by far the commonest marine fish represented in the collections, are only generally accessible to line fishing when they migrate to shallow water to spawn in late winter and spring. Oysters are in poor condition during the summer, but improve during the winter and reach their peak nutritional value during the spring prior to spawning.

As far as the terrestrial resources are concerned, from late spring to early autumn the herbivores would have tended to concentrate on the more open areas of optimum grazing: the edges of the woodland along the littoral as well as around inland lakes and marshes, and perhaps also the area of more open woodland in central and western Jutland associated with the infertile sands and gravels of that region (Iversen 1941). In winter, the lean season for the herbivore population, they would probably have been much more dispersed and less easily exploited, with many subsisting on browse within the woodland itself.

We might thus reasonably expect there to have been a tendency for human groups to concentrate upon the coastal areas from late autumn to early spring, when abundant marine resources as well as terrestrial herbivores could have supported a high human population. The decline in marine resources with the onset of summer will have made it advantageous for at least some of the population to disperse inland to exploit those large herbivores utilising inland grazing and to take advantage at the same time of lake resources. This movement inland is not inconsistent with our previous assumption that the coastal sites were the major foci of settlement and subsistence. The distances moved are unlikely to have been great in the Danish context, and economies may well have been of the mobile-cum-sedentary kind rather than fully mobile ones.

Broadly speaking the seasonal indicators from excavated sites are consonant with this hypothesis. More than half the avifauna at such coastal sites as Ertebølle consists of probable winter migrants (Bay-Petersen 1975). The whooper swan, which is the commonest species, now spends from November to March in the area. Most of the remaining birds are permanent residents, and could have been taken at any time, but are more dispersed in summer. Only occasional remains indicate summer occupation, such as the honey buzzard from Aamølle, and the crane and black stork remains from Villingebaek (Kapel 1969). The shed red deer antlers at Ertebølle imply exploitation during the spring, while the unshed specimens show winter occupation; shed roe deer antlers suggest autumn occupation, and the unshed antlers could come from individuals killed at any time between April and October or November. Other indicators of occupation within the period spanning late autumn to early spring are a tooth of a neonatal grey seal at Aamølle and the juvenile dentition of deer and pig at Ertebølle.

It must be pointed out here that an apparent contradiction arises from our suggestion that the coastal zone was primarily occupied in winter. Our territorial and ecological considerations led us to suggest that the large herbivores would have been dispersed through the woodlands at this season. Yet it has been shown that territorial resources probably contributed as much as 75 per cent of dietary energy at many coastal sites. This conclusion is hard to reconcile with the hypothesis of a major occupation at the season when the dietary staples would have been relatively inaccessible.

One factor is apparent which may account for this anomaly. Winter is very much the lean season for herbivores in the area, and they would at this time have been particularly susceptible to simple measures of control and manipulation. We have already discussed in Chapter 3 the form that such measures may have taken, and some evidence that they may have been in use. It does not seem at all unlikely that in winter herbivore populations were encouraged to remain on the coast by supplying feed in the form of browse collected earlier in the year. Furthermore, as noted above, the evidence from Brovst is strongly suggestive of some system of animal management in Mesolithic Denmark.

Seasonal data from inland sites are scarce, and most of those which are available come from Zealand rather than Jutland and are Maglemosian rather than Ertebølle in date. At that earlier date most of the indicators from sites such as Svaerdborg and Mullerup, including the avifauna, the deer antlers, and the ungulate dentition, show a peak of occupation during the summer. Remains of hazelnuts must indicate some autumn occupation, but there is little evidence that unequivocally suggests winter exploitation (Bay-Petersen 1975). In many cases the location of inland settlements on the edge of lakes or marshes may have precluded winter occupation, as rising water levels in winter would have flooded the settlements (Friis Johansen 1919). If the same pattern of inland exploitation persisted into the Ertebølle period, then we have a situation that is roughly the converse of that on the coast.

As suggested above, however, the pattern is more complex and varied than the picture just presented. The seasonal indicators from some sites give a contrary impression. For example, at Ringkloster, one of the few inland Ertebølle sites to yield substantial evidence, the dentition of the pigs (which are the most commonly represented species) suggests occupation primarily from September to May. The high proportion of unshed to shed red deer antler and the whole pine marten skeletons (presumably killed for their pelts) lends support to the supposition of winter occupation (Andersen 1975). In this case, finds of cached hazelnuts may indicate storage for winter consumption. The neighbouring coastal sites of Norslund, Flynderhage, and Norsminde give signs of a peak of occupation during the summer months and might have been the economic complements to sites like Ringkloster (Figure 26). The location of these three sites gives them greater access than many of the other coastal sites to littoral grazing areas which would have been at their best in summer. Compared to many of the other coastal sites these deposits are poor in winter marine resources such as seals. At Norsminde there are numerous otoliths of young cod, which normally enter the river estuaries only in early summer, and analysis of seasonal growth rings of cockle shells shows both summer and winter collection of shellfish.

The patterns of movement of people appear therefore to have been as complex as the landscape is variegated. As pointed out in the earlier chapters, archaeological data are unlikely to allow us to define in minute detail the individual movements of a specific community from a single site. What long-term pattern does emerge from the evidence does not, however, support the traditional interpretation of the coastal sites as home bases for a sedentary or strandlooping population. The coastal sites probably were indeed home bases, but the on-site seasonal indicators, the inherent limitations of marine resources, the seasonal and geographical distribution of grazing resources, and the typological links between some coastal and inland sites all argue against this hypothesis and for continuing, if not uniform, economic links between the coast and hinterland.

Long-term perspectives

We have discussed the Ertebølle economy and the rôle of coastal resources within it. It is of interest now to relate this evidence to the long-term picture. The first point to make is that there is no firm evidence to show that the Maglemosian exploited marine resources less intensively than the later Ertebølle. The earliest extant coastal sites, such as Carstensmide and Villingebaek, date from the time when the sea first reached approximately its present level. During the Maglemosian period sea levels would have been some 10–20 m lower than at present, so coastal settlements of that time would since have been submerged or destroyed. As we have seen, in as much as there are some hints that existing inland Maglemosian sites were for the most part summer occupations, it is perhaps more likely than not that the coastal area was primarily exploited in winter.

Shellfish, however, seem to make a relatively later appearance. The large shell mounds of the Ertebølle period are consistently associated with the third Litorina transgression, whereas coastal sites associated with the earlier transgressions either have fewer shells or lack them entirely. It is possible that such evidence, along with other indicators discussed in detail by Andersen (1973), shows progressive economic intensification during the final Atlantic period in response to contraction of the terrestrial biomass and/or increasing competition from early farming economies to the south. On the other hand, the major loss of land resources caused by marine transgression and forest expansion would already have been felt in the Maglemosian period long before the earliest evidence of shell-gathering. Moreover the earliest coastal sites, of the Kongemosen or 'Early Coastal Culture' period, are often in different types of locations from the major Ertebølle shell mounds, being on off-shore islands (as at Brovst), or in different areas (mainly in eastern Zealand). The lack of shells may therefore be due to differences in the economic function of the sites or to variations in local ecological conditions, rather than to chronological factors. It is noteworthy that at Brovst, which provides a rare instance of an early shell midden (associated with the second Litorina transgression) stratified beneath a small Ertebølle midden, there is no significant increase in the rate of accumulation of oyster shells in the Ertebølle layers (Bailey, personal observation).

Environmental trends should also be taken into account. Salinity in particular would have shown periodic fluctuations, being lower and more highly variable during periods of marine regression or isostatic uplift because of reduced tidal inflow from the North Sea, and higher and more stable during periods of marine transgression. Characteristically there is also a geographical cline, with highest salinities in the Limfjord and progressively lower figures southwards and eastwards into the Baltic. Today salinities are tolerable for oysters only in the Limfjord. During the Ertebølle period, when salinities were at their most favourable, oysters were more extensively distributed, although even at this period the effects of geographical variation are apparent. Oyster shells show a progressive decrease in size from Ertebølle in the west to Klintesø in the east (Madsen *et al*. 1900), while they are almost entirely absent from the sites in eastern Zealand. The first and second transgressions were several metres lower than the later ones, the precise figure varying locally according to differential earth movements. Although the difference is not great, the effect that even small fluctuations can have in a marginal area is illustrated by events in this century. In 1923 a massive inflow of more saline water from the North Sea brought in large numbers of spawning haddock which led to a temporary ten-fold increase in haddock yields over the next few years (Zenkevitch 1963). It is thus significant that the only shell middens known to precede the third transgression, namely Brovst and Østerjølby, are in the Limfjord. Contemporaneous shell middens elsewhere may conceivably have been lost through differential isostatic uplift, but it seems quite possible that even a small drop in salinity from its peak values could have reduced the range of the oysters to one similar to that of today.

From the end of the classic Ertebølle culture, about 3200–3000 b.c., successive developments took the economy from the characteristic Ertebølle pattern to the establishment of a mixed farming economy as exemplified by Middle Neolithic sites such as Troldebjerg and Bundsø (Higham 1968). Data for the intervening Early Neolithic period are complex, uneven, and controversial. In many cases the nature of the sites is ambiguous, particularly in the case of Barkaer (Madsen 1979). Nevertheless, if one makes the reasonable assumption, based on the cereal remains, that at least some of them represent settlements, then the following trends can be discerned.

In the first place there was some readjustment of settlement distribution. Many of the classic Ertebølle sites, especially the large shell mounds of northeast Jutland, but also other types of site such as Ringkloster and Ølby Lyng, were largely abandoned, leaving only scanty and ambiguous traces of Neolithic settlement at some sites. In their place appear farming settlements based on cereal cultivation, including emmer, einkorn, bread wheat, and barley, and on cattle husbandry at sites such as Barkaer and Store Valby with artefact assemblages of more or less pure Funnel-Beaker material (Becker 1954, Jørgensen 1977). In addition there are a number of sites based on an apparent continuation of the Ertebølle integration of large ungulates and marine resources. Mostly these are coastal sites, sometimes stratified above classic Ertebølle levels as at the coastal midden of Sølager in Zealand and the recently discovered shell midden of Norsminde in eastern Jutland. The inland site of Muldbjerg 1 in the Aamosen bog is in a similar category, although Troels-Smith (1953) has identified evidence of cereal cultivation in association with this material.

A second set of evidence consists of the pollen data. The elm decline, traditional marker of the Atlantic/Sub-Boreal boundary at *c*. 3000 b.c., has been variously interpreted as the result of climatic change or the collection of leaf fodder for livestock (Iversen 1960, Tauber 1965, Troels-Smith 1960). More recently Iversen (1973) retracted his climatic hypothesis, although he continued to view the contemporaneous decline of ivy pollen as evidence of a trend to colder winters at this time especially in northeast Jutland. Clearance of forest for grazing and cereal plots (landnam) is dated to about 2600 b.c., although this may have occurred as early as the elm decline in some areas (Tauber 1967).

It must be stressed that stratigraphical correlation between pollen data and settlement data is rare, and radiocarbon dates are few. Thus three general hypotheses have arisen. The first is that the Early Neolithic period witnessed the coexistence of two separate populations, an 'epi-mesolithic' group of surviving hunters and gatherers and an intrusive group of Funnel-Beaker farmers, mixed artefact assemblages being attributable to trade or other forms of contact between the two groups (Becker 1954, Clark, J. G. D. 1952). Alternatively, a surviving Ertebølle population was seen as having adopted elements of a farming economy and Funnel-Beaker artefactual material alongside its traditional activities. This thus represented a population chronologically, economically, and artefactually transitional between the classic Ertebølle and the fully developed Funnel-Beaker culture (Troels-Smith 1953,

1966). A third alternative is that there was a single intrusive farming population which also used seasonal camps inland and on the coast as 'hunting stations' for the exploitation of naturally occurring resources (Skaarup 1973). On this hypothesis mixed artefact assemblages are explained as the result of stratigraphic disturbance. Crucial to any test of these hypotheses is the interpretation of the coastal hunting stations and of the general rôle of marine resources alongside the farming economy.

The first point to emphasise is that marine resources continued to be generally available during this period. The fourth and highest Litorina transgression occurred at the beginning of the Sub-Boreal and would presumably have maintained conditions of salinity and tidal amplitude at least as favourable as those of earlier transgressions. Abundant remains of cod at Sølager, seal at Hesselø, and molluscs at a number of sites show a continuation at some level of all the major marine exploitation activities of the Ertebølle period. Clark's suggestion (Clark, J. G. D. 1948) that the Sølager evidence indicates an intensification of fishing, however, is not borne out by more recent evidence, resting as it does principally on a comparison with the poor fish remains from the classic Ertebølle shell mounds of Jutland before the discovery of the cod-rich Ertebølle deposits of Ølby Lyng. As pointed out earlier, differential representation of cod probably reflects geographical variations in its availability rather than changes through time.

A second point to consider is the extent to which this abundance of marine resources was exploited by Neolithic farming groups. The actual location of sites, while apparently determined by the arable element in the economy, would still have allowed easy access to marine resources. The known sites are invariably located on the Danish islands or in the coastal areas of Jutland, for it is these areas where the slightly milder oceanic climate provided the best chance of successful crop cultivation in these northerly latitudes, and where easy access could be had to the rich grazing of shore meadows. Barkaer is actually located at the head of a marine inlet, while other sites are inland by a kilometre or so from the coast, where they could maximise the availability of arable resources within the critical 10 minute site territory (see Chapter 2) without losing the general benefits of the littoral zone. Thus the environmental constraints on the optimum location for a mixed farming economy would have tended to maintain settlements within easy reach of marine resources. These farming communities would clearly have had the opportunity to exploit marine resources, and we might

further hypothesise that they had a strong incentive to do so both as a general complement to a diet rich in carbohydrates and as a critical resource at times of poor harvests.

This hypothesis may be examined more closely by considering the evidence from the site of Norsminde (Figure 24). During the Ertebølle period the two large shell mounds of Norslund and Flynderhage, on the northern shore of a small inlet, were in use alongside the smaller site of Norsminde itself. All show evidence of exploitation of terrestrial and aquatic resources, including oysters as the main shellfood species. Neolithic occupation, however, is only recorded at Norsminde, where the upper deposit is associated with Funnel-Beaker pottery, a shellfish fauna in which oysters are replaced by cockles as the dominant species, and the disappearance of fish remains along with a general scarcity of bone remains of all kinds.

These changes were probably the result of a combination of environmental and economic processes. Although the pollen data may be open to question, the suggestion that winter temperatures dropped during the Sub-Boreal period is certainly consistent with the replacement of oysters by cockles as the dominant species, since the latter are more tolerant of lower temperatures. Lowered salinities and altered patterns of sedimentation would also have tended to favour the rise to dominance of cockles. Certainly oysters would have been vulnerable to a number of environmental changes at the edge of their range, and the disappearance of the large oyster beds which formerly supplied the Flynderhage and Norslund mounds must have resulted locally in a marked reduction of the shellfood supply. It remains to be seen whether the picture emerging from the Norsminde data applies elsewhere, but the environmental changes of the Sub-Boreal period may have been detrimental to the extensive oyster beds of the late Atlantic period over a wide area.

A second factor is the apparent change in the economic function of the Norsminde site from a base for the integrated exploitation of several resources in the Ertebølle period to a highly specialised camp site used almost exclusively for the intensive gathering of cockles, most probably on an intermittent basis, during the Neolithic period. One would expect it to have been linked to a nearby farming settlement which, however, has yet to be found. A similar hypothesis was put forward by Jarman, M. R. & Webley (1975) with regard to the site of Coppa Nevigata in southern Italy. This seems to have been visited repeatedly but fleetingly over several millennia, primarily for the exploitation of cockles, and seemed best explained in terms of occasional visits from farmers and/or pastoralists who spent most of the year and the vast preponderance of their economic energy elsewhere in the region.

Given that Danish Neolithic farmers had the incentive to clear areas of forest and locate sites away from the immediate shoreline so as to maximise access to arable resources, the integration of marine resources through small, special-function sites, rather than at coastal home bases on the seashore, may reflect the altered constraints on settlement patterning introduced by a farming economy, rather than any reduced emphasis on marine exploitation. If anything, the sharp fluctuations in the size frequencies of the cockle shells in the Neolithic levels at Norsminde suggest that the cockle beds came under far more intensive exploitation pressure than the shell beds of the Ertebølle period.

The disappearance of fish in the Neolithic levels at Norsminde is less easily explained, although it may reflect local changes in the estuarine environment. Certainly the evidence elsewhere, of fish at Sølager for example, and seal at Hesselø, suggests that these resources continued to be exploited where available, and it seems reasonable to suppose that these sites, like Norsminde, were transitory or seasonal task-specific sites used by local farmers.

The above evidence also suggests an hypothesis to explain the timing of the appearance of mixed farming in Denmark. It seems possible that the environmental changes at the Atlantic–Sub-Boreal transition may have been important factors. While the conditions prevailing during the Atlantic period were obviously favourable to the exploitation of indigenous marine and terrestrial resources by a large mobile-cum-sedentary population, they were probably equally unsuited to the cultivation of cereals. Wheat and barley today do not generally thrive where average annual rainfall exceeds about 900 mm, and Neolithic cereals may originally have been even less tolerant of high rainfall. The Atlantic period was wetter than present-day conditions with 400–700 mm annual rainfall. Although it is not known what the difference would have been, higher rainfall would presumably have made the success of cereal cultivation that much less certain. Provided that environmental and demographic conditions remained stable, an economy with an arable component would have had little chance of providing a viable alternative to the existing system. Radiocarbon dates show that for about 1000 years highly productive Linear Pottery mixed farming sites existed only some 500 km away without having any noticeable economic impact on the Danish economy.

Shellfish, although not a major staple in the Ertebølle economy, were nevertheless persistently exploited, most probably as a critical resource. If environmental changes at the beginning of the Sub-Boreal period were responsible for a general decline in shellfish resources, this could have placed sufficient stress on the existing economy, while providing improved conditions for cereal cultivation, to tip the balance in favour of a mixed farming economy. Lower winter temperatures were probably not critical to crop husbandry, since they can be mitigated to some extent by the selection of local conditions offering a milder microclimate. It is therefore possible that the same set of environmental changes which were detrimental to the shellfish element of the Mesolithic economy were beneficial to the cereal component of the Neolithic economy, the two effects together contributing to the rapid spread of arable agriculture into new areas, regardless of whether this was achieved through immigration of new populations or by local development.

Judging from the evidence at Norsminde we are seeing yet another instance of the association of an important economic change with a period of population stress. While the data are as yet too poor to allow us to follow the process in detail, the intensity with which the cockle beds seem to have been exploited – probably amounting to over-exploitation in some phases – implies that the system was in some difficulty. How much this was due to external forces of population pressure, and how much to the deteriorating marine environment, remains obscure.

CANTABRIAN COAST

Cantabria has a mountainous coastline, and the topography is a primary limiting factor on almost all forms of economic exploitation. The area has, however, the advantage of compressing within a comparatively short distance a variety of ecological conditions ranging from the seashore to the heights of the Cantabrian Alps. The region thus combines characteristics of both highland and coastal exploitation zones, each of which is closely interlinked and is integral to an understanding of prehistoric economic development in the area.

Resources

The shoreline is rocky and exposed, and the continental shelf is narrow at all points. Headlands have been eroded back to form cliffs interspersed with sand or gravel beaches, while river estuaries are steep-sided

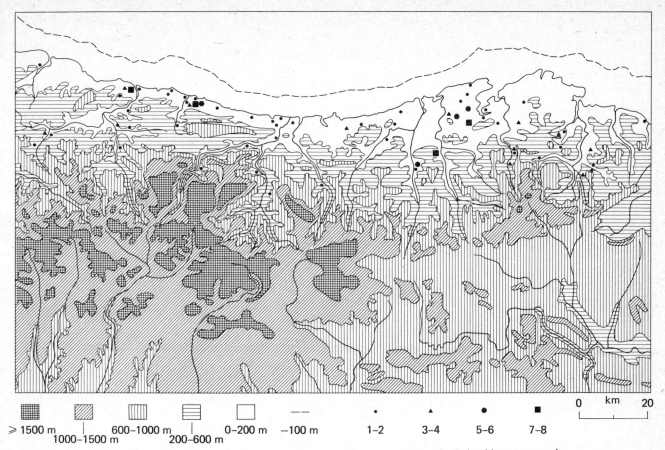

⊞	⊘	⫼	⊟	☐	– –	•	▲	●	■	0 km 20

⩾ 1500 m   600–1000 m   0–200 m   –100 m   1–2   3–4   5–6   7–8
     1000–1500 m   200–600 m

Figure 26. Distribution of archaeological sites in Cantabria showing length of occupation and relationship to topography.

and narrow. Here, as elsewhere in Europe, these features are associated with coastal waters of relatively low productivity and poor accessibility.

The littoral, by contrast, is a key resource zone. It comprises a coastal plain which is usually between about 5 km and 15 km wide, and which extends inland to about the 200 m contour. It owes its economic importance to the fairly level topography, good soil cover, and an almost snow-free winter with temperatures rarely below freezing, thanks to low altitude and the ameliorating effects of the Gulf Stream. The oceanic climate and an evenly distributed annual rainfall of over 1000 mm encourage a lush vegetation with a growing season which extends throughout the year. This zone is of primary importance as a winter grazing area in the modern exploitation system. During the last glacial the maximum lowering of sea level would nearly have doubled the present width of the coastal plain in some places, and exploitation systems based on terrestrial resources are likely to have been particularly sensitive to changes of sea level and to economic pressures induced by the expansion and contraction of this highly productive littoral zone.

Inland the hills rise steeply. The Cantabrian watershed runs roughly parallel with the shoreline, and never

more than 50 km from it, with maximum elevations of between 1000 m and 2650 m. Routes of access are closely confined to the major river valleys. Except in the low-lying valleys, the inland resources are generally of lower economic potential than on the littoral plain, because of steep topography and/or higher altitude. They would have been important mainly as seasonal grazing areas for the larger herbivores, or as a source of chamois and ibex. Generally speaking topography provides a good overall guide to differences in potential grazing productivity and forms the principal basis for distinguishing the two major resources categories of good grazing and rough grazing used in the territorial maps.

Sites

The distribution of the archaeological sites is illustrated in Figure 26. We have confined our attention to Santander and eastern Asturias, which form a self-contained geographical unit with a sample of some 85 prehistoric sites ranging in age from Mousterian to Neolithic. The sites are weighted according to the number of archaeological periods represented (Table 10). Thus, the largest symbols refer to sites with the

Table 10. Periods of occupation represented at Cantabrian sites shown in Figure 26

Site	Acheulean	Mousterian	Aurignacian	Gravettian	Solutrean	Magdalenian Lower	Magdalenian Unspecified	Magdalenian Upper	Azilian	Asturian	Neolithic	Total
Asturias												
Valdedíos							×			×		2
Aviao			(— Unspecified Upper Palaeolithic only —)									1
Ferrán							×				×	2
Collareu			(— Unspecified Upper Palaeolithic only —)									1
Cova Rosa					×	×						2
Les Pedroses										×		1
Cierro					×	×				×		3
Lloseta					×	×				×		3
Cuevona			×							×		2
Viesca							×					1
Rio de Ardines						×			×			2
Tito Bustillo								×				1
San Antonio										×		1
Villa			(— — — Unexcavated — — —)									1
Los Azules									×			1
Buxu			(— Unspecified Upper Palaeolithic only —)									1
Collubil						×			×			2
Cuevas del Mar										×		1
Penicial										×		1
San Antolín										×		1
Coberizas					×		×			×		3
Arnero			×									1
Fonfría							×			×		2
Lledías							×			×		2
Bricia					×					×		2
Cueto de la Mina				×	×	×		×	×	×		6
La Riera					×	×		×		×		4
Tres Calabres						×				×		2
Balmori					×	×		×	×	×		5
Meré							×			×		2
Bulnes							×			×		2
Herrerías										×		1
Vidiago										×		1
Sel			(— Unspecified Upper Palaeolithic only —)									1
Hermida								×	×			2
La Franca										×		1
Colombres										×		1
La Loja			(— Unspecified Upper Palaeolithic only —)									1
Pindal							×			×		2
Santander												
Unquera		×										1
La Mora		×										1

Site		Count
Carranceja		2
Altamira		2
Cuco		1
San Felices de Buelna		1
Hornos de la Peña		5
Castillo		9
Cobalejos		3
Pendo		7
Juyo		1
Liencres		1
Peña Castillo		1
Peña del Mazo		5
Morín[a]		7
Astillero		1
Los Moros		2
San Vitores		1
Mar		3
Fuente Francés		3
Rascaño		1
Bona		4
Salitré		1
Cubillo		4
Otero		1
Chora		1
Cobrantes		3
Valle		1
VentadelaPerra (– Unspecified Upper Palaeolithic only –)		1
La Haza (– Unspecified Upper Palaeolithic only –)		1
Mirón		1
Covalanas (– Unspecified Upper Palaeolithic only –)		—
Peña del Cuco[b]		
Burgos		
Blanca		1
Caballón		1
Penches[b]		

Sites are listed in geographical order from west to east and north to south. Sites are grouped to show dense clusters of sites, represented in Figure 26 either by a single symbol or several adjacent symbols. Sources: Alcalde del Rio et al. (1911), Cabrera & Bernaldo de Quirós (1977), Clark, G. A. (1971, 1975), Clark, G. A. & Straus (1977), Fernández-Tresguerres (1976), García Guinea (1968), González Echegaray (1957), González Echegaray et al. (1963, 1966), Hernández-Pacheco, E. (1919), Hernández-Pacheco, F. (1959), Hernández-Pacheco, F. et al. (1957), Jordá (1955, 1958, 1963), Martínez Santa-Olalla (1925), Obermaier (1925), Straus (1977), Vega del Sella (1923).

[a] Chatelperronian is also represented at this site.
[b] There is no record of habitation at these sites. Dates are based on the rock art.

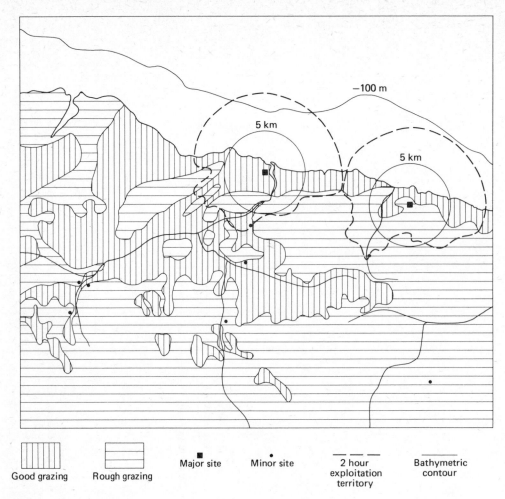

Good grazing   Rough grazing   Major site ■   Minor site •   2 hour exploitation territory   Bathymetric contour

Figure 27. Site exploitation territories of Lloseta (left) and Cueto de la Mina (right).

maximum number of archaeological periods. The largest site in this sense is Castillo with eight periods represented from the Mousterian to the Neolithic. Our weighting of sites according to longevity of occupation is obviously a crude device. It takes no account of the size of sites or of individual strata within them, nor of the different time periods represented by such conventional archaeological entities as the 'Mousterian' or the 'Asturian'. Nor does it take into consideration the inadequacies of the typological sequence, much of which remains uncertain in the absence of corroboration from radiocarbon dates. It is, however, intended purely as a rough and ready guide to one factor which is of significance in the analysis of long-term palaeoeconomic trends.

Two features stand out in Figure 26: the concentration of sites, especially the larger sites, in the favoured littoral zone below the 200 m contour; and the irregularity of the distribution. Many factors have doubtless

influenced this site distribution. Most of the sites are caves or rock shelters, and it might therefore be argued that they form a sample which typifies locations of good archaeological preservation rather than reflecting overall habitation patterns. On the other hand, Lower and Middle Palaeolithic surface scatters or individual tools have been recorded from at least 20 localities in central Asturias (Manuel González 1968), and there are similar well-known examples in eastern Asturias and Santander. If substantial open sites were a significant feature of local settlement patterns, one would therefore expect them to have been found in some numbers by now. Furthermore, less than 10 per cent of the 480 caves recorded in Santander province show clear evidence of prehistoric occupation (Begínes Ramírez 1965). Even excluding those obviously unsuited or inaccessible to occupation, there is ample scope within such a sample for preference of site location to operate. This, and the clear evidence that certain of the caves were foci of

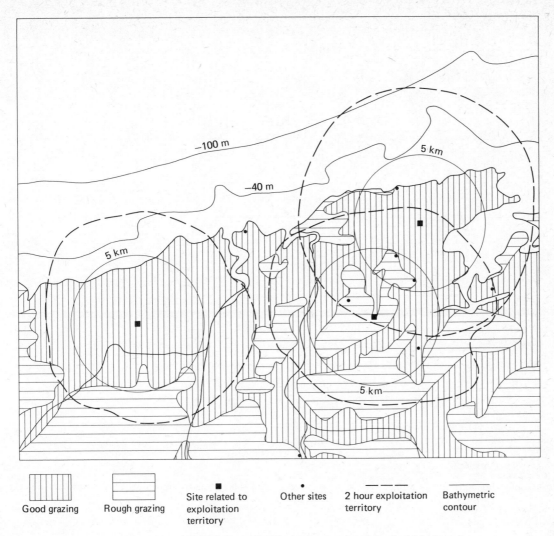

Good grazing	Rough grazing	Site related to exploitation territory	Other sites	2 hour exploitation territory	Bathymetric contour

Figure 28. Site exploitation territories of Altamira (left), Peña Castillo (right upper) and Pendo (right lower).

settlement over very long periods while others had only a transitory occupation, encourages us to believe that it is worth searching for an intelligible pattern in the data.

Site territories

Sites tend to occur in certain characteristic types of location, and their territories can be classified accordingly into four general categories.

Sites on or close to the seashore typically have territories which include a substantial proportion of open sea within the 2 hour limit (Figure 27). The extension of the territorial boundary out to sea does not necessarily indicate that all the area so enclosed was regularly exploited. It is rather a measure of the amount of land that the occupants were prepared to forego by comparison with a site located further inland.

Site territories of this type offer the best opportunity for the integration of marine resources into the terrestrial economy.

A second type of territory is associated with sites located within the littoral zone in such a way that the resources of both marine and upland zones are peripheral to their territories (Figure 28). Sites of this type are well placed to take best advantage of littoral zone resources. They also tend to have the largest territories because of the fairly level topography and ease of movement on the coastal plain.

Other groups of sites are located at the junction of the coastal plain with the upland zone, for example Castillo (Figure 29) and Otero (Figure 30), or in the upland zone itself (as with Valle in Figure 30). These are discussed in more detail in Chapter 6, although their relationship to coastal settlement and economy is

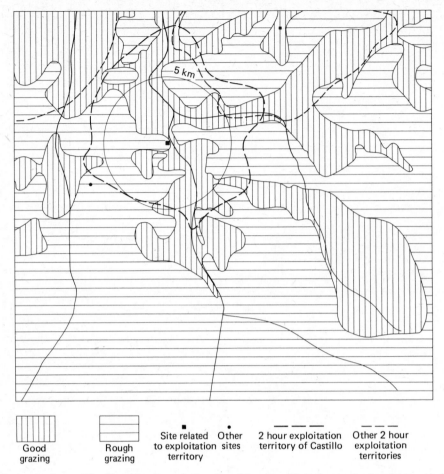

Good grazing | Rough grazing | ■ Site related to exploitation territory | • Other sites | — — — 2 hour exploitation territory of Castillo | – – – Other 2 hour exploitation territories

Figure 29. Site exploitation territory of Castillo. Also shown is the edge of the site exploitation territories of Altamira (left) and Cueva Morín (right).

outlined later in this chapter. Some site territories have a mixture of characteristics, particularly on the narrow coastal plain of Asturias.

Economic niches

Before going on to a more detailed consideration of particular sites and their economic development, it will be useful to comment briefly on some factors affecting the distribution of sites and populations in the area as a whole. As we have seen from Figure 26, there is a strong general correlation between the population and economic potential, with the majority of preferred sites occurring in the favoured coastal plain. It might logically be expected that this relationship would be extended in such a way that the most important sites would be associated with the largest and most productive exploitation territories. Analysis shows this to be only partly the case, with an important additional factor

being the relationship to other sites and resources which lie beyond their site territories.

This may be illustrated with reference to Castillo, a site occupied in almost all the major archaeological periods from the Mousterian to the Neolithic. The richness of the site contents reinforces this impression of its long-standing importance. The Castillo territory is not remarkable, however, being significantly constricted by topographic distortion, and containing approximately equal proportions of good grazing and rough grazing resources (Figure 29). What is unusual about Castillo is its location at the mouth of a valley which provides the major link between the coastal plain to the north and a series of possible routes to the upland zone to the south of the site. The coastal plain is at this point broader than elsewhere in the region, and thus represents an unusually favourable concentration of resources which supported a number of other major sites such as Pendo and Morín. To the south the

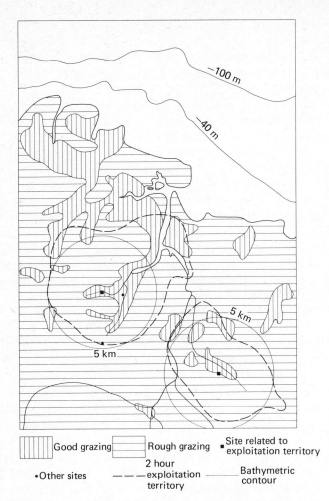

Figure 30. Site exploitation territories of Otero (left) and Valle (right).

Good grazing   Rough grazing   Site related to exploitation territory

•Other sites   — — — 2 hour exploitation territory   Bathymetric contour

In contrast, eastern Asturias has a narrower coastal plain and a steeper and less accessible upland interior. The preferred sites, such as Lloseta and Cueto de la Mina (Figure 27), are much closer to the coast than is Castillo. These sites, and others on the coastal plain, are typically located near valleys linking this zone with intermontane valleys in the immediate hinterland. However, the north–south compression of the system due to the basic environmental limitations mentioned above appears to have resulted in a coastward displacement of the main focus of settlement. Similarly we may expect that the exploitation patterns will have fallen into the short-distance transhumance or mobile-cum-sedentary categories, rather than the long-distance mobility appropriate to the Santander environment.

The Palaeolithic

In Cantabria as elsewhere in Mediterranean Europe, Mousterian occupation is concentrated on and near the coastal plain. There is little evidence in the site locations and territories or from the faunal remains that either marine or upland resources exerted a considerable effect on population distribution or economy.

The great uncertainty which surrounds Mousterian chronology and the related sea levels hampers any interpretation of this evidence. All that can be said is that the existing site distribution indicates a preoccupation with the exploitation of lowland terrestrial resources. A small number of shells from the Mousterian deposits at Cueva Morín (Madariaga 1971) indicates at least a casual exploitation of marine resources, although the site is not well located for intensive shell-gathering (Figure 28). This, and the upland site of La Mora (see Chapter 6), suggest that some use was made of complementary resources beyond the lowland zone, but neither upland nor marine resources appear to have achieved any prominence in the economy. Ibex and chamois are rare or absent in faunal assemblages, and exploitation seems to have been fairly eclectic (and probably fairly opportunistic), relying principally on horse and large bovids and to a lesser extent on red deer (Freeman, L. G. 1973, Straus 1977).

The Upper Palaeolithic seems to show a relatively gradual development from this pattern, and not a sudden break. We have chosen the Solutrean and Lower Magdalenian periods as the focus of our analysis, as these highlight some important aspects of this development. Additionally, the period *c.* 20 000–15 000 b.p. covers the episode of maximum lowering of both sea level and snowlines, and thus provides a useful measure of economic reactions to these important

relatively low-potential uplands are more productive than is the general rule in Cantabria. Their less severe topography results in a better soil and vegetation cover. This area is today one of the most favoured regions of summer grazing for cattle transhumants (de Terán 1947) and is likely to have fulfilled a similar complementary economic role throughout prehistory.

The valley adjacent to Castillo offers, furthermore, one of the shortest and easiest routes across the Cantabrian watershed into the upland grazing on the northern margins of the *meseta*. No other site in Santander provides these combined advantages to the same degree; and we can thus see the importance of Castillo as stemming in part from its suitability for the integration of a whole constellation of widespread seasonal resources, whose effective exploitation would have required a considerable degree of human mobility.

stimuli. We have assumed in our interpretations that the broad outlines of the typologically derived sequence do provide reliable chronological indicators, an hypothesis which seems to be supported by such positive dating evidence as exists.

Significant general features of the Upper Palaeolithic development include the gradual decline in importance (and eventual disappearance in some cases) of the large fauna such as rhinoceros, equids, and bovids, coupled with a corresponding rise in the importance of deer (especially the red deer), pig, chamois, and ibex; a larger number of sites covering a wider area; and evidence of a more intensive exploitation of upland and marine resources.

The twin phenomena of lowered sea levels and lowered snowlines, along with a more severe winter climate than that of today, are of great importance in the consideration of the Cantabrian economy at this period. Together they would have had the effect of increasing greatly the area available for winter grazing, while reducing the availability of summer grazing in the Cantabrian uplands. A maximum marine regression of 100–130 m would in some cases have doubled the width of the coastal plain. Sites which, like Lloseta, Juyo, and Peña Castillo, lie near the modern coast would have had several kilometres of coastal plain between them and the sea at the time of their Lower Magdalenian occupation (Figures 27 and 28). The enhanced value of winter grazing has its counterpart in a distinct drop in upland summer grazing potential due to lowered snowlines and shorter growing seasons. As is discussed further in Chapter 6, it is of some significance that signs of the development of exploitation of the northern *meseta*, and of the long-range integration of this area with the lowland zone through such sites as Castillo, are first apparent during the Upper Palaeolithic when climatic conditions would have placed an increasing strain on the available summer resources.

A number of lines of evidence testify to an increased degree of exploitation of marine resources. Cave art depicts flatfish, salmon, trout and lamprey, and includes the Pindal representation, variously interpreted as a tunny or a sturgeon (Madariaga 1969). Occasional fish vertebrae have been found at a number of sites. The Solutrean level at Altamira produced a seal's tooth, matched by more recently discovered specimens from La Riera and Tito Bustillo (Straus 1976–7), while a number of coastal sites contain limpets.

These data cannot be accurately compared with those from earlier or later periods, but there is clearly more evidence for at least the casual exploitation of marine resources than was the case in the Middle

Palaeolithic. The productivity of marine resources, particularly fish and sea mammals, was probably higher during this period than previously, because of colder temperatures and the southward extension of zoogeographical zones, so that the evidence may simply reflect a response to environmental change rather than any intensification of economic exploitation. The latter possibility is, however, raised by the greater concentration of molluscs in the Upper Palaeolithic deposits despite the fact that during the Solutrean and Lower Magdalenian occupations the shoreline would have been at its maximum distance from the modern coast. We should remember, however, that most of the Lower Magdalenian sites adjacent to the modern coast, such as Lloseta, Balmori, Cueto de la Mina, Juyo and Peña Castillo, would have had the sea at the northern periphery of their territories, at closest (Figures 27 and 28). It therefore seems likely that these sites represent the exploitation of the productive coastal plain made accessible by the lowered sea levels, rather than bases for marine exploitation itself. Even Juyo, which is described as containing 'large numbers' of shells, has a large mammalian fauna dominated by exceptional quantities of red deer bones (Freeman, L. G. 1973). It may well be that sites primarily located for the exploitation of marine resources existed on the contemporary coast, and that the evidence in existing sites represents such material as was occasionally transported back to the lowland home base. The interpretation of these latter sites as being primarily concerned with terrestrial exploitation is supported by the fact that both Juyo and Peña Castillo were abandoned in subsequent periods in favour of more inland locations such as Pendo and Morín. This suggests that the maximum extent of the Late Glacial coastal plain was a crucial factor in their occupation; and that once sea levels rose again, truncating the northern sector of the territory, more advantageous sites were chosen further inland.

This hypothesis is perhaps strengthened by the converse case of the site of Otero (Figure 30). Here a hiatus occurred between the Solutrean and Upper Magdalenian occupations. Local depopulation during the Lower Magdalenian seems an implausible explanation, as the inland site of Valle (which, as we suggest in Chapter 6, may have been linked with Otero) remained in occupation then. The relatively small size of the Otero territory, due to topographic constraints, suggests an alternative explanation. With the sea at its lowest level and the coastal plain at its greatest extent during the Lower Magdalenian it seems likely that site locations nearer the coastline may have offered considerably better access to the lowland resources than did Otero, and that an alternative home base thus awaits discovery (or is submerged) somewhere to the north.

It seems then that during the Upper Palaeolithic there may have been some slight increase in the attention paid to the shoreline, as is attested by the greater incidence of mollusc shells. There is no unequivocal evidence that exploitation of these coastal resources had any significant impact on site locations or overall economic strategies. The main feature of this period is, on the contrary, the evidence for a more intensive and wide-ranging exploitation of terrestrial resources in both the upland and lowland zones. As mentioned in Chapter 6, the evidence for some degree of specialisation on red deer during this period coupled with the pattern of site distribution around some intermontane valleys suggests that we may be dealing with a much closer exploitative relationship than is implied by the conventional term 'hunting'. Although there is insufficient faunal evidence to explore the suggestion further, it is quite possible that the Upper Palaeolithic witnessed developments in the course of which the staple herbivores would have been exploited by some form of herding or herd-following economy.

The Asturian

Economic development through the Upper Magdalenian to the Asturian period seems again to have been largely a matter of continuity. The most outstanding change is the trend to the increasing representation of molluscs at archaeological sites, particularly in eastern Asturias (Clark, G. A. 1971, Vega del Sella 1923).

True midden deposits have been claimed for periods as early as the Magdalenian, notably at Lloseta and Juyo (Clark, G. A. 1971, Straus 1977), but the majority of preserved shell middens, some 20 in all, cluster in the Asturian period dated between about 9000 b.p. and 7000 b.p. Most of these have been severely eroded, and it is thus impossible to make accurate estimates of the actual number of molluscs involved, but rough calculations indicate that even the smallest middens would have contained hundreds of thousands of shells, the largest millions. This provides at least a strong general indication of the increase in the evidence for exploitation of marine resources. Remains of sea urchins, crabs, and fish are also present.

On the other hand, a number of features suggest the continued importance of terrestrial resources. The shell middens are all at the entrances to caves and rock shelters, no large exposed middens on or adjacent to the shoreline (after the Danish pattern) being known.

This, and the frequent representation of terrestrial mammals in the middens, suggests that we are probably dealing with lowland home bases similar to those of earlier periods, rather than temporary camps specialising in marine exploitation. This impression is reinforced by the considerable degree of continuity of site location and territorial factors.

Two immediate questions are raised by these data: what economic changes are implied by the increased evidence of marine, and particularly molluscan, exploitation, and why did these changes occur? Here as elsewhere a close examination does not support the hypothesis that the shell middens resulted from economies primarily based upon marine resources. Middens do not as a rule seem to be correlated differentially with regions of particularly rich shellfish potential, but rather seem to be related to areas favourable for the exploitation of terrestrial ungulates. These conclusions are discussed in detail elsewhere (Bailey 1973, 1975b, 1978), but the evidence on which they rest may be summarised as follows. In the first place the on-site data, although they apparently suggest an overwhelming predominance of molluscs in the diet, also consistently include bone remains, amongst which red deer is usually the predominant species. The data are too poor for detailed numerical analysis of the midden deposits to be fruitful, but when it is remembered that at least 30 000 limpets are required to supply the calorific equivalent of a single red deer carcase, it seems most unlikely that the situation in the Asturias would have been substantially different from that in Denmark. Indeed, when we consider that the economic potential of the steep and rocky Asturian coastline would probably have been considerably less than that of Denmark, while the accessible terrestrial biomas is likely to have been at least as large, it seems that the rôle of marine resources may well have been of even less significance in the former region than in the latter.

The territorial evidence, too, is in accordance with the suggestion that the economic system continued to be centred on terrestrial resources. One of the largest recorded Asturian middens is that at Pendo (Carballo & González Echegaray 1952). The site is 5 km from the nearest modern shoreline, and the sea is thus barely included in the 1-hour exploitation territory (Figure 28). During the occupation of the site the sea would probably have been slightly further away. Any economy focusing upon marine resources would necessarily have involved site locations much nearer the sea, and the midden at Pendo thus seems to exemplify the distance over which the local population was prepared to transport molluscs while conducting a land-based economy. There is little or no evidence to suggest that the marine resources were sufficiently important to attract major settlements or home bases to the coast in this area. Were this the case, it seems most unlikely that so many shells would have been transported back to Pendo. A number of apparently suitable caves and rock shelters exist much nearer the coastline, but with the exception of the Lower Magdalenian deposits at Juyo and Peña Castillo none of these shows signs of more than a scanty and transient occupation. The open site of Liencres which would have been well located for a marine-based economy appears rather to have been a workshop site for the extraction of flint (Clark, G. A. 1975).

In eastern Asturias, where the coastal plain is narrow and the mountains rise steeply close to the shore, there is a greater density of middens than elsewhere in Cantabria. This might appear superficially to suggest a greater economic importance for molluscs. On the other hand, there is nothing to suggest that the molluscan resources of this region of coast are especially rich, and the evidence seems more likely to represent the effect of accommodating a herbivore-based economy to the constricted coastal plain. Any site in this area located so as to take advantage of the lowland terrestrial resources would automatically include within its territory a large area of coast and open sea. In these circumstances it is scarcely surprising that large quantities of molluscs were transported back to the home base. The density of middens may thus be better attributed to the fortuitous inclusion of the marine sector in the exploitation territories of these sites than to significant concentration upon coastal resources.

Taken as a whole, then, the evidence seems to show the continuation of a land-based economy. The changes in site location constitute adjustments to variations in sea level and were undertaken to optimise terrestrial resource potential rather than to include marine resources as an important element in the economy. It should further be noted that our territorial evidence suggests that the archaeological representation of marine resource exploitation may be a misleading guide to economic changes. It is quite possible that molluscs were of a similar importance during the Upper Palaeolithic period as in the Asturian, but that due to the more distant shoreline, fewer shellfish were brought back and preserved in the existing and visible home bases.

Long-term perspectives

When we examine the broader picture, however, there are some indications that there may have been an increasing intensity in the exploitation of shellfish towards the end of the Palaeolithic and in the Asturian period. If variations in visible evidence of exploitation were related solely to changes in sea level and shore position, then we should expect middens to be well represented for periods of high sea level prior to the Postglacial. This does not seem to be so.

There is no evidence whatever for shell middens of Eemian date, despite the fact that uncertainties in the dating of the Cantabrian Mousterian make it difficult to analyse the economy of that period. Suggestions that some of the Asturian middens may have had an Eemian or earlier date (Jordá 1959) seem to have been eliminated by radiocarbon dating. The relative scarcity of shells throughout deposits of the last glacial is entirely what we would expect, given that sea levels were generally lower than today (Geyh *et al.* 1979). On the other hand, it is significant that a general increase in shellfish exploitation seems to have taken place during the maximum of the last glacial, when sea level was at its lowest, although the higher sea levels preceding the maximum of the last glacial (Shackleton & Opdyke 1973) might be expected to have been more favourable to such a development.

It is clear, therefore, that some factor is involved in addition to eustatic change. One possibility is that climatic or other environmental changes may have affected the availability of shellfish at different periods. This seems most unlikely for a number of reasons. The limpet is by far the commonest species represented at all periods, with periwinkles and topshells also fairly common. This is entirely what might be expected on a steep, rocky coastline. Neither the temperature change (which seems in the Asturian period to have caused the replacement of *Littorina littorea* by the ecologically similar but warm-adapted *Trochocochlea crassa*) nor the slight decline in mean limpet size in the Asturian middens seems to have had any appreciable impact on overall availability of shellfish. It is hard to attribute economic significance to those relatively minor ecological adjustments. Nor is it likely that the low sea levels of the maximum regressions would have so changed the nature of the coast as to eliminate limpet habitats. The steep slope to the continental shelf and the fact that Cantabria has a 'high-energy' coastline with intensive wave action mean that the general character of the shore will have remained much the same.

The second obvious hypothesis is that the intensification in the exploitation of coastal resources depended on broader developments than those discussed above. Specifically, it seems quite possible that the trend was stimulated by changes in the exploitation of terrestrial resources. We have already noted general indications of an increasingly complete and intensive pattern of terrestrial exploitation during the Upper Palaeolithic, and it would not be surprising if the use of hitherto neglected resources such as molluscs were part of such a development.

We are hampered in our analysis of the Asturian economy as a whole by the almost complete absence of sites in the hinterland. The standard archaeological explanation of such cases is that the area was therefore unoccupied, and that hence in this case the Asturian would have been a shore-based, strandlooping economy. We have developed above our reasons for rejecting such a hypothesis except under specific conditions. Given that the two main diagnostic features of the Asturian have been the shell middens and the 'pic' – a tool most probably used to detach limpets from their rocks – it is scarcely surprising that this particular facies is closely confined to the coastline. We should bear in mind here the fact that economies exploiting contrasting environments are likely to employ varying toolkits, and that an inland facies contemporaneous with the Asturian and manufactured by 'the Asturian population' might well look very different from the coastal culture. Recent radiocarbon dates from the inland site of Los Azules (Fernández-Tresguerres 1976), near Buxu, show that the Azilian could have been at least partly contemporaneous with the Asturian, and might therefore represent just such a facies.

The apparent absence of a contemporaneous inland industry may alternatively be a problem of archaeological visibility, so commonly encountered in the upland areas. It is hard to argue convincingly that the hinterland would have been uninhabitable, particularly in view of the fact that both Azilian and Neolithic sites are known. The expansion of forest cover due to the postglacial rise in temperature is not likely to have been sufficiently dramatic as to render the hinterland uninhabitable, although it may well have made it a less productive source of terrestrial resources. There is no sign of the regular pattern of site location on river banks, lake shores, and seashores, as there is in the heavily forested environment of Denmark, and many of the existing coastal sites would have been as much affected by the vegetational changes as were the seemingly deserted areas inland. If, as seems quite possible, the uplands were used primarily on a mobile basis during the summer, and if, due to the climatic changes, settlements were mainly insubstantial open camps rather than in caves, then the lack of evidence is hardly remarkable. There can be little doubt that open habitations would have been a perfectly feasible form

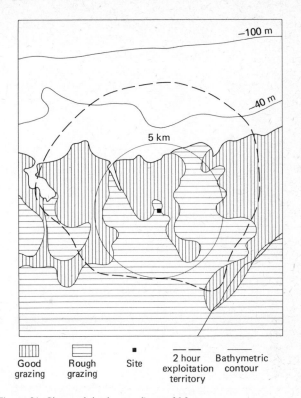

Good grazing   Rough grazing   Site   2 hour exploitation territory   Bathymetric contour

Figure 31. Site exploitation territory of Meaza.

of settlement. Occupation at many of the coastal Asturian sites must have been just outside, rather than actually in the caves, as many of these are filled to the ceiling with midden material.

The nature of inland exploitation thus remains obscure. There are, however, indications in the coastal evidence that important developments were taking place. While there is a strong element of settlement continuity, with Asturian deposits stratified above or adjacent to earlier levels, a number of middens occur in new locations. The area of coastal settlement appears to have expanded, as in the region of the sites at Franca, Meaza, and Cáscaras (Figures 31 and 32). In addition, there is some infilling of the areas between existing major settlements, as at Penicial, Cuevas del Mar, Vidiago, and Herrerías (Figure 32). Whether we view these as indicating a denser packing of home bases, or of increased use of temporary camps in the coastal economy, it amounts to clear evidence of a more intensive exploitation of the coastal strip.

An important factor here is the postglacial rise in sea level, which would have dramatically and progressively reduced the size of the coastal plain, and hence put increasingly severe pressure on the available winter grazing. Winter is the lean period of the year, and winter grazing the prime limiting factor on herbivore

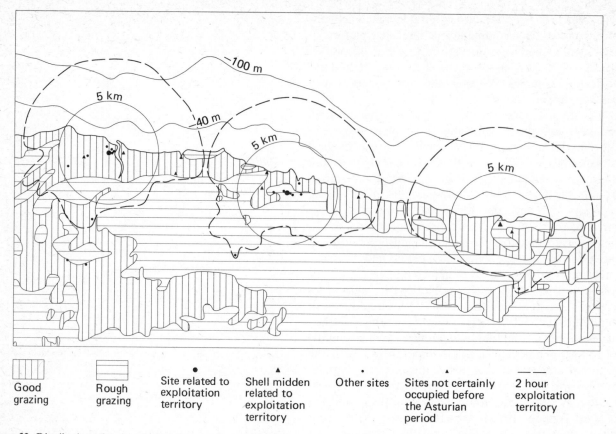

Figure 32. Distribution of archaeological sites on the coastal plain of eastern Asturias, showing the site exploitation territories of Lloseta, Cueto de la Mina and La Franca (from left to right).

populations in the Asturias. As the large herbivores, particularly the red deer, formed the main dietary staple at the time (Clark, G. A. 1971), the economy as a whole would have been particularly sensitive to the contraction of the narrow coastal plain. The steep mountainous topography inland means that the southern margin of the main winter grazing area is relatively in elastic. A certain amount of the loss due to eustatic changes would have been compensated for by rising snowlines and the longer growing season, but this effect would have been counterbalanced by the detrimental effect on the larger herbivore populations of the growth of forested conditions.

All in all, then, there is little doubt that the total amount of winter grazing was considerably reduced. As has been pointed out, the postglacial changes of climate by no means always led to economic advantage, and in this case the rising sea level and increasingly forested environment would certainly have created considerable stress. It is instructive to consider the development of the coastal economy in relation to this factor. It is noticeable that the sites newly occupied in the Asturian period are in marginal locations from the point of view

of terrestrial exploitation, in comparison with the preferred sites of earlier periods. They are either adjacent to inland grazing areas of low productivity, or they are in positions with poor access to the hinterland. The former is exemplified by the coastal strip bounded by the site territories of La Franca and Meaza. The extensive areas of inland grazing which complement coastal grazing resources for the large herbivores elsewhere in Cantabria are lacking in this region. While occupation is also attested at inland sites such as Chufin, La Loja, and Hermida, it appears to have been either of a transitory nature or late in date. The spread of sites within existing regions of settlement is illustrated by such examples as Penicial, Cuevas del Mar, Vidiago and Herrerías (Figure 32), which are cut off from direct access to the intermontane valleys of the hinterland by the steep scarp slope of the coastal hill ranges. Both groups of sites are, however, well placed to intensify exploitation of the coastal strip itself. Remains of terrestrial mammals as well as shellfish testify to the exploitation of marine and littoral resources which would have been peripheral to the territories of previously occupied sites, and which were presumably of little interest to their inhabitants, if indeed they were exploited at all. Such peripheral resources would have become increasingly valuable in the face of the pressure on pre-existing staples.

This adds up to a picture of sustained population pressure in the early postglacial, resulting in a large degree from the rise in sea level. The stress upon the economic system may well have been severe. It is worth remembering that seafood in general, and shellfish in particular, have not infrequently been used to mitigate stress in the terrestrial economy. Ethnographic examples have been quoted earlier in this chapter. One obvious if extreme historical example is the intensive collection of limpets by which means the coastal population of Ireland attempted to ward off starvation during periods of famine in the early nineteenth century (Patterson 1839). We are not implying that an episode of comparable severity was necessarily involved in postglacial Asturias, but it would not be surprising if such were the case.

This still does not explain the lack of evidence for shell-gathering during earlier episodes of high sea level. Here our general hypothesis that, on the long prehistoric timescale, populations will have tended to increase seems relevant. Eemian populations may have been able to adjust to decreased terrestrial resources in the coastal plain either by emigration or by an intensification of terrestrial exploitation, or by a combination of these two. With the higher population levels of the Asturian period, however, emigration would have been restricted by population pressure in adjacent areas, while the possibility of economic intensification would have been limited by an already highly developed pattern of exploitation of the larger herbivores. In these circumstances marine resources may have represented a crucial safety valve, the exploitation of which would have been one alternative to serious population decline. It also seems likely that the economic stress of the Early Postglacial acted as a powerful spur to the general directional forces which eventually brought about the more intensive economies associated with the Neolithic. As the local variant of the farmyard economy developed, so interest in marine resources seems to have declined. We may take this as an indication that the development of the more productive and stable pastoral economy removed the need for the intensive exploitation of such emergency rations as limpets.

THE POLISH LITTORAL

The coastal region of northern Poland shows a number of similarities with Denmark both in its environmental potential and in the sequence of its prehistoric occupation. The landscape is a morainic one with glacial sands dotted with lakes and extensive marsh and peat formations. This extends inland for several hundred kilometres without exceeding 200 m in altitude. Much of the immediate littoral consists of a strip of salt marshes backed by sand dunes and punctuated by marshy river valleys and lagoons, while offshore there is the occasional formation of narrow sand bars. Towards the east, low, steep morainic cliffs are more prevalent. These features are best developed in the Gulf of Gdańsk with its large, sheltered lagoons and occasional cliffs giving way to the extensive marshy deposits of the Vistula delta. Much of the marshy ground has been drained in recent times, especially on the lower reaches of the Vistula, to create an area of highly productive arable. Elsewhere, however, the soils are rather sandy, podsolised and infertile.

Substantial human occupation of the area is recorded from the late Glacial period onwards, as in the other glaciated regions of the North European Plain. Rising sea levels have destroyed any signs of coastal settlement that there may have been at this time, and we have not attempted a detailed analysis of the economy of the Late Glacial or early Holocene. In view of the concentration of inland Mesolithic sites in marshy areas it seems probable that the economies in operation were broadly similar to the contemporaneous Scandinavian systems (i.e. Denmark and Sweden) discussed elsewhere in this chapter.

Neolithic economies

Two general points are of interest when we compare the littoral zone with Poland as a whole. The first is that typical Neolithic economies, as judged by the traditional criteria of possession of pottery and the modern farmyard plants and animals, appear late in the north by comparison with the loess areas of southern Poland. Typologically speaking the first appearance of these is with Late Neolithic Globular Amphora and Corded Ware (Rzucewo) cultures, although the slightly earlier Funnel-Beaker culture (TRB) is also recorded within the study area as at the site of Kosin (Wiślański 1970, Wiślański & Czarnecki 1971). Secondly, the settlements are small and scattered, and it seems likely that population densities would have been much lower than those suggested by the dense clusters of Neolithic sites on the favoured loess (see Chapter 5). This demographic differential is also recorded historically and persists to the present day for the most part.

Agricultural potential

Broadly speaking, the area with which we are concerned can be divided today into two main soil types with widely divergent agricultural characteristics: marsh soils and glacial sands. In their natural state the marshy soils carry highly productive and nutritious pasture. A study of fossil and subfossil peats in northern Poland (Jasnowski 1972) indicates that there have been some changes in the nature and extent of vegetation on these soils since Neolithic times. On the whole, wet grazing resources would have been more widespread in the past; not only have there been numerous drainage projects since mediaeval times, but the ecological succession has consisted of a replacement of the open marsh plant communities with more closed woodland–bog associations, and of sedgelands with drier meadow plant communities. The older marsh soils are, however, readily recognisable in the field and have been mapped as wet grazing on territorial maps.

The extent of coastal salt-marshes has, on the contrary, stayed roughly the same. Unlike Denmark, where the glacio-isostatic uplift since the Neolithic period has contributed to the development of salt-marshes, the Polish coastline appears to have remained fairly stable (Rosa 1963). Given the generally shallow gradient between *terra firma* and open water, it seems reasonable to assume the presence in Neolithic times, as now, of salt-marshes and marshy river deltas.

These areas of seasonally and permanently flooded pasture are capable of supporting two to three cattle per hectare. Even the permanently waterlogged areas are usually relatively easy of access due to their sandy substrate. The most productive species for hay are the hydrophytic rushes and reeds. At peak productivity, just before flowering, they yield more than twice as much as other hay crops, and even in the early growing period they are at least as productive as fully grown sedges and grasses. The sedges, characteristic of much of the marshy and floodplain vegetation, are the other main hay producers, and contain more protein and albumen, and less cellulose, than do the grasses (Larin 1962). Moreover, the rate of regeneration is high, and even unimproved wet grazing commonly gives two to three hay crops per year. The high fertility and good water retention properties of the marsh soils also give them a high arable potential, but they need a considerable investment of labour for this potential to be fully realised. Not only do they require large-scale drainage before they can be exploited as arable, but even when drained they demand heavy equipment to break the soil and produce a tilth. For these reasons we may exclude these soils from any consideration of prehistoric arable farming.

The glacial sands are by contrast very easy to till except where podsolised. Today these support a mixture of woodland, rough pasture, and arable – mainly barley and potatoes. Cereal yields, however, are low as a rule. Not only are the soils infertile, but their poor water retention is also a limitation in an area which suffers from drought from February to April. Rainfall at this time is frequently too low to support spring-sown cereals. Winter crops suffer from sudden temperature changes which produce heavy glazed frosts. To this day farmers often take the precaution of sowing both winter and spring crops, only one of which is expected to reach maturity despite the availability of modern improved varieties. Cereal production thus tends to be concentrated on the small areas of admixture between the sands and clays or silts from the areas of impeded drainage. This produces a tractable soil of higher fertility than that of the pure sands and is more retentive of moisture. These patches would have been the only good arable accessible to a Neolithic technology.

Thus the sandy soils must for the most part be viewed as having a rough grazing rather than an arable potential. Their value even as grazing would have been limited by their extreme permeability, as they would have been too dry during the early spring and most of the summer to sustain much plant growth. In winter, grazing would have been inhibited by glazed frosts. Even at best the carrying capacity of these soils is fairly low, and their main value is that they warm up very rapidly in the spring, and carry an early flush of vegetation which is available towards the end of May. This is about a month earlier than in the wet grazing areas, where the first growth is retarded by cold melt water. The sandy soils may thus have been of considerable importance in providing the first grazing at the end of the winter lean period, but will not have contributed greatly to the year-round grazing requirements.

Site locations and territories

While a few of the sites, notably the Rzucewo sites in the Gdańsk area, are located on or adjacent to the shoreline itself, the majority are situated further inland within the littoral zone and have territories composed primarily of terrestrial resources. The unaccentuated topography, and the ease of movement even in many of the waterlogged areas due to the firm sandy substrate, has resulted in nearly circular exploitation territories.

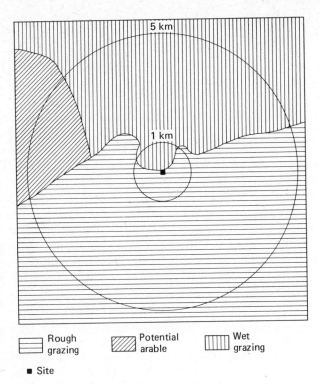

Figure 33. Site exploitation territory of Zielenica.

Figure 34. Site exploitation territory of Tolmicko.

The main exceptions to this are where the sea or the larger lakes impinge upon the territories.

The main unifying feature of settlement distribution is the preference for locations at the junction between marshy depressions and the higher glacial sands. Equally striking is the absence of any evidence for concentration on those few areas with above-average arable potential. Zielenica (Wiślański 1969), for example, has a territory primarily composed of sandy soils and marshland. Starting about 1 km from the site is an area of sandy silt with a much higher arable potential than the other soils within the territory (Figure 33). This area produces good crops of barley and it is here that modern arable production in the region is concentrated. The site is more than 1 km away, however, and is separated from the arable soil by a strip of marshland. The sites of Tolmicko (Ehrlich 1940), Gleznowo (Wiślański 1969) and Oslanino (Engel 1931) similarly have territories that include areas of high arable potential. These are loess deposits which are today under intensive cultivation for spring wheat, but the sites are from 1 to 3 km distant from them (Figure 34). The site territory associated with the Funnel-Beaker (TRB) settlements at Kosin (not illustrated) indicates a closely similar pattern. Other site territories are largely lacking in arable potential.

It seems then, bearing in mind the severe limitations placed upon cereal cultivation by the time–distance factor, that the economy must have been primarily concerned with the exploitation of the grazing potential of the wetlands and the glacial sands. We have already emphasised the richness of the former, and they seem indeed to have played a crucial part in the economy.

Sites are usually located so as to provide immediate access to extensive areas of wet grazing. The typical site location is on a slight elevation at the junction of the low-lying wet grazing and the slightly higher sandy plateaux. Most sites are immediately adjacent to the former zone, none of them being as much as 0.5 km away. The economic importance of this resource is further underlined by the fact that wet grazing usually accounts for from one-third to one-half of the exploitation territories. In some cases, as at Lichnowy (Szymańska 1968), the territory is almost entirely wet grazing. This is a much higher proportion than its distribution in the coastal region as a whole. Wet grazing accounts for 10.5 per cent on average of the four coastal vovoidships, rising to a maximum of only 14.2 per cent in the Szczecin vovoidship. It is thus clear that site location and territories are profoundly influenced by the availability and distribution of the relatively scarce resource of wet-land grazing. The glacial sands are both the dominant soil type and occur in relatively large blocks, but seem to have attracted little settlement except at their periphery.

Economic niches

It appears therefore that the coastal economy must to a large degree have been dependent upon pastoralism. From some sites, it is true, there is evidence that wheat and barley were cultivated. The territorial evidence is unequivocal, however, that arable concerns were at best of minor importance. Those coastal sites of the Gdańsk area which have a large marine territorial element contain the bones of harp seal and fish (mainly bream, ziege, and pike perch) in addition to those of the common farmyard animals which occur at all sites with adequate faunal assemblages. Here again, however, the accent remains on pastoral resources, with the bones of terrestrial herbivores in the majority. Furthermore, the sites in this region are located, like the others, at the junction of wet grazing with sandy soils. Wet grazing is at a premium in the immediate coastal strip, and it is noticeable that settlement here is for the most part restricted to those areas where there is salt-marsh available to fulfil this crucial requirement. The exceptions are some flint and pottery scatters on the Hel and Wislana sand spits, which probably represent temporary fishing and sealing camps.

We must, therefore consider how this primary pastoral economy may have been organised. In many areas where geographical and seasonal variations lead to a considerable spatial imbalance of resources the response both of herbivores and of human groups dependent on them involves seasonal mobility (Chapter 2). We have often been led to argue that this was also the case in the prehistoric past.

In northern Poland, however, the case is altered. The major limiting factor with which any animal-based economy will have to contend is the shortage of winter grazing. The winter is long, with plant growth absent or negligible for about six months from late October to late April. Frozen ground and vegetation greatly restrict the natural winter carrying capacity. In many areas of Europe, coastal regions benefit from the maritime climate, and thus become favoured areas of winter grazing that attract large populations of herbivores and their exploiters at this season. The shallow waters of the southern Baltic cool down rapidly, however, and they commonly freeze over for at least two months. The best of the winter grazing to be had in the vicinity is on the permanently waterlogged pastures, but these too

are of limited nutritional value by the winter, and eventually ice up.

Moreover, these limitations on winter grazing resources cannot be overcome easily by long-range mobility, an expedient resorted to in many other areas of Europe. The nearest area offering a range of complementary resources is in the Carpathian and Tatra mountains of southern Poland. While this, at 500 km and more, is just about within the effective annual range of animal movement, here too the winter is the lean season, most of the pasture being inaccessible under snow. One does not really come to an area with good winter grazing before reaching the Atlantic lowlands to the west. These are not only too distant to be effectively exploited from Poland in an annual cycle, they were in any case doubtless already utilised to capacity by populations much better situated to make use of them.

Left to themselves, the natural reaction of the herbivore populations to this situation would probably have been a pattern of concentration upon the wet grazing areas from late spring until autumn, followed by a dispersal through the region as a whole to make the most of the scanty winter fodder. Human groups depending on such a system would have had to rely on a combination of a heavy autumn cull and the exploitation of other resources to see them through the winter. In the coastal regions marine resources offer themselves as an obvious possible alternative for winter subsistence. Historical records indicate that exploitation of seal was traditionally a winter activity, the animals being taken from the sea ice. As discussed earlier, however, the Baltic is relatively poor in marine resources, and much of what is there is inaccessible during the winter due to icing. Such cereals as were grown would, of course, have provided an additional supplement to the winter diet, possibly both of animals and humans.

A number of indications suggest that the typical exploitation pattern in the Polish littoral may have involved a more intensive use of terrestrial resources than the above picture portrays. Few of the Neolithic sites are located on islets or spurs surrounded by wet grazing, as one might expect of sites located purely for the warm-season exploitation of grazing resources. Similarly, no sites are recorded from the higher sandy plateaux, such as one might expect as evidence of winter occupation. Instead, as we have remarked, sites are characteristically located at the junction of wet grazing with the sands. The main exception is the site of Lichnowy, with its unusually high proportion of wet grazing in its territory. It is perhaps significant that here the absence of structures and the small number of artefacts may well indicate a temporary or subsidiary station rather than a home base.

It seems most likely, given the environmental constraints and the settlement pattern, that the economy was based upon a sedentary occupation, although limited mobility may of course have been employed to gain access to specific resources beyond the territorial limits. If the animal population were not to be limited to the very small number which could survive on the naturally available winter grazing, we must suppose that, in Neolithic times as now, the summer surplus was preserved in the form of hay or foggage for winter use.

Indeed, it seems most unlikely that this was not the case. Where faunal collections are of adequate size, cattle are invariably the predominant species. Cattle do extremely badly on inferior pasture, and with their relatively slow rate of natural increase, the population would have suffered heavily from a stringent autumn cull. By cutting some of the early summer growth – which would in any case certainly have been surplus to requirements – for winter use, the hungry gap would have been at least partly filled, and a higher year-round population maintained. Here, as in many other areas of Europe, the carrying capacity of cattle, and hence the human population ceiling, would have depended to a large extent upon the amount of hay which could be made during the summer.

It is, of course, difficult to demonstrate the practice of hay-making purely from archaeological evidence. The identification of winter cattle stalls in Neolithic Switzerland predicates some source of winter fodder. Pollen diagrams and macrobotanical data have long been interpreted as giving evidence of the collection of browse for animal fodder elsewhere in Europe, and more recently it has been suggested that the practice may well extend back into Mesolithic times (Simmons & Dimbleby 1974). It is therefore perhaps a little unlikely that the Neolithic inhabitants of the coastal zone in Poland did not arrive at this simple and obvious way of increasing the stability of their economy, and of raising the carrying capacity both for themselves and their livestock. An additional advantage of cutting hay would have been that it would also improve the quality of the pasture. The rapidly growing wet grazing would soon become coarse and rank, both unpalatable and low in nutrition, if allowed to grow unchecked. We can probably rule out the control of vegetation by fire, in this area, as there is a serious danger of a permanent peat fire.

The cropping of hay would have resulted in a much more intensive pattern of land use, and would have required a considerably greater investment of labour than would a system relying on naturally available winter fodder. It is hard to compare requirements from one case to another, as the climate, quality of hay, and size of beast are all highly variable. Nevertheless, it is probably fair to estimate that each animal will have required as much as a ton of hay to see it through the winter. A population primarily dependent on cattle pastoralism will thus have needed sufficient labour in the early summer to cut, make and transport very large amounts of hay. Even if horses or wheeled transport were available – and there is no evidence whatever that they were – this would have been a very considerable task, and the early summer would have been the busiest and most critical phase of the annual economic cycle. Transport of hay in Neolithic times may have been facilitated by the same means as it is today in some areas of northern Poland, where it is left stacked in the fields until the autumn freeze and then moved by sledge.

Thus in some senses the intensive cropping of hay has elements of similarity to the cultivation of cereals. In an area of very limited arable potential one might almost say that hay-making fulfils a comparable economic rôle and takes the same pre-eminence in the overall pattern of the economy. Through the investment of a considerable input of labour higher animal and human populations are maintained. As with most arable-based economies the system both permits and demands a degree of sedentism. Because labour and transport costs are high, there is a powerful incentive for the settlement to be located as close as possible to the most intensively utilised resources, in this case the prime hay fields. One might therefore expect there to have been a rudimentary zonation of land use. The main summer grazing for the cattle would have been towards the periphery of the territory (but probably in most cases within the effective radius for daily movement), the wet grazing adjacent to the site being reserved for hay. The drier sandy areas would have provided the critical resource of spring grazing before plant growth commenced in the wet grazing areas. The small arable element in the economy would also have been part of the exploitation pattern of the light sandy soils, probably in the area adjacent to the site.

Despite these analogies between two intensive forms of subsistence economy, it should be remembered that cereal-based agriculture usually has a far higher productive potential than has even the most intensive pastoralism. It is therefore scarcely surprising that Neolithic settlement in the loess areas of southern Poland appears to have been both earlier and consider-

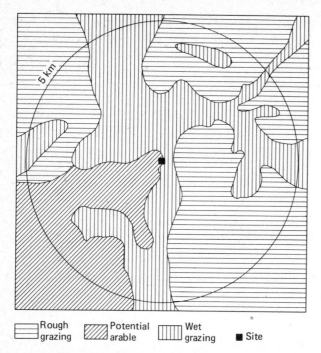

Figure 35. Site exploitation territory of Lubieszewo.

ably denser than that in the coastal region. Moreover, it seems probable that the growth of the basically sedentary economy that we have described in this latter area may have been a direct response to growing population pressures both within the area and elsewhere.

Despite an increasing dependence on arable exploitation (due partly to the greater emphasis on the hardier rye and barley, and partly to the use of the iron plough which permitted effective cultivation of much heavier soils than previously) wet grazing resources continued to be of primary importance throughout the prehistoric periods. In the Drawsko district the Bronze Age and mediaeval settlements are in locations very similar to those of the Neolithic sites discussed above: on light sandy soils adjacent to extensive areas of wet grazing. Some sites, like the La Tène sites of Juszkowo, Cieplewo, and Rozyny (Łuka & Pietrzak 1969, Pietrzak 1968, Podgórski 1971, Woźniak 1970) in the Gdańsk area, and the Roman and medieval Lubieszewo (Wołagíewicz 1970) are located at the junction of wet grazing and heavy fertile arable soils (Figure 35). The sites themselves are usually on patches of much lighter sandy soil, presumably for reasons of drainage. It should, of course, be remembered that the more intensive exploitation of the clays for arable purposes would itself have committed a substantial proportion of the grazing resources to the maintenance of plough teams, as up to eight beasts would have been required to draw a

mouldboard plough through the heavier soils. Indeed, in many cases the wet grazing potential of the marsh soils remains the dominant factor in their exploitation, although this pattern of land use is steadily giving way before the impact of mechanisation and continuing drainage of the wetlands.

NORDFRIESLAND

Neolithic economies comparable to those of coastal Poland developed in the very similar environment of Nordfriesland. Despite the unifying environmental factors, however, there are two crucial differences. The climate is more favourable to cereal agriculture than in Poland, the spring rainfall, in particular, being more plentiful, and usually sufficient to produce a reasonable yield. The strip of coastal marsh is wider and more continuous, and merges gradually into a muddy intertidal zone. This has the effect of making marine resources much less accessible and more expensive to exploit.

The effect of these differences is seen in the pattern of settlement distribution. The characteristic site location is at the junction of an area of wet grazing with light but relatively fertile soils. These latter are usually in small patches, often only 3–4 ha in extent, but their higher arable potential is shown by their higher modern cereal yields when compared with the adjacent sandier soils. Nevertheless, the economy seems, like that of

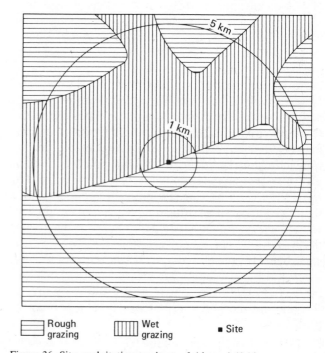

Figure 36. Site exploitation territory of Ahrenviolfeld.

coastal Poland, to have been primarily organised around the pastoral component. The favoured patches of arable soil only attracted settlement when adjacent to appreciable areas of wet grazing. Figure 36 illustrates a typical exploitation territory. The lowered value of marine resources is reflected in the smaller number of sites found adjacent to the coastal marshes. This may also be due in part to the prevalence of infertile sands immediately inland from the zone of salt-marsh, and the extreme exposure of the coast to the prevailing westerly winds. It is notable that sites here tend to be located on the more sheltered easterly facing slopes.

THE MEDITERRANEAN LITTORAL

The information available to us from the Mediterranean littoral is much less satisfactory than that from the other areas discussed in this chapter for a number of reasons. First and foremost the relative poverty of the marine environment has meant that there would have been less exploitation of marine resources. In particular, the shortage of edible shellfish has resulted in few durable and easily recognised shell middens. Many coastal occupations would have been ephemeral open sites with little chance of survival. The general lack of isostatic effects has meant that virtually all of the earlier postglacial coastline is submerged. Because of these limitations we have devoted little time to the study of the exploitation of this zone. There are, nonetheless, some hints that the factors discussed in northern Europe are relevant here, too.

The most striking point is that relatively few of the coastal sites appear to be primarily concerned with the exploitation of marine resources. Fish are generally scarce in the faunal collections, being far outnumbered by the bones of herbivores such as red deer and *Equus hydruntinus* in the earlier part of the Postglacial, and sheep and goat in the later part. Although detailed figures such as those used in the Danish section are not available, it is quite clear that herbivores were the dietary staples at such sites as Francthi Cave in Greece, Sidari on Corfu, Arene Candide in Italy, and Chateauneuf-lez-Martigues in France (except for the numerical dominance of the rabbit in the basal layer at the last site). Exploitation of shellfish such as cockles occurs widely, but rarely with any signs that they contributed a substantial proportion of the diet.

Occasional sites are found, as in northern Europe, which seem to have functioned as specialised locations for the exploitation of fish and molluscs. These, like the shell middens on the Ile de Rion and Ile Maire in the Bay of Marseilles, and the site of Coppa Nevigata in southern Italy, were almost certainly temporary camps occupied fleetingly over many years, and represent occasional inputs of a marine supplement to a basically terrestrial economy, rather than a population substantially dependent upon coastal resources. Even the site of Saliagos on Antiparos, which seems to give evidence of a sedentary community with an economy based to a large extent upon tunny fish, may be misleading in this context. Modern data on tunny migrations suggest that the fish would have been mainly available in the area in late spring or early summer (Bintliffe 1977), and that other resources would have been of prime importance at other times of the year. While it is quite possible that the fish may have been preserved and stored for use at other seasons, it seems equally likely that more use was made of the herbivores, particularly sheep and goat, than is suggested by the small available faunal collection.

The main importance of the Mediterranean littoral for prehistoric economies would thus have lain in its grazing potential. As a general rule this would have been at its best in winter, the dry summers resulting in dessication and cessation of plant growth for four or five months in many areas. The pattern of exploitation would thus have required considerable mobility, as stock and herders transhumed between the coasts and their summer grazing grounds in the uplands (Chapter 6).

Settlements are sometimes closely related to coastal lakes, lagoons, and marshland. This applies to the sites around the Étang de Berre near Marseilles, those on the Roman Maremma, and those around the Lago di Lèsina and the Lago di Varano in Apulia. It is possible that these represent the sedentary exploitation of restricted areas of favoured resources where the high water table maintains some plant growth throughout the year. This is the modern pattern in some cases. A number of considerations suggests that this was probably only a minor element in the exploitation system, if indeed it occurred at all. Firstly, we are unsure in many cases whether or not the relevant wetlands would have been in existence during the prehistoric occupations. Some will almost certainly have been created or greatly enlarged by such factors as the recent silting up of the lower valleys of rivers. Equally, while vegetation does continue to grow to some extent, in many cases the area of enhanced summer productivity is restricted, and its carrying capacity very small. Conversely, the Mediterranean uplands represent a huge area of summer grazing whose potential tends to be underexploited in many areas due to a deficiency of complementary lowland grazing for winter use. Finally, the Mediterranean coastal marshes are often unhealthy for both man and livestock in the summer due to the large number of insects and other parasites. While this is unlikely to have been the overriding constraint, it would certainly have been an added incentive to seasonal movement.

For these reasons it is more probable that the summer use of these areas was, at the most, small, and that the primary adaptation was summer transhumance to the uplands. The marshlands would, perhaps, have been most significant as suppliers of autumn grazing, before the main lowland period of vegetative growth, and in spring, before the move to the mountains.

We have already dealt in passing with a number of lakeside environments in our consideration of the coastal regions of Denmark and Poland. It was felt that in these areas coastal and lakeside habitats, and man's prehistoric exploitation of these, had so many factors in common that they were better dealt with together than separately. In some areas, however, the lakes appear to provide a focus of settlement worthy of analysis as a separate phenomenon, and we have chosen the sub-Alpine region of the Swiss–German border centred on the Bodensee, and the central Norrland of Sweden, as examples for study.

CENTRAL NORRLAND

Central Norrland is an area of about 72 000 km² which extends across the modern provinces of Västernorrland, Jämtland, and parts of Västerbotten and the

Figure 37. Regions of central Norrland.

Norwegian province of Tröndelag (Figure 37). Norrland as a whole has a characteristic taiga environment, with dense conifer forest mainly of pine (*Pinus sylvestris*) and spruce (*Picea abies*). The area shows extreme effects of glaciation, with numerous lakes, swamps, and waterways. The climate is severe, with short summers and long cold winters (mean annual temperature close to 0 °C), and heavy snow cover (>70 cm) from October until April (Wallén, Rodhe & Lindholm 1965). Central Norrland is primarily distinguished from the areas to the north and south by its spruce-dominated forests, lower and narrower mountain ranges, and more productive soils in the interior. Broad physiographic distinctions permit the division of Central Norrland into a number of regions (Figure 37): the mountains, the monadnock plateau (Interior A), plains and undulating hill country (Interior B), the low hill country with extensive pine heaths (Interior C), and the coastlands.

Resources

Like most arctic and subarctic environments, Central Norrland is poor in plant resources directly exploitable by man for food, and subsistence economies tend to be dominated by animal resources. Elk is by far the commonest of the native ungulates. Reindeer were uncommon in the area until the Iron Age (Baudou, personal communication) and red deer do not appear in the prehistoric faunal collections. The distribution and density of elk are profoundly influenced by the availability of deciduous trees, particularly willows. Willows form the bulk of the elk's diet except for brief periods in winter. They have a highly localised distribution, growing profusely in the enhanced light conditions at the edge of the conifer forest, particularly around the edges of lakes, swamps and waterways. Unusually rich ranges may carry as many as five to seven elk per 1000 ha, but densities of one to three animals per 1000 ha are more usual in the European taiga (Heptner *et al.* 1966). Hunting records from Central Norrland indicate that the average density for 1964–73 was about two to five elk per 1000 ha, although this figure will certainly have fluctuated in the past in response to hunting pressure and cyclic population fluctuations.

In North America, Norway, Finland and the U.S.S.R. elk have been shown to undertake seasonal migrations of 50–300 km in response to the availability of complementary browse resources, population pressure, and snow depth. Initial surveys (Andersson 1974, Hopfgarten 1975) indicate that the elk of Central Norrland are also seasonally mobile. Broadly speaking there seem to be two main elk populations in the region. One of these summers in the mountain region, moving down to the Interior A and the western fringe of the Interior B regions in winter. The other moves from its summer range in the hills to the outer coast and islands in winter.

The other principal terrestrial resource would have been beaver. This has been extinct in the area in recent historical times, prior to its recent reintroduction. Analogy with comparable environments in Sweden and America suggests that about 20 beaver per 1000 ha would be a reasonable estimate of prehistoric densities in Central Norrland. They are most easily taken and are at their fattest and best in winter. On the coast the ringed seal would have been available, most easily taken during pupping on the in-shore ice in the later winter and early spring. Salmon are available in the rivers, but the runs are comparatively small, and the rivers are in general too small for many of the fish to have travelled far upstream. The main run is in late summer.

The resident fish such as pike, trout and char, birds such as capercaillie and ptarmigan, and plant foods such as the cloudberries, appear to have had local and occasional importance in historical times, particularly as commercial crops. In no case, however, do they appear to have been of great importance on a regional scale or as staples.

Archaeological sites

The majority of sites in Central Norrland fall into one or another of two main categories. Approximately 1200 *boplatser* (settlement sites) are known from Central Norrland. Characteristically these are poorly stratified or unstratified scatters of stone and bone fragments. Dated sites are rare, but radiocarbon determinations suggest a continuous series from the seventh millennium b.p. down to the Roman or Viking period, or later. Technological change over this period seems essentially to have been limited to the development of a more refined technique of quartzite flaking and the introduction of asbestos-tempered pottery.

The other major category of site is the *fångstgrop*, or trapping pit. Well over 10 000 of these are known, and they seem to cover at least as long a period as the *boplatser*. They continued to be constructed until the second half of the nineteenth century, however, and many of those now known may be relatively recent.

The overwhelming impression is one of uniformity and continuity. Very similar kinds of site and technology are in evidence throughout, and the continuity extends also to site locations and economic evidence as far as the interior is concerned. In the coastal region the introduction of cereals initiated changes in settlement and economy from the mid-third millennium onwards. The *boplatser* are situated almost without exception on the banks of lakes and rivers. The *fångstgrop* is also most commonly found on waterways, particularly where these are narrow, or where deep swamp, topographic barriers, or other natural obstacles present an opportunity to control and direct animal movement. In Central Jämtland, where such situations are few, immense systems of pits have been constructed across the landscape. These are customarily oriented northeast–southwest, and are clearly designed to exploit animals moving at right angles to this axis, as elk do today in their seasonal migrations.

Subsistence

Our brief discussion of the available resources suggests that the economy is most likely to have been based upon the exploitation of elk, with beaver as the next most important resource, and seal perhaps being of some significance on the coast. In view of the invariable waterside location of settlement sites, however, we should perhaps first look a little more closely at the aquatic resources, particularly fish.

While Central Norrland is not especially rich in the migratory species, the trout, char, grayling, pike, perch and bream are abundant in the innumerable lakes and rivers. Moreover, the settlements are most frequently found in locations favourable for fishing: at the inlets and outlets of lakes, on points or islands, or where tributaries meet. Viewed more broadly, however, there seems to be little evidence that availability of fish influenced site location or the overall distribution of population. Probably the best fishing locations of all along the rivers are found at the foot of falls and rapids. Yet many rapids have no known sites nearby; and of the 192 *boplatser* known on the Ångerman river between Nämforsen and Vilhelmina, only 10 per cent are found within 1 km of rapids of falls, and most of these are above rather than below the feature in question. Similarly, the overall distribution of settlements seems to bear an inverse rather than a direct relationship to fishing resources (Figure 38). The richest fisheries are in the 80 km or so coastal strip, where the fewest settlements are found. The mountains – the second richest region for fish resources – have more settlements, but the greatest number comes from the interior hills and monadnock plateau, the region poorest in fish resources.

The on-site data are similarly discouraging to any

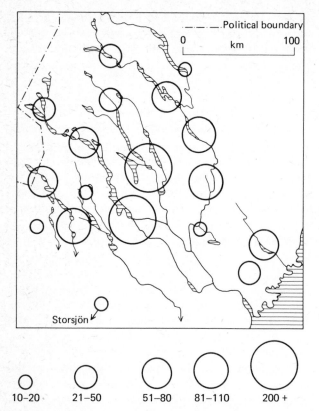

Figure 38. Density of settlement sites in Central Norrland.

hypothesis that fish were exploited as a staple. While we must always bear in mind the possibility of poor preservation, recovery, or recognition of fishing equipment and of fish bones, it remains true that these are conspicuously rare in the Central Norrland sites. There are almost no unequivocal fishing artefacts from our area, and fishbone occurs in only 15 of the 74 available faunal collections (Anderson 1976). Even where they occur, fish are relatively rare in the collections, seldom amounting to more than a few individuals per site. At Ställverket, nine salmon and three other fish count for about half of the estimated meat yield represented by the faunal collection, but in no other case does fish account for more than about 1 per cent of the estimated yield.

The possibility that fish bones were discarded elsewhere is unlikely, both on the grounds that some bones have been found, and also because the identifications were mainly made on cranial parts (Iregren, n.d.) suggesting that preparation occurred on the site. Removal of bone from the region in dried fish used for trade is also unlikely. The Gulf of Bothnia, although it is a poor marine environment, is more productive than any of the inland waters and has many of the same species. The most likely possibility is that fish bones are

rare in sites because the returns from fishing are far lower than from other economic activities. In historical times, for example, the yield of fresh pike meat from eight weeks summer fishing in the best pike waters of the Ume valley was only equivalent to about two elk carcasses (Campbell 1948). More generally, ethnographic evidence suggests that throughout the circumpolar arctic and taiga regions fishing was often regarded as inferior to hunting or reindeer husbandry (Eidlitz 1969). The increased importance of fishing among the Kemi Lapps seems to have been a response to the loss of good reindeer and beaver lands to the invading Finnish farmers (Tegengren 1952).

It seems then that, while fish were doubtless taken where available and may have influenced site location where other factors were equal, they were a relatively minor resource, and that their exploitation had little or no impact on most site locations or on the general distribution of population. This by no means rules out the possibility of their significant exploitation as a critical resource in times of shortage.

Although there is much less available evidence, the situation as regards the place of wildfowl in the economy seems to have been similar. Birds occur in only 11 faunal collections, representing a maximum of two individuals per site. Capercaillie and black grouse are the commonest species, while the ducks and divers which were in historical times taken in large numbers by mass driving (Storå 1968) are rare. It is also worth noting that birds, which figure so prominently in the rock art of eastern Finland and northwestern Russia, are very rare in the art of Norrland.

The hypothesis of an economy based primarily upon elk is supported by a number of arguments. The deciduous forage which provides the prime grazing for elk throughout most of the year is at its most abundant around lakes and rivers, and to a lesser extent in the marshes. Those situations chosen for site location are frequently the favoured crossing places of elk, narrow points of lakes and rivers, inflow and outflow areas where the treacherous thin ice forms later and breaks up earlier, and so on. It is noticeable that trapping pits tend also to be concentrated at those points. It is also true that there is a close relationship between settlement density and areas particularly rich in deciduous browse. Figure 39 plots, for one small area, site density against the distribution of water edge distance, a good measure of availability of this resource. It is clear that there is a strong positive correlation between the two phenomena.

Elk is the commonest species in the archaeological sites. It appears in 45 of the available collections, and

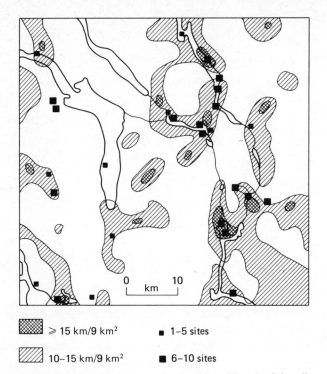

≥ 15 km/9 km²   ■ 1–5 sites

10–15 km/9 km²   ■ 6–10 sites

Figure 39. Relationship between site density and length of shoreline in Central Norrland.

parallel with a lake shore or river, a little way back from the bank. Two hour territories commonly have a maximum radius of only 5–6 km, and territories average 29 km². ranging from 12–54 km².

The small size of these territories, the largest of which are likely to have been regularly exploitable on foot from the sites in question, poses something of a problem. We may assume conservatively that elk provided 75 per cent of the calories in the diet; if we assume further (1) that elk density in prehistory was approximately the same as that of today, (2) that a sustained cropping rate of 25 per cent was achieved in prehistory, (3) that territories were providing on average the subsistence requirements of a family of five, and (4) that the seasonal movements of the elk will have imposed similar movements on their exploiters, each settlement thus representing one half year's rather than a full year's subsistence, then it can be calculated that the minimum area needed to supply the requisite number of elk is greatly in excess of the exploitation territories postulated on the basis of field research. The arguments and figures involved are set out in full by Anderson (1976). The *required territories* vary in size from 190 km² to 78 km² according to the environment and the season.

There are a number of possible explanations of this. The first of these is that our basic theory of exploitation territories is wrong or that our methodology is inadequate. In view of the overwhelming considerations in favour of the general theory, discussed in Chapter 2, and in view of the substantial success which the method has met in many other case studies, we reject this suggestion. A second possibility is that the economy may have been forced by the poverty of the resources to be much more mobile, with more than two home bases being employed annually, thus expanding the annual territory.

We should also bear in mind the possibility that elk densities were raised, and that through some form of controlled relationship the efficiency of exploitation was substantially increased. Modern experiments (Wilkinson 1975) show that this is perfectly possible, and we must also remember the historical records of the use of elk for riding and draught purposes. There are, furthermore, suggestive representations in prehistoric art, including one carving at Nämforsen which, while ambiguous, might well be interpreted as the herding or control of some 40 elk by a group of men. Against this hypothesis it must be admitted that elk densities under natural conditions could well have fallen, from time to time, still lower than those suggested above, and that the ubiquitous *fångstgrop* suggests an economy with at

accounts for more than 90 per cent of the meat weight represented in the Central Norrland faunas. Elk are similarly predominant in the art sites. They occur in 99 per cent of the animal carvings at Nämforsen, and are probably the only species represented in the other Norrland art sites (R. Hensen, personal communication). As is well known from the immense body of historical and ethnographic evidence, the elk retained its economic significance beyond the prehistoric period.

In the winter, at least, beaver would have been an important, if secondary, resource. It occurs in 28 faunal collections, and while its dietary contribution in terms of meat weight was probably not large, it will have played a crucial rôle in the winter economy. At this time of year it is the only inland species providing a substantial amount of fat, of critical importance in the northern winter. Seal will no doubt have fulfilled the same need in coastal areas.

Territories

Thirty-seven sites were subjected to territorial analysis. The territories are for the most part small and distorted due to the difficulty of movement on foot in the heavily forested environment with its frequent lakes, marshes and watercourses. Movement is generally easiest

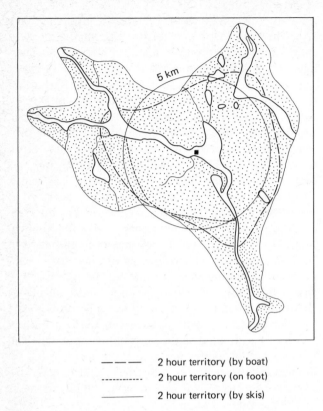

——— 2 hour territory (by boat)
············· 2 hour territory (on foot)
——— 2 hour territory (by skis)

Figure 40. Site exploitation territory of Bellsås.

Table 11. Walking, boating, and skiing territories (km²)

Site	Walking	Boating	Skiing
Frostviken	42	106 (250)	not applicable
Vilhelmina T238	52	95 (180)	not applicable
Vilhelmina 654	30	70 (230)	148 (490)
Åsele	28	70 (250)	123 (440)
Hoting	26	85 (320)	152 (580)
Lesjön	20	58 (290)	126 (630)
Tröms	54	92 (170)	151 (280)
Junsele	37	78 (210)	125 (330)

Figures in brackets represent percentage increase in territory size over walking territory. (Frostviken and Vilhelmina T238 assumed not to be occupied in winter.)

best occasional and rudimentary measures of control and husbandry.

The fourth and most plausible hypothesis takes us back to a reconsideration of the territorial evidence. It is, perhaps, most unlikely that movement would have been exclusively on foot. There is excellent evidence for the prehistoric use of skis, and fair indications that water craft would have been available and in use as well. Although it is difficult to estimate precisely the advantages involved, it is certain that both skiing and canoeing would have been considerably faster and more efficient in this environment than walking (Anderson 1976). Using the fairly conservative estimate of average speeds of 4 km/h by boat and 7 km/h by ski, we have mapped the territories accessible from the site at Bellsås (Figure 40). It can be seen that these alternative forms of travel have a dramatic impact on the size of the exploitation territory, raising it from 23 km² to 76 km² (by boat) and 139 km² (by ski). Figures for other territories are shown in Table 11.

Annual territories and economic niches

The seasonal extremes of the climate, relatively unproductive environment, and the mobility of the primary economic staple all suggest that human economic adaptation must have included an element of mobility. Ethnographic data from comparable environments in northern Fennoscandia and from North America lend support to the view. It is much more difficult to be sure about the size and shape of annual territories, or about the precise ways in which the various seasonal resources were integrated. It is possible to argue with Clark, J. G. D. (1975) that a late winter–early spring coastal occupation, concentrating on sealing, was followed by a gradual movement inland, following the migratory fish up river. By autumn or early winter the groups would have reached the interior forests for winter exploitation of elk and the fur-bearing animals.

A number of points suggest a more complex picture, however. As was mentioned above, there are two substantially separate elk populations in Central Norrland, an inland one which migrates from the mountains to the Interior A region, and a more coastal one. It seems possible that there might equally be two human populations, each primarily dependent upon one of the two elk populations. The theoretical arguments in favour of such a system are substantial (see Chapter 3). There are indeed sites in the mountain region which would probably have been summer bases, for the most part. The elk move down from the mountains which are low in available resources in winter. Clark's hypothesis may also undervalue the important winter resource of beaver, which would probably have been most abundant in the Interior B region (R. Brändtröm, personal communication). It seems quite likely, therefore, that there were two major foci of winter occupation; one on the coast, with a population mainly dependent upon seal and elk; the other in the interior, its population mainly dependent upon beaver and elk. In the summer the human communities would have dispersed more widely, as the elk themselves are spread more widely through Central Norrland at this season. The fish resources would also be widely distributed in summer. So far the only possible archaeological substantiation for this reconstruction comes from Baudou (1973), who has argued that there may be evidence from burial customs that there were separate inland and coastal groups in existence by Bronze Age times, and in an area of such environmental and economic continuity it would be scarcely surprising if the patterns of population distribution and movement proved equally stable.

Long-term perspectives

The Norrland environment, with low temperatures, long winters, dense forest, and infertile soils, imposes severe limitations on any farming economy. Records of pioneer farming in the historical period show that successful agricultural settlement depended primarily on cattle husbandry and naturally occurring resources, and that site locations were chosen for access to natural marshes and water meadows from which hay crops could be cut as animal fodder for the long winter months (Campbell 1948).

The early evidence for prehistoric crop agriculture is confined to the coastal region, where pollen records show the introduction of barley between about 2500 b.c. and 2000 b.c. (Huttunen & Tolonen 1972, Königsson 1970). Sheep were also probably introduced in small numbers at this period. Even here the new economic elements appear to have been subordinated to the seasonal requirements of fur trapping and more especially seal hunting, and the principal impetus for this northward expansion of agriculture may well have been the extension of the habitat of the ringed seal (Broadbent 1978, Christiansson & Broadbent 1975).

Although there are considerably more coastal settlements during the Bronze Age, the principal emphasis of the economy remained essentially unchanged with hunting and fishing as the main occupations (Baudou 1968). It is only in the later Iron Age and Viking periods that there begin to appear permanent settlements with a substantial dependence on crop agriculture and a preferential selection for the best available arable soils such as the alluvial silts of the coastlands or the lime-rich soils of central Jämtland. With the exception of the Storsjön settlement in the latter area, however, agricultural economies were confined almost exclusively to coastal Norrland until the mediaeval

period, and they continued to depend, as before, on a substantial element of fishing and trapping.

In the interior region the elk–beaver economy persisted with little change until the later Iron Age. From this time on the progressive encroachment of farming communities, and the increased demand for beaver skins created by market economies external to Norrland, resulted in progressive depletion of elk and beaver supplies. This in its turn was probably a major factor in the development of the characteristic Lappish type of economy based on reindeer husbandry and fishing. These economies seem to have developed in the northern part of the interior regions by the eleventh century, if not earlier, and reflect above all the development of fish and reindeer milk as substitutes for the traditional supplies of elk meat and beaver fat, as a result of external economic competition.

We seem thus to have evidence of the spread of various kinds of controlled exploitation into a marginal area as a consequence of economic developments elsewhere. The arable agricultural exploitation of Norrland seems always to have been intimately associated with the trapping of fur-bearing animals, and may indeed only have been viable in this context. Conversely, the higher productivity of the arable economy permitted an expansion and intensification of the fur trade. This, with the sustained market forces operating from outside the area, doubtless contributed to the eventual depletion and final extinction of the beaver, and the spread of reindeer husbandry as an alternative.

A broadly comparable picture is gained from other areas around the Gulf of Bothnia and the Gulf of Finland. Recent research into prehistoric economic development in Estonia, Latvia, and southwest Finland (Zvelebil 1978 and personal communication) indicates that elk, beaver, and seal were the staple resources from the earliest postglacial occupation until at least the first two centuries A.D., and that exploitation of these naturally available resources remained of great importance until mediaeval times. Despite the overwhelming preference for site locations on lakes, rivers, and coasts, fish rarely if ever approached the status of staples.

One observation of interest was the evidence of long-term size decrease in the elk, a phenomenon most marked at those sites where this species was of the greatest economic importance. This trend continued until the second millennium b.c., and was then reversed. There are many possible reasons for such size changes (Higgs & Jarman 1969, Jarman, M. R. 1976b, Jarman, M. R. & Wilkinson 1972), among them the effects of climatic change or of worsening browse conditions. We must not forget, however, that size decrease is a frequent concomitant of certain kinds of animal husbandry, and that small individual body size may carry substantial economic advantages, particularly where there are severe seasonal shortages of fodder.

Although barley appeared as early as the mid third millennium, it made little general economic impact until the first two centuries A.D. At this time there was a switch of some site locations to the lighter of the more fertile morainic soils, away from the waterways. The potential of arable crops is severely limited by the climate, with drought frequent in the growing season, rain in the ripening season, and frosts at harvest time. Even barley is thus far too risky a crop to be cultivated as a staple, despite its relatively high productivity in good years.

The main trends of economic intensification relate to the increasing importance of cattle and sheep pastoralism. These can be maintained at 50–100 times the stocking rate of elk, and thus represent a vastly more productive exploitation system. The main limitation is the supply of winter fodder, and the small arable element in the economy was as much concerned with the mitigation of this constraint as with the direct production of cereals for human consumption.

THE BODENSEE

The Alpine and sub-Alpine region of Europe as a whole suffers in an extreme form from the economic limitations of the European uplands. Winters are both cold and snowy. Plant growth ceases altogether for five to six months, and is concentrated in the three months from June to August when warm temperatures promote rapid growth. Steep slopes and high altitudes with their attendant handicaps of poor soil development, poor insolation in many areas, and high transport costs present additional disadvantages. Modern settlement, in consequence, is concentrated in the favoured valley bottoms and on south-facing slopes with good insolation.

The Bodensee (Figure 41) lies at 400 m altitude on the northern margins of the main Alpine block. While it is climatically less extreme than much of the area, it partakes of its general character. Annual precipitation increases from an average of 750 mm at Radolfzell in the northwest to 1500 mm at Bregenz in the southeast. Although much depends on the additional factors of annual distribution of rainfall, evapotranspiration, and drainage, wheat and barley do not generally prosper where annual rainfall exceeds 900 mm. Flax, another frequent Neolithic crop in this area, does not generally

tolerate annual rainfall greater than 750 mm. Thus despite the fact that the Neolithic climate may have been slightly drier and warmer than at present (Sakellaridis 1978), it seems that the area would have been marginal for Neolithic arable agriculture. Average temperatures today range from about −1 °C in January to 18 °C in July, but the point of main significance here is that with only 170–200 frost-free days (Knock 1953), the growing season is necessarily compressed within a relatively short period.

We must take account, however, of the impact of the thermal properties of the lake itself on the climate of its immediate environs. The Bodensee has, indeed, been described as a 'climatic oasis', notable especially for its mild winters (Dickinson 1961). Figure 41 shows the relationship of these climatic effects to the lake. The lake shore as a whole represents a distinctive climatic zone with the smallest diurnal and seasonal temperature range of the region at large. Winter temperatures are on average 1–2 °C warmer on the lake edge, giving a longer growing season with fewer days of frost, and relatively little serious snow cover. These advantages are particularly pronounced on the immediate edge of the water and show a sharp fall-off over quite short distances away from the lake. Within this shore zone the northwest portion is the driest, with average annual rainfall less than 1000 mm, and this area would thus be the most favourable for crop agriculture.

Palynological evidence (Bertsch 1928, Müller 1947) suggests that during the Mesolithic and early Neolithic periods the vegetation would have been dominated by a mixed oak forest community up to about 600 m, with pine, fir and spruce at higher altitudes. More open conditions along the lake shore are indicated by high pollen frequencies of hazel, but extensive natural breaks in the woodland are likely to have been confined to those regions above the tree line (about 1500 m today, but probably slightly higher during the altithermal) or to areas with poor soil cover.

Site location and distribution

The lake basins of southern Germany and Switzerland have attracted settlement from Mesolithic times to the present day. In Switzerland some 367 Neolithic sites are known from the shores of the large glacial lakes, and an additional 97 from the small moraine lakes (Sakellaridis 1978). It is true that their waterlogged condition may have resulted in an unusually good level of archaeological recovery, and that their apparent predominance in the distribution pattern may thus be exaggerated. On the other hand, detailed surveys in other areas have

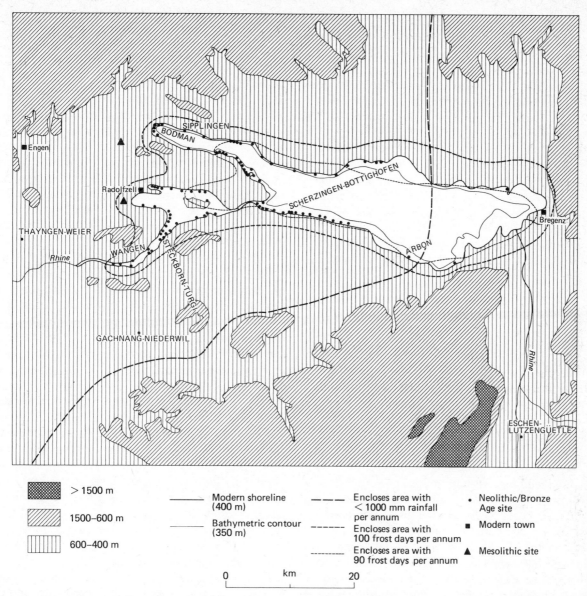

Figure 41. Distribution of archaeological sites in the Bodensee region, showing the relationship with topography, temperature and rainfall.

revealed the existence of sites on river banks and hill tops, demonstrating that these do exist in recognisable form. Although they are quite numerous, their small size and relative artefactual poverty seem to indicate that they were of lesser importance. Many of the Neolithic lake settlements continued in occupation in later prehistoric periods, especially on the large glacial lakes, and indeed pile dwellings are still built on the lake edge at the present day.

About 58 Mesolithic lake-side sites are known from the Bodensee (Reinerth 1931). The lake has receded from the Mesolithic shoreline, so that nothing has survived except the flint artifacts. We thus know little of the precise nature of the settlements, although the distribution of the flints has been claimed to indicate hut outlines. About 110 Neolithic sites are known. Many have been disturbed by wave movement and few are well excavated. The commonest culture represented is the Pfyn, regarded as a distinctive grouping peculiar to the Bodensee region (Driehaus 1960, Winiger 1971). Material of the later Horgen and Corded Ware culture is also present, along with some Bronze Age remains.

Apart from the considerable increase in numbers of Neolithic sites, which may as always be partly a result of archaeological visibility, there is a most striking change in the site distribution (Figure 41). Almost all the Mesolithic sites are concentrated on shallow bays which formerly existed at the northwest end of the lake. Neolithic sites also tend to concentrate at the northwest end, but are distributed far more generally along the lake margins. A similar pattern is discernible in data from elsewhere in sub-Alpine Switzerland and Germany. Mesolithic sites are invariably confined to the small, shallow moraine lakes such as the Burgäschisee in Switzerland, or the Federsee in southern Germany, to the shallow bays of the large glacial lakes, such as the Zugersee, or to marshy regions adjoining the large lakes such as the Grosses Moos of Lake Neuchatel (Sakellaridis 1978). Neolithic sites, while they frequently occur in the same or similar locations, are also distributed more widely and in more varied settings.

Neolithic site location and distribution

One obvious aspect of the overall pattern of Neolithic settlement is the close correspondence with the zone of favoured climatic conditions. The sites are clustered almost without exception in the zone of lower rainfall. Within this zone there is a further preference for the lake edge itself and thus for the mildest winter conditions (Figure 41).

These factors suggest that cereal cultivation may have been a significant element in the economy, and substantial seed remains have indeed been excavated at Sipplingen (Reinerth 1938), Wangen (Neuweiler 1905), and the Steckborn sites (Hartmann 1884). Finds include emmer, einkorn, hexaploid wheat (both club wheat and bread wheat), six-row barley, broomcorn millet, and flax. The Neolithic climate, even though it may have been warmer and drier than now, would still have been marginal for successful cereal cultivation and is unlikely to have reduced the significance of the small advantages offered by the microclimate around the northwestern shores of the lake. The presence and in some cases predominance of barley, club wheat, and millet also points to the importance of climatic variables as limiting factors. Millet with its short growing season, and barley and club wheat with their well-known tolerance of cold and wet growing conditions, are well adapted to such marginal climatic conditions.

Another general attraction of the lake-shore environment would have been the vegetation. Palynological evidence and modern analogy suggest that vegetation would have been more open along the lake margins. This would both have lessened the labour costs of clearance for cereal cultivation and would also have resulted in a richer growth of shrubs and plants offering a variety of resources for human and animal consumption. Bowls of hazelnuts, raspberries, pears and apples were recovered from the site of Wangen, as well as layers of apple seeds and other wild fruits and nuts, while a total of some 180 naturally occurring plant-food species were identified at Sipplingen.

The best of the arable soils are also generally to be found in the vicinity of the lake shore, although this is more a matter of topography and climate than of strictly pedological variables. Within the region as a whole the soils are mostly silts and loamy clays laid down by the Würm glacier. These would have been less favourable than loess for Neolithic cultivators, both in terms of fertility and tractability, but the lighter soils would not be seriously limiting in either respect except in the restricted areas of waterlogging. Then as now the principal limitations would have been steep topography and unfavourable climate. Thus the flat margins, low altitude, and mild climate of the lake shore offer significant advantages over the more steeply undulating and cooler hinterland.

These environmental variables would also have had an impact on animal resources. The milder climate of the lake edge would have been particularly important for livestock in the critical months of food shortage in winter and early spring by reducing snow cover and advancing the onset of the growing season, features which would also have attracted free-ranging deer and pig populations to the lake shore at this season. The more open vegetation along the forest edge would also have provided a richer growth of browse and grazing resources than within the forest canopy, and the water plants and wet grazing along the lake margins would have been an added attraction.

Lake-side locations also offer easy access to fish and other lacustrine resources. Nets, harpoons, and other fishing gear attest exploitation of these, but here as in so many other areas there is remarkably little evidence for a systematic exploitation. Very few fish bones are found in the faunal collections; a single pike bone occurs amongst 1556 identified specimens at Sipplingen (Vogel 1933). Pike bones and fish scales were also recovered at Steckborn-Turgi and Schanz, but they are not abundant here or elsewhere among the lake-side villages of the sub-Alpine zone. In some cases the paucity of fish bones may have been partly due to the inadequacies of excavation, but this cannot explain the evidence from Molino Casarotto (see p. 130), for example, where excavation was careful and where large samples of deposit were sieved and subjected to froth flotation. It may be noted that on the Bodensee the most productive fishing waters are the shallow bays of the Überlinger See and Unter See (Kiefer 1955), where the majority of sites are clustered. The correlation may be incidental to other factors, however, since this is also the zone of favoured climate. As ever, we cannot exclude with certainty the possibility that aquatic resources exerted some pressure on site location, but in general they seem to have been little used, and to have constituted a supplementary attraction rather than a major focus of exploitation.

A similar comment seems appropriate to suggestions that the requirements of defence, trade, or communication may have been key factors. None can be ruled out as a possibility, but none is supported by a significant body of evidence. Water transport was certainly in use, to judge from the archaeological remains, and may well have been a favoured means of movement for people and goods. This will not, however, necessarily have been a sufficient reason for lake-side site locations if the economy was based on the exploitation of terrestrial resources.

It seems that in this case we may make a useful distinction between factors which affect the broad pattern of settlement distribution, and those which relate to the precise locations of sites. A whole range of basic environmental and economic factors discussed above ensures that the immediate environs of the Bodensee are both more easily exploitable and have a higher inherent productive potential than the hills and mountains which surround it, and it is thus scarcely surprising that the lake basin should have attracted early and relatively dense settlement.

It is less easy to arrive at a satisfactory explanation of why Neolithic and subsequent settlements were characteristically situated not just close to the lake but in all likelihood on the very edge of the lake itself, frequently on boggy, unstable ground. The building and maintenance of pile dwellings and of wooden trackways to the dry land must surely have involved much higher labour costs than would the erection of adequate buildings of similar size 100 m or so further from the lake on *terra firma*. Over such short distances the economic advantages of being close to the lake itself, or to the zone of wet grazing, seem most unlikely to have been sufficient to outweigh the disadvantages resulting from the additional construction costs. Another suggestion is that arable soils were of limited extent because of forest cover and steep slopes. Thus settlements were built on the uncultivable lake margin in order to leave free the maximum area for plots of cereals (Sauter 1976). This, while it may have been a contributory factor, is difficult to see as the primary cause in view of the apparent

capacity of Neolithic farmers to clear forest by cutting or burning wherever economic circumstances demanded. Nor can topography be invoked as a limiting factor at many sites, as can be seen from the site territories presented later in this chapter. On the other hand, the additional labour costs of clearing areas for settlement as well as cultivation in a forested environment may have been sufficient to counterbalance the added costs of building and maintaining wooden dwellings on boggy ground (Vogt 1957).

There are, in fact, insufficient data to support adequately or to eliminate any of the possible hypotheses. If, as is probable, the precise site location represents the cumulative effects of a number of factors which may have small individual significance, then it may never be possible to answer the question convincingly. In the mountainous and forested environment water transport may well have been considerably more efficient in many areas than movement on land, and this may have been one of the more important factors. We should also remember that the thermal properties of the lake will have been most pronounced at the lake edge itself, and that even a distance of a few hundred metres may have made a significant difference. During January and December the temperature of the lake water is some 5 °C higher than the air temperature on the lake shore (Kiefer 1955). However, this is a less plausible argument in the many cases of settlements on smaller lakes, as these smaller bodies of water have a much reduced potential for heat storage.

Neolithic territories and economy

We may now examine more closely the economic potential available to lake-side settlements. The exploitation territory of Sipplingen (Figure 42) provides an example. Movement inland is severely restricted by the steep slopes which rise from the lake shore. It can be seen that, while a relatively large proportion (57 per cent) of the 1 hour territory (excluding the opposite shore) would have been suitable for arable agriculture in Neolithic times from the point of view of soil quality, much of this would have been at some distance from the site, towards the edge of the territory. Most of the modern crops (primarily potatoes, maize, and other fodder crops) are grown on the gently undulating plateau on the heights above the lake shore at a distance of some 20 minutes from the site. It is possible that this was also the area used by the Neolithic population for arable agriculture. Instances are certainly recorded where fields lie more than 20 minutes from the main habitation. Hillman (1973) has documented

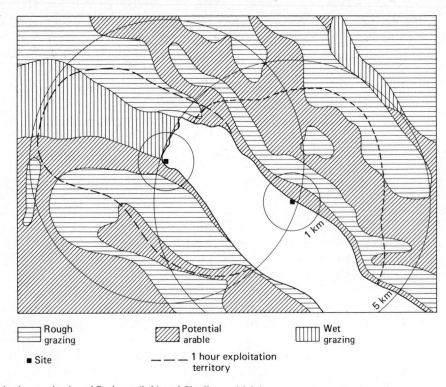

Figure 42. Site exploitation territories of Bodman (left) and Sipplingen (right).

some of the ways in which Turkish villagers cut the costs of cultivating distant fields by not irrigating or manuring them, by a longer fallow period, by fewer ploughings with horses instead of oxen, and by living in temporary shelters in the fields during labour-intensive periods such as harvesting. In this latter case, the farmers are in effect creating a new exploitation territory which brings the distant fields within the economic 10 minute radius. For several reasons it seems more likely that the land actually used as arable at the time would in general have been confined to the strip of flat ground along the lake edge, the slopes and plateau carrying pasture or woodland. The increase, with increasing distance, of the labour and transport costs of cereal cultivation would have been such that, had the plateau been extensively cultivated, we would expect some settlements on the plateau itself, for which there is no evidence. Furthermore, as we have discussed, the microclimate of the area is such that the increased altitude of the plateau and its greater distance from the lake would have resulted in some deterioration in a climate already marginal from the point of view of cereal agriculture. The effective actual arable area for Sipplingen would probably have been much smaller, about 13 per cent of the terrestrial territory.

The other key resource would have been the ground exposed along the lake margins by lowered water level at the time of occupation. This is, of course, now submerged so that its resource potential cannot be directly assessed. However, whatever cereal potential it may have had would have been severely limited by the high water table. The modern situation and the pile structure of the prehistoric settlements suggest an environment sufficiently boggy to rule out affective cereal cultivation. Wheat and barley in particular are especially susceptible to lodging on waterlogged ground. It is true that the height of the water table fluctuates seasonally by as much as 2 m, but it normally reaches its peak in early summer (Collet 1922), when the crop is especially vulnerable. On the other hand, flax and broomcorn millet, both recorded in archaeological deposits, are shallow-rooting plants better able to thrive on the higher water table near the lake edge. However, cereal cultivation of these waterlogged conditions is likely to have been at best patchy, and a more plausible overall use of them would have been as wet grazing. Indeed, the grazing potential of the lake edge is likely to have been generally high, given the better conditions of light penetration at the edge of the woodland. The slopes themselves and the plateau were probably fairly heavily wooded, and while they provided browse and a wide variety of casual resources, they would have had a comparatively low economic potential per unit area. The large proportion of this

124

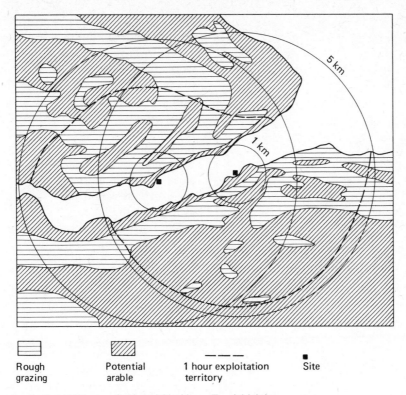

Figure 43. Site exploitation territories of Wangen (left) and Steckborn-Turgi (right).

land use category in the territory, however, may well have meant that its contribution to the economy was considerable.

The faunal data from the site (Vogel 1933) reflect this territorial reconstruction. The commonest species is the pig, which would have been run for the most part in the forested areas away from the lake. Pigs make more effective use of forest than do cattle, which are the other main livestock represented in the fauna. These would presumably have been pastured mainly in the wet grazing area along the lake edge. Sheep are present only in small numbers (8–10 per cent of the identified specimens) as is to be expected in the forested and relatively damp environment. These would have grazed the open areas along the lake edge and any clearings which may have existed on higher ground in the hinterland. The low proportion of red deer (5–7 per cent) is perhaps surprising in view of the wooded environment and when one remembers the staple rôle of the species in the economy of such sites as Burgäschisee Süd (Boessneck, Jéquier & Stampfli 1963). It may perhaps be significant that the steep ridge behind the site denies easy access from the hinterland to the lake at this point. The substantial red deer population which must undoubtedly have existed in the hinterland may generally have sought access to the lake-side

grazing in areas with more gentle topography. On the other hand, it must be remembered that here, as elsewhere (Jarman, M. R. 1972b, 1976b), there would have been a chronological as well as an environmental component to the economic system, and that we have as yet insufficient evidence to pursue this point satisfactorily.

A similar territorial pattern is indicated at Wangen and Steckborn-Turgi (Figure 43). Both have yielded evidence of cereal cultivation, but as at Sipplingen the area of effective arable would have been confined by a steeply sloping hinterland. A similar example of this effect can be seen at Bodman in dem Wiler (Figure 42). The area of potential arable is partly limited by steep slopes and marshy ground. None of these sites, however, would be completely excluded from practising cereal cultivation, if only on a small scale, although the major emphasis must in all cases have been on animal resources.

About 30 of the Bodensee sites have territories closely similar to that of Sipplingen, but rather more than this number have a more even hinterland, and thus a less distorted territory. Figure 44 shows the territory of Scherzingen-Bottighofen, characteristic of this type. There is, however, no evidence that the easily accessible arable land of the hinterland was of sufficient

125

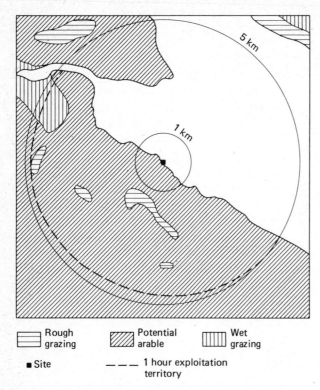

Rough grazing

Potential arable

Wet grazing

■ Site

— — — 1 hour exploitation territory

Figure 44. Site exploitation territory of Scherzingen-Bottighofen.

potential to attract settlement away from the lake-edge location, although a move of about 1 km inland so as to maximise the quantity of potential arable soils within the 10 minute territory could have been achieved without detracting seriously from the exploitation of the lake-side resources. This reinforces our argument that, in so marginal an area for cereals, the climatic deterioration involved in even a small movement away from the lake was sufficient to discourage settlement of the plateau lands. Thus as at sites with the Sipplingen type of territory the area of effective arable exploitation would have been confined to the immediate vicinity of the lake. The apparent increase in arable potential is largely illusory, the more open territories representing rather a slightly increased potential in woodland grazing resources.

The general picture is thus one of a concentration of settlement and exploitation in the narrow band of high productivity potential between the lake itself and the foot of the steep slopes. This represents both the best of the arable resources, for climatic and topographic reasons, and the best of the grazing resources, for climatic reasons and because of the improved conditions of light penetration. How much use would actually have been made of the lower potential areas towards the territorial peripheries must remain conjectural,

although they doubtless were exploited as extensive grazing, and for hunting and gathering, as the lake itself seems to have been. It is most likely that the system would have reduced as far as possible the pressure upon the high-potential lake-side grazing during summer, in order to preserve this for the long winter period of zero plant growth. This would have involved the exploitation as far as possible of the poorer hinterland grazing throughout the summer. The stock may well have been separated in summer into a milking herd (pastured close to the home base) and the rest of the cattle and sheep which would have been taken to graze further away from the lake.

Despite the territorial preponderance of grazing resources, it is notable that all the sites have immediate access to a potentially arable soil on the lake edge. The vast majority of the sites, and all of those with substantial evidence of cereals, are clustered in the zone of lowest rainfall at the west end of the lake. Even here, however, the marginal climate for cereals would have made the cultivation of crops a high-risk enterprise, and the staples throughout the region must surely have been the animal resources. It is indeed quite possible that the arable exploitation was viewed primarily as a way of intensifying the production of fodder, as is mainly the case today. The low values of cereal pollen in the pollen diagrams may provide some support for this interpretation.

Annual territories and economic niches

We have so far considered the economic organisation of these sites as if they had been permanently occupied settlements operating an essentially sedentary economy. This might initially seem improbable, bearing in mind our arguments regarding unevenly distributed resources and human mobility (Chapter 2). The position of the Bodensee in this context is somewhat ambiguous. The region is certainly at its best and offers its highest economic potential in summer, winter being the lean season. It is also true, however, that because of its climatic effect the Bodensee offers the best winter conditions for some considerable distance. Thus one might argue that it was either the summer area for groups wintering elsewhere – perhaps in the Rhine and Danube valleys, or that on the contrary it was the winter base of populations exploiting the high Alpine pastures in summer.

In practice we are arguing that neither of these was the case in general. The economies of the Rhine and Danube valleys, although they almost certainly included a mobile element (see Chapter 5), would have

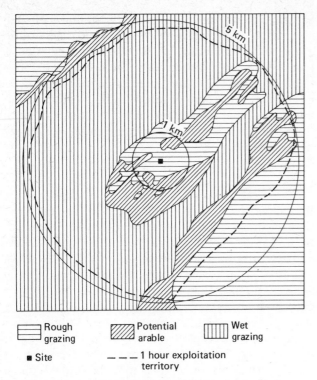

Rough grazing

Potential arable

Wet grazing

■ Site

— — — 1 hour exploitation territory

Figure 45. Site exploitation territory of Eschen-Lutzengüetle.

had ample summer grazing nearer their home bases, such as the Schwabische and Frankische Alb and the Bö Wald. The hypothesis of a summer movement from sites like Sipplingen to the high Alpine pastures cannot be ruled out altogether, although the difficulties of long-distance movement in such an environment will certainly have presented a barrier. In this context it should be remembered that the site locations so far considered have conspicuously poor access to the interior. We can eliminate the possibility of a wholesale summer exodus of human and animal populations, as the cereals would have required tending and harvesting. As we have suggested, much of the stock would probably have been pastured away from the high-quality lake-side grazing during the summer, in order to conserve this scarce resource for winter use. It is by no means unlikely that this system included a mobile-cum-sedentary element, and that sheep and non-milking cattle and their herders may have spent some days or weeks at temporary camps outside the site territory.

It seems less likely, on the other hand, that a system of long-distance transhumance was in operation. The nearest substantial summer grazings available above the tree line are some 50 km to the southeast. While this is by no means an unacceptable distance even in severe topographic circumstances, contemporaneous sites such as Eschen-Lutzengüetle are better placed to

serve as bases from which to exploit these pastures than are sites in the Sipplingen area. Eschen-Lutzengüetle seems to have been in a broadly comparable situation to sites on the Bodensee, on a well-drained, well-insolated inselberg above the marshy floor of the Rhine Valley (Figure 45). There is no indication from the fauna that this would have been a seasonal camp, and it seems rather to have been a home base of the Bodensee type.

If we are right in arguing for a substantially sedentary economy for the Bodensee sites, there would have been a considerable shortage of animal fodder in winter. Today with extensive forest clearance the standard adaptation is short-distance movement of stock in summer and haymaking for winter use, but the restricted areas of open pasture would have limited the efficiency of this response in Neolithic Switzerland. At Neolithic Sipplingen a crucial winter supplement would probably have been leaves of such deciduous trees as ash, elm, and oak. If, as seems likely, however, the elementary step was taken of preserving some of the summer growth for winter use, then some of the rich wetland vegetation from the lake side would also have been available in the form of hay or foggage.

The site of Thayngen-Weier provides a useful comparative example to the Bodensee (Winiger 1971). It lies about 20 km west of the Bodensee at an altitude of 450 m on the edge of a small moraine lake (now filled with peat) in an enclosed valley north of the Rhine. Climatic conditions are similar to those at the western end of the Bodensee. The site consists of three consecutive settlements of the Pfyn culture, separated by periods of abandonment, the total span of time being about 200 years. There are extensive deposits of loess and silt within the 1 hour site territory (Figure 46), but much of this could not have been effectively cultivated because of steep topography and difficulties of access. Club wheat, emmer, and barley were nevertheless grown, and archaeological remains also include flax, poppy, lentil, peas and beans, as well as a variety of fruits and nuts. Cattle and pig predominate over ovicaprids in the faunal remains.

Although the settlements were located on the lake edge, and pike bones and antler leisters were found in the deposits, the lake would have been far too small to provide an abundance of fish or other lacustrine resources, and the economic resources of the lake can still less be invoked as a sufficient explanation of the site location than with the sites along the shores of the Bodensee. As with the Bodensee sites, two factors seem to have been uppermost in the choice of site location: easy access to a combination of plant and

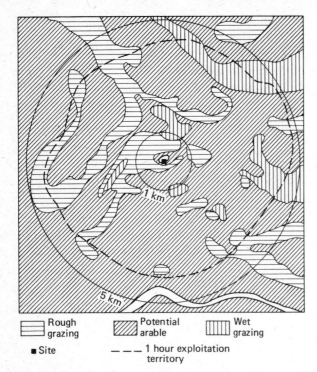

Rough grazing   Potential arable   Wet grazing

■ Site   — — — 1 hour exploitation territory

Figure 46. Site exploitation territory of Thayngen-Weier.

animal resources rather than maximisation of the arable component; and selection of the most favourable microclimate. The lake itself would probably have been too small to have any significant impact on the local climate, but the small valley in which the settlements occur has the advantage of being exceptionally well sheltered from the prevailing winds by the surrounding ridges.

At this site there is also additional corroboration of the hypothesis of sedentary settlement. Ovicaprids were slaughtered between April and October, and cattle between September and January. There is strong evidence for the stall-feeding of the stock in winter, and both pollen and macrobotanical remains point to the collection of leafy fodder. Fishing and plant-food exploitation would have been mainly summer activities.

Thayngen-Weier, therefore, is of particular interest as the high quality of information and the unusually refined chronology give us some hints of the economic and demographic development of a single community. In the earliest settlement, dated to about 3060 b.c., only about 40 per cent of the cattle survived beyond their first winter. By the time of the second settlement, some 40 years later, 80 per cent survived beyond their first year and the proportion of the ovicaprids and pigs surviving their first year also increased. This seems to imply the development from an economy with so severe a shortage of winter fodder as to require a stringent

autumn cull to one in which this limitation had been very substantially overcome. At the same time the size of the settlement increased, with an estimated population of 50 in the first phase, 90 in the second, and 150 in the third. The Thayngen-Weier evidence thus may be interpreted as a record of substantial short-term economic success, and gives an indication of the way in which the Neolithic economic and environmental systems may have evolved.

Long-term perspectives

In comparison with the subalpine Neolithic economy we have discussed, that of the Mesolithic seems to have been characterised by a narrower range of resources and a greater degree of seasonal mobility. The staple resources seem to have been the red deer, pig, and aurochs. Despite the pattern of site location, which is concentrated upon the small moraine lakes and the shallower bays of the larger lakes, there is little direct evidence for the exploitation of fish or other aquatic resources. Faunal remains are rarely preserved, but it is significant that the only faunal material studied from a lake-shore site lacked fish (Stampfli, 1979). It seems that here, as with the Neolithic, it is the terrestrial resources associated with the lake side that are of prime significance. It is worthy of note that the shallower bays tend generally to be associated with a relatively open adjacent hinterland, thus giving improved access to the resources of this area. There is no evidence of a significant degree of dependence on plant foods, although the exploitation of such fruits as the hazelnut is likely at least at a casual level.

Seasonal data are scarce although evidence of spring occupation is present at Schötz 7 on the Wauwilermoos (Stampfli, n.d.). The productive potential of the lake-margin grazing would be highest in spring and summer, and it seems thus reasonable to suppose that the lake-side sites would have been occupied at this season. To the north of the Bodensee, Jochim (1976) has suggested that human groups may have had annual territories of some 500 km², incorporating a summer concentration on the Federsee, and more dispersed winter settlement in the shelters along the Danube. If occupation of the Bodensee was principally in the warmer months, the Mesolithic inhabitants are likely to have moved westwards down the Rhine Valley for more sheltered winter quarters. It must be admitted that there is at present no archaeological confirmation of this suggestion, although the use of raw material from Engen some 20 km to the west (Reinerth 1929) certainly suggests some sort of movement in this direction.

If we are correct in our hesitant suggestion that Mesolithic economies were significantly more mobile and extensive than those typical of the Neolithic in this area, we must briefly consider what was involved in the important economic changes. As so often, the critical stimulus for the intensification of exploitation patterns seems likely to have been population pressure. Not only is there a substantial increase in the number of sites in the Neolithic – and here we must remember that the 'Neolithic' represents a considerably shorter period of time than the 'Mesolithic' – but the significance of factors outside our particular study area must be taken into account. From at least as early as 4500 b.c. onwards the surrounding lowlands were filling up progressively with farmers operating a plant-based form of mixed agriculture (see Chapter 5). The resulting competition for resources would certainly have exerted pressure on those economic systems adapted to postglacial conditions in areas unsuited to agriculture. Not only would lowland resources formerly available have been taken over, but increasing areas of upland grazing would have been required by farmers seeking to mitigate the problems of overwintering their own livestock by summering them outside the site territories of their lowland home bases. By this time the arable crops had probably become better adapted to marginal environments and could facilitate overwintering in the uplands by producing storable surpluses for men and livestock.

As we have seen, the main axis of economic development in the sub-Alpine region concerned the intensification of the pattern of animal exploitation. We have suggested that settlement became more sedentary mainly as a result of the farming of the lakeside grazing resources. In all likelihood this included the provision of hay and other summer-gathered fodder for winter use. The small arable component in the economy may also have been primarily geared to the needs of pastoralism. In this context the discovery of cereal pollen in the Mesolithic levels at Baulmes Abri de la Cure in the Swiss Jura (Leroi-Gourhan & Girard 1971) and Niederwil to the south of the Bodensee (Waterbolk & van Zeist 1966) is of some interest. While it must always be borne in mind that such isolated instances may represent stratigraphic confusions or the long-distance transport of pollen from contemporaneous lowland farming communities, it is by no means implausible that the advantages of the speculative cultivation of small patches of cereals should have been realised at this date.

Developments subsequent to the Neolithic seem to have concerned further intensification of the pattern of pastoral exploitation. There is palynological evidence which implies that during the Bronze Age an increasing amount of permanent pasture became established, as at the site of Arbon Bleiche on the Bodensee (Higham 1967). It is at this stage, too, that we first find substantial evidence of high-altitude settlements, suggesting an increased use of upland pastures (see Chapter 6).

SUB-ALPINE ITALY

A similar pattern of lake-side settlement allied to progressive penetration of upland resource zones under the stimulus of competition from developing lowland economies is indicated by the evidence on the Italian side of the Alps (Jarman, M. R. 1971, 1976b). Here, too, animal-based economies with a marked preference for lake-side locations are conspicuous. Broadly speaking the climatic picture is less extreme, and winter frost and snow are generally less severe limitations. Summers tend to be humid, with considerable precipitation as one moves north into the Alps themselves. While there is much intensive arable production today, most of this is on soils which were unsuitable for Neolithic agriculture. The damp summers also inhibit cereal production, and much of the arable land of today is devoted to fodder crops.

Molino Casarotto is located on a small lake in the Berici Hills on the edge of the Alpine zone (Figure 47).

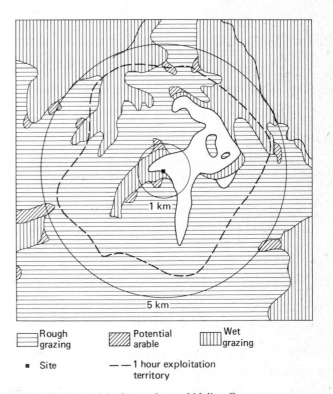

Rough grazing
Potential arable
Wet grazing

■ Site
— — 1 hour exploitation territory

Figure 47. Site exploitation territory of Molino Casarotto.

4. COASTS, LAKES, AND LITTORALS

Like its Middle Neolithic counterparts on the moraine lakes north of the Alps, its economy has a 'Mesolithic' character, with deer and pig as animal staples and water chestnuts as the main source of plant food, with very little evidence of cereals. The paucity of fish remains is striking in view of the lake-side location. Great care was taken in the collection of faunal specimens, but only just over 200 fish bones (mostly of smallish pike) were recovered out of more than 6000 identified specimens. Potentially arable soil is virtually non-existent except for small isolated patches, and the main resource category within the 10 minute territory is the wetland grazing represented by the poorly drained ground around the lake margin.

At other sites in the area the combination of red deer and pig was gradually superseded by the more productive combination of cattle and caprovines as time went on, and as woodland gave way increasingly to more open conditions under the impact of continuous grazing. As is clear from sites such as Fondo Tomollero, the role of cereals in the economy expanded over this period, despite the low level of arable potential. There was also an increasing penetration of upland areas in the higher Alpine zone, culminating in the Bronze Age with the establishment of sedentary communities, as at the Middle Bronze Age lake-side site of Fiavè, located at an altitude of *c.* 650 m (see Chapter 6). As in Switzerland, the stimulus for the increasingly intensive exploitation of the uplands and other areas marginal for crop agriculture stems ultimately from the population pressure exerted by the gradual filling up of the more productive lowland economic niches.

5. THE LOWLANDS

The lowlands of Europe may be viewed as comprising roughly the area that lies under 200 m OD. However, as will be seen in Chapter 6, some areas of low hills function economically as uplands, due either to their geology, soil, or microclimate. Similarly, some plateau regions at altitudes greater than 200 m present broad environmental analogies with the lowlands. Our distinction between uplands and lowland is therefore based partly on economic considerations. In general, lowlands have a milder winter climate than adjacent uplands, a better developed soil profile, and gentler topography. In contrast to most of the uplands, some parts of the lowlands can support highly productive arable agriculture. The lowlands are by no means uniform, however. Figure 48 shows the distribution of lowlands and uplands in Europe, and soils suitable for modern wheat production. It can be seen that not only is very little cereal produced in the upland region, but also certain parts of the lowlands are much more productive than others. On this basis we shall divide the lowlands into (1) the zone of high arable potential and (2) the zone of low arable potential. The dividing line between the two is not always clear-cut, but the distinctions between the two were probably far greater in the past. The zone of high arable potential has relatively gentle topography, low rainfall, high temperatures, a long growing season, and well-drained tractable fertile soils. The zone of low arable potential is lacking in one or more of these qualities; for example, being so far north that it suffers from low temperatures and a

Figure 48. The relationship between the distribution of Neolithic sites and lowlands, uplands, and modern arable potential.

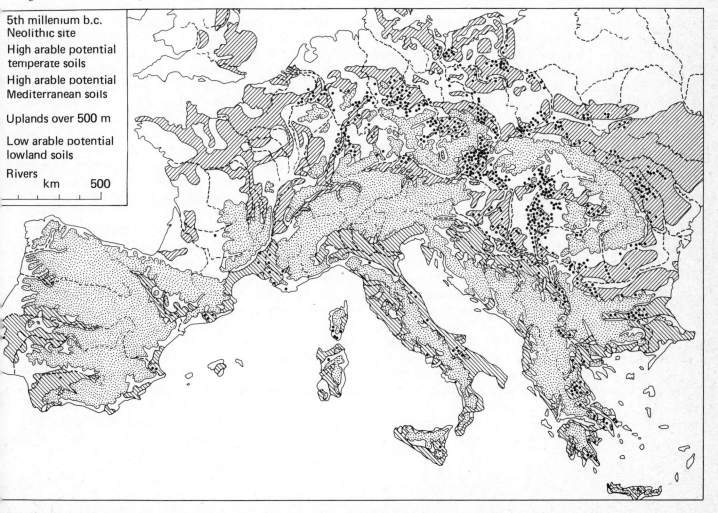

5th millenium b.c. Neolithic site

High arable potential temperate soils

High arable potential Mediterranean soils

Uplands over 500 m

Low arable potential lowland soils

Rivers

km   500

shortened growing season, or being in an area of high rainfall which leads to leached and impoverished soils. The reclamation of large areas of low-lying marsh land from the sea over the past two to three millennia, combined with rapid progress in plant breeding and agricultural technology in the twentieth century have increased arable productivity in the zone of low arable potential by far more than it has affected the zone of high arable potential.

The Netherlands provides an extreme example of the type of changes that have occurred since Neolithic occupation (Monkhouse 1974). The surface deposits today are either heavy soils derived from recent marine clays, sandy peat soils, or heavy river clays. A small loess-covered patch in south Limburg is the most fertile in the country, and carries the earliest Neolithic occupation in the country. Apart from these loess-loams, the best arable soils are the heavy marine clays; the river clays are less productive and are for the most part under permanent pasture. In any case, the clays would have been inaccessible to Neolithic agriculture either by virtue of being below sea level or of being too heavy to be worked effectively. The heathlands have been heavily fertilised, but even then their low arable potential means that they are mostly under permanent pasture. Therefore, from a Neolithic point of view, wheat production is overrepresented in Figure 48, and the zone of low arable potential can in fact be imagined as larger and as being more thoroughly animal-orientated than is apparent from this map.

The prehistoric record suggests that these fundamental variations in economic potential were recognised and had an important impact at least from the early Neolithic onwards. Two primary axes of Neolithic development are frequently recognised. The first of these incorporates the dramatic spread across Europe of the pottery-using, mixed farming economies represented by the Starčevo–Criş–Körös–Linear Pottery culture groups. It can be seen from Figure 48 that this corresponds strikingly to the zone of high arable potential. The other axis is that of the coastal 'Cardial ware' sites, which lie for the most part in the coastal zone discussed in the last chapter. Outside these two main areas of development, in the lowland zone of low arable potential, the classically defined Neolithic traits of polished stone, pottery, cereal agriculture, and sheep and goat tend on the whole to arrive a millennium or more later than in the zone of high arable potential. It is with this latter zone that we shall mainly be concerned in this chapter.

Before we can go on effectively to consider the prehistoric data from our chosen study areas, two general questions must be examined. The first is the effect that surface soil conditions have upon arable farming, and the second is the general nature of the agricultural system which we may suppose to have been in operation.

SOIL AND ARABLE AGRICULTURE

Pedological factors, being among the primary ecological variables, clearly have an important impact upon all subsistence economies. Their especial significance for arable exploitation is a consequence of the fact that, in his attempt to modify qualitatively and quantitatively the naturally occurring vegetational associations, man relies increasingly upon mechanical and chemical manipulation of the soil. The two soil properties of greatest importance for our purposes are its fertility and its texture. Soil fertility is affected by a number of factors, including its chemical composition, particle size, and moisture status. A rough guide can usually be gained from observation of plant growth and information on current agricultural procedures. Soil texture is largely a matter of particle size.

For a number of reasons our analyses of soils exploited in prehistory differ from modern pedological laboratory studies. In particular, we have neither the same objectives nor the capacity for precision and refinement which pedology provides. As we have discussed at length in Chapter 1, the nature of our basic data encourages us to deal in generalities rather than specifics, and the loss of fine detail occasioned by our adoption of rough and ready techniques of analysis is not, therefore, of great significance. The two primary requirements of our assessments of soils are that they should take into account possible geomorphological and pedological changes since the occupation of a settlement, and that they should be widely and rapidly applicable in the field.

There is, of course, a wide range of techniques available for studying changes in land forms. As regards changes in soil quality it is worth remembering that we are necessarily concerned primarily with gross changes in fertility or texture, and that alterations of a scale likely to have had a significant impact on prehistoric land use potential are usually likely to have left unmistakable traces in the prehistoric or geomorphological record.

We therefore adopted the techniques recommended by the Agricultural Development and Advisory Service (1971) for the field assessment of soil texture as our primary criteria for the separation of soils into light, medium, and heavy categories, and supplemented this classification with information on modern and historical land use. We are encouraged in our reliance on such crude methods by the fact that they formed the basis of land potential assessments at least as far back as Roman times and remain so for many subsistence agriculturalists. In cases where more detail is needed the mechanical force required to turn the soil can be measured accurately and quantified by use of a penetrometer (Barker & Webley 1978). This technique can in some cases enable estimates to be made of the number of draught animals which might be needed to till the soil in different agricultural circumstances.

It might at first be imagined that soil fertility would have been the factor of greatest importance for prehistoric arable farming. However, nutrient content is only one aspect of the matter, and other factors such as texture, permeability, and pH may have an equal effect on crop selection and productivity. Population density and technological levels are two additional considerations which affect land use.

Our early field work suggested that, in some cases at least, texture was more important than fertility in determining which soils were cultivated in prehistory, and there are indeed a number of reasons why this should be so for most subsistence farmers. Generally speaking, the finer the soil and the higher its clay content, the heavier it is and thus the greater the force required to cultivate it – whether by hoe, ard, or tractor-drawn plough. The physical difficulties of ploughing the clayier soils are compounded by their poor drainage. When they are only slightly damp, they offer less mechanical resistance to cultivation than when dry, but when wet they become cohesive and sticky, and ploughing is either impossible or causes compaction and puddling. Furthermore, due to their retention of cold winter rain and snow melt, the heavier soils are slow to warm up in spring, and plant growth is often significantly retarded relative to the better drained soils.

Fertility and tractability may thus be viewed as being to some extent in inverse relation to each other. Fertility depends substantially upon particle size, as broadly speaking the finer-grained the soil the more easily and completely its nutrients are accessible to plants. While the high energy and labour costs tend to discourage cultivation of the heavier soils, these are generally sufficiently productive to repay the investment where population levels impel it and technology permits it to be made. Many of the heavier loam soils of Europe appear not to have been settled and ploughed until Roman or Anglo-Saxon times, with the availability of the mouldboard plough (Pounds 1973). In the

Paris Basin the agricultural potential of the heavy loams was not realised until as late as the ninth to twelfth centuries (Clout 1977). The really intractable clays have only begun to come under the plough in this century with the advent of sophisticated drainage systems and heavy farm machinery. Technologically simple economies would not necessarily find these heavy soils absolutely impossible to till, but only a tiny area of such intractable soils could be turned with the available equipment. Under ideal conditions almost any soil can be worked even with hand tools, albeit laboriously. With the more difficult soils this would confine their cultivation to so few days in the year as effectively to prohibit their exploitation as arable land until the equipment was available whereby to deal with them in less than ideal conditions.

As with so many other aspects of prehistory, therefore, we are left with an irreducible area of uncertainty. We cannot demonstrate unequivocally that particular soils were not cultivated at certain periods. Nevertheless, to judge from both ethnographic and historical data, the heavier loams and the still less tractable clayey soils are most unlikely to have come under cultivation in prehistory to any significant extent. In our analysis of prehistoric economies we have therefore excluded the heavier soils from consideration as having any regularly exploited arable potential. We have assumed that arable crops would have been restricted to the light and medium-light soils, the former being the easier to cultivate, the latter generally the more productive. As we shall see, prehistoric economies with a substantial arable element seem to have been attracted primarily to the most fertile soils available within this restricted range of textures.

NEOLITHIC AGRICULTURAL SYSTEMS

The primitiveness of Neolithic agricultural technology has been a persistent theme in the literature dealing with early European farming up to the nineteen seventies. This view has been applied equally with regard to tools, such as the lack of obvious ploughs, and to the general level of know-how. Childe (1929) characterised the Danubian economy as *Hackbau* 'implying cultivation by hoeing without rotation of crops or systematic manuring'. At one time or another it has been generally believed that Neolithic farmers were incapable of dealing with forest vegetation, incapable of recognising suitable arable soils under wooded conditions, and incapable of maintaining adequate soil fertility without resorting to an extensive slash-and-burn regime. The concept of prehistoric man as *Homo ignoramus* has, however, been gradually eroded. His ability to deal effectively with forest vegetation was argued some 30 years ago by Clark, J. G. D. (1945). His intention was to demonstrate that, contrary to the view then current, the forests of Atlantic Europe were of great importance to the spread of agriculture into the continent, rather than a barrier. Clark was able to destroy convincingly and lastingly the hypothesis that it was only a treeless landscape consequent upon a dry oscillation that permitted the Neolithic colonisation. In doing so, he was instrumental in firmly establishing, if not originating, the succeeding model for that process, which suggested that Europe was colonised by communities practising a 'slash-and-burn' or *brandwirtschaft* form of economy, which were to a large degree dependent upon the forest vegetation for the maintenance of their agricultural system. Clark also argued that these early farmers may well have been capable of recognising soil types, in particular loess, on the basis of the vegetation on them.

More recently, the results of animal behaviour studies and ethnographic investigations have made us aware of highly adaptive and complex subsistence systems among other animals and of the great range and depth of knowledge about the natural environment that is possessed by modern hunter–gatherers and peasant farmers. While the demise of the 'ignorant savage' may make the practice of certain subsistence strategies improbable on the basis of their irrationality, it does not automatically point to a particular system as the only possible one for Neolithic agriculture. A system of agriculture is only 'sensible' or 'efficient' in terms of the natural environment in which it functions, the population level it supports, and the technological capability of its practitioners.

The accepted model for the European Neolithic agricultural system is that of shifting agriculture. In certain cases other systems have been proposed for particular areas or circumstances, such as the small-scale *hackbau*-like system suggested by Kruk (1973) for the Polish Linear Pottery settlements. In many cases the matter is not discussed explicitly at all. Nevertheless the shifting cultivation stereotype is well established as the dominant explanatory hypothesis. It is an example of a belief so widely held and of such respectable antiquity as to have acquired the status of unchallengeable fact. Recent developments have, however, led us to re-examine the data, and it will be seen that other conclusions may be drawn for which there is as much support as for the authorised version.

The evidence adduced to support the shifting cultivation theory is diffuse, embracing botanical, agronomic, archaeological, historical, ethnographic, and demographic data. As will become apparent, most of the detailed support comes from Central Europe, in particular from Linear Pottery settlements. The relationship of agricultural systems here with those elsewhere in Europe has never been analysed in detail. Before we discuss the evidence further, it will be helpful to consider what the model implies. European shifting agriculture is also often described as 'slash-and-burn' or *brandwirtschaft* agriculture, while a growing familiarity with the ethnographic literature has added the terms 'swidden', 'long fallow', and 'forest fallow'. These have been variously described and defined, but seem generally to involve a number of elements. Fire is used as a tool to assist in forest clearance and weed and pest regulation, and to provide a top dressing of wood ash. Plots are cleared in primary or secondary forest vegetation for relatively short periods of cropping. With falling soil fertility yields drop so far as to be uneconomic, the plot is abandoned and allowed to go back to forest. No permanent fields are maintained, and the period of fallow, though variable, is always greater than the maximum period of cropping. Thus the areas of cultivation, and sometimes the settlement itself, are not stationary, but move from year to year. It is important that, imprecise though they are, the terms imply more than simply the clearance of forest by fire for agricultural purposes. A complex of agronomic practices is involved; and, by implication, the absence of others is equally suggested.

Botanical evidence

For our immediate purposes there is no need to become involved in the debate concerning the precise nature of the 'natural' vegetation of Holocene Europe. Opinions vary as to the degree and density of forest cover, but the consensus at least is that most of the lowlands would have included a substantial amount of woodland, which would presumably have been denser upon the heavy and poorly drained soils, and more open upon the lighter and drier soils. The composition of the woodland flora would, of course, have varied tremendously with latitude and other factors.

There is not a great deal in the way of macroscopic remains which bears directly upon our present considerations. Collection of plant remains from excavations has been at best sporadic, and can only provide a few general hints. Cereals (especially einkorn and emmer) and pulses (especially peas and lentils) occur commonly enough to indicate that part at least of the subsistence depended upon arable agriculture. Charcoal is present on many sites, and this along with the widespread

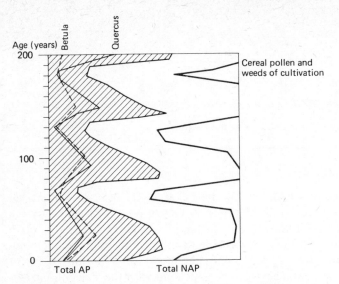

Figure 49. Pollen diagram expected from shifting agriculture under conditions of fine chronological control.

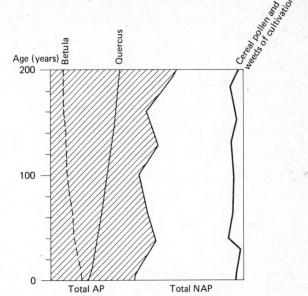

Figure 50. Pollen diagram expected from shifting agriculture under conditions of poor chronological control.

evidence of substantial timber-framed buildings in Central Europe shows that woodland existed within economic range of the sites, and that some initial clearance of croplands may well have been necessary in some cases.

The critical information comes from pollen cores. Let us take the Bohemian Linear Pottery site of Bylany as typifying the agricultural system of the loesslands, and accept for the moment Soudsky's contentions (Soudsky & Pavlů 1972) regarding the nature of the site and the system of which it is a part. Bylany is held to have been occupied for periods of *c* 10–15 years at a time, with gaps in between the settlement phases of *c* 30–50 years, during which time other sites in a fixed cycle would be occupied. The total period of occupation at Bylany appears to have been a minimum of about 700 years.

The palynological evidence that one might expect from this situation would vary, depending on its capacity for refinement and detail of interpretation. If it were possible to distinguish chronological units of only a few years' duration the pollen core should indicate a repeated cycle of short phases of clearance separated by longer periods of forest regeneration (Figure 49). An overall decline of species which are slow to reproduce or colonise, and a corresponding increase in colonising species, might also be expected. Cereal pollen and that of weeds of agriculture should be fairly sharply restricted to, or at least markedly peaked during, the clearance phases. If on the other hand the chronological control is poorer, and only phases of 50 or 100 years can reliably be distinguished, no such periodicity could be expected to appear. Instead, a zone in which pollen

of forest species was predominant would precede one in which it was less so, but the degree of change need not necessarily be very great (Figure 50). Cereal pollen would presumably put in an appearance in the second zone, and would be present throughout its duration.

Evidence such as that discussed in the first hypothetical instance would provide powerful support for a theory of slash-and-burn agriculture. The second instance could not be considered evidence for or against the theory, as it gives no indication at all of events taking place on the short time scale of shifting cultivation. Many other explanations of the evidence could be proposed.

In fact, the palynological evidence usually presented in favour of the slash-and-burn theory is customarily like neither of the two hypothetical examples. A much-quoted example is that of Ordrup Mose (Iversen 1941). A pollen core adjacent to a Neolithic occupation shows a period of drastic decline in the levels of arboreal pollen, followed by a period in which the proportion of arboreal to non-arboreal pollen rises to similar levels to those prior to the original decline. Within the arboreal pollen spectrum there is a dramatic increase in the ratio of birch to oak during and just after the overall decline of tree pollen. At this same level cereal pollen and that of plants commonly occurring as weeds of agriculture put in their first appearance, and a striking increase in the amounts of charcoal in the deposit is seen (Figure 51).

This is interpreted as showing the clearance by fire of

5. THE LOWLANDS

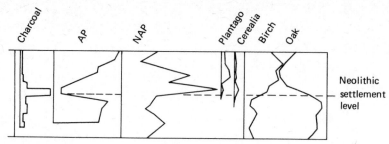

Figure 51. Pollen diagram from Ordrup Mose. After Iversen (1941).

the forest surrounding the site, which, after a period of cultivation, was abandoned and the forest permitted to regenerate. Birch, as a colonising species, made the first major impact upon the area once agriculture had ceased, the oak recovering from the effects of clearance more slowly.

Certainly pollen diagrams such as that at Ordrup Mose can reasonably be viewed as showing the impact on local vegetation of clearance by fire (or with its help) and the subsequent practice of arable agriculture. The use of fire in this way should occasion no surprise; it remains one of the primary methods of forest clearance in Europe, frequently for the purpose of arable agriculture. But does this amount to, or even point strongly towards, slash-and-burn agriculture? The duration of the agricultural episode is unknown, and there is no specific evidence that a repetitive form of long-fallow extensive agriculture was in operation. On the contrary, there appears in the Ordrup Mose pollen diagram to have been a single period of cultivation prior to the return of forested conditions.

There are unfortunately no substantial pollen samples directly related to Linear Pottery sites. By and large cores come either from the uplands or from the lowland zone of low arable potential. The agronomic conditions of these areas are entirely different from those of the loesslands and would have favoured different agricultural systems. Thus even if existing pollen data were best interpreted in terms of 'slash-and-burn' agriculture, it would not necessarily give an accurate indication of the system in operation in the zone of high arable potential.

Other considerations warn us to be cautious of too easily interpreting palynological evidence in agronomic terms. Until relatively recently it was commonly assumed *a priori* that it was only with the Neolithic and 'food production' that man first began to have a serious impact upon his environment. Increasing research is beginning to indicate the limitations of this assumption. The interesting thing in terms of the present discussion is the nature of some of the evidence which has

accumulated for man's effect on his surroundings in pre-Neolithic times. A classic case is provided by the well-known Acheulean site at Hoxne, Suffolk. Here West (1956) was able to show on the basis of palynological evidence the likelihood of a period of forest clearance by fire, coinciding with the Palaeolithic settlement. In some of its details the Hoxne pollen diagram is quite remarkably similar to Holocene diagrams such as that at Ordrup. Among those features are the appearance of *Artemesia* and *Plantago* pollen for the first time at the deforestation horizon, and an increase in the importance of birch relative to oak following the deforestation. Current estimates place the Hoxne pollen diagram as approximately 400 000 years old, and it is thus well beyond the time range within which any prehistorian would be prepared to suggest an agricultural economy, slash-and-burn or otherwise. If the point is accepted that the pollen diagrams bear substantial and significant similarities to each other, then it follows that we should hesitate before proposing the evidence of one diagram as a corroboration of an hypothesis which is excluded *a priori* as a possible explanation for the other.

It is becoming clear that such episodes may by no means be infrequent in pre-Neolithic pollen diagrams. Simmons (1964) notes signs of deforestation on Dartmoor in pollen zone VI, which may well have been caused by the activities of Mesolithic man. Dimbleby (1967) has noted a number of other comparable instances in Western Europe.

There is nothing intrinsically surprising in these records. Man was in possession of fire for tens, if not hundreds, of thousands of years prior to the Neolithic. Historical and ethnographic records indicate that the use of fire to manipulate the natural environment was well known to some groups practising an entirely non-agricultural economy. It appears to have been in widespread use as a means of game driving, but also more interestingly as a way of controlling vegetation and providing optimum grazing conditions for the local herbivore populations. There are indications that the use of these techniques can be traced back into prehistory (Jones 1969).

Archaeological, ethnographic, and historical evidence

The archaeological remains have often been held to support the hypothesis of shifting agriculture. Since the interpretation usually depends to some extent on ethnographic or historical analogy we shall attempt to deal with these three classes of information together.

The toolkits of European Neolithic man are lacking in certain evidence of ploughs or ards. The earliest certain find of such a tool is the Hvorslev ard in Denmark, radiocarbon-dated to 1490 b.c. (Fowler 1971). While Glob (1951) and others have suggested that the plough may be of much greater antiquity in Europe, there is no positive evidence one way or the other. On the other hand, tools which could have served as axes, adzes, or hoes, are not infrequent. It has been suggested that the much discussed 'shoe-last celt' of the Linear Pottery assemblages may have acted in these capacities, and chipped and polished celts are indeed widespread and common in the European Neolithic. While most of these would have been at best ineffective as tools for the felling of mature hardwood trees, their interpretation as tools for woodworking and hoeing seems perfectly reasonable.

The inference of a simple hoe and digging-stick agriculture for Neolithic Europe has been extended by reference to some recent and modern examples of simple agricultural economies exploiting forested environments. In many areas of the humid tropics swidden agriculture is the norm or was so until the past few decades. Until recently these economies frequently relied upon stone tools, although iron axes and hoes have made an increasing impact in this century. This technological simplicity has encouraged elaborate analogies between the modern inhabitants of New Guinea, for example, and those of Central Europe during the Atlantic pollen zone. The former are frequently described as being at a 'Neolithic' stage of development, and much attention has been paid to the striking, if enigmatic, parallels between the long houses of many Indonesian swidden agriculturalists and those of the Linear Pottery sites.

Similar use has been made of historical evidence. Manninen's (1932) discussion of slash-and-burn methods among the Finno–Ougrian peoples has been much quoted, and comparable evidence comes from some areas of Russia and northern Germany. Similarly, in the early land-rich days of the European colonisation

of America vast areas of forest were cleared for arable exploitation by use of fire and the axe.

These examples have led many to the assumption that technologically primitive agriculture is *ipso facto* a land-extensive system employing slash-and-burn methods. This is a viewpoint which has been fostered by Boserup's (1965) suggestion that agricultural economies in all regions went through a relatively inflexible development from forest fallow through increasing intensifications to annual cropping and yet more intensive modes of exploitation. She explicitly hypothesises, furthermore, that agricultural organisation 'in sparsely populated regions of underdeveloped countries with systems of extensive land use, give a more or less faithful picture of the pattern and degree of agricultural employment which existed in past times in the now densely populated regions.'

Justification, indeed, is here for the classic stereotype of the Danubian farmer slashing-and-burning his way from Szeged to Liège. As has been pointed out by Bronson (1972), however, so rigid a scheme takes insufficient account of local and regional environmental variations, whatever its broad validity may be. Not only are there many examples of tropical agriculturalists operating highly intensive agricultural systems which are 'essentially hardware free', but there are some basic ecological circumstances which are not conducive to highly land-extensive methods in the first place. Similarly, for all the *landnam* methods of the early American colonists, Bronson found that 'the non-plantation section of the American colonial period was based on farming techniques just as intensive and labour demanding as those of the teeming mother countries.' It therefore seems that the easy assumption that all farmers went through an early slash-and-burn stage, and that in the remnants of this stage among surviving swidden agriculturalists we see preserved the agricultural organisation of Neolithic Europe, bears re-examination. We return to this topic in the next section.

Other types of archaeological evidence have been interpreted as showing abandonment and reoccupation of sites and thus as providing strong support for the slash-and-burn model. The prime example is Bylany (Soudsky & Pavlů 1972). At this site a number of features were taken as indicating a regular cyclic occupation of the settlement. Horizontal stratigraphy of both houses and pits certainly shows that it was occupied for a considerable period. Apparent discontinuities occur in the details of the pottery typology, as regards the fabrics, the forms, and the decoration. Soudsky has in addition distinguished a number of changes in the precise orientation of the houses, and infers from all these that the site must have been periodically abandoned.

A proposition of this nature is inherently as difficult to establish as to contest, as it depends so heavily upon individual opinion in the selection of key criteria and their assessment. An analysis could doubtless be constructed which, by selecting different attributes, would emphasise continuity. Suffice it to say that such data are subject to a number of possible explanations, even if it be satisfactorily established that they represent genuine and significant patterning of the prehistoric material. Tringham (1971) has, for instance, pointed out that Soudsky's interpretation relies upon the assumption that each local population conducted its settlement cycle uninfluenced by contacts with neighbouring groups; which seems logically, historically, and ethnographically implausible. Indeed there is considerable prehistoric evidence of large-scale movement of materials, and therefore of contact between populations, in Europe at and before this period. House orientation provides similarly inconclusive data. Differences in orientation between phases was as low as 5°, and the proposition that all buildings of a single period ought to show precisely the same orientation is not one which can be tested with the available data. Rebuilding of structures cannot of itself be taken as evidence for periodic abandonment. Rebuilding could have been a continuous activity as existing houses decayed naturally. It should perhaps be stressed that we are not at present attempting to disprove the specific interpretations of the Bylany material. We are simply trying to show that this evidence in itself is but a weak support for the hypothesis that the Linear Pottery economy, much less all early Neolithic economies, was based upon slash-and-burn agriculture.

Looking elsewhere within the Linear Pottery culture area evidence appears to be accumulating to the contrary. Studies on the Aldenhovener Platte of northwest Germany (Kuper *et al.* 1974 and personal communication) give a number of pointers to the nature of settlement in that area. An analysis of the pottery failed to show any discontinuities in its development, and the analysts have interpreted the assemblage as representing a continuous long-term development with all Linear Pottery pits containing sherds of all phases. Clearly, the same considerations apply to this finding as to Soudsky's at Bylany, and we must view it with equal caution. The Aldenhovener Platte material does at least make the point, however, that not all Linear Pottery settlements can easily be accommodated to the Bylany model.

Of more interest, perhaps, is the evidence of the overall settlement distribution on the Aldenhovener Platte. Large-scale open-cast lignite mining has given the opportunity for the recovery of unusually detailed information on the location and extent of settlements. From the Linear Pottery period onwards we have evidence of remarkably regular and complete settlement of the plateau. Broadly speaking, settlements appear to be concentrated on the terraces overlooking the minor tributaries and streams, rather than related to the main river valleys. Individual stream valleys appear to carry large numbers of settlements but adjacent river valleys will only be so occupied if they lie at a minimum of about 1 hour's walk from each other. This gives a picture of the actual range of exploitation from the settlements. Furthermore, on the basis of their data the workers in this area suggest that the so-called Linear Pottery 'villages' represent multiple rebuildings of smaller farmsteads, with a maximum of two or three buildings existing at any one time, rather than villages in the modern sense. Thus, in contrast to Bylany, we seem to have a picture of the stable development of small communities, rather than the cyclic habitation of villages.

Longevity of settlements, their permanence or seasonality, and local and regional population levels can only be assessed speculatively and imprecisely from archaeological data. The main value of the Aldenhovener Platte material for our purposes is that it offers an alternative series of explanations to those proposed by Soudsky for the Bylany material. In each case a number of different models fit the data, and there is no reason to assume that a satisfactory explanation for the one instance need necessarily embrace the other. The very regularity of site location on the Aldenhovener Platte implies a considerable degree of inter-site contemporaneity. As we have seen, the on-site archaeological data can also be seen in terms of long-lived, small-sized settlements. Of course, other explanations are possible, but this hypothesis must clearly be borne in mind in any consideration of Linear Pottery economic exploitation patterns. It should also be pointed out that the Aldenhovener Platte, while providing perhaps its most complete documentation, is by no means unique in supplying support to the hypothesis of a permanent, rather than cyclic, Linear Pottery pattern of occupation. Kruk (1973) found no reason to propose cyclic habitation of Linear Pottery sites in southern Poland and Jankuhn (1969) suggested that permanent occupation was probably the system generally in existence, at least as far as the German portion of the Linear Pottery distribution is concerned.

So far we have restricted our discussion of the archaeological data exclusively to the Linear Pottery area. This is because it is here, almost without exception, that support for the slash-and-burn model has been sought. Little attempt has been made to integrate the hypothesis thus derived with other European data, and indeed it is hard to tell if the general belief that early Neolithic agriculture was based on shifting cultivation extends to the Balkans and Near East, or not.

As far as the zone of high arable potential is concerned, the Neolithic settlements of these latter areas are predominantly tell sites. For a number of reasons it seems unlikely that these represent the kind of highly land-extensive economy envisaged for Central Europe. While we must not fall into the trap of assuming that substantial settlements necessarily demonstrate sedentary populations, it seems nevertheless unlikely that tells the size of Samarra and Hassuna, of Karanovo, Argissa, and Vinča, would arise from such peripatetic land use. Furthermore, stratigraphic and dating evidence suggest long-term continuity of occupation at many of these sites. In general the stratigraphic evidence supports the interpretation of continuous deposition of occupational debris, and there is certainly no established pattern of erosional phases. It could, of course, be argued, that while the settlement was stationary, the site territory was very large, only a small proportion of it being cultivated in any one year. Some such cases are reported in the ethnographic literature. This does not seem a likely explanation here, though. Recorded shifting agriculturalists are often constrained to rest land for a minimum of ten years between crops, partly to allow a restoration of soil fertility, partly to permit sufficient regrowth of vegetation. The fallow period is in many cases much greater than this. When we look at the density of settlement in the areas in question, it seems that such an extensive system would have been insufficient to support the estimated populations. Thus Dennell & Webley (1975) found that inter-site distance was on average *c* 5.2 km, giving a radius of exploitation of *c* 2.6 km. On the assumption that the majority of arable agricultural effort would have been concentrated within the first 2 km of the site, they found that with half the available arable land under cereals in any one year (the other half being rested or carrying legumes) enough cereals could probably have been grown to support the likely populations of the settlements. It can be seen that a fallow period of anything from ten to thirty times the cropping period would reduce the arable productivity of the territories to virtual insignificance. Similarly, on the Tavoliere in southern Italy (Jarman, M. R. & Webley 1975) some

hundreds of Neolithic sites are distributed in an area of about 400 000 hectares. Only about 20 per cent of this area was suitable for Neolithic arable exploitation, and even assuming that only a relatively small proportion of the sites were contemporaneous, it seems doubtful whether such extensive methods would have sufficed to feed the substantial populations implied by these large 'ditched' villages.

We must not push the argument too far, as all the crucial factors involved are only putatively to be inferred from archaeological data. We cannot be sure how many of the sites were in occupation simultaneously, how large their populations were, how productive the agriculture was, or how large a proportion of the economy it constituted. It seems nevertheless that such evidence as there is fits more readily the hypothesis of a short-fallow than that of a long-fallow agricultural system.

If it is accepted, then, that the high arable potential areas of the Balkans and Near East were probably exploited by relatively intensive forms of arable agriculture, we must ask why this should have suddenly changed as the economy spread into Central and Western Europe. Or, conversely, if one is to argue that the agricultural system in this latter region was that of shifting agriculture because this was the system most appropriate to colonising Neolithic economies, then we must ask why this appears not to have been the case further to the south and east. It seems most unlikely that adequate answers can be found for this anomaly in an inherent drop in potential productivity from one area to the other; that in Central Europe shifting cultivation was forced on the populations by the poverty of the arable resources. As will be seen in subsequent sections of this chapter, the groups concerned were exploiting some of the richest arable land in Europe. This leads us on to a consideration of the agronomic factors in the argument.

Agronomic considerations

The agronomic arguments in favour of slash-and-burn agriculture in Neolithic Europe may be expressed simply as follows. Repeated cropping of the same area would rapidly result in declining yields and a build-up of weeds and parasites. In a few years the effect of these disadvantages would have been sufficiently severe to require some preventative response. Neolithic man, technologically restricted to hand tools and lacking knowledge of the potential benefits of manuring and crop rotation, would have been forced to employ long-fallow methods, clearing new areas in primary

139

Table 12. Cultivation of emmer and einkorn (after Schiemann 1956)

Region	Soil	Climate	Altitude (m)
T. monococcum			
Sluny	sour, karst	rough winters, dry summers	338
Herzegowina (Posusje)	alluvial		–
Herzegowina (Mostar)	alluvial, coarse rubble-stone, worst soil	Mediterranean	38
Macedonia (Kumanova)	heavy, without Ca	eastern continental	340
T. dicoccum			
Brinje	sandy, very permeable, sour, karst	mountain	630
Sluny	sour, karst	rough winters, dry summers	338
Perušić	little sour, karst	–	400–500
Gospić	karst, high tableland	continental	500
Gospić	sandy loam, on many years fallow ground	continental	500
Gospić	karst, plough land without manure	continental	500
Herzegowina (Mostar)	alluvial, coarse rubble-stone, worst soil	Mediterranean	38
Bosnia (Sanski Most)	hills (good yield)	–	200
Montenegro (Nikšić)	worst soil, skelettoid alluvial	subalpine	610–30

forest every few years as the only means of maintaining yields at economically viable levels. Clearance by burning would have had the additional advantage of providing a top dressing of wood ash and of clearing the ground of weeds and insect pests.

Each of these points justifies further discussion. There are two aspects to the question of fertility, for apart from the basic structure and nutrient content of the soil itself, we must also consider the capacity of the crop to respond to these. Broadly speaking, the primitive wheats are hardy and well adapted to both unfavourable climatic conditions and poor soils. They are low yielding compared with the selectively bred wheats of today, and have a limited response to richer and heavily fertilised soils. Table 12 shows the results of Schiemann's (1956) analysis of the conditions in which einkorn (*Triticum monococcum*) and emmer (*T. dicoccum*), the commonest cereals on early Neolithic sites in Europe, were grown in Yugoslavia. They were usually sown on poor, light soils, sometimes without manure. Their climatic tolerance ranged from coastal Mediterranean to inland continental and subalpine regimes. Percival (1921) noted that while einkorn was of poor quality, ripened late, and had a low yield, compared to modern hexaploid wheats, it resisted frost and rust

diseases better, its awns and thick glumes protected it from bird predation, and it could be grown without manure on poor sandy, chalky, and rocky soils where higher quality wheats failed. Similarly, experiments in the United States at the turn of the century showed that under relatively dry, continental conditions emmer produced a more reliable yield than any other cereal under cultivation at that time (Carleton 1901). Thus einkorn and emmer make fewer demands upon soil fertility than do the more productive wheats like *T. aestivum*, which correspondingly deplete soil nutrients at a greater rate. Furthermore, the more primitive wheats often cannot take advantage of the richest soils. Arnon (1972) notes that in dry regions improvement of soil fertility in the past was largely self-defeating, as beyond a certain level all the available traditional varieties of *durum* wheat lodged heavily, making them difficult to harvest and reducing the yield.

As to the soil itself, it is of course incontestable that under almost all circumstances monocropping a piece of land for long periods will result in some reduction in basic soil fertility, and hence in yields. Different soils react in different ways to similar treatment, however. Poorly structured soils, poorly developed soils, and those with low base fertility will be most prone to rapid

140

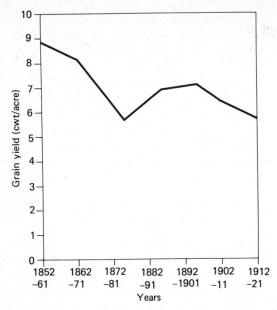

Figure 52. Ten-year means of grain yields from unmanured plot in the Rothamsted Broadbalk continuous wheat experiment (Garner & Dyke, 1969).

deterioration, and will thus require the most care to ensure that lasting damage does not occur. Thick soils, rich in nutrients, are less subject to these particular hazards.

It is a commonplace that a great majority of Linear Pottery sites are found on loess deposits of central and western Europe. This correlation has probably been exaggerated, as in some areas where loess soils are rare, Linear Pottery sites are found on soils which, while pedologically quite different, have comparable agronomic properties. Nevertheless it remains a valid generalisation that the majority of Linear Pottery settlement appears on the loess. Many factors influence the fertility of loess soils, but as a group they are characterised by high levels of base fertility and considerable soil depths. They are extremely fine-grained deposits, which makes a high proportion of the nutrients readily available to plants. Due to their high calcium and magnesium content, they are virtually unique among soils of such small particle size in being freely draining, and maintaining a loamy texture which makes them easy to cultivate (Berg 1964). While their fineness and light texture makes them to some degree susceptible to erosion, they occur commonly in such great depths that this is rarely a significant agricultural problem, at least under today's conditions.

Experiments conducted on loess and other chalk-rich loams indicate that many of them are surprisingly robust in terms of their reaction to long periods of monocropping. Data from the Rothamsted Broadbalk continuous wheat experiment indicated that, even without manure or fertiliser, average yields of grain showed only a very gradual decline over 60 years (Figure 52). Writing about the loess-based chernozem soils of the Soviet Union, Gerasimov & Glazovskaya (1965) say: 'Moreover, for several centuries the chernozems were most often exploited without fertilizing. Their high natural fertility, inherited from previous stages of the soil's development, together with periodic fallowing, were sufficient to ensure high crop yields in years of satisfactory humidity.'

The argument that the reliance on hoes or digging sticks for tillage will also have tended to enforce long fallow periods has probably been exaggerated. It is true that modern intensive agriculture relies on deep ploughing to release soil nutrients that lie below the depth of shallow-rooting plants like wheat and barley. However, a horse-drawn ard does not penetrate much below the depth of cereal root systems, and it is not until the appearance of the metal-bladed mouldboard plough that this limitation is overcome. In this particular respect hoe agriculture is probably not significantly at a disadvantage compared to ard-based cultivation.

The importance of the fertilising effects of wood ash may likewise be queried. The only significant nutrient which this contributes to the soil is potash. While this is a good source of the soluble potassium required by many crops, potassium is not usually a limiting factor to the yield of cereals in the temperate zone of Europe. Furthermore, chernozems and red-brown forest soils are particularly rich in potentially available potassium, and cereals grown under traditional cropping systems show little response to potassium fertilisers (Davidescu et al. 1975 and other papers in the same Proceedings). The observation commonly made that yields are much higher in the first year after the burning of forest in an area with fragile soils may possibly be attributable in part to the wood ash, but measured solely as a technique of fertilisation in temperate Europe, forest burning is far less cost effective than fallowing or manuring.

In summary, then, we may say that the supposed pressures enforcing long fallow systems may have been substantially mitigated by the combination of relatively undemanding crops, and the choice of stable fertile soils.

This leads us to a consideration of the ways in which soil fertility may have been maintained or enhanced. Whatever assumptions may in the past have been made to the contrary, the basic methods in use up until the advent of chemical fertilisers (manuring and crop rotation) were no less available to prehistoric farmers. In the very nature of archaeological data it is virtually impossible to demonstrate conclusively the existence of such practices until there is supporting literary evidence. Much is made of the writings of Roman agronomists such as Columella, who advocate particular agricultural systems and practices, including crop rotation. It is frequently assumed from this that prior to Roman times the benefits of crop rotation were unknown.

This may be the case, of course, but we should be wary of so important an assumption until alternatives have been considered. An interesting feature of almost all substantial Neolithic plant assemblages, from the earliest times onward, throughout Europe and the Near East, is the great frequency with which cereals and pulses are found together. Because of their property of replacing and fixing nitrogen in the soil, the pulses are the classic rotation crops for combination with cereals. The historical practice of growing cereals and pulses together as a mixed crop has among its advantages the effect of helping to maintain nitrogen levels in the soil while extracting a cereal yield, normally expensive of nitrogen. Renfrew, J. (1973) has suggested that this practice (maslin) may go back into prehistoric times. The constant association of these two crop groups strongly suggests that their capacity for integration into a unified system of great economic potential was realised at least from early in the Neolithic. Even if the advantages of crop rotation were not formally and consciously appreciated, it must have happened frequently by chance that they were grown in alternate years on the same patch of ground. The results would have been sufficiently dramatic that they must have been noticed, and it is hard to believe that once noticed they were not incorporated into the standard battery of agricultural techniques. Some evidence for its practice comes from the Linear Pottery site of Hienheim in Bavaria, where Bakels (1978) found that remains of peas were more numerous than those of emmer and einkorn, though they were found in fewer pits. This is in contrast to collections from sites in the Rhineland, where legumes are poorly represented. It appears that two different types of husbandry practice were in operation in the two regions, with Hienheim possibly using some form of cereal–legume rotation. Knörzer (1971) has nevertheless inferred a continuous cropping system for the Rhineland from the assemblages of weed seeds found with the cereals. As has already been stated, one of the lessons that can be learnt from the study of modern 'primitive' agriculturalists is their sophistication and detailed knowledge and awareness of their environment and its economic potential.

Even if Neolithic farmers had been unlucky enough or stupid enough not to discover the efficacy of growing cereals and pulses in rotation, a long fallow would still not necessarily have been essential to restore the fertility of the loess-type soils. The rate of recovery of the soils would have depended greatly upon their structure and fertility; a short fallow system may well have sufficed. In experiments at Rothamsted it was found that after four years of continuous cropping, a single year of fallow resulted in a 34 per cent increase in grain yield over the fourth year crop (Garner & Dyke 1969).

The other obvious means of maintaining soil fertility which would have been available to Neolithic man is the practice of manuring. Here again it is commonly supposed that the beneficial effect of manuring was only recognised comparatively recently. This, too, is an untested – indeed an untestable – assumption. As with the question of crop rotation it is hard to imagine an archaeological demonstration one way or the other, but commonsense suggests that it is at least as reasonable to suggest *a priori* that a degree of manuring took place and that its value was perceived. In fact it is difficult to see how some manuring could have been avoided. There is good evidence that the Neolithic economic systems combined animal husbandry with arable farming. The balance of these two elements is difficult to assess, but bone remains and territorial studies indicate a substantial involvement with animal exploitation. Much has been written about the rôle of herbivorous animals in the establishment and maintenance of the clearings which were used for arable crops, and in their grazing they must obviously have manured the soil, albeit in a haphazard fashion. It seems reasonable to suggest that the herds might have been pastured on fallow ground as a regular practice of animal husbandry. Harris, D. (1972) has argued that, while the grazing would have been heavy enough to reduce the effectiveness of swidden regeneration, yet the manuring would be too scanty and irregular to be of much agronomic value. To a large extent these arguments are in direct opposition to each other, however. An interesting additional point is raised by those Neolithic sites where there is evidence suggesting that cattle were stalled at some seasons of the year. This would lead to considerable concentrated accumulations of dung which could then have been applied more systematically to the fields. Features on some of the Linear Pottery sites have been interpreted as cattle corrals (Soudsky & Pavlů 1972), and these could have provided similar reservoirs of manure. It is difficult to use archaeological data to explore this suggestion, but it contains nothing inherently unlikely, and is no less plausible than categorical assertions to the contrary.

Our conclusions from this inquiry into the agronomic properties of early Neolithic settlement zones and of possible farming practices within them calls into question the usual parallels drawn with modern and historical examples of slash-and-burn agriculture. It is striking that these economies are as a group characteristic of areas with poor and fragile soils. This is clearly true of the tropical forest zone, and indeed much of the energy expended by agriculturalists such as the Hanunóo is devoted to making sure that the soil is physically protected from the deleterious effect of sun, wind, and rain for as long as possible. In addition, most tropical forest soils are of very low base fertility. Once the immediate surface horizon is exposed to the elements, and its humic content is lowered by cropping, these soils take many years to recover, and thus inherently require a long-fallow system. It is also interesting to note a further response to this poverty of resources. Much of the subsistence agriculture in these areas is based on root crop staples, which make relatively low demands on soil fertility, compared with those made by the protein-rich seed staples of European agriculture. As Allan (1972) puts it, 'these systems are often ingenious adaptations to unfavourable environments, based on a remarkably complete knowledge of local ecology and soil potential'.

Similar inherent limitations seem to apply to most, if not all, of the areas of recent and extant European slash-and-burn agriculture. They are characteristically either at the northern fringes of viable crop agriculture, such as Karelia, where they are in addition in areas of predominantly poor soils; or in mountainous areas such as the Polish Carpathians, where again climatic and pedological constraints severely limit the range of possible arable systems. In the same way, during mediaeval times, temporary fields were cleared and cultivated for short periods in times of stress on marginal land at the periphery of the permanently cultivated areas (Slicher van Bath 1963).

As far as the main group of tropical swidden systems is concerned a further observation is of interest. Few if any of these are totally without an animal husbandry component, but it is a valid generalisation that they are heavily plant-based economies. This is probably for sound ecological reasons, as many of these areas are equally lacking in large populations of indigenous wild animals suitable for intensive economic exploitation. It is therefore not surprising that manuring is of little importance among agronomic practices. It seems scarcely reasonable to transpose this limitation unthinkingly to the very different European ecosystems, many of which both naturally and under cultivation carried large herbivore populations which were thoroughly integrated into the systems of exploitation.

One further step in the agronomic argument must also be considered. So far we have only dealt with the question of potential productivity, and that is as much as most analyses attempt. But this, of course, is only part of the story, and an important aspect of all economic systems is the input–output relationship; the cost of operating the system in terms of capital, labour, or energy. Viewed in these terms it can be seen that it is not sufficient to consider only whether or not there is increased productive potential resulting from a slash-and-burn economy. The extra cost involved must also be borne in mind.

Allan (1972) has emphasised the importance of distinguishing between shifting agricultural systems based upon a permanent village with land-extensive exploitation of its surroundings, and systems in which the settlement itself is moved. In the former case the extra cost is primarily that of movement and the labour of transport. Such a system will clearly be very difficult to distinguish archaeologically from a shorter fallow system. The fields themselves will seldom have left any traces, and one can only deal in terms of speculations arising from the settlement itself, or from the economic potential of its exploitation territory. Soudsky's interpretation of Bylany, on the other hand, which forms the basis of the usual stereotype of Linear Pottery economies, assumes that the arable resources were so dispersed or of so poor a quality that all those within an economic distance of the site were fairly rapidly exhausted. The labour of exploiting at an ever greater distance from the site became too great, and the settlement itself had to be moved. This kind of system would have been extremely land-extensive. To the extra cost of exploitation at considerable distances from the settlement must be added the cost of repeated forest clearance and of building an entirely new settlement relatively frequently: about every 14 years at Bylany, according to Soudsky. Without putting an exact figure on the labour costs, it is obvious that they must have been considerable when one takes into account the size of the structural timbers used in the settlements. In order for the move to have been worthwhile, the advantages of an increased yield for a few years must therefore have more than outweighed the extra costs of the movement.

It is sometimes inferred that tropical swidden cultivators are impelled to move by the build-up of weeds and parasites and the consequent additional labour involved in producing satisfactory yields. Results of such detailed studies as are available suggest that, while these are indeed contributory factors, it is serious decline in soil fertility and thus in yields that exerts the controlling influence. For while the former can be mitigated in various ways, the latter can only be overcome within the local environmental constraints by long fallowing. As we have pointed out, the same is not the case in the European zone of high agricultural potential.

Demographic arguments

The work of Boserup (1965) has given a powerful impetus to considerations of the demographic factors involved in patterns of settlement and exploitation. Her basic thesis that population levels exert a profound influence upon agricultural organisation and technology can scarcely be contested. Some of her specific hypotheses, and, more particularly, the use which has been made of them by some archaeologists, seem less valid. The belief that all agricultural systems must have been bound by, and have developed through, a rigid series of steps of increasing intensification seems logically dubious and ignores many concrete examples to the contrary. The particular form of land-extensive economy we are discussing under the names long-fallow, shifting agriculture, and so on, while they tend to be correlated with low population levels for obvious reasons, cannot automatically be assumed to represent a necessary stage through which all agricultural systems developed when their population was appropriately low. As we have noted, there is the ratio of input to output to be taken into account. In addition, not only will some environments favour more intensive systems from their first agricultural exploitation, but there is no certainty that all areas will have carried sufficiently low populations as to permit such land-extensive methods, even at an early stage. The European zone of high arable potential may well have been above this threshold from the beginning of its colonisation by Neolithic economies.

It has been suggested from time to time that shifting agriculture provides a particularly appropriate economic framework to explain the rapid colonisation of Neolithic Europe which the radiocarbon dates seem to show. It is felt that the mobility inherent in the system would in some way encourage the rapid dispersal of new communities, and that the speed of the spread is hard to account for in any other terms. Analogies are drawn with the colonisation of North America, and of New Guinea and Borneo. As we have noted, however, the latter lie in an area of totally different ecological circumstances, which set a very real limit on the capacity for agricultural intensification. As far as America is concerned, while there has, of course, been considerable intensification of land use since the days of the early colonists, there is little evidence that forest fallow methods ever had much widespread importance.

More fundamentally, we may question whether there really need be any particular correlation between a mobile economy and an inherent tendency towards rapid colonisation of new environments. Mobility is clearly a necessary factor in any colonisation process, be it by foot, horse, or aircraft. But, as is apparent from reflection on historical examples, this does not necessarily stem from a mobile economy at the point of emigration, nor tend to one on arrival. Colonisation seems generally to be a response to high population levels and/or severe population pressure. For a number of reasons mobile economies, both plant-based and animal-based, tend to support low levels of population, and whereas this may well represent a considerable degree of population pressure relative to the available resources, they are unlikely of themselves to provide conditions specifically and particularly conducive to rapid population increase and enforced emigration.

We may furthermore query the impression one gets from some of the literature that the early Neolithic spread involved the inexorable wholesale occupation of very large areas of Europe. Figure 49 suggests how little of the total area of Europe may actually have been occupied by early Neolithic sites. Rather than a thin and continuous spread of population – the pattern to be expected from the 'Brownian motion' model of Ammerman & Cavalli-Sforza (1971, 1973) – we find relatively small, isolated pockets of apparently fairly dense population. One might imagine such a pattern resulting from colonisation by people impelled by relatively dense populations and a high rate of population increase in newly settled regions, looking for specific environmental conditions suited to a productive agricultural economy. The relatively small pockets of prime arable land (in Neolithic terms) make the rapid spread of the new economy much less remarkable than has sometimes been supposed. The agronomic conditions related to Linear Pottery settlement have already been discussed and will be elaborated further in the discussion of particular areas. But the point has been made that they are precisely those conditions which would allow intensive and permanent agricultural exploitation. The blank spaces in between the areas of primary settlement might indeed have required slash-and-burn techniques in order to maintain arable productivity with a primitive technology, or may have been unsuitable for arable agriculture altogether.

These areas seem to have been ignored by arable-based economies until much later in the prehistoric record.

Integration

So far this consideration of the prehistoric agricultural system in lowland Europe has been largely destructive, picking holes in existing hypotheses, and only hinting at alternative possibilities. When one brings together the individual pieces of evidence – the inconclusiveness of technological and ethnographic arguments, the robustness of Neolithic varieties of cereals, the constant association of cereals with pulses and of those plant crops with cattle, pig, sheep, and goat, the high population density correlated with areas of high arable potential – the picture which emerges looks remarkably similar to descriptions of European peasant agriculture from mediaeval times up to the Second World War, and later in some places. It cannot, needless to say, have been identical; but we are unable, in any case, to produce more than an impressionistic image of the prehistoric conditions, and thus differences in detail are of secondary interest. As we have argued earlier, archaeological investigation is far more suited to the perception of long-term factors and here we will highlight those which seem to have been of prime importance in the several millennia of agricultural development in Europe.

Territorial studies everywhere emphasise the importance of soils to European Neolithic exploitation patterns in the lowlands. This is scarcely to be wondered at when we are dealing with subsistence agriculturalists, and is entirely borne out by studies of prehistoric peoples elsewhere in the world, and by studies of modern agriculturalists at a low level of technological development. Thus locational analysis of Mayan settlements (Green 1973) has shown that one of the main determinants of site location was the proximity of fertile but cultivable soil. Similar factors tie the villages of the Mississippi period in the southeastern United States to a specific series of soil types (Ward 1965, Larson 1972). Soil remains today one of the primary determinants of agricultural practice and settlement location, although technological advance to some extent mitigates and blurs its direct impact.

This preoccupation with soil quality is strongly pronounced in Neolithic Europe. Almost the only recognition of this has been that of the celebrated association of Linear Pottery sites with loess. As our territorial studies show, the reality is both more complex than this and much more interesting. Settlement is neither confined to the loess, nor is it as uniform on loess soils as is often supposed. In areas with little loess, soils of comparable agricultural potential are chosen. In areas with large expanses of loess soil particular areas are more heavily colonised than others.

We have seen that much of the accepted picture of Linear Pottery agriculture stems from speculations as to the capacity of the available resources to sustain permanent settlement. Territorial analysis has so sharpened our focus on the nature of resources actually available to occupants of particular settlements that it is worth re-examining this question. On average, Linear Pottery sites from the many areas we have studied are located so that at least half the area within 10 minute's walk of the site is of high agricultural potential in Neolithic terms. This means that within something just under 1 km from the site there was a minimum of about 114 ha of good arable land. The area of such soil in the next 10 minutes from the site is about 344 ha, but of course the labour cost of exploiting the land increases rapidly as one moves further from the site.

It is reasonable, and in line with observations of modern subsistence agriculture, to assume that attention would have been focused primarily upon the area accessible within 10 minutes of the site. On the basis of a simple five-year rotation (two years of wheat followed by barley, a legume, and a fallow year), this area could have produced 23 metric tons of wheat yearly given a very modest average yield of five quintals per hectare (q/ha). (Farmers growing unimproved varieties of cereal under pre-industrial conditions quoted yields of 10–20 q/ha adjacent to mechanised farms growing improved varieties and producing 20–40 q/ha.) After extracting 1 q/ha as seed corn, this would provide 1 kg of wheat per day per person (3000 kcal) for 50 people. Were use to be made of arable land at even a slightly greater distance from the site, then productive potential would clearly be greatly raised. We cannot, of course, treat these specific figures as if they have any precise validity. Their significance is rather in their demonstration that, even choosing minimal values, an effective agricultural system would have been quite feasible given a rudimentary crop rotation, without resorting to a swidden cycle. Obviously it is possible that less than two-fifths of the area cultivated would have been under wheat at any one time, that is, that the fallow period would have been longer. Equally it is possible that average yields may have been higher than 5 q/ha, and that some arable use was made of areas beyond the 10 minute threshold. Also, it must be remembered that occasional bad crops will have been inevitable, and probably had a considerable effect on population levels, as was discussed in Chapter 1. All in all, however, given the high base fertility and stability of the loess and the temperate climatic conditions of the area, it seems most unlikely that the basic situation would have been so different from that suggested above as to have enforced such a land-extensive pattern of exploitation as slash-and-burn agriculture.

This conclusion may be extended beyond the loess regions. Sites on the Tavoliere of southern Italy (Jarman, M. R. & Webley 1975) and the Nova Zagora region of Bulgaria (Dennell & Webley 1975) seem to have had sufficient arable resources available within their exploitation territories to sustain sizable populations without the need to resort to land-extensive agriculture. As we shall see below, this is a pattern which seems to be repeated throughout the lowland zone of high arable potential.

We have now completed our introductory ground clearance, and can proceed to the consideration of specific case studies. We shall be concentrating our attention for the most part on the zone of high arable potential. Lakes and littorals form a major focus of settlement in the zone of low arable potential, which thus comes under consideration in Chapter 4. The bulk of the rest of this chapter therefore consists of analyses of the settlement patterns and economies of prehistoric sites in the arable-rich lowlands of the Balkans, southern Italy, and central Europe. By way of contrast we have included at the end of the chapter brief studies of areas with lower prehistoric arable potential, in northern Italy and France.

GREECE

We have studied in some detail the major concentrations of Neolithic sites in Thessaly and Macedonia, and also the site of Knossos in Crete. Together these give us a picture of the kinds of environmental conditions exploited by the practitioners of the first recognisably 'modern' farming in Europe. Local variations notwithstanding, these areas (and those discussed elsewhere in the Balkans and in southern Italy) experience a broadly Mediterranean climatic régime. The microclimatic details vary considerably, but the climate of the Mediterranean basin as a whole is characterised by hot, dry summers and cool, wet winters, with moderate temperatures and rainfall around the equinoxes.

The relatively polarised seasonal regime has important economic repercussions which can be observed throughout the Mediterranean, though modified in places by local conditions. Arable agriculture must be based for the most part upon autumn- and winter-sown crops, as spring-sown crops receive insufficient rainfall to develop before summer drought halts plant growth. Cereal yields show a close correlation with spring rainfall, and total failure can even now occur in the not infrequent years of spring drought. The other main class of crop consists of those plants which, like vines and olives, can survive the summer dry season and are harvested in the autumn and early winter. As far as the pastoral aspect of subsistence agriculture is concerned, the principal effect of the climate is to create a severe shortage of summer grazing in the lowlands. In many areas plant growth essentially ceases between May and October, and the lowland population of herbivores is limited to those which can be pastured on the small areas of water-retentive and marshy soil and those subsisting on irrigated fodder crops and hay. Perforce, therefore, the dominant form of pastoral exploitation is mobile to a greater or lesser degree, the lowlands providing the bulk of the winter grazing but being largely deserted by herbivores in summer in favour of the uplands.

Just as there are today geographical variations within this broad climatic pattern, so there have doubtless been chronological variations in the past. To judge from the evidence that is available, such as the faunal collection from Franchthi Cave and the pollen diagram from the Ioannina lake basin (Bottema 1967), the current climatic regime replaced the cooler conditions of the Late Pleistocene fairly early in postglacial times. The radiocarbon dates from such early sites as Knossos, Nea Nikomedeia, and Argissa seem to indicate, therefore, that the new economy colonised the area shortly after the crucial climatic changes which made cereal agriculture and sheep and goat pastoralism a practical proposition.

Crete

We shall here focus on a single site, Knossos. Not only is it the only settlement on the island known to have a sequence of habitation throughout the prehistoric occupation of the island, but both the cultural and economic data have been studied relatively completely.

Crete as a whole is a mountainous island of extremely limited arable agricultural resources. That remains the case today, despite the great increase in the area under the plough due to the use of mechanised equipment and the growing importance of olives and grapes as commercial crops. Well over 50 per cent of Crete is over 400 m above sea level, and much of the lower lying land is infertile. Good arable soils are confined to less than 7 per cent of the island, and of these most are

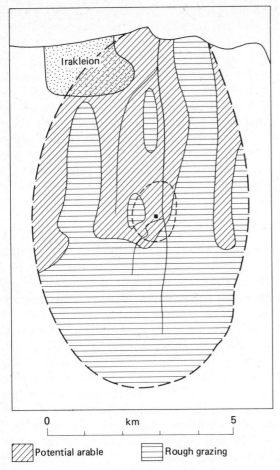

0   km   5

///// Potential arable   ≡≡ Rough grazing

Figure 53. Schematic one hour exploitation territory of Knossos.

situated on the Mesara Plain in the south (Allbaugh 1953).

The location of Knossos is of interest in that it lies at the edge of one of the largest arable areas, the plain to the south of the modern town of Irakleion. Most of this region of central Crete is covered with a varied deposit of Tertiary marine sediments, including conglomerates and marls. Their agricultural potential is highly variable, depending on topography and pebble content. In the immediate vicinity of Knossos the soil is primarily a light, fine-grained, friable marl, which provides a highly workable and relatively fertile tilth. While erosion is considerable on the steeper slopes, relatively stable arable areas are established over most of this deposit. Further north there is much more conglomerate, and the soil is less productive, while to the south of the site arable agriculture is largely confined to vines, as the more broken topography and steeper slopes are unsuited to cereals (Figure 53).

A second feature of importance is the presence of a permanent stream immediately below the site. This

flows, albeit sluggishly, throughout the summer. Crete experiences considerable summer drought with little available surface water. There are no large permanent rivers on the island, and it is not surprising to find the focus of early settlement at one of the relatively rare permanent streams. Until fairly recent volcanic activity, there was in addition a permanent spring adjacent to the site, but it is not known whether this would also have been present in prehistoric times.

The settlement therefore has colonised one of the relatively few areas of prime agricultural land, from a Neolithic point of view. Much of the territory would have been utilised as rough grazing, however. The limestone ridges which run roughly north–south in the northern part of the territory carry very little soil cover, and support only a scanty scrub vegetation. Slopes are sufficiently steep that, even allowing for a certain amount of denudation, they cannot at any time have offered other than a grazing potential. Large areas to the south of the site would also have been exploited as grazing prior to their recent clearance and cultivation for vines.

As elsewhere in the Mediterranean the lowlands are so desiccated and short of surface water in summer that some form of mobile pastoralism will almost certainly have been employed to integrate the summer grazing of the uplands further inland with the high winter potential of the lowland and coastal grazing. As on mainland Greece we lack at present the Neolithic upland sites to demonstrate the case conclusively, but it is nonetheless overwhelmingly likely that some type of transhumance will have been in operation.

The organic remains from the site indicate that a relatively stable and developed system of mixed farming was established at the site from its first occupation at about 6000 b.c. Bread wheat is the commonest Neolithic cereal, with lentils providing the pulse element in the rotation. The huge faunal collection is in all levels dominated by the common farmyard animals, which between them account for 97.5–99.5 per cent of identified specimens from the Neolithic and Bronze Age deposits.

The only major trend visible in animal husbandry over this period is a steady decline in the importance of sheep and goats on the one hand relative to cattle on the other, from the Aceramic Neolithic to the Middle Neolithic. This trend is reversed in the Late Neolithic. This is paradoxical from an ecological point of view, as Crete then as now must have been little suited to cattle. Furthermore, both naturally and humanly induced vegetational changes in the first millennia of the post-glacial period seem more likely to have favoured sheep and goats than bovids. No entirely satisfactory explanation has emerged so far. The low initial levels of cattle may plausibly be seen in terms of the greater difficulty of transporting them to the island, coupled with their slower rate of natural increase. By the Middle Neolithic, however, they account for about 50 per cent of the large sample of 14 000 identified specimens of cattle, caprines, and pigs. Even assuming a high degree of overrepresentation due to the size and robustness of their bones, this seems to imply a significance which is environmentally inappropriate. Differential distribution of bones on the site may be producing undetected sampling errors; or undocumented microenvironmental changes, such as the drying up of springs, may have made the site territory less suitable to cattle from the Late Neolithic onwards. It is just possible, theoretically, that in the buffered and protected environment of an uninhabited island the first inhabitants were able to indulge a preference for beef for as long as 2500 years, before being forced in Late Neolithic times to adjust more closely to basic ecological constraints. Conversely it may be – although there is no evidence that it was so – that as early as this Knossos became the pinnacle of an economic, commercial, and political hierarchy, and that the food remains represent a creaming off of wealth from a wide area, rather than the general subsistence picture. This alternative is made perhaps less likely by the fact that, in Minoan times when Knossos certainly was such a 'central place', the faunal sample conforms much more closely to apparent ecological sense. In our view there will almost certainly have been economic or ecological factors underlying the apparent anomalous importance of cattle, but the data may never be sufficiently satisfactory to demonstrate this.

Two considerations seem worthy of further comment. The colonisation of the previously apparently uninhabited island of Crete so early in the Holocene testifies to the considerable population pressure which, we have suggested, was one of the most potent forces lying behind the phenomenon of 'the Neolithic' and its spread into Europe. The selection of the Knossos area demonstrates the high level of agricultural know-how available to the colonists. For it is remarkable that, despite many attempts to find others, Knossos remains the sole example of a substantial Aceramic and Early Neolithic site on Crete. It seems to have been located where it is in response to a very particular combination of circumstances.

The main candidate for another possible Neolithic site of some size is Phaistos. So far, excavation has concentrated on the impressive Minoan palace and related habitation, and the discovery of Late Neolithic material in one of the trenches has not been followed up with deeper or more extensive soundings. Therefore a detailed territorial analysis was not undertaken for the site, but in two important respects its location is similar to that of Knossos: lying on the Mesara plain, it is in one of the areas of high arable productivity today, and it has a permanent source of water. Although further work is required to assess the Neolithic arable potential of the plain, it is of some interest that the only available evidence which hints at a Neolithic occupation at all on the lines of that at Knossos comes from another lowland area with relatively high modern cereal productivity.

The Plain of Thessaly

The Plain of Thessaly in eastern Greece is remarkable today as a focus of cereal agriculture. From the beginning of the century it has, together with Macedonia and eastern Thrace, provided the bulk of the wheat produced in the country, and it has had a reputation as a rich granary since Classical times. As in so many areas, much of the modern arable potential is a recent development, relying upon selective breeding of plants, mechanical equipment, and sophisticated management of water resources. Much of the plain carries heavy, clayey-silt soils which would not have been accessible to Neolithic agricultural technology. Furthermore, the area of the plain around the modern town of Larissa has until recently been much subject to floods, as has a more substantial area in the upper plain to the west. This constituted another factor limiting arable potential until the development of drainage and irrigation schemes this century.

The surface geology is complex and poorly studied, and we cannot at present be sure of the dating of specific surface deposits. Stratigraphic evidence of the relationship between Neolithic settlements and the modern land surface does not suggest that there has been much change in the relevant period, and the modern situation can probably be taken as a rough indication of pedological conditions at the time. The deposits are mostly riverine, being derived from fans originating from the mountains which form the western border of the plain. Broadly speaking, the upper plain, with its faster flowing rivers, has the coarser deposits, soils tending to become finer-grained in the lower eastern plain, and between the major rivers. This generalisation obscures a welter of local variation, however, which, as will be seen, is likely to have exerted a considerable effect on settlement location. Here, as on the Tavoliere of southern Italy, despite the greater areal extent of heavy silts and clayey soils, Neolithic settle-

GREECE

Table 13. Analysis of land use potential in territories of sites in Thessaly and central Macedonia

Sites	1 hour territory					10 minute territory				
	total (km²)	light arable (%)	heavier arable (%)	rough grazing (%)	wet grazing (%)	total (km²)	light arable (%)	heavier arable (%)	rough grazing (%)	wet grazing (%)
Thessaly										
Sesklo	45.7	25.84	–	74.16	–	1.2	80.67	–	19.23	–
Dimini	50.5	44.29	–	55.71	–	1.7	64.07	–	35.93	–
Argissa	64.8	24.87	66.77	–	8.35	1.4	87.59	–	–	12.41
Otzaki	69.7	27.21	67.06	–	5.73	2.0	96.08	3.92	–	–
Central Macedonia										
Pylaia	52.2	7.54	–	92.46	–	0.7	6.15	–	93.85	–
Thermi	59.4	15.32	33.51	48.53	2.65	1.0	91.92	–	8.08	–
Nea Raidestos	65.4	29.13	47.47	16.85	6.55	1.9	38.14	61.86	–	–
Vasilika C	68.0	55.16	12.70	30.57	1.57	2.4	100.00	–	–	–
Mesimeriani Toumba	68.2	60.10	15.65	24.25	–	1.7	61.45	–	38.55	–
Mesimeri	73.5	77.84	5.26	16.90	–	1.4	100.00	–	–	–
Kritsana	43.0	88.36	2.79	3.33	5.52	0.9	57.45	26.60	–	15.96
Nea Kallikratia	37.1	56.27	16.98	25.16	1.59	1.4	80.14	–	19.86	–
Veria	38.0	74.09	19.10	6.81	–	1.3	85.61	14.39	–	–
Nea Syllata	63.2	57.99	9.41	32.59	–	1.8	98.30	–	1.70	–
Nea Triglia	57.2	56.63	0.26	43.11	–	1.9	49.73	–	50.27	–
Phloyita	39.4	46.65	48.94	4.41	–	1.9	100.00	–	–	–

ment is concentrated upon those rarer exposures of more tractable soils. In Thessaly these are usually sandy silts.

Two main types of site location may be distinguished among early Neolithic sites. Some, like Argissa Magula, Otzaki, and Gediki are out in the main area of the plain itself, located on or adjacent to substantial areas of the lighter arable soils (Figure 54, Table 13). Others, such as Dimini and Sesklo, are in the classic mobile-cum-sedentary position at the edge of the hills. All the sites have relatively good access to water, an important factor in an area of high summer temperatures and aridity. Most of the sites are immediately adjacent to permanent streams (even if these are reduced to a very feeble flow in August and September).

Figures 54 and 55 illustrate some of the site territories. It will be seen that those sites out on the plain appear to have a greater arable potential than those at its edge. These latter thus may well have had a larger animal component in the economy. A number of considerations, however, suggest that such variations will have been relatively minor adjustments within a fairly uniform pattern of subsistence. Firstly, despite the differences in detail, each of the 10 minute exploitation territories incorporates a far greater proportion of good potential arable than is present in the 1 hour territories, and each 1 hour territory includes a substantial area which could only have been used as lowland

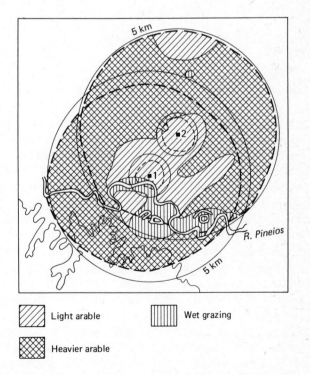

Light arable Wet grazing

Heavier arable

Figure 54. One hour exploitation territories of (1) Argissa and (2) Otzaki.

149

5. THE LOWLANDS

Table 14. Representation of cereal and legume remains from Neolithic sites in Greece (Renfrew, J. 1973)

	Knossos	Franchthi	Gediki	Achilleion	Sesklo	Argissa	Soufli	Nea Nikomedeia
Wheat (mainly emmer)	+	+	+	+	+	+	+	+
Barley	+	+	+	−	+	+	−	+
Peas	−	−	+	−	+	−	−	+
Vetch	−	−	+	−	−	−	−	+
Lentils	+	−	+	−	−	+	+	+

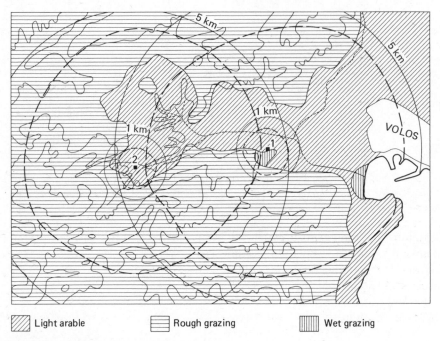

Light arable   Rough grazing   Wet grazing

Figure 55. One hour exploitation territories of (1) Dimini and (2) Sesklo.

grazing. The site of Sesklo is of great interest as an illustration of the recognition and exploitation of the unusual arable qualities of a very restricted area of Tertiary lacustrine marls. These provide a very easily worked soil, and, together with the soils produced by admixture with the local limestone hill-wash, form a small and unique area of much higher quality arable soil than any other available within the territory.

The plant remains from the sites (Table 14), despite the limitations of the available samples, suggest a substantial degree of economic similarity over the plain as a whole. No plant remains are available from Dimini or Otzaki, but it seems almost certain that this is because the data were not preserved or recovered rather than because these sites genuinely lacked arable agriculture. Emmer, barley, and a pulse of some sort occurs at all the other sites as a concrete indication of the important arable element.

As far as the pastoral component is concerned, sheep and goats, cattle, and pigs are found at all the sites, and between them constitute the overwhelming preponderance of the fauna. Where the information is available, the caprovine group as a whole consistently predominates numerically over the others, at least as far as the early and middle Neolithic are concerned.

The discussion of the animal remains brings us to a consideration of the overall site system and economic pattern which these few sites represent. In common with most Mediterranean lowlands, the Plain of Thessaly experiences such severe desiccation between May and September that plant growth ceases altogether except for a few favoured narrow strips along such rivers as the Pineios. For this reason summer carrying capacity for herbivores is extremely low, and, with the exception of those few that eke out the summer on stubble grazing and commercially produced fodder, the

150

sheep and goats spend this period in the Pindos mountains which lie immediately to the west of the plain. In winter, by contrast, the plain is at its best for pasture after the autumn rains; while the mountains have poor grazing conditions due to cold and snow cover.

This has led in historical times to a system of transhumance which is of great, though unknown, antiquity. While a few animals have probably always spent the summers on the plains, the vast majority of the local sheep and goat populations travel yearly between seasonal pastures which may be as much as 200 km apart. Characteristically these movements are conducted by a distinct social and ethnic group of pastoralists, the Vlachs. Today, as elsewhere in Europe, the system is in decline due largely to the capacity of modern technology to convert previously marginal arable or rough grazing land into highly productive arable. Since the Second World War this has so impinged on the lowland winter grazing resources of the Plain of Thessaly, the limiting factor in the local transhumance system, as to force a drastic reduction in the number of animals, while large numbers of Vlachs have become urbanised (Institute of Animal Breeding, Giannitsa, personal communication). Many of the remaining pastoralists now overwinter their stock in the Pindos through the use of hay, lucerne, and commercially produced concentrates. Data from other parts of Europe indicate a similar trend to year-round occupation of the uplands and breakdown of long-range transhumance, often at a much earlier date (see Chapter 6).

It seems reasonable to suggest that the Neolithic sites of the Plain of Thessaly were the lowland home bases of a similar mobile exploitation pattern, in addition to their more sedentary arable rôle. This would indeed have been the only way in which to integrate effectively the upland and lowland resources, and would merely have echoed the natural response of the herbivores to the environmental conditions. In the case of Epirus, to the west of the Pindos, Higgs *et al.* (1967) have argued strongly for the operation of a similar economic system, based primarily upon deer, in the Late Glacial period. It seems most unlikely that so successful and long-established an adaptation would be discarded in favour of the inefficient and uneconomic alternative, that of abandoning the uplands altogether, and limiting the animal population to the small numbers that could be maintained on the Plain of Thessaly in high summer.

It might be argued, on the basis of the scarce palynological evidence, that the Neolithic environment was very much more heavily forested and the climate less seasonally polarised. Stocking levels might thus

have been very low in Neolithic times, and the historical transhumance system inappropriate. Furthermore, it must be admitted that there are as yet no upland sites to lend support to our hypothesis.

On the other hand, all the lowland sites which have been sufficiently well excavated have yielded very substantial faunal samples. Furthermore, these invariably prove on examination to be dominated by sheep in the earlier levels, suggesting a more open environment than might be supposed from a superficial reading of the pollen diagrams. Indeed, it seems strange that with the passing centuries the proportion of goats in the Greek faunas generally rises rather than falls. This is the farmyard animal best adapted to browse, and one would have expected the converse situation were it simply a case of a steady denudation of an unbroken aboriginal forest. Much more likely is that there were always substantial open areas of grazing, as the high initial levels of sheep indicate, and that the numbers of goats increased as the woodland areas were degraded into scrubland.

As to the apparent blank in the uplands prior to the Bronze Age, this may be attributed to a number of factors. The Pindos as a whole has been very poorly surveyed archaeologically, and it would be surprising if some evidence did not emerge when this has been rectified. At the same time it should be remembered that erosional forces in the area are severe, and that the summer camps of shepherds characteristically leave little in the way of permanent traces. The sandstones and shales which form much of the Pindos do not lead to the frequent cave formation of many limestone areas, and thus these locations of favoured archaeological preservation are not commonly available.

From the very first it is thus likely that pastoralism played a crucial economic role in the Neolithic economy of Thessaly, and that some form of mobility would have been a necessary part of the system of animal husbandry. Figure 56 illustrates the vulnerability of modern cereal yields to climatic variation in the area. In prehistory, with fewer technological resources, and lower yielding varieties (and in all probability a far smaller margin between an adequate return and crop failure), the animal component in the economy would have provided an indispensable insurance against cereal loss, being better able to take advantage, through mobility, of transient and localised climatic variability.

Southern Macedonia

The only Early Neolithic site in southern Macedonia is Nea Nikomedeia. While the on-site data appears typic-

5. THE LOWLANDS

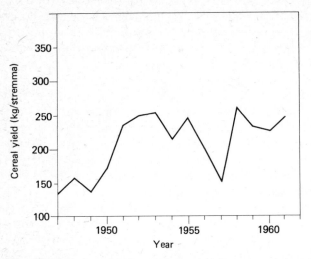

Figure 56. Annual variability of yields of indigenous varieties of wheat.

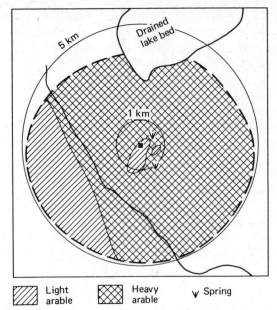

Light arable   Heavy arable   v Spring

Figure 57. One hour exploitation territory of Nea Nikomedeia showing present-day land use.

al of Greek Early Neolithic sites, it is difficult to reconcile the off-site data with what is known of Early Neolithic economy elsewhere in Greece or with later developments in the same area. As far as the on-site data is concerned, the cultural material indicates an aceramic to early ceramic Neolithic occupation. The economic data are closely comparable with those from the sites in the Plain of Thessaly, with caprines dominating a fauna composed almost exclusively of the farmyard species, and a flora including emmer, einkorn, and some pulses. If the modern situation is anything to go by, there would have been a good permanent water supply, as a spring flows strongly today about five minutes' walk to the northeast of the site, even in August.

The territory (Figure 57) does not, on the face of it, conform to the same pattern as that of Greek sites of similar age, and again there is a choice of explanations. The modern territory is dominated by the heavy clays and silts of the drained Lake Yiannitsa. Today the area is under intensive irrigated agriculture, having been extensively drained and cultivated with heavy equipment. These soils would have been way beyond the capacity of Neolithic agricultural technology to cultivate, even after they had been drained. But here again there is good reason to suppose that much of the heavy alluvium postdates the occupation. In Bintliff's (1975) reconstruction of the recent geomorphology of the area most of Nea Nikomedeia's exploitation territory would have been under Tertiary marls, sands, and conglomerates, like those of Knossos. As we have seen, these are much lighter and more easily cultivated than the surface deposits of today. Bintliff sees the serious silting up of the area as commencing only in Roman times.

If this were the case, however, it is hard to explain satisfactorily the relatively small and short-lived settlement at Nea Nikomedeia, and the near absence of substantial Late Neolithic and Bronze Age sites. In Thessaly, Crete, and Central Macedonia there is ample evidence of increasing populations through this period. Assuming that a large arable potential such as is represented in the Nea Nikomedeia area is most unlikely to have been abandoned for long, it is perhaps more likely that the silting up of the region started earlier than envisaged by Bintliff, and had reached a stage sufficient to inhibit arable agriculture and large-scale settlement during the later Neolithic and Bronze Age periods.

As we have suggested elsewhere, from the point of view of pastoralism, the Greek lowlands must be considered as primarily a winter grazing area. The area of plain around Edhessa is richer in summer water resources than many parts of lowland Greece, but has nonetheless a low summer carrying capacity for herbivores. We must suppose that, here as elsewhere, the human response to this involved some form of mobile pastoralism. Nea Nikomedeia is exceptional, however, in that there is a little more than usual in the way of corroborative on-site evidence for this hypothesis. Much of the flint toolkit has been traced to sources in the upland area around Konitsa near the modern Albanian border (R. J. Rodden, personal communication). We cannot, of course, assume that this specific region was necessarily the precise summer grazing

152

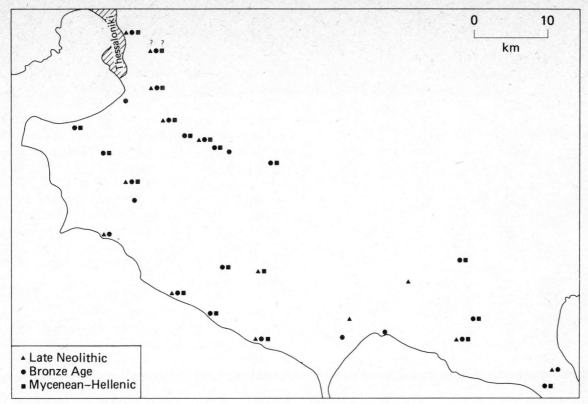

Figure 58. Distribution of Neolithic and Bronze Age sites in the Vasilika valley and Chalkidiki.

range to which the Nea Nikomedeia livestock were taken, but contact that clearly existed between the two areas may well have been a result of regular pastoral activities.

Central Macedonia

Prehistoric settlement is concentrated mainly in the Vasilika, Ghalliko, and Axios valleys. No Early or Middle Neolithic sites are known from central Macedonia, but the territories of over 50 sites representing all periods from the Late Neolithic to Classical times were analysed. The Vasilika valley and western Chalkidiki have the greatest concentration of Late Neolithic sites and will therefore form the basis of discussion of this area.

The region as a whole is hilly and is dissected by numerous small stream and river valleys, most of which are dry during the summer months. One notable exception is the Vasilika valley, where an abundance of water throughout the summer has allowed the development of large-scale irrigation.

The valley is a small catchment opening to the sea on the west and bounded to the north and east by mountains with a complex mixture of bedrocks, including limestone, metamorphic, and igneous formations. The valley soils vary from moderately heavy waterlogged patches to those that are sufficiently light in texture to have had a reasonable Neolithic arable potential, while the limestone hills everywhere provide rough grazing, with very poor soil cover and scrub vegetation. To the

south of the valley the bedrock is covered by thick lacustrine sediments with friable soils developed in most parts. The main limitations to arable exploitation today are steep slopes along stream and river valleys, and summer aridity.

On the whole, sites are located so as to take advantage of areas of high quality arable with tractable soils. Vasilika C in the Vasilika valley, Mesimeriani Toumba to the south, and Nea Kallikratia on the coast are all examples of sites whose 1 hour and 10 minute territories are more than 50 per cent light arable (Table 13). The other unifying aspect of site location is that all the sites investigated had a permanent water source within 5 minutes' walk, again a phenomenon related to summer drought. Even today, water supply is rationed in some areas during the summer.

French's survey (1967) gives us information on enough sites to permit the analysis of an unusually wide range of site locations (Figure 58). The site of Pylaia (Figure 59) has only an insignificant amount of potential arable in its territory, being on a narrow limestone ridge in low hills to the north of the Vasilika valley, above a small, but permanent stream and surrounded by similar precipitous topography. The territory is dominated by thin limestone soils, steep slopes, and rough scrub vegetation with occasional olive groves. It can only have been a herding station of some description, and it may have been a corral, such as are still seen in the hills in this area today. They are used mainly

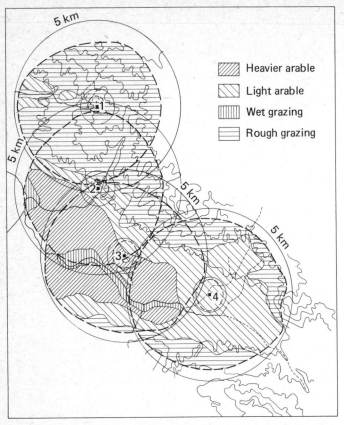

Figure 59. Exploitation territories of (1) Pylaia, (2) Thermi, (3) Nea Raidestos and (4) Vasilika C.

as summer bases for those small herds kept in the lowland throughout the summer, and the availability of a permanent water supply suggests that the site of Pylaia may possibly have fulfilled the same function in Neolithic times. If so, it probably represents the mobile-cum-sedentary element in the economy of one of the arable-oriented lowland home bases such as Vasilika C.

The three Neolithic sites of Thermi, Nea Raidestos, and Vasilika C form a line along the valley floor and are separated from each other by roughly an hour's walk (Figure 59). The exploitation territory of each must therefore have been considerably smaller than that defined by a 1 hour radius, as settlements would have been in competition for resources at the edges of their territories. The same spacing of sites with similar territories has been noted by Dennell & Webley (1975) in Bulgaria and will be shown later in this volume to occur elsewhere in lowland Europe.

The territory of Nea Raidestos, with its high proportion of heavy arable soils, appears anomalous, but this is probably more apparent than real. Nea Raidestos is located on the bank of the Anthemous river, further out in the alluvial plain than other sites in the valley. Therefore its territory will have been more apt to have been affected by recent alluviation and may well have

contained a higher proportion of light arable during its Neolithic and Bronze Age occupation.

Three further sites (Kritsana, Nea Kallikratia, and Phloyita) are evenly spaced along the southwest coast of Chalkidiki, so that their territories are truncated by the sea and are only half the size of those in the Vasilika valley (Figure 60). However, in this case the sites are more than 2 hours apart, so that none will have impinged on its neighbour's territory, and the area available is thus not dissimilar to that of the Vasilika valley sites. The 1 hour territories of the archaeologically contemporaneous inland sites of Mesimeriani Toumba and Nea Triglia overlap only slightly with the coastal sites.

By the Early Bronze Age this particular area had become much more crowded and actual exploitation territories must have been greatly reduced. Without evidence from excavations, however, it is impossible to assess what the greater density of sites implies. From the size of many of the sites it seems likely that this represents a real increase in population, rather than simply a division of groups into smaller units. The economic changes that must have come with and supported the population increase cannot be elucidated until more excavation has been done. It seems likely, however, that here as elsewhere, the extraction of an arable return from marginal areas through the cultivation of vines and olives will have been of considerable importance.

The two other centres of prehistoric occupation in central Macedonia lie to the northwest in the Ghalliko and Axios valleys of eastern Kambania. Here, however, very little trace of Neolithic settlement has been found, and as in the Vasilika valley and Chalkidiki, what does exist is all Late Neolithic. In the Ghalliko valley only one out of twelve sites has yielded Late Neolithic material, and in the Axios valley four, or possibly five, out of seventeen. This compares to four, or possibly five Late Neolithic sites out of a total of ten known sites in the Vasilika valley, and eleven out of twenty-two in the Chalkidiki. The location of sites of all ages is more uniform than that discussed above. Characteristically they are located on the upper terraces of the rivers, which provide soils of medium to medium–light texture. The floodplains would presumably have been utilised as wet grazing areas. Many of the territories are truncated by the Axios and Ghalliko rivers, which are wide enough to have seriously affected the practicality of regular exploitation of the opposite bank, during the rainy season at least. Sites are spaced characteristically less than 1 hour apart. This suggests that, at least for the period of densest settlement

154

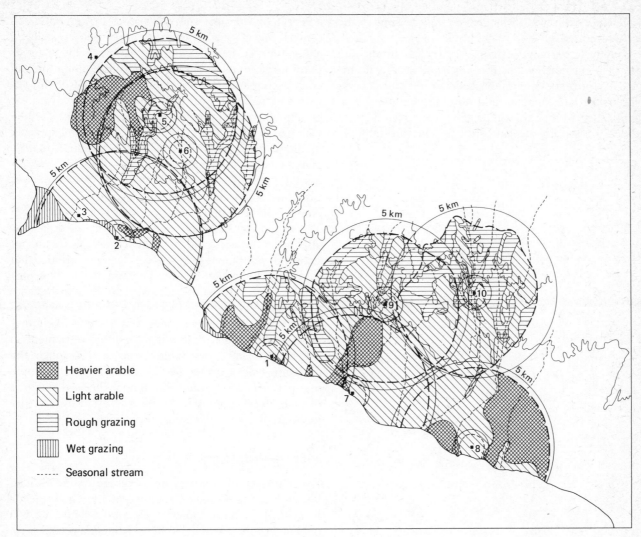

Figure 60. One hour exploitation territories of (1) Nea Kallikratia, (2) Kritsana, (3) Apanomi C, (4) Playiari, (5) Mesimeriani Toumba, (6) Mesimeri, (7) Veria, (8) Phloyita, (9) Nea Syllata, (10) Nea Triglia.

between the Late Bronze Age and the Proto-Geometric periods, exploitation territories would have been considerably smaller than the theoretical 1 hour limit, assuming contemporaneity of sites (Figure 61).

Two general factors are of interest in the overall pattern of settlement in central Macedonia. The first is the striking absence of any Early or Middle Neolithic sites in the area, in contrast with other important modern cereal-producing areas such as the Plain of Thessaly. The second is the evidence of a shift in the emphasis of settlement within Macedonia. Whereas the majority of Late Neolithic sites are found in the Vasilika valley and the Chalkidiki, the Axios and Ghalliko valleys become much more significant foci during the Bronze Age and subsequently. The high modern cereal potential of the area combined with the

medium to light textured soils might lead us to expect a substantial Early and Middle Neolithic population. Several limiting factors seem likely to have been of significance in this delay of large-scale agricultural exploitation. The soils tend to be slightly heavier and require additions of nitrogen or longer fallow periods to produce their best yields. Summer water shortage is even more severe here than in other areas of high arable production in Greece; total annual rainfall is usually less than 500 mm. With the exception of the floodplains of the major river valleys, the water table is usually too inaccessible to permit commercial irrigation. Many of the sites are conspicuously located adjacent to the single small perennial spring or stream for some kilometres, in an otherwise dry landscape, while a large proportion of modern settlements depends upon deep wells which could only be sunk in the fairly recent past.

Equally important, perhaps, are the persistent and often violent north winds for which the area is notorious. These render central Macedonia hot and uncomfortable in late summer and autumn, but their real significance is that in winter they are so cold as to reduce the season of plant growth. This substantially

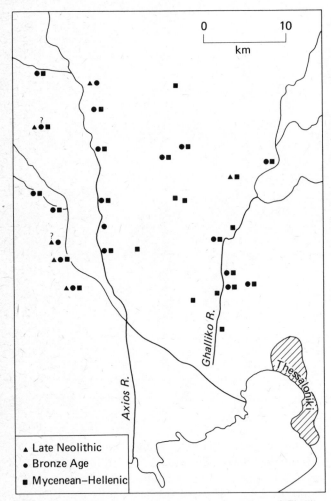

Figure 61. Distribution of prehistoric sites in the Axios and Ghalliko valleys.

reduces the average crop yields, and the chances of serious crop failure are higher, by comparison with areas to the south. This factor may also be of importance in the apparent trend in the pattern of settlement within central Macedonia itself. The Vasilika basin is much more protected from these winds than are the broadly north–south orientated Axios and Ghalliko valleys.

As we have noticed, however, after the appearance of the few Late Neolithic sites, the eastern Kambania

area rapidly became the main focus of population in central Macedonia, with sites fairly densely packed along the Axios and Ghalliko valleys. This suggests that, once the initial barriers to arable exploitation had been accommodated, the greater potential of this region was realised. Not only does the area have a far greater expanse of cultivable soil than the Vasilika valley or the Chalkidiki, but, being for the most part a medium loam, the soil is of better potential quality, given ideal management. Since this would have required greater labour and more precise timing of activities, it may be that it was only the larger Bronze Age populations that made such soils worth cultivating. The expansion of arable agriculture to this area may also have required the gradual, conscious or unconscious, development of cereal and legume varieties that were more resistant to drought and the cold winter winds. There are at the moment no data to indicate whether the climatic factors were more or less important than the pedological ones, but it seems likely that both contributed to inhibiting Neolithic settlement in the area. What does seem clear is that, once the difficulties were overcome, we have another example of a pattern encountered throughout the lowland zone of high arable potential: of a dense prehistoric settlement in an area of high cereal productivity.

THE NORTHERN BALKANS

For a variety of reasons our coverage of the Balkan lowlands to the north of Greece is patchy. The Project's work in Bulgaria has already been published, and will only be briefly summarised here. Romania is dealt with in more detail, but we were unable to conduct any field work in Yugoslavia, and have thus been confined to commenting upon published data, particularly those of Barker (1975a).

Bulgaria

The work of Dennell & Webley (1975) may be condensed as follows. The settlements examined, of Neolithic and Bronze Age date, appear to have been supported by an economy with a significant arable element. In a region with very restricted Neolithic arable resources, by far the majority of the sites were found to be on or immediately adjacent to those soils with the greatest Neolithic arable potential. Large expanses of soils which have only a seasonal grazing potential do not appear to have attracted settlement. Furthermore, site density and size of site both seem to be broadly correlated with prehistoric arable potential. The northern part of the Nova Zagora region, where the arable soils are most widespread, carries noticeably more sites than the southern area. In the Čelopeč study area to the west, where both climatic and other environmental factors are less favourable to crop agriculture, sites are still rarer. Thus exploitation territories are most extensive in the least productive arable areas, becoming more compressed as arable potential rises. It was also found that the larger tells, and those with long-lived occupations, were generally associated with the exploitation territories with the highest arable potential. Thus the indications are that the economy was substantially influenced by the requirements of arable agriculture, which affected both the distribution and density of population. This is not to say that pastoralism would not have played an important economic rôle; indeed, given the nature of the environment in general, it is inevitable that the animal component should have been of significance. Nonetheless, the arable aspect seems to have exerted a crucial influence on settlement patterns and the human carrying capacity.

The same broad pattern is evident in the Early Bronze Age as in the Neolithic period. Two principal changes are evident. A deterioration in the soil conditions in the lower-lying parts of the plain had led to a decrease in the arable potential of the area. At the same time the number of sites had slightly increased, leading to more closely packed territories in some areas. Both these factors will in all probability have exerted perceptible population pressure. The response to this may perhaps be seen in the larger number of sites in marginal locations on the non-arable soils, and in the colonisation of even very small patches of potentially arable soil, as with the sites of Södievo and Lubenova Mahla.

Romania

As far as the lowlands of Romania are concerned, much of the detailed field work and excavation to date has been carried out in the area around Bucharest and Olteniţa, and these points were used as the foci for the present study. The study area encompasses the zone between the Romanian capital and the Danube, a distance of some 60 km, and has been confined to the floodplain and interfluves of the rivers Argeş, Dimvoviţa, and the Danube. The main feature of this zone is the wide gently undulating loess plain, rising in terraces of between 60 m and 80 m above the courses of the rivers. Along the Danube in this area the width of the floodplain varies between 5 km and 10 km. Formerly an area of marshy meadowland and extensive shallow

lakes, much of it has been recently drained to form a low-level irrigated plain, between 4 m and 7 m above the level of the Danube.

Over 50 Neolithic sites are known from this area. On close examination the lack of early sites is striking, with Criş material occurring only in two areas near Bucharest itself. As a general rule, Early Neolithic sites in Romania do not occur below the 100 m contour. Since there appears to be no environmental reason for this absence, it is probable that unknown factors have acted to give us an inaccurate record of settlement in the area. In this regard, the site at Bassarabi, a middle Criş site in Oltenia is of interest. The site was accidentally discovered beneath 2 m of alluvial sand and gravel 40 m from the river, some of the deposits lying below the water table (Nica 1971). This, and the occurrence of Criş material eroding from the island of Boian seem to suggest that Early Neolithic site location in the area may have centred on the floodplains, and that the apparent blank on the map at this period denotes a spurious archaeological invisibility rather than a genuine absence of settlement.

In this study we have concentrated, therefore, on the major settlements of the later Neolithic and Eneolithic periods, especially those which have been excavated. The nature of these sites varied from single-period deposits such as that of Jilava to multi-layered 'tell' settlements.

As has been mentioned, the main feature of the lowland landscape is the gently undulating plain. This is formed of a mass of gravels, overlain by alluvial and loess soils, in all up to as much as 80 m thick at Marculeşti. A large proportion of the surface area of the region is formed by the terraces and floodplains of the rivers which dissect the area. The climate of this region is markedly continental, with cold winters, short springs, and hot summers. The average annual temperature is 11.1 °C in the centre of the study area, with a July maximum of 22.5 °C. In general, fewer than 50 days, between mid-December and mid-February, have temperatures below freezing. Early summer has the most rainfall, with as much as 90 mm falling in June out of an average annual precipitation of 580 mm in the north of the region. Areas closer to the Danube tend to be drier, and Olteniţa has an annual average of 540 mm.

This climatic regime has acted on the soils to produce a range from slightly leached chernozems to red-brown forest soils. The former are predominantly distributed to the east of the Ialomiţa and Argeş, while red-brown forest soils are concentrated to the west. Though slightly leached, the chernozems have a high level of natural fertility (Chiţu 1975), and the traditional agriculture in the area produced a cereal yield averaging between 8 and 14 q/ha (Warriner 1964). However, violent fluctuations in yield occurred from one year to the next, as is shown in the 13-bushel discrepancy between the 1913 production of 21 bushels per acre and that of 8 bushels in 1914 (Admiralty 1920).

The primary cause for the variability of the yields is the susceptibility of crops to drought on the highly permeable loess plateau. Although the annual average of between 580 mm and 540 mm is sufficient for dry agriculture, the pedology of the area and the rainfall distribution combine to make the area at times marginal for cereal cultivation. Much of the spring and early summer precipitation takes the form of violent thunderstorms, which is rapidly absorbed by the freely draining soils, and flows out in springs in all the great river valleys which dissect the region.

A study of present-day settlement distribution shows a strongly marked tendency to follow the line of the major river courses. Population densities in the centres of the interfluves are very much lower, and indeed the history of permanent settlement in these regions is very recent. It was only the increased technological capacity of the early nineteenth century, and the rising demand for grain, that enabled the necessary wells to be sunk and resulted in large areas of this land being put under arable exploitation. Between 1837 and 1916 the area of ploughland increased from one to six million hectares (Matley 1970), principally at the expense of pasture land that had been used by Transylvanian shepherds wintering their flocks in the Danube lowlands.

A further reason for the concentration of settlement on the river courses was due to the nature of the floodplain of these rivers and the Danube. Because the regime of the Danube caused high water levels in the spring and early summer months (de Martonne 1904), this low-lying area was inundated by floodwaters and acted as a crucial source of moisture-rich vegetation for livestock during the summer lean season. Stretching from Calafat eastwards the floodplain, or *lunca*, provided a valuable strip of wet grazing varying from 10 to 20 km in width. From the late summer months onwards, the fall in the river level progressively caused new areas of vegetation to become available for grazing until late autumn and early winter. Meanwhile on the loess plateaux, the low rainfall in late summer, the rapid absorption of any water, and the strong drying effect of the *austral* wind, which blows northeast along the corridor between the Black Sea and the Carpathians, make these areas unsuitable for livestock. In response to the poor quality of summer grazing on the

plains, animals are moved up into the foothills of the Carpathians or onto the *lunca*. Thus today the summer grazing resources of the *lunca* of the Danube and the floodplains of the other major rivers are an important factor affecting settlement location. Furthermore the large areas of lateral lakes, little more than 1 m deep, provide an additional resource in their large stocks of fish.

From this discussion it is evident that location of settlement near the major rivers was related to the presence of sufficient water, fodder, and other resources. The similar settlement pattern in the mediaeval period seems likely to have been related to these same factors, to judge from the seventeenth-century description quoted in Tappe (1972): '. . . the country is all campaign . . . and . . . the land lies uncultivated . . .

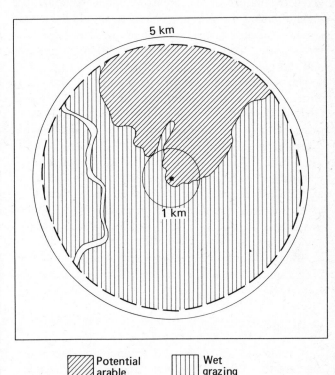

Figure 62. One hour exploitaţion territory of Gumelniţa.

while along the Danube is the most culture and pasture everywhere'.

An initial examination of the distribution of the later Neolithic and Bronze Age settlements indicates a closely similar pattern, and it appears thus that they, too, were located so as best to exploit the complementary resource areas of loess plateaux and the floodplain.

As has been described above, sites with Criş pottery are absent from this area, and it is difficult to explain this in any other terms than of deficiencies in the data. The evidence from outside our main study area at Bassarabi (Dobj), Locurile Lungi, and Moldova Veche in the Banat, indicates that Criş settlement occurred close to the river courses. The locations of most of the later Neolithic and Eneolithic settlements in the area, such as Gumelniţa (Figure 62) and Cascioarele (Figure 63), are ecotonal. The settlements are placed on the edge of the high terrace above the floodplain or on small eminences at the edge of the floodplain. They are thus in locations well suited to integrate the complementary resources of the dry plateau and alluvial *lunca*. One site stands out as an exception to this rule. The 'tell' near the village of Chiselet is sited on a slight eminence in the floodplain, only 1 km from the Danube. Its exploitation territory (Figure 64) is thus

The majority of the sites, however, with their territories divided between the dry loess plateau and the floodplain, offer more varied resources and seem likely to be the permanent home bases of a mixed agricultural economy with a considerable arable element. There is little in the way of botanical remains to testify to the arable element in the economy, but finds of wheat, barley, and millet indicate that the loess resources were indeed being exploited. Faunal remains are also rare, but such collections as have been studied suggest a livestock economy based upon cattle, with pigs and sheep present in smaller proportions.

We may thus envisage a broad economic pattern as follows. The loess areas adjacent to the site would have been exploited as arable, winter-sown cereals probably being the main crop. These would probably have been

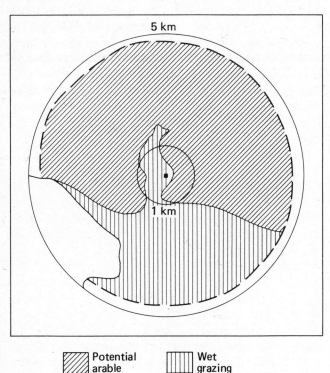

| Potential arable | Wet grazing |

Figure 63. One hour exploitation territory of Cascioarele.

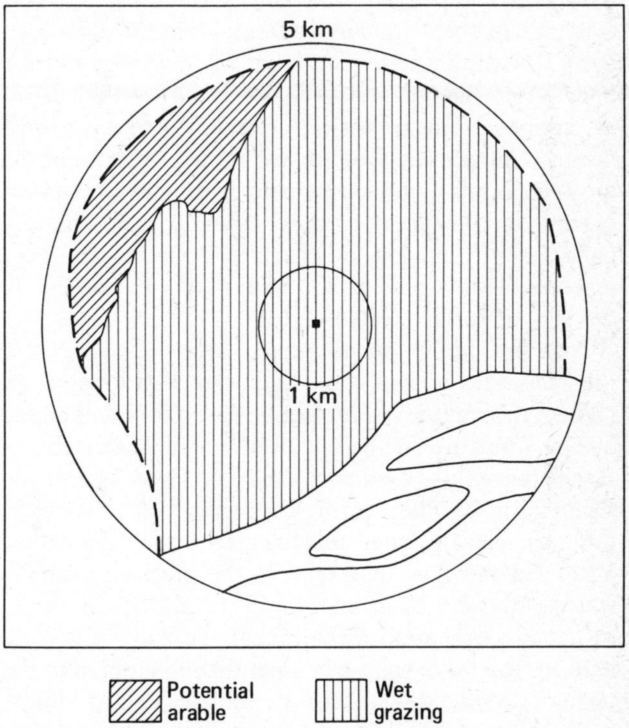

Figure 64. One hour exploitation territory of Chiselet.

overwhelmingly dominated by the floodplain soils, waterlogged or flooded for most of the growing season. Any significant arable element in the economy of Chiselet can thus be eliminated, and it must be interpreted as primarily a herding site. It seems likely that it would have been occupied principally on a seasonal basis, in late summer and autumn, when the rich wet grazing would have been at a premium in an area dominated by the dessicated loess plateau.

harvested in July or August, after the early summer peak in rainfall. The importance of cattle testifies to the quality of the wet grazing on the *lunca* and other floodplain areas. These would have provided a succession of grazings from the time that the floods started to recede in July, through into the autumn. Some of the wetland grazing may well have been preserved, or cut as hay, for use in the coldest part of the winter, but in the late autumn and in spring and early summer there was probably sufficient fodder on the drier parts of the loess interfluves to support the cattle in these seasons. The sheep may well have been pastured on these drier grazings throughout the year, perhaps with supplementary grazings on stubble and fallow land, or on the fringes of the floodplains, at the peak of the summer drought. The pigs would have made good use of the forested areas which would have existed where the water table permitted and clearance had not taken place.

The economy may thus be categorised as basically sedentary, but with a minor, short-distance mobile element. Sites such as Chiselet probably represent seasonal late summer herding stations, which may have acted as temporary home bases for a part of the community for this limited period. It is also possible that the sheep were pastured away from the main home base for some periods, but there is certainly no direct evidence of this. In many situations superficially comparable with that described here, we have argued for a much more significant degree of mobility in the pastoral economy. The necessity for recourse to such long-distance mobility is avoided in this case because of the local availability of an unusually large area of wetland grazing on the floodplains, combined with large expanses of dry grazing on the interfluves, which were inaccessible to arable exploitation at that period due to the lack of surface water.

A feature in the faunal remains from the very end of the Neolithic period requires some additional comment. Whereas the earlier Neolithic fauna is dominated by the farmyard animals with very few specimens of *Bos primigenius*, *Cervus elaphus*, or large pig, in the Gumeiniţa B fauna from Cascioarele, for instance, these species account for over half the specimens. Whatever view we may take of the precise economic status of these zoologically 'wild' animals, this apparent reversal of economic development is worthy of consideration, the more so as a comparable phenomenon has been observed elsewhere in the Balkans and in Moldavia.

As far as our particular Romanian data are concerned, two factors are apparent which may, singly or in concert, have contributed to the changes. There is both geomorphological and archaeological evidence of a number of substantial transgressions and regressions in the average level of the Danube. Thus the sites of Cascioarele and Chirnogi have deposits which lie below the modern water table, and also show signs of later alluviation at higher levels. One transgression of approximately 5 m occurred sometime in the later Neolithic (Banu 1971), and may in part have coincided with the faunal change. The effect of the transgression would have been progressively to inundate the floodplain and thus to remove the wet grazings so crucial to the livestock sector of the economy. One possible short-term response to this economic crisis would have been an intensification of the exploitation of hitherto neglected resources, such as red deer and 'wild' pigs and cattle.

The second factor is more specifically economic, rather than environmental, in its nature. At the same level as that in which the faunal change is observed, there appear in some quantity the bones of horses that are morphologically indistinguishable from those classified as 'domestic' horses in the subsequent Bronze Age period. If one is to infer from this that domestic horses had already begun to make an impact by the final Neolithic period, then it is possible that these may have had a significant impact on the faunal representation. Not only is it likely that hunting on horseback may have increased the efficiency with which large animals such as deer and cattle could be exploited. It may be of even greater significance that the use of the horse as a draught animal will have facilitated the transport of whole carcasses back to the home base, thus increasing their representation in the faunal collection even if the intensity of exploitation remained unaltered.

The data from the period transitional to the Bronze Age are scant and both that period and the Bronze Age itself are incompletely studied. We shall therefore confine ourselves to the consideration of one major question. It is usually suggested (e.g. Gimbutas 1970) that these periods saw the colonisation of the area from the east by nomadic horse-based pastoralists, whose culture and economy took over from that of the 'settled' Neolithic and Eneolithic communities which preceded them. Condurachi & Daicoviciu (1971) write that 'all the sites excavated in eastern and southern Romania have produced clear evidence of a radical change in the economy and an increasing importance of stock rearing'. In fact, there is remarkably little direct economic evidence one way or another, there being no plant remains known, and few faunal collections; and the 'new culture' is inferred largely from the appearance of material related to the comb-marked, shell-tempered Cucuteni C pottery on some sites.

As far as the evidence of site location is concerned, there is a definite suggestion of continuity. Although there are few settlements, they are for the most part still located on the edge of floodplain and plateau, and seem to offer access to the same range of resources as the home bases of previous periods. If there is a development in the settlement pattern, then it consists of the abandonment of the few sites on the *lunca* itself, and a corresponding move up the drier valleys of the tributaries. It seems likely, therefore, that the arable element in the economy remained relatively unchanged.

On the other hand, there may well have been a dramatic change in the pastoral element in the economy. We have already noted evidence for periodic high levels of the Danube and discussed the possible initial economic response to this. The total absence of sites on the *lunca* in the Transitional and Bronze Age periods may mean that a transgression was at this time rendering the floodplains inaccessible to regular exploitation. The strain that this would have imposed on the Neolithic pastoral system that we have hypothesised could in the long run be relieved only by finding alternative sources of summer grazing. These would have to be sought in the complementary resource zone of the Carpathians, some 150 to 200 km to the north. These long-distance movements may help to explain the appearance in the Transitional period of exotic pottery styles on the lowland sites simply as a result of greater contact with foreign groups of people. From the Bronze Age onwards it is revealing to note that there does indeed seem to be evidence, discussed in Chapter 6, for a more intensive and complete exploitation of these upland pastures. The integration of the Carpathian uplands with the lowlands to the south is particularly strongly indicated by the uniformity of ceramic styles associated with Glina/Schneckenberg (named after the eponymous lowland and upland sites respectively) and Noua cultures.

Thus while there seems at the moment to be little justification for the inference of a takeover by nomadic and war-like pastoralists, it may nonetheless be that the existing agricultural economy was forced by environmental changes to incorporate an increasingly mobile element in its pastoralism, a development which culminated in historical times in the virtual separation of the arable and pastoral elements in the subsistence economy.

Yugoslavia

As far as Yugoslavia is concerned we are in the paradoxical position of having to rely almost entirely on work which employs a form of our technique of territorial analysis, but with the interpretation of which we largely disagree. Barker (1975a) examined the soils and land use potential within the 5 km territories of Starčevo sites from a number of different areas. With fairly rare exceptions his reconstructions place arable concerns as of little or no importance in the economy of the settlements, and he emphasises throughout the variability of both the territories and the prehistoric economies, and the severe restrictions in the arable potential which would have been available in Neolithic times.

It is indisputable that different sites and areas will have presented varying economic opportunities, and that in prehistory, as today, this will have resulted in variations, often quite large, in economic orientation. This does not mean, however, that we may not look for some pattern and predictability in Starčevo site location. We have already argued that elsewhere in the Balkans where there was any significant Neolithic arable potential this was sought out by the early Neolithic populations; and that consequently a high proportion of the lowland settlement and land use was organised around these areas. We shall see later that the same appears to be broadly true elsewhere in the environmentally appropriate areas of central and western Europe. These are not sufficient reasons for us to assume that the same was necessarily the case in Yugoslavia, but they do seem to justify our looking again at Barker's data to see whether sites there may not have been more closely comparable in economic terms to those of similar date and nature elsewhere.

The Project has no first-hand field experience in Yugoslavia on which to rely, and thus can only make the most tentative alternative suggestions to those put forward by Barker. Enough of the Starčevo sites have now yielded botanical evidence of arable farming to indicate that lowland Yugoslavia was producing substantial amounts of crops at the time. The groups of sites studied by Barker are the major known concentrations of sites for the area and period, and in some cases the density of settlement implies considerable lowland populations. Yet in most cases, as mentioned above, the territories are interpreted as having little or nothing in the way of arable potential.

We cannot, on the basis of evidence available to us, exclude Barker's hypothesis that the increasing amount of evidence of crop agriculture represents the relatively small-scale exploitation of isolated pockets of relatively low potential arable soils; and that the population of the enormous and long-lived tell at Vinča, for instance, was supported by pastoral resources and the restricted arable resources of the Belečica valley. On the other hand, it requires only a minor, but crucial, reinterpretation of a few environmental variables for the picture of settlement and land use to take on a more readily comprehensible pattern.

Two issues are central to the interpretation of

Neolithic land use potential in the areas in question. The near absence of arable potential at many of the sites depends substantially upon the view taken of the chernozem and smonitsa deposits which are prominent among the modern surface soils in some areas. Barker characterises these as being too heavy for Neolithic agriculture in general, and adduces evidence that they would have been in existence in Neolithic times. Both these points are open questions, however. While there seems every reason to believe that chernozem and smonitsa formation started early in the Postglacial, there is also clear evidence that, in some areas at least, it continued throughout the Neolithic and later. Indeed, it has been argued that in southern Poland, for instance, chernozems formed on loess as a result of Neolithic exploitation (Kruk 1973). Furthermore, although the smonitsas are all more or less heavy in texture, many chernozems are relatively light, and would have been well within the scope of Neolithic arable capabilities. It must also be remembered that these soils often form the focus of modern intensive farming in Yugoslavia, and that here, as in Hungary, years of heavy mechanised cultivation in some areas may have affected the soil structure and made the soils heavier than they were. Their previous condition can often be ascertained from ethnographic and historical records.

In the Vojvodina much of the area is classified by Barker as having little or no arable potential because of either aridity or liability to flooding. Climatic and hydrological conditions are not substantially different to those on the Hungarian portion of the Great Plain to the north. As we shall see, there are excellent reasons for interpreting contemporaneous Hungarian populations as relying on an economy with an important arable element. While it is quite true that, from the viewpoint of the expectations of modern commercial farming, much of the area is on the dry side for cereal farming, this does not mean that it was necessarily so marginal for subsistence production; particularly if, as is often suggested, the climate of the Atlantic period was rather moister than that of today. It must be remembered after all that cereals were naturally adapted to and successfully grown in much more arid areas to the south and east. The large number of sites in those areas liable to modern flooding of the Danube and Tisza rivers seems hard to accommodate within any rational economic scheme, but here we must remember two important deficiencies in our data. The distribution map supplied by Barker is at too small a scale to permit the indication of localised but crucial variations in topography. He notes that here as in Hungary sites tend to be on drier 'islands' within the alluvium, and it seems quite possible that the sites themselves and their immediate surroundings were less flood-prone than the general zone in which they are situated. In addition, we have only a very broad knowledge of the river courses and regimes during the Neolithic. The main rivers are and were highly volatile, changing course on a short time scale. It seems highly probable that they would have flooded large areas in prehistory as today, but much of the alluvium has certainly been laid down in post-Neolithic times, and the floods may thus well have been less widespread and destructive than those of the recent historical past.

It seems quite possible therefore that when more field data are available, it will appear that here, as to the north, much of the Early Neolithic settlement of the Vojvodina was concentrated upon small patches of the best available arable soils, and that cereals were an important element in the economy. The close relationship of sites to the river and stream valleys is characteristic of settlement distribution in many loessic landscapes. Away from the rivers the permeability of these soils results in very low water tables, and drinking water for stock and humans was thus inaccessible until deep wells could be sunk.

Further south, in the region of the Ovče Polje in the Bregalnica basin, evidence has come to light since Barker's work which suggests that here, too, arable potential may have been greater than he suggests. Sites such as Rug Bajr and Anzabegovo are interpreted by him as having access to arable resources only in the narrow alluvial plains of the modern streams. Data from Gimbutas (1976), however, show that a band of chernozems some 2 km wide was available adjacent to the sites, and it seems highly probable that these provided the focus of the arable agriculture for which there is botanical evidence at the latter site at least.

THE TAVOLIERE

This area has been discussed in some detail elsewhere (Jarman & Webley 1975), and the results will therefore only be summarised here. The Tavoliere is a large lowland plain in northern Apulia, bordered to the north by the limestone promontory of the Gargano, to the west and south by the foothills of the Apennines, and to the east by the Adriatic. The surface is far from featureless, a series of ridges running roughly west–east declining from the Apennine foothills to the coast. The area is characterised by hot dry summers and warm moist winters. Vegetative growth is maintained throughout the winter, and frost and snow do not occur with sufficient frequency to be significant economic factors. Critical climatic factors with respect to land use are the mildness of the winters and the summer drought. Between them these ensure that while the Tavoliere provides excellent winter grazing it is nearly devoid of summer fodder; and that cereals must be winter-sown (there being too little summer rainfall to produce crops from spring-sown wheat). Cereal yields are highly dependent upon the adequacy of the uncertain spring rainfall. Modern land use concentrates on cereal production; olives and vines occupy the poorer arable soils; irrigation and drainage have between them extended the range of crops grown and the area under the plough. Thus the traditional role of the Tavoliere as a winter grazing area for sheep that summered in the Apennines is in decline, though the practice continues to a reduced extent.

Two groups of soils are of particular importance for the agricultural exploitation of the area. Much of the plain is covered with a mixture of silts and clays, heavy in texture and requiring mechanised equipment for their effective cultivation. Some of these are even today coming under the plough for the first time due to progressive drainage of the heaviest soils in the valleys and to the availability of caterpillar tractors. The second major soil type is formed of a mixture of the above soils with the *crosta*, a calcium carbonate crust which forms within the soil profile. These soils are much more friable, well drained, and lighter in texture than the former, and occur characteristically on the tops of ridges and on even quite minor and visually insignificant eminences. To judge from dates obtained for comparable phenomena elsewhere, *crosta* formation is likely to have been initiated early in the Holocene, perhaps in response to drier soil conditions. Neolithic features (ditches and pits) on many sites are cut into considerable depths of *crosta*, indicating that its formation was far advanced by the fifth millennium b.c. Relatively small areas of rendsinas, Terra Rossa, and coastal dunes are also present.

Very few finds of the Palaeolithic and Mesolithic periods have been made on the plain itself, and such as have been made are isolated and ambiguous specimens. This apparent absence of regular exploitation may be illusory to some extent. Progressive valley alluviation has certainly obscured some of the Pleistocene land surfaces, and erosion of the hill slopes may have further destroyed the evidence. As is always the case, we must also take into account the possibility that littoral occupations were submerged by the Late Pleistocene and Holocene rises in sea level. It seems most unlikely, however, that these factors are entirely to blame for the

paucity of evidence. Extensive archaeological exploration coupled with a long history of drainage and other civil engineering projects mean that much is known of the subsurface features of the plain, and if there had been any substantial or prolonged occupation more evidence would surely have come to light. Lowland settlement is concentrated at the junction of the plain with the Gargano, and is exemplified by such cave sites

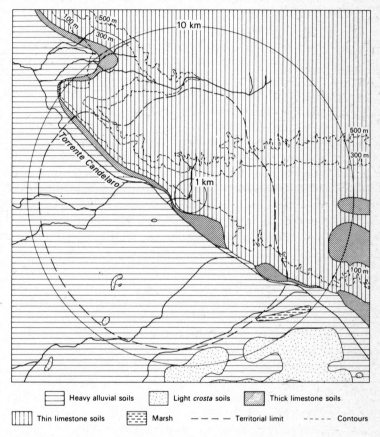

Figure 65. Two hour exploitation territory of Grotta Paglicci.

as Grotta Paglicci (Figure 65) and Grotta Spagnoli. These sites are in a typical mobile-cum-sedentary location, and probably served as home bases for the exploitation of the whole Gargano–Tavoliere region. They offer both the resources of the plain and those of the lower limestone slopes within their 2 hour exploitation territories. Some, like Grotta Paglicci, are situated on access routes to the higher ground further to the north. The isolated finds from the Tavoliere and the surface scatters of Palaeolithic material from the central Gargano presumably indicate temporary winter and summer camps respectively. The economy would have been based on large herbivores, such as the red deer, *Bos*, and equids found at Grotta Paglicci. There is a lack of data that might give us an indication of the relative importance of different species or of the type of exploitation pattern.

The overall picture, then, is of a restricted population practising a mobile-cum-sedentary economy, small-scale movements from a single home base sufficing for the most part to integrate the available resources. The paucity of sites from the plain seems to indicate that it may have had a relatively low carrying capacity under Late Pleistocene winter conditions. This may have been a consequence of extensive marsh and waterlogging. The Gargano is sufficiently small that it might well have been exploitable by such a population from temporary camps, without the necessity of establishing a separate upland home base.

The first and most striking feature of Neolithic site distribution is the evidence of a dramatic change relative to previous periods. Not only are the bulk of the known sites now from the Tavoliere plain itself, but they are present there in very large numbers. Well over a thousand sites are known from the plain from aerial photography, and of these it is thought that at least 300 are of Neolithic date. A further phenomenon of great interest is that 18 out of the 20 Early and Middle Neolithic sites analysed were located on *crosta* soils, which only cover about 20 per cent of the plain as a whole. This bias is confirmed by an analysis of the proportion of different soil types found within 1 km of the sites. From 27 to 99 per cent of this area carries *crosta* soils, the average figure being *c* 65 per cent. This is in contrast to the 1 hour territories as a whole, for which the area of *crosta* is less than 40 per cent, much closer to the proportion on the plain as a whole. Given the nature of the soils, two obvious explanations of this bias present themselves. Firstly, the *crosta* soils are more freely drained; while secondly they are much easier to plough than the heavy alluvia. These latter have indeed only come under the plough in historical times in many cases, and may be considered as being effectively beyond the range of Neolithic arable technology. It seems likely that the arable potential of the *crosta* soils was more important than drainage in attracting Neolithic settlement. Well-drained but infertile limestone soils at the edge of and within the Tavoliere did not attract settlement at this period. Furthermore, the dramatic change in the site distribution pattern at this time seems most likely to be related to the impact of a cereal-based economy. We know from Passo di Corvo (Follieri 1971) that arable crops were being exploited during the Neolithic, and they would seem to be the only element in the economy so different from that of the Palaeolithic as to occasion

such a change. The Neolithic herbivores, and any new measures of husbandry that may have accompanied them, are unlikely to have been sufficient in themselves to cause the change. The upland areas of Europe (see Chapter 6) give many examples of long-term continuity in site location in areas where herbivores remain as the subsistence base. There thus seems to be a strong argument that Neolithic sites were located with respect to arable resources.

Two other features require comment. Sites are rarely placed in the centre of the larger patches of *crosta* (which would have maximised their Neolithic arable potential). They are much more frequently to be found close to the junction of *crosta* and alluvium, a feature echoed in site distributions in many areas of lowland Europe. This indicates that, while the availability of arable resources exercised a clear influence on site location, access to the wet grazing of the bottom lands was also a factor of significance. Secondly, a number of occupations are situated very close to patches of grey gleyed marsh soil, showing areas of seriously impeded drainage. Such locations are today favoured sites for the sinking of wells, as the water table is frequently more accessible here. It seems likely that this was also a factor of significance in Neolithic times. Figure 66 shows the exploitation territory of San Lorenzo, which may be taken as characteristic.

The two exceptions to the general rule should also be briefly discussed. Monte Aquilone is a substantial ditched settlement like those already discussed. It is situated on rendsina soils formed by a mixture of limestone-derived slope soils and heavy alluvium. The soil contains sufficient coarse particles from the limestone for it to be relatively light in texture, providing a tilth much more closely comparable with that of the *crosta* soils than of the alluvia. From an agronomic point of view we may therefore treat Monte Aquilone as being similar to the main group of sites.

Coppa Nevigata (Figure 67) is a very different case. The site is a small mound without evidence of substantial structures. Unlike the larger Neolithic sites, it shows signs of Bronze Age and Iron Age settlement as well as the original Neolithic occupation. It is located on heavy alluvial soils, and would have been adjacent to a large saline or brackish lagoon during its occupation. There are no *crosta* soils, or indeed any soils suitable for Neolithic agriculture, within the exploitation territory. We can thus dismiss any suggestion of a considerable arable element in the economy practised at the site. The territory would have been roughly composed half of lagoon and marsh, half of rough grazing. This latter is today only of value during the wetter months, and is abandoned from about May to October. Figure 67 shows the position of one of the permanent shelters which are today used in winter by transhumant shepherds who spend the summer in the Gargano or the Apennines. There is no reason to suppose that Neolithic climatic conditions were sufficiently different to alter this basic pattern. Coppa Nevigata may thus plausibly be viewed as an ephemeral

that arable agriculture was of very great importance in the economy of much of the lowland population of the Tavoliere. The significance of pastoralism is also suggested by a number of considerations, however. Site location, while favouring the arable element, does not maximise the arable potential, thus indicating the impact of other concerns. The available resources on the Tavoliere are such that very large areas at that time

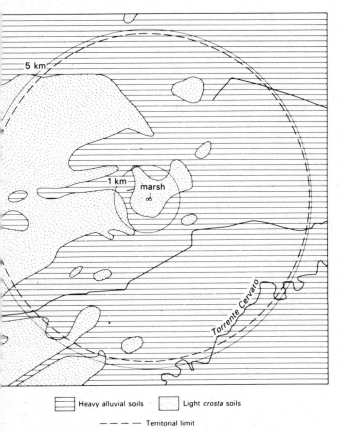

Figure 66. One hour exploitation territory of San Lorenzo.

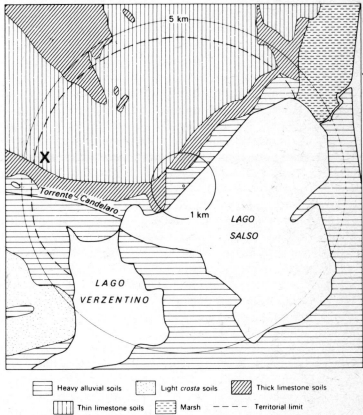

Figure 67. One hour exploitation territory of Coppa Nevigata. × = modern herding shelter.

but repeatedly occupied site which was partly concerned with the exploitation of coastal resources. Large numbers of cockle shells occur in the deposits. As discussed at length in Chapter 4, however, we do not believe that the coastal resources are likely in themselves to have been sufficiently important in the economy entirely to explain the settlement location. The site seems most likely to represent some of the winter activities of pastoralists who may well have included other lowland sites within their winter territory, although depending on its extent, the marshland grazing may also have been utilised during the summer.

As we have seen, there is every reason for arguing

could only have been utilised for pastoralism or less intensive forms of exploitation. We know from faunal collections that the common farmyard animals were present in the Neolithic. Climatic conditions are such that, with the exception of a few favoured areas along the major water courses, herbivores could not be pastured on the plain during the summer, as plant growth ceases for several months. Despite the absence of unequivocal proofs, seasonal inequality of resources must have been accommodated by human and animal mobility. The majority of the flocks would have spent the summers in the surrounding upland areas, the Gargano and the Apennines. Small numbers of animals could doubtless have been maintained as 'killing herds' on the Tavoliere to serve the needs of whatever proportion of the population may have stayed there to reap and process the cereal harvest. The site of Coppa Nevigata, discussed above, represents the winter aspect of this seasonal pastoralism.

It has been widely accepted until recently that the Tavoliere was virtually abandoned during the Eneolithic and Bronze Age. Theoretical arguments have been put forward (Jarman, M. R. & Webley 1975) for rejecting this interpretation. Coincidentally, renewed field work seemed to be indicating that, at the very least, the degree of change had been greatly exaggerated (Delano Smith & Smith 1973). On the face of it, lowland occupation at this time appears to avoid the bulk of the plain proper, and to concentrate on the fringe areas such as that surrounding the Lago di Varano and the Lago di Lèsina. Coppa Nevigata continues in occupation at this period. The sites themselves are very different from those of the Neolithic, consisting mainly of surface flint scatters with some rather rough pottery. Colle Tauro (Figure 68) is one example. It can be seen that despite the location of the site on a small patch of *crosta* soil, there is very little soil of arable potential within the territory. Even allowing for the possibility that recent alluviation may have covered some areas of lighter soil, it is clear that the territory is of low arable potential compared with most of the Neolithic sites. Other sites in the area and on the coastal fringes of the Gargano have even less arable potential.

It is difficult to reconstruct the pattern of land use at this time with any confidence. It seems very likely that some substantial sites will now be recognised on the Tavoliere proper, and that these will be in comparable situations to those of the preceding Neolithic occupations. On the other hand, the inescapable abundance of Neolithic sites contrasted with the overt paucity of Eneolithic and Bronze Age sites over much of the plain does argue for a considerable change between the two periods.

The climate of the Tavoliere is such that it may reasonably be termed 'marginal' with respect to cereal agriculture. Even today, with modern technology and improved varieties of crops at their disposal, one year in four is considered by local farmers to be a year of crop failure, due to spring drought. The effect is so severe that there is sometimes almost no yield at all. These disaster years are offset by the fact that average yields in good and moderate years are very high by comparison with much of southern Italy. A comparatively minor climatic fluctuation, to less rainfall, or less

dependable rainfall, or a change in its seasonal distribution, might in these circumstances have a disproportionate effect upon the viability of a cereal-based economy. There is no positive evidence that the Tavoliere did undergo a period of desiccation at this time; all that can be said is that such an oscillation would explain the available evidence without doing violence to our

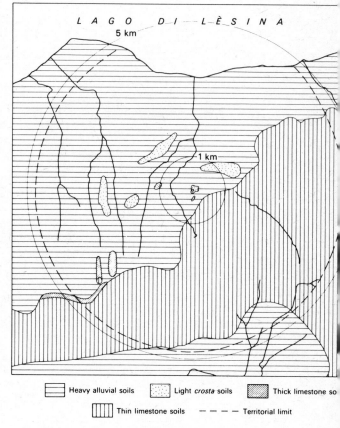

Figure 68. One hour exploitation territory of Colle Tauro.

basic theoretical propositions concerning human economic behaviour. Two consequences of a shift to an increasingly animal-based economy would have been a considerable decline in the size of the population, and the possibility of a more mobile lowland settlement pattern leading to more ephemeral sites.

The settlement pattern of classical and mediaeval times is substantially the same as that of the Neolithic. The majority of sites are found on *crosta* soils, the heavy alluvia being avoided (as indeed they still are today, for the most part). Both large settlements like Arpi and small farms show this locational preference. It seems reasonable to infer from this that arable crops were again playing an important rôle in the economy.

Despite the overwhelming emphasis laid in the literature upon the importance of the Tavoliere in the long-range, large-scale, commercial sheep transhumance of the period, there are also hints that this was only one aspect of the economy of the area. Both from Imperial Rome and from later mediaeval records there are references to the export of wheat from Apulia. Apulia comprises much more than the Tavoliere, of course; but the Tavoliere is by far its most significant wheat-producing area, both actually and potentially. Aerial photographs show areas of centuriated fields and of mediaeval cultivation, and the very substantial urban populations of such settlements as Arpi and, later, Foggia would have required large areas of cultivation to serve them. The continuous mediaeval litigation between transhumant herders and peasant farmers says as much for the numbers and importance of the latter as the former. Contrary to the usual construction placed upon this literary evidence, one might almost argue that it was only the pressure placed upon winter grazing by an expansion of arable exploitation that occasioned the friction.

However this may have been, it is clear that the seasonal mobile element in the economy remained of great importance throughout the period. It does seem, too, that sheep transhumance may have changed its nature somewhat. The system certainly became highly organised, run on a commercial rather than a subsistence basis, and involved the movement of very large numbers of stock from the Tavoliere to the best high Apennine pastures, up to 200–300 km away. How early such a system first came into being is unknown. From Varro's writings it seems to have been in operation during the first half of the first century B.C. but may well have originated much earlier.

One noteworthy change in land use which seems to have come about in the early Classical period is the commercial production of vines and olives. This is demonstrated by the evidence of aerial photographs, which clearly show the regular lines of pits and trenches that were cut through the solid *crosta* to aid root penetration. Many of these traces are datable to the first century B.C. Large-scale olive and vine production is of interest in that, as in many other areas of the Mediterranean, it represents a way of extracting a cultivated crop from areas unsuited to cereals, and which would otherwise be given over to rough grazing. Thus it would have resulted in raising the productivity of the Tavoliere and in reducing its carrying capacity for livestock.

The Tavoliere is one of the largest areas of lowland in Italy south of the Po. The coastal plains of peninsular Italy are very narrow, by and large, and are deeply dissected by river valleys. The overriding influence is that of the Apennines. Only the Campanian lowlands rival the Tavoliere in arable potential and extent. There are, however, isolated areas which appear to show prehistoric man–land relationships comparable to those of the Tavoliere. The Matera area of Basilicata, for instance, is another region of concentrated Neolithic settlement, though not as densely populated as the Tavoliere. Here again the Neolithic sites keep primarily to the lightest of the fertile soils, avoiding the heavy clays of the lower Bradano valley. Significantly this is another area of high modern wheat production. Similar observations apply to the ditched villages of the Stentinello group on Sicily, and may also be applicable to sites on the small areas of coastal lowland such as Favella, on the plain of Sibari. As is discussed in Chapter 6, there are good reasons for arguing that lowland sites like Favella were integrated by means of mobile pastoralism with the seasonal upland resources which are so dominant a feature of the region. In central Italy it is apparent from Barker's (1975b) work that the majority of the large lowland sites are situated on low terraces or plateaux overlooking river valleys. This gives them the same broad locational characteristics as the Tavoliere sites, with a combination of light arable and heavy pasture soils. Examples are Santa Maria in Selva (Figure 69) in Marche, and Pianaccio in Abruzzi.

A second type of site is found on the heavy and (in winter) damp lowlands of the Maremma. Soil texture makes this area entirely unsuitable for Neolithic arable agriculture, and many areas have only recently been drained and put under the plough. The area is desiccated and agriculturally worthless for much of the summer. Its prime economic value in the past, and for much of it today, has been as winter grazing for stock (especially sheep) which spend the summer in the high Apennines. One must postulate a broadly comparable system for prehistory; the Apennines cannot easily or effectively be exploited in winter, while the Maremma cannot in summer. The logical and advantageous economic response is to employ some form of transhumance between those two complementary areas, which are within a few days travel of each other. A number of sites, both from the Neolithic and Bronze Age periods, are found along the edge of the plain, others being in the middle of the Maremma itself (Barker 1975b). The former, like Palidoro and Tre Erici, could possibly have combined winter pastoralism on the plain with an element of arable exploitation on the adjacent slopes to the east. The relatively small size of the occupations makes it perhaps more likely that they were primarily herding stations, perhaps mainly utilised in spring and autumn, or as transit camps on the way down to the plain itself. Those sites more centrally placed in the

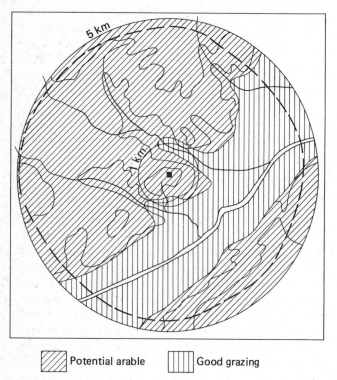

Figure 69. One hour exploitation territory of Santa Maria in Selva.

Maremma can only have had a herding function, given the constraints upon its economic potential.

We have so far been concerned with economic developments in the Mediterranean and sub-Mediterranean environments of southern Europe and the Balkans. In moving to the loesslands of central and western Europe we encounter a different set of key environmental variables. Thus, while there are, of course, substantial variations within this large region, those areas which formed the foci of early agricultural exploitation are unified by a number of features which merit brief comment as a preliminary to studies of specific groups of sites.

Körös and Linear Pottery settlements are characteristically grouped in clusters, each of which is loosely related to a major river valley. As will be seen later, however, the individual sites show no consistent relationship to the large rivers themselves. The relatively dense groups of sites are commonly separated by wide expanses of loess, which seem to have attracted little or

no early agricultural settlement, and only a few contemporaneous sites are known from the adjacent areas of upland.

Major concentrations of sites are all closely related to loessic soils or agronomically similar soils. Far from the impression frequently given in the literature, the loess areas are characteristically neither flat nor uniform. Their surface varies from a gently undulating plain, with a relief of 1–2 m; to low, rolling hills, sometimes with steeply sloping sides, and rising to 20–30 m; to a more extreme topography with heights of 200 m and steep slopes sometimes amounting to cliffs. The surface is dissected by small streams which would in Neolithic times probably have lain in wider, more pronounced valleys. Thus a soil map shows the loess-based soils cut by ribbons of more recent alluvium, and in the areas of greatest relief the pre-Quaternary bedrock is sometimes exposed on the surface.

The modern land use tends towards a monotonous expanse of cereals chequered with green squares of sugar beet, potatoes, or irrigated fodder crops such as lucerne. The valley bottoms of the larger streams support for the most part a rich moist pasture and often some trees. Modern settlement is concentrated in small villages, which usually lie in the valleys.

Annual rainfall in the loesslands tends to be low relative to surrounding areas, though it varies from about 450 mm to 850 mm. It is, however, adequate for tree growth, and the general lack of trees, apart from occasional small patches of woodland on poor soils, is due primarily to the suitability of the loesslands for agriculture rather than their unsuitability for woodland. The current botanical consensus is that in the warm, moist Atlantic period, during which the Linear Pottery sites appear in Central Europe, the loesslands would have supported a mixed deciduous woodland. It seems unlikely that forests of equal density stretched over the whole area, but there seems to be no general agreement as to the precise nature and density of forest cover.

HUNGARY

The boundaries of modern Hungary enclose an area of great environmental and archaeological diversity. We shall be focusing our attention upon the Körös and Linear Pottery settlement of the Alföld (the Great Plain) in eastern Hungary and in particular on the area of the Tiszazug. The concentrations of Neolithic sites in western Hungary seem to be a part of distributions which reach into Burgenland and Niederösterreich in eastern Austria, and we have assumed them to be broadly similar to these in their economic patterning and development.

Agricultural environment

As Figure 70 shows, the distribution of Körös sites is wholly confined to the Alföld, and almost entirely to the Tiszantul, the area east of the Tisza river. As is the case in many other areas of Europe, there is virtually

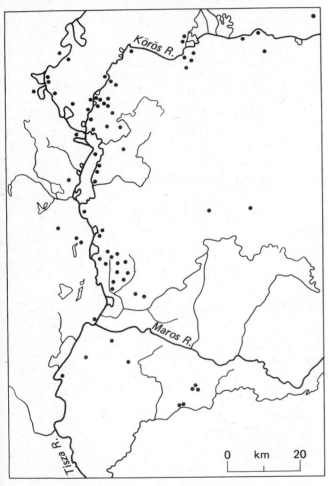

Figure 70. Distribution of Körös sites in Hungary.

no overlap between the distributions of Palaeolithic and Mesolithic sites on the one hand, and the first Neolithic sites on the other.

The Great Plain has in modern times gained a reputation as a treeless and windswept expanse of grassy steppe and sandy waste, largely from reports of travellers and historians of the eighteenth and nineteenth centuries. Today, however, it is largely under cultivation, wheat and maize being the dominant crops. Areas of steppe and *puszta* (waste) are relatively

small. The general consensus among botanists now seems to be that the Great Plain belongs to a forest–steppe zone, with open, mixed-oak woodland forming the dominant plant association (Pécsi & Sárfalvi 1964, Somogyi 1971). More open vegetation probably existed on the sandy Danube–Tisza interfluve and on the alkaline solonetz soils. Conditions permitting tree growth have existed ever since the beginning of the Holocene, particularly on the loess-based soils east of the Tisza. The fact that large areas of the plain have at one time or another become grassy steppe and sand dunes may be taken as evidence that at least some of the area must be considered as a fragile environment which may have deteriorated, even in prehistoric times, under intensive or misdirected use. East of the Tisza, however, there are large areas of stable Late Pleistocene loess deposits still exposed on the surface of the plain. It is thought that chernozem soils developed on the loess deposits before the appearance of the earliest Neolithic in Hungary, and it is on those soils that the Körös settlements occur.

Compared to the rest of Hungary this area shows many similarities with the more Mediterranean climates to the south. Figure 71 shows that the annual precipitation is low – 500–550 mm. More than half the rain falls in the summer months from May to August, and therefore the main part of the growing season for winter wheat is even drier than these figures might suggest. The climate during the Atlantic period, however, may have been somewhat wetter than that of today. As is usual in areas of relatively low rainfall, percentage variations from year to year are great. Table 15 gives monthly totals for rainfall at Szarvas for the years 1931–35. The variation from month to month, and in the same month of successive years, is enormous and is critical for the winter wheat yield. Excess rain causes the most damage in June, when the grain is ripening, and in September to October, when ploughing and sowing take place. Drought is particularly critical in May, when the ears are filling. Pécsi & Sárfalvi (1964) say that 'droughts exhibit a fair degree of periodicity in that they occur on the average every 3 to 5 years . . . Years with an excess of precipitation (700–900 mm) are similarly frequent'.

The timing of the annual floods prevents their being of any help in alleviating drought conditions for cereals. There are two floods every year, one in early spring, due to snowmelt in the Carpathian and Transylvanian mountain ranges, and a second, higher flood in early summer, due entirely to rainfall. Winter cereals planted on the floodplains would be ruined or swept away by floods at this time of year.

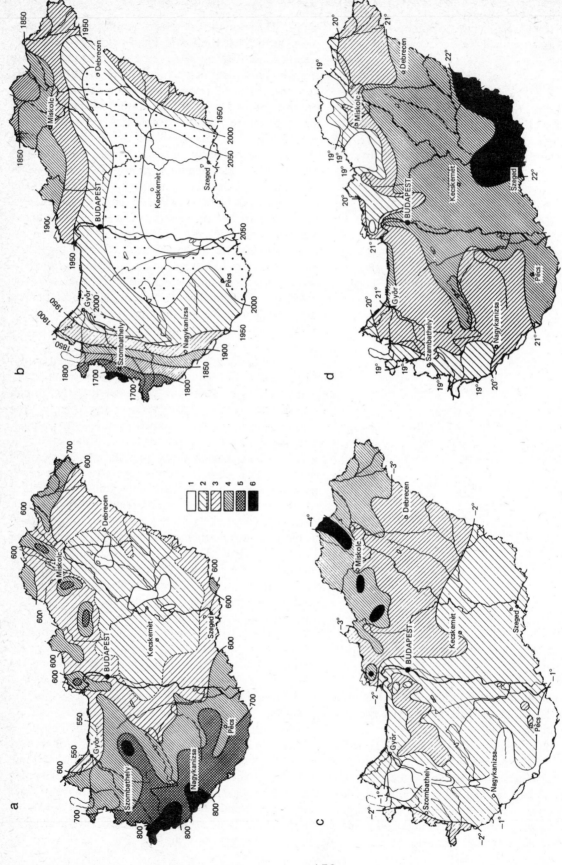

Figure 71. (a) Total annual precipitation. (1) Under 500 mm, (2) 500–550 mm, (3) 550–600 mm, (4) 600–700 mm, (5) 700–800 mm, (6) over 800 mm. (b) Total annual sunshine (h). (c) Mean temperature in January (°C). (d) Mean temperature in July (°C). From Pécsi & Sárfalvi (1964).

HUNGARY

It should be noted that despite the variability in cereal yields from year to year, the Tiszantul remains one of the most important wheat producing areas in Hungary (Figure 72): it is one of the three principal growing areas, one of the four regions producing the largest crops, and the Middle Tisza and southern portions of the Tiszantul produce the highest quality crops. The agricultural productivity of the Tiszantul is not uniform. Not only is the quality of wheat higher in the central and southern sections, but the whole level of agricultural production is greatest south of the Körös river (Enyedi 1971) – the area within which most of the Körös sites are found.

Other climatic factors which affect crop yields also tend towards a Mediterranean character. The area lies in the zone of the greatest annual total of sunshine (Figure 71b), the next to warmest mean temperature for January (Figure 71c), and the highest and next to highest mean temperatures for July (Figure 71d).

The Körös sites are thus distributed in a zone of high

centred in the Balkans to the south. It seems likely that the crops and economy in general originated in and were adapted to Mediterranean climatic and environmental conditions, and that beyond the Alföld, changes in these factors reached critical thresholds which presented very real barriers to further expansion. Only a small number of sites has been excavated, and plant remains have not as a rule been systematically sought. It is therefore of interest to note that cereal remains were found at the one Körös site where flotation was used (Kutzian, personal communication).

Bökönyi (1974), on the other hand, emphasises other environmental factors in his discussion of prehistoric stock-rearing in the area. In particular he argues that the large areas of marsh and seasonally flooded land would have been ill-suited to the high proportion of sheep and goat usually found upon Körös sites both in Hungary and to the south. Bökönyi suggests that the inhabitants of the Körös settlements had acquired a 'cultural preference' for caprines so strong that they

Table 15. Annual rainfall for 1931 to 1935 measured at Szarvas in the Great Plain (Gróf 1936)

	1931	1932	1933	1934	1935
January	51	18	17	7	17
February	19	20	11	1	24
March	77	40	44	0	22
April	27	79	26	28	73
May	53	43	47	8	66
June	49	50	46	69	18
July	14	69	27	100	22
August	87	63	25	17	50
September	96	14	52	35	14
October	38	55	55	16	17
November	35	16	72	76	38
December	29	21	46	18	53
Total	575	488	468	375	414

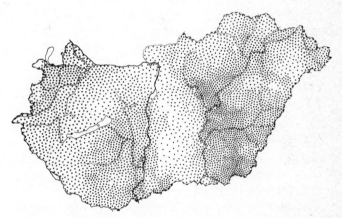

Figure 72. Distribution of wheat production (1 dot = 290 ha). From Pécsi & Sárfalvi (1964).

arable potential. It must be remembered that if the Atlantic climate was indeed, as is supposed, wetter than that of today, the danger of crop failure through drought would probably have been less, although this may have been counterbalanced by increased losses caused by too frequent rainfall during the harvest. It is of interest that the sites are sharply restricted to the area with the most Mediterranean-like climate available in the country. We may view the Körös sites in the Alföld as the northernmost extension of distributions

continued to maintain them as best they could in an unfavourable environment. He argues that they were so poorly adapted to the local ecology that it would have been necessary, for a period of some 500 years, to import breeding stock in substantial numbers from further south.

On purely economic grounds, it seems unlikely that so gross an economic maladaptation would have survived so long, particularly in view of the evidence, discussed below, for the accurate and sensitive adjustment of the arable sector of the economy to local conditions. As we argued in Chapter 1, while our basic

171

viewpoint does not demand that there should be perfect economic adaptation at all times, we nonetheless would expect such long-term maladjustments to be very unusual.

A more plausible explanation for the predominance of caprines is that the Tiszantul was better suited to those species than Bökönyi allows. During the Boreal period, prior to the appearance of Körös sites in Hungary, arid conditions had caused the formation of large areas of alkaline solonetz soils, which supported

number of pigs is dependent to a substantial degree on an intensive rearing system based on supplies of maize and barley for feed, and is therefore a relatively recent phenomenon. The numerical importance of sheep in these figures belies the suggestion that Hungary is basically unsuited to caprines, as do the distribution maps in Figure 73. Due to the greater milk and meat yield per head of cattle, equality of numbers between cattle and caprines nevertheless leaves cattle the more important animals in the economy of this century.

Table 16. Numbers of livestock in Hungary (thousands) (Pécsi & Sárfalvi 1964)

Year	Cattle	Pigs	Horses	Sheep	Goats	Buffaloes	Donkeys	Mules	Poultry
1935	1910	4670	890	1450	39	7.1	3.9	1.1	21900
1942	2360	4670	900	1710	71	n.d.	5.3	1.4	n.d.
1946	1100	1330	400	370	88	n.d.	3.9	1.0	n.d.
1949	1940	3320	600	910	n.d.	n.d.	n.d.	n.d.	n.d.
1951	2010	4300	700	1140	132	3.5	4.3	1.8	n.d.
1953	2240	4980	680	1640	189	3.5	4.2	1.7	n.d.
1955	2130	5820	710	1860	186	3.1	3.7	2.1	22800
1957	1970	5000	720	1870	129	3.2	3.7	1.6	23900
1958	1940	5340	720	2050	n.d.	n.d.	n.d.	n.d.	n.d.
1959	2003	6225	717	2154	n.d.	n.d.	n.d.	n.d.	n.d.
1961	1957	5921	463	2643	n.d.	n.d.	n.d.	n.d.	n.d.

short, salt-tolerant grasses. Even areas that were seasonally flooded dried out in late summer leaving a salt-rich surface. Despite the fact that they were usually wet or damp, these would not have been good pastures for cattle, who find salt-rich vegetation unpalatable. On the other hand the coastal salt-marshes of the Landes, the polders, Romney Marsh, and East Anglia make some of the finest sheep pasture in Europe. Pécsi & Sárfalvi (1964) write of Hungarian pastures: 'Owing to poor quality, a considerable proportion of the grazing grounds – such as the stony, sparsely grown pastures of Transdanubia, the alkaline or sandy tracts of the Great Plains, and the poor mountain pastures of the Northern Mountains – are unsuited for anything but sheep farming'. And further: 'In former times, sheep farming used to be of far more importance than it is today. At the beginning of the last century, Hungary was one of the leading wool producing countries in Europe, but she was eventually beaten by the much finer wool from overseas'. Table 16 shows the numbers of cattle, pigs, horses, and sheep in the whole of Hungary for a number of years between 1935 and 1961. The large

Despite this conclusion, there seems to be no support for the contention that caprines are poorly adapted to survive and reproduce in the Tiszantul.

The Tiszazug sites

The Tiszazug is a peninsula of 450 km² lying in the fork formed by the confluence of the Tisza and Körös rivers. Large areas of low-lying marsh encroach along the edges of the peninsula, and these would have been even more widespread prior to the regulation of the rivers in the past century. The nearly flat centre of the peninsula is covered by soils of varying degrees of tractibility and fertility, ranging from pure sand through loess to waterlogged clays.

The earliest occupation yet discovered in the area is of the Körös period, and settlement seems to have been more or less continuous from that time to the present. Sites of all periods are strung out along either the modern or ancient river channels, the interior of the peninsula having produced no trace of prehistoric settlement, and remaining virtually deserted to this day. The relationship between this pattern of settlement and the prevailing economic system will be discussed after a description of individual site territories and of the probable geomorphological and vegetational changes during the past 7000 years.

a

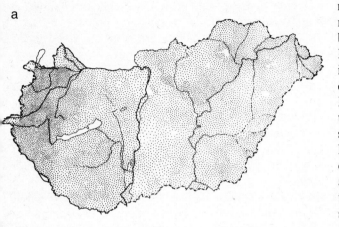

b

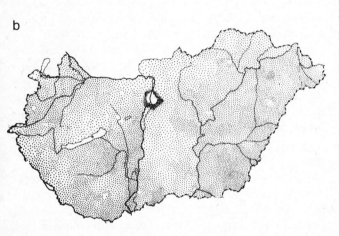

Figure 73. Distribution of (a) cattle and (b) sheep (1 dot = 200 animals). From Pécsi & Sárfalvi (1964).

The area appears as a gently undulating plain, the only noticeable relief being the Pleistocene sand dunes and the steep banks down to disused river channels. Thus topography is not at present a constraint on land use, nor is there any evidence that it has changed since Pleistocene times.

The soils and the course of the two rivers have undergone major transformations during the Holocene period. Because of the shallow gradient of the Tisza and Körös, they have followed continually changing, meandering courses. Furthermore, the spring snow melt and a rainfall peak in early summer combined to cause annual flooding of large areas of land prior to regulation of the river-beds. A geological study of the remnants of ancient meanders (Nagy 1954) has divided them according to the period of their formation: those of the early Holocene (probably pre-Boreal), those more than 1000 years old, and those cut off by the recent regulation of the river. Figure 74 shows in broken line all meanders formed later than the pre-Boreal but more than 1000 years ago. It is obviously impossible from this information to reconstruct the course of the river at any one prehistoric period. However, it will be noted that every Körös site lies on the bank of one of these meanders, which strongly suggests that those meanders, at least, show the Early Neolithic river course. No prehistoric sites have been discovered to have been truncated by these meanders, and therefore it seems probable that they formed prior to the Körös settlement of the area. The two river-beds seem to have been steadily diverging since the Pleistocene, and thus if we delimit the area between the present-day riverbed and the innermost meander, we will have defined the maximum area within which the rivers might have flowed. The precise changes in the course of the river in the intervening periods are not traceable. However, it is necessary to make some assessment of how such changes might have affected the exploitation territories available to the sites. There are two possible ways in which the territories may have changed. Firstly, Pleistocene and Early Holocene deposits on the river side of the sites may have been eroded away, thus leaving a smaller amount of good arable soil than actually existed when the site was occupied. This will be discussed in reference to particular sites below. Late Holocene fluviatile deposits are found only as fill in earlier meanders and do not appear to encroach upon earlier wind-blown deposits. The other possible alteration is that areas of present-day low-lying pasture may well not have existed or may have been separated from the sites by the rivers. Thus one must bear in mind that the site territories based on the modern, or even the best possible reconstruction of, riverine configuration probably minimise the amount of available arable and maximise the grazing resources. The distortion is of course greater in the land use proportions of the 1 km territories than those of the 5 km territories, because of the consistent proximity of the sites to the rivers.

Despite these uncertainties, regularities in site locations are perceptible. The first point, which has been observed frequently before, is that all the sites lie on high banks overlooking old meanders in the river. Secondly, as Figure 74 shows, all the sites lie on light fertile soil, primarily Upper Pleistocene loessic soils. The light but infertile soils of the central portion of the interfluve, and small, scattered patches of heavy clay are avoided at all periods. The medium to moderately heavy silts were only settled during later periods, as were the fragile soils liable to solonisation. Evidence from modern farmers suggests that the Early Neolithic people were aware of even slight differences in soil texture. For example, the sites of Csépa-Csipsárpart III and V lie at opposite ends of a continuous and apparently uniform loess ridge. Farmers who have worked the ridge with horse-drawn ploughs stated that the ridge is one of the easiest areas near Csépa to plough – two-horse land as opposed to three- or four-horse land in the lower-lying districts – and that the end at site III, the larger of the two, was lighter than the end at site V. A farmer at Szelevény-Brena reported that the ridge on which the site lies is far easier to plough than the surrounding land. Szelevény-Hosszúhat, the location of another large Körös settlement, was named as equally tractable soil. At Nagyrév the soil along the ridge was pronounced easy to plough except for that on the northwestern end of the ridge near the modern village; while there are two large Körös sites in the areas of the lightest soil, there are none in this northwestern area. A disadvantage of the light soils is that yields are more affected in dry years than are those on heavy soils. However, in an area with a rainfall peak in June and with excess rainfall as frequent as drought, heavy soils produce as variable yields as the light soils. One farmer reported that in the wet year of 1974 he harvested 36 q/ha from fields with heavy soil and 43 q/ha from light soils. The probable higher rainfall during the Atlantic would have put an even greater premium on light soils.

Tractability, however, was obviously not the sole criterion of site location, or the sand deposits would have been equally sought after. Instead they are the only areas not completely covered by 5 km territories. The sites are uniformly on stable soils of high inherent fertility. Fragile soils, difficult to manage and subject to solonisation were avoided, despite the fact that the initial yield from them would have been high.

There does not appear to be any correlation between Körös sites and depth of the water table, despite suggestions to the contrary by Nandris (1972). The depth of the water table at sites varies from 3–4 m up to 8–9 m, covering virtually the entire possible range (1–10 m) existing in the area. It is true that there are

only small areas where the water table lies at a depth greater than 8 m, and some of the sites are located on or near these spots. However, when the soil overlying the low water table is sand, there are no sites, whereas several sites are correlated with water tables at 3–4 m depths where the overlying soil is loess-loam. We may conclude that the soil, rather than the water table, is the influential factor.

The characteristics of the territories discussed so far seem to indicate that cereal agriculture formed a significant part of the economy of the Tiszazug in Körös times. Abundant animal bones from Körös sites in other regions lead us to assume that animal husbandry probably formed part of the economy in this area as well; indeed, animal bones as well as pottery can be picked up from the surface of most of the Tiszazug Körös sites. The usual cattle, caprines, and pigs are certainly represented. In the absence of excavated sites, however, one can only guess at the composition of the fauna on the basis of modern environmental conditions in the site territories. Today in the region as a whole cattle are by far the most important animals, with pigs and poultry following. Horses used to be kept for ploughing, but are rare today. Sheep are important only in a small area around Szelevény which supplies winter pasture for sheep that summer near Kecskemet, some 40 km to the northwest. Although this short-distance transhumance is restricted today, it may well have been a major aspect of animal husbandry in prehistoric times. The present-day importance of cattle is based on pastures on late Holocene and modern fluviatile deposits, which would not have existed in Körös times. Although some areas of wet riverine grazing would doubtless have existed, the majority of the available grazing would have been patches of poor and acid soil near the sites and the dry land at the centre of the interfluve and further away from the sites. Cattle pastured in that area today must be watered from wells, as there is insufficient surface water for their needs. Furthermore, cattle can only be kept in the area throughout the winter by providing additional fodder. Such a practice would not have been impossible in Early Neolithic times; nor would a system of transhumance in which the cattle were moved further south for the winter. It seems more likely, however, in view of the nature of the grazing resources under Early Neolithic conditions, that caprines formed the basis of the livestock economy, perhaps with transhumance to the Danube–Tisza interfluve or to the Bükk Mountains to the north, and that cattle only surpassed them in importance when high-quality pasture became avail-

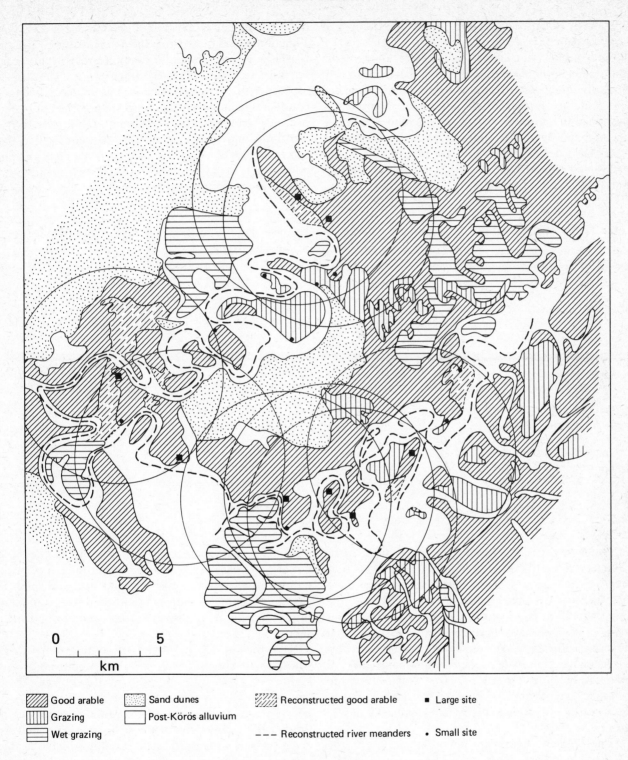

Good arable   Sand dunes   Reconstructed good arable   ■ Large site
Grazing   Post-Körös alluvium
Wet grazing   - - - Reconstructed river meanders   • Small site

Figure 74. Distribution and potential land use of Körös sites in the Tiszazug.

5. THE LOWLANDS

able locally in sufficient quantities with the changes in river courses.

Neither plant nor animal remains are known from Körös sites in the Tiszazug. We have therefore to rely primarily on evidence from the exploitation territories to provide any further insight into the economic organisation at that time. Even here we are hindered by the fact that movements in the courses of the Tisza and Körös have destroyed much of the information in the vital region adjacent to the sites. Something can nevertheless be done. As we have noted, site location occurs

quently a higher proportion of good arable land within 1 km of the sites than within the 5 km territory or within the Tiszazug as a whole, for example in the exploitation territory of Csipsarpart III (Figure 75). The arable aspect of the economy thus seems to have been of considerable importance, a suggestion borne out by the overall predominance of potential arable soils in the territories and the avoidance of those areas, like the central region of sandy soils, which have only a grazing potential. It may further be noted that sites tend to be related to the best available arable soils within the light

Table 17. Percentages of potential land use categories in reconstructed 1 km and 5 km exploitation territories of large Körös sites in the Tiszazug

		1 km territory					5 km territory			
Site	total area (ha)	good arable (%)	poor arable/ grazing (%)	wet grazing[a] (%)	sand dunes (%)	total area (ha)	good arable (%)	poor arable/ grazing (%)	wet grazing[a] (%)	sand dunes (%)
1 Csépa-Csipsarpart III	204	77.94	–	22.06	–	4475	45.84	3.20	27.78	23.18
2 Nagyrév-Zsidóhalom V/IV	314	55.12	–	35.04	9.84	4239	46.71	6.40	28.38	18.50
3 Nagyrév-Zsidóhalom	292	83.97	–	12.66	3.38	5809	47.68	11.92	23.39	17.01
4 Szelevény-Brena	237	41.67	20.83	37.50	–	4475	45.66	9.18	39.80	5.36
5 Szelevény-Hosszúhát	294	32.35	–	67.65	–	3454	47.50	7.54	37.20	7.75
6 Szelevény-Kisasszonypart I	314	31.89	–	68.11	–	4789	45.53	8.38	30.00	16.09
7 Tiszasas-Körösi Imre kertje	287	53.88	–	46.12	–	3847	49.07	–	25.96	24.97
8 Tiszazug-Tópart II	246	83.92	–	16.08	–	2669	56.01	–	30.61	13.38

[a] Includes post-Körös deposits.

with such regularity upon the banks of those river meanders dated to post-Boreal times, but before 1000 years ago, that it seems reasonable to assume that these represent a part of the course of the rivers during the Early Neolithic. The rivers are very substantial bodies of water, and we have therefore further assumed that they were sufficient barriers to movement as to discourage regular exploitation on their farther banks. Where land has been lost to recent river movements and hydraulic engineering schemes we have attempted as far as possible to estimate the probable area and nature of this.

Table 17 shows figures for potential land use of the reconstructed Körös 1 km and 5 km territories. We have already observed that Körös sites as a whole are differentially associated with one of the best cereal-producing areas in Hungary. We see here that this bias is equally visible at a more local level. There is fre-

loess-loam texture category. Thus some of the best wheat land lies on the Nagyrév peninsula, with two large Körös sites, whereas the land in the vicinity of Tiszainoka and Tiszakürt is slightly less fertile and has produced only a few small surface scatters of Körös sherds.

Nevertheless, all the territories contain some areas which could not profitably have been cultivated (see Figure 74): the waterlogged and flood-prone river margins, the heavy soils, and those too infertile or too poorly retentive of water. These would have provided the grazing component of the economy. The heavier and river-side soils would have been invaluable in the summer, when the vegetation on the more freely draining soils was of little value. We must also remember our earlier suggestion that use would probably have been made of transhumance in order to pasture as much stock as possible outside the area during summer.

176

If this was the case, the annual territories of the populations based in the Tiszazug may have had as much as 75 per cent grazing resources.

The Tiszazug illustrates well the possibilities for short-fallow and simple rotation cropping systems on loessic soils, and weighs against the suggestion that the high arable potential of such soils derives purely from prolonged and careful management. Indeed, the farming practices of mediaeval and later Hungarian peasantry have on occasion been roundly condemned, as by

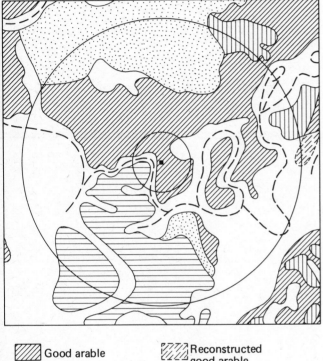

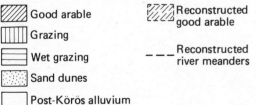

Good arable   Reconstructed good arable

Grazing

Wet grazing   Reconstructed river meanders

Sand dunes

Post-Körös alluvium

Figure 75. One hour exploitation territory of Csépa–Csipsarpart III.

Warriner (1964). One farmer interviewed by us used to apply 600 q of manure per hectare once every six or seven years. Another stated that because of the shortage of manure he applied only 200–250 q/ha every fourth year. Both used a rotation system combining wheat, barley, and maize, but no fallow. Their yields of wheat and barley ranged from 6–8 q/ha in a bad year up to 28 q/ha in good years, high yields for subsistence agriculture. One informant calculated that without any manure the yield in a good year would be 8–10 q/ha.

While inadequate by modern standards, this is double that quoted in many sources as average mediaeval yields in Western Europe. It therefore seems that these soils are well able to withstand prolonged periods of cereal cropping with only modest measures to preserve soil fertility. It seems highly unlikely that the prehistoric farmers of the area would have been forced into extensive long-fallow methods to maintain yields.

The riverside location of the sites raises the question of the rôle of fishing in the site economies and in that of the region as a whole. Fishing was unanimously declared by our informants to be of secondary importance in the modern economy of the region, whether from the point of view of commercial fishing or from that of contribution to the local diet. We have already argued in Chapters 3 and 4 that fish are on the whole poorer sources of calories than large mammals, and there are no special circumstances here that suggest an exception to that general rule. Even at a site such as Röszke-Ludvár near Szeged, where fish bones account for 20 per cent of the fauna, only two bones are certainly from large fish that would have contributed a significant amount of food to the diet.

If fishing was not an important element in the economy, we are left with the question as to why all the sites are located on the river banks rather than centrally within the best of the potential arable soils available. This would have maximised access to the cereal land which we have argued to be a dominant factor in the economy. This is not a question which we can answer unequivocally, but a number of factors are probably relevant. We may first note that some of the most fertile of the tractable loess soils are found on the high banks along the old river courses. Furthermore, here as elsewhere in Europe (see other sections of this chapter and Chapter 4) the high quality wet-land grazing was a rich but scarce resource, which probably exerted a considerable economic attraction, possibly extending to site location. To this may be added the value of drinking water for both human and animal populations in an area where surface water was narrowly restricted to the river valleys. The grazing resources will have been all the more important in view of the slightly capricious climate from the point of view of cereal farming. Spring drought affects cereal yields more or less severely about once every four years today. While this may have happened less frequently under Atlantic climatic conditions, it seems likely that it would have been a factor which it was necessary to take into account. Where complete or near crop failure is threatened once per generation subsistence farmers cannot afford to place all their economic eggs in the

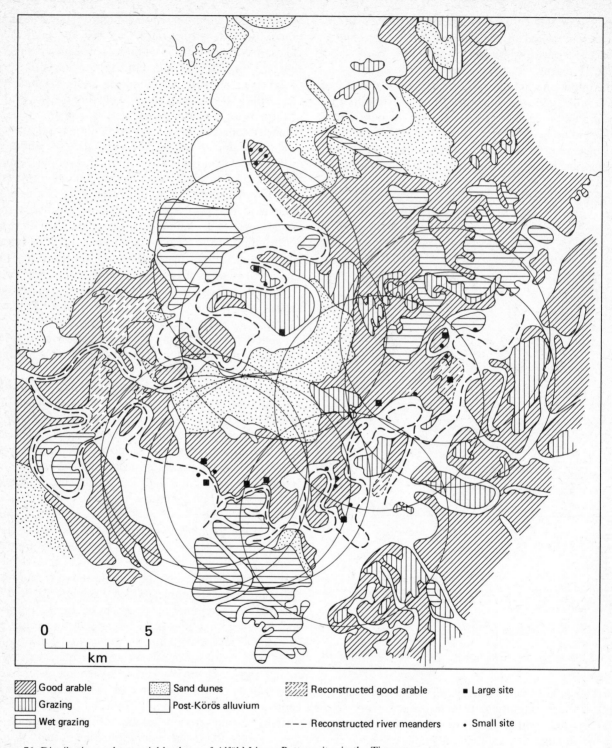

Figure 76. Distribution and potential land use of Alföld Linear Pottery sites in the Tiszazug.

0   5

km

▨ Good arable	⠿ Sand dunes	▨ Reconstructed good arable	■ Large site
▥ Grazing	☐ Post-Körös alluvium		
▤ Wet grazing		--- Reconstructed river meanders	• Small site

arable basket, and other resources which may have buffered fluctuations in the cereal yield thus have considerable significance. The grazing animals in all likelihood have been chief among these, although doubtless the riverine resources would also have been useful in this capacity.

That the river, whether as a source of food, travel, or protection, was not the primary locational directive is confirmed by the distribution of sites in the Endröd-Gyoma region, to the east of the Tiszazug in the Körös river valley. In this area there is a broad band of heavy, clayey soils running adjacent and parallel to the river, with light loessic soils lying several kilometres to the south. If the river had been more important than access to tractable arable soils, one would expect to find Körös sites on the heavy soil near the river. Instead they are all on the light, loess-loam soils, judged by modern farmers to be the best in the area for wheat cultivation. No ancient river meanders cut this area. However, there are small valleys and depressions which may have carried streams in Körös times and provided an easy source of water and small amounts of rich grazing, but no large fish. Thus it appears that where fertile, tractable soils could be integrated with riverside resources in the same territories, these were the preferred site locations. However, when such a combination was impossible, the arable sector of the economy dictated the location of sites.

Alföld Linear Pottery and Late Neolithic sites

Figure 76 clearly shows the many points of similarity between the distribution and territories of the Körös and the Alföld Linear Pottery sites. The focus of settlement and exploitation remains in the southern part of the area, concentrating on the Pleistocene loess soils. There are only five sites at which both Körös and Linear Pottery material are found together. At three of those the Körös finds consist of only scattered sherds, and at the other two the Linear Pottery identification is insecure. It thus appears that Körös settlements were for the most part avoided as places for Linear Pottery settlements. Many of the sites of the two periods are only a few hundred metres apart, however, and they would thus have had access to virtually identical exploitation territories. This suggests that the same basic factors governed site location, with a minor factor prompting a small shift in the precise locations. It may well be that the 500 years or so of Körös exploitation had slightly but noticeably lowered the productivity of the immediate surroundings of the Körös sites through loss of fertility or deterioration of soil structure. Many other phenomena, both economic and non-economic, could be suggested as causative agents, but the archaeological data do not at present permit us to arrive at a preferred hypothesis. A similar minor shift in site location occurs between the Linear Pottery and Funnel-Beaker occupations in southern Poland (see pp. 194–7).

There are some sites in entirely new locations, however, which must be explained differently. These are the sites lying on poor solonetz soils, on medium heavy fluviatile silts, and on low-lying marshy or seasonally flooded areas. No Körös sites occur on these soils apart from a few small scatters of sherds on the solonetzes of the northwest part of the region. There are two possible explanations for this development in the settlement pattern, each of which probably played some part. The first involves climatic and hydrological alterations which would not only have influenced the relationship between areas of land and water, but also had an effect on soil development.

Nagy (1954) has suggested that under Atlantic conditions in the Tiszazug development of chernozems and calcification (solonetz formation) ceased and the undesirable salts began to be washed from the upper seasonally flooded surfaces down onto the alluvial plain. Subsequently the Tisza River began downcutting and a new terrace was formed below the existing Early Holocene terrace. At this time the Tisza took on roughly its modern course prior to regulation. Excess salts continued to be washed out of the solonetzes which had formed during the Boreal phase. Thus this period witnessed the creation of one new land surface, the lower terrace, and the improvement of another, the Early Holocene solonetz soils.

At the moment the chronological correlation of changes in settlement pattern with geomorphological development cannot be demonstrated. However, the new site locations are precisely those which might be expected to result from the environmental changes described. Settlement expanded on to the two newly created areas. Neither could be considered to be as attractive for cereal agriculture and permanent settlements as the earlier Körös settlement areas. Despite their improvement, the solonetz soils would have required careful management. In years with adequate rainfall during the growing season, they could have produced reasonable cereal yields, though they would always have been more safely utilised as pasture. The decreased salination may have made them suitable as cattle pasture, whereas previously they would only have been exploitable by sheep. Such a change has been recorded for the North Sea polders and East Anglian fenlands in mediaeval times, which first supported sheep and later, as the salt was leached from the meadows, were used for cattle (Duby 1968). The lower terrace would have been subject to annual flooding in spring and early summer and so could only have been used for seasonal grazing. With this increased wet grazing potential one would expect a livestock balance rather more like that of today, with cattle assuming a dominant economic role. Figures of the livestock distribution in four Tiszazug villages for the year 1895 are shown in Table 18. There is great variability from

Table 18. Distribution of livestock in the Tiszazug in 1895

	Csépa	Tiszainoka	Tiszasas	Szelevény	Total
cattle	380	249	580	1714	2923
caprines	142	1587	23	1285	3037
pigs	1486	742	926	3099	6253
horses	512	191	451	668	1822

village to village, but the total number of cattle and caprines is nearly equal. Given the higher meat and milk yield of cattle, they must have been economically more important. The variation from village to village is due primarily to the amount of solonetz pasture in its territory. It remains for future excavations and faunal analyses to discover whether cattle do increase in importance in the Tiszazug at this period. If such a change is confirmed, it seems far more probable that it was due to an increase in the availability of grazing suitable for cattle than to the 'alien' nature of the Körös livestock (Bökönyi 1974) and the conservatism of the Körös people.

It may be that these marginal environments would not have been utilised at all had it not been for a contemporaneous increase in population. There are 50 per cent more Linear Pottery sites than Körös sites in the Tiszazug, and the expansion of settlement is precisely into those areas which would have appeared more attractive under the combined influence of desalinisation and increasing population pressure. These areas were used in mediaeval times, also a period of high population, for huts of herdsmen and shelters for animals.

Very few settlements are known which contain the relatively short-lived Late Neolithic pottery types. This is hard to explain in the current state of knowledge. It seems most unlikely that there was a total absence of a local population during the 300 years or so that the Tisza 'culture' is thought to span. It is possible that the high population levels of the preceding period placed an unsustainable demand on the resources, and that the more brittle sectors of the environment suffered as a consequence, causing the collapse of a part of the economy and demographic stagnation. This seems unlikely as far as the more stable and fertile arable soils are concerned, however; unless a substantial unfavourable climatic oscillation occurred concurrently, of which we have no evidence. We must remember that in the absence of excavations from the area we know little of the details of the local ceramic sequence. This ignorance, and the strong possibility of Late Neolithic deposits existing under large Bronze Age tells, may eventually prove more relevant to the ostensible lacuna in occupation during the Late Neolithic.

It is appropriate to comment here upon the observation by Bökönyi (1974) that in other areas of Hungary some sites, particularly in the Late Neolithic Herpály culture, have an unusually high proportion of 'wild' animals in their fauna. On the sites in question it is only in a few instances that wild animals contribute more than 50 per cent of the animal resources on the site (Figure 77a). In most other instances the contribution of wild animals is much smaller, especially if one takes into consideration the actual meat weight contributed by the various species. The most important of the larger animals is the aurochs, which may in fact be confusing the figures for wild and domestic species. Bökönyi reports that on Middle and Late Neolithic sites there are not only bones of aurochs and domestic cattle, but also specimens that are transitional between the two. He himself suggests that the livestock was increased 'by capturing and domesticating wild animals'. If the aurochs on the sites were 'domesticated', as Bökönyi postulates, then they cannot be included in the percentages of 'wild' animals, nor can they be considered a 'hunted' species. Forms intermediate between 'wild' and 'domestic' pig also occur on these sites, and it seems probable that they, too, should be added to the husbanded species, as it appears they were kept under identical conditions. If we examine Figure 77b with this in mind, it can be seen that Körös sites have the largest number of what were probably casually hunted animals, mainly fish and terrapins, small mammals and birds, which would have contributed little to the diet overall. The main interest in the phenomenon of the exploitation of large cattle and pigs (and, to some

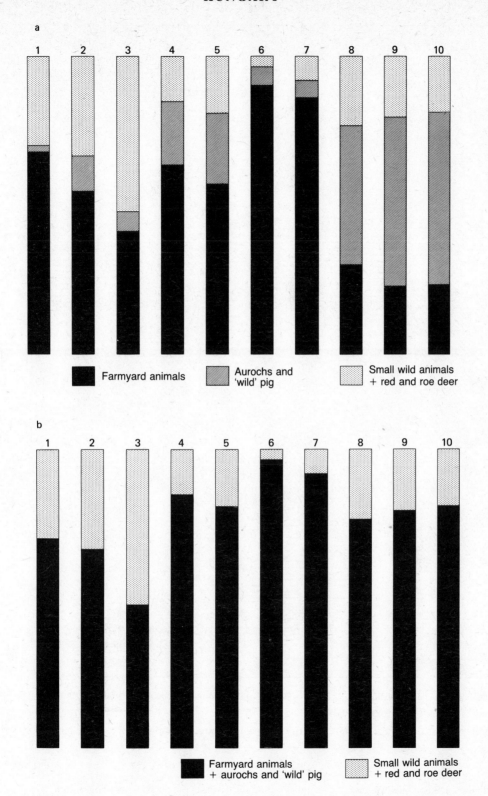

Figure 77a and b. Frequencies of species in Hungarian Neolithic faunas. (1) Maroslele-Pana, (2) Gyálarét, (3) Röszke-Ludvár, (4) Lebö, (5) Szegvár-Tüzköves, (6) Györ-Pápai vám, (7) Neszmély-Tekeres patak, (8) Polgár-Csöszhalom, (9) Berettyószentmárton, (10) Berrettyóúöjfa-lu. After Bökönyi (1974).

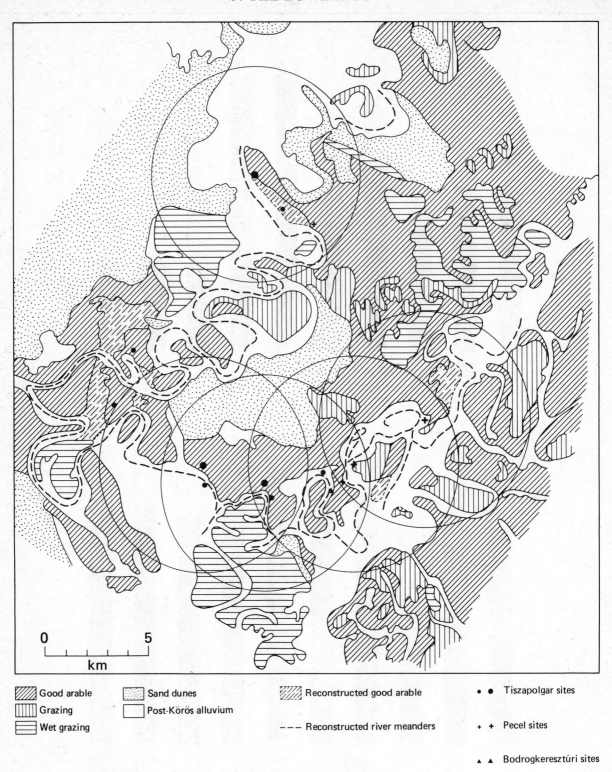

Figure 78. Distribution and potential land use of Eneolithic sites in the Tiszazug (larger symbol = larger site).

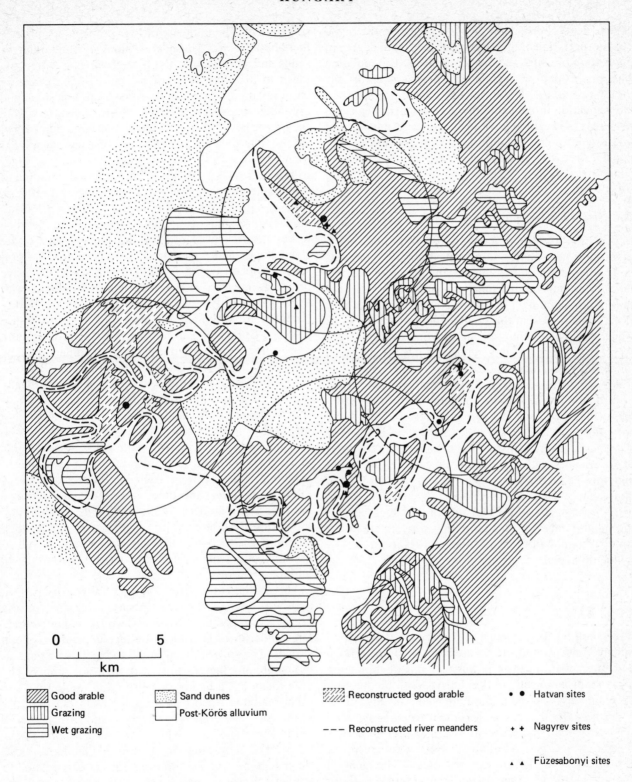

Figure 79. Distribution and potential land use of Bronze Age sites in the Tiszazug (larger symbol = larger site).

0   5
km

Good arable	Sand dunes	Reconstructed good arable	• ● Hatvan sites
Grazing	Post-Körös alluvium		
Wet grazing		– – – Reconstructed river meanders	+ + Nagyrev sites
			▲ ▲ Füzesabonyi sites

extent, deer), in the later Neolithic, may be the possible interpretation of this as another index of a degree of population pressure and economic stress. If population was, by this period, beginning to press uncomfortably on the resource ceiling, it may well have prompted an intensification in the exploitation of hitherto neglected resources. This could have included the establishment of close economic relationships with previously wild populations, and also the clearance of woodland for additional grazing.

Post-Neolithic developments

Information from subsequent prehistoric periods in the Tiszazug is very poor, and we have only the rudiments of a settlement pattern. This may be due in part to the far shorter duration of individual pottery styles, and thus the small number of sites of any particular culture. It may also represent the small amount of survey work which has been done specifically on these periods. Apart from the large Hatvan tells, we rarely have much in the way of evidence of the sizes of sites. Nevertheless it is possible to see an increasing tendency with time towards a more highly agglomerated pattern of settlement (Figures 78 and 79). Sites are clustered into small concentrations located so that virtually the whole of the Tiszazug is covered by the 5 km exploitation territories of known sites, again excluding the central sand dunes and the Tiszakürt-Tiszainoka area to the east as in Körös times. This total coverage of the area, combined with the large size of the Hatvan tell sites suggests that the small number of sites represents a relatively minor shift in population distribution rather than a low population level.

AUSTRIA

The Neolithic settlements of Austria are overwhelmingly concentrated in the areas of Niederösterreich and Burgenland in eastern Austria. This phenomenon is most pronounced in the Early Neolithic period, becoming less marked in the Late Neolithic and subsequent periods. We lacked the time to conduct detailed surveys of exploitation territories and therefore concentrated on a general analysis of the relationship of site location to agricultural resources. The general picture is strikingly reminiscent of that found in those areas of central Europe which we have examined more intensively.

Niederösterreich is characterised topographically by rolling hills, of no great height, but with steep slopes in some areas. The majority of the area is under broadly loess-based soils. These are commonly underlain by sands and gravels, and the topsoil varies greatly from place to place as different amounts of these are incorporated into the loess. In some areas limestone and crystalline bedrock lies very close to the surface, and the loessic cover is absent or contains large numbers of stones. The only substantial areas of heavyish soil are found in the valleys of the Danube and its larger tributaries, where the lower terraces and floodplains are frequently composed of a silty redeposited loess. Modern land use is predominantly arable, with woodland and rough grazing taking over where bedrock leaves insufficient depth for the plough, and where steep slopes make ploughing impracticable. The present floodplain of the Danube is subject to extensive flooding, and carries a wet deciduous woodland with some pasture. All in all, topography and land use potential are strikingly reminiscent of the Little Polish Upland. Burgenland is for the most part flatter and more intensively agricultural, and is similar in many respects to the middle Danube valley in Lower Bavaria.

Linear Pottery settlements are characteristically located close to tributaries to the Danube. The apparent avoidance of the main valley may be genuine, but may reflect the extent to which post-Neolithic deposition has obscured traces of settlement. Sites at Tulln and Schwechat show that some of the valley was indeed exploited, but the river itself may well have had a different course at the time, and not been as close to the sites as the modern situation suggests. Exploitation territories are dominated by light loessic soils of high Neolithic arable potential, while small areas of valley-bottom wet grazing are usually contained within the 10 minute territories.

The settlement distribution thus follows the pattern seen elsewhere. The concentration of sites in the northeastern corner of Niederösterreich and in Burgenland underlines the Linear Pottery dependence upon cereals. The soils are well suited to Neolithic technology, combining high fertility with high tractability. The area today has a higher proportion of arable than any other region in Austria and supplies by far the majority of the country's home-grown wheat and barley, consistently giving the best yields (*Atlas der Republik Österreich*). We may note, furthermore, that here, as in other regions, the Neolithic sites are closely related to the very best of the arable resources available to them. Thus all of the sixteen sites we were able to locate precisely lie in the zone of optimum rainfall for cereals during the growing season. To the west lies a large area of mountainous country which receives 300 mm or

Table 19. Periods represented at sites analysed on the Lower Bavarian plateau

	Site	Periods
1	Burgweinting 'Islinger Weg'	Linear Pottery
	'Langer Weg'	Linear Pottery
2	Gailsbach	Linear Pottery
3	Hagelstadt	Linear Pottery, Stroke-Ornamented Ware, Rössen, Urnfield, La Tène
4	Harting	Linear Pottery
5	Mangolding	Linear Pottery, Bronze Age, La Tène
6	Mintraching	Linear Pottery, Stroke-Ornamented Ware, Münchshöfen Gravefield
7	Oberhinkofen	Linear Pottery, Stroke-Ornamented Ware, Rössen
8	Scharmassing	Linear Pottery
9	Taimering	Linear Pottery
10	Untermassing	Linear Pottery

more in May and June. The sites are restricted to the zone receiving 200–250 mm in these months. Cereals in the zone which receives less than 200 mm at this crucial season are vulnerable to drought, exacerbated by the highly permeable soils. Spring and summer temperatures are also substantially higher in this area than in the highlands to the west, again promoting rapid growth and maturation of arable crops.

It may also be noted that climatic and agronomic conditions in northeastern Niederösterreich are very similar to those in the Regensburg–Straubing region of Bavaria, the two areas being separated by a large tract of land environmentally much less well suited to arable agriculture. The notable concentrations of early Neolithic sites in these two regions may reasonably be contrasted with the relative absence of substantial Neolithic settlement in the 300 km intervening.

We must not, of course, infer that these less productive uplands will have been deserted and unexploited. The climatic constraints will certainly have ensured that exploitation will have been predominantly pastoral and seasonal, however, and we should not therefore be surprised that the traces of early permanent settlement are restricted to the more favoured lowlands. The Linear Pottery finds at the Merkensteinhöhle near Gainfarn suggest that the alpine foothills to the west were indeed being exploited at this date. It is worth remembering that the relatively warm and snow-free area around the Neusiedler See in Burgenland would have been ideally suited to act as complementary winter grazing for animals which were grazed in the mountains during the summer.

LOWER BAVARIAN PLATEAU

The gently undulating plateau of Lower Bavaria is surrounded by regions characterised by higher altitudes and more pronounced relief. These and other associated factors have their effect upon economic potential and land use, and the area appears as an island of intensive high quality arable agriculture in a sea of more pastoral and forested aspect. We chose for study the small area immediately to the south of Regensburg, between the Danube and its tributary the Grosse Laaber.

The surface soil in the area is dominated by a highly variable series of loess-based loams. Most of these have a medium loam texture, but admixture with silts and clays on the one hand, and sands and gravels on the other, produces soils of both heavier and lighter character. The lower Danube terrace is composed almost entirely of sands and gravels. Soil fertility is equally variable but generally high on the loess soils, the best of which are among the highest yielding in Germany. Land use is dominated by cereals and sugar beet, with potatoes important as a rotation crop.

Fourteen Linear Pottery sites were subjected to territorial analysis. We present here the data from ten that form a coherent group. The other four were consistent with the pattern suggested by these ten, but were not contiguous with them. Table 19 shows the cultural attributions of the sites, and it will be seen that some continue in occupation in later periods.

Site territories

The nature of the local soils, with most of the area falling between the light loam and heavy loam texture categories, has led us to distinguish a category of land use potential additional to those employed in most of our study areas. The heavier loams could probably have been tilled with the early forms of animal-drawn ard and plough, but would have required more time and traction power than the large areas of lighter loams

5. THE LOWLANDS

Table 20. Percentages of potential land use categories in 10 minute and 1 hour exploitation territories of Linear Pottery sites on the Lower Bavarian plateau

	Site	10 minute territory				1 hour territory				
		arable (%)	wet grazing (%)	good grazing (%)	rough grazing (%)	arable (%)	wet grazing (%)	good grazing (%)	rough grazing (%)	unclass-ified (%)
1	Burgweinting	68.2	31.8	–	–	41.3	16.3	19.6	9.1	13.7
2	Gailsbach	78.5	14.8	6.7	–	71.7	14.1	13.7	0.5	–
3	Hagelstadt	62.0	15.8	22.2	–	78.1	10.2	11.2	0.5	–
4	Harting	49.1	28.0	22.8	–	46.0	14.9	9.9	20.8	8.4
5	Mangolding	72.3	27.7	–	–	72.9	16.2	10.9	–	–
6	Mintraching	49.8	20.4	29.8	–	61.8	31.0	7.2	–	–
7	Oberhinkofen	65.2	21.5	13.3	–	73.9	10.0	7.7	8.5	–
8	Scharmassing	65.7	23.4	10.9	–	69.1	11.1	11.2	8.6	–
9	Taimering	40.2	8.6	51.1	–	44.5	42.8	12.7	–	–
10	Untermassing	73.8	22.4	–	3.9	70.5	10.9	–	18.6	–

available. It thus seems most unlikely that these would have actually been tilled in Neolithic times even if we assume the technological competence, particularly in view of the abundance of lighter textured soils. In all likelihood the arable potential of the heavier loams would not have been effectively realised until post-Neolithic times. Accordingly we have classified these areas as good grazing, distinguishing them both from the poorer quality pasture on the relatively infertile sands and gravels and also from the wet grazing on seasonally flooded land. Its value as pasture would have been felt both during the winter months, when it would provide better drained grazing than the stream valleys and marshes, and during the summer months, when it would retain more moisture and thus produce richer grazing than the lighter loams and sandy soils in the region. The wet grazing is the land which used to be subject to seasonal flooding and which even today, after it has been extensively drained, is still used only for pasture and hay.

Even in the hilliest parts of the plateau the relief is not great enough to distort significantly the 1 hour territories, and all but two of them, which are slightly truncated by the Danube, are essentially circular. The sites and their territories show no consistent relationship to the Danube and its lowest terrace. The only territories that intersect with the river at all are those in the northeastern part of the plateau where the high quality loess-loam soils extend nearly to the river's edge. Table 20 shows the percentages of various types of potential land use within the 10 minute and 1 hour territories of the walked sites. At all ten sites potentially arable soils are the commonest land use type in the

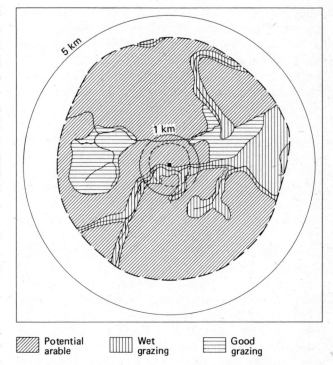

Potential arable   Wet grazing   Good grazing

Figure 80. One hour exploitation territory of Mangolding.

territory, ranging from 41 to 78 per cent of the 1 hour territories. The wet and good grazing categories account for most of the remaining area. Each site is located adjacent to a stream valley so that there tends to be a higher proportion of wet grazing in the 10 minute territory than in the 1 hour territory.

Mangolding (Figure 80) is a characteristic example in the flat northeastern part of the region. It is located on

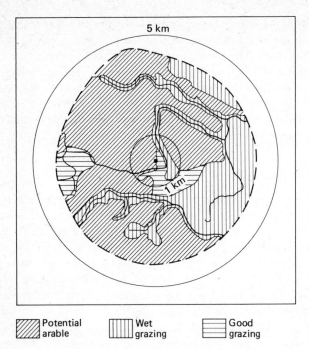

Potential arable   Wet grazing   Good grazing

Figure 81. One hour exploitation territory of Mintraching.

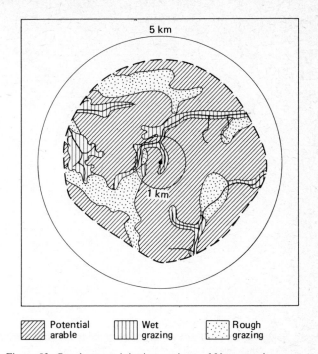

Potential arable   Wet grazing   Rough grazing

Figure 82. One hour exploitation territory of Untermassing.

the north bank of a small stream, whose south bank is low-lying and marshy. Nearly three-quarters of both the 10 minute and 1 hour territories is covered in a light loess-loam which today supports high-yielding crops of cereals, sugar beet, lucerne, and potatoes.

Mintraching (Figure 81), only 25 minutes from Mangolding, is an example of a site with a high proportion of good and wet grazing in its territory. It is located on the western edge of a relatively large area of heavy or waterlogged soils. Within living memory these areas were either permanent marsh or subject to seasonal flooding and were primarily cut for winter fodder. To the west of the site there stretches an almost uninterrupted patch of highly fertile, easily worked loam soil. The 10 minute territory includes the best arable soil in the area, judged by modern yields.

Untermassing (Figure 82) lies at the extreme southwestern edge of the region and is an example of a territory whose arable potential is curtailed by exposed sands and gravels and excessive slopes. In fact, its arable potential is probably somewhat poorer than it appears from the territorial map, as it was impossible to assess adequately in our brief survey the effect on yields of the continuously changing slope and aspect. Nevertheless, with nearly three-quarters of the territory being covered in tractable loess-loams, the location of the site conforms to others in flatter portions of the plateau and shows a preoccupation with areas of high arable potential.

Economy

The only on-site evidence of the Linear Pottery economy in this area comes from the site of Hienheim (Modderman 1977) on the left bank of the Danube, just to the west of our main study area. It is unusual in its proximity to the river, but in this instance the loess plateau on which it is located is separated from the Danube by a low-lying river terrace only about 200 m wide. Thus, on the side away from the river the site is surrounded by a semi-circle of arable and dry grazing land, with the strip along the river providing wet grazing (Figure 83).

Bakels (1978) has discussed in detail the reconstruction of the Linear Pottery landscape, including soils and vegetation. She concludes that the soils would have been substantially the same as today and that the area would have carried a variety of woodland associations depending on the substrate. Few animal bones were preserved at Hienheim, but it is clear that cattle were the most numerous species, with caprines, pigs, and red deer also represented in significant numbers. The bulk of the plant material from the site consists of wheat (*Triticum monococcum* and *T. dicoccum*) and peas (*Pisum sativum*), with a few specimens of lentil and linseed.

The loess-based soils adjacent to the site would probably have been used as fields for the arable crops, possibly grown in some sort of cereal–legume rotation

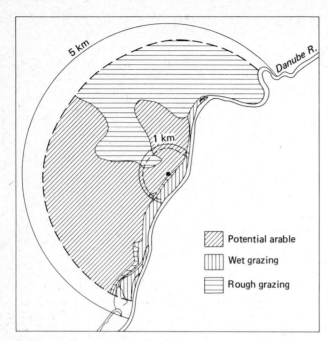

Figure 83. One hour exploitation territory of Hienheim.

bringing sheep down to the area around Regensburg during the winter months. Caves to the north in the Frankische Jura have produced Linear Pottery material (Freund 1963, C. Gamble personal communication), and although much of the evidence was destroyed without being analysed, it seems likely that the sites would have been occupied only seasonally for summer grazing resources.

Interpretation

Two aspects of site location emerge, both emphasising the importance of arable agriculture in the Linear Pottery economy. The 1 hour territories are all composed of more good arable than any other single category of land use, with good and wet grazing forming the bulk of the rest of the territories in all but one case. The wet grazing category is emphasised in the 10 minute territories, being better represented than in the 1 hour territories in all but two instances. Particularly well illustrated here is the ability of the Linear Pottery farmers to select optimal conditions for arable exploitation. Tractable soils include sandy and gravelly soils in addition to the very fertile loess-loams, but the sites are invariably located so as to include the latter soils in their 10 minute territories.

Moving away from the individual sites and looking at regional distribution of the sites, Figure 84 illustrates the striking uniformity in the location of sites on or near the edges of the most fertile soils in the plain. The effect of such locations at the individual site level is to reduce the quantity of the highest grade arable in each site's territory, but at the regional level the overall effect is to maximise the potential number of sites with access to prime agricultural soils. The 5 km territories of the walked sites completely cover the area of high-quality arable soils accessible to a Neolithic technology. Furthermore, the relatively dense Neolithic settlement of the region may be compared with the great scarcity of sites known from the surrounding areas. In these latter not only is the proportion of potentially arable soils much smaller, but the crops are today usually up to a month or so behind those of Lower Bavaria in development, with a consequent drop in yields. From evidence in areas that have been more systematically surveyed, such as the Aldenhovener Plateau, the Little Polish Upland, and the Nova Zagora region of Bulgaria, the spacing of Early Neolithic sites suggests that similar settlements subsisted on considerably less than a 1 hour territory. Extrapolating from those areas, it seems likely that the Bavarian plateau could have accommodated a somewhat greater number of contem-

system. The soils further to the north and west of the site are considerably heavier and would not only have been intractable with Neolithic technology, but are even today considered worse because they warm up slowly in spring and make the harvest about a fortnight later than at Hienheim itself. The terrace of the Danube would have provided good wet grazing for the cattle during the summer, and both cattle and the other livestock could have been grazed at most times of the year on the area of heavier soils that were unsuited to arable exploitation, as well as on stubble and fallow fields. Winter grazing could have been supplemented with cut hay or foggage from the river terrace, and gathered deciduous tree foliage. There is some slight evidence of the latter practice at Heinheim from a nearby pollen core, in which the beginning of an elm decline is correlated with the first Linear Pottery settlement in the area.

Present-day animal husbandry of the Lower Bavarian plateau consists almost entirely of intensive rearing of cattle and pigs. Although farmers still recall the earlier period when animals occupied a more important position in the economy and when more of the land was devoted to pasturage and fodder crops, cereals have historically always dominated the agriculture of the plateau. This relatively small region is, however, surrounded by vast blocks of upland grazing to which the lowland farmers could easily have gained access. A system of transhumance operates today with herders

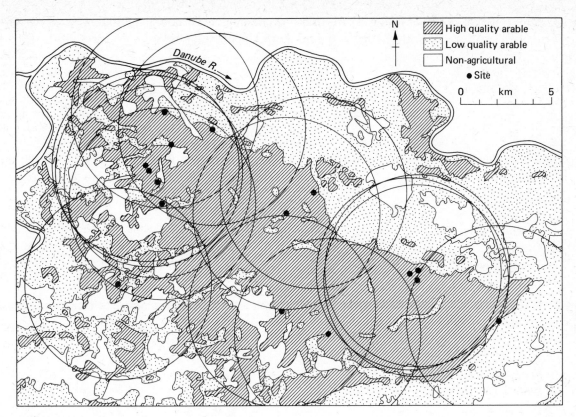

Figure 84. Distribution of Neolithic sites in Lower Bavaria.

poraneous settlements, and it is to be expected that more will be found when an intensive survey is carried out.

THE NORTHERN UPPER RHINE VALLEY

Territorial analysis was carried out on 46 sites on both sides of the Rhine in the Wormsgau, Rheinpfalz, Mannheim, and Heidelberg areas. Detailed information will be presented here on 20 Linear Pottery sites on the left bank of the Rhine, some of which also have subsequent occupations. Due to sand dune movement on the right bank around the mouth of the Neckar after the Early Neolithic, it is considerably more difficult to reconstruct the Neolithic territories from the modern situation than in the case of the left bank, where surface geology has not altered appreciably since the Pleistocene. Sielmann (1971) and Maier-Arendt (1966) have assigned many of the sites to one or more of five time periods, but others can at present only be designated as undifferentiated Linear Pottery.

Table 21 shows the percentage representation of potential land use categories for 10 minute and 1 hour territories. The arable category is composed primarily of gently rolling hills covered with tractable loess-based loams. We have assumed that all the loess soils would have had an arable potential. Under today's conditions some areas carry soils with a medium or medium-heavy loam texture, but it seems likely that decades of mechanised agriculture have altered the picture of soil texture to some degree. It was also found that today's yields are affected by aspect, north-facing slopes giving poorer yields than others. We have not taken this factor into account, and our figure for Neolithic arable potential may thus be taken as a maximum.

In addition to steeply sloping land, the rough grazing category covers the Alzey hills with their poor mountain soils and other areas which would have produced poor yields due to the extreme sandiness of the soil. The wet grazing lies primarily in small stream valleys and on the Rhine floodplain. Detailed geomorphological work in the loesslands of the Aldenhovener Platte and of the Little Polish Upland shows that post-Neolithic erosion has washed soil from hilltops into the stream valleys and has caused the valleys to become shallower, less pronounced, and drier. Only the larger valleys remain today a good source of wet grazing, whereas in Neolithic times many of the smaller valleys

5. THE LOWLANDS

Table 21. Percentages of potential land use categories in 10 minute and 1 hour exploitation territories of Linear Pottery sites in the northern Upper Rhine valley

Phase	Site	10 minute territory					1 hour territory				
		territory type[a]	arable (%)	wet grazing (%)	rough grazing (%)	good grazing (%)	territory type	arable (%)	wet grazing (%)	rough grazing (%)	good grazing (%)
I	Worms 'Untere Platt'	B	42.1	57.9	–	–	B	35.4	60.1	4.5	–
II	Flomborn	A	82.4	17.6	–	–	A	92.7	4.5	2.8	–
	Mölsheim	A	76.1	9.5	14.3	–	A	84.5	7.6	7.8	–
	Monsheim	A	75.2	24.8	–	–	A	83.1	8.1	8.8	–
	Weinsheim	A	86.6	13.4	–	–	A	64.6	35.2	0.1	–
	Worms 'Untere Platt'	B	42.1	57.9	–	–	B	35.4	60.1	4.5	–
II/III	Osthofen	A	80.1	18.2	1.7	–	B	53.6	40.9	5.5	–
III	Worms 'Untere Platt'	B	42.1	57.9	–	–	B	35.4	60.1	4.5	–
III/IV	Bolanden	A	61.9	6.2	32.0	–	C	42.6	7.5	50.0	–
	Dannstadt	A	78.7	17.1	–	4.2	B	43.0	31.0	8.5	17.5
	Fussgönheim	A	71.2	28.8	–	–	B	39.5	41.0	19.5	–
	Insheim	A	90.7	9.3	–	–	A	72.1	22.3	5.7	–
	Mölsheim	A	76.1	9.5	14.3	–	A	84.5	7.6	7.8	–
	Monsheim	A	75.2	24.8	–	–	A	83.1	8.1	8.8	–
	Wachenheim	A	62.5	–	37.5	–	A	81.5	9.0	9.6	–
	Weisenheim	C	–	17.7	82.3	–	C	12.5	16.4	71.1	–
IV	Worms 'Untere Platt'	B	42.1	57.9	–	–	B	35.4	60.1	4.5	–
Indet.	Biedesheim	A	93.2	6.8	–	–	A	75.9	11.5	12.6	–
	Dautenheim	B/C	42.6	21.0	36.5	–	A	83.2	8.5	8.2	–
	Dintesheim	A	92.2	7.8	–	–	A	85.0	8.0	7.0	–
	Herxheim	A	74.9	25.1	–	–	B/C	48.6	21.6	29.9	–
	Kallstadt	C	21.8	–	78.2	–	C	23.0	–	77.0	–
	Mörzheim	A	71.1	28.9	–	–	A	77.9	22.1	–	–
	Rüssingen	A	87.2	12.8	–	–	A	78.0	10.2	11.9	–
	Schauernheim	A	66.3	33.7	–	–	A/B	59.1	28.8	5.8	6.3

[a] A, greater than 60 per cent potentially arable; B, arable less than 60 per cent and wet grazing greater than rough grazing; C, arable less than 60 per cent and rough grazing greater than wet grazing.

would also have provided this resource. An estimated reconstruction of Neolithic conditions has been used in calculating the percentages of land use categories.

Given these limitations in the data, it can nevertheless be seen that the 1 hour territories fall into three major categories: A, greater than 60 per cent potentially arable; B, arable less than 60 per cent and wet grazing greater than rough grazing; C, arable less than 60 per cent and rough grazing greater than wet grazing. A few sites do not fit clearly into any one category and these have been classed as intermediates. Class A is the predominant type of territory, containing 11 out of 20 sites. Only four of the sites fall into Class B and three into Class C.

Monsheim (Figure 85) is a good example of a typical Class A site. It is located on a south-facing slope just above the Pfrimm river valley. Two other watercourses

cross the territory, each flanked by a narrow band of wet grazing. There are small patches of rough grazing on steep slopes. At other sites, such as Flomborn (Figure 86), the potentially arable sector forms an even greater proportion of the total territory.

Class B is well illustrated by Dannstadt, one of several sites lying in a string along the junction between the loess terrace and the low-lying alluvial deposits of the floodplain of the Rhine. The territory is a mixture of good arable on the loess slopes, heavy wet soils supporting pasture in stream valleys and on the Rhine floodplain, interspersed with patches of sand and gravel.

Three Linear Pottery exploitation territories fall into Class C. Bolanden (Figure 87) and Kallstadt both lie on the western edge of the Rhine upper terrace, and their territories are divided between arable land on the

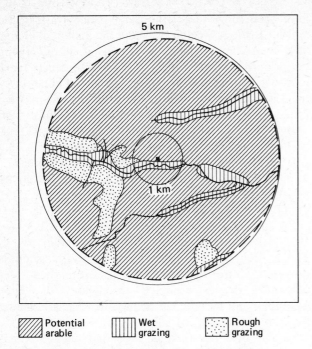

Potential arable | Wet grazing | Rough grazing

Figure 85. One hour exploitation territory of Monsheim.

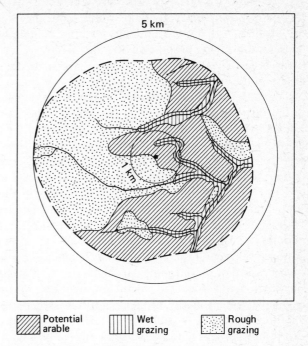

Potential arable | Wet grazing | Rough grazing

Figure 87. One hour exploitation territory of Bolanden.

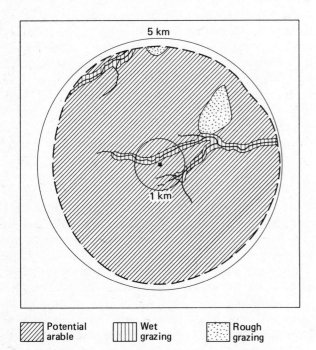

Potential arable | Wet grazing | Rough grazing

Figure 86. One hour exploitation territory of Flomborn.

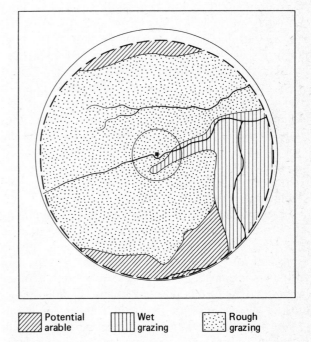

Potential arable | Wet grazing | Rough grazing

Figure 88. One hour exploitation territory of Weisenheim-Eyersheimer.

terrace and rough grazing in the hills. Weisenheim-Eyersheimer (Figure 88) lies on old alluvial sands and gravels, with good arable soils occurring only at the very periphery of the 1 hour territory. Only a Linear Pottery grave has been found at Herxheim, the settlements being of Rössen and Michelsberg date.

If one now concentrates upon the 10 minute territories, it is found that an even greater proportion fall into Class A, which has 16 out of the 20 sites, with only one example in Class B and two in Class C. In other words, even in cases where the 1 hour territory is composed of less than 60 per cent potentially arable land, the sites are located so that the 10 minute territory contains a considerably higher proportion of arable. Here, as in so many areas, sites are located so as to give immediate access to the best arable soils available.

Sielmann (1971) has discerned a number of changes in the distribution of sites from the early to the later Linear Pottery period in several areas of central Germany. Settlement expanded from the optimal loess-type soils and low rainfall zones in his Phase I onto poorer soils and into areas of higher rainfall in later phases. The composition of 1 hour territories in our study area shows a similar trend. The Worms 'Untere Platt' site seems to have an anomalous territory, due perhaps to its proximity to the Rhine, which may either have caused geomorphological changes since the site was occupied or played some part in the function of the site while it was inhabited. Sielmann suggested that it may have been primarily a trading, not subsistence site, but it seems equally possible on the territorial evidence that it may perhaps have been a seasonal site located to take advantage of the seasonal grazing resources. If we omit 'Untere Platt', then the area had no other Phase I sites; in Phase II there were four Class A 1 hour territories and one in Class B; whereas by Phase III there were four Class A, but five Class B or C 1 hour territories. The 10 minute territories, which would have had the greatest significance for the arable component of the economy, show less sign of change. In Phase II five out of five sites have Class A 10 minute territories; in Phases III and IV eight out of nine are Class A. Thus while the evidence of the 1 hour territories indicates the exploitation of increasingly marginal conditions overall, it is noteworthy that site locations nevertheless continued to give optimum access to the best available arable adjacent to the settlements.

The importance of arable agriculture in determining site locations is further indicated by Sielmann's data on sites from other areas in Germany. Sielmann divides the region of Linear Pottery settlement into two environmental zones, Ecology Region A and Ecology Region B. The former possesses many climatic characteristics in common with the Mediterranean conditions to which einkorn and emmer were originally adapted: low rainfall, high summer temperatures, and a large number of frost-free days. The latter has higher rainfall combined with lower temperatures, and probably would have been in general less well suited to Mediterranean adapted crops. It is thus significant that in Ecology Region A a considerable number of sites (13–27 per cent) are to be found on less permeable soils than loess, but still within the range of soils which could have been cultivated at the time. By contrast, in the moister Ecology Region B, where the high rainfall may have been a limiting factor for cereal agriculture relying on primitive wheats, the sites have a much more narrowly restricted distribution. Thus 100 per cent of the Linear Pottery sites in the Heidelberg area, for instance, are located on loess-based soils, whose high permeability allowed their arable potential to be realised even with the crop species then available.

It seems highly likely, therefore, that the areas of primary Linear Pottery settlement were selected by agriculturalists who relied sufficiently upon arable exploitation to seek out and locate their sites on the best arable potential land, even in areas such as Ecology Region B where these were narrowly circumscribed. The accuracy of their original agronomic assessment is proved in retrospect, as many of the earliest sites continued to be occupied throughout the later Neolithic; and they lie, of course, in what are among the primary areas of cereal production even today.

All the evidence thus suggests that the settlement and economy of the area were primarily organised around the requirements of arable agriculture. A substantial proportion of the area as a whole would not have been suitable for arable purposes, however, and even given the dearth of relevant data, it is worthwhile to speculate how this may have been exploited and integrated into the economic system as a whole. The northern upper Rhine is remarkable for its mild winters. Frost and snow are rare; today winter wheat is sometimes incompletely vernalised and some vegetative growth usually continues throughout the winter. For this reason it was a favoured area of winter pasture in the recent historical past when pastoralism played a much greater part in the local economy than under today's conditions of intensive arable exploitation. The pastoral system combined a relatively sedentary or mobile-cum-sedentary element with transhumance which encompassed summer pastures as far south as the Vosges and the Schwarzwald. Characteristically, the cattle would mostly be maintained in the Rhine valley throughout the year. They would graze the dry sandy areas in spring when these carried the first flush of grass, and the wetlands in summer and autumn. In winter they would subsist mainly on hay cut from the wet pastures. The area also saw a huge winter influx of stock, mainly sheep, which grazed the rougher pastures and fallows from October to March, and returned for the summer to their grazings in the uplands to the south.

From a theoretical viewpoint it seems more likely than not that some such system, or a variant of it, would have been in operation in Neolithic times, although there is as yet no specific evidence of it from our study area. Little in the way of bone remains has survived on the sites here, and there are few upland sites known with Linear Pottery material. Nevertheless there can be little doubt that the Linear Pottery economy incorporated a pastoral element here, as it did elsewhere. We can, similarly, expect that some adjustment would have been made to the local seasonal fluctuations in the availability of grazing resources. Even if there was adequate year-round grazing for some lowlands herds, we know from sites such as those on the upper Danube, Felsdach Lautereck (Taute 1966) for example, and the Grotte de la Baume at Gonvillars that the uplands were also exploited at this time. These areas would have experienced winters sufficiently severe strongly to encourage, if not to require, a move to the adjacent lowlands at this season. Indeed, Pétrequin (1974) found substantial evidence of a spring–summer occupation at the Grotte de la Baume, and the large numbers of fish bones from Felsdach Lautereck probably also indicate summer occupation.

The influence of population growth on site location and economic exploitation has been a recurrent theme in our writings, and nowhere is it better illustrated than in Sielmann's (1971) study of the Neolithic settlement of southwest Germany. We have already discussed the Early Neolithic spread of sites onto non-loess soils and into areas of higher rainfall, that is, from areas optimal for cereal-based agriculture to less optimal areas. Sielmann's mapping of later sites shows this trend continuing through the Middle and Late Neolithic. The Hinkelstein, Grossgartach, and Rössen settlements all continue to occupy the optimal loess–low rainfall zones in some parts of their distribution, but a higher proportion of sites begins to appear on poorer soils and in lower or higher rainfall zones. The greatest concentration of Hinkelstein sites is still on loess soils but in the lowest precipitation zone, previously avoided for settlement in Linear Pottery times. The Grossgartach distribution is very similar to that of the Linear Pottery except that those sites not on loess soils are much further from any good arable soils than their Linear Pottery counterparts had been. Settlements with Rössen material appear slightly later, but overlap chronologically with the Grossgartach sites. They mostly avoid areas occupied by the Grossgartach sites and therefore in some parts of their distribution are forced more onto non-loess soils and into more extreme and less favourable rainfall zones, from the point of view of arable agriculture.

Before the disappearance of the Grossgartach and Rössen sites, Michelsberg sites appear. During the Michelsberg occupation one can trace a development similar to that of the Linear Pottery period. The earliest sites are densest on loess soils. Later sites see the first expansion into previously unoccupied or sporadically occupied areas ill-suited to cereal agriculture. There are Michelsberg sites in Hegau, the non-loess areas of Bavaria, the rainier and colder areas of the southern upper Rhine, the loess deposits of the Schwarzwald foothills, and on the western side of the Bodensee.

The distribution of the Late Neolithic Corded Ware sites (mainly graves), and Bell Beaker sites, shows another increase in the occupation of non-loess soils. In the Mannheim area about 40 per cent of the Corded Ware sites are on sandy soils, and between 60 per cent and 80 per cent of the Bell Beaker sites are on the wet soils of the outer edges of the Rhine terrace.

These changes in site distribution patterns may be seen as the most visible manifestation of alterations in the economic system under the promptings of sustained population increase. The changes probably included adaptations in the environmental tolerances of plant and animal crops, the adoption of new crops or changes in proportions of existing crops, and the permanent occupation of the lowland zone of low arable potential and the uplands, which appear previously to have been exploited on a sporadic or seasonal basis. Conscious or unconscious selection for field varieties of cereals that yielded best under conditions of slightly higher rainfall could easily have brought zones of increased precipitation within the optimal arable sphere, especially for those sites located on permeable loess soils. By the time Michelsberg sites appear in the uplands, such as those on the Bodensee, cereals must have become adapted to even higher rainfall and colder temperatures, since, as was discussed in Chapter 4, the evidence from plant remains in the area suggests strongly that cereals were grown there. We have already pointed out the significance cereals would probably have had for the lake-side sites in allowing the production of an adequate storable surplus to permit year-round occupation of areas that were previously exploited only on a seasonal basis, even if the arable aspect of the economy remained relatively small in quantitative terms. The stimulus for permanent occupation of the uplands at this period seems clear when viewed from the standpoint of the lowlands of the middle and upper Rhine valley. Continual population increase had resulted in a filling up of the attractive lowland zone of high arable potential. With arable exploitation spreading onto marginal land, which would previously have been available as winter grazing for pastoralists, more and more would have been forced to find means other than transhumance to cope with seasonal shortages.

THE LITTLE POLISH UPLAND

The Little Polish Upland, along with Upper Silesia, was the site of the earliest classic Neolithic settlement north of the Carpathians. Detailed archaeological surveys in the Upland have been carried out by Kruk (1969, 1970) and his colleagues, which have produced evidence for sites of all periods from the Neolithic to mediaeval times. Our work in this area was designed to serve as a comparison to the detailed studies carried out in Hungary and Germany and therefore concentrated on the broad outlines of Neolithic economic development as revealed by the territories of a few representative sites.

Its geographical name notwithstanding, the Little Polish Upland is a region of low, rounded, loess-covered hills lying northeast of Kraków and bounded on the south by the Vistula river valley (Figure 89). While the maximum altitude of the hills is just over 300 m OD, they rise only 120 m above the alluvial plains of the Vistula and its tributaries. The area receives 700–750 mm of rain per year, compared to the 1100 mm that fall on the mountains to the south. Winters are milder and shorter. It is one of the three major wheat-producing areas in Poland, mainly due to the high fertility of its loess soils. Yields are high despite the fact that farms in this area are still for the most part very small, privately owned, and largely unmechanised. Agronomically the region has much in common with the Hungarian, Bavarian, and Upper Rhine areas of Linear Pottery settlement, and territorial analysis produced similar results.

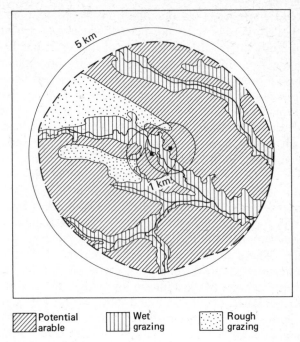

Potential arable Wet grazing Rough grazing

Figure 90. One hour exploitation territory of Niegardów and Piotrkowice Wielkie.

The area may conveniently be divided into three zones. The valley bottoms have high water tables, are often marshy, and carry wet cattle pasture. Towards the valley edges and on slight eminences the better drained soils carry intensively cultivated arable crops. The slopes, where much of the modern settlement is, are highly variable in both gradient and land use. The more gentle slopes have arable crops with garden crops around the villages; the steeper and less accessible slopes are under scrub woodland and rough grazing. The wide expanse of rolling hills behind and between the river valleys, the interfluves, are almost exclusively exploited as arable, with wheat, sugar beet, and potatoes being the dominant crops.

The 1 hour territories were analysed for three sites, and 10 minute territories were walked for 11 other sites. Figure 90 shows the adjacent sites of Niegardów and Piotrkowice Wielkie (pow. Proszowice). Both 1 km territories are marked, but as their 1 hour territories are virtually identical, we have only plotted that of the former. Table 22 summarises the potential land use information of all the walked sites. As in most lowland areas, the topography is too gentle to distort the territories significantly, and they are roughly circular. Site locations follow the pattern characteristic of Linear Pottery sites in other areas; the sites tend to be located along river or stream valleys so that their 10 minute territories are divided between good arable land (usual-

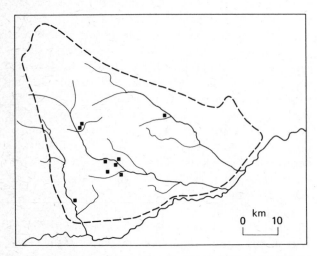

Figure 89. Distribution of Neolithic sites in the Little Polish Upland.

Table 22. Period of occupation and percentages of potential land use categories in 10 minute and 1 hour exploitation territories of sites in the Little Polish Upland

Site	Age						10 minute territory			1 hour territory		
	Linear Pottery	Lengyel	Funnel-Beaker (TRB)	Corded Ware	Bronze Age II	Lusatian	good arable (%)	wet grazing (%)	rough grazing (%)	good arable (%)	wet grazing (%)	rough grazing (%)
Szczepanowice 3 (Miechów district)	+						69.4	30.6				
Ksiazniczki II (Kraków district)	+						72.0	28.0				
Wysiólek Niegardowski 2 (Proszowice district)	+						85.0	15.0				
Niegardów 2 (Proszowice district)	+	+	+	+	+		44.3	55.7		63.0	25.1	11.9
Piotrkowice Wielkie 1 (Proszowice district)	+	+	+		+		58.3	41.7		61.8	26.6	11.6
Przesławice 1 (Proszowice district)	+		+		+	+	29.9	70.1		69.1	27.0	3.9
Brończyce 1 (Miechów district)	+		+		+	+	68.0	32.0				
Sławice 1 (Miechów district)	+				+	+	85.8	14.2				
Kepa 2 (Miechów district)	+				+	+	60.0	40.0				
Szczepanowice 9 (Meichów district)	+				+	+	83.3	16.7				

ly loess-based loams) and wet grazing. The amount of arable varies from a maximum of nearly 86 per cent to a minimum of 30 per cent with most of the sites having at least 60 per cent arable within the 10 minute radius. Przesławice, with only 30 per cent arable, is an unusual extreme, which the territorial data are insufficient to explain. The site has produced material of the Linear Pottery, Funnel-Beaker (TRB), and Lusation periods, which indicates that its occupation was not simply a short-term 'mistake'. It may be that it was a specialised base for stock-rearing, or that it served some other function not directly related to the economic potential of the surrounding land. Information from excavation may help to solve this problem in the future.

The other sites have territories characteristic of the arable-based mixed farming economies that we have observed in Hungary, Austria, and Germany. Although organic remains were not available from the walked sites, other Neolithic sites such as Strzelce (Bakker, Vogel & Wislanski 1969) in the same region have produced cereals as evidence of the arable portion of the economy, and cattle, pigs, and caprines (in that order of abundance) on the animal side. Cattle bones predominate in all the collections, as might be expected from the high quality of the pasture. Cattle are equally the basis of modern animal husbandry in the area.

The distribution of Linear Pottery sites here illustrates yet again the process of the rapid colonisation by the new economy of the very best of the available arable resources. The settlements occur mainly on small eminences in or at the edge of the valleys of larger tributaries of the Vistula, such as the Nida. This gives immediate access to the highest quality arable and grazing resources. The soils of the lower slopes benefit both from the high water tables and from the continual recharging of nutrients which wash down from the surrounding slopes. Furthermore, the valleys have higher average temperatures and a longer growing season. Cereal yields are thus substantially higher here than on the tops, and cropping can be more intensive. As the difference between valley and plateau is frequently only a matter of 3–5 minutes' walk, access is also available to a wide area of drier, but still highly fertile, loess-based chernozems and brown forest soils within an easily exploitable distance of the site. The valley bottom grazing is by far the most productive, most nutritious, and most palatable available in the region.

It may seem strange, in view of their high modern arable potential that the interfluves show no signs of settlement or intensive exploitation at this period. This gap may be seen as a result of the severe shortage of surface water in the area. The surface loess deposits lie on Cretaceous marls, a combination of permeable soils which creates karst-like conditions with the water table often tens of metres deep. This lack of surface water for human and animal drinking effectively limits exploitation to areas within easy striking distance of the water sources in the valleys, despite the fact that there is ample rainfall for cereal growth. In many parts of the interfluves there are no traces of habitation until mediaeval times, when technology permitted and high population levels demanded the digging of deep wells. Even today many of these dry up in summer, and water has to be imported.

The economy may thus reasonably, if speculatively, be reconstructed as follows. The better drained eminences in the valleys and the more gentle hill slopes would have carried arable crops, as would the plateau edge immediately overlooking the valley. In all likelihood the former area would have been cropped more intensively. The central areas of the interfluves, farther away from the settlements, would have carried dry scrub grazing and woodland.

Grazing probably would have been divided between the waterlogged valley bottoms and the high interfluves, perhaps alternating seasonally between the two. Probably the only appreciable quantity of fodder available for cattle in the winter would have been in the valleys, which would have meant keeping the cattle as much as possible on the drier tops in summer. A more productive system would involve moving the bulk of the herd south to mountain pastures in the Tatras in summer, while conserving the lowland meadow for use as winter fodder either in the form of hay or foggage. There is ample evidence of contacts with people to the south in imports of obsidian from the Bükk Mountains on several sites (Kulczycka-Leciejewiczowa 1970), a sherd with Slovakian decoration at Olszanica (Milisaukas 1976), and Polish flint found on sites in Slovakia and Moravia (Kozłowski 1971). Trading of goods and ideas could have occurred as a result of communication between transhumant herders from dispersed lowland areas. The main Vistula valley may also have served as a source of rich summer grazing for cattle. The only sites with Linear Pottery material that have been found in areas with predominantly grazing potential are caves in the Olkusz district to the west of Kraków. These sites could be the remains of seasonal herding camps used during the summer for short-distance stock transference.

The pigs would probably have been grazing within a much more restricted area. The plateau woodland may have provided rich autumn pannage, and more scattered resources at other seasons. The pigs may well, indeed, have been an important factor in the early establishment and maintenance of clearings for arable use. At other times they would have exploited the marshier patches in the valley bottoms. Such caprovines as there were would probably have kept mainly to the drier grazings of the slopes and plateaux.

As in other parts of Europe, Linear Pottery sites here are often very close together at distances of only 10–20 minutes apart. It seems likely that excavations will show that in most cases each site is equivalent to one or two farmsteads, as has been found in the Aldenhovener Platte. The overall pattern of settlement is a logical adaptation to the situation we have described, in which sites are packed so as to make fullest use of a relatively restricted zone of highly productive resources.

The distribution of Lengyel sites strongly suggests an increase in the local population. Sites continue to be mainly located in the large valleys, but now smaller sites also occur in small side valleys and on the interfluves. Both of these locations represent a slight worsening of conditions: the side valleys are narrower and therefore provide smaller areas of both prime arable and grazing; the interfluves are further from water and do not share the especially favourable microclimate of the valleys. However, as indicated above, the plateaux offer in general conditions with considerable arable potential. The rolling hills are covered with a great depth of fertile and tractable loess-loam, interrupted only by small patches of poorer rendzinas. It seems likely that the site distribution of the Lengyel period reflects the success of the Linear Pottery mixed farming economy, with the consequent rise in population and its expansion into other suitable locations.

The subsequent Funnel-Beaker (TRB) phase of settlement apparently sees a continuation of the same trends of rising population and an increasingly intensive exploitation of the available resources. Occupation continues in the location characteristic of the Linear Pottery and Lengyel phases, but there is a shift of emphasis in the pattern. Whereas settlement on the interfluves was virtually absent in the former period, and restricted to small sites in the latter, the largest Funnel-Beaker (TRB) sites are situated on the edges of the interfluves, overlooking the valleys. Moreover, many more Funnel-Beaker (TRB) sites are found deeper in the interfluves, away from the streams and rivers. The available evidence is insufficient to explain the change of settlement pattern satisfactorily. As we have noted, the distance between the bottom and top of the slopes at the edge of the valleys is frequently a matter of a very few minutes, a difference which would only slightly change the exploitation territories. We must always remember that such relatively small changes in site location may have been motivated largely or entirely by non-economic reasons. Some economic factors can be suggested, though. The increased size of the Funnel-Beaker (TRB) sites may partly have prompted the move. Land on the lower slopes suitable for occupation is limited in extent, and is also the prime agricultural land. The need to conserve this scarce and highly productive resource may have restricted the degree of settlement expansion in this zone. A more powerful factor is likely to have been the fact that, with rising population and expanding agricultural development on the plateaux, an increasing ergonomic pull would have been exerted away from the valley. The associated phenomenon of an increase in the number of sites on the interfluves away from the valleys inclines us to favour this second suggestion as the primary influence. These usually take the form of surface scatters some 2.0–2.5 km away from the main settlements, and may represent temporary huts associated with working the most distant fields, and/or those used in the course of pastoral exploitation.

It is during the Funnel-Beaker (TRB) period that the first evidence of cereal agriculture and cattle rearing comes from northern Poland in the lowland zone of low arable potential. Economic exploitation in this region has already been discussed in Chapter 4, but it is worthwhile here drawing the parallel with the similar developments just discussed in the upper Rhine and Bodensee regions. Again it appears that cereals had become adapted to colder and wetter conditions, and under the stimulus of continued population increase were grown in climatically unfavourable areas.

There is also at this time more evidence that could be interpreted as resulting from a long-distance transhumance system. The later part of the Funnel-Beaker (TRB) phase sees a proliferation of 'Corded Ware' graves in locations similar to the Funnel-Beaker (TRB) sites, and often actually associated with Funnel-Beaker (TRB) settlements. Partial contemporaneity of the two material assemblages has been argued by Kruk (1973) on typological grounds and by analogy with other areas in Central Europe. The usual hypothesis to explain this phenomenon is that the graves represent an influx of foreign mobile pastoralists, and this is certainly possible. It also seems possible that in the course of pasturing cattle in the Tatra mountains in summer, Polish Funnel-Beaker (TRB) shepherds will have encountered groups who buried their dead in 'Corded Ware' graves, and may have acquired the practice from them. The 'invasion of pastoralists' model seems the less likely in view of the evidence that the Little Polish Upland was probably being exploited to near capacity already. We may also note that even if the 'Corded Ware' burials do indeed represent a separate social and cultural entity, with an economy based entirely upon mobile pastoralism, they would have been forced by the identical environmental pressures operating on the TRB population to integrate the same complementary upland and lowland resources. The economic effect of the two forms of organisation would thus have been similar: the maintenance of larger numbers of stock to support higher human populations.

It will be apparent that the outline of economic and population development suggested here differs fundamentally from that of Kruk (1973). We do not have the space to evaluate Kruk's hypotheses in detail, but some specific points of conflict require consideration.

Kruk argues that the Linear Pottery and Lengyel economy was based upon intensive horticulture in the valleys, with some small areas of cereal cultivation. The seasonally flooded land is seen as a critical arable resource, rich in nutrients, cultivated intensively using mattocks or hoes, and producing a wide variety of vegetables. The later phases of settlement are interpreted as showing the gradual spread of agriculture on to the interfluves, where a slash-and-burn, long-fallow system was practised. Animal husbandry is thought to have grown in importance throughout the Neolithic, restricted initially by the forest vegetation, and growing with the increasing clearance. This process is seen as culminating in the entirely pastoral-based Corded Ware 'culture', with the mobile economy as an explanation of the apparent lack of settlements to go with the graves. We believe, on the contrary, that the only basic development was the long-term trend to population increase, and that the settlement data can be accommodated to the hypothesis, set out above, of the steady spread of agricultural exploitation from the most favourable to increasingly marginal conditions. The Kruk hypothesis fails in particular to take account of a number of factors which seem to us to be crucial.

The first question is how productive horticulture could have been in the circumstances; or, rather, how productive of any of the dietary constituents which are essential in large quantities and are provided by our staple foods. As we have noted in the introductory chapters, the European flora was lacking in the root and tuber crops which are the basis of most tropical horticultural economies, or even in their close relatives. It is, of course, perfectly true that there are rhizomes and tubers which could have been grown. That they have not been cultivated in historic times is certainly not sufficient evidence that they were not so in the prehistoric past. However, while their productive potential and nutritional value are for the most part unknown, as a group they seem most unlikely to have been promising as staple crops. What is of much more significance is that they would have been competing with cereals and legumes, infinitely more suitable crops, both high-yielding and extremely nutritious, which we know were available and to which the environment was ideally suited. We must not forget that root-based horticulture flourishes today exclusively in environments which for one reason or another are ill-suited to the more demanding seed crops.

Secondly, as was discussed in the introduction to this chapter, there seems to be considerable doubt as to whether extensive slash-and-burn agriculture would ever have been needed or advantageous in the European lowland zone of high arable potential. It is especially doubtful whether such a system would have evolved in an area of deep, fertile loess soils receiving ample rainfall, such as the Little Polish Upland.

Thirdly, and perhaps most important, is the fact that in Kruk's hypothesis the economic and demographic trends appear to run in contrary direction. All the settlement evidence suggests substantial population increase during the Neolithic, although as always it is not possible to arrive at authoritative figures with prehistoric data. The economic development proposed by Kruk, on the other hand, consists in a decline of intensity and thus in productivity per unit area. The most intensive system is that proposed for the earliest phase with, almost certainly, the lowest population. While the later expansion of the area under cultivation may have compensated to some extent for the trend to more land-extensive exploitation, it seems unlikely to have done so sufficiently to accommodate the popula-

tion increases. Certainly it seems most implausible that the mobile pastoralism proposed for the final phase would by itself have supported the population then in existence. We may wonder, moreover, why the more usual relationship between population and economy, with increases in the former encouraging intensification in the latter, should have been reversed in the Neolithic of southern Poland.

ALDENHOVENER PLATTE

Surveys were also carried out on the group of sites on the Aldenhovener Platte just to the northeast of Aachen on the German side of the Dutch border. They may probably be viewed as part of the distribution which extends westwards into Dutch and Belgian Limburg. The pattern of settlement is unusually well known due to the collaboration between archaeologists and the open-cast lignite mining companies in the area (Farruggia *et al.* 1973, Kuper *et al.* 1974, etc.).

Site locations, and the economic scheme which may be inferred from these, repeat in all essentials those observed elsewhere in the European loesslands, and we have furthermore already referred to the evidence from this area earlier in this chapter and in Chapter 2. We will therefore confine ourselves to a statement of the barest essentials of the data.

The area is dominated by loess-based soils on a gently undulating plateau, the only heavier deposits being formed of redeposited alluvial silts derived from the loess, found in the river and stream valleys. Modern land use is thus dominated by intensive agriculture, with wet grazing and woodland in the valley bottoms. Reconstruction of conditions in Neolithic times (Göbel *et al.* 1973) suggests that the valleys would have been slightly deeper and moister and that the soil profile may have altered slightly, but that otherwise modern conditions would have obtained in general.

The settlements are situated mainly on terraces overlooking small tributaries of the larger rivers, like the Rur. In general, locations overlooking the main valleys are avoided. In an area of abundant and widespread Neolithic arable potential the sites thus seem to be distributed so as to maximise access to the relatively scarce resource of rich wetland grazing. The nature of the area as a whole is such that any location on the edge of the valleys will automatically provide access to large areas of high-quality arable potential soils close to the site.

The unusually complete record available of settlement distribution, and the comparative regularity of site location, encourage us to speculate that we may have a picture close to that of the actual settlement pattern in Linear Pottery times. We have discussed before reasons for supposing that many of the sites were indeed contemporaneous farmsteads. The pattern which emerges is of a relatively closely packed distribution along individual stream valleys. However, adjacent valleys only attracted settlement if they were a minimum of 1 hour's walk from each other. This may eventually give us a rather closer estimate of the actual exploitation territories in use than is usually possible, and thus some clue as to local population levels. It seems that, in an arable-rich but dryish environment, the twin resources of wetland grazing and surface water for drinking constituted an important factor affecting the precise site locations. Nevertheless, the choice of the general region for settlement and the density of occupation re-emphasise the concern for rich but tractable arable soils which we have observed in so many of our study areas.

THE LOWLAND ZONE OF LOW ARABLE POTENTIAL

We may now turn briefly to the lowland zone of low arable potential. As was mentioned earlier in the chapter, this is discussed tangentially but at some length in Chapter 4. We will close this chapter by consideration of two areas of reduced Neolithic arable potential in Western Europe: northern Italy and the Paris basin. Two factors seem above all to link together these and other areas in the zone, while distinguishing them from the zone of high arable potential. These are (1) the relative lateness with which the full complement of 'Neolithic' traits (artefactual and economic) puts in an appearance, and (2) the dominance of the animal rather than the arable sector of the economy.

Northern Italy

Prehistoric settlement in the lowlands of and surrounding the Po plain can be divided into two main groups. Most of the substantial, primary sites are to be found along the edges of the hills which surround the plain, but there is also a second group of sites to be found out on the plain itself.

The geomorphological history of the Po valley is highly complex and poorly known. This presents a very real obstacle to the reconstruction of prehistoric land use and potential. It seems reasonable to suppose that much of the present land surface of the plain is due to relatively recent deposition, but how much effect this has had is uncertain. As far as the tableland on the

fringes of the plain is concerned, this is less likely to be a serious factor, although again a certain amount of material has certainly been washed down off the hills. At Chiozza the first Neolithic level is encountered at only c. 50 cm below the modern surface, however, and there is no hint in the sections or excavation reports that the prehistoric land surface was notably different from today's. Much the same can be said of the sites around Vho di Piàdena. Thus, while it is perfectly true that the environment of the sites may have been different in detail during their occupation from that of today, it seems unlikely that sufficient change will have taken place to invalidate our very general conclusions.

As far as the Neolithic is concerned, the first group of sites is best exemplified by the 'Fiorano' settlements of the southern edge of the Po valley. A string of sites runs along the edge of the hills roughly between Reggio nell'Emilia and Bologna. These include Fiorano itself, Chiozza, and Albinea. All these sites are located on a low tableland a few tens of metres above the level of the plain, but before the hills start to rise steeply to the south.

The interesting feature of the location of these sites is that they occupy perhaps the one area in the whole region which offers any arable potential to an economy with a Neolithic technology. The soils of the plain itself are heavy and frequently waterlogged, and require considerable technological sophistication for arable exploitation. The Neolithic land surface may have included a few areas with lighter, sandier soils, but there is no evidence that these were of any great extent, if they did exist. The hills to the south have a very choppy topography with short, steep slopes which present a considerable barrier to cultivation. Even more important in this respect is that the surface of much of the hills is covered with very heavy soils. These soils are in many cases pure, fine clays, which provide the source for the many commercial potteries in the area, such as those at Scandiano, Fiorano, Casalgrande, and Sassuolo. Seeing that much of the tableland soil is derived from this parent material, these are frequently on the heavy side, too. On the other hand, in certain areas they are mixed with a sufficient quantity of coarser material from the underlying bedrock of the hills to provide a much more workable tilth. It seems reasonable to argue that the Neolithic settlements were attracted mainly by this (albeit modest) arable potential in an area which was otherwise conspicuously lacking in this resource. The discovery of traces of barley at the sites of Albinea and Chiozza (Evett & Renfrew 1971) may suggest that some use was being made of this potential. The same area shows signs of continued occupation in the Bronze Age, as do comparable areas in the Berici Hills, where the site of Torri is in a similar relationship to the wet bottomlands of the Fimon lake basin (Jarman, M. R. 1976b).

About 15 km north and northeast of Albinea lies a group of sites (S. Ilario d'Enza, Calerno, Campegine, and Castelnuovo di Sotto) in the Po plain itself. A similar occupation is to be found west of Mantova, at Vho di Piàdena. Although superficially different (the area around Vho is under intensive arable exploitation, while that to the south of the Po is primarily under improved pasture), the land use of the two areas is subject to the same constraints and limitations. The soils are uniformly heavy and frequently waterlogged despite centuries of careful management. With elaborate drainage and heavy machinery the soils can be ploughed, and under such a regime produce a very good return. They would not have been accessible to a Neolithic technology, however, and must have provided grazing resources at that time. Today the pastures around the Campegine group of sites are of exceptionally high quality, and supply cattle grazing for the production of *parmigiano* cheese. Under the less intensive management of prehistoric times the environment would have contained more marsh and open water than at present, which would have offered aquatic resources. There is little evidence that these were intensively exploited, however.

In the Berici Hills the Neolithic site of Molino Casarotto and the Bronze Age site of Fondo Tomollero (Jarman, M. R. 1976b) are closely comparable to those just discussed. In an area which is now under intensive arable exploitation, Neolithic exploitation of the lake basin would have been confined for the most part to the hunting and husbandry of herbivores.

It is necessary, finally, to consider briefly the interrelationship of the two groups of sites. It is possible, of course, that there was no real connection between the sites at the edge of the plain and those more centrally placed. Conventional archaeological explanation would suggest that these sites are most likely to have been autonomous, permanently occupied settlements, each population exploiting a different set of resources. The group of settlements at the southern margin of the Po plain do indeed seem likely to have been home bases which may well have had a permanent population. Apart from their arable potential already discussed, they are well situated to take advantage of the complementary grazing resources both of the hills to the south and the plain to the north. The sites further out on the plain seem more plausibly viewed as seasonal occupations than separate home bases. It is not possible

to be sure of this in the absence of more geomorphological information, but in winter the plain is likely to have been flooded, or at least so waterlogged as to present considerable barriers to occupation. The Fimon lake basin was inundated over a considerable area in winter prior to the drainage of the nineteenth and early twentieth centuries. This would almost certainly have precluded winter occupation of Molino Casarotto and Fondo Tomollero, and it seems likely that a similar situation would have obtained out on the Po plain proper. If these sites were indeed primarily summer stations, their populations must presumably have retreated to higher ground in winter. It seems by no means unlikely that the Campegine group of sites thus represents summer occupations of groups whose home bases lay on the southern margins of the plain. These home bases may have carried a small permanent population which was augmented in winter by groups which exploited the complementary resources both of the Po plain and of the hills to the south.

One further feature is worthy of note. The valley bottom sites are generally characterised by high levels of 'wild' fauna – particularly red deer – with the common farmyard domesticates present only in small numbers (Jarman, M. R. 1971, 1976b, Bagolini & Biagi 1975). In the sites at the margins of the plain, however, a much higher proportion of sheep, goat, and small cattle is characteristic (Malavolti 1953), although red deer frequently remain of considerable economic importance. The caprines in particular would have been most unsuited to the marshy environment of the plain, and it is therefore no surprise that they are scarce in those sites. These species are most likely to have been grazed to the south, away from the lowlands. As has been discussed in more detail elsewhere (Chapter 2, Jarman, M. R. 1972b, 1976b), there is no reason to believe that red deer were not at this time also a herded and husbanded resource, and it is thus possible that we should view the Po plain sites as summer herding stations despite the low incidence of 'domestic' animals. As has already been pointed out, the pedological and technological limitations inherent in the situation make it unlikely that the occasional grains of cereals found at some of the valley bottom sites were grown immediately adjacent to the site. In the case of the single grain of einkorn from Vho, it is hard to imagine that it came from within the site territory at all.

Paris Basin

A number of sites, mainly with *Rubané*, Rössen, and Chassey pottery, was studied in the Yonne and Essonne valleys to the south of Paris, and in the Oise valley to the north. There are considerable difficulties in classifying these from the point of view of land use potential and in making useful generalisations about their past economic orientation. The difficulties arise from two principal causes. The soils of the region, and thus both modern and past vegetation and land use, are highly complex, and vary greatly over short distances. Additionally, the best of the arable soils in the region today are medium-textured loams. To what extent these would have been cultivable in prehistory depends on factors which are difficult to assess, such as the precise methods of tillage, availability of labour, and distribution of rainfall. The soils are not as a rule sufficiently tractable to have been obvious targets for Neolithic arable agriculture, but nor are they all so heavy as to be easily eliminated from consideration in this respect. For these reasons, and because in the Paris region so much of the land use potential is obscured by industrial and residential development, this proved a more difficult area to analyse satisfactorily than many others in the lowland zone. There are nonetheless reasons for viewing the area as a whole as one of low Neolithic arable potential, however much small patches within it may seem to contradict this view.

The southernmost sites, like those at Sermizelles and Saint-Moré on the Cure (a tributary of the Yonne), lie in an area which even today is dominated by woodland. Thus the Chassey site of La Varenne just north of Sermizelles is located in the river valley, which provides a strip of light sandy soils. Steeply sloping valley sides lead up to a rolling plateau which carries the heavy clay soils of the *Terre Plaine*. Modern land use consists of a mixture of arable and pasture in the valley bottom, the slopes and plateau being predominantly under deciduous woodland and scrub, with occasional patches of pasture and arable. In prehistory the plateau would certainly not have been cultivable at all because of the intractability of the soils, and any arable exploitation would have been confined to the small area of better drained soils in the river valley. The Chassey, Bronze Age, and Iron Age sites at Saint-Moré, a little to the north, have territories which are similar to that of La Varenne in all essentials.

The sites around Auxerre, like those at Vaux and Augy, have territories with lighter soils for the most part, but these are mostly thin stony, limestone soils of low fertility. Much of the cultivated area is today given over to vines, Chablis lying only a few kilometres to the east. Further north one passes through the Gault clay lands of *Champagne humide*, much of which remains woodland today, and where the existing arable potential has for the most part been reclaimed from marshland and needs heavy equipment to be ploughed. The territories of sites such as those at Sougères-sur-Sinotte and Cheny thus have little in the way of Neolithic arable potential. Further north again the Yonne traverses the *Pays d'Othe*, at the western end of the *Champagne pouilleuse*. Here, prehistoric arable potential improves somewhat, as the sites have access in places to the light chalky soils which characterise the area. The increase is probably only marginal, however; in the *Pays d'Othe* the chalk is in many areas mantled with heavy clays which are still predominantly forested. Furthermore, while the chalk soils are tractable, they are infertile and poorly retentive of water. Historically they were almost entirely given over to sheep pasture, and it is only since 1945 that heavy applications of artificial fertilisers have raised yields sufficiently to encourage arable exploitation.

In the Essonne and Oise valleys the territories of sites such as Buno-Bonnevaux, Cerny, Saint Maximin, and Jonquières contain a mixture of light sands which are wooded for the most part, and medium to medium-heavy loams, intensively cultivated today. In these areas the arable potential is considerable for economies able to deal effectively with the heavier plateaux soils; but, as is so frequently the case, fertility is to a large degree correlated with soil texture, increasing as particle size and tractability decrease. The highly tractable sandy soils of the area give very meagre yields of arable crops, hence their largely wooded condition today.

Taking the study area as a whole, then, the only zones of substantial arable capacity are those just mentioned, whose Neolithic land use potential is ambiguous. A number of considerations suggest that these soils were indeed beyond the reach of the arable technology of the time. The large exposures of the best soils do not seem to have attracted much settlement except at their edges. While there certainly are exceptions, the majority of sites is found in the river valleys or in other areas where the heavier soils give way to sands. Many of the heavier soils seem not to have been settled until the introduction of wheeled mouldboard ploughs in the late Middle Ages (Clout 1977), prior to which rural settlement concentrated on the best of the lighter soils. It is notable that almost all the territories have areas of sandy soil close to the site, and many were actually discovered in the workings in sand pits. Additionally, some of those in the *Champagne pouilleuse* have light chalky soils accessible. These highly tractable soils seem to provide the main unifying feature among the sites, and their substantially riverine distribution seems likely to be related to the associated soil conditions. This suggests that it was these relatively poor but easily cultivated soils which were the focus of the subsistence economy, rather than the more difficult but rewarding soils which are the basis of the modern agricultural system.

The likelihood thus seems to be that the Paris Basin as a whole, and these sites in particular, had a low arable potential in Neolithic times, and certainly much lower than that at present. The Neolithic economy would have been primarily animal-based, although the selection of sandy soils for settlement suggests that the population was distributed to make the best of the small crop potential which did exist. It is not surprising, in view of the relative arable poverty of the area, that classic Neolithic economies developed rather late in comparison with the main zone of high arable potential. Not only are the earliest Neolithic sites typologically late (being classified as *Rubané récent*), but it is also noticeable that the animal sector of the economy shows

strong continuity with that of earlier postglacial economies. This is hard to pursue further as reports on the biological on-site data are rare, and detailed economic analyses non-existent. One substantial Neolithic fauna is reported from the site at Videlles les Roches, in the Essonne valley. This is dominated by species classified as 'wild', particularly red and roe deer and large pigs, only 30 per cent of the specimens coming from the domestic farmyard animals. This is a pattern familiar from many other areas of low arable potential, and encourages us in our belief that cereals would have occupied only a minor position in the Neolithic economy in the Paris Basin. The frequent association of plant-based economies with a highly developed animal sector may be taken to some extent as an index of the high degree of interdependence between the two economic components. The importance of their capacity for mutually beneficial integration has been alluded to in Chapter 3.

6. THE UPLANDS

It is integral to the approach pursued in this volume that the different economic zones are crucially inter-related. It is in the very nature of the upland zone that its resources can often only be utilised effectively in conjunction with the exploitation of the lowland and littoral zones. For this reason our discussion of upland economies revolves around the ways in which upland resources have been integrated with those com-plementary to them, and the economic mechanisms that have developed increasingly to overcome the limitations inherent in upland environments.

As far as postglacial Europe is concerned the charac-teristic resource offered by the upland zone is that of summer grazing. Snow cover, long periods of low temperatures with the resulting cessation of plant growth, steep slopes with poor soil development and rapid erosion, these factors tend as a whole to produce an environment which is low in both arable and winter grazing potential. High levels of summer rainfall and relatively low temperatures frequently lead to lush summer growth, however, and a high grazing potential at this season. Even today the European uplands are primarily exploited for their grazing and forestry re-sources. Moreover, it must be remembered that the modern situation is the product of millennia of agri-cultural development (both botanical and technologic-al) and of sustained population increase over the same period. The current picture thus gives generally an exaggerated view of the arable resources of the uplands compared with their prehistoric land use potential. Many upland areas are also rich in mineral resources. Minerals are often more easily accessible to surface exploitation here than in the lowlands, and the uplands have a different range of minerals from the adjacent lowlands in many cases. Evidence for the exploitation of a wide range of upland mineral resources, such as hard fine-grained rocks for ground-stone axes and metal ores, is ubiquitous in prehistoric Europe.

We have discussed in Chapter 2 the mechanism of mobility which represents the principal economic adapta-tion to the seasonal constraints embodied in upland environments. The pattern and degree of mobility vary with individual circumstances, from the mobile-cum-sedentary economic niche up to long-range trans-

humance where the seasonal ranges may be separated by hundreds of kilometres and many weeks of travel-ling. In one sense the scale of mobility is at the same time a scale of decreasing favourability. Economies occupying the key mobile-cum-sedentary niche are commonly situated on the junction of upland and lowland areas. They are in a position to tap the complementary resources of each zone with a minimum of movement and often without the need to establish a second home base. The small-scale movements which are needed to exploit the upland resources can fre-quently be accomplished within one or a few days. This permits a highly flexible and sensitive exploitation, easily adjusted to annual and local fluctuations in conditions. Energy loss in movement and in the trans-port of upland goods such as dairy products is at a minimum. With the need for long-distance mobility, it is less easy to make accurate allowances for yearly varia-tions, and contact between the upland and lowland zones becomes more difficult and tenuous other than at the time of the main seasonal movements. Further-more, reproductive levels of the stock tend to be lower, while losses due to predation, disease, and accident are generally much higher. On the other hand, economies employing long-distance mobility constitute one of the few ways of integrating effectively far distant com-plementary grazing resources. They are thus a vital adaptation to the pattern of resource distribution. Without such a mechanism, the upland zone could not be exploited with any degree of efficiency, and would have remained largely uninhabited.

This leads us to a further consideration which is of some importance. A casual glance at the archaeological picture of many regions and periods might lead one to suppose that the uplands were indeed for the most part uninhabited and unexploited. There are good reasons, however, for doubting the reality of these prehistoric empty spaces. It is, of course, true that the uplands will almost always have been less densely populated than the lowlands. The lack of any substantial potential for cereal agriculture severely restricts the population ceil-ing. In addition, a combination of factors (including the extremely large areas of upland in Europe, the high rate of plant growth through much of the summer in many of these areas, and the existence of important competing forms of economy for the lowland resources) tends to produce a situation in which the uplands are undergrazed. There are, of course, exceptions to this, but it is nevertheless true on the whole that upland grazing is exploited at considerably under its full potential, the limiting factor being the restriction of lowland grazing during the season when the uplands are inaccessible or economically unviable.

The uplands certainly were occupied and exploited, however. Where the necessary work has been done the evidence is available to demonstrate such occupation, although it is frequently difficult to interpret satisfactorily. Given the nature of upland economies – largely pastoral and mobile, involving a dispersed and relatively low population with little need of technological sophistication – it is perhaps not surprising that the evidence should be so exiguous. Equipment needed for pastoralism is negligible, and the constraints of mobility militate against the erection of elaborate settlements. Add to this the greater tendency of natural forces such as erosion to destroy traces of settlement, and the greater difficulties (and smaller rewards) of conducting effective archaeological survey work, and one has perhaps sufficient to account for the apparent paucity of evidence for upland occupation by comparison with the lowlands. It seems quite probable that the numerous typological discontinuities which exist between the two zones may be explicable in similar terms.

We realise, of course, that 'the uplands' is a most general term, comprising a very heterogeneous collection of physical and environmental types. Despite this great range of variation, however, it was felt that broad similarities are apparent which unite the uplands, and the way in which they have been exploited, into a significant unity.

CANTABRIA

The coastal topography of this area is such that the upland and littoral zones are in extremely close proximity. It is therefore particularly difficult to discuss the two areas in isolation, and a degree of overlap will be apparent between this section and some passages of Chapter 4. The Cantabrian mountains rise steeply from the narrow coastal plain, the watershed running roughly parallel with the coast and not more than 50 km inland (Figure 26). Considerable areas of land lie at over 1000 m and many peaks rise to over 2000 m. The steepness of the topography means that access to the uplands is primarily along the river valleys, some of which lead to passes sufficiently low to offer reasonably

good communication with the high central plateau of the *meseta*.

The modern winter snowline is about 1650 m, and passes are usually blocked for some months above about 1400 m, or sometimes as low as 1000 m. During the last glacial the permanent snowline dropped to about 1300–1500 m, and the winter snowline must have fallen correspondingly. Obermaier (1925) compared the situation of glacial Cantabria with that of modern Scotland, where the winter snowline is at *c.* 400–600 m. While the influence of the ocean probably maintained relatively snow-free conditions on the coastal plain, there would presumably have been a minimum of several weeks in every year in which the whole of the upland zone would have been inaccessible to exploitation. On the *meseta* to the south modern climatic conditions are continental, characterised by cold winds and below zero temperatures in winter, and hot arid summers. The annual rainfall of *c.* 600 mm is concentrated in spring and autumn. Under a glacial climatic régime winter conditions would have been more severe and would probably have discouraged occupation, while summer would have been more favourable to pastoral exploitation than at present.

Upland resources vary according to altitude and terrain. The lower and shallower slopes of the Cantabrian highlands, up to a maximum of about 1000 m, would have provided spring and summer grazing resources for the large herbivores. On steeper ground and at higher altitudes chamois and ibex would have been the principal resources. Similar conditions are likely to have prevailed on the *meseta*.

Upland resources of Cantabria were often exploited from sites at the junction of upland and lowland zones. These sites are frequently located at the debouchement of major river valleys from the hills, and thus have considerable potential for controlling the seasonal movements of animals, particularly in an area characterised by severe topography. On the narrow littoral of Asturias, with its steeply mountainous hinterland and compressed ecological zonation, preferred sites such as Cueto de la Mina and Riera offer easy access to winter grazing resources on the coastal plains, ibex or chamois in the immediately adjacent coastal hills, and control over major routes to the upland interior (Figure 27). There can be little doubt that this combination of advantages was a major attraction to repeated settlement over long periods. Transit or temporary sites also occur in the uplands proper, with site territories severely circumscribed by steep terrain and faunal remains dominated by the alpine species, as at Collubil and Rascaño.

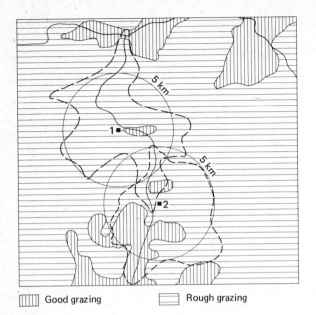

Good grazing   Rough grazing

Figure 91. Two hour exploitation territory of (1) Hermida and (2) La Mora.

Most of the Mousterian sites in the area are on the coastal plain or in the lower foothills. As was found in parts of both Italy (Barker 1975b) and Greece (Higgs 1966), Mousterian economies appear to concentrate on the lower and middle altitudes. There is no evidence of systematic exploitation of the high mountain zone, and the economy is relatively broadly based with little sign of the specialisation on one or two species which so frequently characterises later patterns of exploitation. Only the site of La Mora, at over 500 m, is an exception to the pattern. The single faunal identification is of ibex (Altuna 1971), which suggests an alpine element in the economy. As will be seen from the exploitation territory (Figure 91), however, a considerable area accessible to exploitation lies in the sheltered Deva valley, and this may well help to explain the unusual site location.

In contrast to the more northerly site of Hermida, La Mora is separated from the coast by steep mountains and almost impassable ravines. It is, however, easily accessible from the south, and its location and economic function would appear to have more relevance to Mousterian sites on the *meseta*, rather than being linked to sites on the Cantabrian coast. Evidence for the integration of coastal lowland and upland resources, so apparent for later periods, thus seems to be lacking during the Mousterian period. The relatively low density of fauna and artefacts in the Mousterian levels of Castillo is consistent with the view that this site had not yet realised its full potential. Indeed, when one takes into account the long time period which, presum-

ably, the Mousterian deposits represent, the impression is gained of a much lower population and much less intensive exploitation of resources than those found subsequently. We must remember, however, that the evidence at present is very thin, and it would not be altogether surprising if future research indicated at least some integration of the littoral and upland resources in the earlier part of the last glacial.

In the upper Palaeolithic, notably during the Solutrean and Magdalenian periods, developments are evident in the economy here as in many other areas of Europe. These include changes in the species exploited and in the overall patterns of site distribution. Large bovids and equids decline in importance, and there are signs of an increasing dependence on red deer, and of a more intensive exploitation of the higher parts of the upland zone and the resources (such as ibex and chamois) which these offer. Two main groups of sites concern us here, illustrating contrasting situations.

In eastern Asturias annual territories were bounded by the Cantabrian watershed. The steepness with which the mountains rise from the coast and the absence of low-level passes mean that the summer grazing of the *meseta* would have been inaccessible from the coast. The route which passes the site of Collubil would have been just passable, given the theoretical position of the permanent snowline. However, even under today's climatic conditions, the topography here presents a severe barrier to movement across the watershed. The addition of low-lying snow and ice during the last glacial would almost certainly have maintained an effective permanent barrier. This is reflected in the location and probable function of Collubil. Although apparently well-placed to exploit long-distance seasonal movements of animals (Figure 92), it was apparently used mainly as a temporary camp for the local exploitation of ibex. Other upland sites are similarly ephemeral transit or hunting camps.

An alternative summer range is provided by the intermontane valleys of the immediate hinterland, which form a large, relatively enclosed and fairly shallow basin – a productive and easily accessible complement to the extensive winter grazing on the enlarged coastal plain of the time (Figure 26). Although lying within the modern winter grazing zone, these inland valleys would have been marginal for winter use during the last glacial. Numerous topographical barriers enclose this basin except at certain well-defined exit points, and the area seems ideally suited to provide an extended territory of the kind discussed by Sturdy (1975), in which herd animals could be left to graze freely during the summer with a

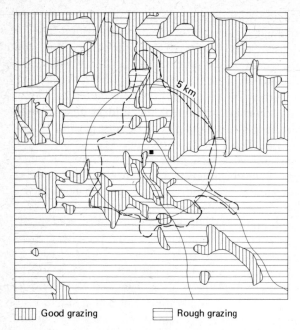

☐☐☐ Good grazing   ☐☐☐ Rough grazing

Figure 92. Two hour exploitation territory of Collubil.

minimum of interference from the human population. Sites such as Collubil, Ferran, Buxu, and Meré are so located that they could have performed the function of observing and controlling movement out of this area. The largely treeless vegetation believed to have prevailed during the last glacial would have assisted in this.

This pattern of site location is reminiscent of similar groupings of late glacial sites studied by Sturdy in central and northern Europe. This and the rise to dominance of red deer in the Solutrean and Magdalenian faunas of coastal deposits suggests that, as with the contemporaneous economies of northern Europe, we may be dealing with some form of specialised loose herding or herd-following economy, rather than a 'hunting' economy in the accepted sense. The contiguity of summer and winter zones would have greatly facilitated the flexible and controlled manipulation of animal resources, and may have allowed the human population to maintain a mobile-cum-sedentary pattern of settlement. The coastal home bases may have supported almost continuous human occupation, perhaps involving the maintenance of small killing herds in the lowland zone during the summer. Visits to the interior could have been undertaken by small parties to control deer movements and exploit other resources.

In Santander the case is somewhat different. Most of the major passes across the watershed would have been open in summer during the last glacial. The easiest routes lie south of Castillo and Hornos de la Peña, and

south of Otero and Valle through the twin passes controlled by the group of sites which includes Covalanas, Mirón, La Haza, Sotarriza, and Venta de la Perra (Figure 26). The clear relationship of major sites to such routes certainly encourages consideration of the possibility of long-distance seasonal mobility. Even so, the mountain passes are approached only by a steep ascent, and the degree to which herd animals would have made regular seasonal traverses would have depended on the pressure on summer grazing resources.

Two factors would have heightened the pressure on summer grazing during the maximum of the last glacial in the Santander region. Herbivore populations would, in all probability, have been limited by the availability of winter grazing. The considerable extension of the winter grazing zone by the lowered sea level would have allowed populations to rise, with a concomitant increase in the requirement for complementary summer grazing. At the same time the lowering of snowlines would have reduced considerably the availability of summer grazing in the mountain chain itself.

Evidence of occupation on the northern *meseta* at this time is scanty. A number of Upper Palaeolithic cave deposits have been identified, particularly in the vicinity of Oña on the upper reaches of the Ebro, in direct line of communication with the Cantabrian mountain passes. Faunal remains, including deer and equids were found here in association with stone tools (Martínez Santa-Olalla 1925). These claims have recently been questioned on the basis that the artefacts are not diagnostic and that the faunal remains appear to be carnivore accumulations (Clark, G. A. *et al.* 1975). The evidence is not, however, incompatible with the sort of transient human occupation that would be associated with a highly mobile seasonal exploitation. The widely acknowledged stylistic similarities of the cave art on the northern *meseta* with the classic sites of lowland Cantabria certainly suggests some connection between the two areas during the late glacial period.

It is possible however that, as in Asturias, the watershed remained a substantial natural barrier, and that exploitation of the *meseta* was occasional and limited. A good case can certainly be made for regarding Castillo as an inland home base served by natural corrals in its immediate vicinity and exploiting an extended territory comprising the major valleys leading up to the watershed (Figure 29). A similar pattern may be represented by the sites inland from Otero, while upland sites such as Rascaño (Figure 93) indicate the seasonal exploitation of ibex, as in Asturias. It seems likely, however, that a greater degree of seasonal

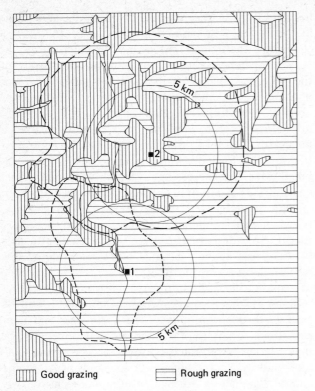

Good grazing   Rough grazing

Figure 93. Two hour exploitation territory of (1) Rascaño and (2) Fuente Frances.

mobility both of animals and human groups would have been necessary for effective exploitation than in this latter area, where the complementary zones are in such close proximity.

Despite the scantiness of the data, the hints in the record of a more intensive exploitation of upland resources and of the possible sophisticated management of red deer are of interest in view of the apparent population increase compared to Mousterian times. The larger population, coupled with the contraction in the area of summer grazing, may well have been instrumental in the development of a more controlled exploitative relationship with the primary food animals, and in the economic integration of the more widespread resources on which these depended.

Little is known of the Mesolithic period in the Cantabrian mountains. A number of inland sites have upper levels assigned to the Azilian, an ill-defined and poorly dated entity which appears to fill the gap between the end of the Magdalenian and the beginning of the Asturian period. Red deer persisted as the principal species throughout the transition to postglacial conditions. Los Azules shows a continued exploitation of the hinterland during the Azilian period, most

probably by means of seasonal movements from the adjacent coast, contacts with which are indicated by finds of mussel shells (Fernández-Tresguerres 1976). The Azilian level of Castillo yields a Mediterranean species of mollusc (Fischer 1925) which indicates contact of some sort with populations based on the Mediterranean littoral. In all likelihood they would have been encountered during summer exploitation of the *meseta*.

The apparent absence of inland occupation during the Asturian period (9000–7000 b.p.) is probably illusory, due to the association of the Asturian type-fossil with shellfish exploitation and the inadequate dating of Azilian levels in the hinterland, many of which are stratified beneath Neolithic finds. Economic changes would certainly have been necessitated by environmental change, but total abandonment of the hinterland is unlikely, although its economic potential may have been reduced to some extent by the spread of forest vegetation.

As in so many areas of upland, the Neolithic is characterised by economics closely comparable with those of the Upper Palaeolithic. Site distributions are frequently similar, and indeed many Palaeolithic caves show signs of reoccupation during the Neolithic. In Asturias, for instance, the Magdalenian site of Ferrán is reoccupied in the Neolithic; while similar evidence comes from Rascaño and Venta de la Perra in Santander, and Atapuerca in the northern *meseta*. In addition, there are many new Neolithic occupations in this region, such as the Poblado de Milagro and the Cueva de la Miel in the vicinity of Oña. The broad similarity of site distribution suggests that in the Neolithic, as in the Upper Palaeolithic, these sites represent summer grazing activities for the most part, although of course the milder Holocene climate and the possibility of small-scale arable agriculture may have permitted a degree of winter settlement. Whereas in some cases there is a faunal change, with the first appearance of the modern farmyard domesticates, in many instances there is substantial continuity, with red deer remaining an important resource. As is also the case in many other areas, the Neolithic shows signs of a larger population and much more intensive exploitation than hitherto. This is indicated both by the larger numbers of sites and by the expansion into new areas in addition to those previously exploited. This is particularly clear in the upland zone where many of the higher alpine areas show their first trace of intensive exploitation during the Neolithic. We return to a consideration of some of the Neolithic site locations and economic evidence in the next chapter.

THE FRENCH PYRENEES

The Pyrenees form a mountain chain some 400 km in length, which ascend in a series of steps from the Basse Montagne (600–1000 m) to the Moyenne Montagne (1000–1600 m) and the Haute Montagne (over 1600 m). In addition, the chain as a whole is tilted, the peaks being lower and the descent to the plain conspicuously more gentle in the west than in the east.

The modern permanent snowline is at *c.* 2800 m, while snow lies on average for six months at 1650 m, three months at 1170 m, and one month at 650 m. Snow depths are often very considerable, tending to increase from west to east. Snow and frost are relatively infrequent at the base of the mountains and have no importance as limiting economic factors at this altitude. Precipitation is high, most of it falling between autumn and spring. The Atlantic end of the chain receives fairly frequent summer rain, the Mediterranean end very little. As in most mountainous regions isolation is a critical factor in local climatic variation; the *soulanes* (sunny side) of the valleys being greatly favoured in terms of plant growth and settlement relative to the *bachs* (shady side).

Differences in altitude, geology, and aspect produce a highly variable vegetation. Plant growth tends to be extremely rapid, particularly at the moister and warmer western end. About a quarter of the French Pyrenees remain under forest cover today, despite continuous clearance. In the east the vegetation passes from evergreen oak woodland in the foothills to pines above, while in the central Pyrenees the lower altitudes are dominated by beech, with mixed conifers above. At the Atlantic end the mixed deciduous forest includes ash, beech, and chestnut among its common species. Above the forest zone, broadly speaking at over 1500–2000 m, lies an extensive zone of alpine vegetation which is of critical economic importance. On limestone soils in particular this zone produces highly nutritious summer grazing for sheep, while cattle do better on the crystalline and siliceous rocks.

Modern land use is overwhelmingly dominated by pastoralism and forestry. Arable agriculture is limited, as in other mountainous regions, by meteorological and pedological constraints. Crops are effectively limited to the valley floors (which form the main focus of human occupation) and to artificially created terraces at the lower altitudes. Prior to the introduction of the potato and maize, with their wide climatic tolerance, the area under the plough would have been yet smaller. Seldom, if ever, have the Pyrenean valleys been self-sufficient in their carbohydrate staples, and a series of market towns has grown up at the junction of mountain and plain, like Foix and Mauléon, which act as centres of exchange for the upland and lowland products.

As elsewhere in Europe, the historical dominance of the sheep as the main pastoral animal is less pronounced today, and cattle are found in much larger numbers than formerly. This is partly due to the large urban market for dairy products and technological means for their large-scale preservation and transport. Pressure on lowland winter grazing resources, combined with the increasing availability of maize and concentrates as alternative winter feeds, has also been an important factor. Despite these modern changes, transhumance remains an important and necessary aspect of pastoral practice. Very large areas, particularly in the central and eastern Pyrenees, are under snow for months at a time in winter, and are thus inaccessible to exploitation. These form a gigantic reservoir of summer grazing resources whose potential can only be realised through mobility of the herbivores and their exploiters. A pattern of regular seasonal movement has thus become established between these summer pastures and winter grazings in the lowlands of Aquitaine and the Languedoc. Spring and autumn are customarily spent at the junction of mountain and plain, and it is here that the main Pyrenean market towns, usually incorporating annual livestock fairs, have grown up.

Prehistoric land use must have been subject to the same basic constraints, as is indeed borne out by the fact that modern settlement patterns are broadly comparable to those of long periods of prehistory. The Pyrenees are undoubtedly experiencing a greater degree of arable exploitation now than at any time in the past. This is partly due to the availability of modern crop varieties and equipment, and partly due to population increase and economic development in western Europe as a whole. In earlier periods, and particularly in prehistoric times, pastoralism must have shaped and dominated land use and settlement to an even greater extent than today. Very similar factors will have operated in Pleistocene as in Holocene times. The effect of a colder, more continental climate will have been primarily to emphasise the seasonal aspect of settlement and exploitation patterns, and thus to reinforce the crucial importance of mobility. This will have been the case regardless of whether the herbivorous animals which formed the dietary staples were fully domesticated, or were the objects of a hunting or herd-following economy.

The impact of these fundamental directives can be clearly seen in the long-term continuity of settlement patterns, and, where the evidence is available, of the basis of subsistence. Most of the caves which contain significant Palaeolithic occupations show signs of subsequent use. Often such sites were used as burial areas in Neolithic, Eneolithic, and Bronze Age times, while many continued in use through the Iron Age and into the Roman and mediaeval periods. As elsewhere in Europe, there is little detailed evidence available of these occupations, as excavators were customarily only interested in the more spectacular Palaeolithic finds below. Many instances are thus merely recorded without comment, while others doubtless failed even to achieve this limited recognition. The most obvious exceptions to this continuity of occupation are caves which collapsed or were sealed up at earlier periods.

At all periods settlement concentrates at the junction of upland and lowland, in the foothill zone which historically was the focus of spring and autumn grazing for animals which summered in the high Pyrenees and wintered on the plains to the north. To some extent this pattern may be a consequence of geological factors, as it is in this zone that most of the caves are to be found. However, such open sites and surface scatters that are known are also most frequent in the same area, and it therefore seems likely that a genuine distribution of settlements is represented.

Sites in the area of Foix (Ariège) may be taken as exemplifying the situation as a whole. The Mas d'Azil, occupied from the Aurignacian period to protohistoric times and later, lies at about 300 m in a basin between the Montagnes du Plantaurel and the Massif de l'Arize which rises to over 1500 m some 20 km to the south. The exploitation territory (Figure 94) reveals it to be a characteristic herding site, with the steep-sided gorges forming potential natural corrals along much of the valley of the Arize. Indeed, much of the small basin around the modern village of Maury, to the south of the site, is sealed off by topographic barriers. As far as arable agriculture is concerned, even the few relatively flat areas carry poorly drained soils derived from the limestone hill slopes. These vary greatly in texture, but by and large those which are sufficiently fine-grained to be attractive to agriculture are far too heavy to have been accessible to a Neolithic technology. These are in any case of so small an extent as to be of little general significance in the area. Modern land use is dominated by pasture, rough grazing, and forestry. Other sites, such as those at Foix itself and those (like Ussat, Fontanet, Bédeilhac, and Pradières) around Tarascon about 13 km to the south, also cluster around intermontane basins, with similar land use and potential, and show long-term continuity of occupation.

If it is accepted that the area must in prehistory as

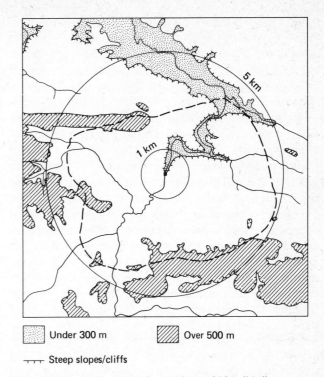

Under 300 m   Over 500 m

Steep slopes/cliffs

Figure 94. One hour exploitation territory of Mas d'Azil.

today have been exploited primarily through economies dependent upon herbivores, the seasonal nature of exploitation is an inevitable conclusion. The Massif de l'Arize is under snow for many weeks of every year, falls being fairly frequent as late as April and as early as October. Winter occupation of the Massif by pastoralists is thus out of the question unless the animals are to be fed on stored fodder. In Pleistocene times the whole area was probably under snow for months at a time, and the area would then, as in recent historical times, have been primarily a spring and autumn grazing ground. Occupation of this zone would also have been possible during the summer, but it seems perhaps more likely that sites served as bases from which movements were made to temporary summer camps at higher altitudes. This is suggested by the importance of ibex in the Palaeolithic levels at many sites, as it seems unlikely that large numbers of ibex would have descended quite so low at high summer, even under Pleistocene climatic conditions.

The above-mentioned line of market towns at the junction of mountains and foothills thus represents the historical development from the clusters of prehistoric sites at the same positions. These locations are important not only as junctions of ecological zones, but also as points where valleys come together, and, above all, where stock-routes from the mountains converge before scattering across the lowlands. The main gatherings of humans and herds occurred here at the equinoxes, a situation often reflected in the faunal material from the sites and in the clustering of evidence of socio-religious activities, such as cave art or funerary monuments.

A classic example of this type of location can be seen where the Garonne emerges from the mountains and converges with the river Neste. The occupation of both Gargas and Gourdan began in the Middle Palaeolithic, but after the collapse of the former, the latter became the major site of this area. After the more broadly based economies of the earlier periods, its Magdalenian occupation shows an almost total predominance of reindeer. This economic specialisation, and the relationship of sites to natural barriers such as major rivers and steep slopes, emphasises the similarity of this situation to that of many sites in the Dordogne (see Chapter 3), and suggests strongly that some form of herd control or corralling may have been in use. These junction sites may have had some winter occupation, as is implied by reindeer remains at both Gargas and Gourdan, but the principal winter occupation occurred farther out on the lowland at sites like Duruthy and Isturitz, and, no doubt, along the littoral (Bahn 1977).

The pivotal settlements at the crucial junction of upland and lowland continued in use throughout the prehistoric and historic periods, despite the demographic and economic changes which took place. The red deer–pig economy that developed in the early post-glacial seems to have persisted into the late Bronze Age in some areas. The transition to an economy based on the modern farmyard animals is still very poorly known, but certainly occurred first at the Mediterranean end of the chain. This is to be expected. As we have noted, cattle-based economies in the Pyrenees depend heavily on commercially supplied winter foods and urban markets. The sheep, better adapted to the environmental limitations, is well suited to the drier Mediterranean conditions of the eastern Pyrenees, but would have experienced considerable economic competition from indigenous species in the moister and lusher environment of the central and western Pyrenees. Both red deer and pig maintained a high degree of importance in most areas; particularly the pig, which was one of the dominant Pyrenean resources even as late as mediaeval times.

The Neolithic and post-Neolithic periods saw an expansion in terms of numbers of sites (although many are merely sepulchral caves) and in terms of penetration of the high mountain zone. This can be seen most clearly in the distribution of funerary monuments and

in scattered finds on high cols and passes (well over 2000 m). However difficult it may be to quantify, it seems clear that this period witnessed a considerable increase in the upland population and in the intensity of exploitation. Most sites, monuments, and finds occur on crests and along known stock-routes, and it is evident that settlement and economy remains throughout firmly anchored by the constraints of mobile pastoralism.

Thus the severity of the overall environmental limitations has led to a pattern of pastoral exploitation of very great antiquity, and to substantial continuity in many aspects of life. The importance of mobility is emphasised by the many extant permanent drove-ways for sheep and cattle, some of which are known to date back at least as far as the earliest written records. Where these converge at nodal points in the foothill zone one finds the concentrations of prehistoric sites, the mediaeval (and more recent) spring and autumn sheep fairs, and the modern market towns. However dramatically the economic minutiae have changed, it is clear that some fundamental aspects have been constant for many millennia.

THE APENNINE CHAIN

Peninsular Italy is dominated by the Apennines. This is true not only in a crude topographic sense; their influence is felt profoundly in climate, vegetation, economy, and communications. South of the Po plain by far the majority of Italy lies at over 200 m in altitude, and large areas at over 500 m, while many of the peaks in the high Apennines rise over 2000 m. The relatively rapid ascent from the Tyrrhenian lowlands in the west and the Adriatic lowlands in the east up to the central spine has an important impact on climate and vegetation, and hence upon economic potential. The limited areas of coastal lowland provide the best arable resources available in peninsular Italy and also supply winter grazing. With increasing altitude, precipitation rises, average temperatures decrease, and the natural vegetation changes from a typical Mediterranean flora of conifers, evergreen oak, and macchia scrub, through mixed deciduous woodland, beech woodland, and finally to the more open vegetation of the highest peaks. A similar broad zonation is to be seen in the pattern of modern land use. As one climbs from coasts to the high Apennines, so conditions become increasingly marginal for arable agriculture, and cereals, vines, and olives give way to pasture and forestry. Figure 95 shows the topography of peninsular Italy, and the location of the main features referred to in the text.

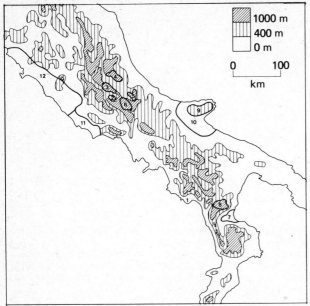

Figure 95. Relief of peninsular Italy with the location of areas referred to in the text. (1) Camerota caves, (2) Fucine Lake basin, (3) Monte Velino, (4) Gran Sasso, (5) Maiella, (6) Piano delle Cinquemiglia, (7) Plain of Sibari, (8) Sierra Dolcedorme, (9) Gargano, (10) Tavoliere, (11) Pontine lowlands, (12) Maremma.

In our attempt to envisage the prehistoric landscape and its resources we must never forget that the modern picture is the end result of sustained exploitation over many centuries. In general this means that upland areas will have been increasingly put under the plough, as population pressure demands that ever more marginal regions should yield an arable return, and as technological progress makes this possible. It is generally the case in Europe, therefore, that present areas of pasture and woodland represent minima, except where commercial afforestation has begun to reverse this trend in the past few decades. The degree of change since prehistoric times is probably especially large in Italy, for a number of reasons. In the first place, with its early development of high population levels and an urbanised society, the Italian environment has undergone a much longer period of the consequent degree of pressure upon resources than have many areas of Europe. Furthermore, the hot dry summers go some way towards mitigating the effects of altitude, with field crops producing acceptable yields at higher levels than is the case in many other regions. This factor is accentuated by the fact that many of the hills of medium height, such as the Tuscan hills and eastern foothills, have unusually stable and well-developed soils for upland areas. Additionally, the widespread importance of the olive and the vine, with their tolerance of relatively infertile soils, has enabled many areas to yield worth-

while arable returns in environments which could not do so under more demanding crops outside the climatic range of these characteristic Mediterranean cultivars. This is a process which, as we shall see, probably has its roots in prehistory.

Settlement and economy

Pre-Neolithic

A general survey of the pre-Neolithic exploitation of Central Italy (Barker 1975b) indicated a number of features which are of significance for our analysis of later economies. It was observed that, as in Greece, there seems to have been a shift in the distribution of sites, coupled with evidence of an economic change, between the Middle and Upper Palaeolithic. Middle Palaeolithic sites are primarily restricted to the lowlands and the valleys of the foothill zones, while the area of Upper Palaeolithic settlement extends further inland and to considerably greater altitudes. Coupled with this phenomenon is the fact that, while throughout the period red deer appears to have been the staple source of animal protein, the Middle Palaeolithic economy seems in general to have been more broadly based than the more specialised Upper Palaeolithic pattern. A number of factors would have been involved in this change. Firstly, a change in the nature of the available resources is involved. Such species as *Elephas antiquus*, *Dicerorhinus merckii*, and *Hippopotamus amphibius* were available and exploited regularly, if in small numbers, during the Middle Palaeolithic. With the possible exception of small relict populations in the extreme south of the peninsula, these had become extinct in Italy by the Upper Palaeolithic. Underlying this faunal change was presumably the onset of more extreme climatic conditions which characterised the latter half of the Würm glacial period, and this in itself probably contributed significantly to the change in settlement pattern. Lowered snowlines, longer periods of winter snow cover in the uplands, with the attendant cessation of plant growth, would have had the effect of increasing the degree of seasonal polarity with which the human and animal populations had to contend. The low sea levels which coincided with glacial conditions would have exposed important areas of coastal lowland in some areas. These would have provided crucial winter grazing resources, and would have been incorporated into the seasonal pattern of exploitation witnessed by the appearance of sites in the high Apennines.

Our basic demographic hypothesis suggests that

there is likely to have been a substantial population increase over a period as long as the Upper Pleistocene. Indeed, if one accepts as indicative the admittedly crude data of site density and distribution, there is good evidence of a population increase between the Middle and Upper Palaeolithic periods. We could expect this to be reflected in economic behaviour, and it seems reasonable to view the signs of a more efficient and complete exploitation of the total available resources in this light.

The evidence of economic change does not rest entirely upon the faunal spectrum and upon an expansion in the area of settlement. Barker (1975b) points to evidence that, although scanty, can be taken as suggesting a more controlled exploitation of the primary food source, the red deer, during the Upper Palaeolithic. In view of the evidence discussed above it seems reasonable to follow Barker in suggesting that, under the promptings of resource and demographic change, an increasingly close economic relationship was established with the red deer, depending on the close association of human with animal populations, and which may have amounted to herd following. The details of site location lend some weight to this interpretation. In some areas, at least, sites appear to be located in accordance with Sturdy's extended territory concept (1972, 1975). That is to say that many of the site locations can best be explained in terms of control of animal movement and of access to large areas of seasonal grazing, rather than in terms of direct exploitation of whole animal ranges. Thus in the Camerota area the site of Cala delle Ossa is located in a position which affords maximum potential control over animal movements between the upland summer pastures of the Monte Alburno massif and the winter pastures on the coastal lowlands.

The important group of Upper Palaeolithic sites in the Fucine lake basin (Figure 96) at c. 650–700 m in the central Apennines will serve as our main example. Of the six important known sites, the conspicuously larger faunal and artefactual collection from the Riparo Maurizio indicates that this was the most likely home base. Despite arguments to the contrary, Barker (1975b) was able to show that even a late Würm winter snowline conservatively estimated at 750 m would have left little in the way of exploitable resources at this time of year. Certainly the sites are not located to take best advantage of what land there is below 750 m. Furthermore, most of the sites are oriented with a north or northeast aspect, most inappropriate for inhabitants planning regular winter occupation during the last glaciation. It must therefore be concluded that the sites

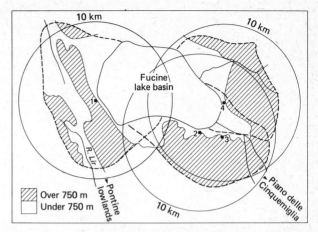

Figure 96. The Fucine Lake basin showing Epigravettian sites and their relationship to topography and routes of access to primary areas of upland and lowland grazing. The two hour exploitation territories of (1) Grotta di Ciccio Felice, (2) Grotta Maritza and (3) Riparo Maurizio are delimited. Grotta di Ortucchio (4) is also shown. After Barker (1975b).

were primarily, if not exclusively, occupied during the summer. Due to variations in orientation and topography, the Riparo Maurizio territory contains more high-quality upland grazing than do the sites along the southern edge of the basin under today's conditions, and there is no reason to think that it was otherwise during their period of occupation. This factor was presumably of importance in the selection of Riparo Maurizio as the main summer home base; and the ruggedness of much of the area within the exploitation territory of the other sites is reflected in the presence of ibex and chamois in their faunal samples.

Today high quality summer grazing is found in the high Apennines surrounding the Fucine lake basin; particularly the Monte Velino massif to the north and the Piano delle Cinquemiglia and Maiella area to the south and east. The dense scatter of Upper Palaeolithic sites in this latter area (see Barker 1975b, Figure 20) indicates a significant degree of exploitation. Barker suggests that this may have been exploited mainly as an extended territory, and it would in this case be unsurprising that more substantial signs of occupation are lacking. With this perspective the sites in the Fucine basin can be seen as having as much to do with the manipulation and control of animal movements as with subsistence purely in terms of their own exploitation territories. Some details of the Fucine sites are suggestive in this context. With the approach of winter weather conditions in the high pasture area the stock would begin to move downwards towards their winter grazings. As we have noted, red deer is the staple resource of the economic system, and this species is well known to be extremely sensitive to weather conditions (Darling 1937). Some of the animals would doubtless have travelled north and east to the Adriatic coastal lowlands, but others would have moved south and west to the Pontine lowlands of Lazio. Many of these would necessarily have passed through the Fucine basin *en route*.

A conspicuous feature of the location of the Fucine sites is that they offer, by reason of topographic constraints and their proximity to the lake, maximum opportunities for the control of the movement of animals entering the basin from the south or east. The details of the location and the toolkit at Grotta Maritza led Barker to suggest that it was probably the specialised autumn killing station of those groups whose deer were moving to their winter grazing grounds, having summered in the high Apennines. It is of particular interest to note that there is no sign that the lake contributed any significant resources to the diet at this period. The Fucino sites are clustered so close to the (Late Pleistocene) lake shore that, in the absence of signs of exploitation of the lake itself, it seems more than reasonable to infer that a crucial factor was the strategic value of lake-side location in terms of regulation of animal movements.

Neolithic

We have seen that there is good evidence for the operation of controlled economic systems involving large-scale seasonal mobility during the Upper Palaeolithic period. The Neolithic situation in the upland zone is in many ways closely comparable; a fact which is scarcely surprising in view of the environmental constraints which ensure that subsistence must have been based upon the exploitation of seasonally mobile herbivores in both periods. Indeed, as Barker has pointed out, there are striking continuities of flint typology and site location, as there are also between the Neolithic and Bronze Age. We can distinguish two main groups of upland sites. The first group is located characteristically at the point where valley routes debouch from the main summer grazing areas. These sites are of varying potential according to local topographic and soil conditions, but do not seem to be concerned primarily with arable exploitation. Even those which, like Maddalena di Muccia and the Grotta del Orso, contain considerable arable potential within their one hour territories, are not optimally located to exploit this. Others in this group have only small territories without a high economic potential even in terms of grazing resources. These are probably best viewed as

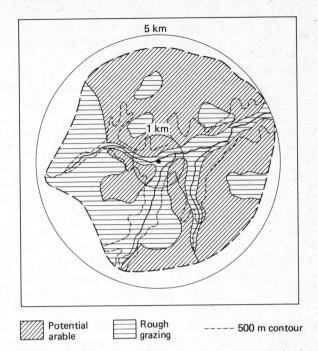

Figure 97. One hour exploitation territory of Maddalena di Muccia.

spring and autumn transit camps, unlikely to have been occupied for long periods in any one year. It is impossible to demonstrate the absence of year-round occupation on the available evidence, but as we shall see below, there are good reasons to suggest that this was the case. The second group of sites comprises summer grazing camps with little or no arable potential, and with very considerable climatic obstacles to winter occupation and exploitation.

We may take Maddalena di Muccia, Marche, as one example of the first group of sites (Figure 97). The site itself is at *c*. 400 m in the Chienti river valley where it emerges from the Apennines; but nearly all the one hour exploitation territory is over 500 m. One might interpret the site as being a permanently occupied mixed arable and stock farm. On the other hand, the site itself is in the valley bottom, away from the best available potential arable soils, although an area of these lies fairly close to the west of the settlement. There is certainly no direct evidence of cereals at the site, and this combined with the territorial evidence suggests that they would have had at best a subsidiary economic importance. The best summer grazing in the region lies to the west of the territory on the slopes of Monte Pennino. There is little winter grazing potential due to cold and snow cover, and local farmers are forced to stall-feed their cattle at this season. Sheep are today sometimes sent to the coastal lowlands to the east in winter.

In view of these factors it seems reasonable to suggest that the site was primarily occupied in spring and autumn, and that it was mainly concerned with the exploitation and control of herbivores moving between the winter grazings on the coast and their summer grounds in the uplands. It is also possible, however, that the economy was a mobile-cum-sedentary one, with at least a small sedentary or semi-sedentary population subsisting mainly upon resources available within the exploitation territory, while the rest of the population moved with the animals. Although the evidence available at present is inconclusive, it might be argued that the faunal data favour the latter interpretation. Pig and red deer dominate the faunal collection, caprovines and cattle being present in relatively small numbers. Pigs are poorly adapted to long-distance transhumance, but would have been well suited to the deciduous woodland and river bottom lands in the immediate vicinity of the site. Thus we may argue either that the faunal spectrum reflects the exploitation of locally available resources by the sedentary portion of the population, or that despite the overall economic importance of the mobile stock, they were not heavily cropped during the spring and autumn occupations of the site. We should always bear in mind that the picture gained from a single element in a mobile economy may be incomplete to the point of being misleading as to the nature of the system as a whole.

It is also worth remembering, however, that in some instances there seems to be good evidence for the persistence of economies based substantially upon red deer and pigs well into the Neolithic. This certainly seems to be the case at Molino Casarotto in northern Italy (Jarman, M. R. 1971, 1976b) in an environment unsuited to the Neolithic farmyard economy. The high proportion of red deer bones in such upland Neolithic sites as Valle Ottara and Capo d'Acqua in central Italy suggests the same maintenance of close economic relationships with a species which had been largely superseded by more productive alternatives in other areas.

Broadly speaking, the Grotta dei Piccioni (Abruzzi), Grotta dell'Orso (Toscana), and Grotta Lattaia (Umbria) have comparable exploitation territories and economic data to those of Maddalena di Muccia. Details can be found in Barker (1975b). A slightly different kind of site in the first group can be recognised on the basis of the exploitation territories. Grotta dei Baffoni and Grotta del Mezzogiorno (Marche), for example, are restricted to small exploitation territories by topographic factors, while their altitude places them

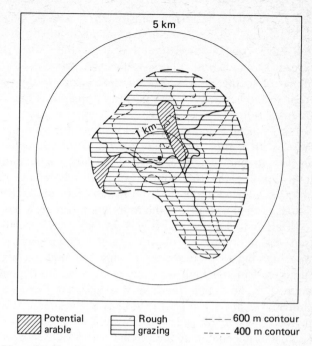

Figure 98. One hour exploitation territory of Grotta dei Baffoni.

Potential arable — Rough grazing — --- 600 m contour — ----- 400 m contour

in the same intermediate zone as Maddalena di Muccia, as far as seasonal grazing is concerned. It seems certain that such sites as these would have been temporary herding stations occupied for only very short periods during the spring and autumn movement. They do not give access to sufficient grazing resources to have encouraged long periods of occupation. Figure 98 illustrates the impact of topography upon the territory accessible from Grotta dei Baffoni.

The second group can be exemplified by such sites as Grotta la Punta and Paterno in the Fucine lake basin (Figure 96), Grotta Sant'Angelo and Capo d'Acqua (Abbruzzi), Norcia (Umbria), and Valle Ottara (Lazio). These sites are characteristically located at the lower edge of the main summer grazing areas, as we have seen in the Fucine basin in earlier periods. They are thus well suited as summer home bases from which small short-term movements could be made into the adjacent grazing areas. It is certain that there would have been temporary camps at higher altitudes in the heart of the summer grazing, but in the nature of things these would have been ephemeral and unlikely to survive in recognisable form. The Grotta Cola II di Petrella, at 1000 m in the Monti Simbruini (Abruzzi), provides one example of such a site, and, as Barker (1975b) notes, it is remarkable for the poverty of its archaeological assemblage.

Eneolithic to Bronze Age

The continuity of site location and economic behaviour is again striking. Many sites continue in occupation from the Neolithic, and the constraints upon upland exploitation would have been substantially the same. Attiggio and Monte San Croce in Marche have territories which are closely comparable with that of Maddalena di Muccia, while the territory of the site of Belverde is identical with that of Grotta Lattaia (see above). Grotta dei Baffoni and Grotta del Mezzogiorno continue in occupation, as do Grotta la Punta Grotta dei Piccione, Grotta del Orso, Valle Ottara, and others.

There are, however, some significant signs of change. The faunal evidence is patchy in the extreme, and yields little in the way of a general pattern. One feature which does emerge, however, is the decrease in importance of red deer with time. One of the main staples at many sites in the Neolithic, it declines to insignificance in the Bronze Age. This is a commonplace in European economic evolution, and can be related to the development of a more efficient and productive integration of resources, particularly through the development of mixed cereal and livestock farming (Jarman, M. R. 1971, 1976b).

Of more importance in the present context is the increasing evidence of exploitation of the highest upland pastures, and some hints at more intensive exploitation, perhaps including permanent settlement, of the intermediate altitudinal zone towards the upper limit of viable arable farming. Good examples of the former are Collarmele (Figure 99) and Blokhaus in Abruzzi, and Campo Pericolo (Figure 100) on the Gran Sasso. As regards the latter phenomenon, the site of Belverde (Figure 101) contains substantial evidence of both cereals and pulses; as does the Tara del Diavolo, which has a comparable exploitation territory. Belverde is distinguished by the richness of its Bronze Age assemblage. Similar evidence is available from the Val di Varri, and Barker (1975b) may be right in arguing that even the Grotta a Male, at nearly 1000 m on the Gran Sasso, became a permanently occupied site by the end of the Bronze Age. As always, it is difficult to be categorical about seasonal interpretations, but the substantial nature of the assemblages, and the evidence of cultivated crops, can plausibly be interpreted in terms of an increasingly intensive and stable pattern of exploitation. It should be remembered, of course, that the plants could in some or all cases have been imported from lower altitudes. In the present context this is not a crucial issue. The plant foods, even if imported,

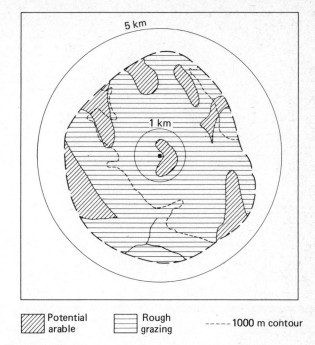

Potential arable   Rough grazing   ----- 1000 m contour

Figure 99. One hour exploitation territory of Collarmele.

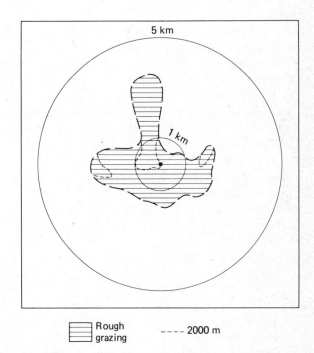

Rough grazing   ---- 2000 m

Figure 100. One hour exploitation territory of Campo Pericolo.

are more likely to have been employed as winter staples, when other food resources were inaccessible, rather than consumed in summer when alternatives were plentiful. This is particularly so in the case of the beans from Belverde and Val di Varri, which, like

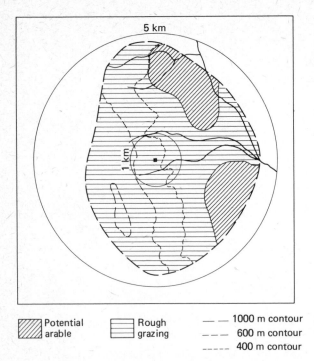

Potential arable   Rough grazing   — — 1000 m contour
— — — 600 m contour
— — — — 400 m contour

Figure 101. One hour exploitation territory of Belverde.

those on so many other Apennine Bronze Age sites, were almost certainly used as animal fodder.

These developments visible in settlement and land use can reasonably be attributed to adjustments made in the face of rising population levels. There is evidence in the plant remains from sites such as Belverde that during the Bronze Age there may already have begun to develop the system of intensive polyculture which in many areas typified Mediterranean agriculture for much of the Classical period. This not only has the effect of greatly increasing the productive potential of the intermediate altitude zone, but it tends to polarise transhumant pastoralism. Increased utilisation of this area for crops necessitates more controlled and larger scale movements for stock, and eventually results in the more intensive use of both upland and winter grazings. Among the developments which may be expected under such circumstances is the maintenance of some stock all the year round in the summer grazing area by the use of stored fodder crops and hay as winter supplements. Although there is no positive evidence of stall-maintained animals in the upland zone of central Italy during winter at this period, the presence there of fodder crops makes this a reasonable assumption. Where the summer limitation on drinking water can be overcome, similar expedients are possible in the lowlands. A further development over this period is of course that of bronze technology. Barker (1972) has discussed the possible rôle of mobile pastoralism in exploiting and dispersing copper from the upland zone, and it is most likely that this process was an additional factor in the increasingly intensive exploitation of this area.

Rigorous demonstration that population levels rose over the period in question, let alone of a causative relationship between this and the economic phenomena observed, must elude us in the present state of knowledge. Both are reasonable assumptions, however, and are supported by what little evidence there is. The number of known Bronze Age sites in the area under consideration certainly exceeds that of Neolithic sites, and some of the former considerably exceed the latter in size and substance. As Barker (1975b) points out, detailed survey work in the *Ager Veientanus* area of southern Etruria clearly illustrates the continuation of this trend into later periods. Substantial population increase would of itself require economic adjustments of the type observed to have been made, and signs of other possible causative agents are lacking so far. The relationship between the two is of course a complex one, but there seems to be sufficient reason for postulating their correlation in this case.

We must also say something of the rest of peninsular Italy. Our evidence is considerably better in the area just discussed, for it has seen the most intensive research as far as palaeoeconomic analysis is concerned. There is sufficient information from elsewhere to suggest that the same basic patterns are visible, and that the same critical factors were in operation.

A rather different kind of upland situation is illustrated by the Gargano promontory, in Apulia. This is a relatively small, isolated area of upland, which, with maximum altitudes of just over 1000 m, presents its exploiters with different constraints and potentials. In this case upland sites proper seem to be restricted to surface scatters, there being no sign so far of home-base sites in the central Gargano region. Palaeolithic settlement seems to be concentrated around the edge of the hills, exploiting the mobile-cum-sedentary economic niche. Some factors which may have influenced the situation were discussed by Jarman, M. R. & Webley (1975). There is an almost total absence of Palaeolithic data from the Tavoliere plain to the south of the Gargano. It is always impossible to be confident of hypotheses based upon such negative evidence, but one possible explanation of this is in terms of the low winter carrying capacity of the area. This combined with the small size of the Gargano upland block, could have led to a situation in which it was possible to exploit the Gargano summer grazing as far as was necessary from a series of peripheral home bases, in conjunction with a number of ephemeral transit camps in the interior. Subsequent occupation follows the same lines, with the home-base sites located on the periphery of the Gargano, upland sites proper being mainly restricted to surface scatters, betokening considerable exploitation, but an occupation which was insubstantial in terms of its archaeological traces. Although winter climatic conditions are less severe on the Gargano than in many areas of the central Apennines, they are sufficient seriously to have inhibited exploitation at this time of year. The Gargano offers very little in the way of arable resources, and must have been primarily if not exclusively a source of summer grazing for animal populations which wintered on the Tavoliere.

A similar emphasis upon seasonal factors is evident in upland exploitation elsewhere. Thus the site of Grotta Sant'Angelo (Calabria) is clearly a short-term transit camp for mobile pastoralists moving from their winter grazings on the Plain of Sibari to the uplands of the Serra Dolcedorme (Jarman, M. R. 1972b). This interpretation is supported by the nature of the site (a small cave with only a shallow deposit despite an occupation spanning Middle Neolithic to Bronze Age) and its territory (small, and not particularly well located for pastoralism, let alone for arable farming). Grotta Sant'Angelo is, significantly, located immediately adjacent to one of the main modern transhumance routes. The site is thus closely comparable to those of Grotta dei Baffoni and Grotta del Mezzogiorno, discussed above.

A brief elaboration should be made concerning the emphasis upon seasonal factors in the interpretation of the upland sites. The theoretical aspects of the question have been discussed at length (Chapter 2), but it is worth pointing out that the arguments do not rest on hypothesis alone. It is, of course, rare for archaeological evidence to survive which conclusively demonstrates a case of this nature, but indications are sometimes there when they are sought. Faunal evidence strongly implies an emphasis on winter occupation in the Palaeolithic exploitation of the Camerota region, and by the same token implies summer sites elsewhere in a zone of complementary resources. In a number of areas there are unequivocal signs of links between upland and lowland sites and areas, quite apart from the more enigmatic artefactual and stylistic parallels. Thus a number of central Italian upland sites, including Grotta dei Baffoni and Grotta del Mezzogiorno, are linked to sites on the eastern lowlands by the presence of pottery with an identical mica fill. Bauxite in the pottery at Val di Varri probably came from the area of the main

summer pastures on Monte Velino. Where its source has been identified, the flint on the Tavoliere sites proves to have come from the Gargano. Furthermore, many of the sites identified by us as spring and autumn sites lie close to modern and historically known transhumance routes.

NORTHERN ITALY

The area that we will be considering comprises parts of the Veneto and Trentino-Alto Adige provinces. So large an area includes, needless to say, a wide variety of environments, but many of the factors show a broad cline of variation from south to north. As one proceeds from the Po plain towards the Austrian border, winters become colder and snowier, and summers wetter and cooler; soils become increasingly stony and skeletal; vegetation varies from dense deciduous scrub and woodland, through beech forests to conifer forests, with open pasture on the high plateaux. This broad vegetation pattern represents, of course, the combination of human exploitation and other environmental factors. Modern human land use becomes increasingly dominated by pastoralism as one goes north, but some crops are grown practically wherever there is settlement. Maize is the dominant arable crop, grown almost exclusively for fodder, and yielding well in the warm wet summers of the Alto Adige. Few cereals are grown for human consumption in the northern part of the region, although further south summers are hot and dry enough to give reasonable yields where other conditions permit. Potatoes become an increasingly important crop as agricultural conditions become more marginal with the higher altitudes and less favourable climate.

Taken as a whole, however, the area is low in arable potential, and would have been yet more so in prehistoric times, prior to the effects of lowland drainage, technological advances, and the introduction of maize and potatoes. Even in the southern part of the region, in the most favourable area for arable crops from a climatic and pedological viewpoint, the majority of the uplands are under scrub woodland and pasture. The pasture is often improved by occasional ploughing and sowing of fodder plants, and indeed much of such arable exploitation as exists is geared to livestock farming, as it is dominated by the cultivation of fodder crops. Despite the fact that winter is the lean season, winters are mild by comparison with those further north, with few serious snowfalls or severe frosts. As one moves first into the foothills, and thence into the Alps proper, winter conditions present ever more

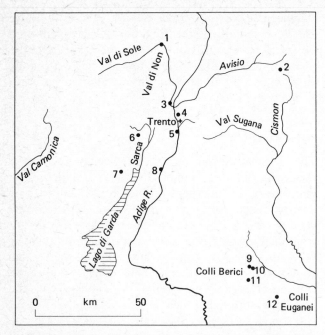

Figure 102. North Italian location map showing key sites and features mentioned in the text. (1) Castellaz di Cagno, (2) Colbricon, (3) Vatte di Zambana, (4) Riparo Gaban, (5) Romagnano, (6) Fiavè, (7) Ledro, (8) Isera, (9) Molino Casarotto, (10) Fondo Tomollero, (11) Monte Tondo, (12) Castelnuovo di Teolo.

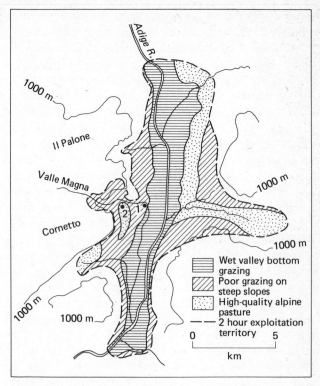

Figure 103. Two hour exploitation territory of (1) Romagnano. Also shown is (2) Garniga.

stringent limitations, and become the factor around which the economy revolves. Economies must overcome this period of low or zero productivity either by mobility, or (increasingly) by the storage of summer surpluses and/or the buying in of fodder. With the move northwards conditions for arable crops deteriorate, and the landscape and economy are increasingly given over to pastoralism and forestry, the main crops being hay and timber.

The upland sites of the area can conveniently be divided into three main groups: sites in the Adige valley, sites higher up on the *altipiani*, and sites in the Berici and Euganei hills, which lie further south isolated from the Alps by the northern fringe of the Po plain (Figure 102). More detailed descriptions of individual sites and their environments can be found in Jarman, M. R. (1971, 1975, 1976b).

The Adige valley sites

The group of sites at Romagnano (Perini 1971, 1975) is crucial to any consideration of this group. Between them they cover a substantially complete range of Epipalaeolithic and Neolithic occupations, while graves testify to continued exploitation of the locality in the Bronze Age. The shelter of Romagnano III, in particu-

lar, has a long Epipalaeolithic and Neolithic succession, and was clearly a preferred site. Figure 103 illustrates the exploitation territory.

We must mention here a difficulty which arises with all the Adige valley sites: to what degree did the river present an obstacle to movement and exploitation? Today, in summer at least, the river can be negotiated with ease in a number of places, but it must be remembered that until the relatively recent historical regulation of the river and drainage of the marshes which characterised its floodplain in many places, the valley would have presented a far more imposing obstacle. The view is therefore taken here that significant exploitation of resources to the east of the river is unlikely in prehistoric times from sites to its west, and *vice versa*. We have shown the whole exploitation territory of each site, but it seems almost certain that sites were concerned predominantly with resources on their own side of the Adige. It must be borne in mind, moreover, that while we have shown the present-day course of the Adige, there is evidence of considerable movement within the area of the modern valley bottom. The exact position of the river during the occupation of the sites is unknown, and thus both this and the precise distribution of floodplain resources must be regarded as an approximation.

Romagnano lies at just over 200 m, with slopes rising rapidly to over 1000 m to the west. They are in places so steep as to be to all intents and purposes inaccessible. The territory is thus essentially a long corridor running north–south along the Adige, with lateral extensions where there are side valleys, indicating the severe constraints imposed by topography. These limitations apply more stringently on the west of the Adige, leading to the paradoxical situation that there is in theory a larger area accessible for exploitation to the east of the Adige than to the west where the site is located. It is also notable that the eastern portion of the territory has a higher proportion of relatively productive rough grazing resources, again due to the slightly gentler topography.

Nevertheless, as has been argued, the sites must for practical reasons have been primarily concerned with resources on their own side of the valley, and in the case of Romagnano a number of features here are noteworthy. Firstly its site location gives immediate access to the resources of the valley bottom. Today this is largely exploited for intensive vine and fruit production, with some small areas of field crops. Prior to the drainage of the floodplain and regulation of the river this area would have had little or no arable potential, however, and must have been used mainly for wet pasture and hay. Such arable potential as existed would have been confined to the small areas of more freely drained slope soils at the foot of the valley sides, where these were not too steep or too stony. There is no direct evidence that this small arable potential was being exploited from Romagnano in prehistoric times. In view of this, and, more significantly, of the important general limitations on arable exploitation in the area, it seems probable that the site was predominantly concerned with the exploitation of animals.

The territory as a whole, and particularly the more accessible portion to the west of the Adige, is poor in good upland grazing resources outside the floodplain zone. Not only does topography seriously limit the area available, but the steep slopes have generally little soil cover and often receive little insolation. These factors reduce substantially the grazing potential, and the slopes are largely unproductive of anything except timber. As Figure 103 shows, only two small areas of better quality rough grazing lie within the western portion of the territory, both at a considerable walking distance from the site. Romagnano is, however, located so as to provide two advantages to an animal-based economy. The Valle Magna offers one of the few routes up to the large area of good upland grazing immediately to the west of the territory on Il Palone and the Cornetto. Furthermore, the very topographic severity which limits the potential of the territory lends itself to the use of the area around Romagnano as a natural corral, with the exploitation of the good upland grazing to the west as an extended territory.

Riparo Gaban, a little to the north, has an Epipalaeolithic to Bronze Age succession, and seems to have been a preferred site comparable to Romagnano III. It lies to the east of the Adige at the northern limit of the Romagnano two hour territory, and has a similar territory and resources. Again, the valley-bottom grazing seems to be the most significant resource within easy distance, but the site has upland grazing resources available to the northeast and is also in a position to control access to the rich and extensive grazings of the upper Val Sugana (Figure 102).

In addition to these preferred sites there are a large number of sites which seem to have been occupied on a more transient basis, or which appear, at least, not to show a comparable degree of long-term preference. These occupy very similar positions and have similar territories. The Mesolithic site of Vatte di Zambana (Broglio 1971) shows the familiar picture of a highly distorted territory with little beyond valley-bottom resources, but offering access to rich upland grazings just beyond the western territorial limit, in this case the *piano* around the modern village of Fai, and the southern Val di Non (Figure 104). Again, a valley close to the site provides a route through what is otherwise a virtually unbroken line of cliffs. Isera (Barfield 1971, Jarman, M. R. 1976b) exemplifies a comparable site location during the Neolithic, from which access would have been gained to the upland grazing on the gentler slopes below the summit of Monte Stivo.

As far as we can tell from the available evidence, sites were situated in smaller locations elsewhere in northern Italy. The Neolithic site of Calodri, in the Sarca valley just to the west of our main study area, and the Bronze Age site of Montesei di Serso in the upper Val Sugana have similar territories and resources to those discussed in the Adige valley itself. The group of sites based on the preferred site of Riparo del Belverde, with its Middle Palaeolithic to Neolithic succession, in the Sesia valley to the west of Lago Maggiore (Fedele 1973), suggests the existence of comparable patterns of settlement elsewhere in the north Italian subalpine and alpine zone.

To judge from the number of sites known, there seems to have been considerable long-term population increase in the prehistoric occupation of the Adige

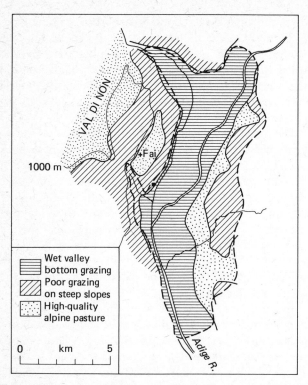

Figure 104. Two hour exploitation territory of Vatte di Zambana.

the authors suggest a date of *c*. 6000 b.c. for the occupations. The area has a characteristically alpine environment, with conifer forests on the steep slopes and pasture on the more accessible and open areas. There is deep snow cover throughout the winter, and falls can occur as early as October and as late as May. The area must thus have been exploited exclusively as a high summer grazing area in prehistory, as it indeed remained until the recent development of forestry and tourism as competing aspects in the economy. The sites are in the vicinity of two small lakes. Much of the area to the west, south, and east is extremely severe topographically, and the exploitation territories are thus highly restricted. The sites give access mainly to the more gentle areas of grazing to their north and northwest. They lie close to the headquarters of the Avisio and Cismon rivers, which would have provided easy routes of travel to complementary lowland bases south of Trento (in the former case) or on the northern margins of the Po plain further east.

Elsewhere in northern Italy an Epipalaeolithic industry was found at over 900 m on the Altipiano di Coriadeghe, between Brescia and Lago di Garda (Biagi 1972); while at Piancavallo, in Friuli, a similar (but typologically slightly earlier) industry has been found at over 1200 m (Guerreschi 1975).

In the Neolithic there are again occasional signs of exploitation of the upland valleys. The site of Garniga (Figure 103) is close to Romagnano, but is located in an upland basin at *c*. 750 m. The site seems to have been a single hut (Bagolini & Biagi 1975). The territory is very similar to that of Romagnano, but the more westerly position of Garniga gives it easier access to the extensive upland grazing in the Bondone basin at the foot of Il Palone. There is also a small patch of good pasture in the Garniga basin adjacent to the site. A similar small Neolithic site is known from Castel di Cagno, at over 600 m in the Val di Non. The territory provides almost exclusively upland grazing resources in the northern Val di Non basin.

Comparable Bronze Age settlements are relatively common; one may cite Doss Mion, Doss de la Cros, and San Biagio from the Val di Non, while elsewhere in Trentino, Doss Casteler/Pinza in the Val di Sole and Passo Sella at the head of the Avisio are in similar positions from the point of view of exploitative potential.

valley. A casual survey of the literature suggests that there may be as many as twice the number of Neolithic sites as Epipalaeolithic to Mesolithic sites; much shorter Bronze and Iron Ages are also better represented, and there is, in addition, evidence discussed below for a substantial expansion in the area of settlement in the later prehistoric periods.

Sites of the high plateaux and valleys

This group of sites is best subdivided into a number of categories. Some may reasonably be interpreted as ephemeral or short-term sites on the basis of their positions, small size, paucity of remains, or the absence of signs of substantial structures. Others, for a variety of reasons, may be argued to result from a more substantial, even year-round, occupation. Finally, a number of sites are best treated separately – art sites, tombs, and centres of mineral extraction.

Ephemeral sites

Ephemeral sites are known from at least the Mesolithic period onwards. At Colbricon there have recently been excavated (Bagolini *et al*. 1975) a number of small encampments at 1900–2200 m. The industry is microlithic, and by a comparison with similar assemblages

Permanent settlements

There is no indication that there was any long-term or year-round occupation of the upland valleys prior to the Bronze Age. Presumably the disincentives involved in severe winter weather and the problems of over-wintering animals were sufficiently potent to discourage the establishment of a permanent alpine population. With the Bronze Age, however, there are signs that this may have started to change. The site of Fiavè (Perini 1975) is a substantial lake-side settlement, with impressive structures which, along with other organic remains, have been excellently preserved by the water-logged conditions. The site is at *c.* 650 m and climatic constraints would certainly have presented great difficulties to human and other animals attempting to overwinter in the lake basin. On the other hand, the area is permanently occupied today (the animals being stall-fed), and evidence from the slaughter patterns of all the primary food animals suggested strongly that the site was occupied all the year round. The hypothesis was advanced (Jarman, M. R. 1975, 1976b) that this was the result of increasing competition for alternative sources of lowland (winter) grazing, which forced increasingly intensive use of the upland resources, including stall-feeding in winter and, almost certainly, the intensive exploitation of meadows and fodder crops for winter use. The subsequent historical development of these trends has recently been discussed in some detail by Cole & Wolf (1974). The well-known Bronze Age lake-side settlement at Ledro is in a comparable environmental position to that of Fiavè and has a similar exploitation territory. It seems reasonable to view it as a permanent upland settlement of the Fiavè type, although the economy has not been analysed in detail.

Other sites

It is interesting to note that the exploitation of minerals in northern Italy appears to go hand in hand with the increasingly intensive use of alpine resources discussed above. A recent analysis (Preuschen 1973) of Bronze Age mining in Trentino has shown the extent to which the increasing importance of copper ores must necessarily have involved high human population levels in the upland zone, at least periodically. The half dozen mining sites known in the Tione area are within 10–15 km of Ledro and Fiavè. Many more are known from the Valle dei Mòheni area, to the north of the upper Val Sugana. It is not our purpose to speculate at length as to the precise socio-economic configuration involved in the exploitation of the various upland resources. No doubt many different systems are arguable. Nonetheless, the coincidence of accessible mineral deposits with long-used areas of upland grazing is significant, and it

may even be that the increasing importance of the former was in some measure involved in the tendency to a more permanent, as well as a more intensive exploitation of the upland zone. The significance of upland art sites, such as the notable concentrations of carvings in the Val Camonica, is similarly obscure. Again, however, these are in environmental contexts which strongly suggest the involvement of herders in their summer grazings, and the subject matter of many of the representations support this supposition.

The Colli Berici and Colli Euganei

Basic environmental variations create a rather different economic situation in this area. Not only does it lie some 60–80 km south of Trento, but these hills are isolated from the main body of alpine foothills by an area of lowland. A consequence of this has been a very different set of factors affecting winter settlement and exploitation. Very little snow falls in the area, and frosts are not generally severe. This removes the main critical factor determining winter economic strategies in the alpine area proper.

The economic prehistory of the Berici Hills is discussed in some detail in an earlier paper (Jarman, M. R. 1976b). Here we may take the Bronze Age site of Monte Tondo (Figure 105) as an example of an upland site location. This site is at just below 400 m, the exploitation territory being almost entirely rough grazing. The nearest potential arable, in small patches along the eastern edge of the hills, lies some 1.5–2 km from the site, and arable agriculture is thus unlikely to have been of great significance in the economy, which would have been based upon pastoralism. The Neolithic site at Castelnovo in the Euganei Hills (Figure 106) is comparable as regards location and potential resources. The highly complex mosaic character of land use and potential in the Euganei Hills makes it almost impossible to map these accurately other than at very large scales. Land use here depends primarily upon the linked factors of slope and soil cover, which vary widely on a very local scale. In Figure 106 we have classified those parts of the territory with greater than 50 per cent of the area having reasonable arable potential as 'potentially arable', those dominated by pasture, woodland, and scrub as 'rough grazing'. It can be seen that the site is in the centre of an area of dominantly grazing potential, and that with the exception of a small patch to the west, the nearest area of high arable potential is some 20 minutes from the site.

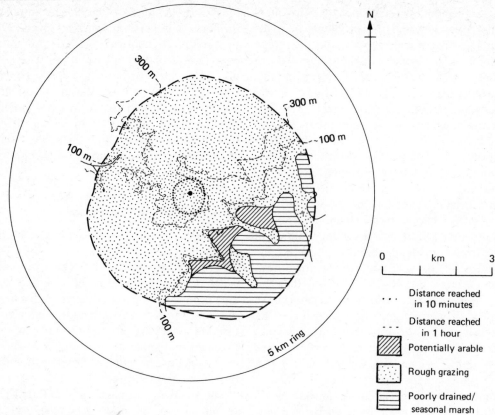

Figure 105. One hour exploitation territory of Monte Tondo. From Jarman, M. R. (1976b).

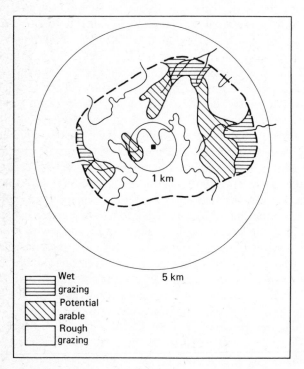

Figure 106. One hour exploitation territory of Castelnovo di Teolo.

Integration

We are now in a position to take a more general look at the settlement and exploitation of the upland areas of northern Italy to see what patterns and trends may emerge. A first stage is the consideration of the inter-relationship of the different categories of site discussed above. As we have noticed, at a general level the picture is striking for its continuity rather than for dramatic change. Not only do certain sites such as Romagnano III act as foci of settlement repeatedly over long periods, but throughout the period surveyed here the overall pattern of settlement is based upon a series of sites strung along the sides of the main Adige valley and a series of complementary, ephemeral, upland sites in areas of rich summer pasture. This picture begins to change significantly with the Bronze Age, when there are signs of an increasingly intensive use of upland resources, including not only a closer management of the grazing potential, but also the systematic exploitation of minerals.

The climatic conditions in winter are such that occupation of the upland valleys and plateaux at this season requires major economic adjustments which

222

affect the whole subsistence cycle. If we are correct in suggesting that these are first to be observed in the Bronze Age, then we must see in the earlier upland sites, such as Colbricon, Garniga, and Castel di Cagno, the summer stations of human groups subsisting (whether by pastoralism or hunting) on animal populations which spent the winter at lower altitudes, below the snowline. Historically the main axis of transhumance was between the Adige valley, which was the wintering area, and such upland areas as the Val di Non. There are many factors involved in the pattern. Throughout most of the historical period population levels in the region were high, and rising (Cole & Wolf 1974). One consequence of this was the exertion of considerable pressure upon the available winter grazing, the principal limiting factor. This competition for lowland grazing, coupled with the gradual expansion of the area under arable crops as opposed to pasture, had the effect of decreasing the viability of long-range transhumant systems operating between the Po valley and the southern foothills of the subalpine zone. As population levels rose in this southerly area, and the exploitation of the local winter grazing resources increased to capacity, increasingly intensive use therefore had to be made of the resources of the alpine zone proper.

Accordingly, while it seems perfectly plausible that some human and animal populations remained throughout the winter in the Adige valley in prehistoric as in historic times, it seems most likely that a high proportion used the valley as an autumn and spring grazing area, and as a route south to the main winter grazings on the Po plain, or its northern margins. The capacity of the Po plain itself to support winter populations would have depended primarily upon the degree of flooding; it is possible (Jarman, M. R. 1976b) that much of the area was too wet for exploitation in the winter, though doubtless some of it was so used. The Adige valley itself would not have had a sufficiently high carrying capacity to overwinter all of the stock summering in the upper valleys, and thus a combination of the short- and long-range transhumant systems seems likely. Similarly it is probable that the Sarca valley to the west acted as a route for stock from the uplands to the lowland grazings around and to the south of Lago di Garda.

Along with, and intimately bound up with, the development of the more intensive exploitation patterns in the alpine zone, one can perceive certain specific economic adaptations. There are few faunal or botanical studies from archaeological sites in the area, but there are sufficient to give us some hints as to the general nature of the trends. Again, the picture is striking for its basic continuity. Far from the Neolithic economy depending principally upon the integration of a new series of introduced animal and plant staples, as is the case in some areas of Europe, the earlier Neolithic faunas are dominated by red deer and pig. These species, the former in particular, are important in the Mesolithic/Epipalaeolithic economy, the chamois being the other main staple. Cereals, where they exist at all at Neolithic sites, are conspicuous for their rarity. The development of the stereotyped Neolithic subsistence economy, based on sheep, goats, cattle, domestic pigs, and cereals, was a gradual process, because the potential for this kind of system was initially very low. Furthermore, the potential only increased as a result of, and was maintained by, long-term population pressure (Jarman, M. R. 1976b). Table 23 illustrates some of the trends in the developing economy; and it can be seen that it is only with the Bronze Age that the modern farmyard animals became firmly established as the sole animal staples, and that cereals came to have any significance in the economy of the upland zone proper. The expansion of cereal growing into basically unfavourable and marginal environments such as those at Fiavè and Ledro is of great significance. Not only does this in itself illustrate the considerable population pressure which had built up in the area as a whole by this date, but it seems probable that, even if many of the cereal crops were grown for animal fodder rather than human consumption, it was only through the successful extraction of some arable yield from the upland valleys that they became habitable on a year-round basis. It seems more than possible that the contemporaneous development of mineral resources in the area, with its concomitant trading opportunities, also contributed to the feasibility of maintaining a permanent alpine population in the Bronze Age, as it was known to do in the historical period.

The factor of long-term population pressure is clearly of paramount importance in the foregoing discussion, and requires some explicit (if brief) discussion. Even accepting the difficulties inherent in any attempt to gauge past population levels, it is clear that in relative terms the period under review witnessed considerable population increase. Both the numbers of sites per unit of time, and the area of occupation can be seen to rise in the long term. Furthermore, many of the economic adaptations we have observed – the increasing importance of the modern farmyard animals; the gradual spread in area and increase of importance of cereal growing in marginal areas; the permanent settlement of regions which could only be thus settled at the cost of

Table 23. Economic trends in subalpine Italy as seen in faunal and botanical remains from archaeological sites

Site	Age	Fauna							Flora		
		ibex	chamois	red deer	roe deer	pig	cattle	sheep + goat	wheat	barley	other plants
Berici and Euganei hills											
Molino Casarotto	M. Neolithic			49.8%	5.0%	37.5%	0.9%	0.4%	trace		water chestnut dominant
La Fontega	Eneolithic/ Bronze Age			3		1	4		n.d.	n.d.	n.d.
Val Liona	Eneolithic/ Bronze Age			18		11	8	6	n.d.	n.d.	n.d.
Castellon del Brosimo	Eneolithic/ Bronze Age			present	present	10	5	9	n.d.	n.d.	n.d.
Arqua	Eneolithic/ Bronze Age			present		present	present	present	n.d.	n.d.	n.d.
Monte Tondo	Bronze Age			7.7%		34.1%	24.9%	27.3%	no plant remains		
Torri d'Arcugnano	Bronze Age			2.2%	0.2%	25.6%	24.1%	38.3%	n.d.	n.d.	n.d.
Fondo Tomollero	Bronze Age			2.4%	2.3%	26.2%	13.4%	45.4%	present		Cornelian cherry present
Adige valley and Alpine foothills											
Romagnano	Epipalaeolithic/ Mesolithic	rare	present	common	common	rare			n.d.	n.d.	n.d.
Zambana	Epipalaeolithic/ Mesolithic	rare	common	common	rare				n.d.	n.d.	n.d.
Busa dell'Adamo	Mesolithic/ E. Neolithic			present		present	?	present	n.d.	n.d.	n.d.
Romagnano	E. Neolithic			common	present	rare	present	rare	n.d.	n.d.	n.d.
Vela	E. Neolithic			dominant					n.d.	n.d.	n.d.
Romagnano	M. Neolithic			present	present	present	present	present	n.d.	n.d.	n.d.
Vela	M. Neolithic			present		present	present		n.d.	n.d.	n.d.
Rivoli	Middle/Late Neolithic		trace	6.9%	1.5%	30.5%	22.7%	22.3%	cereal impressions		
Isera	Middle/Late Neolithic			29.7%		23.8%	27.5%	19.0%	n.d.	n.d.	n.d.
Colombare	Eneolithic			7.0%		26.1%	37.2%	24.8%	n.d.	n.d.	n.d.
Alle Giare	Bronze Age/ Iron Age	present		present	present	present	present	present	n.d.	n.d.	n.d.
High-level sites											
Fiavè	Bronze Age		trace	1.4%	0.5%	6.5%	28.5%	51.9%	dominant	present	pulses, wide variety of fruits
Ledro	Bronze Age			2.2%		8.0%	23.2%	65.2%	present	present	
Naturno	Bronze Age					common	common	common	n.d.	n.d.	n.d.

considerable technological expenditure and economic adjustment – can only be satisfactorily explained in terms of sustained population pressure. There would have been no incentive for the year-round occupation of the Fiavè and Ledro lake basins until alternative and less labour-demanding solutions to the problems of shortage of winter fodder became inadequate. Conversely, the creation, cultivation, and harvesting of upland hay meadows, inherent in such a system as these sites reflect, is highly expensive of labour and thus requires a relatively high population for their maintenance. Significantly, these factors remain crucial in the historic and modern exploitation of the area as Cole & Wolf (1974) have clearly shown. They demonstrate that the permanent settlement of the Val di Non in mediaeval times was directly correlated with popula-

tion pressure; and, conversely, that in some areas under today's conditions of rural depopulation the upland livestock economy is beginning to break down due to a lack of labour to maintain the intensively exploited meadows. Similarly, it is evident that, just as we have hypothesised for the prehistoric period, population growth is a long-term constant in historic times. Table 24 illustrates this phenomenon at both the regional and local level.

It was pointed out earlier that the Colli Berici and Colli Euganei differ from the main part of our study area in one crucial respect. The absence of prolonged winter snow or cold weather removes the major limiting factor which operates on settlement and economy further north. Thus, despite the many overriding similarities between the two areas, the precise way in which

Table 24. Historical population increase in the Tyrol, and in two villages in the Val di Non
(data from Cole & Wolf 1974)

Date	Total Tyrol population	Date	Population of village of St Felix	Date	Population of village of Trets
1312	240 000				
1427	360 000				
		16th century	100–125		
1650	500 000	17th century	250–275	early 17th century	c. 110–120
1754	593 000	end 18th century	275–300		
1835	719 000	late 19th century	c. 350	1800	c. 160
1910	947 000			1900	c. 200–250
1951	1 170 000			1960	238

the varying resources were integrated is likely to have been different. It was argued (Jarman, M. R. 1976b) that the valley-bottom settlements in the Berici Hills were probably primarily summer occupations. If recent historical conditions are any guide, there would have been substantial lowland flooding in winter, and sites such as Molino Casarotto and Fondo Tomollero could not have been occupied at this season. In view of this, it was argued that upland sites such as Monte Tondo may represent the winter habitation. We thus have the reverse pattern to that of the alpine zone; of lowland summer occupation, followed by a short-range movement to higher winter territories. Certain features of the Monte Tondo faunal collection such as the very low percentage of first-year animals in the cull, which are otherwise curious, become more readily explicable in the light of this hypothesis (Jarman, M. R. 1976b). If this pattern of restricted mobility was indeed in operation in prehistoric times in the Berici Hills, it is likely that a comparable system functioned in the Euganei Hills as well; but there is little evidence either to support or combat this suggestion.

THE CARPATHIANS

The Carpathians form a sickle-shaped mountain chain, rising in places to over 2500 m, which exerts a crucial influence upon the economy and settlement of parts of Romania, the Soviet Union, Czechoslovakia and Poland. We have chosen the Braşov Depression, in Transylvania, as an area for detailed treatment. It is an essentially enclosed basin which lies within the Carpathian arc, immediately inside its southeastern angle (Figure 107). The basin, its floor at about 500 m, covers about 500 km², and is bordered on the south by the Bucegi massif through which a number of valley routes

permit relatively easy access to the Wallachian plain to the south. Further west lies the more massive Făgăraş range. To the east of the Depression the deeply dissected mountains of Buzau and Vrancea, seldom higher than 1500 m, allow access to the loess plains of southern Moldavia.

The Depression is generally divided into three physiographic zones which have some relevance for this study. The first of these zones forms the floor of the basin, lying between 490 m and 550 m. This occupies the central area and consists of Miocene and Pliocene deposits which are drained by the River Olt and its main tributary the Riu Negru. The northern edge of the basin is delimited by the Olt where it is forced by the mountain massifs to flow in a strongly arched meander northwards and westwards before finding a passage south through the Făgăraş range. Surrounding this central area is a piedmont zone. Here grassy slopes and gentle rounded summits rise abruptly from the basin floor to a height of 750 m. The piedmont is particularly extensive in the southern and western sections of the Depression. Above 750 m is the third zone, formed by a range of limestone mountains which dominates the Depression, reaching heights of between 1300 m and 2000 m in the south.

The climate of the Depression is continental; it is characterised by cold winters and hot summers, with a rainfall peak in June. Altitude plays an important rôle in determining the local climate within the Depression. In the basin, at Bod (508 m), the average annual precipitation is 592.4 mm; while Braşov, 100 m higher in the piedmont zone, receives 744.9 mm. Seasonal variations in temperature are also affected by altitude, though not always in the way that might be expected. Average July temperatures are nearly the same in the plain and the piedmont, being 17.9 °C at Bod and 18.0 °C at Braşov,

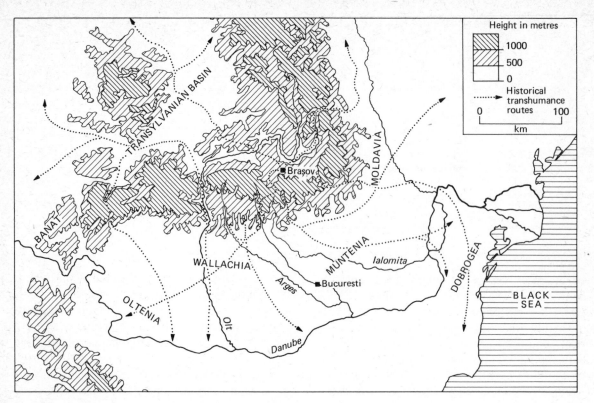

Figure 107. Map of Romania showing the Braşov depression, historical transhumance routes from Braşov to the lowlands, and other key features mentioned in the text.

but the average January temperatures are lower in the plain (−5.6°C at Bod) than on the piedmont (−4.2°C at Braşov). This temperature inversion is produced by the proximity of the mountains which causes cold air masses to collect in the bowl of the Depression. As a result the plain suffers a large number of days of frost, on average 135 per year, and a winter minimum temperature of −38.5°C was recorded at Bod, the lowest ever in the entire country. Sharp frosts begin as early as September and snow cover usually lasts from November to March, though owing to the low winter precipitation snow only actually falls on 30 days per year on average. It can form drifts of some depth in valleys exposed to the prevailing northeast–southwest winds, and generally remains until the fairly rapid spring thaw.

Altitude and climate act to produce a marked zonal distribution of soil types and land use. Hydromorphic soils – humic grey meadow soils and pseudo-gleys – occupy the low-lying areas of the basin floor and the poorly drained floodplains of the rivers. They have their widest extent in the floodplains of the Olt and the Riu Negru. The characteristics of these soils are their high moisture content owing to the presence of ground-water close to the surface, and their heavy texture. In the rainy periods of spring and early summer they are frequently inundated and in some areas the water can lie for considerable periods. Under drier conditions and a lower water table, these soils evolve towards the range of strongly leached chernozems. The humic content of these soils is moderate, but they are not attractive for arable agriculture because of the difficulty in ploughing them and their exposure to flooding.

On the better drained areas of the plain and the lower parts of the piedmont there are developed pod-zolised soils, typical of cool humid climates elsewhere. Though their humic level is reduced, they have a lower moisture content than the first group and have some potential for arable agriculture.

In the high piedmont zone the soils are predominant-ly brown earths. These soils are associated with a land surface originally covered with deciduous forest, in this area beech and oak. Basically loessic in character, these soils have been subjected to considerable but variable amounts of leaching in the Depression, produced by the high levels of precipitation. They tend to have a low humus content, but are well-drained and relatively easy to till.

On the higher slopes, the soils tend to be thin and poorly developed because of steep slopes and erosion.

However, on the summits of the mountains a rendzina-type soil forms on the calcareous marls. This is a shallow soil, rich in organic matter and biological activity, with a stable crumb structure. Because of their shallowness, these rendzina soils may not have supported heavy vegetation in the past and today they produce a rich summer growth of pasture which is utilised by large herds of sheep brought into the area from the drier loessic plain to the south and east of the Carpathians, and by cattle cooperatives which generally employ a more restricted seasonal movement, the animals being stall-fed in winter in the Braşov Depression.

Prehistoric settlement and land use

As in many upland areas of Europe, parts of the Braşov Depression are today under arable cultivation, despite the environmental limitations on this form of exploitation. There are good reasons for supposing that the degree of reliance upon the arable component of the economy was less in prehistory, however. Two important groups of factors act as primary limitations on the development of crop agriculture: climatic and physiographic conditions.

The overall climatic regime is most inappropriate for the successful cultivation of cereal crops. The peak of rainfall in early summer, which, coupled with snowmelt, causes regular June flooding of the Olt and the Negru valleys, damages the crops and encourages fungus disease. Early frosts start in the second half of September, and intensify in October. Much of the growth of the crop, and especially the critical formation and ripening of the head must thus be accomplished within about ten weeks. In good years some grain fit for human consumption can indeed be harvested, but the low average yields and high risks involved mean that this is unlikely to have been an important prehistoric economic objective. Moreover much of the area is in any case unsuitable for arable exploitation. The low-lying valley soils are very heavy in texture and were waterlogged prior to modern drainage schemes; many of them remain so today for the critical spring and early summer period. These may certainly be ruled out as having any arable potential in prehistoric times. Many of the higher areas are covered with thin, poorly developed soils of low fertility, and steep slopes frequently rule out any heavy involvement with crop agriculture. This leaves the intermediate zone of better drained loessic brown soils as the sole area in which some cereals may perhaps have been grown in prehistory.

Under modern conditions a number of important influences tend to mitigate these limiting factors and to obscure their impact. Drainage of low-lying soils and heavy machinery for cultivation have recently made some areas available for arable use. Developments in plant breeding and agronomic practice have gone a long way towards reducing the effect of adverse climatic conditions. The introduction of that most adaptable of cereals, maize, has proved of great significance in this respect. It is of interest to note that, prior to the appearance of maize, millet was the principal cereal of the region rather than wheat. This crop, *Panicum miliaceum*, is especially well-adapted to the conditions in the Braşov area by its very short growing season, as little as 60–65 days. In modern times elsewhere it is planted as late as the second half of June, and in areas where it is still an important crop it is characteristically 'a late seeded, short-season summer catch crop' (Martin & Leonard 1967) following cereals or other crops harvested earlier in the summer. The modern growing of wheat and maize in the Depression, as opposed to less demanding cereals, has further been encouraged by the availability of chemical fertilisers.

Perhaps most significant, the development of cattle breeding on a commercial, rather than a subsistence, basis has greatly stimulated the cultivation of fodder crops. Much of the value of these lies in their vegetative growth, and the crop can be cut green. Production of cereals for human consumption relies entirely on the successful ripening of the crop, both in terms of the value of the harvest and the need to provide viable seed grain for the future. Commercial production of cattle fodder can afford flexibility as regards both these requirements. The impact of these factors may be seen in recent and modern land use. As just one example, the parish of Sacale in 1939 cultivated 215 ha of maize as against only 12 ha of wheat.

All in all then, it seems most unlikely that cereal production played an important part in the prehistoric subsistence economy of the Depression. This inference is borne out by a number of observations. Many of the known sites are not located so as to take full advantage of the better drained brown soils, which would have provided the best arable potential. The Neolithic sites are, on the whole, remarkable for their relatively small size and little depth of deposit, and it has been suggested (Tringham 1971) that they may therefore represent seasonally occupied settlements. No archaeological evidence for the exploitation of cereals is found until the transitional period between the Eneolithic and Bronze Age. A few sites are located where they have access to some of the more tractable soils, however, and doubtless cereals played a part in the economy at least from Bronze Age times onwards, as will be discussed in more detail below.

Aside from the question of arable exploitation, the major limiting factor on settlement and land use in the Depression is the winter climate, described above. Severe conditions bring a complete cessation to plant growth for well over a third of the year, and for much of this period whatever herbage may remain from the summer is rendered inaccessible by snow cover.

Historically there were two main responses to these conditions. Many cattle were taken to high alpine pastures in the mountain ranges surrounding the basin for the summer; they returned to the basin to graze stubble in the autumn, and were maintained in stalls on hay and fodder crops such as maize throughout the winter. In addition, many animals and their herders left the Depression altogether in September, and spent the winter months on the lowlands to the south and east of the Carpathians. Braşov and Sibiu (a little to the west) have long been considered the two main centres of this long-distance transhumance. Eighteenth-century documents record the yearly movement of nearly 100 000 sheep and 5000 cattle from the Braşov region into Wallachia, figures which must certainly represent minima in view of the fact that they came from taxation records, and that considerable effort was indubitably made to evade as far as possible the statutory *per capita* levy.

Figure 107 shows the recent historical transhumance routes linking the Braşov Depression with the lowlands. A similar pattern of mobility was in operation between the Apuseni mountains and the lowlands of the Tisza valley. This was instrumental in the decision in 1918 to ignore the wishes of the predominantly Hungarian-speaking lowland population, and to make the Tisza the national boundary. The alternative would have been to divorce the two complementary resource zones by a national boundary, to the economic detriment of both areas.

Under today's conditions the emphasis is increasingly upon the former adaptation, and the long-range transhumance system is declining or breaking down. This is a commonplace in modern Europe. Among the reasons for this is the increasing pressure upon the lowland winter grazing from competing forms of exploitation. Land hitherto unsuitable for any other use is being drained, or is made accessible to more profitable patterns of land use by the availability of advanced agricultural technology. A parallel trend to the more intensive exploitation of the upland zone, with the growing importance of fodder crops and of food con-

centrates, makes it possible to continue exploiting the summer grazing potential of the uplands. Conversely, it is probable that the further one goes back into the historical period, the more important was the system of long-range transhumance and the less significant the practice of overwintering in the uplands. Prior to the availability of maize as a most productive source of winter fodder, the winter carrying capacity must have been very severely constrained by the amount of hay which could have been harvested during the short summer.

Two important conclusions emerge from this general discussion of modern and recent conditions. Firstly, whatever the particular balance of the economy at specific sites, arable crops were unlikely to have been of much significance in the prehistoric exploitation of the area. We must consequently envisage a subsistence economy based primarily upon pastoralism. The second point is that any pastoral economy must have incorporated a measure of mobility in order to accommodate the seasonal imbalance of resources, in particular to cope with the severity of the winter.

It was noted above that the Neolithic sites in the area are, characteristically, insubstantial and with little depth of deposit, or sign of structures. These fit well with the hypothesis of summer seasonal exploitation, and sites such as Harman and Eresteghin probably functioned primarily as summer herding home bases. How much use was made at this time of the higher alpine areas must be a matter of speculation. It is unlikely that these resources were totally ignored, but grazing may have been concentrated on the basin itself, and traces of exploitation at the higher altitudes may have been too ephemeral to have been recovered. Cernatu de Sus at least indicates that settlement was not entirely restricted to the basin floor. The site of Leţ is the main apparent exception to this picture, in that the site is more substantial, forming a mound on a low terrace of the Riu Negru. Here the area available for settlement is very small, and the superposition of layers may well therefore be a result of the lack of room for much lateral expansion rather than because the settlement was permanently occupied.

None of the Neolithic sites has yielded evidence of plant exploitation; and, while such negative evidence is ambiguous and must be treated with caution, we have already noted that the area does not lend itself to the production of plant staples. In addition it may be pointed out that the site locations do not as a rule show an attempt to maximise what small arable potential there is. We are not much better served as regards faunal remains, but the handful of bones from Leţ has been studied (Necrasov 1961). Caprine bones dominate the tiny sample, and while no statistical significance can be attached to this, their presence strengthens the case for the seasonal occupation of the area. Sheep were the primary transhumant animal in historic times, and would have been very difficult to maintain in the region in winter. Further indications of an upland–lowland link are given by the typological similarities between the two zones noted by Tringham (1971). The complementary lowland zone of the Mizil area, just to the south of the Carpathian arc (see Figure 107), is a likely region to have provided winter pasture for flocks summering in the Braşov Depression. The sites there are located on a dissected loess plain of high arable potential and with a climate much more conducive to cereal production than that of the uplands. Away from the river valleys, however, large areas of the plain were too dry in summer to support permanent populations (of men or stock), prior to the sinking of deep wells. (This situation is encountered over much of the Wallachian and Moldavian plain, and a similar case in southern Poland is discussed in Chapter 5.) These areas, and fallow fields, would have provided good winter grazing, however, and thus constituted an ideal zone of complementary resources. Access between the two regions is relatively easy, along the Buzau valley.

By the Eneolithic and Transitional Neolithic/Bronze Age periods (represented by the Ariuşd, Coţofeni, and Glina/Schneckenberg pottery types in the local cultural sequence) a number of interesting features emerge in the land use and settlement pattern. The first and most obvious feature is an expansion in the area and density of settlement. Not only are more sites known, but they are beginning to be found in locations which for one reason or another may be thought of as marginal, or at least as less than optimal, in an economic sense. An example of this is the occupation of such situations as the modern town of Braşov, which lies in the sun-shadow of the Carpathians, and is thus much less attractive for any subsistence economy than the more favoured south-facing slopes. Continued occupation of such sites as Harman, Leţ, and Eresteghin shows that this should be viewed as an expansion of settlement rather than merely a shift in its focus. A comparable increase is witnessed in the occupation of cave sites in the mountains immediately to the north of our main study area (Marcu, personal communication).

Another new feature is the evidence of substantial timber-and-daub structures on many Ariuşd sites. It might be argued that this represents an architectural response to the needs imposed by year-round settlement in an area of severe winter climate. This argument

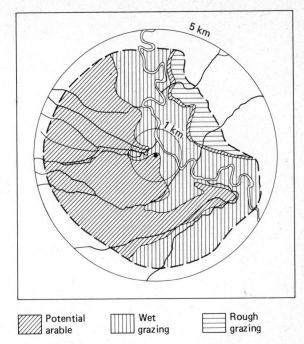

Potential arable   Wet grazing   Rough grazing

Figure 108. One hour exploitation territory of Rotbav.

is weakened, however, by the fact that the structures are equally a feature of archaeologically contemporaneous lowland sites; and also by the absence of evidence for similarly robust structures in the Bronze Age of the area. A more significant phenomenon is that from the Coţofeni levels at Rotbav there is evidence of cereals in the form of a few carbonised wheat grains. At the same site the fauna is dominated by pigs and caprines, with cattle present but in small numbers.

In general, then, there is good evidence for an expansion of upland population, and hence an increasingly intensive use of the upland resources at this time. Although one cannot be unequivocal on the basis of the available evidence, it is quite possible that the period saw the first year-round settlement of the Braşov Depression. The high proportion of pigs in the Rotbav fauna might be held to point in this direction; pigs, although they can be driven, are not very suitable as a long-range transhumant species, and their importance might thus be taken as an indication of a degree of sedentism. The presence of cereals is ambiguous, but might again be linked to a more permanent upland population. The quantities of grain are so small that one should bear in mind the possibility that they were imported from the lowlands rather than grown in the area. The exploitation territory of the site (Figure 108) does include some soil with arable potential, however, and it is perhaps more likely that small quantities of cereal were produced in the Depression than that it was

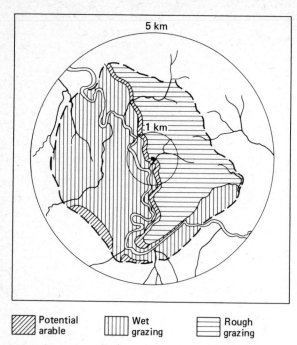

Figure 109. One hour exploitation territory of Ariuşd.

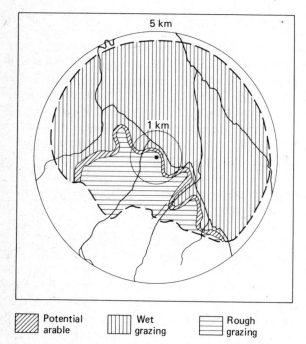

Figure 110. One hour exploitation territory of Dealul Melcilor.

animal staple apart from pigs, would almost certainly have been in the area during the summer only, spending the winters on the lowlands to the south and east. Thus whether or not we believe that the Braşov Depression saw its first year-round occupation as early as this, it seems clear that there remained a substantial mobile element in the pattern of exploitation.

It is tempting to comment here upon a curious anomaly which appears in the faunal remains from the Depression. The Neolithic and subsequent faunas from most of Romania show a strong tendency to be dominated by cattle. This is not an invariable rule: drier areas such as the Dobrogea have sites which show a greater concentration upon caprines; but it is generally the case. The only two pre-Bronze Age faunal samples from the Braşov area show, on the contrary, little evidence of concentration upon cattle. This may be due to sampling distortion, since there are some signs that at the Unghiul Gardului site at Rotbav differential distribution of the bones of different species in the site may well be influencing their apparent proportions. In any case, on so few data it is impossible to offer firm interpretations, but one possible explanation concerns the nature of the overall exploitation of the Depression. The undoubted quality of summer cattle pasture available in the area is most easily exploited by a population established on a year-round basis, employing only limited mobility between the basin and the adjacent alpine pastures. Cattle can be employed as long-distance transhumant animals, but they are not so well-suited to this form of economy as are sheep. As long as the exploitation of the Depression was primarily concerned with summer occupation only, there would therefore have been a built-in factor favouring the dependence upon sheep rather than cattle. With the development of an increasing year-round element in the economic system, the cattle would become increasingly appropriate.

Many sites elsewhere in Romania at this transitional period seem to give some evidence for increased exploitation of 'wild' animals – red deer, and large pigs and cattle. One possible explanation of this phenomenon is discussed briefly earlier in this volume (Chapter 5). The Unghiul Gardului site again looks like an exception to this general picture, but it is possible that, as could be the case with the low percentage of cattle bones, this will eventually prove to be due to sampling bias.

In the Bronze Age, site location and distribution patterns are substantially the same as those of the immediately preceding period, but again with evidence of more sites and further colonisation of economically

found economically worthwhile to transport it from the lowlands. By contrast with Rotbav, some of the sites first occupied in this period, such as Ariuşd itself and Dealul Melcilor, occupy hill-top locations with very little arable potential in their exploitation territories (Figures 109 and 110). The sheep, the other main more marginal areas. Two features are of particular interest. Unghiul Gardului shows evidence of an expansion in the importance of cereals in the economy. Again, one could argue that these represent imports, but some considerations point to an alternative hypothesis. There is an increase in the amount of carbonised grain recovered, and significantly millet (*Panicum miliaceum*) is the commonest species of cereal. The appearance of this and of barley (the second commonest species) may reasonably be interpreted as signs of economic adaptation to the severe limitations of climate on arable production. We have already commented upon the appropriateness of millet to local conditions, and it is well known that barley is the most dependable cereal under a wide range of adverse conditions. At Unghiul Gardului and elsewhere the numerous bell-shaped pits have plausibly been interpreted as being for grain storage, again suggesting an increased exploitation of what small cereal potential existed locally. The two Bronze Age faunas from the Depression, from Unghiul Gardului and Părăuti indicate a second point of interest. By this period the cattle are certainly of considerable numerical significance, as is usual elsewhere in Romania. As was suggested above, this in addition to the evidence for an increased arable component in the economy, strongly supports the hypothesis that a year-round population was established in the Depression by this date. As is discussed earlier in this chapter, there is evidence which suggests that a comparable intensification and expansion in the exploitation of upland resources also took place elsewhere in Europe at about this time.

Nevertheless, mobility of at least a part of the human and animal population must have remained an important aspect of the economic system, as indeed it did throughout the historic periods, and does to a lesser extent today. Even with the provision of hay and millet, lack of winter fodder constitutes the main limiting factor which must be overcome by any pastoralist adaptation to the area. Given that by the Bronze Age the population was already seeking to do so partly through an increasingly intensive management of locally available resources, there is no reason to suppose that they ceased to make use of the long-established transhumance system which integrated the complementary resources of upland and lowland. Indeed, the strong links in pottery typology between sites such as Feldioara and Risnov with others in the lowlands of Muntenia may reasonably be viewed in this light.

The hypothesis of the establishment of a permanent upland population has important general implications. The development of prehistoric settlement in the Bra-şov Depression seems to provide a clear if crude record of long-term population increase. Numbers of sites rise, they expand into more marginal locations, and economic adaptations emerge which are most easily explained in terms of rising population levels, demanding increasingly productive subsistence systems. The system of long-distance transhumance which, we have argued, was in Neolithic times the primary (probably the sole) economic adaptation to the uneven distribution of resources, would have remained so as long as sufficient lowland grazing was available for a reasonably full use to be made of the summer grazing resources of the upland zone. The signs that by the Bronze Age the transhumance system was increasingly being augmented by a more sedentary and intensive system of upland exploitation seem to indicate that the pressure on areas of lowland grazing was such as to exclude from them an increasing proportion of those human and animal populations that summered in the Carpathians. To a degree, then, we may take the permanent settlement of the Braşov Depression as an index of a rise in the population of lowland Romania as a whole, and thus an increase in competition for winter grazing resources. Matley (1970) has documented a more recent and more severe, but closely comparable, phenomenon with shepherds who summered in the Carpathian uplands being forced by increasing agricultural exploitation of the Danube lowlands in the eighteenth and nineteenth centuries to search ever further eastward for alternative winter grazing.

Our survey of the exploitation of European uplands has concentrated upon phenomena which may have seemed repetitious to the point of tedium. It is worth re-emphasising in conclusion that this springs from the basic environmental constraints which govern the patterns of exploitation, and from man's successive economic adaptations designed to mitigate the impact of these limitations in the face of rising populations. The strong pastoral bias to upland economies, and the accommodation of seasonal extremes through mobility are there to be seen in most areas today, as are the end products of the millennia of attempts to overcome, to some degree, their effect and thus to raise the upland carrying capacity. These attempts commonly incorporate the terracing of hillsides for agricultural use, the selection of crops which are unusually tolerant of poor soils or harsh climates, the intensive management and storage of the best pasture resources, and the increasing integration of non-dietary resources, such as textiles and minerals, as supplements into the subsistence economy.

6. THE UPLANDS

We may also point out that the association of the complementary resources of upland and lowland, and the trend to an increasingly intensive use of the uplands under the spur of population pressure, seem to be equally well exemplified in those areas we have not studied in detail as in those discussed above. In Greece the upland massif of the Pindhos, while clearly exploited seasonally at least from the Upper Palaeolithic onwards, shows little signs of substantial settlement, with, perhaps, year-round occupation, until Bronze Age times. Similar evidence comes from Crete, although here the first convincing signs of colonisation of the island come with the Neolithic. At another geographical extreme, strong cases have been made by Clark, J. G. D. (1972) and Webley (1976) for the seasonal exploitation of upland and lowland resources in various parts of Britain. It is also notable that here, as elsewhere, substantial evidence of a more intensive exploitation of the upland zone, such as that documented by Simmons (1964) on Dartmoor and Fleming (1971) in Yorkshire, is a feature of the later prehistoric record.

7. THE MEGALITHS: A PROBLEM IN PALAEOETHOLOGY

Megalithic monuments have attracted a great deal of archaeological attention at all stages of the development of prehistoric studies. Their conspicuous size, implications of mechanical sophistication, and the intimations they give of spiritual consciousness have made them a primary target of interest from the days of Stukeley to the present. Their illustrious archaeological pedigree makes the megaliths a tempting area of study for any new approach. There are many who will feel that this chapter is anomalous in this volume, and that there is little relationship between this and the foregoing chapters. We are confident, however, that the general importance of palaeoeconomy, and the significance of the principles we have been discussing, are such that their relevance to other branches of the subject will eventually become apparent, whether or not the case is conclusively demonstrated here.

In the past the megaliths have been treated as objects of classification, as indicators of a unified religious movement or of prospectors for metals, as evidence of the study of mathematics and astronomy, and as symbols of community solidarity. Here we have chosen a different approach; not through any conviction that previous views are necessarily wrong, but in order to see whether a new perspective will add something to the composite picture that has already accumulated. It has never been a part of our thesis that prehistoric studies should deal solely with economic data, only that these give crucial clues about some of the important constants and long-term factors which govern human behaviour. We would argue that most, if not all, aspects of behaviour have a relationship to the evolutionary performance of the species, and that thus even phenomena without apparent connection with the economy may well have had evolutionary significance. The difficulty lies in perceiving and understanding these often tenuous and obscure links, whether in prehistory or today. With this in mind we decided to study megaliths from a palaeoeconomic viewpoint in an effort to recognise any consistent relationships which might exist between these (apparently purely funerary) monuments and the economic constraints operating on the populations that produced them. To this extent this chapter may be viewed as an experiment in palaeoethology; a crude attempt to take into account a wider range of human behaviour than we have encompassed hitherto in this volume.

An immediate difficulty encountered is that we know little of the precise geographic relationship between the tombs and the settlements of their makers. Few of the latter are known, and it could be argued that they might therefore have been in situations sufficiently different from those of the tombs to invalidate palaeoeconomic analysis based on a territorial approach. We agree with Clark's lucidly expressed contrary arguments, however (Clark, J. G. D. 1977). Furthermore, as will be seen, we are in many cases dealing with areas where movements of a kilometre or two do not generally involve significant changes of palaeoeconomic potential.

We have studied in some detail the distributions of megaliths in some areas of Spain, France, Ireland, and northern Europe. We have not attempted an exhaustive survey of all the European megaliths, nor have we employed a detailed classification of them whether by typological or chronological criteria. We have considered tombs and monuments, alignments and menhirs. In those areas, like Cantabria, where there is reason to believe that many of the megaliths originally had tumuli covering them, and that many of the unexcavated tumuli may contain megalithic cists, we have boldly lumped the two phenomena together. There are many who will be dissatisfied with this cavalier treatment, and who may feel that such crudity negates our conclusions. It is our view, however, that we are dealing with relationships sufficiently fundamental and widespread to override these considerations.

CANTABRIA

An outline of the Cantabrian environment has already been given in the relevant sections of Chapters 4 and 6. Of especial interest here is the fact that arable potential, as far as the Old World cereals are concerned, is essentially confined to the narrow coastal strip, and is very limited even here. The mountain chain immediately inland, while it supports a certain amount of maize and other crops grown as cattle fodder, is too wet in

7. THE MEGALITHS

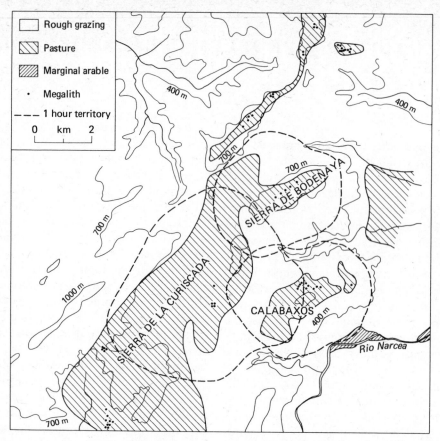

Figure 111. Relationship of megaliths to land use potential in central Oviedo. Sample one hour territories plotted to indicate the impact of steep slopes.

summer, too poor in soils, and too rugged to encourage arable-based economies.

Detailed surveys were made of the site locations and territories of some sixty sites in the central part of the province of Oviedo. The number of individual tombs involved is much larger, as they often occur in groups, sometimes of ten or more. They are spread, if not evenly, at least in widely ranging situations from the mountainous interior to the coastal lowlands. We have chosen some groups of tombs to the north and east of Tineo as characteristic examples (Figure 111).

The main concentrations of sites are found on ridges and upland plateaux such as the Pevidal group and those on the Sierra de Bodenaya. The topography of the region is complex with narrow tortuous valleys surmounted by steep slopes. The Sierra de Bodenaya and the hill of Calabaxos just to the west of Pevidal provide two of the relatively few areas of more gently undulating upland. Each of these is surrounded for most of its perimeter by steep and inaccessible slopes down to river valleys. Other sites are found along the system of narrow ridges which runs north of the Sierra

de Bodenaya, and more on the rolling plateau of the Sierra de la Curiscada to the southwest.

Soils in the area are varied, but are for the most part light and sandy. They have a high but variable stone content, which depends on such factors as slope and proximity of bedrock to the surface. Generally their light texture makes them easy to till, but they are low in arable potential due to limited fertility, excessive stoniness, and steep slopes. A few areas, in particular the valley bottoms of the larger rivers and rare natural basins, carry heavier soils of much finer particle size, which are harder but more rewarding to cultivate.

Modern land use reflects the broad outlines of topographic and pedological constraint. The steeper slopes carry a mixture of coniferous pine plantations and an unproductive rough grazing with gorse, bracken, and heather prominent in its species composition. In some places the slopes take the form of steep cliffs with much exposed rock-face. The plateaux and more gently sloping areas are primarily given over to a better pasture with a high proportion of grasses. Sometimes the quality has been improved by stone clearance and

234

ploughing. Some small natural basins carry relatively impermeable soils with impeded drainage, leading to marshy and wet pasture plant associations. A few areas, almost exclusively in narrow bands around modern settlements, include fairly high proportions of arable land. Maize (for animal fodder) and potatoes are the main crops; other fodder crops and vegetables are also grown. The only areas of more intensive land use are the floodplains and lowest terraces of the larger rivers, which have substantial amounts of land under cultivation. Maize, hay, and vegetables are the main crops here.

Taken as a whole the agricultural economy of the area is largely dependent upon animals, particularly upon cattle. This pastoral basis would have been yet more pronounced in the past. It is notable that the only arable crops of real significance are potatoes and maize, both species imported in the relatively recent historical past. The Cantabrian chain is climatically, topographically, and pedologically unsuited to arable exploitation and to cereals in particular. Rye and oats could no doubt be grown to some degree, but the staples of any prehistoric diet must surely have been animal products. There is no apparent association of sites with the few areas of enhanced arable productivity in the river valleys. On the contrary, the sites are all found on the tops, and often in areas where access to and from the valley bottoms is extremely difficult.

Clearly the exploitation territories of the sites have a much less precise analytic value than in the case of settlements. They serve nevertheless as a useful index of the economic potential of the area as a whole and of the relationship of the existing sites to this. A few sample one hour territories have been plotted in Figure 111. They clearly show the restricting effect that topography has on movement, and emphasise the negative correlation of sites and alluvial valley soils.

Elsewhere in the study area sites occupy broadly similar positions in a comparable environment. Such differences as there are seem to be largely a consequence of topography and altitude. Some of the sites in the more low-lying coastal area, like Pruvia and Cobertoria to the northeast of Oviedo, have much larger and more regular exploitation territories due to the more open country. Others, however, like Monte de Cobertoria and Riforque have territories greatly restricted by topography despite lying at only just over 300 m. At the other extreme are sites such as La Corona, La Escrita, La Forcada, and Balbona, on the Cordal de Porcabezas ridge to the east of the Rio Pigueña, just south of Belmonte. These all lie at 1000 m or more on a narrow ridge running north–south, and separated from the

valleys to the east and west by extremely steep and rugged country.

Despite these variations the overall economic orientation remains the same. Even the flatter lowlands of the Oviedo area have light, coarse, sandy and stony loams which are under hay and pasture for the most part, with marshland in areas of impeded drainage. A few areas carry maize for fodder and garden crops, while the eminences are under a rough scrubby grazing. Nearer the coast the land use is dominated by rough pasture and eucalyptus plantations, with small areas under maize and potatoes. The sites on the higher mountains to the south of Belmonte, on the other hand, have territories that are almost exclusively of grazing potential. The steep slopes carry a mixture of rough pasture and exposed rock with some patches of woodland – very hard of access in many places – while the tops of the ridges carry a much more open pasture. A few small patches in the Pigueña valley bottom are cultivable, but these are both too small and too distant (in time) from the crest to have much palaeoeconomic significance as far as the sites in question are concerned.

Asturias as a whole is thus an area of low arable, but high pastoral potential; and, as we have seen, the megalithic tombs or tumuli seem to be consistently related to grazing resources rather than to those few areas which may have supplied a small arable component in the economy. We may also note certain features of site location that seem to operate within this broad pattern. A large proportion of the tombs are found on relatively discrete blocks of upland grazing, like those on Calabaxos and Sierra de Bodenaya. These are characteristically delimited by very steep slopes along large portions of their perimeters. In the extreme case of Monsacro, the sites are on a small upland plateau cut off from the enclosing valleys on almost all sides. Many other sites follow the ridges, which were the main communication routes until the advent of motor transport and modern road engineering. In the case of the Cordal de Porcabezas, the line of sites conspicuously follows the route of the old road from Oviedo to Estremadura. Tombs such as these, and those on the ridges running north from Sierra de Bodenaya towards the Pico de Corcinera are usually sited in cols, often in flatter areas carrying unusually good pasture. These naturally defined blocks of upland grazing frequently carry large numbers of untended stock (mainly young cattle and horses) in the summer months.

No consistent pattern was discovered in the orientation of the tombs. There is a tendency for sites to have a broadly northern aspect, but there are many contrary

235

7. THE MEGALITHS

examples and sites on flat ground with no particular aspect at all. There is no apparent choice of false crest sitings, and indeed most of the sites are invisible from more than a couple of hundred metres. It is difficult to know whether or not the sites were more conspicuous in the past, as much would have depended upon the original height of the mounds and the degree to which their colour contrasted with their surroundings. Still more would have depended upon the nature of the local vegetation at the time. It can be said, however, that there is little or no attempt to choose especially prominent or conspicuous locations, and that the tombs would probably only have been visible from afar where they were overlooked by higher ground.

The availability of the construction material, also, seems to have exercised little influence over site location. Asturias as a whole has plentiful and widespread resources of stone accessible at or near the surface, but the sites are rarely if ever located adjacent to particularly rich or accessible sources. Thus the stone from the megalithic cists in the Pevidal group is identical with that available locally on the Calabaxos hill, but the sites are not in any case located at, or even very close to, the many exposures.

We may now consider briefly the economic implications of the site distribution we have discussed. The modern economy is based upon cattle and potatoes. Wheat is not generally grown as it does not do well, normal summer conditions being too damp to fill and ripen the ears. Cattle are customarily stall-fed in winter on hay which is cut in July. At altitudes such as Pevidal and Sierra de Bodenaya, there is some winter snow, but cattle can be put out to graze during fine spells. Further south and at higher altitudes the winters are severer and the snow more persistent, and stock must be stall-fed for months at a time. The present-day emphasis upon cattle is largely a result of the commercial market for dairy products. In the historical past the dependence upon pastoralism was greater, but the importance of cattle was less, as sheep were also present in large numbers. Prior to the introduction of potatoes the arable input into the human diet was further restricted, and the absence of maize reduced the carrying capacity for cattle. The naturally available grazing is not of very high quality in many areas and much of it was exploited by the better suited sheep. While one might possibly argue for a small arable element in the economy of the coastal plain, and might associate the tombs with this element by assuming no locational relationship between tombs and settlements, for most of the area under consideration even this tenuous possibility must be dismissed on environmental

grounds alone. It can only be inferred that the tombs were the product of pastoralist populations.

As discussed in Chapters 4 and 6, while modern economic and commercial pressures have introduced a considerable degree of sedentism into the Asturian exploitation system, in historic (and, we have argued, necessarily in prehistoric) times, it was largely exploited through mobile economies of various kinds. The distribution of resources and historical records both argue for two main patterns of prehistoric exploitation. Some groups would have used a relatively short movement exploiting the coastal grazing in winter, with its preferential maritime climate, and moving inland to the northern slopes of the mountains in summer. Historically the high Asturias and the southern slopes were used by transhumant groups travelling much longer distances; some from as far as Estremadura, 400 km away. This was in part because much of the intervening area was by that time being exploited primarily by arable farmers, and it is likely that in prehistory the distances involved will not often have been so great. Nevertheless it seems highly probable that the Asturian mountains were a summer focus and meeting point for pastoralists who moved away both north and south to their winter grazing areas. It may reasonably be suggested that the sites of the coastal strip represent the winter terminal of economic systems which encompassed much of the northern slopes of the mountain chain. Sites higher up, closer to and on the watershed may rather be associated with groups who travelled south in the winter to exploit the vast reservoir of winter grazing in the interior. While sites comparable with those in Asturias are not common in Leon, further south there is a chain of megalithic tombs in the provinces of Zamora, Salamanca, Caceres, Badajoz, and Huelva. The strip of Portugal contiguous with those provinces has a notable concentration of similar monuments.

Surveys of selected sites in Salamanca, Caceres, Badajoz, and Huelva suggest that here too association of tombs with pastoral rather than arable resources may be a general rule. This area of western Iberia is geographically very different to Asturias, particularly in its much drier climate with little summer rainfall. Topographically it is less extreme. The landscape is characterised by dissected plateaux and rolling hills rather than the more severe mountains of the Cantabrian chain.

In so large an area economic potential must obviously vary enormously, but the climate is in most cases more favourable for cereal production than in the moister Asturias, and winter wheat and barley are commonly grown today where soil conditions permit and spring rainfall is sufficient. Nevertheless the arable production of the region as a whole is low, and it has primarily a grazing potential. The sites surveyed show no consistent association with the areas of better arable soil. Some, like the Nava del Hito and Dolmen de Ralida in Salamanca and La Alqueria in Huelva, are indeed located in areas where some cereals are grown. Wheat is grown in widely spaced rows in some areas close to Nava del Hito, but yields are poor (less than 10 q/ha in an average year). Most of the site exploitation territory carries pasture or rough scrubby grazing, however. The area to the west of the Dolmen de Ralida carries wheat and barley in rotation with fodder crops and a fallow year. The soil is easy to cultivate but yields are low, with a maximum of 13 q/ha and a minimum of 3 q/ha for wheat. La Alqueria lies in a patch of arable land growing wheat, olives, vines, and squashes. Cereal yields are moderate in good years but unreliable because of climatic vagaries. This arable area gives way in a short distance from the site to much poorer stony soils with rough grazing and forestry. Most of the sites surveyed lack even this very modest arable potential, and their exploitation territories are given over today almost entirely to a mixture of rough grazing and forestry.

It is also of interest that further west in the Portuguese province of Alentejo, where there are some hundreds of megalithic tombs, while the modern arable potential is somewhat greater than that for most of the Spanish sites analysed, the prehistoric arable potential would have been very restricted. The soils of Alentejo tend to be better developed over wider areas, and topographic constraints are less severe. The soils are primarily limestone-derived red beds and rendsinas, many of which have a fairly high clay content and require heavy machinery to produce a good tilth. Even the modern exploitation of Alentejo, however, relies to a large extent upon pastoralism and arboriculture. About half the area has bedrock so close to the surface as to make cultivation impracticable. These areas carry pasture and cork oaks. Olives and cork oaks are also frequently intermingled with cereals and squashes on the better soils. It is noticeable, furthermore, that there is an inverse correlation between megalith density and modern arable productivity. Thus the area immediately around Elvas, which has the most productive arable potential of the area surveyed, has no sites at all, while they are especially frequent in the poor areas such as between Elvas and Monforte and between Reguengos and Mourão.

In general, then, the megaliths of western Iberia are in an area of low and unreliable arable potential, and the individual sites show no tendency to be differentially associated with the best arable areas available. Whereas the modern rural economy incorporates many elements, including viticulture, olive production, and increasing amounts of forestry, the majority of the land is given over to rough grazing. The dry summers severely limit the carrying capacity for stock at this season. Not only is there a shortage of water, but the grazing is of poor quality. This is increasingly overcome by the use of irrigated fodder crops and concentrates, and the technological capacity to tap groundwater at much greater depths than formerly. Nevertheless, large numbers of sheep continue to transhume to the Cantabrian mountains in summer, and many more did so in the recent past. In the winter, on the contrary, the pastures of western Iberia are at their best. Plant growth resumes with the autumn rains, which usually reach a peak in November. Pastoral potential is particularly high in the more westerly area, where the oceanic influence moderates winter temperatures, and where the water-retentive and lime-rich soils ensure a highly nutritious pasture. The temperature rarely falls below freezing on the Portuguese littoral, and plant growth continues virtually unchecked throughout the winter. On the *meseta*, however, winters are always cold, with prolonged spells of sub-zero temperatures, and sometimes periods of exceptional cold. This continental effect becomes more pronounced as one moves eastwards from the Portuguese/Spanish border towards the central *meseta* around Madrid and Ciudad Real. This area is essentially devoid of naturally available grazing in mid-winter, as in high summer, and is at its best for pasture in spring and autumn. The pronounced decline in the numbers of megaliths found to the east of the Portuguese border may well be related to these circumstances.

It seems reasonable to suggest therefore that during the periods of megalithic construction western Iberia was primarily exploited as winter grazing grounds for stock which for the most part moved elsewhere in the summer. Iberia is unusual in Europe in that it had until fairly recently a relative abundance of winter grazing, but restricted areas of summer grazing. The prehistoric human and animal populations wintering in the areas just discussed must surely have been constrained in many cases to travel north to Asturias for the summer, as many of their historic successors did.

CATALONIA

The region of Catalonia lies in the northeastern corner of Spain, and comprises the modern provinces of

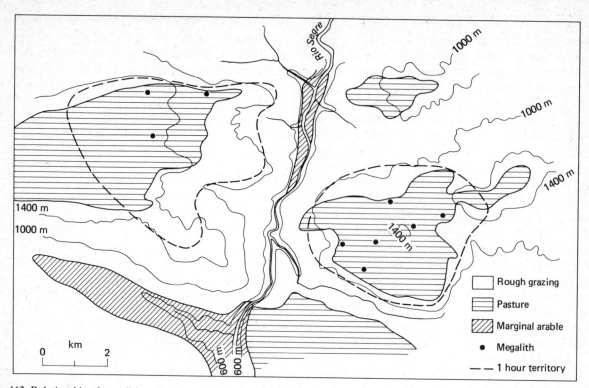

Figure 112. Relationship of megaliths to land use potential in northern Catalonia. Sample one hour territories plotted to indicate the impact of steep slopes.

Gerona, Barcelona, Tarragona, and Lérida. Environmentally it is very varied. To the north the Pyrenees are sufficiently high to receive 1000–2000 mm of rain per year. The altitude also modifies the temperatures and the high Pyrenees are consequently green and lush in summer, with good pasture and plantations of *Pinus sylvestris*. A relatively small movement south or east into the foothills occasions major changes. Rainfall is lower, and is more severely restricted to the autumn and winter months. Pastures dry out rapidly in the summer, being at their best from spring to early summer. The vegetation is characterised by oak scrub and plantations of more xerophytic conifers, such as *P. nigra* and *P. halepensis*. In the coastal region itself winters are warm, and pasture is at its best at this season. Olives, vines, cork oaks, and umbrella pines (*P. pinea*) occur commonly. About sixty tombs or groups of tombs were surveyed, some from each of these three broad zones.

Sites in the Organa area in the Pyrenees to the south of Andorra have situations reminiscent of many site locations in the Cantabrian region. Some, like the Noves and Montant groups (Figure 112) and the Col de Creus sites are on topographically isolated blocks of upland grazing, hard of access and delimited on most or all sides by cliffs or very steep slopes. The Montanisell

sites and the Serrat de les Cobertrades are in the converse situation, an upland valley with steep slopes rising on all sides. Further north the tombs in the Castellbó area tend to be located on narrow ridges, usually in cols. Although modern forestry frequently makes it difficult to analyse in detail the visibility of these tombs, there is certainly no systematic siting for maximum visibility. Peaks and false crests seem often to be avoided, and many of the tombs are only visible from within a few hundred metres or less.

Modern land use is very heavily weighted towards pastoralism and forestry, as one might expect from the environmental limitations. The sites analysed lie at 900–1500 m. Small areas around villages are cultivated. Lucerne and potatoes are the primary crops, with some cereals being grown and cut green as cattle fodder. The soils are for the most part poor, thin and very stony, and much too cold for the successful cultivation of cereals for human consumption. The vast preponderance of the area is under pasture, rough grazing, and coniferous forest. There are, in addition, considerable areas of exposed bedrock. Winters are cold and snowy, and the pasture is both inaccessible and of little value from the autumn through to spring, being at its best from June to September. In the northern part of the area, around Castellbó and the Noves sites, winter snow is sufficiently deep and prolonged to require a small-scale mobility in the modern local pastoral exploitation. The stock summers on the tops and winters in stalls in the valleys. A little to the south, around Montanisell, animals are sometimes kept in stalls on the hills throughout the winter. The whole area, as far north as Andorra and the French frontier, also receives a colossal summer influx of animals which spend the rest of the year outside the area, notably on the coastal lowlands of Barcelona and Tarragona.

The exploitation territories of the tombs show no tendency to maximise access to such exiguous arable resources as there are. As we have seen, sites seem mainly to be related to relatively enclosed areas of grazing. Today these frequently carry large numbers of untended stock in summer. These are characteristically sheep, and calves, heifers, and yearling bullocks (i.e. non-milking stock) among the cattle. While in some cases (as with the Montant sites, for instance) territories include areas now cultivated to produce winter fodder for stock this is by no means always the case. The exploitation territories of the Castellbó and Noves sites contain virtually no arable potential at all, even today. Modern settlement and arable exploitation are both very largely restricted to the bottoms of the larger river valleys, with which megalithic tombs show if anything a negative rather than a positive correlation.

The Solsona-Cardona region to the southeast is much less extreme topographically and less restricted in economic potential. The whole area is below 1000 m, and while steep slopes occur, it is much less rugged than around Organa. Sites tend to be located on spurs, ridges, and knolls, and to avoid river valleys, but in the less accentuated landscape there is no obvious association with isolated plateaux. The visibility of the tombs is highly variable, but the more open topography again results in their being visible in some cases over longer distances than is the case further to the north.

The better soil development and less extreme climate result in a far higher arable potential than has the Organa area. Nevertheless, even under today's conditions some 50 per cent of the region is unsuitable for cultivation, and carries a mixture of coniferous and scrub oak woodland, and rough pasture. Much of the existing ploughland has only recently been cleared, and has in most cases required the investment of much labour and the use of heavy machinery to remove stones and woodland. The arable potential is further limited by the fact that in many areas the soils are heavy limestone-based *terra rossas* which would have been inaccessible to Neolithic arable agricultural technology. Soils around the Cal Passavant site, for instance,

require several (mechanised) ploughings to produce a tilth. Penetrometer readings confirm that many areas now under the plough could not have been successfully cultivated prior to the introduction of tractors. Modern cereal yields are very variable, depending on soil conditions. Average yields (with the use of chemical fertilisers) range from 10 to 30 q/ha in a good year. The area is marginal for wheat cultivation, however; shortage of spring rainfall causes fairly frequent crop failure. Furthermore, the best modern yields come from the heaviest and most intractable soils. The light stony soils which would have been accessible to Neolithic economies give poorer yields because of their lower fertility and greater permeability.

The large uncultivated area is today primarily exploited by forestry, with some sheep on the areas of rough grazing. The animal component of the present economy is dominated by intensive pig and veal calf raising. Prior to modern demographic and commercial conditions the region carried small permanent populations of sheep and cattle which had to be stall fed, both during the winter cold period, and during the summer when the pasture dries out. The area also served as late spring pasture for sheep which spend the winter in the coast and the summer in the Pyrenees. The grazing is at its best in May and June, although it is locally available both earlier and later in the year. This practice is less common now than in the past, both because of the increasing use of railways and lorries for transhumance and because of the growing pressure of arable and forestry exploitation on the available grazing.

Our coastal study area, between the Golfo de Rosas and the French frontier, has the densest scatter of coastal megaliths. Here we have entered a characteristically Mediterranean environment. Precipitation is concentrated in autumn and winter. The summers are long, hot, and dry, the winters virtually free of snow. The coastal hills do not attain any great altitudes, rising to a maximum of less than 1000 m on the frontier, most of the peaks being less than 700 m. The topography is very tortuous, however, with steep, eroded hill slopes, and many deeply incised and winding stream valleys. Soils tend to be poorly developed, particularly on the hills. Olives, vines, and cork oaks are common crops.

As with the areas discussed above, there is little discernible pattern of individual site location. Some tombs, like those east of Rosas, are in relatively flat and low-lying situations, but are surrounded by steep hills. Others, like the Mas Girolles are halfway up hillsides (but not in false crest locations). Yet others, such as the Cabaña Arqueta and Puig d'Asquer lie on the crests of ridges or the summits of hills. In the majority of cases the tombs are but poorly visible, even assuming a denuded vegetation. The Puig Balaguer and Puig d'Asquer sites, for instance, are invisible outside a radius of some 50–100 m.

Today the region as a whole is dominated by rough grazing and forestry, with pine plantations on many of the hills and cork oaks in the flatter areas. There is little soil cover, and many areas have large exposures of bedrock. Much of what little cultivation does take place is only possible through the terracing of the lower valley slopes, as the valleys themselves are rarely wide enough to provide substantial floodplains. A little wheat is grown in the few patches with sufficient depth of soil, but fertility is low, resulting in poor yields (only c. 12–13 q/ha in a good year). The soils are generally coarse and highly permeable, and hence arable crops are greatly affected by the frequent dry springs. Vines and olives, with their deep rooting systems and tolerance of poor and stony soils, are much more important crops than cereals. The only important exception to these generalisations is the coastal plain which lies just to the south of the study area, southwest of Rosas and east of Figueras. Inland from a strip of coastal salt marsh, the plain is intensively cultivated. Maize is the main crop, with other cereals, lucerne, and vines also grown. Soil texture and quality is very variable, but cereal yields are generally fairly good.

Most of the area, then, is exploited through pastoralism and forestry. The grazing is too poor and coarse for cattle to do well, and in summer it rapidly dries out, being of little value in most places from spring until late autumn. The traditional economy was dominated by sheep transhumance. After wintering in the coastal hills, herds moved west to the Pyrenees from March until June, after which some of them moved back down to the strip of coastal marsh for the rest of the summer. This system still operates to some extent but is declining due to the increasing afforestation of the winter grazing area and commercial development of the coastal strip.

As elsewhere, there is no indication whatsoever that sites were differentially located close to what arable resources were available. There is, rather, a negative correlation between sites and areas of arable potential. While a few sites lie at its northern edge, no tombs at all are known from the plain of the lower Rio Fluvia between the Pyrenees and the coast. In the relatively small area between the plain and the French Frontier, by contrast, there are fifty or more. We must bear in mind the likelihood that some, at least, of the coastal plain has been deposited recently. We thus cannot be sure that either its existing arable resources or the

salt-marsh grazing were available to the builders of the megalithic tombs.

Taking Catalonia as a whole, therefore, we have a pattern not unlike that seen in Cantabria. While it cannot be said that the whole region is devoid of arable potential, it is certainly true that it is dominated by pastoral resources. In the prehistoric past this bias would have been yet more pronounced. Not only are grazing resources being steadily replaced by commercial forestry operations, but many of the areas now cultivated would have been inaccessible to a Neolithic technology or unprofitable without the use of imported crops and chemical fertilisers.

Given this overwhelming pastoral bias, and the absence of any consistent association between sites and the few arable resources which do exist, we must surely conclude that here, as in Cantabria, the builders of the megalithic tombs were pastoralists. They would necessarily have been largely transhumant, dependent upon sheep that spent the summers in the high Pyrenees and the winters on the coast. In this connection, it is of some interest that dolmens have frequently been used as shepherds' huts, or have had these built on to them. Other hints at an association with pastoralism may be seen in the frequency with which monuments are found on or close to cañadas, the traditional transhumant stock routes.

In both Cantabria and Catalonia it was noted that many of the largest groups of tombs are found on topographically isolated blocks of upland grazing. The significance of this may possibly be seen in the 'extended territory' concept of Sturdy (1975), discussed briefly in Chapter 3. Modern economies of the herd following and loose herding type frequently make extensive use of natural barriers such as very steep slopes, rivers, and marshes to control the movement of their stock.

Extended territories are in essence natural corrals which may have been well beyond the limits of the exploitation territory of the main settlement of a human group, and may have been only visited by a few individuals for brief periods during a season. Given sufficient grazing, relative freedom from interference, and the existence of substantial natural barriers to movement, the animals would have tended to stay put rather than to stray beyond the topographically delimited range. Once there, whether as a consequence of established natural movements or introduced there by human herders, stock could have been maintained at the expense of very little human labour, through the blocking of natural exits. This could have been achieved either by guards or by the erection of physical barriers. The animals upon which the bulk of the human group depended for day-to-day subsistence would have been maintained and exploited within the exploitation territory of the home base.

An essentially similar system is now in operation in some of the areas discussed above, and indeed is widespread in Europe today. Where circumstances permit, large numbers of stock which are not needed immediately and which do not require day to day attention, are summered on discrete blocks of upland grazing. They frequently are left to their own devices for long periods, human contact being confined to occasional checks. As we have noted, populations of untended stock are commonly found on upland pastures rich in megalithic remains. The association is interestingly underlined by the coincidence of such place names as Alto de los Corrales and Sierra de Prada.

FRANCE

It is clear from the work of de Barandiarán (1953), Blot (1974), and de Pous (1967), that the megalithic monuments of the French Pyrenees bear a relationship to pastoral resources that is similar to that already discussed for Spain. The dolmens, cromlechs, and tumuli of the Basque provinces are characteristically found on ridges and crests, frequently in a col. It is notable that the monuments tend to face east where they have any aspect at all, particularly in the more low-lying regions. Thus Blot found that some 73 per cent of dolmens in the Basque provinces (which are concentrated between 100 m and 600 m) face broadly eastwards.

As in Spain the megaliths are frequently associated with modern and historical pastoral features. The dolmens and cromlechs are always near tracks used by pastoralists in their seasonal movements, and sometimes follow the routes precisely. The main axis is roughly north–south, from the coastal lowlands of the southern Landes to the summer pastures of the higher Pyrenées Atlantiques. Many of the sites, especially the non-funerary mounds known as *fonds de cabanes*, have modern shepherds' huts built close to them, or indeed incorporate them. The main concentrations of megaliths are invariably in areas of good pasture, whereas areas of poor pasture have none. As in Spain, there is sometimes a linguistic link as well; Larraona (Basque 'good pastures') and Artzamendi ('mountain of the shepherds') are both notably rich in megaliths.

Megalithic monuments are also often associated with areas which traditionally have been used as meeting places by transhumant pastoralists, whether for annual sheep and produce fairs or prior to setting out for the summer or winter pastures. 'No es raro que importantes grupos de dólmenes ocupen precisamente los territorios de facérias y se hallen en sitios enque los pastores celebran sus tradicionales asambleas' (Barandiarán 1951). A similar point is made by Arambourou & Mohen (1977): '. . . les zones de concentration de tumulus correspondent assez bien aux zones fréquentés par les transhumants tels qu'on les connaît encore dans les temps historiques'. The highest megaliths known in France are the dolmens of La Pierre St Martin (Pyrenées Atlantiques) at 1700 m. On the border with Spain, this has been for centuries the site of a major sheep fair attended from both France and Spain. A megalithic 'table' of unknown antiquity marks the location of a similar fair at the Col de Lizuniaga. Sites, or groups of them, are commonly found at nodal points where pastoralists and their stock were forced to congregate by geographical factors, as at Buzy and on the Laneplaa to the east of Bayonne.

Elsewhere in southern France the general relationship between megaliths and pastoral resources is no less striking. Half of the known French megaliths are in the Midi, and it is here that one finds the '*loi du calcaire*' best exemplified. Temple (1936) found that in the *départements* of Aveyron, Hérault, and Gard between 82 per cent and 91 per cent of the dolmens then known were found on the Jurassic limestone *Causses*. In Lozère, Prunières (1872) only found one monument out of a sample of more than 100 which was not in the area of calcareous rocks. These distributions are highly biased, as the calcareous areas only account for one-third or less of the area of these *départements*.

The factors responsible for this markedly asymmetrical distribution seem most likely to be concerned with the high quality of pasture available on the *Causses*. The climate does not vary sufficiently between these and the other regions in the *départements* for this to provide a plausible explanation, nor is there an absence of surface stone for building purposes outside the limestone regions. Here the pasturage is of exceptionally high quality, particularly on the lower '*petits Causses*' where the climate is less severe. Today these produce the ewe's milk for Roquefort and the cow's milk for *Bleu des Causses*, as well as stock raised for meat. Aveyron still carries over half a million sheep, mostly in the dolmen-rich areas. The main difficulty in the exploitation of the *Causses* is their aridity, but this is mainly felt in its restriction of drinking water for humans and cattle, as the sheep derive sufficient moisture from their fodder. By contrast with the *Causses*, the soils of most of the region are mainly granite and schist based. While these can produce a good growth of woodland and herbage, they are deficient in lime. Pasture is poor in quality and stock does not do well on it, tending to be small and inadequately fleshed, and to suffer from mineral-deficiency diseases.

Here, as in the Pyrenees, the monuments are closely related to the *drailles*, the local transhumance routes. These tend to follow the crests, and dolmens are characteristically found in cols and where ridges and tracks join each other. For example, the Draille d'Aubrac in Lozère is marked by a succession of menhirs and Bronze Age hoards, and passes furthermore through two of the densest distributions of dolmens. The antiquity of many of the *drailles* is unknown, but some in Aveyron are at the very least pre-Iron Age, as they are overlain by tumuli of this date. Traditional resting places of pastoralists are again favoured locations for monuments. Another feature reminiscent of many of the Spanish megaliths is that the topography of the *Causses*, with its upland plateaux separated from each other by deeply incised and steep-sided valleys, means that a very large proportion of the monuments are situated on topographically isolated blocks of upland grazing. These are frequently used today as natural corrals.

Another striking concentration of French megaliths is in the Morbihan area of Brittany. Here the environment presents a great contrast to those discussed so far, but it remains nevertheless one which favours a strong pastoral bias to the subsistence economy. While some areas of Brittany, in particular the coastal regions of the Côtes du Nord and Finistère, and the plain around Rennes, have considerable areas of good arable soil and the potential for good cereal yields, in Morbihan less than 50 per cent of the area is cultivated even under today's conditions when a lucrative market for *primeurs* and dairy products has greatly increased the area under the plough. Much of the arable is sown with fodder crops, and is thus geared to the pastoral side of the economy. In general the combination of acid infertile soils and moist summers limits the cereal potential, as is indicated by the prominence of oats, rye, potatoes, and buckwheat in the traditional economy. In the past the emphasis was more heavily upon pastoralism than today. The picture given by William of Poitiers of the mediaeval subsistence pattern places milk as considerably more important in the diet than bread (Pounds 1973). Travellers such as Arthur Young commented disparagingly on the great extent of wasteland (i.e. uncultivated and unenclosed rough grazing) in Brittany in the eighteenth century. At this time only just over half the area of the bishoprics of Quimper and Vannes

was cultivated land, a figure which probably includes land carrying improved permanent pasture (Sutton 1977). As late as the beginning of the nineteenth century Morbihan is distinguished on the cadastral maps as having among the lowest proportions of arable land and the highest proportions of wasteland in all of France (Fel 1977). It is thus especially noteworthy that the major concentration of Breton megaliths lies in the area of Brittany with the lowest arable potential.

On the other hand, however, the oceanic climate with its warm winters and evenly distributed rainfall makes Brittany a highly favoured area for grazing. 'One important factor in the agricultural economy is the early spring, indeed in many years the temperature rarely falls below 6 °C . . ., and meadow grass hardly ceases to grow' (Monkhouse 1974). One great advantage of the mild winters is that stock can for the most part be pastured out of doors throughout the year. Today the pastoral economy is dominated by intensive dairying, with little movement of stock into or out of the region. In the past, however, the unusually good winter grazing conditions would in all probability have attracted pastoralists to Brittany from considerable distances.

A few monuments were also surveyed from the relatively small distribution to the west of Nancy in Lorraine. Here, in another very different environment, the same basic pattern is repeated. The area as a whole is low in arable resources, and historically it has always tended to have a small and dispersed population. The soils present considerable problems to cultivation, being for the most part a mixture of heavy, glutinous, poorly drained clays and light but relatively infertile sandy soils. The former are certainly beyond the capacity of prehistoric arable technology, and the latter rarely repay cultivation. Cereals are grown in places on the better soils today, but the elevation and high levels of precipitation, especially in early summer, are significant limitations, as is suggested by the importance of oats and potatoes among the arable crops. Fifty per cent or more of the modern land use consists of woodland and permanent pasture.

Sites such as the *allées couvertes* of the Bois l'Eveque and the Ferme de Saucy, and the menhirs such as the Damechonne at St Mihiel and those at Montplonne exemplify these conditions. They are in heavily wooded areas, with permanent pasture for cattle also of importance in their territories. There is more arable in the vicinity of the Montplonne sites than in the territories of the other Lorraine sites. Even here only about 50 per cent of the land is cultivated, and huge piles of stones in all the fields testify to the labour that is needed to extract even this meagre arable potential. The majority of the soils of the area are in any case extremely heavy, and most of the existing arable has only recently come under the plough. Furthermore, this continuing clearance is but an index of modern population pressure, as cereal yields are low, and even the quality of the pasture is not particularly good (George 1973). During the period of erection of the megaliths the area as a whole can only have been exploited for its pastoral and woodland resources. It is notable that there is no evidence whatever of any relationship between the monuments and those few areas of soil sufficiently tractable to have been successfully cultivated at the time.

The broad outlines of megalithic distribution in the areas of France considered above are thus very similar to those analysed in Spain. In no case can the hypothesis be sustained that the local subsistence depended to any appreciable extent upon arable crops, and we must suppose therefore that these particular 'megalith builders' relied primarily upon pastoral resources. Other specific features reminiscent of the Spanish megaliths are the choice of locations in cols on ridges, or on isolated blocks of upland grazing; and the association with routes along crests, particularly with the traditional transhumance routes and meeting points, and with modern shepherds' huts.

In Brittany and Lorraine, where the modern pastoral economies are largely sedentary or semi-sedentary, it is unclear to what degree prehistoric pastoralism would have relied on transhumance. However, we have pointed out the attractions of Brittany as a winter grazing area, and it seems unlikely that these qualities did not result in a substantial winter influx of stock and their herders, even if there was a permanent population in addition. One hint of support for this argument may perhaps be seen in the distribution of polished axes of dolomite and hornblende. These, mined in Brittany, are found widely in western and central France. While there are, of course, many possible mechanisms for such a spread, the distribution shows that wide-ranging contacts did exist. One possible explanation is that they may represent, in part at least, the seasonal movements of pastoralists. The megaliths of Lorraine are situated between the highlands of the Vosges to the east and the lowlands of Champagne and the Paris Basin to the west. The Vosges suffer the characteristic limitations of the European uplands as far as winter grazing potential is concerned, and the two areas are well-suited for exploitation on a complementary seasonal basis. Even Lorraine itself receives sufficient snow and frost in winter to have discouraged permanent occupation by

pastoralists until stall-feeding for long periods during the winter became established. Movement westwards to the Paris Basin is perhaps the most likely adaptation until pressure on the lowland grazing resources enforced a more intensive use of the resources of the Lorraine area. We have no positive evidence of such contact in prehistory, but we should remember the existence of the well-known concentration of megalithic tombs in the northern and eastern Paris Basin in the valleys of the Aisne, Oise, and Seine. We have already noted briefly (Chapter 5) that this area is not as a whole of high Neolithic arable potential.

In the Pyrenees and the Midi regions the situation is clearer, and there is every reason to believe that in prehistory as in the historical past (and today, also, to a substantial degree) pastoralism was primarily dependent upon seasonal mobility. In the Pyrenees the summer pastures become snowed up for long periods in winter, and a move to the lowlands is an inevitable response for any economic system unable to stall-feed its stock throughout the winter months. In the Midi the main factor impelling transhumance is the summer aridity in the lowlands which desiccates the pasture at this season. The only means of maintaining large numbers of stock at this period, short of the provision of hay, is by movement to higher pastures with more rain and lower temperatures. To this day the higher *Causses* receive a vast summer influx of animals from Languedoc, while many others go to pastures higher up in the Massif Central and the Alps.

IRELAND

Ireland is another country conspicuously rich in megalithic monuments, with many hundreds of tombs as well as menhirs, stone circles, and the like. Detailed surveys in the counties of Mayo and Clare alone revealed well over two hundred tombs, the estimated number for the country as a whole being over one thousand (de Valéra & Ó'Nualláin 1961, 1964).

The basic environment of Ireland is such that we may well expect the general pattern of association between megaliths and pastoral resources, observed elsewhere in Europe, to be repeated. The climate of the country as a whole is markedly oceanic. Its salient features include mild winters, low annual temperature variation, moderate, evenly distributed precipitation with rain falling on about 150–200 days per annum, and a high degree of cloud cover. The soil, another factor of great economic significance, is highly varied, but very large areas are covered with acid soils of low productive potential – peats, gleys, and acid brown earths. The higher potential calcareous soils are frequently very shallow.

As far as our present interests are concerned, the main impact of the environment is seen in the stringent limitations it imposes on arable agriculture. Today, very little of the country is under arable exploitation. In some areas as little as 40 per cent of the land is farmed at all, while some 90 per cent of this area is under permanent pasture and hay. Wide areas of peat bog and hill land are barely exploited except for low-intensity rough grazing, and, increasingly, forestry. The combination of frequent rainfall, poor drainage, and poor insolation are particularly inimical to successful cereal growth. 'Conditions for wheat are minimal, and those for barley little better' (Mitchell 1976). 'Oats and potatoes are the only crops of significance, though wheat production was encouraged during the two wars, and almost completely abandoned between them' (Freeman, T. W. 1950). On the other hand, the same factors that restrict the cereal potential are largely beneficial to pastoralism. Moist summers and warm winters result in year-round vegetative growth, and reduces the need for stall-feeding. The major economic emphasis is thus on pastoralism, especially dairy cattle today, with sheep of importance on the poorer soils and higher pastures.

In the past, while the precise balance of the subsistence economy fluctuated in response to variations in both internal and external economic, commercial, demographic, and environmental pressures, the broad outlines were substantially the same as those of today's pattern of land use. The traditional diet of the rural Irish in the eighteenth and nineteenth centuries was overwhelmingly based upon milk and potatoes. The great importance of the potato in Ireland lies in its capacity to yield an arable return in conditions of soil and climate that will not support other crops. In the earlier historic periods the very much smaller population would have been yet more heavily dependent upon pastoral resources, supplemented by such cereals as could be grown. Giraldus Cambrensis, visiting Ireland in the late twelfth century, writes that 'Only the granaries are without their wealth . . . For here the grains of wheat are shrivelled and small . . . What is born and comes forth in the spring . . . can scarcely be reaped in the harvest because of the unceasing rain' (quoted in Mitchell 1976). The difficulties of successful wheat cultivation at this period are of especial interest in view of the fact that it was probably during a warmer interstadial, and represented the best conditions for cereal growth which Ireland has enjoyed throughout the last millennium.

Before we turn to the relationship of the megaliths to the distribution of resources, we must briefly consider the ever-present question of the degree to which recent environmental changes will have distorted the situation. There is, unfortunately, no entirely satisfactory answer to this. It is certain that the peat bogs and other areas of impeded drainage have increased, sometimes dramatically, since the Neolithic. There is some evidence that in certain areas a major phase of bog formation succeeded, and may have been partially caused by, woodland clearance associated with increasing human exploitation. On the other hand, it is clear that in many cases the peat formation was initiated prior to the building of the megaliths, and it seems in some instances to have been a fairly continuous process since the early postglacial. We must remember, furthermore, that the low permeability of the soils and substrate will have meant that prior to bog formation the areas would in any case have had at best a wet pasture potential. In the present context the issue is of less importance than might at first appear, as the megaliths tend in any case to be negatively correlated with these areas of impeded drainage. It might similarly be suggested that denudation of the drier hill slopes has changed their character, degrading arable potential areas into pasture and rough grazing. While some erosion has doubtless occurred in places, all that can be said is that there is little or no evidence to suggest a general or catastrophic alteration of land use potential. Even on the denuded limestone plateaux such little stratigraphic evidence as exists suggests that the relevant prehistoric land surface was substantially the same as that of today.

Our general expectations as to the economic orientation of the Irish megaliths are amply confirmed by detailed field survey. Counties Mayo and Clare were chosen as study areas because of the relatively complete information on site location available from the work of de Valéra & Ó'Nualláin (1961, 1964). In Mayo sites such as those at Lecarrowtemple are set in a mixture of improved pasture and poor quality grazing with high percentages of heather, gorse, and sedge. The only arable in the whole exploitation territory of these sites consists of small family plots of potatoes and oats in the coastal strip at its northern extremity. It is true that the overwhelming dependence upon dairy farming rests largely upon its nationwide commercial development over the past two decades. Nevertheless northern Mayo, which carries by far the majority of the sites, has very little in the way of arable potential. Furthermore megalithic sites seem to be quite unrelated to the best of such poor arable resources as are available, in the low-lying plain around Ballina. By and large there is an avoidance of basins and low-lying situations, most of the sites being found on hill slopes. Other sites in northern Mayo are almost all in pasture or rough grazing areas, like those at Lecarrowtemple. There is an evident locational preference for the well-drained soils. This suggests that the avoidance of much of the low-lying area may have to do with the poor conditions of drainage and boggy conditions frequently found there. Today this is increasingly overcome by artificial drainage.

The case is, if anything, more clear-cut in County Clare. The Burren, which carries the majority of the tombs (and by far the densest distribution) is a well-drained limestone plateau. In many areas there is little soil depth, much of the surface consisting of exposed bedrock. The area is overwhelmingly dominated by rough grazing, with some improved pasture in the more favoured and sheltered basins. By contrast, the flag-stone and slate formations which cover almost half the county have only seven known tombs out of a total of about 120 for Clare as a whole. There is a general avoidance of low-lying and valley situations and other areas with waterlogged soils and bog formation. The higher and more rugged mountain tops are also avoided, and tombs are typically located in well-drained situations on the plateaux and hill slopes. Similar concentrations of tombs are to be found on upland limestone soils in Limerick, Kerry, Tipperary, and Cork, while the heavy soils of the valleys and basins and the shale and flagstone exposures are gener-ally avoided.

It should be mentioned that some other authors have laid much less emphasis upon the pastoralist bias to the Irish prehistoric economy. Aalen (1978) points to the preference for light, well-drained slope soils, the palynological evidence for woodland clearance, and the concentration of the largest passage graves in the drier eastern coastlands, and infers a mixed farming eco-nomy in which cereals were of considerable importance in determining settlement patterns. Indeed, it is not our intention to suggest that arable farming had no place in the economy, as pollen and macroscopic plant remains clearly indicate that cereals and other plants were certainly cultivated where conditions permitted. The basic climatic limitations are such, however, that this can hardly ever, if at all, have outweighed the signifi-cance of pastoralism. Aalen himself notes a number of points with which his interpretation is difficult to reconcile. In northeastern Ireland surveys by Watson (1956) indicated that 'areas of light, well-drained soils away from mountain masses failed to attract their fair share of settlement'. The largely settled mixed farming communities envisaged by Aalen seem to have left remarkably little in the way of settlements to go with their impressive funerary monuments; while the well-known megalithic cemetery at Carrowkeel in County Sligo (and the adjacent 'village' of hut emplacements which may well be associated with it) lies at c. 250 m on a limestone hillside, and seems in a most implausible location for a population operating a plant-based eco-nomy. It may further be noted that despite the slight locational preference of the passage graves for the drier eastern half of the country, these seem rather to avoid the most favoured areas for arable production, the littoral zone of the southeast. Instead they are concen-trated for the most part in the colder and wetter areas – Ulster to the north, and the Wicklow mountains to the south.

In our view, then, there is every reason to view the Irish megaliths as the product of a subsistence economy primarily based upon pastoralism. To what extent this would have been transhumant in nature is unknown. Ireland, like Brittany, is remarkable for the mildness of its winters and the quality of the naturally available grazing at this season. It is thus by no means impossible that some areas carried largely sedentary human and animal populations in prehistory as they do today. Grazing resources do fluctuate seasonally in value and accessibility, however, and it is to be expected that such variations will have been accommodated through the mobile or mobile-cum-sedentary adaptations, which in historical Ireland were termed 'booleying'. These may very well have been generally on a more local scale than conditions permit in some of the more extreme seasonal environments elsewhere in Europe.

Another local feature of some interest is that the direction of seasonal movement will, in some areas at least, have been reversed relative to what might be expected. The significance of the association of tombs with limestone plateaux was discussed by de Valéra & O'Nualláin (1961), and we cannot do better than to quote them on the subject directly. 'It is abundantly clear that (in the Burren) the tombs correspond very exactly to the presence of what is now good winterage land. In fact the general rule is the better the winterage the greater the concentration of sites.' The Burren has for centuries been of crucial importance in providing win-ter pasturage for stock. Some of these animals summer in the immediately surrounding lowlands, while others are drawn from considerable distances by the well-drained soils and the mild winters. Lack of frost and snow and high mean winter temperatures ensure that most of the animals can overwinter outside without supplementary fodder. The thin limestone soils are very freely draining, and are thus not subject to the winter flooding which is widespread on the heavier lowland soils. They are, on the other hand, so permeable as to become fairly desiccated in the occasional dry summer spells, and they are therefore little grazed at this season. As with the limestone pastures of the *Causses*, pasture quality is extremely high and cattle grazed on the Burren in winter have a justifiably high reputation for their general condition and resistance to disease.

In Ireland, as in the other areas discussed, there is little sign of a precise formula for individual tomb locations. We have noted the general preference for upland plateaux and hill slopes. Many of the tombs have a broadly southwesterly orientation. Here, as was noted in France and Spain, it is an open question in some cases as to whether one is dealing with a megalithic monument or with the huts and enclosures of historic – and prehistoric – pastoralists. Doubtless the same structure has served both purposes in some instances.

NORTH GERMANY

A small number of megaliths is known from the Münster and Kassel regions of West Germany. Some of these appear to be in locations which suggest a different relationship to resources from that which emerged elsewhere, and so we include a brief discussion of these sites here despite the cursory survey that was all we were able to conduct.

Within this area there may be distinguished five more or less discrete groups of sites: (1) in the area where the Teutoburger Wald meets the North German Plain, (2) in the lower Lippe valley, (3) around Soest on the southern edge of the Münster Bay, (4) around Paderborn at the eastern extremity of the Münster Bay, and (5) to the west of Kassel.

Even in this relatively small area environment and land use potential vary tremendously in accordance particularly with changes in soils and relief. Of especial relevance to our interests is the narrow band of loess which lies along the southern margin of the Münster Bay, and a similar tongue of loess which extends from the Bördeland of Saxony down the Weser as far as Kassel. These provide areas of high modern arable potential close to the Soest and Kassel megaliths, and we should thus consider what their Neolithic potential would have been and what we may infer as to the economy of the populations involved.

The loess deposits are not extensive in the area, but where they do exist they and the loams derived from them are tractable, well drained, and fertile, producing good yields of a variety of arable crops today. Furthermore, there is a long history of prosperous arable exploitation of the soils, and indeed there are Linear Pottery sites known from the Kassel area which probably were here, as elsewhere, exemplars of an arable-based economy. There thus seems good reason on the face of it to argue that the later Wartburg settlements and the megalithic tombs associated with them, and those of the Soest area, were also primarily arable-oriented.

A number of considerations suggest that, at the very least, this is but part of the picture. Taking the north German megaliths as a whole, there is no consistent association with soils of arable potential. On the contrary, the vast majority are on poor soils with a rough grazing or wet pasture potential. The North German Plain is for the most part relatively poor in arable resources. Infertile, acid sands and gravels are the dominant soil types, heath and bog the natural vegetation. Even within the southerly distribution under discussion here it is only two of the groups which are located in the arable-rich areas. Moreover, of the seven megaliths in the Soest group, three are located on, and have territories dominated by, heavy clayey soils with a wet pasture land use potential. The other three groups are all in areas dominated by rough grazing and pasture. Thus only 15 tombs (out of the 38 dealt with here) have territories with an appreciable arable component, and rather than any general association of tombs with local arable resources there seems to be a general scatter through a number of land use zones, the most southerly of which coincides with some small arable-rich areas.

It is also noteworthy that the settlements hypothetically linked with the Kassel tombs show a minor shift in site location relative to the earlier Linear Pottery sites. The latter are characteristically on flat and gently sloping loess exposures giving immediate access to high quality arable soils, while the former are on small eminences, the slopes of which are usually too steep to permit effective cultivation. Their 10 minute territories tend thus to be predominantly of rough grazing potential, despite the undoubted arable potential of the area as a whole.

We may also wonder how attractive these small areas really were from an arable viewpoint at the time in question, despite the undoubted suitability of the soils. The loess soils produce good crops of cereals and sugar beet today, but barley, oats, rye, and potatoes are of importance in the local rotation. While there are many different factors involved in this system, it is significant that these are all crops which yield successfully in poorer growing conditions than wheat, which tends to be the favoured crop where it can be grown successfully. Indeed, the climatic conditions for cereal growth are poorer here than in the most favoured areas of Germany, such as the Rhine Rift valley and the middle Danube valley east of Regensburg, with spring coming later, the growing season thus being shorter and cooler, and the cereal harvest delayed. This is of some importance in an environment with a peak of rainfall in summer, and it seems significant that both of the climatically favoured areas carry substantial concentrations of Linear Pottery sites (see Chapter 5).

We must not, of course, overemphasise the obstacles to arable agriculture on the loess of northwest Germany. As we have already mentioned, some Linear Pottery sites do indeed occur in the Kassel area, and are likely to have had substantially plant-based economies. It is perhaps significant that these are not of the earliest phase of Linear Pottery spread, and represent a later spread into more marginal areas due to population pressure. Another factor of interest is the rôle of possible climatic change between the mid fifth millennium and mid third millenium b.c. The data are poor, but it seems certain that the climate would have been cooler, and perhaps also moister, by the time of tomb construction, than it was during the Linear Pottery period at and shortly after the altithermal. The sites concerned lie at the very edge of the Linear Pottery distribution, and thus presumably represent the limits of environmental tolerance to which their agronomic capacities and economic requirements were adapted. It would in those circumstances be less than surprising if a minor deterioration in climate from the point of view of cereal production should have tilted the economic balance in favour of pastoralism.

There are, clearly, insufficient data with which to reach firm conclusions on the subject. It is perfectly possible that the Soest and Kassel megaliths represent a small arable-based population despite the contrary indications in many of the major areas of megalithic distribution. Nevertheless, it is a striking fact that these few particular tombs lie both on the extreme southern edge of the main north European area of megaliths, and also on the extreme northern edge of the main area of early Neolithic plant-based economies. This, and the other factors discussed above, incline us to believe that they may prove less anomalous than might at first appear when compared with the other areas discussed in this chapter.

SWEDEN AND GREAT BRITAIN

The megaliths of southern Sweden provide an example very similar to those just discussed. At first sight they appear to be related primarily to arable resources. Indeed, Clark, J. G. D. (1977) has recently considered them from an economic viewpoint, applying lines of argument like those followed here. One group of tombs was found to be associated closely with the best arable soils in the region, the lime-rich and relatively tractable soils such as those of the Baltic end moraine and parts of Västergötland. Clark argues reasonably for a considerable arable element in the economy of the tomb builders, a conclusion which seems to be confirmed by the grain impressions found in the pottery from the tombs. Significantly, wheat dominates the (admittedly very small) sample to the tune of 80–90 per cent. The second, Bohuslän, group has a pronounced coastal distribution, with half the tombs within 1 km of the coast and three-quarters within 2 km. The area as a whole is poor in arable potential, and the coastal strip particularly so. On the other hand, the adjacent waters of the Skagerrak are rich in fish resources. Fishing was the mainstay of the traditional economy, and to judge from the faunal remains in Mesolithic and Neolithic sites, the prehistoric economy showed a similar bias.

Let it at once be admitted that there is good evidence for an arable and a marine component respectively in the subsistence of the two areas discussed. We feel nevertheless that there are some factors which may have been given insufficient consideration in Clark's analysis, although without first-hand experience of the region in question we can clearly only make some tentative suggestions.

The first point is that for all the fertility of small patches of soil, southern Sweden as a whole is not a region of high arable potential. Even today the area under the plough is relatively small – about one-third of the southern Swedish lowlands, although this does rise to 70–80 per cent in the most favoured coastal areas of Skåne. Crop yields can be good, but it is noteworthy that seasonal variations are such that the government levies a compulsory crop insurance for indemnities in years of failure. The rural economy everywhere retains a substantial pastoral element, and indeed nearly 80 per cent of the area classified as arable is in fact geared to pastoralism, growing fodder crops and grassland rotation crops. It is quite true that megaliths are found in two of the areas favoured for modern arable agriculture, but it is equally the case that these areas, Västergötland and Skåne, carry the largest cattle populations in Sweden. As we have already noted with respect to parts of France and Ireland, there are other reasons than the demands of cereal cultivation for seeking out lime-rich soils, reasons that seem to have been of relevance in the distributions of megaliths. Indeed, it should always be remembered that in general soils that have a high arable potential will also produce excellent grazing. If technological or environmental circumstances discourage arable exploitation, then those areas will frequently be sought after for their grazing potential.

The obstacles to successful crop agriculture are indeed substantial, as even the areas with suitable soils suffer from the severe winter climate which cuts the effective farming year to about 240 days in southern Skåne and 200–210 days in Västergötland. In the past, when many of the richer but heavier clay soils would not have been cultivable, and with plant breeding in rudimentary stage at best, the importance of cereals must have been less than it is today. Some of the megaliths are located in the narrow sandy coastal strip, where the soils would have been accessible to the Neolithic arable technology. Others, however, are further inland on clayey and morainic soils which would have been difficult to work or totally intractable at the time. Clark himself notes the palynological evidence that suggests that cereals were of little importance until the Iron Age, by which time the mouldboard plough and animal traction may well have been in use. Even as late as the eighteenth century, with better technology and more suitable crops, such as rye, the small Swedish population of about 1 500 000 was not self-sufficient in cereals. Contemporary accounts stress the difficulties of cereal cultivation, one writer recording crop failure in two to three years out of every ten, with full ripening in only the same proportion of harvests (East 1966). It may be significant, therefore, that a high proportion of the Neolithic cereal impressions are of einkorn, a crop that is of poor quality and low yield compared with more advanced wheats, but which is frost and disease resistant, and will yield a crop on poor soils.

As for the Bohuslän sites, there do indeed seem to be good grounds for inferring a significant marine element in the economy. The pastoral potential of the area goes without comment, however, in Clark's analysis, and it is worth recalling here the discussion in Chapter 4 of the limitations which attend communities with a year-round marine-based economy. It is notable that by far the most important fish in the coastal sites of the area are the bottom-feeding cod, ling, and haddock. As Clark notes, these would have been at their most accessible to Neolithic technology during their winter spawning runs. It is surely possible that fishing was

more a seasonal activity of pastoralists in their winter grazing grounds than the main economic orientation of the system as a whole. Any animal-based economy is likely to have been at least partially mobile due to climatic constraints. The lowlands, and in particular the westward facing coast with its relatively short and mild winters, would have been the favoured winter pasturage area.

Shortage of time has precluded our pursuing field surveys in Great Britain, but general environmental considerations and work already published suggest that the broad picture is the same as that which has emerged elsewhere. The overwhelming predominance of British megalithic monuments is found in the west and in the uplands; that is, specifically in the zone which has primarily a grazing potential rather than an arable potential. Webley (1976) has discussed the importance of mobile pastoralism in the historic and prehistoric economies of southern Wales and Fleming (1971) has argued persuasively that the barrows and other monuments of Bronze Age Wessex may have been related to the seasonal grazing territories of transhumant pastoralists. Other important megalithic groupings are found in the Peak District, famous for the quality of its lime-rich pastures, and western Scotland and the Orkneys. It may or may not be that in these latter areas crops were grown on the small patches of land that Renfrew, C. (1976) defines as being of arable potential, and to which the tombs are often adjacent. On the other hand, these areas suffer from much the same kind of environmental limitation as does Ireland, and in a more extreme and adverse form as regards climate, due to their more northerly position. Yields would certainly have been low and uncertain, particularly as there is little sign that the hardier oats and rye were being cultivated at the time. Renfrew makes only the most casual reference to the grazing potential of the area, which is the crucial resource. Pastoralism forms the mainstay of the modern and traditional subsistence economy, and would in all probability have played a yet more important stabilising part in prehistory when seasons of poor yield or total crop failure could not easily be made good from outside the area. Marine resources, unmentioned by Renfrew, probably fulfilled an important secondary rôle in coastal areas.

We have demonstrated the strongest likelihood that, in a number of important centres of European megalithic distribution, the subsistence economy of the builders of the monuments was based upon mobile pastoralism. There is indeed a striking negative correlation between areas of dense megalithic distribution and areas of high arable productivity. There are localised exceptions, it is true; but generally the crops of the major megalithic areas are those characteristic of poor environments: rye, oats, buckwheat, potatoes. Conversely, megaliths tend to be densely distributed in areas rich in pastoral resources. A concomitant of this is the relatively low population level that would have obtained in many of the megalithic areas. These correlations would doubtless have been much more pronounced in the past. In those areas, such as Denmark and Brittany, where important concentrations of megaliths coincide with high modern population densities, these latter have little to do with the productive potential of traditional agriculture. When we extract from the picture those areas of high arable productivity which only became viable with the availability of modern varieties and/or of mechanical equipment, it becomes apparent that the zones of highest arable productivity in prehistoric Europe are mutually exclusive of the primary areas of megalithic concentration.

This conclusion is directly contrary to the premise commonly employed that the megalith builders were arable agriculturalists. It has long been clear that the larger monuments represent a very considerable investment of human labour, and in a sense may thus be viewed as indices of dependable economic surplus which permitted the expenditure of labour in spheres considerably removed from the primary concerns of subsistence. It is usually assumed, though often not explicitly stated, that it is only with the development of economies based upon the modern farmyard species of plants and animals, dependent to a large extent on the unprecedented productive potential of cereals, that population levels can have risen sufficiently to supply the necessary labour.

One of the most recent and most explicitly stated arguments involving this hypothesis is that of Renfrew, C. (1976). He assumes *a priori* that the economy had an arable basis and suggests that this may well have been of the 'shifting agriculture' type. He goes on to speculate as to the social significance of the tombs and the social framework within which they came to be built. The conclusion is drawn that megaliths may be viewed as a response to increases in population density consequent upon the adoption of a farming economy along the 'Atlantic façade' of Europe. This is seen as leading to 'a developing scarcity of land, accompanied by a greater concern for establishing and defining community territories and boundaries'. The megaliths are seen as concrete and abiding symbols of community strength and solidarity, and thus as being of adaptive value in a situation of population stress. This demographic crisis

is thought to have been exacerbated by the existence of substantial Mesolithic populations in the main megalithic areas.

Parts of this synthesis are more appealing than others. Monuments of the size of the larger megaliths undoubtedly bespeak substantial human agglomerations; and thus presumably the social mechanisms for their organisation, at least at a rudimentary level. Renfrew may well be right in his speculations about the enhanced social value of the tombs, although the ethnographic analogies used to support his inferences are surely too distant and too disparate to carry much conviction. As we have seen, however, the basic assumption concerning the economic basis of the builders seems to us in many cases demonstrably false. This is not simply a quibble on a minor point of interpretation. It is from his premise regarding the subsistence economy that Renfrew is able to draw his conclusions about land-hunger and population pressure.

All the concrete evidence that we have suggests that, as we would expect intuitively, population levels would have been much higher, and rates of population growth much faster, in the areas such as the European loesslands, which are conspicuously lacking in megaliths for the most part. Here, and in the relatively constricted pockets of suitable environment in the Mediterranean lowlands, such as the Tavoliere, there is abundant archaeological evidence of rapid population growth and of high densities. There are probably more settlements known from a few square miles of the Tiszazug, let us say, or of the Tavoliere, than there are from all the major megalithic areas put together. It would be absurd, of course, to infer directly from numbers of known settlements to population levels. Nevertheless the extraordinary rarity of house or village sites attributable to the megalith builders must surely lend weight to our hypothesis that population was relatively thinly spread and that the economy incorporated an important element of mobility. The oft-remarked paucity of grave goods associated with megaliths is also consonant with this view, as it seems likely that a mobile economy would tend to discourage the acquisition of expendable symbols of material wealth.

We cannot infer from the evidence that *population pressure* was necessarily lower in these mainly pastoralist areas, as this is a relative concept depending on the relationship of the population to the available resources rather than on absolute population levels themselves. All that can be said is that these latter, and the rates of population growth, were surely considerably higher in the primary areas of arable production and of drastic economic change. It is therefore perhaps unlikely that population pressure would have been unusually high in the main megalithic areas, where the pastoralist economy would have been in many ways similar to, and adapted to the same basic environment as, the preceding Mesolithic economy. Renfrew's argument to the contrary, the significance of the Téviec evidence quoted by him is perhaps to be seen simply in the essential economic – and for all we know social – continuity in the megalithic areas between Mesolithic and Neolithic times. We should not forget that skeletal studies in the Basque provinces indicate substantial anthropometric continuity from Palaeolithic to Neolithic, and indeed to modern, times (Bahn, personal communication).

Not only is it doubtful that the megalithic areas experienced especially high population pressure; it is also questionable whether the dashing of the 'Neolithic wave of advance' against an 'Atlantic façade' populated with an indigenous Mesolithic population was a significant factor. It is only by great elasticity of imagination, coupled with the use of very small-scale maps, that one can encompass the megaliths of the *Causses*, Lorraine, and Hesse-Kassel within an Atlantic façade. This view also leaves unremarked the general absence of megaliths from the Low Countries and much of lowland Britain. Similarly, while it is true that much of the loesslands of central and western Europe have little trace of Mesolithic settlement (whether because they were genuinely little exploited or because subsequent erosion has destroyed most of the traces), there is little reason to assume the whole region to have been as devoid of population as Renfrew implies; or that, hence, contact between Mesolithic and colonising Neolithic populations will not have occurred. Relatively dense scatters of Mesolithic sites are known from the sands of Czechoslovakia and southern Poland, for example, in areas too close to distributions of Linear Pottery sites for us easily to countenance the divorce proposed by Renfrew's hypothesis. Nandris (1972) has pointed out the absurdities raised by the argument that the Mesolithic and Early Neolithic populations of Central Europe were so narrowly confined to the sandy heaths and uplands, and the loess-clad river valleys respectively.

If we reject, then, the suggestion that megaliths are to be associated with (and to be seen as in part a consequence of) arable agricultural economies with relatively high population levels, we are faced with the problem of how to explain the assembly of sufficient man-power potential for their erection. It may first be pointed out that while it is quite true that the larger

monuments would have required the expenditure of many thousands of man-hours, the majority of monuments are on a much smaller scale. They remain formidable evidences of the available labour resources, nonetheless.

Two recurrent features of transhumant pastoralist economies are of interest here. The first is the occurrence of regular – often annual or bi-annual – meetings of large numbers of pastoralists from different groups. These usually have multiple purposes, being produce fairs, livestock sales, social and religious festivals, occasions of trade with other more sedentary communities, re-establishment of land and grazing rights and agreements, and so on. The other factor is the highly seasonal nature of the labour requirements of mobile pastoralism. This means that there are often periods in the annual cycle when much time is available for other activities, and the seasonal festivals are frequently arranged to coincide with these predictable 'slack periods'. We have already mentioned a number of instances of notable concentrations of monuments in areas known to have been important as meeting points for pastoralist groups. These regular seasonal concentrations of large numbers of pastoralists seem to offer a reasonable explanation of how the necessary labour force may have been assembled for even the larger monuments.

Perhaps two main conclusions spring from this enquiry into the economic context of megalithic monuments. Neither is new or original in the sense that they have never been touched upon before, or indeed considered in detail within the framework of a particular centre of distribution. However, the general surveys which exist have tended to concentrate upon chronological and typological phenomena. Ours, while far from exhaustive, has attempted to generalise features of location and the economic implications of these.

The first conclusion is that, assumptions about labour costs notwithstanding, the primary economic orientation of the megalith builders was towards mobile pastoralism. In some areas – the Catalonian Pyrenees, the *Causses*, and Co. Clare, for example – the case seems demonstrated as conclusively as one may hope for in view of the nature of archaeological evidence. In other areas the question remains more open, for despite an overall pastoral bias which results from environmental factors, one cannot exclude the possibility of other forms of subsistence entirely. The customary dictum that only a crop-growing population could produce a sufficiently large and reliable economic surplus to support the necessary expenditure of labour is certainly based upon a misunderstanding of transhumant communities and an underestimation of their wealth. It is true that many transhumant groups have little in the way of solid artefactual 'symbolic' wealth. Given their way of life it is only objects of high value but low weight and bulk which are of use; others would be merely an encumbrance. Inevitably most of their wealth resides in their stock; 'fields on the hoof' in Ekvall's (1968) evocative phrase.

In fact pastoralists are frequently very well-off, both in terms of convertible wealth and in terms of spare time (i.e. surplus labour, at least at some seasons). Although they are often viewed with scorn by peasant farmers, as 'little better than gypsies', this springs from their arduous and relatively unfettered way of life rather than their poverty. For the Greek farmer or urban dweller the word *Vlachos* is a contemptuous and abusive epithet, but towns such as Trikkala are largely composed of Vlach families who have sold out for considerable fortunes in today's economic circumstances, which are increasingly adverse to mobile pastoralism. Those Vlachs still pursuing their traditional economy also have much more uncommitted time at their disposal than does the average lowland peasant. In the same way, the affluence of Tibetan pastoralists is legendary and 'is an acknowledged factor in the wealth collection policies of the religious establishment' (Ekvall 1968).

A second conclusion which seems justified concerns the multifariousness of the monuments, in function and significance as much as in typology. While many are clearly funerary in their primary purpose, and others seem to have a definite if obscure astronomical significance, the repeated association of monuments with stock routes, hill tops, cols, and boundaries seems to hint at a further dimension. At a practical level it is also clear that in many cases they have been used as pastoralists' huts and as stock-pens. Many dolmens in the Midi are surrounded by stone-built 'parcs à bestiaux' of unknown antiquity, recalling the celebrated church painting at St Merri in Paris depicting Ste Geneviève in a cromlech with a flock of sheep.

It seems clear that in certain instances megalithic monuments acquired specific significance as markers, meeting places, and boundary points, quite apart from their general relationship with areas of pasturage. Of course they may for the most part have developed this meaning long after their construction. We can at present only speculate about the antiquity of this aspect, but to say the least the recurrent association of monuments with historically known stock droves and traditional pastoralist gatherings is highly suggestive. It does not seem at all fanciful to suppose that the development of

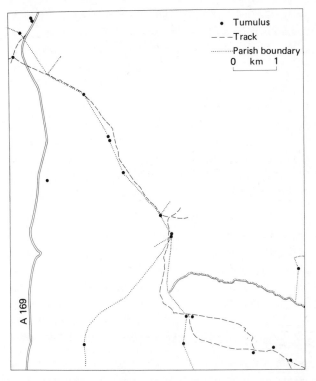

Figure 113. Tumuli used as markers for parish boundaries and tracks on Fylingdales Moor, Yorkshire. Many other tumuli are present in the area but are not included on this map.

the more spectacular large monuments and alignments may have had a similar link with mobile pastoralists. Monuments frequently retain a comparable significance today, as witness the tumuli marking trackways and parish boundaries on Fylingdales Moor in Yorkshire (Figure 113), for example. Fleming (1971) and Grinsell (1953) have convincingly argued for a similar function for Bronze Age and Anglo-Saxon barrows.

Needless to say, the monuments which do not have an obvious demarcation value are far more numerous than those which do. As we have stressed, they clearly have complex and varied meanings. Nevertheless we may recall here Renfrew's view (Renfrew, C. 1976) of megaliths as permanent and substantial symbols of stability in a shifting agricultural economy. While we reject his economic reconstruction in favour of the hypothesis of a much more extensive and widely mobile system, his insistence upon the latent social import of the monuments is of interest. Broad areas of seasonal grazing are commonly exploited jointly by different groups of pastoralists. Any significant degree of competition for grazing will inevitably have given rise to the need for recognised territorial limits, with recognisable boundaries. It is perhaps hard to imagine a more satisfactory means of establishing rights to graze a particular area than by the erection there of the conspicuous tombs of the ancestors of the community.

We may thus indulge a reasonable, if undemonstrable, conviction that the European megaliths not only arose within the context of mobile pastoralism, but also that they performed the vital function of regulating access to grazing resources and of demonstrating ownership of land or usufruct. Such a supposition makes a little more understandable the repeated expenditure of enormous amounts of labour on apparently non-productive enterprises. It illustrates, furthermore, the kind of way in which a wider range of behaviour than the narrowly economic aspects may yet be integrated into the overall pattern of adaptation.

It must be admitted that we are not in a position to answer Renfrew's question as to 'Why, in a specific area – Western Europe – do we find such a concentration of megalithic tombs, while in other regions of Europe and the Near East there are hardly any comparable monuments?' We cannot claim that all megaliths were necessarily built by transhumant pastoralists, although the general link seems clear. Some groups are certainly equivocal in their economic potential, and it is in any case to be expected that then as now transhumant economies will have incorporated secondary arable or other subsistence elements where possible. Still less can we suppose that all prehistoric mobile pastoralists will have built megalithic monuments, and that absence of these is thus to be taken as indicative of an arable-based economy. There are, on the contrary, many areas of Europe where environmental constraints must have imposed a basically pastoralist economy, but where there are few or no known megaliths. A matter worth consideration is whether this particular question is one which can effectively be answered. For all their economic relevance, we are after all discussing monuments of which the immediate and overt functions were probably funerary and religious. If we were to make a modern analogy and inquire into the reasons for geographical differences in church architecture or tomb form, it would immediately be apparent that many of the crucial factors involved concern historical events and 'cultural preferences' which are most unlikely to have left explicable traces in an archaeological record. As we argued in the opening chapter, these seem at the moment to be among the less fruitful avenues of prehistoric research.

CODA

Conclusions all too frequently tend to emerge as tedious reiterations of what has gone before. In the hope of avoiding this particular pitfall we will confine ourselves to an attempt to isolate the central themes and propositions which motivated the work of the Project, and perhaps to hint at possible directions for future development.

Our brief, the study of early European agriculture, inevitably directed our minds at the outset to matters of a rather narrow economic interest. The rôle of agriculture as a 'cultural variable' (to use an accepted archaeological jargon) had been analysed and discussed too thoroughly for us to have much to add beyond the documentation of specific detail. We therefore pursued an alternative course, treating the economy as a dominant force. This led us to a consideration of the relationship between patterns of human subsistence and the ways in which other animals get their living. Broadly speaking, those who study man are impressed with the differences between human and animal behaviour, whereas those approaching man from a biological background more readily see significance in the similarities. One might leave the matter there, and put it down to a question of taste. It is hard to see, however, how a unified study of human behaviour can spring from an approach so selective as to ignore or dismiss the biological component. We have concluded that much that is of importance in human economic behaviour can only be understood by reference to the behaviour of other animals.

This hypothesis is in direct opposition to that espoused by many sociologists, psychologists, and others. For some there exists the firm conviction that, to quote Medawar (1976), 'it is by studying human beings themselves that we learn about their behaviour' rather than by analysing the relationships between our behaviour and that of other animals. But this, surely, is like insisting that no insight into celestial mechanics may be derived from the behaviour of smaller bodies, and that Darwin would have done better to stick to butterflies. Medawar's viewpoint comes into sharper focus when we realise that the phenomena which interest him (and which by implication loom largest among the behavioural patterns he considers worthy of

study) are the distinctive behavioural patterns which contribute to the differences between individuals and groups. 'What is interesting about our human dietetic habits', Medawar asserts, 'is . . . why any one human being will eat this and not that, here and not there, and now and not then'. Other animals exhibit individual preferences too, of course, and are we to suppose that pussy's preference for liver-flavoured Kit-e-Kat is necessarily a more illuminating aspect of its behaviour than its propensity for catching mice?

The same limitations in the basic data which in part prompted our extensive use of studies of animal behaviour confirmed us in our growing belief that there was a need for a branch of archaeology which concentrated upon long-term factors, upon the predictability of some aspects of behaviour, with a view to the establishment of some basic principles which might be seen to unite our present behaviour with that of prehistoric man. For while we can all agree that much of the attraction of individuals and societies lies in their particular personality quirks, yet we should not be blind to the fact that much of human behaviour is governed by biological laws which are nonetheless powerful for their frequently subconscious operation. We feel, furthermore, that archaeological information is peculiarly well fitted to such a generalising rôle, but that it is hopelessly inadequate in almost all cases to deal effectively with the particular.

With this in mind it seemed to us that the nature and development of subsistence economies could usefully be viewed in terms of the interplay between three primary variables: the population, the available resources, and the technology for their exploitation. These have an obvious significance in shaping economic systems at all levels of complexity, and thus provided an appropriate framework for our attempt to view early agricultural systems in their relationship to forms of subsistence which preceded and succeeded them.

The great majority of the work of the Project, both in this volume and elsewhere, has been devoted to our attempts to devise means of dealing with these factors in archaeological terms and with archaeological data, and to the application of those methods to a large sample of study areas in Europe. One might reasonably have expected that, given the nature of its basic data, archaeology would be able to deal effectively with the factor of technology, but less so with the other two primary variables. On the contrary, however. For all the overwhelming predominance of, and significance attached to, artefactual remains in archaeological sites, these usually yield little or nothing in the way of unambiguous information on levels of technology. We know that ploughs were in existence in Europe by 1500 b.c. and that the practice of castrating animals is found by 3000 b.c. We do not know how much earlier either of these phenomena may have occurred, nor how common their practice, nor even the extent of their impact on subsistence economies. Broad technological levels have for the most part, therefore, been inferred indirectly from biological and geographical information. Population and resources, on the other hand, can each be studied by a wide variety of techniques which, while not without their difficulties, provide at least some basic data from which to work. We have in general eschewed precise numerical estimates of both these factors, feeling that our objectives are better served by broad analyses of relative levels and trends than by detailed computations of uncertain accuracy.

In our first volume we discussed means of collecting and analysing biological remains from archaeological sites which represent improvements, in some respects at least, on those otherwise available. Attention was also directed to the need for some way of analysing the off-site data in a more precise way than existing environmental studies offered, and of relating the off-site to the on-site data. From this sprang a series of locational and territorial studies which provide much of the factual basis for the current volume.

Our basic division of this book into coastal, lowland, and upland sections was designed to highlight factors that unified areas within each one of these resource zones even though they might be geographically far apart and very different in their environmental details. It may be worth summarising the main features which emerged as having significance in this context.

Perhaps the most interesting conclusion regarding the coastal zone is that its importance seems almost certain to have been overestimated in the past. This was due to a combination of causes. The great importance in some areas of marine resources today, coupled with their erstwhile near-inexhaustibility, seems to make it a plausible hypothesis that they would have been of comparable significance in prehistory. Furthermore, the archaeological remains of some coastal sites, the shell mounds in particular, are most impressive in

their size and solidity contrasting with the exiguous and flimsy remains which are often all that are encountered elsewhere. What has to be remembered, on the other hand, is the highly sophisticated technology and the investment of labour necessary for the commercial exploitation of deep-sea fisheries. For while the evidence of the early Holocene colonisation of Mediterranean islands testifies to substantial craft and an impressive knowledge of seamanship, this is a far cry from an exploitation of marine resources sufficient to make a substantial impact on the economies of prehistoric Europe.

In some restricted areas, of course, the evidence is that marine resources were of considerable importance, at least at particular sites. It is also true to say that there is a broad relationship between coastal sites and marine and coastal productivity, such that there tend to be more and larger coastal sites in areas of relatively high marine potential. This seems only to be so on a crude zonal level, however, and it is perhaps more interesting from our point of view to note that analysis of individual site locations seems to give little indication that particular sites or groups of sites were situated with a view to gaining preferential access to the resources of sea or coast. Within areas there is rarely any sign that populations were influenced either in their density or distribution by these factors. On the contrary, in some areas at least the details of site location and the exploitation territories can be more easily accommodated to the hypothesis that the population was primarily concerned with the coastal seasonal grazing resources rather than the alternative suggestion of a strandlooping coastal economy. Furthermore, detailed analysis of the contents of shell middens seems to suggest that these, for all their impressive bulk of shells, represent economies which were primarily dependent upon terrestrial resources.

The lowland zone may conveniently be divided into two categories, one of high, the other of low arable potential. The former category emerges overwhelmingly as the region of primary Neolithic expansion into eastern and central Europe. How much this represents movement of people, how much an adoption of a new economy with its attendant demographic and artefactual changes, remains very much an open question. Doubtless both factors were involved. The evidence suggests, however, that the populations identified by their use of Proto-Sesklo, Starčevo–Körös–Criş, and Linear Pottery were mixed agriculturalists whose economy relied sufficiently upon arable agriculture for this to be the dominant factor affecting site location. Again and again the picture is repeated of a conspicuously dense pattern of settlement differentially associated with restricted areas where high fertility combines with amenable soil texture to produce agronomic conditions of high Neolithic arable potential.

A concomitant of this phenomenon is the frequency, in this zone, with which the Neolithic represents a dramatic shift in settlement location and distribution when compared with the preceding Palaeolithic and Mesolithic periods. We may reasonably attribute this change to the economic importance of cereals. As we have argued, pre-Neolithic European economies seem likely to have relied predominantly upon animal products as far as staples are concerned, and a measure of broad continuity of site location might reasonably be expected from the similar constraints to which herd following and pastoral economies were adjusted. The development of plant, particularly cereal, staples was the single major behavioural change in the subsistence economy. They represent the one means by which the productivity of a small section of the environment could be raised, not just by a few degrees but out of all recognition. Conversely, in the areas of low arable potential in both lowlands and uplands we see much more continuity of settlement location, indicating the continuance of animal-based economies.

Even in the lowland zone of high arable potential, however, it is clear that livestock retained a significant place in the economy. This is indicated both by the site contents and also by the frequency with which exploitation territories give good access to areas of rich wetland grazing. Indeed, mixed economic strategies seem to have been vital throughout the zone, even in the areas of richest arable potential. On the extensive loess plateaux, where one might think there would be scope for economies based almost entirely upon the extremely productive arable element, these do not seem to occur. Several factors are concerned in this. We must remember first of all that while the maximum advantage of a single group or settlement might be best served by optimum access to the richest arable, powerful demographic forces will have tended to distribute settlements to the best advantage of the population as a whole. As far as the loesslands are concerned, where water accessible from the surface is commonly restricted to the river valleys, it may well be that lack of drinking water elsewhere was the major factor which tied prehistoric populations predominantly to the valleys. Of more general significance is the consideration that subsistence farmers colonising a new economic niche would have been ill-advised to depend too heavily on a single element in their exploitative armoury. We have no means of assessing accurately the success of Neolithic

husbandry, nor how prone the crops may have been to periodic failure due to climate, pests, or disease. It seems scarcely likely, however, that these were of no significance. Clearly, any population which spread its options by exploiting the available grazing potential as well as the more productive arable potential would greatly enhance its chances of survival in years of crop failure, even if these occurred as seldom as once every generation or so.

It is also relevant, as we have pointed out before, that one of the strengths of the farmyard economy lies in its highly integrated yet flexible structure. The livestock has considerable value for the arable sector as suppliers of manure and in the maintenance of clearings, while the livestock benefits from the grazings available on the fallows and from waste products and surplus from arable production. It was remarked above that we are ignorant of the effectiveness, in many respects, of Neolithic agriculture. At a general level, however, its success is strikingly apparent. The dramatic impact of this powerful combination of cereals, pulses, and the modern farmyard livestock is nowhere better exemplified than by the repeated association of these with high site densities and with evidence of the rapid spread of the new economy.

The nature of this spread has received considerable archaeological attention, to which some of our findings are relevant. It is generally accepted that the agricultural system in operation was a slash-and-burn or long-fallow system, thought to be particularly appropriate to rapid colonisation of new areas. The population movement is thought to have involved a general 'wave of advance', with 'random walk' and 'Brownian motion' models being applied by some to the behaviour of individual communities in their movement to new territories. Our evidence suggests that nothing could be farther from the truth. There is no direct evidence of a slash-and-burn economy, while a number of ethnographic, ecological, and archaeological considerations suggest that a short-fallow crop rotation system may have been in operation. Moreover, what emerges from the study of individual site locations and of patterns of settlement distribution is that specific and precise environmental conditions were sought and recognised by the relevant communities. There is a belief, fostered by the frequent use of distribution maps which reduce most of Europe to the size of a postcard, that Linear Pottery sites are scattered widely and fairly evenly throughout the European loesslands. Gaps are often explained in terms of destruction of sites or lack of research in the relevant areas. Closer examination of particular groups of settlements, coupled with the

CODA

insight which territorial theory gives us into exploitation thresholds, reveals this as a fallacy and emphasises the patchiness of the distributions. Large areas of the loess seem to have been devoid of permanent settlement, like the central areas of the dry plateaux of the Little Polish Upland and the wetter areas of the Middle Rhine.

This selectiveness of colonisation not only gives the lie to the picture of an inexorable 'Neolithic Invasion' rolling through Europe, impelled by whatever forces, but bespeaks a sophisticated knowledge of the relevant aspects of the environment. These were no hopeful travellers into the unknown, but people reliably able to locate and exploit particular sets of conditions. We are reminded of the frequency with which technologically primitive agriculturalists are able to assess accurately agronomic potential from existing vegetation. We do well to remember not only the sophisticated and accurate ecological knowledge, which plays a frequent and important part in the subsistence of many 'simple' economies, but also the abstract, quasi-scientific spirit of enquiry which sometimes accompanies it, albeit haphazardly for the most part. While we cannot, of course, assume anything directly from this as far as prehistoric Europe is concerned, it should nevertheless warn us to beware the easy assumption that the Linear Pottery farmers were economic babes in the Neolithic wood.

A related factor of some interest is the evidence for the *economic opportunism* of the Neolithic populations of Europe. A good example of this is provided by the Tavoliere of southern Italy. An area of conspicuously dense Neolithic settlement, it seems to have been thinly occupied if at all for most of the preceding periods. Field analysis (Jarman, M. R. & Webley 1975) suggested that Neolithic exploitation was dependent upon soil changes which probably took place in the early Holocene. With the earliest dates for Neolithic settlements being as early as the late sixth millennium B.C., it seems that advantage was taken of this newly available arable potential very shortly after it became available. The colonisation of chernozems of high arable potential in Hungary shortly after their formation, and the expansion of the Neolithic farmyard economy onto the North European Plain during what was probably a drier phase may well be comparable examples.

The category of low arable potential presents a very different picture. Two interrelated features seem to dominate here. For the most part the traditional Neolithic economy is late in appearing, and, while artefactual traits such as pottery sometimes occur at relatively early dates, the economic development from

characteristically early Holocene economies to those more typical of the late Holocene tends to be gradual and delayed. Along with this goes a pronounced tendency towards strongly animal-based economies, unsurprising in view of the environmental limitations. Thus typically in Mediterranean Europe there is an evolution from economies based on red deer plus *Equus hydruntinus* to those based on sheep plus goat. Further north economies dominated by red deer, pig, and cattle are gradually supplanted by those in which, with gradual deforestation, the caprines take the place of the deer.

Convenient though it is, we must not overemphasise the distinction between the high and low arable potential categories, for they are cross-cut by crucial links with each other and with the other primary resource zones. These economic links involve the movements of men and their animals, and are primarily designed to accommodate and to profit from the seasonal variation in grazing resources.

Just as the importance in prehistory of coastal and marine resources seems consistently to have been overestimated, that of the upland zone has surely been greatly underestimated. For a variety of reasons which involve the deposition, preservation, and recovery of archaeological data, very little is known in most instances about upland settlement and subsistence in prehistory. As we have emphasised many times, however, the obstinate blanks on archaeological distribution maps need to be examined carefully before we are justified in concluding that they were not occupied or exploited. The uplands of Europe represent a colossal reservoir of summer grazing. While they are unlikely to have carried large permanent human populations in prehistory, their rôle in providing a summer range for innumerable herbivores and their herders is of importance both in itself and for the light which it throws upon the contemporaneous lowland economies. Not only do the enormous areas of upland in some degree compensate for their low human carrying capacity per unit area by their very vastness; we must also remember that many of the lowland grazings could only be exploited very inefficiently were it not for their incorporation in a mobile economy with the complementary upland resources. The mobility of most of these exploitation systems is one of the most important factors contributing to their archaeological underrepresentation. Mobile herdsmen often have shelters which are themselves mobile or ephemeral, and possess a minimum of artefactual clutter. Where belongings must habitually be carried for long distances, unnecessary equipment is an expensive luxury indeed.

CODA

We have discussed elsewhere the fact that, despite some apparent recent evidence to the contrary, human populations tend to increase in irregular jumps, and not smoothly. The same general point may be made of technological progress, and, hence, the level of available resources dependent upon this. When we come to examine the all-important arable element in European farming as we now know it, it can be seen to have developed in a series of steps. The evolution of the Holocene exploitation of lowland Europe may be viewed as the successive overcoming of the thresholds presented by environmental barriers.

The general picture is simple enough. Where it is environmentally suited arable agriculture is so much more productive than pastoralism that whenever there was any incentive to increase production man will, given the opportunity, have grown plants rather than animals. Until recently, at least, there has always been a sufficient superfluity of land which could only be used for non-arable purposes for a real shortage of animal products not to have been an important issue in Europe. Thus the whole prehistoric and historic development of lowland agriculture has been dominated by the ever increasing areas under the plough, and the ever more sophisticated means to maintain and increase crop yields.

Given the nature and origin of the dominant plant species of the farmyard economy it is scarcely surprising that their early successful cultivation in Europe was limited to areas of light and easily tilled soils in the southern Balkans. Subsequent thrusts saw the economic system expand first onto the suitable soils of the climatically sub-Mediterranean areas within the northern Balkans and central Europe, and then throughout the prime cereal producing areas accessible to the available technology in central and northwestern Europe. We have already remarked the selectiveness of the exploitation of arable land. Sielmann (1971) documents in some detail the narrow climatic limits within which Linear Pottery agriculture operated, and has shown how these were gradually expanded with passing time and rising population. Later still the lower arable potential fringes, and the many interstices in the existing pattern of exploitation, began to attract arable farmers until, by 3000 b.c. or shortly after, the small arable potential of even such unpromising areas as the sub-Alpine region and southern Scandinavia were being exploited. The process has continued to the present day. By the middle of the Bronze Age, as we have seen, continuing population pressure had necessitated the permanent occupation of some of the upland fringes. As Fox pointed out long ago, advances in agricultural technology allowed the Anglo-Saxons to exploit much heavier soils than could have been tilled effectively before. Even today, every year sees a record area of Europe under the plough, as waterlogged soils are drained, forests cleared, and areas of low fertility treated with chemical fertilisers.

The time gaps which intervened between these various developments represent the natural and inevitable delays in the evolution of the varied and complex adaptations which permitted the geographical spread of arable agriculture. For while some of these were technological, others would have involved changes in the crops themselves, as through conscious human selection or natural selection they became better adapted to their new environments. One aspect which would have been of increasing importance as time went on is that of the investment requirement as technology became more sophisticated and an increasingly dominant factor in the subsistence equation. Thus the 'Neolithic invasion' may be viewed as the rapid colonisation by a species of a rapidly changing economic niche (as opposed to a new territory) pretty much as soon as circumstances permitted. The process was facilitated and reinforced by the adaptability that springs from man's technological capacity, permitting both greater intensification and diversification than are commonly available to animals.

It is very tempting to close the volume with a bang, rather than a whimper, and to make resounding claims for the future developments of the approaches outlined here. We toyed for some time with the idea of entitling this volume *Palaeoethology*, and of using our data as the basis for a formulation of that subject. This seemed an attractive notion because of the close parallels between our preoccupation with certain aspects of human behaviour and that of ethologists with the behaviour of other animals. We abandoned the scheme for a number of reasons. Despite our attempt to show, in the last chapter, that our views might have relevance beyond the strict confines of economic behaviour, archaeology does not yet seem in a position to make the synthesis which would be implied by such a title. Ethology itself is disunited on the proper focus and framework for its studies and also on the question of the applicability of its theories and procedures to human behaviour. Furthermore, so much of the ethology with which archaeologists and anthropologists are familiar is narrowly concerned with the social and psychological behaviour of primates that there seemed a danger that we might mistakenly be identified with

CODA

this *genre*. We do well, therefore, to temper a justified optimism with caution.

We nevertheless feel that it is in this direction that one branch of archaeological studies may usefully develop and we begin to see the possibility of making some headway. We started the book with the suggestion that one important objective of archaeology was to provide the basis for a scientific study of past human behaviour; and furthermore, that such a study would have inevitable repercussions on our views of our present-day behaviour. Other rapidly developing disciplines focus on the elucidation of modern human behaviour, but these for the most part lack time depth, and thus a crucial evolutionary perspective. Many aspects of our data, on the other hand, lend themselves most appropriately to this viewpoint. For we must not forget that we are as archaeologists above all studying an evolutionary record of *success*. Failure will rarely have survived sufficiently to be preserved intelligibly in our exiguous record, and we are in general faced almost by definition with the evidence of those populations and economies which achieved long-term fitness.

We should perhaps re-emphasise the phrase '*one important objective*'. For we have returned to our starting point here, and to the primacy of the question of what kind of archaeology it is that we wish to pursue. Doubtless the traditional objectives of archaeology will continue to attract adherents. One can play chess with artefactual attributes, or construct and substantiate a kind of prehistorical mythology. We have chosen as our central aim the analysis of those aspects of human behaviour which have long-term biological significance. The disciplines which seem at present to offer the most suitable framework for such a study are variously described as ethology, behavioural ecology, evolutionary biology, and sociobiology.

We are confronted here with a paradox. As we have argued, we cannot satisfactorily study archaeology primarily in terms of models developed by these disciplines as they stand. These customarily require a degree of control over the data and a rigorous level of testability which are not in prospect for our subject. Archaeological data are inadequate to support the complex theoretical structures which will be necessary to produce a synthesis of present biological, anthropological, and sociological interests, along with those of other disciplines concerned with a coherent science of human behaviour. This means that in the long run much of archaeology seems destined to be cannibalised by other disciplines better suited to this task, leaving perhaps a residue of historically and ethnologically orientated studies.

But this is for the future. There exist repeated, but often inadequate, discussions of the prehistory of economic development, warfare, demography and territoriality, and of the relationship of these factors to cultural development in the work of those concerned to formulate a human ethology. These should assure us that there is much to be done, and that there remains a secure, indeed a vital, place for bioarchaeological studies. The inevitable difficulty experienced by specialists in other fields in synthesising accurately the welter of relevant archaeological information highlights the great importance of an archaeological approach which is itself inherently biologically based. As is clear from recent exploratory essays into the area (see for example Tinbergen 1976, Wilson 1975), any attempt to relate human behaviour to biological principles absolutely requires a consideration of data which only archaeology can provide. The subject thus has a significant contribution to make to a science of human behaviour.

REFERENCES

Aalen, F. H. A. (1978) *Man and the Landscape in Ireland*. London: Academic Press.

Admiralty (1920) *A Handbook of Rumania*. London: Naval Intelligence Division, Admiralty.

Agricultural Development and Advisory Service (1971) *Soil Field Handbook*. London.

Albrethsen, S. E. & Brinch Petersen, E. (1977) Excavation of a Mesolithic cemetery at Vedbaele, Denmark. *Acta Archaeologica* **47**, 1–28.

Alcalde del Rio, H., Breuil, H. & Sierra, L. (1911) *Les Cavernes de la Région Cantabrique (Espagne)*, 2 vols. Monaco: Imprimerie Vve A. Cherie.

Allan, W. (1972) Ecology, techniques and settlement patterns. In *Man, Settlement and Urbanism*, ed. P. J. Ucko, R. Tringham & G. W. Dimbleby, pp. 211–26. London: Duckworth.

Allbaugh, L. G. (1953) *Crete (A Case Study of an Undeveloped Area)*. Princeton: Princeton University Press.

Allee, W. C., Emerson, A. E., Park, O., Park, T. & Schmidt, K. P. (1949) *Principles of Animal Ecology*. Philadelphia: Saunders.

Allen, W. L. A. & Richardson, J. B. (1971) The reconstruction of kinship from archaeological data: The concepts, the methods and the feasibility. *American Antiquity* **36**, 41–53.

Altuna, J. (1971) Los mamíferos del yacimiento Prehistórico de Morín (Santander). In *Cueva Morín: Excavaciones 1966–1968*, by J. González Echegaray, L. G. Freeman *et al*. Santander: Patronato de las Cuevas Prehistóricas.

Ammerman, A. J. & Cavalli-Sforza, L. L. (1971) Measuring the rate of spread of early farming in Europe. *Man* **6**, 674–88.

Ammerman, A. J. & Cavalli-Sforza, L. L. (1973) A population model for the diffusion of early farming in Europe. In *The Explanation of Culture Change: Models in Prehistory*, ed. C. Renfrew, pp. 341–57. London: Duckworth.

Andersen, S. H. (1973) Overgangen fra aeldre til yngre Stenalder I Sydskandinavien set fra en Mesolitisk synsvinkel. In Bonde-Veidemann Bofast-Ikke Bofast I Nordisk Forhistorie, ed. P. Simonsen & G. Stamsø Munch, pp. 26–44. *Tromsö Museums Skrifter* 14.

Andersen, S. H. (1975) Ringkloster: en jysk inlandsboplads med Ertebøllekultur. *Kuml* **1973–4**, 10–108.

Anderson, A. J. (1976) *Prehistoric Competition and Economic Change in Northern Sweden*. Unpublished Ph.D. Thesis, University of Cambridge.

Andersson, B. (1974) Flyinventering av älgstammen inom Strömsunds kommun, Jämtlands Län. Unpublished manuscript.

Arambourou, R. & Mohen, J.-P. (1977) Une sépulture sous tumulus du VIIᵉ siècle avant notre ère à St Vincent-de Tyrosse (Landes). *Bulletin de la Société Préhistorique Française* **74**, 91–5.

Arbos, P. (1922) *La Vie Pastorale dans les Alpes Françaises: Etude de Géographie Humaine*. Paris: Librairie Armand Colin.

Arnon, I. (1972) *Crop Production in Dry Regions*, 2 vols. London: Leonard Hill.

Ascher, R. (1962) Ethnography for archaeology: a case from the Seri Indians. *Ethnology* **1**, 360–9.

Bagolini, B. & Biagi, P. (1975) L'insediamento di Garniga (Trento) e considerazioni sul neolitico delle Valle dell'Adige nell'ambito dell'Italia Settentrionale. *Preistoria Alpina* **11**, 7–24.

Bagolini, B., Barbacori, F., Castelletti, L. & Lanziger, M. (1975) Colbricon (scavi 1973–1974). *Preistoria Alpina* **11**, 201–35.

Bahn, P. G. (1976) Les Bâtons Troués: réveil d'une hypothèse abandonnée. *Bulletin de la Société Préhistorique de l'Ariège* **31**, 47–54.

Bahn, P. G. (1977) Seasonal migration in S.W. France during the late Glacial period. *Journal of Archaeological Science* **4**, 245–57.

Bahn, P. G. (1978) The 'unacceptable face' of the West European Upper Palaeolithic. *Antiquity* **52**, 183–92.

Bailey, G. N. (1973) Concheros del norte de España: Una hipótesis preliminar. *Actas del XII Congreso Nacional de Arqueología (1971)* **12**, 73–83.

Bailey, G. N. (1975a) The role of molluscs in coastal economies: the results of midden analysis in Australia. *Journal of Archaeological Science* **2**, 45–62.

Bailey, G. N. (1975b) *The Role of Shell Middens in Prehistoric Economies*. Unpublished Ph.D. Thesis, University of Cambridge.

Bailey, G. N. (1977) Shell mounds, shell middens and raised beaches in the Cape York Peninsula. *Mankind* **11**, 132–43.

Bailey, G. N. (1978) Shell middens as indicators of postglacial economies: a territorial perspective. In *The Early Postglacial Settlement of Northern Europe*, ed. P. Mellars, pp. 37–63. London: Duckworth.

Bakels, C. C. (1978) Four Linearbandkeramik settlements and their environment: a paleoecological study of Sittard, Stein, Elsloo and Hienheim. *Analecta Praehistorica Leidensia* **11**, 1–244.

REFERENCES

Bakker, J. A., Vogel, J. C. & Wislanski, T. (1969) TRB and other C14 dates from Poland. *Helinium* **9**, 3–27.

Balikci, A. (1968) The Netsilik Eskimos: adaptive processes. In *Man the Hunter*, ed. R. B. Lee & I. DeVore, pp. 78–82. Chicago: Aldine.

Banu, A. E. (1971) *Delta Dunării (Studiu de geographe fizica)*. Ph.D. Thesis, Bucharest.

Barandiarán, J.-M. de (1951) En el Pirineo Vasco – Crónica de Prehistoria. *Enski-Jakintza* **5**, 243–56.

Barandiarán, J.-M. de (1953) *El Hombre Prehistórico en el País Vasco*. Buenos Aires.

Barfield, L. H. (1971) *Northern Italy; Before Rome*. London: Thames & Hudson.

Barker, G. W. W. (1972) The conditions of cultural and economic growth in the Bronze Age of central Italy. *Proceedings of the Prehistoric Society* **38**, 170–208.

Barker, G. W. W. (1975a) Early Neolithic land use in Yugoslavia. *Proceedings of the Prehistoric Society* **41**, 85–104.

Barker, G. W. W. (1975b) Prehistoric territories and economies in central Italy. In *Palaeoeconomy*, ed. E. S. Higgs, pp. 111–75. Cambridge: Cambridge University Press.

Barker, G. W. W. & Webley, D. (1978) Causewayed camps and Early Neolithic economies in central southern England. *Proceedings of the Prehistoric Society* **44**, 161–86.

Barth, F. (1959–60) The land use pattern of migratory tribes of South Persia. *Norsk Geografisk Tidsskrift* **17**(1–4), 1–11.

Baudou, E. (1968) Forntida bebyggelse i Ångermanlands Kustland: Arkeologiska undersökningar av Ångermanlandska Kuströsen. *Arkiv för Norrländsk hembygdsforskning* 17. (Härnosand).

Baudou, E. (1973) A programme for archaeological and ecological research of prehistoric and historical material from northern Sweden II: The cultural concept in the north Swedish Stone Age. In *Circumpolar Problems: Habitat, Economy and Social Relations in the Arctic*, ed. G. Berg, pp. 15–20. Oxford: Pergamon Press.

Baumhoff, M. A. (1963) Ecological determinants of Aboriginal California populations. *University of California Publications in American Archaeology and Ethnology* **49**, 155–236.

Bay-Petersen, J. (1975) *Pre-Neolithic Faunal Exploitation in Southern France and Denmark*. Unpublished Ph.D. Thesis, University of Cambridge.

Bay-Petersen, J. (1978) Animal exploitation in Mesolithic Denmark. In *The Early Postglacial Settlement of Northern Europe*, ed. P. Mellars, pp. 115–45. London: Duckworth.

Becker, C. J. (1954) Stenalderbebyggelsen ved Store Valby i Vestsjaelland. Problemer omkring tragt-baeger kulturens aeldste og yngste fase. *Aarbøger for nordisk Oldkyndighed og Historie*, 127–83.

Begines Ramírez, A. (1965) Avance al catálogo de cavidades de la Provincia de Santander. *Cuadernos de Espeleología* **1**, 43–6.

Berg, L. S. (1964) *Loess as a Product of Weathering and Soil Formation*. Jerusalem: Israel Programme for Scientific Translations.

Bertsch, K. (1928) Waldgeschichte des Württembergischen Bodenseegebiets. *Schriften des Vereins für Geschichte des Bodensees* **56**, 221–68.

Biagi, P. (1972) Il giacimento sopra Fienile Rossino sull'Altipiano di Cariadeghe (Serle-Brescia). *Preistoria Alpina* **8**, 177–97.

Bigalke, E. H. (1974) The exploitation of shellfish by coastal tribesmen of the Transkei. *Annals of the Cape Provincial Museums, Natural History* **9**, 159–75.

Binford, L. R. (1968) Post-Pleistocene adaptations. In *New Perspectives in Archaeology*, ed. S. R. & L. R. Binford, pp. 313–41. Chicago: Aldine.

Bintliff, J. L. (1975) Mediterranean alluviation: new evidence from archaeology. *Proceedings of the Prehistoric Society* **41**, 78–84.

Bintliff, J. L. (1977) Natural environment and human settlement in prehistoric Greece. Part 1. *British Archaeological Reports, Supplementary Series* 28 (1).

Bird, J. (1938) Antiquity and migrations of the early inhabitants of Patagonia. *Geographical Review* **28**, 250–75.

Bird, J. (1946) The Alacaluf. In *Handbook of South American Indians, Vol. 1: The Marginal Tribes*, ed. J. H. Steward. *Smithsonian Institution. Bulletin of the Bureau of American Ethnology* **143**, 55–80.

Birdsell, J. B. (1968) Some predictions for the Pleistocene based on equilibrium systems among recent hunter-gatherers. In *Man the Hunter*, ed. R. B. Lee & I. De Vore, pp. 229–40. Chicago: Aldine.

Birket-Smith, K. (1929) The Caribou Eskimos. *Report of the 5th Thule Expedition 1921–24*, Vol. 5, Part 1. Copenhagen: Gyldeddalske Boghandel, Nordisk Forlag.

Birket-Smith, K. (1953) The Chugach Eskimo. *Nationalmuseets Skrifter Etnografisk Række* **6**, 1–262.

Blot, J. (1974) Contribution à la protohistoire en Pays Basque. Nouveaux vestiges mégalithiques en Pays Basque (I–VII). Collected work from *Bulletin du Musée Basque*.

Boessneck, J., Jéquier, J.-P. & Stampfli, H. R. (1963). Seeberg, Burgäschisee-Süd: Die Tierreste. *Acta Bernensia* **2** (3).

Bökönyi, S. (1974) *History of Domestic Mammals in Central and Eastern Europe*. Budapest: Akadémiai Kiadó.

Boserup, E. (1965) *The Conditions of Agricultural Growth. The Economics of Agrarian Change Under Population Pressure*. London: Allen & Unwin.

Bottema, S. (1967) A late Quaternary pollen diagram from Ioannina, North-Western Greece. *Proceedings of the Prehistoric Society* **33**, 26–9.

Bouchud, J. (1966) *Essai sur le renne et la climatologie du Paléolithique moyen et supérieur*. Perigueux, Imprimerie Magne.

Bowen, T. (1976) Seri prehistory: the archeology of the central coast of Sonora, Mexico. *Anthropological Papers of the University of Arizona* 27.

Bowes, A. de P. & Church, C. F. (1966) *Food Values of*

REFERENCES

Portions Commonly Used, 10th edn London: Pitman Medical.

Bradfield, R. M. (1971) The changing pattern of Hopi agriculture. *Royal Anthropological Institute Occasional Paper 30*.

Braidwood, R. J. (1960) The agricultural revolution. *Scientific American* **203**, 130–48.

Braithwaite, R. B. (1953) *Scientific Explanation; a Study of the Function of Theory, Probability and Law in Science*. Cambridge: Cambridge University Press.

Brandon-Cox, H. (1969) *The Trail of the Arctic Nomads*. London: William Kimber.

Broadbent, N. D. (1978) Prehistoric settlement in northern Sweden: a brief survey and a case study. In *The Early Postglacial Settlement of Northern Europe*, ed. P. A. Mellars, pp. 177–204. London: Duckworth.

Brody, H. (1976) Inuit land use in north Baffin Island and northern Foxe Basin. In *Inuit Land Use and Occupancy Project*, ed. M. M. R. Freeman, Vol. 1, pp. 153–71. Ottawa: Department of Indian and Northern Affairs.

Broglio, A. (1971) Risultati preliminari delle ricerche sui complessi epipaleolithici della Valle dell'Adige. *Preistoria Alpina* **7**, 135–241.

Bronson, B. (1972) Farm labor and the evolution of food production. In *Population Growth: Anthropological Implications*, ed. B. Spooner, pp. 190–218. Cambridge, Mass.: MIT Press.

Brookfield, H. C. & Brown, P. (1963) *Struggle for Land: Agriculture and Group Territories among the Chimbu of the New Guinea Highlands*. Melbourne: Oxford University Press.

Browman, D. L. (1976) Demographic correlations of the Wari conquest of Junin. *American Antiquity* **41**, 465–77.

Burch, E. S. (1972) The caribou/wild reindeer as a human resource. *American Antiquity* **37**, 339–68.

Burkill, I. H. (1960) The organography and the evolution of Dioscoreaceae, the family of the yams. *Journal of the Linnaean Society (Botany)* **56**(367), 319–412.

Cabrera, V. & Bernaldo de Quirós, F. (1977) The Solutrean site of Cueva Chufín (Santander, Spain). *Current Anthropology* **18**, 780–1.

Campbell, A. (1948) Fran Vildmark till Bygd: En etnolgisk undersökning i Lappland före industrialismens genombrott. *Skrifter utgivna Genom Landsmals – och Folkminnesarkivet i Uppsala Ser. B*, **5**.

Campbell, A. H. (1965) Elementary food production by the Australian Aborigines. *Mankind* 6, 206–11.

Carballo, J. & González Echegaray, J. (1952) Algunos objetos inéditos de la cueva de El Pendo. *Ampurias* **14**, 37–48.

Carleton, M. A. (1901) Emmer: a grain for the semiarid regions. *Farmers Bulletin* 139. Washington: Government Printing Office.

Carneiro, R. (1961) Slash and burn cultivation among the Kuikuru and its implications for cultural development in the Amazon Basin. In *The Evolution of Horticultural Systems in Native South America: Causes and Consequences*, ed. J. Wilbert, pp. 47–67. *Anthropologica Supp. Publication No. 2*.

Carr, E. H. (1961) *What is History?* London: Macmillan.

Chagnon, N. A. (1968) *Yanomamö: the Fierce People*. New York: Holt, Rinehart & Winston.

Childe, V. G. (1929) *The Danube in Prehistory*. Oxford: Oxford University Press.

Childe, V. G. (1952) *New Light on the Most Ancient East*, 4th edn. London: Kegan Paul, Trench, Trubner.

Chisholm, M. (1968) *Rural Settlement and Land Use*, 2nd edn. London: Hutchinson.

Chiţu, C. (1975) *Relieful şi Solurile României*. Craïova.

Christiansen, C. H. & Skelmose, K. (1963) Gudenåkulturen ved Varde å. *Kuml* **1962**, 144–56.

Christiansson, H. & Broadbent, N. D. (1975) Prehistoric coastal settlement on the Upper Bothnian coast of northern Sweden. In *Prehistoric Maritime Adaptations of the Circumpolar Zone*, ed. W. Fitzhugh, pp. 47–55. The Hague: Mouton.

Clark, C. & Haswell, M. (1967) *The Economics of Subsistence Agriculture*, 4th edn. London: Macmillan.

Clark, G. A. (1971) The Asturian of Cantabria: subsistence base and the evidence for Post-Pleistocene climatic shifts. *American Anthropologist* **73**, 1244–57.

Clark, G. A. (1975) Liencres: una estación al aire libre de estilo Asturiense cerca de Santander. *Cuadernos de Arqueología* **3**, 1–59, 71–84.

Clark, G. A. & Straus, L. G. (1977) La Riera Paleoecological Project: preliminary report, 1976 excavations. *Current Anthropology* **18**, 354–5.

Clark, G. A., Straus, L G. & Fuentes de M. C. (1975) Preliminary site survey of the Meseta del Norte, northern Burgos Province, Spain. *Current Anthropology* **16**, 283–6.

Clark, J. G. D. (1945) Farmers and forests in Neolithic Europe. *Antiquity* **19**, 57–71.

Clark, J. G. D. (1948) The development of fishing in prehistoric Europe. *The Antiquaries Journal* **27**, 45–85.

Clark, J. G. D. (1952) *Prehistoric Europe: the Economic Basis*. London: Methuen.

Clark, J. G. D. (1972) Star Carr: a case study in bioarchaeology. Reading, Mass.: *Addison-Wesley Modular Publications* 10.

Clark, J. G. D. (1975) *The Earlier Stone Age Settlement of Scandinavia*. Cambridge: Cambridge University Press.

Clark, J. G. D. (1977) The economic context of dolmens and passage-graves in Sweden. In *Ancient Europe and the Mediterranean*, ed. V. Markotic, pp. 35–49. Warminster: Aris & Phillips.

Clarke, D. L. (1968) *Analytical Archaeology*. London: Methuen.

Clarke, D. L. (1972) Models and paradigms in contemporary archaeology. In *Models in Archaeology*, ed. D. L. Clarke, pp. 1–60. London: Methuen.

Clarke, D. L. (1976) Mesolithic Europe: the economic basis. In *Problems in Economic and Social Archaeology*, ed. G.

REFERENCES

de G. Sieveking, I. H. Longworth & K. E. Wilson, pp. 449–81. London: Duckworth.

Clastres, P. (1972) The Guayaki. In *Hunters and Gatherers Today*, ed. M. G. Bicchieri, pp. 138–74. New York: Holt, Rinehart & Winston.

Clout, H. D. (1977) *Themes in the Historical Geography of France*. London: Academic Press.

Cohen, M. N. (1977) *The Food Crisis in Prehistory*. New Haven: Yale University Press.

Cole, J. W. & Wolf, E. R. (1974) *The Hidden Frontier: Ecology and Ethnicity in an Alpine Village*. New York: Academic Press.

Collet, L. W. (1922) Alpine lakes. *Scottish Geographical Magazine* **38,** 73–101.

Collier, S. & White, J. P. (1976) Get them young? Age and sex inferences on animal domestication in archaeology. *American Antiquity* **41,** 96–102.

Condurachi, E. & Daicoviciu, C. (1971) *The Ancient Civilisation of Romania*. London: Barrie & Jenkins.

Conklin, H. C. (1957) *Hanunóo Agriculture*. Rome: United Nations FAO.

Cook, S. F. (1972) Prehistoric demography. Reading, Mass.: *Addison-Wesley Modular Publication* 16.

Coull, J. R. (1972) *The Fisheries of Europe*. London: Bell.

Crisler, L. (1956) Some observations on wolves hunting caribou. *Journal of Mammalogy* **37,** 337–46.

Crook, J. H. (1968) The nature and function of territorial aggression. In *Man and Aggression*, ed. F. M. Ashley Montague, pp. 183–220. New York: Oxford University Press.

Damas, D. (1972) The Copper Eskimo. In *Hunters and Gatherers Today*, ed. M. G. Bicchieri, pp. 3–50. New York: Holt, Rinehart & Winston.

Darling, F. F. (1937) *A Herd of Red Deer*. London: Oxford University Press.

Dart, R. A. (1967) Mousterian osteodontokeratic objects from Geula Cave (Haifa, Israel). *Quaternaria* **9,** 69–140.

Davidescu, D., Davidescu, V., Crisan, I. & Reichbuch, L. (1975) Potassium and the nutritive balance of plants. In *Potassium Research and Agricultural Production. Proceedings of the 10th Congress of the International Potash Institute, 1974*, pp. 171–87. Bern: Der Bund.

Davidson, S., Passmore, R. & Brock, J. F. (1972) *Human Nutrition and Dietetics*, 5th edn. Edinburgh: Churchill Livingstone.

Degerbøl, M. & Krog, H. (1959) The reindeer (*Rangifer tarandus* L.) in Denmark. *Biologiske Skrifter udg. af det Kongelige Danske Videnskabernes Selskab*. **10,** 4.

Delano Smith, C. & Smith, C. (1973) The Bronze Age on the Tavoliere, Italy. *Proceedings of the Prehistoric Society* **39,** 454–6.

Dennell, R. W. & Webley, D. (1975) Prehistoric settlement and land use in southern Bulgaria. In *Palaeoeconomy*, ed. E. S. Higgs, pp. 97–109. Cambridge: Cambridge University Press.

DeVore, I. & Washburn, S. (1963) Baboon ecology and human evolution. In *African Ecology and Human Evolution*, ed. F. Clark Howell & F. Bourlière, pp. 335–67. Viking Fund Publications in Anthropology 36. Chicago: Aldine.

Dickinson, R. E. (1961) *Germany: a General and Regional Geography*. London: Methuen.

Dimbleby, G. W. (1967) *Plants and Archaeology*. London: John Baker.

Documenta Geigy (1962) *Scientific Tables*, 6th edn. Macclesfield, Cheshire: Geigy (U.K.) Ltd.

Donald, L. (1970) Food production by the Yalunka household, Sierra Leone. In *African Food Production Systems*, ed. P. F. M. McLaughlin, pp. 165–91. Baltimore & London: John Hopkins Press.

Driehaus, J. (1960) *Die Altheimer Gruppe und das Jungneolithikum im Mitteleuropa*. Mainz: Römisch-Germanisches Zentralmuseum.

Duby, G. (1968) *Rural Economy and Country Life in the Medieval West*. London: Edward Arnold.

Duckham, A. N. & Masefield, G. B. (1970) *Farming Systems of the World*. London: Chatto & Windus.

Ducos, P. (1969) Methodology and results of the study of the earliest domesticated animals in the Near East (Palestine). In *The Domestication and Exploitation of Plants and Animals*, ed. P. J. Ucko & G. W. Dimbleby, pp. 265–75. London: Duckworth.

Ducos, P. (1976) Communautés villageoises et origine de la domestication en Syro-Palestine. *Union Internationale des Sciences Préhistoriques et Protohistoriques, IXe Congrès*. Nice, Colloque XX, pp. 145–52.

Dyson-Hudson, N. (1972) The study of nomads. *Journal of Asian & African Studies* **7**(1–2), 2–29.

Earle, T. K. (1976) A nearest-neighbor analysis of two formative settlement systems. In *The Early Mesoamerican Village*, ed. K. V. Flannery, pp. 196–223. New York: Academic Press.

East, W. G. (1966) *An Historical Geography of Europe*, 5th edn. London: Methuen.

Ehrlich, B. (1940) Schnurkeramische Pfostenhäuser bei Tolkemit Kr. Elbing. *Mannus* **32,** 44–56.

Eidlitz, K. (1969) Food and emergency food in the circumpolar area. *Studia Ethnographia Upsaliensia* 32.

Ekvall, R. B. (1968) *Fields on the Hoof*. New York: Holt, Rinehart & Winston.

Emperaire, J. (1955) *Les Nomades de la Mer*, 2nd edn. Paris: Gallinard.

Engel, C. (1931) Zur Vorgeschichte der Kurische Nehrung. *Mannus* Ergänzungsband 8.

Enyedi, G. (1971) Economic geographical problems of the Great Hungarian Plain. In *The Changing Face of the Great Hungarian Plain*, ed. B. Sarfalvi, pp. 9–33. Budapest: Akadémiai Kiadó.

Estes, R. D. & Goddard, J. (1967) Prey selection and hunting behaviour in the African wild dog. *Journal of Wildlife Management* **31,** 52–70.

Evans, J. D. & Renfrew, A. C. (1968) *Excavations at Saliagos near Antiparos*. British School of Archaeology at

REFERENCES

Athens, Supplementary Volume No. 5. London: Thames & Hudson.

Evans-Pritchard, E. E. (1940) *The Nuer*. London: Oxford University Press.

Evett, D. & Renfrew, J. (1971) L'agricoltura neolitica italiana: una nota sui cereali. *Revista di scienze preistoriche* **26**, 403–9.

FAO (1979) *1978 FAO Production Yearbook*, Vol. 32. Rome: FAO.

Farruggia, J. P., Kuper, R., Lüning, J. & Stehli, P. (1973) Untersuchungen zur neolithischen Besiedlung der Aldenhovener Platte III. *Bonner Jahrbücher* **173**, 226–56.

Fedele, F. (1973) Un vaso a bocca quadrata sul Monfenera, Valsesia (scavi 1969–72). Rapporto preliminare. *Preistoria Alpina* **9**, 223–92.

Fel, A. (1977) Petite culture 1750–1850. In *Themes in the Historical Geography of France*, ed. H. D. Clout, pp. 215–45. London: Academic Press.

Fernández-Tresguerres, J. (1976) Enterramiento Aziliense en la Cueva de Los Azules I. *Boletín del Instituto de Estudios Asturianos* **87**, 273–88.

Firth, R., ed. (1967) *Themes in Economic Anthropology*. (Association of Social Anthropologists Monograph 6.) London: Tavistock.

Fischer, P.-H. (1925) Mollusques Quaternaires récoltes dans la grotte de Castillo (Espagne, province de Santander). *Journal de Conchyliologie* **68**, 320–3.

Flannery, K. V. (1969) Origins and ecological effects of early domestication in Iran and the Near East. In *The Domestication and Exploitation of Plants and Animals*, ed. P. J. Ucko & G. W. Dimbleby, pp. 73–100. London: Duckworth.

Flannery, K. V., ed. (1976) *The Early Mesoamerican Village*. New York: Academic Press.

Fleming, A. (1971) Territorial patterns in Bronze Age Wessex. *Proceedings of the Prehistoric Society* **37**, 138–66.

Follieri, M. (1971) Researches on prehistoric agriculture. Paper presented at Third International Congress of the Museum of Agriculture, Budapest.

Fowler, P. J. (1971) Early prehistoric agriculture in Western Europe: some archaeological evidence. In *Economy and Settlement in Neolithic and Early Bronze Age Britain and Europe*, ed. D. D. A. Simpson, pp. 153–79. Leicester: Leicester University Press.

Freeman, L. G. (1973) The significance of mammalian faunas from Paleolithic occupations in Cantabrian Spain. *American Antiquity* **38**, 3–44.

Freeman, M. M. R., ed. (1976) *Inuit Land Use and Occupancy Project*, 3 vols. Ottawa: Department of Indian & Northern Affairs.

Freeman, T. W. (1950) *Ireland, a General and Regional Geography*. London: Methuen.

French, D. H. (1967) *Index of Prehistoric Sites in Central Macedonia*. Athens: unpublished manuscript.

Freund, G. (1963) Die ältere und die mittlere Steinzeit in Bayern. *Jahresbericht der bayerischen Bodendenkmalpflege* **4**, 9–167.

Friis Johansen, K. (1919) En boplads fra den aeldste Stenalder i Svaerdborg Mose. *Aarbøger for nordisk Oldkyndighed og Historie* (Series 3), **9**, 106–235.

Fuller, W. A. (1962) The biology and management of the bison of Wood Buffalo National Park. *Wildlife Management Bulletin, Ottawa* **1**, 1–52.

García Guinea, M. A. (1968) *Los Grabados de la Cueva de la Peña del Cuco en Castro Urdiales y de la Cueva de Cobrantes (Valle de Aras)*. Santander: Publicaciones del Patronato de las Cuevas Prehistóricas de la Provincia de Santander, **3**.

Gardner, P. M. (1972) The Paliyans. In *Hunters and Gatherers Today*, ed. M. G. Bicchieri, pp. 404–47. New York: Holt, Rinehart & Winston.

Garner, H. V. & Dyke, G. V. (1969) The Broadbalk yields. *Rothamsted Experimental Station Report for 1968*, Part 2, pp. 26–49.

Gates, W. L. (1976) Modeling the ice-age climate. *Science* **191**, 1131–44.

Geist, V. (1971) *Mountain Sheep. A Study in Behavior and Evolution*. Chicago: Chicago University Press.

George, P. (1973) *France; a Geographical Study*. London: Martin Robertson.

Gerasimov, I. P. & Glazovskaya, M. A. (1965) *Fundamentals of Soil Science and Geography*. Jerusalem: Israel Program for Scientific Translation.

Geyh, M. A., Kudrass, H. R. & Streif, H. (1979) Sea-level changes during the late Pleistocene and Holocene in the Strait of Malacca. *Nature* **278**, 441–3.

Gifford, D. P. (1978) Ethnoarchaeological observations of natural processes affecting cultural materials. In *Explorations in Ethnoarchaeology*, ed. R. A. Gould, pp. 77–101. Albuquerque: University of New Mexico Press.

Gimbutas, M. (1970) Proto-Indo-European Culture: The Kurgan Culture during the fifth, fourth and third millennia B.C. In *Indo-European and Indo-Europeans*, ed. G. Cardona, H. M. Hoenigswald & A. Senn, pp. 155–97. Philadelphia: University of Pennsylvania.

Gimbutas, M., ed. (1976) *Neolithic Macedonia. Los Angeles Monumenta Archaeologica* 1. Los Angeles: Institute of Archeology, University of California.

Gleave, M. B. & White, H. P. (1969) Population density and agricultural systems in West Africa. In *Environment and Land Use in Africa*, ed. M. F. Thomas & G. W. Whittington, pp. 273–300. London: Methuen.

Glob, P. V. (1951) *Ard og Plov i Nordens oldtid*. Århus: Universitetsforlaget.

Göbel, W., Knörzer, K.-H., Schalich, J., Schütrumpf, R. & Stehli, P. (1973) Naturwissenschaftliche Untersuchungen an einer späthallstattzeitlichen Fundstelle bei Langweiler, Kr. Düren. *Bonner Jahrbücher* **173**, 289–315.

González Echegaray, J. (1957) La cueva de la Mora: un yacimiento Paleolítico en la region de los Picos de Europa. *Revista del Centro de Estudios Montañeses* **1**, 3–26.

REFERENCES

González Echegaray, J., García Guinea, M. A., Begines Ramírez, A. & Madariaga de la Campa, B. (1963) Cueva de La Chora (Santander). *Excavaciones Arqueológicas en España* **26**.

González Echegaray, J., García Guinea, M. A. & Begines Ramírez, A. (1966) Cueva del Otero. *Excavaciones Arqueológicas en España* **53**.

Graham, A. (1969) Man–water relations in the east central Sudan. In *Environment and Land Use in Africa*, ed. M. F. Thomas & G. W. Whittington, pp. 409–45. London: Methuen.

Green, E. L. (1973) Location analysis of prehistoric Maya sites in northern British Honduras. *American Antiquity* **38**, 279–93.

Greengo, R. E. (1952) Shellfish foods of the Californian Indians. *Kroeber Anthropological Society Papers* **7**, 63–114.

Grinsell, L. V. (1953) *The Ancient Burial Mounds of England*, 2nd edn. London: Methuen.

Gróf, I. (1936) Natural conditions. In *Békés Vármegye*, ed. G. Markus. Budapest.

Grubb, P. & Jewell, P. A. (1966) Social grouping and home range in feral Soay sheep. In *Play, Exploration and Territory in Mammals*, ed. P. A. Jewell & C. Loizos, pp. 179–210. London: Academic Press.

Guerreschi, A. (1975) L'Epigravettiano di Piancavallo (Pordenone). *Preistoria Alpina* **11**, 255–93.

Gulliver, P. H. (1955) *The Family Herds*. London: Routledge & Kegan Paul.

Gusinde, M. (1931) *Die Feuerland-Indianer 1: Die Selk'nam*. Vienna: St Gabriel-Mödling.

Hardy, A. C. (1959) *The Open Sea. Part II. Fish and Fisheries*, revised edn. London: Collins.

Harris, D. R. (1972) Swidden systems and settlement. In *Man, Settlement and Urbanism*, ed. P. J. Ucko, R. Tringham & G. W. Dimbleby, pp. 245–62. London: Duckworth.

Harris, M. (1979) *Cannibals and Kings*. London: Collins.

Hartmann, H. (1884) Die Pfahlbau-Ausgrabungen in Steckborn. *Mitteilungen der Thurgauischen Naturforschenden Gesellschaft*, 61–9.

Hawkes, J. G. (1969) The ecological background of plant domestication. In *The Domestication and Exploitation of Plants and Animals*, ed. P. J. Ucko & G. W. Dimbleby, pp. 17–29. London: Duckworth.

Hegsted, D. M. (1964) Proteins. In *Nutrition*, Vol. 1, ed. G. H. Beaton & E. W. McHenry, pp. 116–79. New York: Academic Press.

Helbaek, H. (1960) The paleoethnobotany of the Near East and Europe. In *Prehistoric Investigations in Iraqi Kurdistan*, ed. R. J. Braidwood & B. Howe, pp. 99–118. *Studies in Ancient Oriental Civilization* 31. Chicago: Chicago University Press.

Helbaek, H. (1966) Pre-pottery Neolithic farming at Beidha. *Palestine Exploration Quarterly* **98**, 61–7.

Helbaek, H. (1970) The plant husbandry of Hacılar. In *Excavations at Hacılar*, by J. Mellaart, pp. 189–244. Edinburgh: Edinburgh University Press.

Heptner, V. G., Nasimovic, A. A. & Bannikov, A. G. (1966) *Die Säugetiere der Sowjetunion*. Jena: Gustav Fischer Verlag.

Hernández-Pacheco, E. (1919) La caverna de la Peña de Candamo (Asturias). *Comisión de Investigaciones Paleontológicas y Prehistóricas*, Memoria 24. Madrid.

Hernández-Pacheco, F. (1959) La morena peri-glaciar de Peña Vieja, Picos de Europa (Santander). *Trabalhos de Antropologia e Etnologia* **17**, 227–34.

Hernández-Pacheco, F., Llopis-Lladó, N., Jordá-Cerdá, F. & Martinez, J. A. (1957) Livret – Guide de l'Excursion N2 – Le Quaternaire de la Région Cantabrique. *Inqua: Vème Congrès International*. Oviedo: Diputación Provincial de Asturias.

Hickerson, H. (1965) The Virginia deer and intertribal buffer zones in the Upper Mississippi Valley. In *Man, Culture and Animals*, ed. A. Leeds & A. P. Vayda, pp. 43–65. Washington D.C.: American Association for the Advancement of Science.

Hickling, C. F. (1971) *Fish Culture*, 2nd ed. London: Faber.

Higgs, E. S. (1966) The climate, environment and industries of Stone Age Greece: Part II. *Proceedings of the Prehistoric Society* **32**, 1–29.

Higgs, E. S., ed. (1975) *Palaeoeconomy: Papers in Economic Prehistory, Vol. 2*. Cambridge: Cambridge University Press.

Higgs, E. S. & Jarman, M. R. (1969) The origins of agriculture: a reconsideration. *Antiquity* **43**, 31–41.

Higgs, E. S. & Jarman, M. R. (1972) The origins of animal and plant husbandry. In *Papers in Economic Prehistory*, ed. E. S. Higgs, pp. 3–13. Cambridge: Cambridge University Press.

Higgs, E. S. & Vita-Finzi, C. (1972) Prehistoric economies: a territorial approach. In *Papers in Economic Prehistory*, ed. E. S. Higgs, pp. 27–36. Cambridge: Cambridge University Press.

Higgs, E. S., Vita-Finzi, C., Harris, D. R. & Fagg, A. E. (1967) The climate, environment and industries of Stone Age Greece, Part III. *Proceedings of the Prehistoric Society* **33**, 1–29.

Higham, C. F. W. (1967) Stock rearing as a cultural factor in prehistoric Europe. *Proceedings of the Prehistoric Society* **33**, 84–106.

Higham, C. F. W. (1968) Prehistoric research in western Southland. *New Zealand Archaeological Association Newsletter* **11**, 155–64.

Hillman, G. (1973) Agricultural resources and settlement in the Aşvan region. *Anatolian Studies* **23**, 217–40.

Hillman, G. (1975) The plant remains from Tell Abu Hureyra: a preliminary report. *Proceedings of the Prehistoric Society* **41**, 70–3.

Hodder, I. & Orton, C. (1976) *Spatial Analysis in Archaeology*. Cambridge: Cambridge University Press.

Hoffman, D. (1976) Inuit land use on the Barren Grounds. In *Inuit Land Use and Occupancy Project*, Vol. 2, ed. M. M. R. Freeman, pp. 69–100. Ottawa: Department of Indian and Northern Affairs.

REFERENCES

Holmes, R. T. (1970) Differences in population density, territoriality, and food supply of dunlin on arctic and subarctic tundra. In *Animal Populations in Relation to their Food Resources*, ed. A. Watson, pp. 303–19. Oxford: Blackwell Scientific Publications.

Hopfgarten, P.-O. (1975) *Undersökning av ett höjdlägesområdes älgstam och dess vandringar mellan sommar och vintervisten inom Västerbottens län*. Unpublished manuscript.

Hull, D. (1974) *Philosophy of Biological Science*. Englewood Cliffs, New Jersey: Prentice-Hall.

Huttunen, P. & Tolonen, M. (1972) Pollen-analytical studies of prehistoric agriculture in nothern Ångermanland. In *Palaeoecological Investigation in Northern Sweden, Early Norrland I*, ed. P. Huttunen, I. U. Olsson, K. Tolonen & M. Tolonen, pp. 9–34. KVHAA Publication.

Ingold, T. (1974) On reindeer and men. *Man* N.S. **9,** 523–38.

Iversen, J. (1941) Landnam i Danmarks Stenalder. *Danmarks Geologiske Undersøgelse*, Ser. 2, **66,** 1–68.

Iversen, J. (1960) Problems of the early Postglacial forest development in Denmark. *Danmarks Geologiske Undersøgelse*, Ser. 4, **4,** 1–32.

Iversen, J. (1973) The development of Denmark's nature since the Last Glacial. *Danmarks Geologiske Undersøgelse*, Ser. 5, **7c,** 7–125.

Jacobi, R. M. (1976) Britain inside and outside Mesolithic Europe. *Proceedings of the Prehistoric Society* **42,** 67–84.

Jankuhn, H. (1969) *Vor- und Frühgeschichte vom Neolithikum bis zur Völkerwanderungszeit. Deutsche Agrargeschichte*, Band I. Stuttgart: Eugen Ulmer.

Jarman, H. N. (1972) The origins of wheat and barley cultivation. In *Papers in Economic Prehistory*, ed. E. S. Higgs, pp. 15–26. Cambridge: Cambridge University Press.

Jarman, M. R. (1971) Culture and economy in the north Italian Neolithic. *World Archaeology* **2,** 255–65.

Jarman, M. R. (1972a) A territorial model for archaeology: a behavioural and geographical approach. In *Models in Archaeology*, ed. D. L. Clarke, pp. 705–33. London: Methuen.

Jarman, M. R. (1972b) European deer economies and the advent of the Neolithic. In *Papers in Economic Prehistory*, ed. E. S. Higgs, pp. 125–47. Cambridge: Cambridge University Press.

Jarman, M. R. (1975) The fauna and economy of Fiavè. *Preistoria Alpina* **11,** 65–73.

Jarman, M. R. (1976a) Early animal husbandry. *Philosophical Transactions of the Royal Society, London B* **275,** 85–97.

Jarman, M. R. (1976b) Prehistoric economic development in sub-Alpine Italy. In *Problems in Economic and Social Archaeology*, ed. G. de G. Sieveking, I. H. Longworth & H. E. Wilson, pp. 523–48. London: Duckworth.

Jarman, M. R. (1976c) Rivoli: The fauna. In *The Excavations on the Rocca di Rivoli, Verona 1963–1968*, by L. H. Barfield & B. Bagolini, pp. 159–73. *Memorie del Museo Civico di Storia Naturale di Verona (1la Serie) Sezione Scienze dell'Uomo*, N.1.

Jarman, M. R., Vita-Finzi, C. & Higgs, E. S. (1972) Site catchment analysis in archaeology. In *Man, Settlement and Urbanism*, ed. P. J. Ucko, R. Tringham & G. W. Dimbleby, pp. 61–6. London: Duckworth.

Jarman, M. R. & Webley, D. (1975) Settlement and land use in Capitanata, Italy. In *Palaeoeconomy*, ed. E. S. Higgs, pp. 177–221. Cambridge: Cambridge University Press.

Jarman, M. R. & Wilkinson, P. F. (1972) Criteria of animal domestication. In *Papers in Economic Prehistory*, ed. E. S. Higgs, pp. 83–96. Cambridge: Cambridge University Press.

Jasnowski, M. (1972) Threat to peatlands and their protection in Poland. *Proceedings of 4th International Peat Congress* **1,** 149–58. Finland: Otavieni.

Jenks, A. E. (1900) The wild rice gatherers of the Upper Lakes. A study of American primitive economies. *Smithsonian Institution Annual Report of the Bureau of American Ethnology* **19**(1), 1013–137.

Jewell, P. A. (1966) The concept of home range in mammals. In *Play, Exploration and Territory in Mammals*, ed. P. A. Jewell & C. Loizos, pp. 85–109. London: Academic Press.

Jochim, M. A. (1976) *Hunter-Gatherer Subsistence and Settlement*. New York: Academic Press.

Jones, R. (1969) Fire-stick farming. *Australian Natural History*, September 1969, 224–8.

Jones, R. (1974) Tasmanian tribes. Appendix in *Aboriginal Tribes of Australia*, by N. B. Tindale. Berkeley: University of California Press.

Jordá Cerdá, F. (1955) Notas sobre el Musteriense de Asturias. *Boletín del Instituto de Estudios Asturianos* **25,** 209–31.

Jordá Cerdá, F. (1958) Avance al estudio de la Cueva de la Lloseta (Ardines, Ribadesella, Asturias). Oviedo: *Servicio de Investigaciones Arqueológicas*, Memoria 3.

Jordá Cerdá, F. (1959) Revisión de la cronología del Asturiense. *Actas del V Congreso Nacional de Arqueología (1957)*.

Jordá Cerdá, F. (1963) El Paleolítico Superior Cantábrico y sus indústrias. *Saitabi* **13,** 3–22.

Jordan, P. A., Shelton, P. C. & Allen, D. L. (1967) Numbers, turnover, and social structure of the Isle Royale wolf population. *American Zoologist* **7,** 233–52.

Jørgensen, G. (1977) Et kornfund fra Sarup: Bidrag til belysning af tragtbaegerkulturens Agerbrug. *Kuml* **1976,** 47–64.

Kapel, H. (1969) En boplads fra tidlig-Atlantisk tid ved Villingebaek. *Nationalmuseets Arbejdsmark*, 85–94.

Kelsall, J. P. (1957) Continued barren ground caribou studies. *Wildlife Management Bulletin* Ser. 1, No. 12.

Kelsall, J. P. (1968) *The Migratory Barren-Ground Caribou of Canada*. Ottawa: Queen's Printer, Department of Indian Affairs and Northern Development, Canadian Wildlife Service.

REFERENCES

Kiefer, F. (1955) *Naturkunde des Bodensees*. Lindau & Konstanz: Jan Thorbecke.

Knock, K., ed. (1953) *Klima-Atlas von Baden-Württemberg*. Bad Kissingen: Deutscher Wetterdienst.

Knörzer, K.-H. (1971) Urgeschichtliche Unkräuter im Rheinland. Ein Beitrag zur Entstehungsgeschichte der Segetalgesellschaften. *Vegetatio* **23**, 89–111.

Königsson, L. K. (1970) Traces of Neolithic human influence upon the landscape development at the Bjurselet settlement, Västerbotten, northern Sweden. *Kungliga Skytteanska Samfundets Handlingar* **7**.

Kroeber, A. L. & Barrett, S. A. (1960) Fishing among the Indians of northwestern California. *Anthropological Records of the University of California* **21**, 1–210.

Krog, H. & Tauber, H. (1974) C-14 chronology of late- and post-glacial marine deposits in North Jutland. *Danmarks Geologiske Undersøgelse Arbog* **1973**, 93–105.

Kruk, J. (1969) Badania poszukiwawcze i weryfikacyjne w dorzeczu Dłubni. *Sprawozdania Archeologiezne* **21**, 347–73.

Kruk, J. (1970) Badania poszukiwawcze i weryfikacyjne w gornym i srodkowym dorzeczu Szreniawy. *Sprawozdania Archeologiezne* **22**, 271.

Kruk, J. (1973) *Studia Osadnicze nad Neolitem Wyżyn Lessowych*. Wroclaw: Polska Akademia Nauk.

Kulczycka-Leciejewiczowa, A. (1970) The Linear and Stroked Pottery Culture. In *The Neolithic in Poland*, ed. T. Wiślanśki, pp. 14–75. Wrocław: Institut Historii Kultury Materialnej Polskiej Akademii Nauk.

Kuper, R., Löhr, H., Lüning, J. & Stehli, P. (1974) Untersuchungen zur neolithischen Besiedlung der Aldenhovener Platte IV. *Bonner Jahrbücher* **174**, 424–508.

Lack, D. (1954) *The Natural Regulation of Animal Numbers*. Oxford: Clarendon Press.

Laevastu, T. (1961) Natural bases of fisheries in the Atlantic Ocean: their past and present characteristics and possibilities for future expansion. In *Atlantic Ocean Fisheries*, ed. G. Borgstrom & A. J. Heighway, pp. 18–39. London: Fishing News (Books) Ltd.

Larin, I. V. (1962) *Pasture, Economy and Meadow Cultivation*. Jerusalem: Israel Program for Scientific Translations.

Larson, L. H. (1972) Functional considerations of warfare in the southeast during the Mississippi period. *American Antiquity* **37**, 383–92.

Lathrap, D. W. (1968) The 'hunting' economies of the tropical forest zone of South America: an attempt at historical perspective. In *Man the Hunter*, ed. R. B. Lee and I. DeVore, pp. 23–9. Chicago: Aldine.

Lee, R. B. (1968) What hunters do for a living, or, how to make out on scarce resources. In *Man the Hunter*, ed. R. B. Lee & I. DeVore, pp. 30–48. Chicago: Aldine.

Lee, R. B. (1972a) The !Kung Bushmen of Botswana. In *Hunters and Gatherers Today*, ed. M. G. Bicchieri, pp. 326–68. New York: Holt, Rinehart & Winston.

Lee, R. B. (1972b) Work effort, group structure and land-use in contemporary hunter-gatherers. In *Man, Settlement and Urbanism*, ed. P. J. Ucko, R. Tringham & G. W. Dimbleby, pp. 177–85. London: Duckworth.

Lee, R. B. (1976) !Kung spatial organization: an ecological and historical perspective. In *Kalahari Hunter-Gatherers. Studies of the !Kung San and their Neighbors*, ed. R. B. Lee & I. DeVore, pp. 73–97. Cambridge: Harvard University Press.

Lee, R. B. & DeVore, I. (1976) *Kalahari Hunter-Gatherers. Studies of the !Kung San and their Neighbors*. Cambridge: Harvard University Press.

Leeds, A. (1961) Yaruro incipient tropical forest horticulture – possibilities and limits. In *The Evolution of Horticultural Systems in Native South America: Causes and Consequences. A Symposium*, ed. J. Wilbert, pp. 13–46. *Anthropologica, Supp. Publication No. 2*.

Leeds, A. (1965) Reindeer herding and Chukchi social institutions. In *Man, Culture and Animals*, ed. A. Leeds A. P. Vayda, pp. 87–128. Washington, D.C.: American Association for the Advancement of Science.

Legge, A. J. (1972) Prehistoric exploitation of the gazelle in Palestine. In *Papers in Economic Prehistory*, ed. E. S. Higgs, pp. 119–24. Cambridge: Cambridge University Press.

Leroi-Gourhan, A. & Girard, M. (1971) L'Abri de la Cure à Baulmes (Suisse) – analyse pollinique. *Jahrbuch der Schweizerischen Gesellschaft für Urgeschichte* **56**, 7–15.

Levin, M. G. & Potapov, L. P., eds (1964) *The Peoples of Siberia*. Chicago: University of Chicago Press.

Lothrop, S. K. (1928) The Indians of Tierra del Fuego. *Contributions from the Museum of the American Indian* **10**, 5–244.

Lubbock, J. (1865) *Prehistoric Times*. London: Williams & Norgate.

Lubell, D., Ballais, J. L. & Hassan, F. A. (1975) The prehistoric cultural ecology of Capsian escargotières. Preliminary results of an interdisciplinary investigation in the Cheria-Télidjène region. *Libyca* **23**, 43–121.

Łuka, L. J. & Pietrzak, M. (1969) A habitation site from the turn of the Bronze and Iron Ages at Będzieszyn, district of Gdańsk. Report on the 1966 excavations. *Sprawozdania Archeologiczne* **20**, 83–93.

Lynch, T. F. (1973) Harvest timing, transhumance and the process of domestication. *American Anthropologist* **75**, 1254–9.

Macan, T. T. & Worthington, E. B. (1972) *Life in Lakes and Rivers*, revised edn. London: Collins.

McLoughlin, P. F. M., ed. (1970) *African Food Production Systems; Cases and Theory*. London: John Hopkins.

Madariaga de la Campa, B. (1969) *Las Pinturas Rupestres de Animales en la Región Franco-Cantábrica*. Santander: Institución Cultural de Cantabria.

Madariaga de la Campa, B. (1971) La fauna marina de la Cueva Morín. In *Cueva Morín: Excavaciones 1966–1968*, ed. J. González Echegaray & L. G. Freeman, pp. 401–15.

REFERENCES

Santander: Patronato de las Cuevas Prehistóricas de la Provincia de Santander, **6.**

Madsen, A. P., Müller, S. & Neergaard, C. (1900) *Affaldsdynger fra Stenalderen i Danmark.* Copenhagen: C. A. Reitzel.

Madsen, T. (1979) Earthen long barrows and timber structures: aspects of the Early Neolithic mortuary practice in Denmark. *Proceedings of the Prehistoric Society* **45,** 301–20.

Maier-Arendt, W. (1966) Die bandkeramische Kultur im Untermaingebiet. *Veröffentlichungen des Amtes für Bodendenkmalpflege in Regierungs bezirk Darmstadt* **3.** Bonn: Habelt.

Malavolti, F. (1953) Appunti per una cronologia relativa del Neo-eneolitico emiliano. *Emilia Preromano* **3–4,** 1–68.

Manninen, I. (1932) *Die Finnisch-Ugrischen Völker.* Leipzig.

Manuel González, J. (1968) El paleolítico inferior y medio en Asturias: nuevos hallazgos. *Archivum* **18,** 75–90.

Martin, J. H. & Leonard, W. H. (1967) *Principles of Field Crop Production.* New York: Macmillan.

Martínez Santa-Olalla, J. (1925) Prehistória Burgalesa. *Butlettí de l'Associacio Catalana d'Antropología, Etnología i Prehistória* **3,** 147–72.

Martonne, E. de (1904) La vie pastorale et la transhumance dans les Karpathes méridionales. *Zu Friedrichs Ratzels Gedachtnis,* pp. 227–45. Leipzig: Seele & Co.

Matthiassen, T. (1937) Gudenaa-Kulturen: en Mesolitisk inlands-bebyggelse i Jylland. *Aarbøger for nordisk Oldkyndighed og Historie,* 1–186.

Matley, I. M. (1970) Traditional pastoral life in Romania. *Professional Geographer* **22,** 311–5.

Meagher, M. (1973) *The Bison of Yellowstone National Park.* National Park Service, Scientific Monograph. Series No. 1.

Mech, L. D. (1970) *The Wolf: The Ecology and Behaviour of an Endangered Species.* New York: Natural History Press.

Medawar, P. B. (1976) Does ethology throw any light on human behaviour? In *Growing Points in Ethology,* ed. P. P. G. Bateson & R. A. Hinde, pp. 497–527. Cambridge: Cambridge University Press.

Meehan, B. (1975) *Shell Bed to Shell Midden.* Unpublished Ph.D. Thesis. Australian National University.

Meehan, B. (1977) Man does not live by calories alone: the role of shellfish in a coastal cuisine. In *Sunda and Sahul,* ed. J. Allen, J. Golson & R. Jones, pp. 493–531. London: Academic Press.

Mellars, P. A. (1976) Fire ecology, animal populations and man: a study of some ecological relationships in prehistory. *Proceedings of the Prehistoric Society* **42,** 15–46.

Mellars, P. A. & Payne, S. (1971) Excavation of two Mesolithic shell middens on the island of Oronsay (Inner Hebrides). *Nature* **231,** 397–8.

Milisaukas, S. (1976) *Archaeological Investigations on the Linear Culture Village of Olszanica.* Wrocław: Akademii Nauk.

Mitchell, G. F. (1976) *The Irish Landscape.* London: Collins.

Modderman, P. J. R. (1977) Die neolithische Besiedlung bei Hienheim, Ldkr. Kelheim. *Analecta Praehistorica Leidensia,* **10.**

Møhl, U. (1971a) Oversigt over dyreknoglerne fra Ølby Lyng. *Aarbøger for nordisk Oldkyndighed og Historie* **1970,** pp. 43–77.

Møhl, U. (1971b) Fangstdyrene ved de Danske strande: den zoologiske baggrund for harpunerne. *Kuml* **1970,** 297–329.

Monkhouse, F. J. (1974) *A Regional Geography of Western Europe,* 4th edn. London: Longman.

Moore, H. B. (1938) Algal production and the food requirements of a limpet. *Proceedings of the Malacological Society* **23**(3), 117–18.

Morel, J. (1967) Découverte d'une pierre à gorge dans une escargotière capsienne de la région de Tébessa. *Libyca* **15,** 125–37.

Morgan, W. B. (1969) The zoning of land use around rural settlements in tropical Africa. In *Environment and Land Use in Africa,* ed. M. F. Thomas & G. W. Whittington, pp. 301–19. London: Methuen.

Müller, I. (1947) Der pollenanalytische Nachweis der menschlichen Besiedlung im Federsee- und Bodenseegebiet. *Planta* **35,** 70–87.

Murdock, G. P. (1967) *Ethnographic Atlas.* Pittsburgh: University of Pittsburgh Press.

Nagy, M. A. (1954) Talajföldrajzi Megfigyelések a Tiszazugban. *Földrajzi Értesitö* **3**(3), 507–43.

Nandris, J. (1972) Relations between the Mesolithic, the first temperate Neolithic, and the Bandkeramik: the nature of the problem. In *Aktuelle Fragen der Bandkeramik,* ed. J. Fitz & J. Makkay, pp. 61–70. Budapest.

Necrasov, O. (1961) Sur les restes des faunes subfossiles datant de la culture Starçevo/Criş et le problème de la domestication. *Anǎlele Ştiinţifice ale Universitǎtii Al. I. Cuza. Din Iaşi* [S.N.] Sect. 2, **10,** 167–78.

Neuweiler, E. (1905) Die prähistorischen Pflanzenreste Mitteleuropas mit besonderer Berucksichtigung der Schweizerischen Funde. *Vierteljahrsschrift der Naturforschenden Gesellschaft in Zürich* **50,** 23–134.

Nica, M. (1971) O Aşezare de Tip Starčevo-Criş Lîngă Basarabi (Jud. Dolj). *Studii şi Cercetǎri de Istorie Veche* **22,** 547–56.

Noe-Nygaard, N. (1974) Mesolithic hunting in Denmark illustrated by bone injuries caused by human weapons. *Journal of Archaeological Science* **1,** 217–48.

Obermaier, H. (1925) El Hombre Fósil. *Comisión de Investigaciones Paleontológicas y Prehistóricas,* Memoria 9 (2nd edn). Madrid: Museo Nacional de Ciencias Naturales.

Osborn, A. J. (1977) Strandloopers, mermaids, and other fairy tales: ecological determinants of marine resource utilization – the Peruvian case. In *For Theory Building in Archaeology,* ed. L. R. Binford, pp. 157–205. New York: Academic Press.

Pales, L. & St Péreuse, M. T. de (1966) Un cheval-prétexte: retour au chevêtre. *Objets et Mondes* **6,** 187–206.

Parkington, J. E. (1972) Seasonal mobility in the Late Stone Age. *African Studies* **31,** 223–43.

REFERENCES

Parmalee, P. W. & Klippel, W. E. (1974) Freshwater mussels as a prehistoric food resource. *American Antiquity* **28**, 421–34.

Passmore, R., Nicol, B. M. & Narayana Rao, M. (1974) *Handbook on Human Nutritional Requirements*. Rome: FAO & WHO.

Patterson, R. (1839) On the common limpet (*P. vulgaris*), considered as an article of food in the north of Ireland. *Annals of Natural History* **26**, 231–4.

Pécsi, M. & Sárfalvi, B. (1964) *The Geography of Hungary*. Budapest: Corvina.

Percival, J. (1921) *The Wheat Plant*. London: Duckworth.

Perini, R. (1971) I depositi preistorici di Romagnano-Loc (Trento). *Preistoria Alpina* **7**, 7–106.

Perini, R. (1975) La palafitta di Fiavè-Carera (nota preliminare sugli scavi del 1972). *Preistoria Alpina* **11**, 25–64.

Perkins, E. J. (1974) *The Biology of Estuaries and Coastal Waters*. London: Duckworth.

Peterson, W. (1975) A demographer's view of prehistoric demography. *Current Anthropology* **16**, 207–26.

Pétrequin, P. (1974) Interprétation d'un habitat néolithique en grotte: le niveau XI de Gonvillars (Haute-Saône). *Bulletin de la Société Préhistorique Française* **71**(2), 489–534.

Pietrzak, M. (1968) Report on rescue excavations of a habitation site of the Venedian culture at Różyny, district of Gdańsk. *Sprawozdania Archeologiczne* **19**, 95–8.

Piggott, S. (1965) *Ancient Europe*. Edinburgh: Edinburgh University Press.

Podgórski, J. T. (1971) Excavations at Juszkowo (Będzieszyn) district of Gdańsk in 1967–69. *Sprawozdania Archeologiczne* **23**, 79–92.

Poiner, G. (1976) The process of the year among Aborigines of the central and south coast of New South Wales. *Archaeology and Physical Anthropology in Oceania* **11**(3), 186–206.

Pounds, N. J. G. (1973) *An Historical Geography of Europe 450 B.C.–A.D. 1330*. Cambridge: Cambridge University Press.

Pous, A. de (1967) L'Architecture de Pierre Sèche dans les Pyrénées Méditerranéennes. *Bulletin Archéologique* N.S. **3**, 21–115.

Preuschen, E. (1973) Estrazione mineraria dell'Età del Bronzo del Trentino. *Preistoria Alpina* **9**, 113–50.

Prothero, R. M. (1957) Land use at Soba, Zaria Province, Northern Nigeria. *Economic Geography* **33**, 72–86.

Prunières, D. (1872) Distribution des dolmens dans la Lozère. *Matériaux pour l'histoire primitive et naturelle de l'homme*, pp. 475–86.

Rappaport, R. (1968) *Pigs for the Ancestors*. New Haven: Yale University Press.

Reichel-Dolmatoff, G. (1961) The agricultural basis of the sub-Andean Chiefdoms of Columbia. In *The Evolution of Horticultural Systems in Native South America: Causes and Consequences*, ed. J. Wilbert, pp. 83–100. *Anthropologica, Supp. Publication No. 2*.

Reinerth, H. (1929) *Das Federseemoor als Siedlungsland des Vorzeitmenschen. Führer zur Urgeschichte 9*. Augsburg: Verlagt Bei Benno Filser.

Reinerth, H. (1931) Wohnplätze der mittleren Steinzeit am Bodensee. *Nachrichtenblatt für Deutsche Vorzeit* **7**, 43–44.

Reinerth, H. (1938) *Das Pfahldorf Sipplingen*. Leipzig: Kurt Kabigsch.

Reining, P. C. (1970) Social factors and food production in an East African peasant society: the Haya. In *African Food Production Systems*, ed. P. F. M. McLoughlin, pp. 41–89. Baltimore: John Hopkins Press.

Renfrew, C. (1972) Patterns of population growth in the prehistoric Aegean. In *Man, Settlement and Urbanism*, ed. P. J. Ucko, R. Tringham & G. W. Dimbleby, pp. 383–99. London: Duckworth.

Renfrew, C. (1976) *Before Civilization: The Radiocarbon Revolution and Prehistoric Europe*. London: Penguin.

Renfrew, J. (1973) Agriculture. In *Neolithic Greece*, ed. D. R. Theocharis *et al.*, pp. 147–64. Athens: National Bank of Greece.

Robson, J. R. K., Larkin, F. A., Sandretto, A. M. & Tadayyon, B. (1972) *Malnutrition. Its Causation and Control*, 2 vols. New York: Gordon & Breach.

Roe, F. G. (1972) *The North American Buffalo: a Critical Study of the Species in its Wild State*, 2nd edn. Newton Abbot: David & Charles.

Rogers, E. S. (1972) The Mistassini Cree. In *Hunters and Gatherers Today*, ed. M. G. Bicchieri, pp. 90–137. New York: Holt, Rinehart & Winston.

Rosa, B. (1963) Über die morphologische Entwicklung der Küste Polens im Lichte det alten Strandformes. *Torunensis* **5**, 3–174.

Rossman, D. L. (1976) A site catchment analysis of San Lorenzo, Veracruz. In *The Early Mesoamerican Village*, ed. K. V. Flannery, pp. 95–103. New York: Academic Press.

Rust, A. (1943) *Die Alt- und Mittelsteinzeitlichen Funde von Stellmoor*. Neumünster in Holstein: Archäologisches Institut des Deutschen Reiches.

Sahlins, M. (1972) *Stone Age Economics*. Chicago: Aldine.

Sakellaridis, M. (1978) *Economic Exploitation of the Swiss Area in the Mesolithic and Neolithic Periods*. Unpublished Ph.D. Thesis, University of Cambridge.

Salzman, P. C. (1972) Multi-resource nomadism in Iranian Baluchistan. *Journal of Asian and African Studies* **7**(1–2), 60–8.

Sauer, C. O. (1952) *Agricultural Origins and Dispersals*. New York: American Geographical Society.

Sauer, C. O. (1962) Seashore – primitive home of man? *Proceedings of the American Philosophical Society* **106**, 41–7.

Sauter, M. R. (1976) *Switzerland*. London: Thames & Hudson.

Sauvy, A. (1969) *The General Theory of Population*. London: Weidenfeld & Nicolson.

Saxon, E. C. (1976) The evolution of domestication. A

REFERENCES

reappraisal of the Near Eastern and North African evidence. *Union Internationale des Sciences Préhistoriques et Protohistoriques, IXe Congrès, Nice, Colloque XX*, 180–226.

Schiemann, E. (1956) New dates for recent cultivation of *Triticum monococcum* and *Triticum dicoccum* in Jugoslavia. *Wheat Information Service* 3, 1–3.

Shackleton, N. J. & Opdyke, N. D. (1973) Oxygen isotope and palaeomagnetic stratigraphy of Equatorial Pacific core, V28–238. *Quaternary Research* 3, 39–55.

Sielmann, B. (1971) Der Einfluss der Umwelt auf die neolithische Besiedlung Südwestdeutschlands. *Acta Praehistorica et Archaeologica* 2, 65–197.

Silberbauer, G. B. (1972) The G/Wi Bushmen. In *Hunters and Gatherers Today*, ed. M. G. Bicchieri, pp. 271–326. New York: Holt, Rinehart & Winston.

Simmons, I. G. (1964) Pollen diagrams from Dartmoor. *New Phytologist* 63, 165–80.

Simmons, I. G. & Dimbleby, G. W. (1974) The possible role of ivy (*Hedera helix* L.) in the Mesolithic economy of Western Europe. *Journal of Archaeological Science* 1, 291–6.

Sinha, D. P. (1972) The Birhors. In *Hunters and Gatherers Today*, ed. M. G. Bicchieri, pp. 371–403. New York: Holt, Rinehart & Winston.

Skaarup, J. (1973) *Hesselø-Sølager: Jagdstationen der Südskandinavischen Trichterbecherkultur*. Arkaeologiske Studier 1. Copenhagen: Institute of Prehistoric Archaeology, University of Copenhagen.

Slicher van Bath, B. H. (1963) *The Agrarian History of Western Europe, A.D. 500–1850*. London: Edward Arnold.

Slobodkin, L. B. (1962) *Growth and Regulation of Animal Populations*. New York: Holt, Rinehart & Winston.

Smith, C. C. (1968) The adaptive nature of social organization in the genus of tree squirrels *Tamiasciurus*. *Ecological Monographs* 38(1), 31–63.

Somogyi, S. (1971) Natural endowments of the Great Hungarian Plain. In *The Changing Face of the Great Hungarian Plain*, ed. B. Sárfalvi, pp. 35–77. Budapest: Akadémiai Kiadó.

Soudsky, B. & Pavlů, I. (1972) The Linear Pottery Culture settlement patterns of Central Europe. In *Man, Settlement and Urbanism*, ed. P. J. Ucko, R. Tringham & G. W. Dimbleby, pp. 317–28. London: Duckworth.

Southern, H. N. (1955) Nocturnal animals. *Scientific American*, October 1955, pp. 88–98.

Spooner, B. (1972) The Iranian deserts. In *Population Growth: Anthropological Implications*, ed. B. Spooner, pp. 245–68. Cambridge, Mass.: MIT Press.

Spurway, H. (1955) The causes of domestication: an attempt to integrate some ideas of Konrad Lorenz with evolutionary theory. *Journal of Genetics* 53, 325–62.

Stefánsson, V. (1914) The Stefánsson–Anderson Arctic expedition of the American Museum: preliminary ethnological report. *Anthropological Papers of the American Museum of Natural History* 14(1), 1–395.

Stenning, D. J. (1959) *Savannah Nomads: A Study of the Wodaabe Pastoral Fulani of Western Bornu Province, Northern Region, Nigeria*. London: Oxford University Press.

Steward, J. H. (1929) Irrigation without agriculture. *Papers of the Michigan Academy of Science, Arts & Letters* 12, 149–56.

Stora, N. (1968) Massfångst av Sjöfagel i Nordeurasien: En etnologisk undersökning av fångsmetoderna. *Acta Academiae Aboensis, Humaniona* 34(2). Abo Akademi.

Straus, L. G. (1976–7) The Upper Palaeolithic cave site of Altamira (Santander, Spain). *Quaternaria* 19, 135–48.

Straus, L. G. (1977) Of deerslayers and mountain men: Paleolithic faunal exploitation in Cantabrian Spain. In *For Theory Building in Archaeology*, ed. L. R. Binford, pp. 41–76. New York: Academic Press.

Streuver, S. (1962) Implications of vegetal remains from an Illinois Hopewell site. *American Antiquity* 27, 584–6.

Sturdy, D. A. (1972) The exploitation patterns of a modern reindeer economy in West Greenland. In *Papers in Economic Prehistory*, ed. E. S. Higgs, pp. 161–8. Cambridge: Cambridge University Press.

Sturdy, D. A. (1975) Some reindeer economies in prehistoric Europe. In *Palaeoeconomy*, ed. E. S. Higgs, pp. 55–95. Cambridge: Cambridge University Press.

Suttles, W. (1968) Coping with an abundance: subsistence on the northwest coast. In *Man the Hunter*, ed. R. B. Lee & I. DeVore, pp. 56–68. Chicago: Aldine.

Sutton, K. (1977) Reclamation and wasteland during the eighteenth and nineteenth centuries. In *Themes in the Historical Geography of France*, ed. H. D. Clout, pp. 247–300. London: Academic Press.

Swidler, W. W. (1972) Some demographic factors regulating the formation of flocks and camps among the Brahui of Baluchistan. *Journal of Asian and African Studies* 7, 69–75.

Szymańska, A. (1968) Neolithic settlement at Lichnowy, Malbork district. *Pomerania Antiqua* 2, 177–87.

Tappe, D. (1972) The Swedish Baron Rolamb in the Balkans. *Actes du IIème Congrès; Etudes S. E. Européen, Tome II Histoire*. Athens, p. 523.

Tauber, H. (1965) Differential pollen dispersal and the interpretation of pollen diagrams: with a contribution to the interpretation of the elm fall. *Danmarks Geologiske Undersøgelse* ser. 2, 89.

Tauber, H. (1967) Danske Kulstof-14 Dateringer af Arkaeologiske Prøver II. *Aarbøger for nordisk Oldkyndighed og Historie* 1966, 102–30.

Taute, W. (1966) Das Felsdach Lautereck, eine mesolithisch–neolithisch–bronzezeitliche Stratigraphie an der oberen Donau. In *Neolithic Studies in Atlantic Europe*, ed. J. D. van der Waals. *Palaeohistoria* 12, 483–504.

Tegengren, H. (1952) Et Utdöd Lappkultur i Kemi Lappinarle: Studier i Nordfulands Kolonisations – historia. *Acta Academiae Åboensis Humaniora* 19(4).

Temple, P. (1936) La préhistoire du Dépt. de l'Aveyron.

REFERENCES

Cahiers d'Histoire et d'Archaeologie (Nîmes), 6e année, **11**.

Terán, M. de (1947) Vaqueros y cabañas en los montes de Pas. *Estudios geográficos* **28**, 493–536.

Thomson, D. F. (1939) The seasonal factor in human culture: illustrated from the life of a contemporary nomadic group. *Proceedings of the Prehistoric Society* **5**, 209–21.

Tinbergen, N. (1976) Ethology in a changing world. In *Growing Points in Ethology*, ed. P. P. G. Bateson & R. A. Hinde, pp. 507–27. Cambridge: Cambridge University Press.

Tindale, N. B. (1972) The Pitjandjara. In *Hunters and Gatherers Today*, ed. M. G. Bicchieri, pp. 217–68. New York: Holt, Rinehart & Winston.

Tringham, R. (1971) *Hunters, Fishers and Farmers of Eastern Europe. 6000–3000 B.C.* London: Hutchinson.

Troels-Smith, J. (1953) Ertebøllekultur-Bondekulture: resultater af de sidste 10 aars undersøgelser i Aamosen. *Aarbøger for nordisk Oldkyndighed og Historie*, 5–62.

Troels-Smith, J. (1960) Ivy, mistletoe and elm, climate indicators – fodder plants. A contribution to the interpretation of the pollen zone border VII–VIII. *Danmarks Geologiske Undersøgelse* ser. 4, **4**.

Troels-Smith, J. (1966) The Ertebølle culture and its background. *Palaeohistoria* **12**, 505–28.

Truswell, A. S. & Hansen, J. D. L. (1976) Medical research among the !Kung. In *Kalahari Hunter-Gatherers. Studies of the !Kung San and their Neighbors*, ed. R. B. Lee & I. DeVore, pp. 166–94. Cambridge, Mass.: Harvard University Press.

Valéra, R. de & Ó'Nualláin, S. (1961) *Survey of the Megalithic Tombs of Ireland. Vol. I. County Clare.* Dublin: The Stationery Office.

Valéra, R. de & Ó'Nualláin, S. (1964) *Survey of the Megalithic Tombs of Ireland. Vol. II. County Mayo.* Dublin: The Stationery Office.

Vayda, A. P. (1961) Expansion and warfare among swidden agriculturalists. *American Anthropologist* **63**, 346–58.

Vega del Sella, Conde de la (1923) El Asturiense; nueva industria Pre-Neolitica. *Comisión de Investigaciones Paleontológicas y Prehistóricas*, Memoria Núm. 38 (Serie Prehistórica Núm. 19). Madrid: Museo Nacional de Ciencias Naturales.

Vita-Finzi, C. (1974) Age of valley deposits in Périgord. *Nature* **250**(5467), 568–70.

Vita-Finzi, C. (1975) Related territories and alluvial sediments. In *Palaeoeconomy*, ed. E. S. Higgs, pp. 225–31. Cambridge: Cambridge University Press.

Vita-Finzi, C. (1978) *Archaeological Sites in their Setting.* London: Thames & Hudson.

Vita-Finzi, C. & Higgs, E. S. (1970) Prehistoric economy in the Mount Carmel area of Palestine: site catchment analysis. *Proceedings of the Prehistoric Society* **36**, 1–37.

Vogel, R. (1933) Tierreste aus vor- und frühgeschichtlichen Siedlungen Schwabens. Teil 1. Die Tierreste aus den Pfahlbauten der Bodensees. *Zoologica* **82**.

Vogt, E. (1957) Swiss pile-dwellings. *Antiquity* **31**, 68–72.

Wallén, C. C., Rodhe, B. & Lindholm, F. (1965) Rainy and frosty days, hours of sunshine, variability of precipitation and temperature, ice conditions, temperature in Stockholm 1756–1963. *Atlas över Sverige*, 33–4.

Ward, T. (1965) Correlation of Mississippian sites and soil types. *Southeastern Archaeological Conference* **3**, pp. 42–8.

Warriner, D. (1964) *Economics of Peasant Farming*, 2nd edn. London: Frank Cass.

Watanabe, H. (1972) The Ainu. In *Hunters and Gatherers Today*, ed. M. G. Bicchieri, pp. 451–84. New York: Holt, Rinehart & Winston.

Waterbolk, H. T. & van Zeist, W. (1966) Preliminary report on the Neolithic bog settlement of Niederwil. *Palaeohistoria* **12**, 559–80.

Watson, E. (1956) Geographical factors in the Neolithic colonisation of North-East Ireland. *Transactions of the Institute of British Geographers* **22**, 117–38.

Webley, D. P. (1976) How the west was won; prehistoric land-use in Southern Marches. In *Welsh Antiquity*, ed. G. C. Boon & J. H. Lewis, pp. 19–35. Cardiff: National Museum of Wales.

Weinstein, M. (1979) In *Alaska Highway Gas Pipeline. British Columbia Public Hearings*, Vol. 17, pp. 1775–1803. Unpublished transcripts of hearings held by the Northern Pipeline Agency.

Wendorf, F. (1968) Late Paleolithic sites in Egyptian Nubia. In *The Prehistory of Nubia*, Vol. 2, ed. F. Wendorf, pp. 791–953. Dallas: Fort Burgwin Research Center & Southern Methodist University Press.

West, R. G. (1956) The Quaternary deposits at Hoxne, Suffolk. *Philosophical Transactions of the Royal Society B* **239**, 265–365.

White, C. (1968) Report on field survey, June–August 1968. *Australian Institute of Aboriginal Studies. Document 68/738.* Canberra.

White, C. & Peterson, N. (1969) Ethnographic interpretations of the prehistory of western Arnhem Land. *South-West Journal of Anthropology* **25**, 45–67.

Wilkinson, P. F. (1972) Current experimental domestication and its relevance to prehistory. In *Papers in Economic Prehistory*, ed. E. S. Higgs, pp. 107–18. Cambridge: Cambridge University Press.

Wilkinson, P. F. (1975) The relevance of musk ox exploitation to the study of prehistoric animal economies. In *Palaeoeconomy*, ed. E. S. Higgs, pp. 9–53. Cambridge: Cambridge University Press.

Wilkinson, P. F. (1976) 'Random' hunting and the composition of faunal samples from archaeological excavations: a modern example from New Zealand. *Journal of Archaeological Science* **3**, 321–8.

Wilson, E. O. (1971) *The Insect Societies.* Cambridge, Mass.: Belknap Press, Harvard University Press.

Wilson, E. O. (1975) *Sociobiology. The New Synthesis.* Cambridge, Mass.: Belknap Press, Harvard University Press.

Winiger, J. (1971) *Das Fundmaterial von Thayngen-Weier im*

REFERENCES

Rahmen der Pfyner Kultur. Monographien zur Ur- und Frühgeschichte der Schweiz, 18. Basel.

Wiślański, T. (1969) *Podstawy Gospodarcze plemion Neolitycznych w Polsce Północno-Zachodniej*. Wrocław.

Wiślański, T. (1970) *The Neolithic in Poland*. Institut Historii Kultury Materialnej Polskiej. Wrocław: Akademii Nauk.

Wiślański, T. & Czarnecki, M. (1971) Eine Siedlung der Trichterbeckerkultur aus Kosin, Kreis Pryrzyce (Fundstelle 6). *Materialy Zachnodniopomorskie* **16**, 73–106.

Wołagiewicz, R. (1970) The investigations at Lubieszewo in Pomerania in 1964–68. *Sprawozdania Archeologiczne* **22**, 103–15.

Woodburn, H. (1968) An introduction to Hadza ecology. In *Man the Hunter*, ed. R. B. Lee & I. DeVore, pp. 49–55. Chicago: Aldine.

Woźniak, Z. (1970) A survey of the investigations of the Bronze and Iron Ages in Poland in 1969. *Sprawozdania Archeologiczne* **22**, 303–9.

Wright, H. E. (1976) The environmental setting for plant domestication in the Near East. *Science* **194**(4263), 385–9.

Wrigley, E. A. (1967) Demographic models and geography. In *Models in Geography*, ed. R. J. Chorley & P. Haggett, pp. 189–215. London: Methuen.

Wynne-Edwards, V. C. (1962) *Animal Dispersion in Relation to Social Behaviour*. Edinburgh: Oliver & Boyd.

Yarnell, R. A. (1964) Aboriginal relationships between culture and plant life in the Upper Great Lakes region. *Anthropological Papers from the Museum of Anthropology, University of Michigan* **23**.

Yellen, J. E. (1976) Settlement patterns of the !Kung: an archaeological perspective. In *Kalahari Hunter-Gatherers. Studies of the !Kung San and their Neighbors*, ed. R. B. Lee & I. DeVore, pp. 47–72. Cambridge, Mass.: Harvard University Press.

Yellen, J. E. & Lee, R. B. (1976) The Dobe-/Du/da environment: background to the hunting and gathering way of life. In *Kalahari Hunter-Gatherers. Studies of the !Kung San and their Neighbours*. ed. R. B. Lee & I. DeVore, pp. 27–46. Cambridge, Mass.: Harvard University Press.

Young, E. G. (1964) Dietary standards. In *Nutrition*, Vol. 2, ed. G. H. Beaton & E. W. McHenry, pp. 299–350. New York: Academic Press.

van Zeist, W. & Casparie, W. A. (1968) Wild barley and einkorn from Tell Mureybit in northern Syria. *Acta Botanica Neerlandica* **17**, 44–55.

Zenkevitch, I. (1963) *Biology of the Seas of the U.S.S.R.* London: Allen & Unwin.

Zeuner, F. E. (1963) *A History of Domesticated Animals*. London: Hutchinson.

Zipf, G. K. (1965) *Human Behaviour and the Principle of Least Effort*. New York: Hafner.

Zvelebil, M. (1978) Subsistence and settlement in the northeastern Baltic. In *The Early Postglacial Settlement of Northern Europe*, ed. P. A. Mellars, pp. 205–41. London: Duckworth.

GENERAL INDEX

NAME INDEX

INDEX OF ARCHAEOLOGICAL SITES AND CULTURES

INDEX OF ARCHAEOLOGICAL SITES AND CULTURES

283